DING DONG DEDDY
FROM DINGBURG

by Bill Griffith

Zippy the Pinhead

DING DONG DADDY FROM DINGBURG

September 2008 – June 2010

ZIPPY / Ding Ding Daddy From Dingburg
Zippy Annual – Volume 10

FANTAGRAPHICS BOOKS

7563 Lake City Way NE, Seattle WA 98115
www.fantagraphics.com
Call 1-800-657-1100 for a full color catalog of fine comics publications.
First Edition: September 2010
Designed by Bill Griffith
Production managed by Kim Thompson
Production by Paul Baresh
Cover production by Paul Baresh
Associate Publisher: Eric Reynolds
Published by Gary Groth and Kim Thompson

Printed in Malaysia
ISBN: 978-1-60699-389-7

The comic strips in this book have appeared in newspapers and on
newspaper websites in the United States and abroad, distributed by
King Features Syndicate, 300 W. 57th St., New York NY 10019.
www.kingfeatures.com

For more on Zippy (including the Zippy Store, Zippy Strip Search,
Letters page, Newsroom and extensive free Zippy Archives), visit:
www.zippythepinhead.com

The "pindex" for this book (location and/or other factoids on strips) may be found
online at: zippythepinhead.com/pages/aarealday.html
Thanks and a tip o' th' pin to: American Color, Gary Groth and Kim Thompson.

Dedicated to Diane Noomin.

Books by Bill Griffith:
Zippy Stories • *Nation of Pinheads* • *Pointed Behavior* • *Pindemonium*
Are We Having Fun Yet? • *Kingpin* • *Pinhead's Progress* • *Get Me A*
Table Without Flies, Harry • *From A To Zippy* • *Zippy's House Of Fun*
Griffith Observatory • *Zippy Annual #1* • *Zippy Annual 2001*
Zippy Annual 2002 • *Zippy Annual 2003* • *ZIPPY: From Here To*
Absurdity • *ZIPPY: Type Z Personality* • *ZIPPY: Connect The Polka Dots*
ZIPPY: Walk A Mile In My Muu-Muu • *ZIPPY: Welcome to Dingburg*

To contact Bill Griffith:
Pinhead Productions, LLC, P.O. Box 88, Hadlyme CT 06439
Griffy@zippythepinhead.com

"My job is to lighten the
burden of rationality."

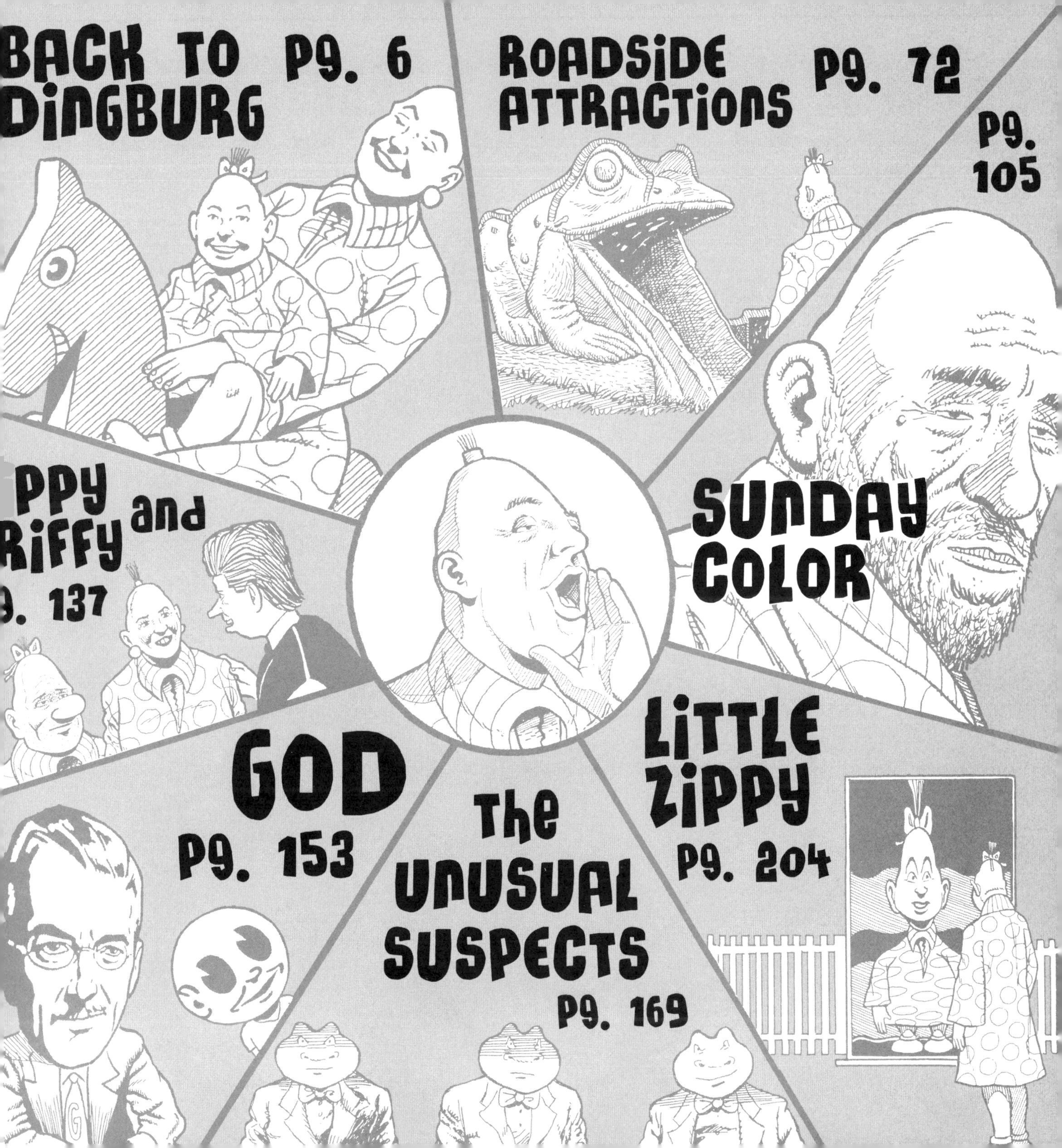
BACK TO DINGBURG
Pg. 6
ROADSIDE ATTRACTIONS
Pg. 72
Pg. 105
SUNDAY COLOR
PPY
RIFFY and
137
GOD
Pg. 153
The UNUSUAL SUSPECTS
Pg. 169
LITTLE ZIPPY
Pg. 204

BACK TO DINGBURG

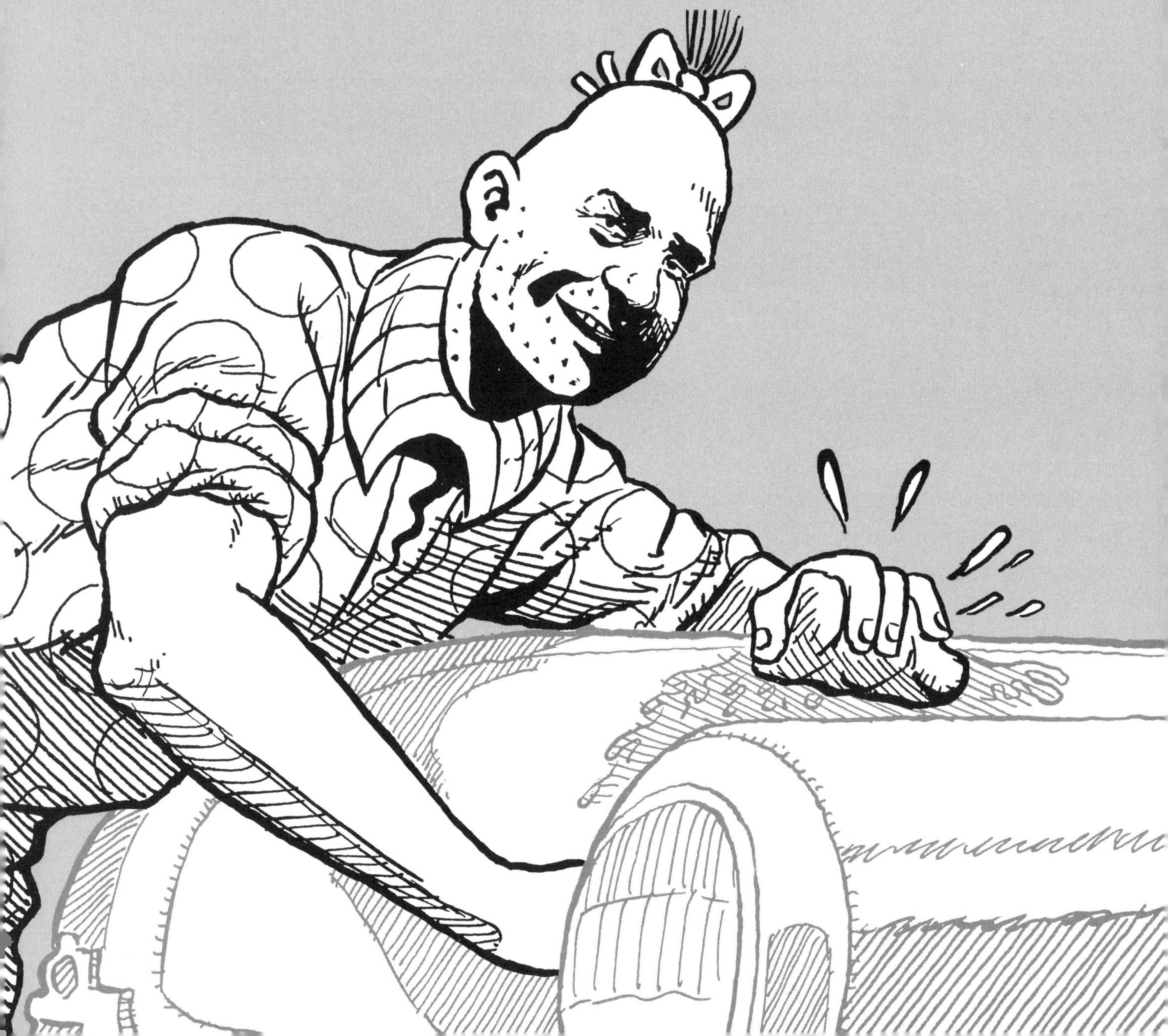

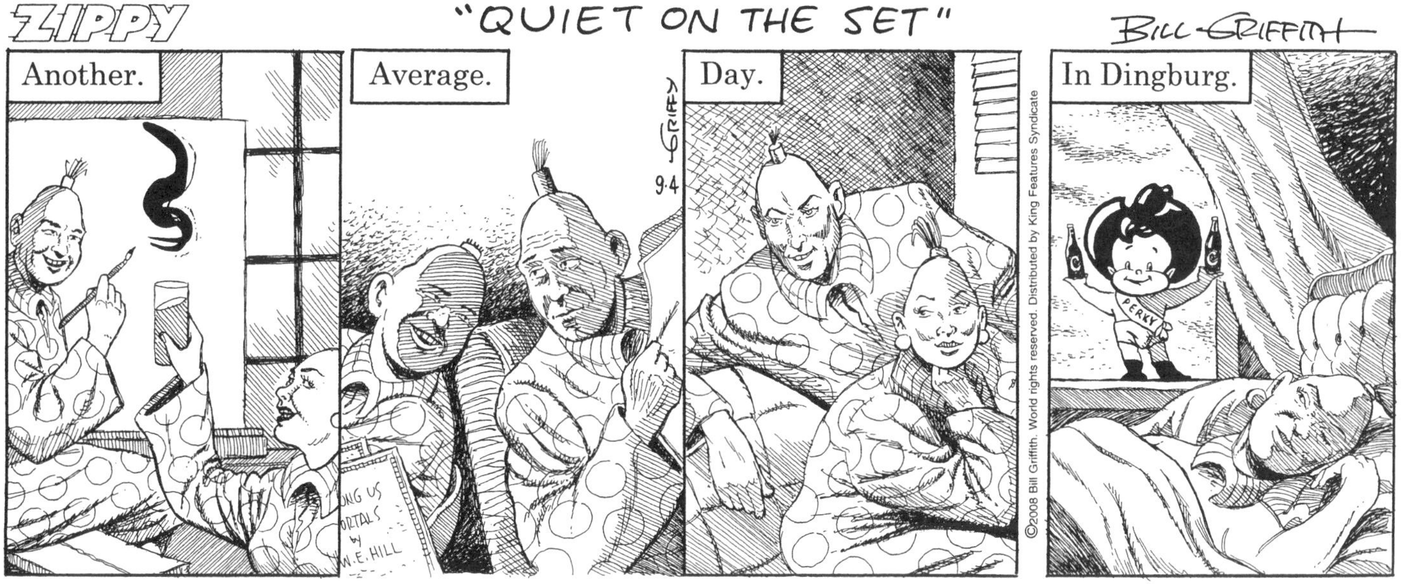
ZIPPY
"QUIET ON THE SET"
BILL GRIFFITH
Another.
Average.
GRIFFY
9·4
Day.
©2008 Bill Griffith. World rights reserved. Distributed by King Features Syndicate
In Dingburg.
PERKY

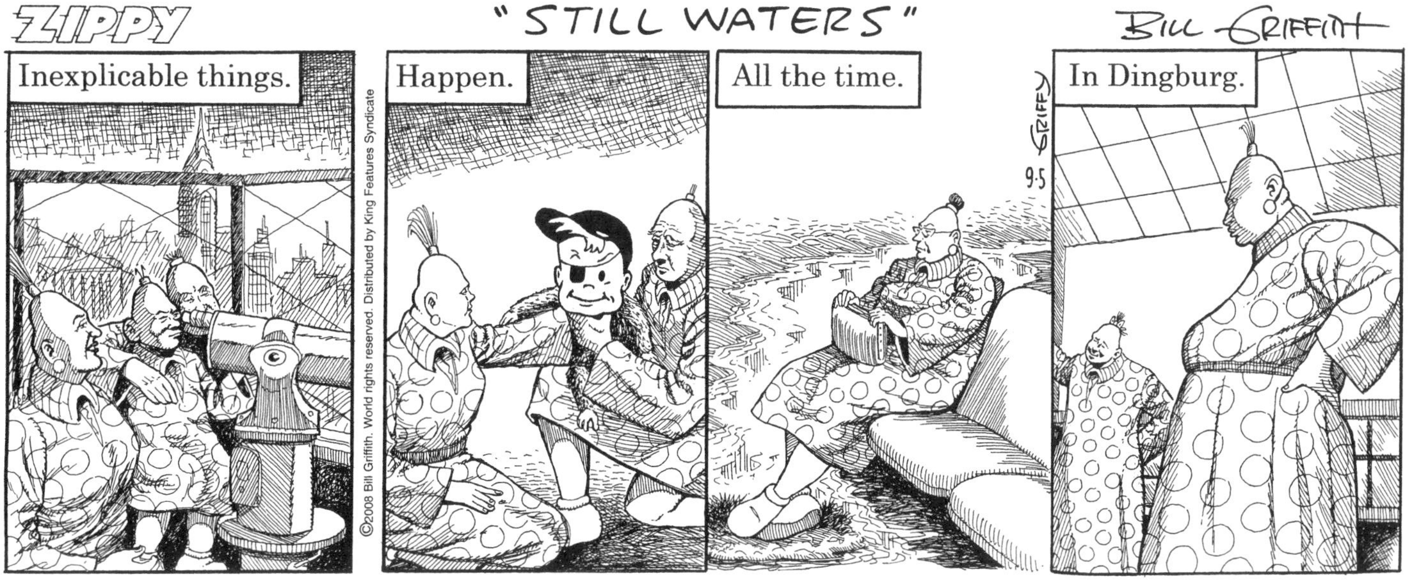
ZIPPY
"STILL WATERS"
BILL GRIFFITH
Inexplicable things.
©2008 Bill Griffith. World rights reserved. Distributed by King Features Syndicate
Happen.
All the time.
GRIFFY
9·5
In Dingburg.

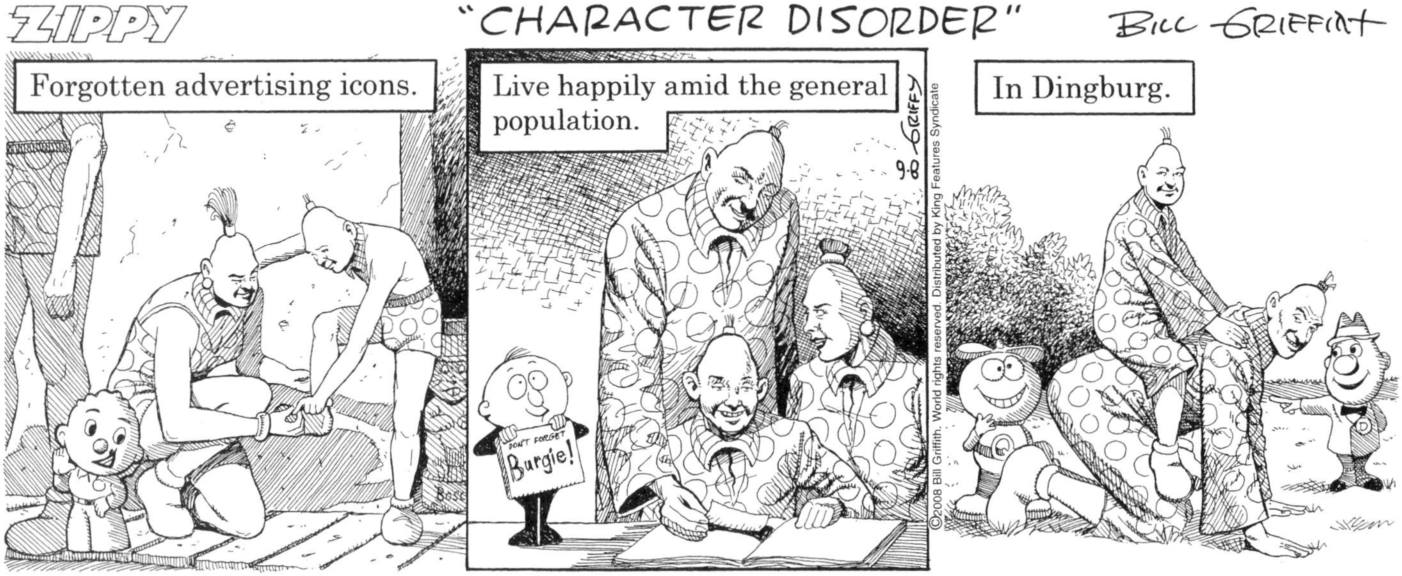
ZIPPY
"CHARACTER DISORDER"
BILL GRIFFITH
Forgotten advertising icons.
Live happily amid the general population.
DON'T FORGET Burgie!
GRIFFY 9-8
©2008 Bill Griffith. World rights reserved. Distributed by King Features Syndicate
In Dingburg.

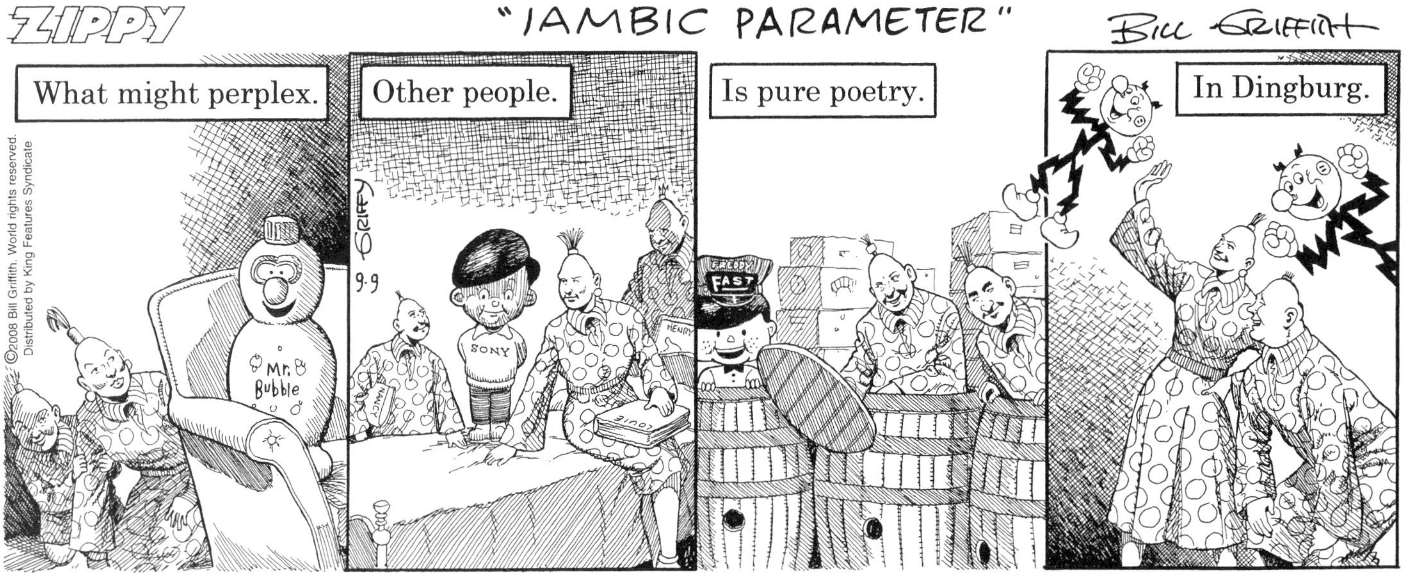
ZIPPY
"IAMBIC PARAMETER"
BILL GRIFFITH
©2008 Bill Griffith. World rights reserved. Distributed by King Features Syndicate
What might perplex.
Mr. Bubble
Other people.
GRIFFY 9-9
SONY
Is pure poetry.
FAST
In Dingburg.

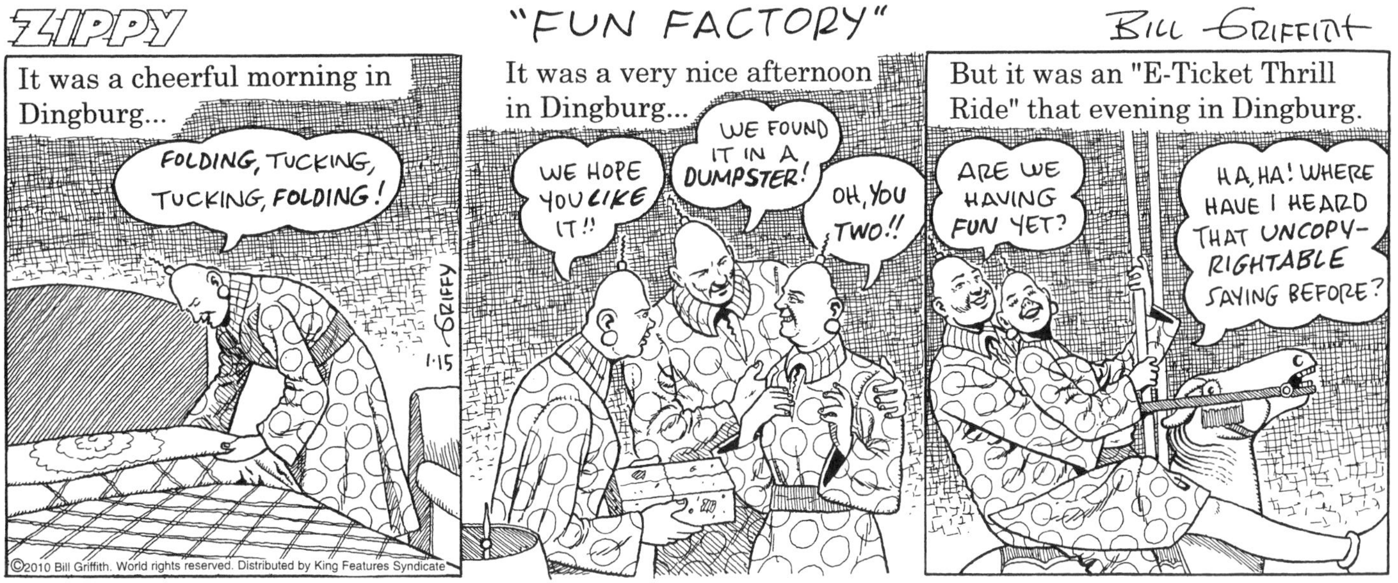
ZIPPY
"FUN FACTORY"
BILL GRIFFITH
It was a cheerful morning in Dingburg...
FOLDING, TUCKING, TUCKING, FOLDING!
GRIFFY 1·15
©2010 Bill Griffith. World rights reserved. Distributed by King Features Syndicate
It was a very nice afternoon in Dingburg...
WE HOPE YOU LIKE IT!!
WE FOUND IT IN A DUMPSTER!
OH, YOU TWO!!
But it was an "E-Ticket Thrill Ride" that evening in Dingburg.
ARE WE HAVING FUN YET?
HA, HA! WHERE HAVE I HEARD THAT UNCOPYRIGHTABLE SAYING BEFORE?

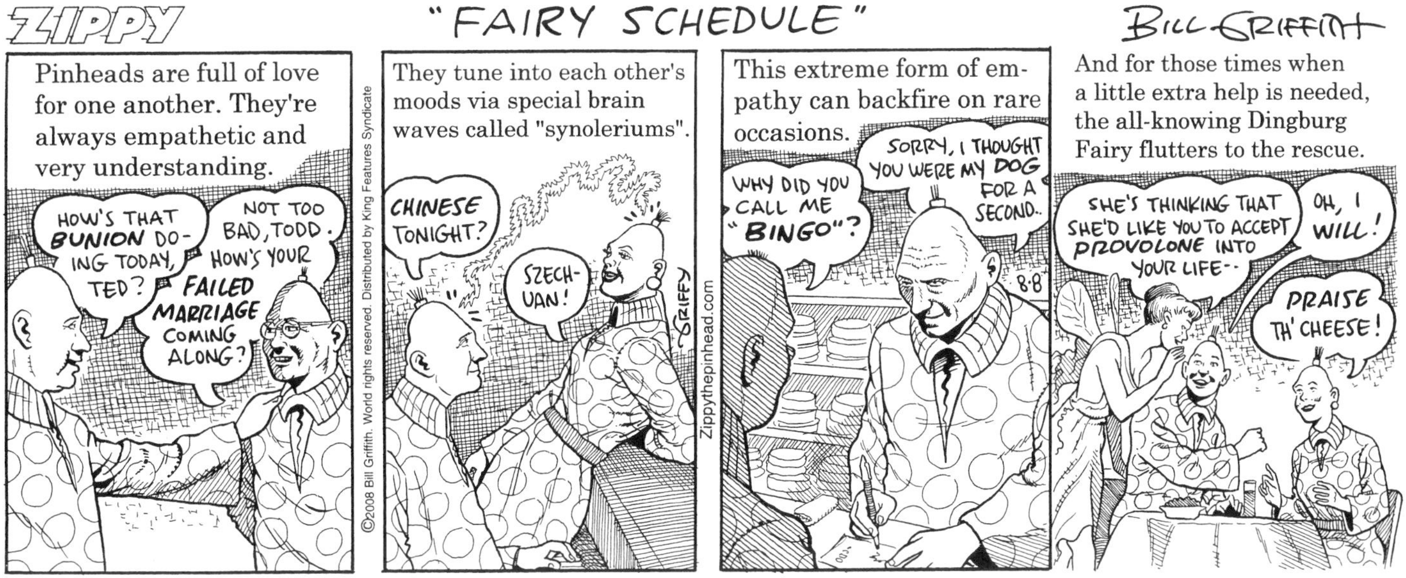
ZIPPY
"FAIRY SCHEDULE"
BILL GRIFFITH
Pinheads are full of love for one another. They're always empathetic and very understanding.
HOW'S THAT BUNION DOING TODAY, TED?
NOT TOO BAD, TODD. HOW'S YOUR FAILED MARRIAGE COMING ALONG?
©2008 Bill Griffith. World rights reserved. Distributed by King Features Syndicate
They tune into each other's moods via special brain waves called "synoleriums".
CHINESE TONIGHT?
SZECHUAN!
GRIFFY
Zippythepinhead.com
This extreme form of empathy can backfire on rare occasions.
WHY DID YOU CALL ME "BINGO"?
SORRY, I THOUGHT YOU WERE MY DOG FOR A SECOND..
8·8
And for those times when a little extra help is needed, the all-knowing Dingburg Fairy flutters to the rescue.
SHE'S THINKING THAT SHE'D LIKE YOU TO ACCEPT PROVOLONE INTO YOUR LIFE--
OH, I WILL!
PRAISE TH' CHEESE!

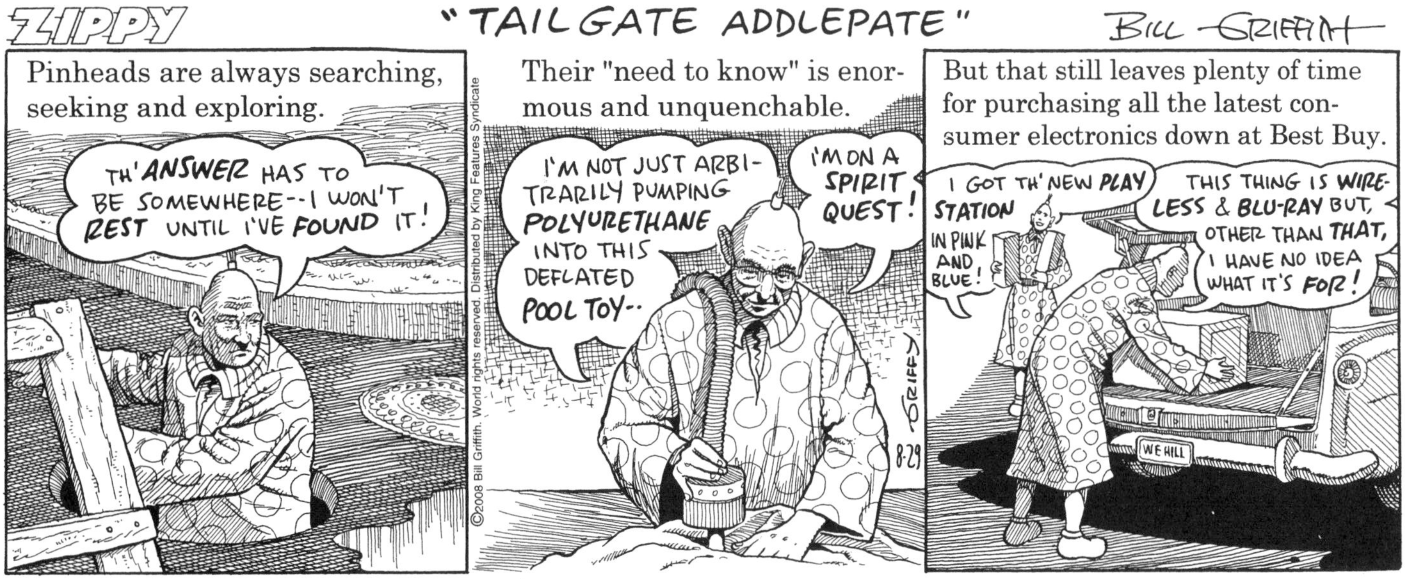
ZIPPY
"TAILGATE ADDLEPATE"
BILL GRIFFITH
Pinheads are always searching, seeking and exploring.
TH' ANSWER HAS TO BE SOMEWHERE--I WON'T REST UNTIL I'VE FOUND IT!
©2008 Bill Griffith. World rights reserved. Distributed by King Features Syndicate
Their "need to know" is enormous and unquenchable.
I'M NOT JUST ARBITRARILY PUMPING POLYURETHANE INTO THIS DEFLATED POOL TOY..
I'M ON A SPIRIT QUEST!
GRIFFY
8-29
But that still leaves plenty of time for purchasing all the latest consumer electronics down at Best Buy.
I GOT TH' NEW PLAY STATION IN PINK AND BLUE!
THIS THING IS WIRELESS & BLU-RAY BUT, OTHER THAN THAT, I HAVE NO IDEA WHAT IT'S FOR!
WE HILL

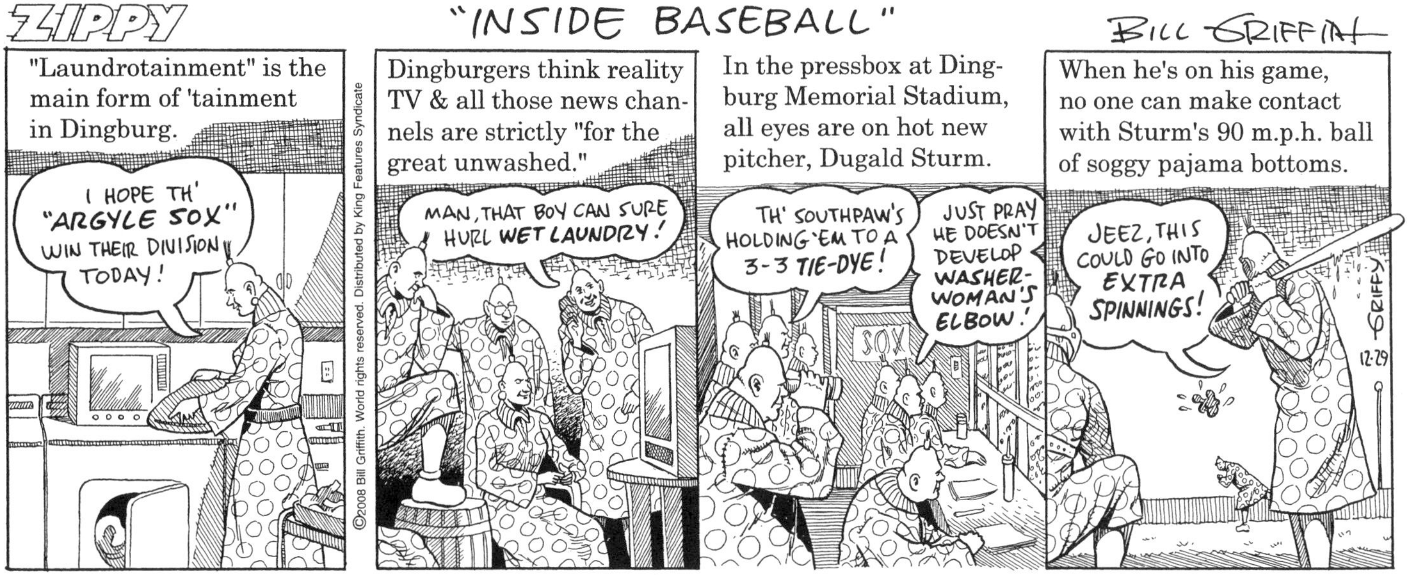
ZIPPY
"INSIDE BASEBALL"
BILL GRIFFITH
"Laundrotainment" is the main form of 'tainment in Dingburg.
I HOPE TH' "ARGYLE SOX" WIN THEIR DIVISION TODAY!
©2008 Bill Griffith. World rights reserved. Distributed by King Features Syndicate
Dingburgers think reality TV & all those news channels are strictly "for the great unwashed."
MAN, THAT BOY CAN SURE HURL WET LAUNDRY!
In the pressbox at Dingburg Memorial Stadium, all eyes are on hot new pitcher, Dugald Sturm.
TH' SOUTHPAW'S HOLDING 'EM TO A 3-3 TIE-DYE!
JUST PRAY HE DOESN'T DEVELOP WASHER-WOMAN'S ELBOW!
SOX
When he's on his game, no one can make contact with Sturm's 90 m.p.h. ball of soggy pajama bottoms.
JEEZ, THIS COULD GO INTO EXTRA SPINNINGS!
GRIFFY
12-29

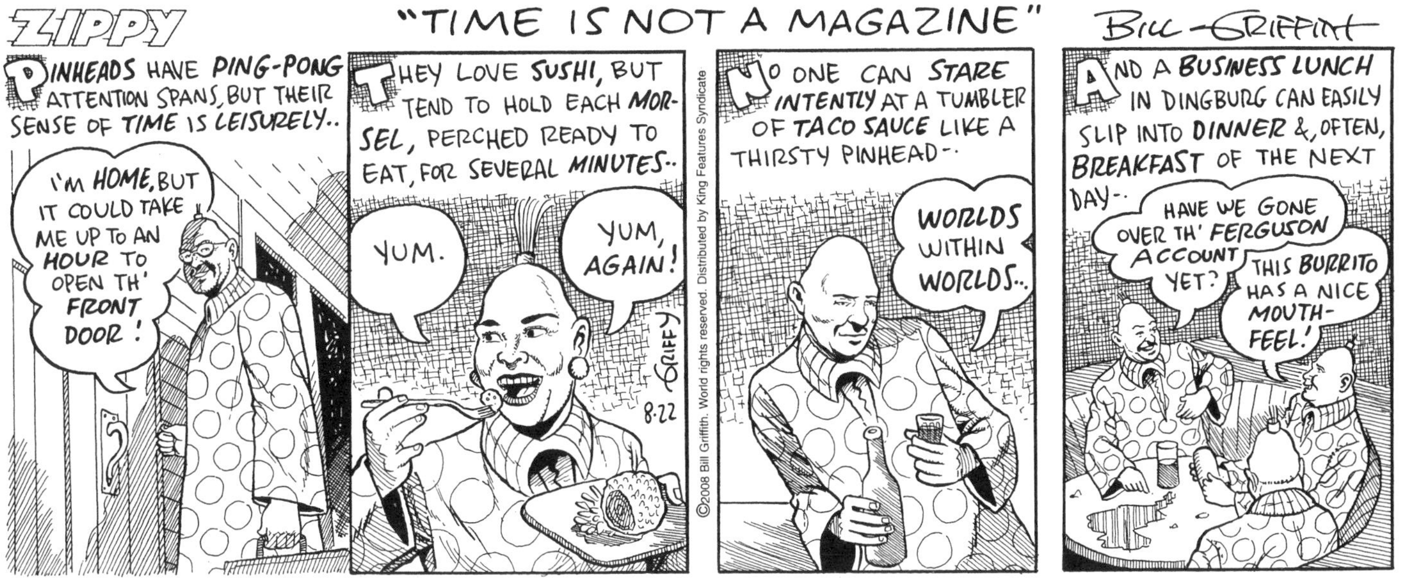
ZIPPY
"TIME IS NOT A MAGAZINE"
BILL GRIFFITH
PINHEADS HAVE PING-PONG ATTENTION SPANS, BUT THEIR SENSE OF TIME IS LEISURELY..
I'M HOME, BUT IT COULD TAKE ME UP TO AN HOUR TO OPEN TH' FRONT DOOR!
THEY LOVE SUSHI, BUT TEND TO HOLD EACH MORSEL, PERCHED READY TO EAT, FOR SEVERAL MINUTES..
YUM.
YUM, AGAIN!
GRIFFY
8·22
©2008 Bill Griffith. World rights reserved. Distributed by King Features Syndicate
NO ONE CAN STARE INTENTLY AT A TUMBLER OF TACO SAUCE LIKE A THIRSTY PINHEAD..
WORLDS WITHIN WORLDS..
AND A BUSINESS LUNCH IN DINGBURG CAN EASILY SLIP INTO DINNER &, OFTEN, BREAKFAST OF THE NEXT DAY..
HAVE WE GONE OVER TH' FERGUSON ACCOUNT YET?
THIS BURRITO HAS A NICE MOUTH-FEEL!

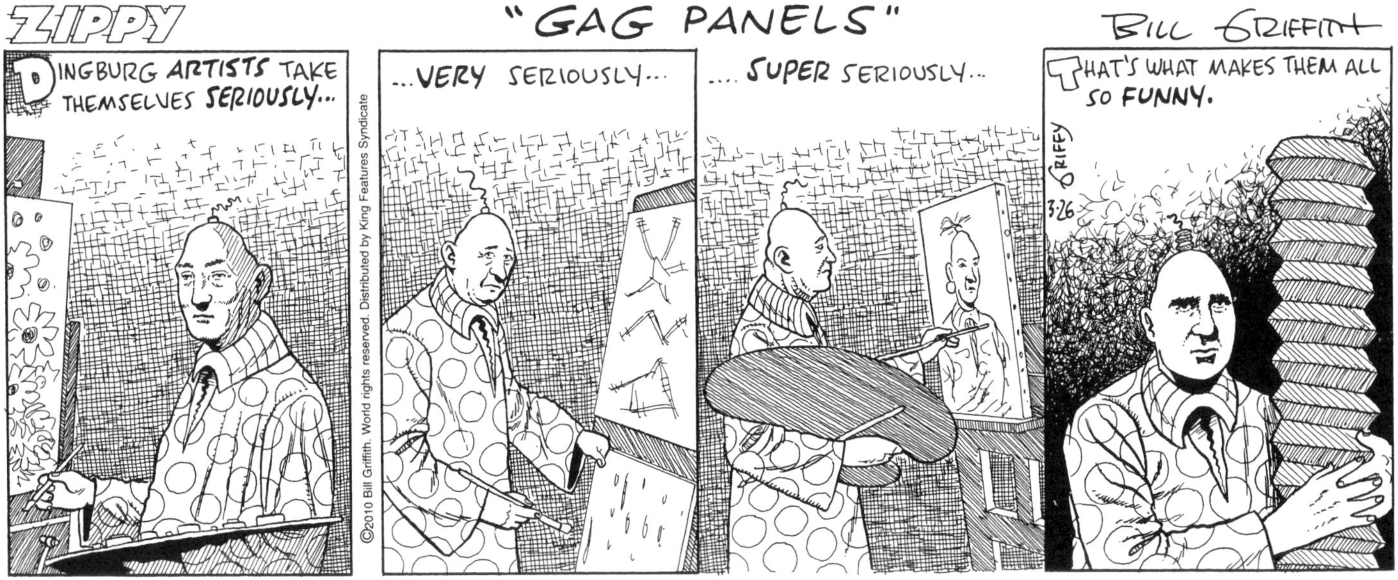
ZIPPY
"GAG PANELS"
BILL GRIFFITH
DINGBURG ARTISTS TAKE THEMSELVES SERIOUSLY...
©2010 Bill Griffith. World rights reserved. Distributed by King Features Syndicate
...VERY SERIOUSLY...
.... SUPER SERIOUSLY...
THAT'S WHAT MAKES THEM ALL SO FUNNY.
GRIFFY
3·26

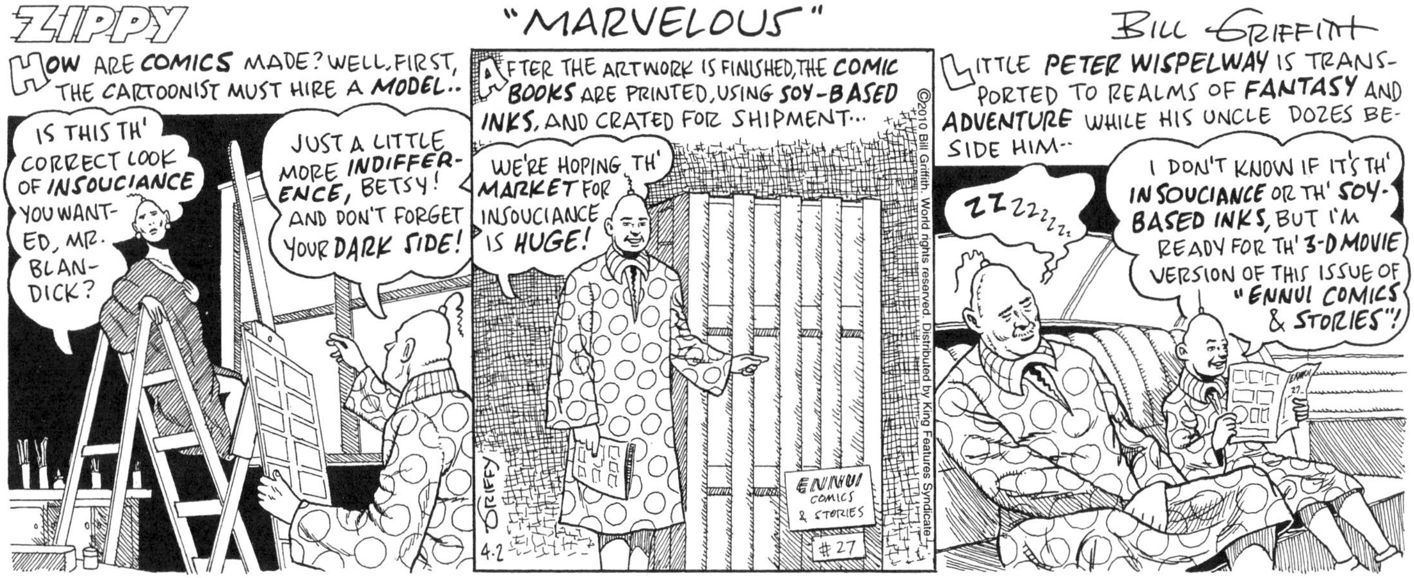
ZIPPY
"MARVELOUS"
BILL GRIFFITH
HOW ARE COMICS MADE? WELL, FIRST, THE CARTOONIST MUST HIRE A MODEL..
IS THIS TH' CORRECT LOOK OF INSOUCIANCE YOU WANTED, MR. BLANDICK?
JUST A LITTLE MORE INDIFFERENCE, BETSY! AND DON'T FORGET YOUR DARK SIDE!
AFTER THE ARTWORK IS FINISHED, THE COMIC BOOKS ARE PRINTED, USING SOY-BASED INKS, AND CRATED FOR SHIPMENT..
WE'RE HOPING TH' MARKET FOR INSOUCIANCE IS HUGE!
ENNUI COMICS & STORIES
#27
GRIFFY 4·2
©2010 Bill Griffith. World rights reserved. Distributed by King Features Syndicate
LITTLE PETER WISPELWAY IS TRANSPORTED TO REALMS OF FANTASY AND ADVENTURE WHILE HIS UNCLE DOZES BESIDE HIM..
ZZZZZZZZ
I DON'T KNOW IF IT'S TH' INSOUCIANCE OR TH' SOY-BASED INKS, BUT I'M READY FOR TH' 3-D MOVIE VERSION OF THIS ISSUE OF "ENNUI COMICS & STORIES"!

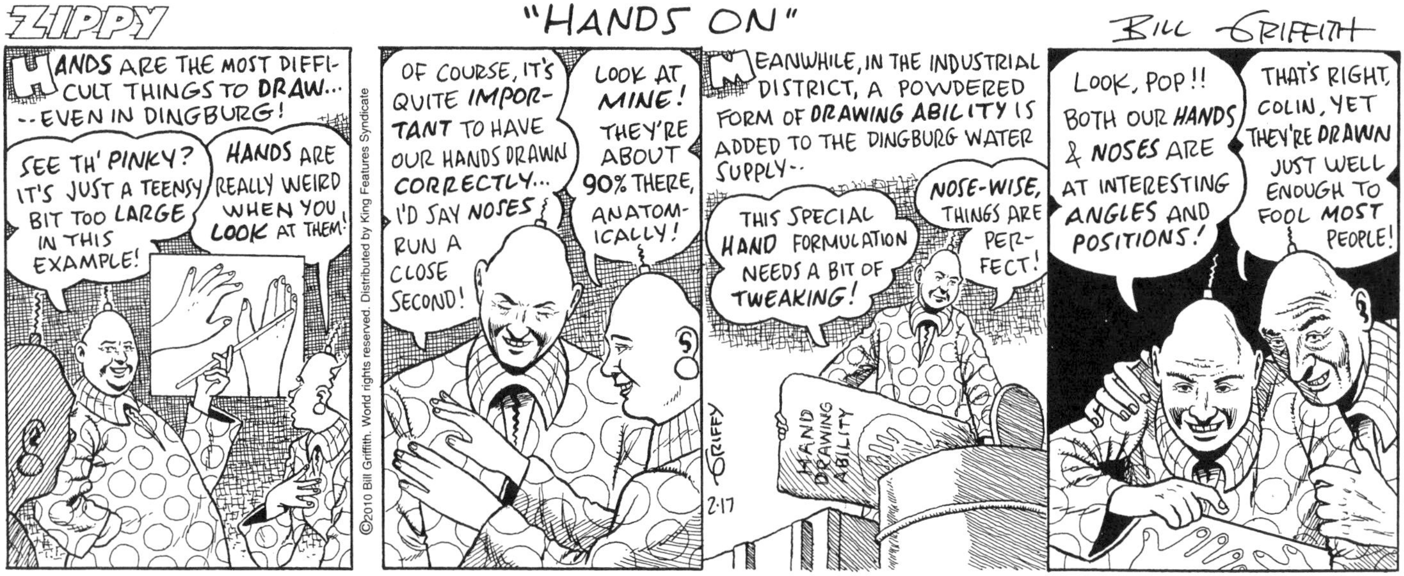
ZIPPY
"HANDS ON"
BILL GRIFFITH
HANDS ARE THE MOST DIFFICULT THINGS TO DRAW... ..EVEN IN DINGBURG!
SEE TH' PINKY? IT'S JUST A TEENSY BIT TOO LARGE IN THIS EXAMPLE!
HANDS ARE REALLY WEIRD WHEN YOU LOOK AT THEM!
©2010 Bill Griffith. World rights reserved. Distributed by King Features Syndicate
OF COURSE, IT'S QUITE IMPORTANT TO HAVE OUR HANDS DRAWN CORRECTLY... I'D SAY NOSES RUN A CLOSE SECOND!
LOOK AT MINE! THEY'RE ABOUT 90% THERE, ANATOMICALLY!
GRIFFY 2·17
MEANWHILE, IN THE INDUSTRIAL DISTRICT, A POWDERED FORM OF DRAWING ABILITY IS ADDED TO THE DINGBURG WATER SUPPLY..
THIS SPECIAL HAND FORMULATION NEEDS A BIT OF TWEAKING!
NOSE-WISE, THINGS ARE PERFECT!
HAND DRAWING ABILITY
LOOK, POP!! BOTH OUR HANDS & NOSES ARE AT INTERESTING ANGLES AND POSITIONS!
THAT'S RIGHT, COLIN, YET THEY'RE DRAWN JUST WELL ENOUGH TO FOOL MOST PEOPLE!

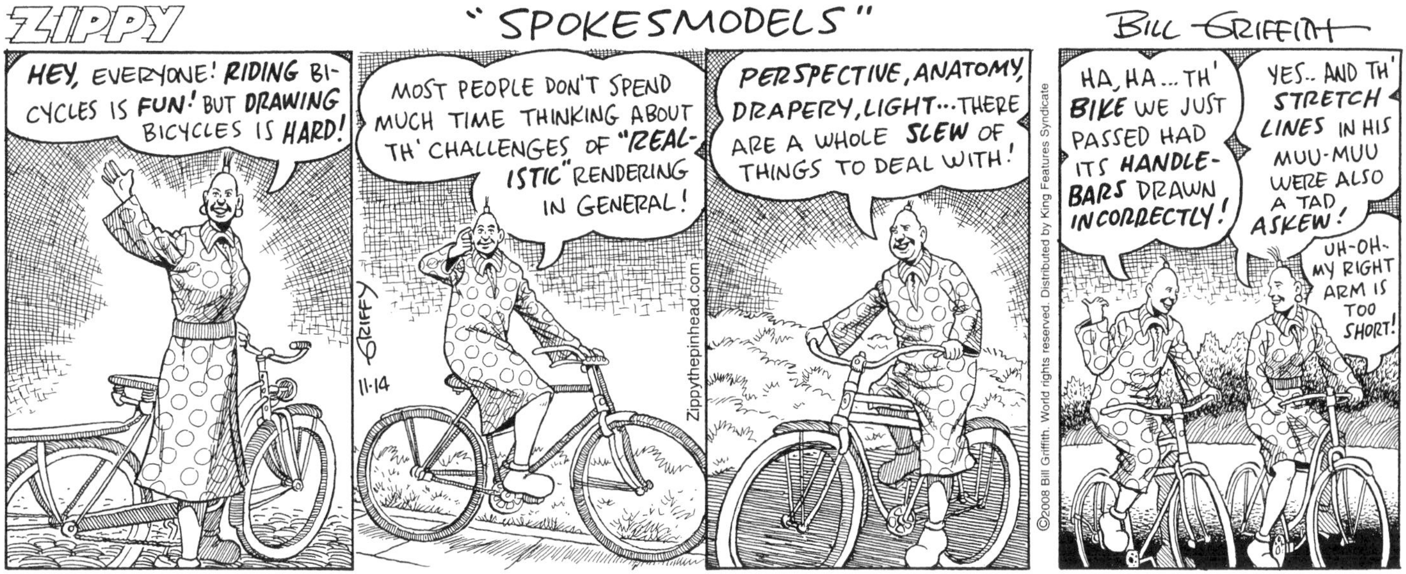
ZIPPY
"SPOKESMODELS"
BILL GRIFFITH
HEY, EVERYONE! RIDING BICYCLES IS FUN! BUT DRAWING BICYCLES IS HARD!
MOST PEOPLE DON'T SPEND MUCH TIME THINKING ABOUT TH' CHALLENGES OF "REALISTIC" RENDERING IN GENERAL!
GRIFFY
11·14
Zippythepinhead.com
PERSPECTIVE, ANATOMY, DRAPERY, LIGHT... THERE ARE A WHOLE SLEW OF THINGS TO DEAL WITH!
©2008 Bill Griffith. World rights reserved. Distributed by King Features Syndicate
HA, HA... TH' BIKE WE JUST PASSED HAD ITS HANDLEBARS DRAWN INCORRECTLY!
YES.. AND TH' STRETCH LINES IN HIS MUU-MUU WERE ALSO A TAD ASKEW!
UH-OH- MY RIGHT ARM IS TOO SHORT!

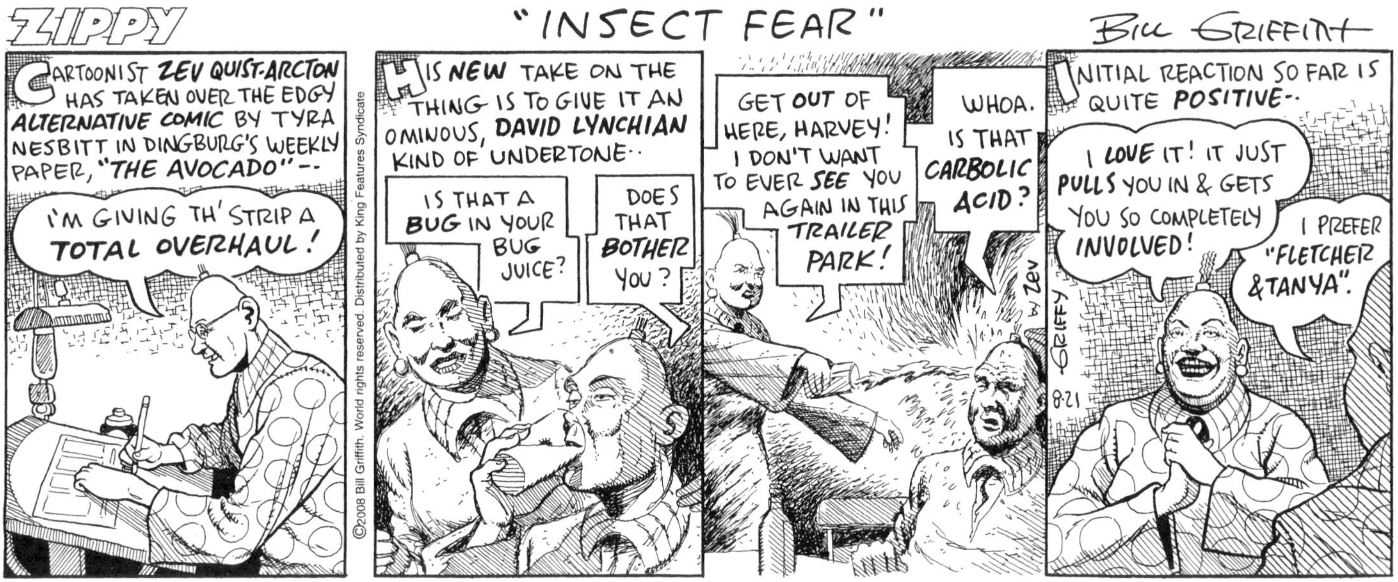
ZIPPY
"INSECT FEAR"
BILL GRIFFITH
CARTOONIST ZEV QUIST-ARCTON HAS TAKEN OVER THE EDGY ALTERNATIVE COMIC BY TYRA NESBITT IN DINGBURG'S WEEKLY PAPER, "THE AVOCADO"--
I'M GIVING TH' STRIP A TOTAL OVERHAUL!
©2008 Bill Griffith. World rights reserved. Distributed by King Features Syndicate
HIS NEW TAKE ON THE THING IS TO GIVE IT AN OMINOUS, DAVID LYNCHIAN KIND OF UNDERTONE..
IS THAT A BUG IN YOUR BUG JUICE?
DOES THAT BOTHER YOU?
GET OUT OF HERE, HARVEY! I DON'T WANT TO EVER SEE YOU AGAIN IN THIS TRAILER PARK!
WHOA. IS THAT CARBOLIC ACID?
w/ ZEV
GRIFFY
8·21
INITIAL REACTION SO FAR IS QUITE POSITIVE..
I LOVE IT! IT JUST PULLS YOU IN & GETS YOU SO COMPLETELY INVOLVED!
I PREFER "FLETCHER & TANYA".

ZIPPY "NEGATIVE FEEDBACK LOOP" BILL GRIFFITH

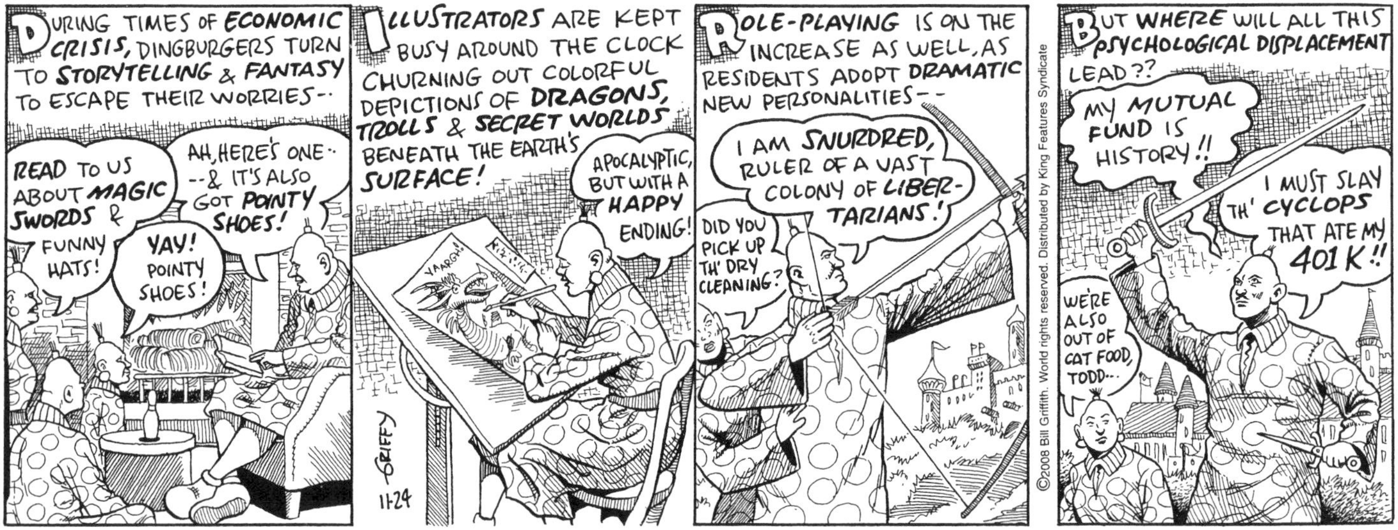

DURING TIMES OF ECONOMIC CRISIS, DINGBURGERS TURN TO STORYTELLING & FANTASY TO ESCAPE THEIR WORRIES--
READ TO US ABOUT MAGIC SWORDS & FUNNY HATS!
AH, HERE'S ONE-- --& IT'S ALSO GOT POINTY SHOES!
YAY! POINTY SHOES!
ILLUSTRATORS ARE KEPT BUSY AROUND THE CLOCK CHURNING OUT COLORFUL DEPICTIONS OF DRAGONS, TROLLS & SECRET WORLDS BENEATH THE EARTH'S SURFACE!
APOCALYPTIC, BUT WITH A HAPPY ENDING!
GRIFFY
11-24
ROLE-PLAYING IS ON THE INCREASE AS WELL, AS RESIDENTS ADOPT DRAMATIC NEW PERSONALITIES--
I AM SNURDRED, RULER OF A VAST COLONY OF LIBERTARIANS!
DID YOU PICK UP TH' DRY CLEANING?
©2008 Bill Griffith. World rights reserved. Distributed by King Features Syndicate
BUT WHERE WILL ALL THIS PSYCHOLOGICAL DISPLACEMENT LEAD??
MY MUTUAL FUND IS HISTORY!!
I MUST SLAY TH' CYCLOPS THAT ATE MY 401K!!
WE'RE ALSO OUT OF CAT FOOD, TODD...

ZIPPY "WAITING FOR JEFFY" BILL GRIFFITH

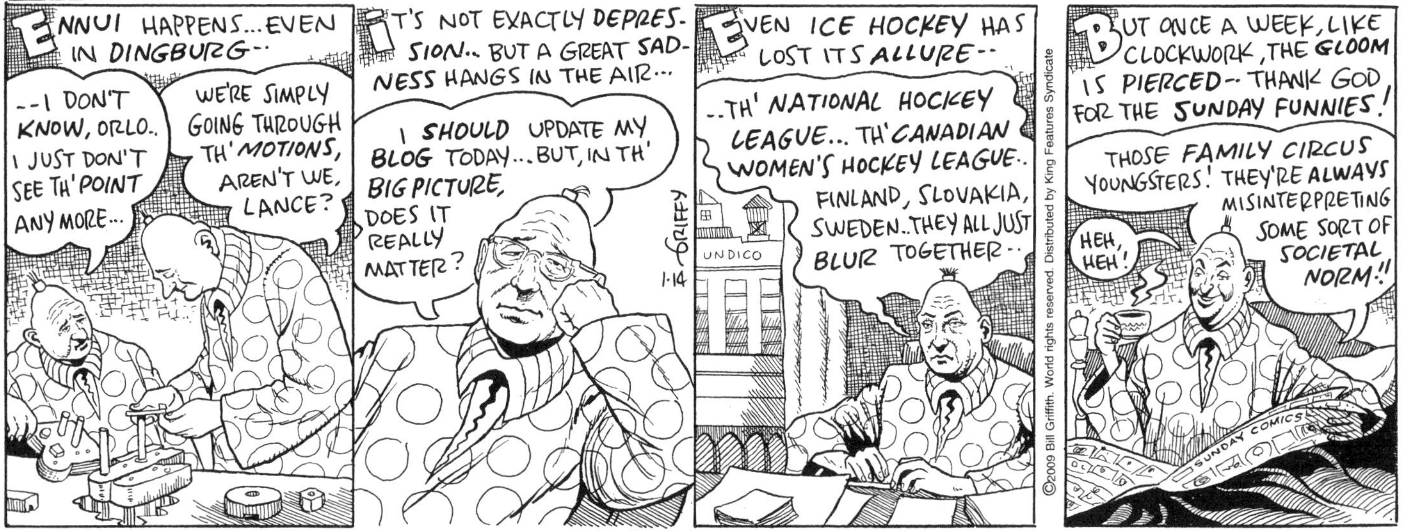

ENNUI HAPPENS...EVEN IN DINGBURG--
--I DON'T KNOW, ORLO.. I JUST DON'T SEE TH' POINT ANY MORE...
WE'RE SIMPLY GOING THROUGH TH' MOTIONS, AREN'T WE, LANCE?
IT'S NOT EXACTLY DEPRESSION.. BUT A GREAT SADNESS HANGS IN THE AIR...
I SHOULD UPDATE MY BLOG TODAY...BUT, IN TH' BIG PICTURE, DOES IT REALLY MATTER?
GRIFFY
1-14
EVEN ICE HOCKEY HAS LOST ITS ALLURE--
--TH' NATIONAL HOCKEY LEAGUE... TH' CANADIAN WOMEN'S HOCKEY LEAGUE.. FINLAND, SLOVAKIA, SWEDEN..THEY ALL JUST BLUR TOGETHER--
UNDICO
©2009 Bill Griffith. World rights reserved. Distributed by King Features Syndicate
BUT ONCE A WEEK, LIKE CLOCKWORK, THE GLOOM IS PIERCED-- THANK GOD FOR THE SUNDAY FUNNIES!
THOSE FAMILY CIRCUS YOUNGSTERS! THEY'RE ALWAYS MISINTERPRETING SOME SORT OF SOCIETAL NORM!!
HEH, HEH!
SUNDAY COMICS

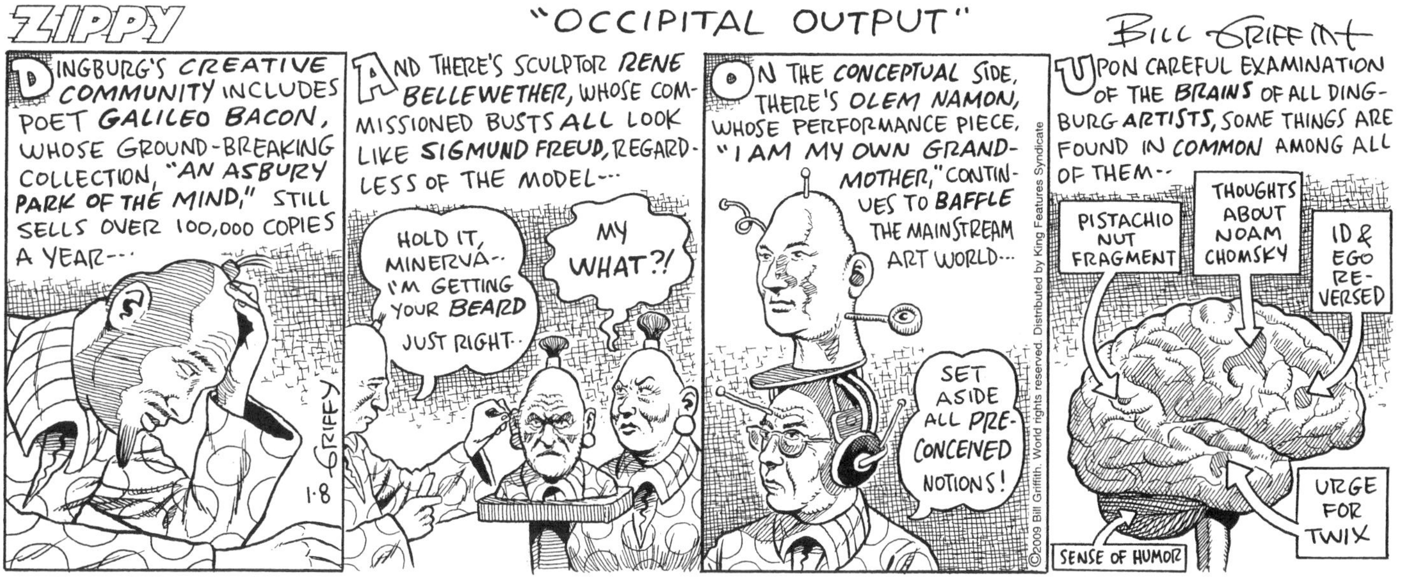
ZIPPY
"OCCIPITAL OUTPUT"
BILL GRIFFITH
DINGBURG'S CREATIVE COMMUNITY INCLUDES POET GALILEO BACON, WHOSE GROUND-BREAKING COLLECTION, "AN ASBURY PARK OF THE MIND," STILL SELLS OVER 100,000 COPIES A YEAR---
GRIFFY
1·8
AND THERE'S SCULPTOR RENE BELLEWETHER, WHOSE COMMISSIONED BUSTS ALL LOOK LIKE SIGMUND FREUD, REGARDLESS OF THE MODEL---
HOLD IT, MINERVA-- I'M GETTING YOUR BEARD JUST RIGHT--
MY WHAT?!
ON THE CONCEPTUAL SIDE, THERE'S OLEM NAMON, WHOSE PERFORMANCE PIECE, "I AM MY OWN GRANDMOTHER," CONTINUES TO BAFFLE THE MAINSTREAM ART WORLD---
SET ASIDE ALL PRECONCEIVED NOTIONS!
©2009 Bill Griffith. World rights reserved. Distributed by King Features Syndicate
UPON CAREFUL EXAMINATION OF THE BRAINS OF ALL DINGBURG ARTISTS, SOME THINGS ARE FOUND IN COMMON AMONG ALL OF THEM--
PISTACHIO NUT FRAGMENT
THOUGHTS ABOUT NOAM CHOMSKY
ID & EGO REVERSED
URGE FOR TWIX
SENSE OF HUMOR

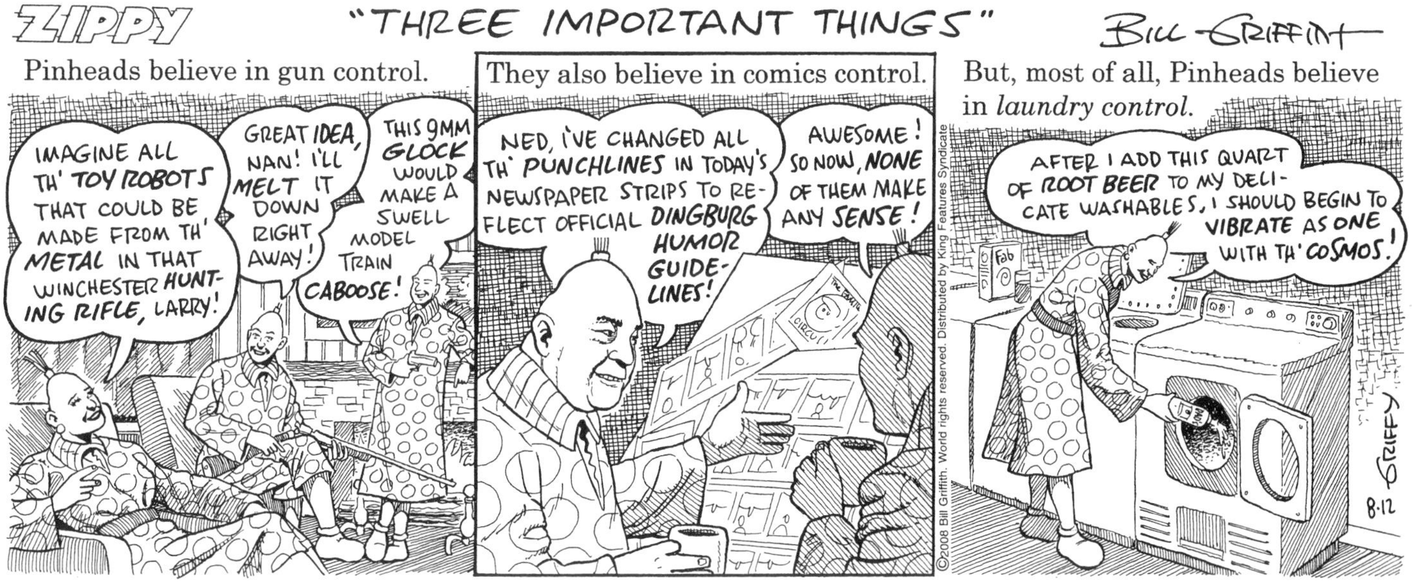
ZIPPY
"THREE IMPORTANT THINGS"
BILL GRIFFITH
Pinheads believe in gun control.
IMAGINE ALL TH' TOY ROBOTS THAT COULD BE MADE FROM TH' METAL IN THAT WINCHESTER HUNTING RIFLE, LARRY!
GREAT IDEA, NAN! I'LL MELT IT DOWN RIGHT AWAY!
THIS 9MM GLOCK WOULD MAKE A SWELL MODEL TRAIN CABOOSE!
They also believe in comics control.
NED, I'VE CHANGED ALL TH' PUNCHLINES IN TODAY'S NEWSPAPER STRIPS TO REFLECT OFFICIAL DINGBURG HUMOR GUIDELINES!
AWESOME! SO NOW, NONE OF THEM MAKE ANY SENSE!
©2008 Bill Griffith. World rights reserved. Distributed by King Features Syndicate
But, most of all, Pinheads believe in *laundry control*.
AFTER I ADD THIS QUART OF ROOT BEER TO MY DELICATE WASHABLES, I SHOULD BEGIN TO VIBRATE AS ONE WITH TH' COSMOS!
GRIFFY
8·12

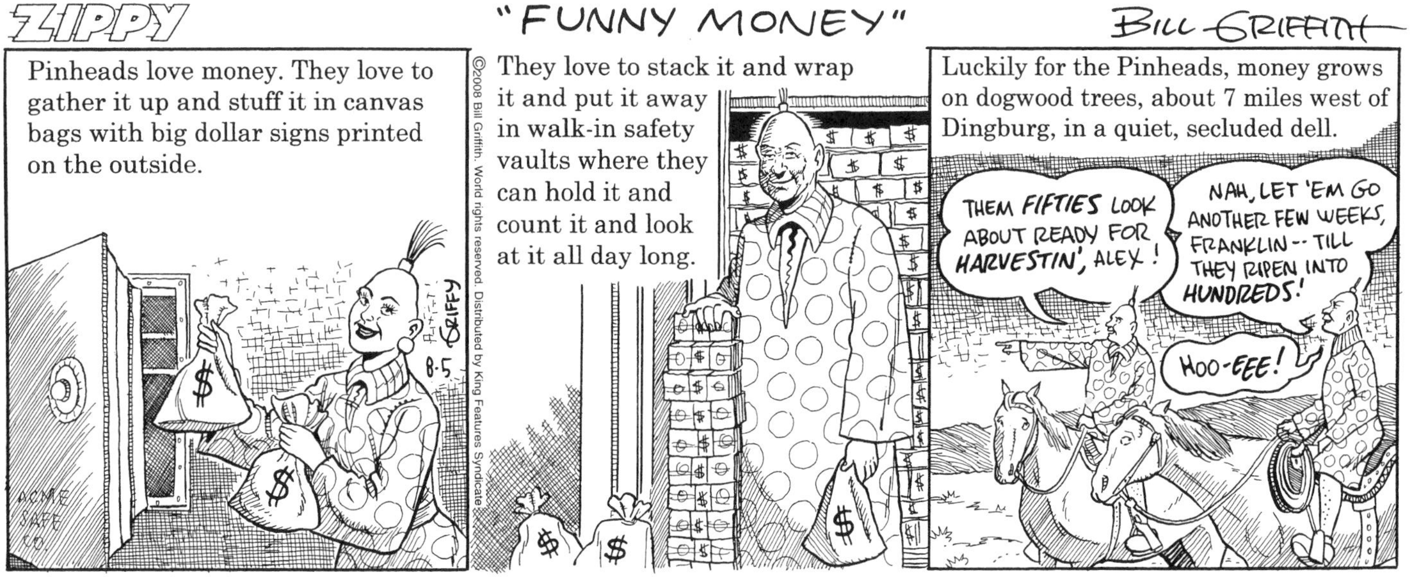
ZIPPY
"FUNNY MONEY"
BILL GRIFFITH
Pinheads love money. They love to gather it up and stuff it in canvas bags with big dollar signs printed on the outside.
ACME SAFE CO.
GRIFFY 8·5
©2008 Bill Griffith. World rights reserved. Distributed by King Features Syndicate
They love to stack it and wrap it and put it away in walk-in safety vaults where they can hold it and count it and look at it all day long.
Luckily for the Pinheads, money grows on dogwood trees, about 7 miles west of Dingburg, in a quiet, secluded dell.
THEM FIFTIES LOOK ABOUT READY FOR HARVESTIN', ALEX!
NAH, LET 'EM GO ANOTHER FEW WEEKS, FRANKLIN -- TILL THEY RIPEN INTO HUNDREDS!
HOO-EEE!

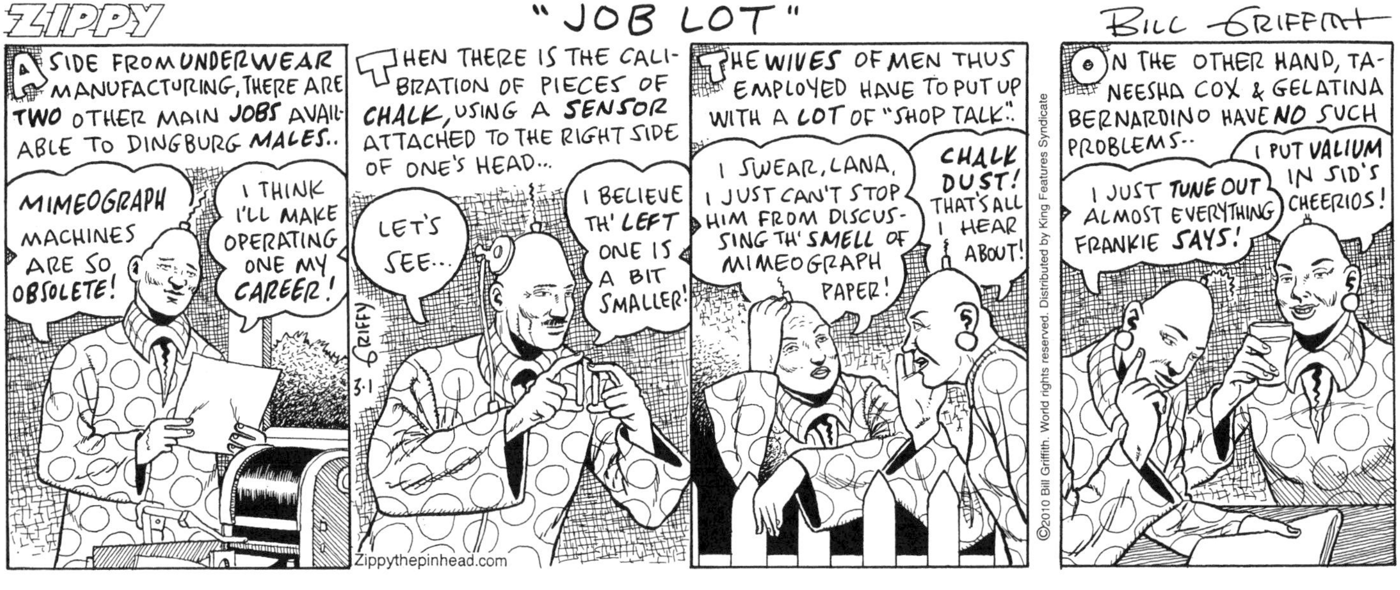
ZIPPY
"JOB LOT"
BILL GRIFFITH
ASIDE FROM UNDERWEAR MANUFACTURING, THERE ARE TWO OTHER MAIN JOBS AVAILABLE TO DINGBURG MALES..
MIMEOGRAPH MACHINES ARE SO OBSOLETE!
I THINK I'LL MAKE OPERATING ONE MY CAREER!
THEN THERE IS THE CALIBRATION OF PIECES OF CHALK, USING A SENSOR ATTACHED TO THE RIGHT SIDE OF ONE'S HEAD...
LET'S SEE...
I BELIEVE TH' LEFT ONE IS A BIT SMALLER!
GRIFFY 3·1
Zippythepinhead.com
THE WIVES OF MEN THUS EMPLOYED HAVE TO PUT UP WITH A LOT OF "SHOP TALK".
I SWEAR, LANA, I JUST CAN'T STOP HIM FROM DISCUSSING TH' SMELL OF MIMEOGRAPH PAPER!
CHALK DUST! THAT'S ALL I HEAR ABOUT!
©2010 Bill Griffith. World rights reserved. Distributed by King Features Syndicate
ON THE OTHER HAND, TANEESHA COX & GELATINA BERNARDINO HAVE NO SUCH PROBLEMS..
I JUST TUNE OUT ALMOST EVERYTHING FRANKIE SAYS!
I PUT VALIUM IN SID'S CHEERIOS!

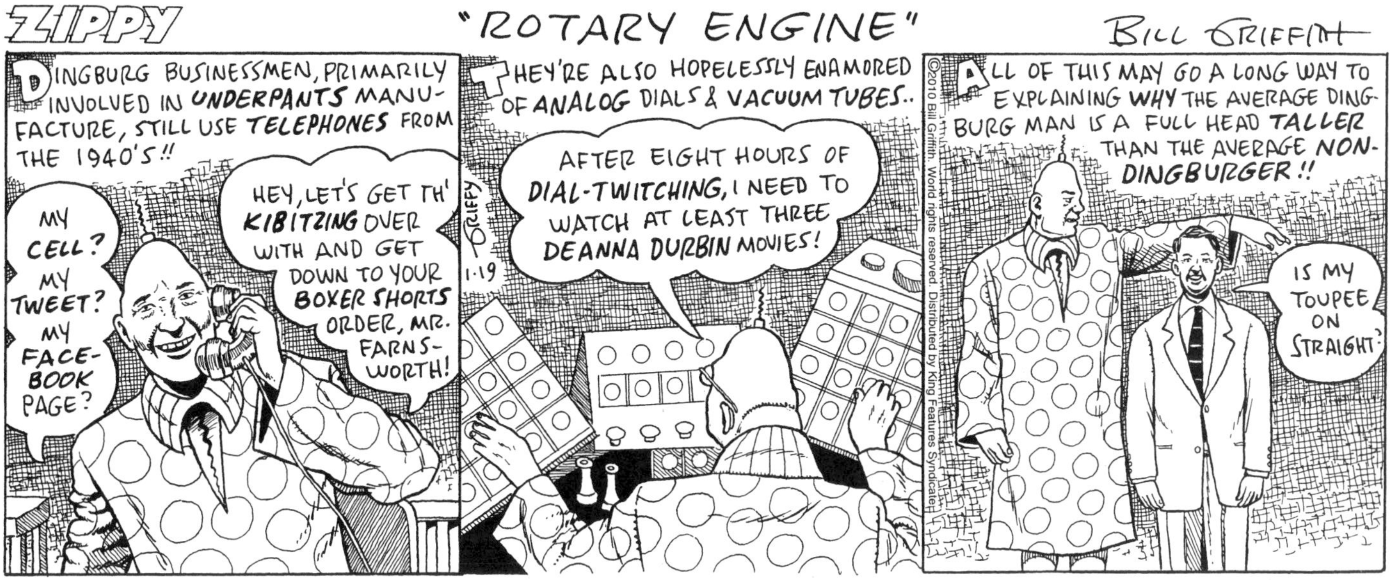
ZIPPY
"ROTARY ENGINE"
BILL GRIFFITH
DINGBURG BUSINESSMEN, PRIMARILY INVOLVED IN UNDERPANTS MANUFACTURE, STILL USE TELEPHONES FROM THE 1940'S!!
MY CELL? MY TWEET? MY FACEBOOK PAGE?
HEY, LET'S GET TH' KIBITZING OVER WITH AND GET DOWN TO YOUR BOXER SHORTS ORDER, MR. FARNSWORTH!
GRIFFY 1-19
THEY'RE ALSO HOPELESSLY ENAMORED OF ANALOG DIALS & VACUUM TUBES..
AFTER EIGHT HOURS OF DIAL-TWITCHING, I NEED TO WATCH AT LEAST THREE DEANNA DURBIN MOVIES!
©2010 Bill Griffith. World rights reserved. Distributed by King Features Syndicate
ALL OF THIS MAY GO A LONG WAY TO EXPLAINING WHY THE AVERAGE DINGBURG MAN IS A FULL HEAD TALLER THAN THE AVERAGE NON-DINGBURGER!!
IS MY TOUPEE ON STRAIGHT?

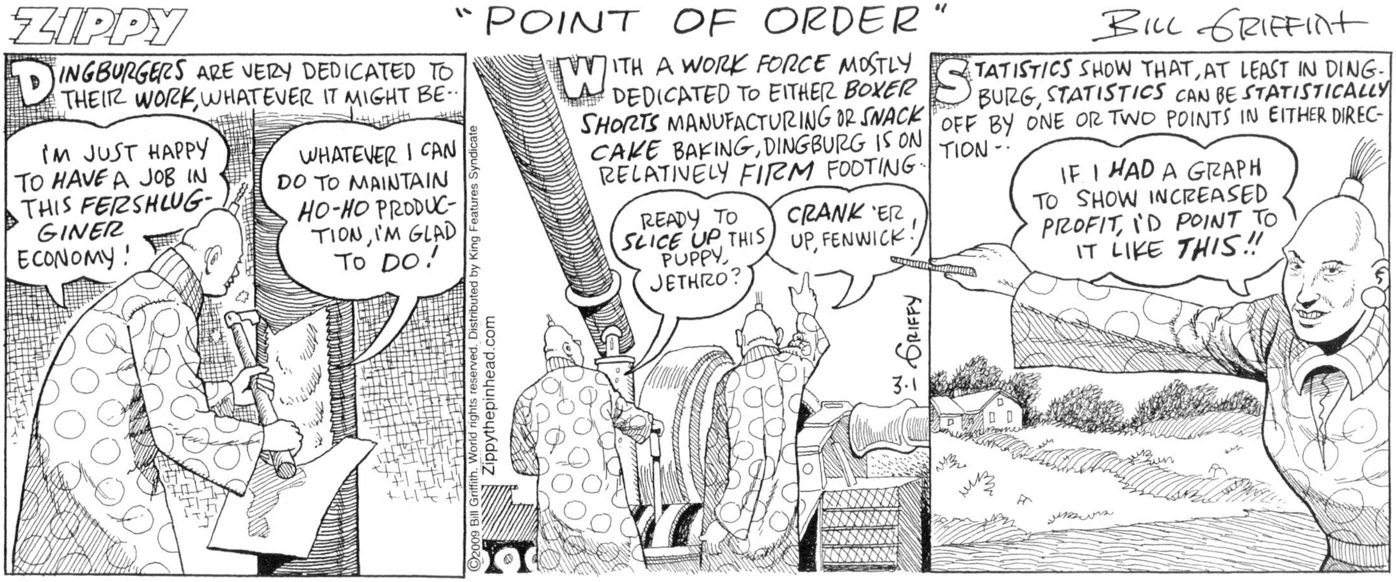
ZIPPY
"POINT OF ORDER"
BILL GRIFFITH
DINGBURGERS ARE VERY DEDICATED TO THEIR WORK, WHATEVER IT MIGHT BE..
I'M JUST HAPPY TO HAVE A JOB IN THIS FERSHLUGGINER ECONOMY!
WHATEVER I CAN DO TO MAINTAIN HO-HO PRODUCTION, I'M GLAD TO DO!
©2009 Bill Griffith. World rights reserved. Distributed by King Features Syndicate
Zippythepinhead.com
WITH A WORK FORCE MOSTLY DEDICATED TO EITHER BOXER SHORTS MANUFACTURING OR SNACK CAKE BAKING, DINGBURG IS ON RELATIVELY FIRM FOOTING..
READY TO SLICE UP THIS PUPPY, JETHRO?
CRANK 'ER UP, FENWICK!
GRIFFY 3-1
STATISTICS SHOW THAT, AT LEAST IN DINGBURG, STATISTICS CAN BE STATISTICALLY OFF BY ONE OR TWO POINTS IN EITHER DIRECTION..
IF I HAD A GRAPH TO SHOW INCREASED PROFIT, I'D POINT TO IT LIKE THIS!!

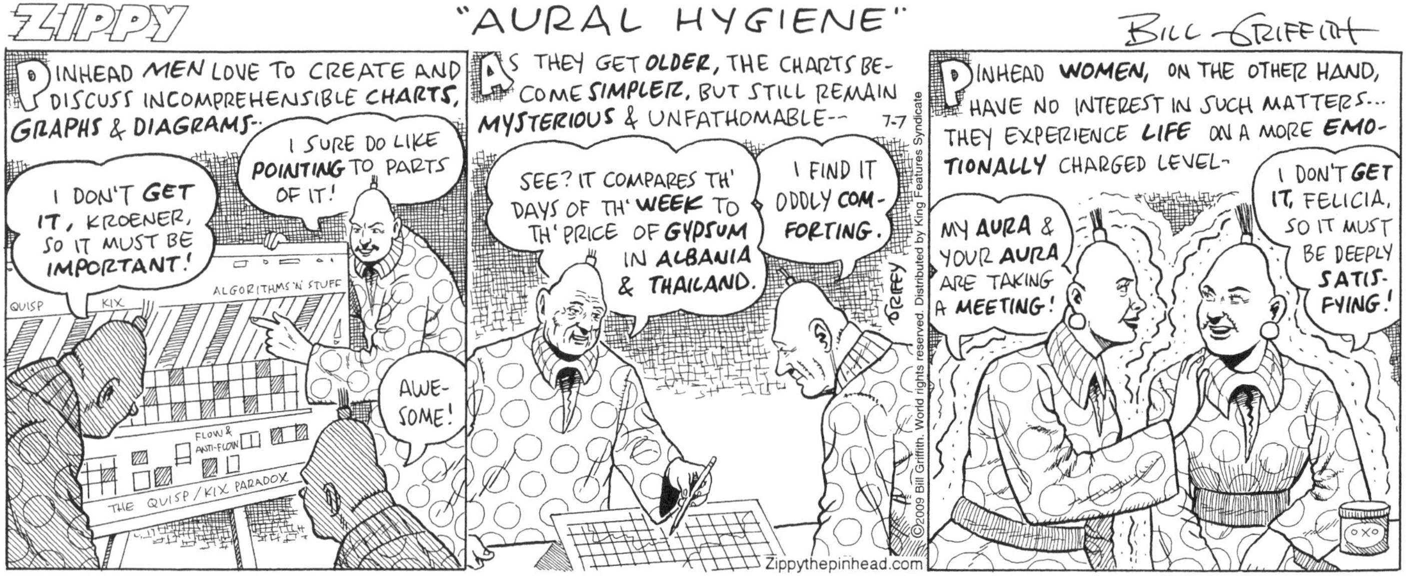
ZIPPY
"AURAL HYGIENE"
BILL GRIFFITH
PINHEAD MEN LOVE TO CREATE AND DISCUSS INCOMPREHENSIBLE CHARTS, GRAPHS & DIAGRAMS--
I SURE DO LIKE POINTING TO PARTS OF IT!
I DON'T GET IT, KROENER, SO IT MUST BE IMPORTANT!
ALGORITHMS 'N' STUFF
QUISP
KIX
FLOW & ANTI-FLOW
THE QUISP / KIX PARADOX
AWE-SOME!
AS THEY GET OLDER, THE CHARTS BECOME SIMPLER, BUT STILL REMAIN MYSTERIOUS & UNFATHOMABLE--
7-7
SEE? IT COMPARES TH' DAYS OF TH' WEEK TO TH' PRICE OF GYPSUM IN ALBANIA & THAILAND.
I FIND IT ODDLY COMFORTING.
GRIFFY
©2009 Bill Griffith. World rights reserved. Distributed by King Features Syndicate
Zippythepinhead.com
PINHEAD WOMEN, ON THE OTHER HAND, HAVE NO INTEREST IN SUCH MATTERS... THEY EXPERIENCE LIFE ON A MORE EMOTIONALLY CHARGED LEVEL-
MY AURA & YOUR AURA ARE TAKING A MEETING!
I DON'T GET IT, FELICIA, SO IT MUST BE DEEPLY SATISFYING!
OXO

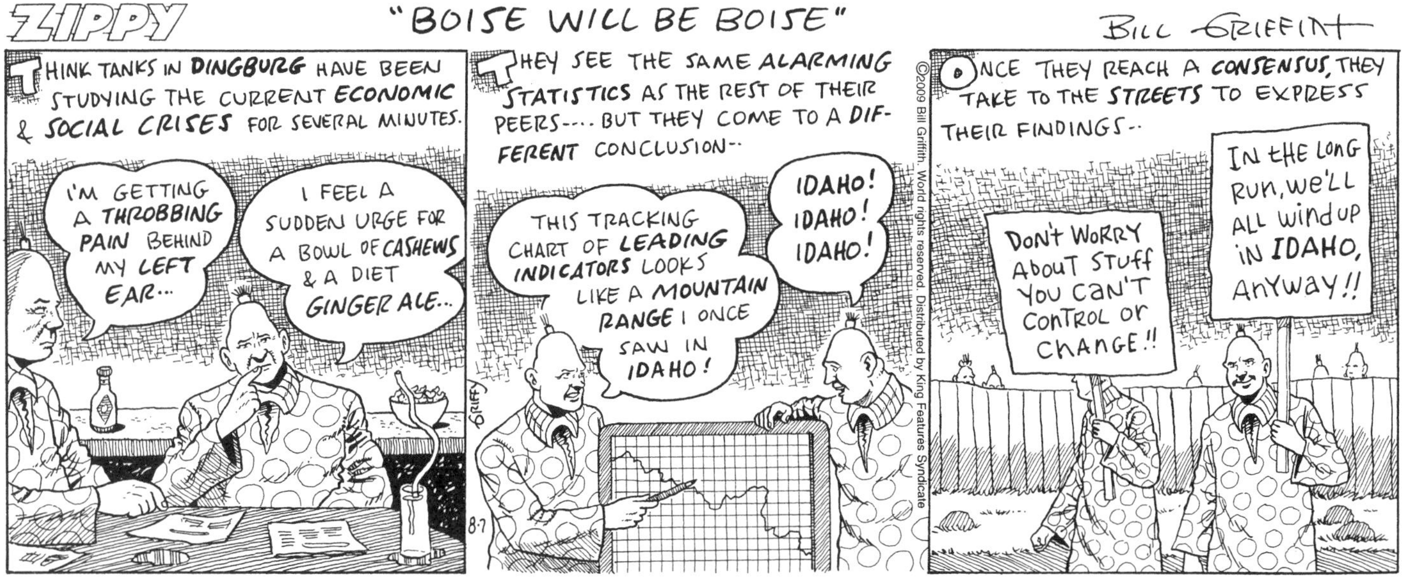
ZIPPY
"BOISE WILL BE BOISE"
BILL GRIFFITH
THINK TANKS IN DINGBURG HAVE BEEN STUDYING THE CURRENT ECONOMIC & SOCIAL CRISES FOR SEVERAL MINUTES.
I'M GETTING A THROBBING PAIN BEHIND MY LEFT EAR...
I FEEL A SUDDEN URGE FOR A BOWL OF CASHEWS & A DIET GINGER ALE...
GRIFFY
THEY SEE THE SAME ALARMING STATISTICS AS THE REST OF THEIR PEERS---. BUT THEY COME TO A DIFFERENT CONCLUSION--
THIS TRACKING CHART OF LEADING INDICATORS LOOKS LIKE A MOUNTAIN RANGE I ONCE SAW IN IDAHO!
IDAHO! IDAHO! IDAHO!
8-7
©2009 Bill Griffith. World rights reserved. Distributed by King Features Syndicate
ONCE THEY REACH A CONSENSUS, THEY TAKE TO THE STREETS TO EXPRESS THEIR FINDINGS--
DON'T WORRY ABOUT STUFF YOU CAN'T CONTROL OR CHANGE!!
IN THE LONG RUN, WE'LL ALL WIND UP IN IDAHO, ANYWAY!!

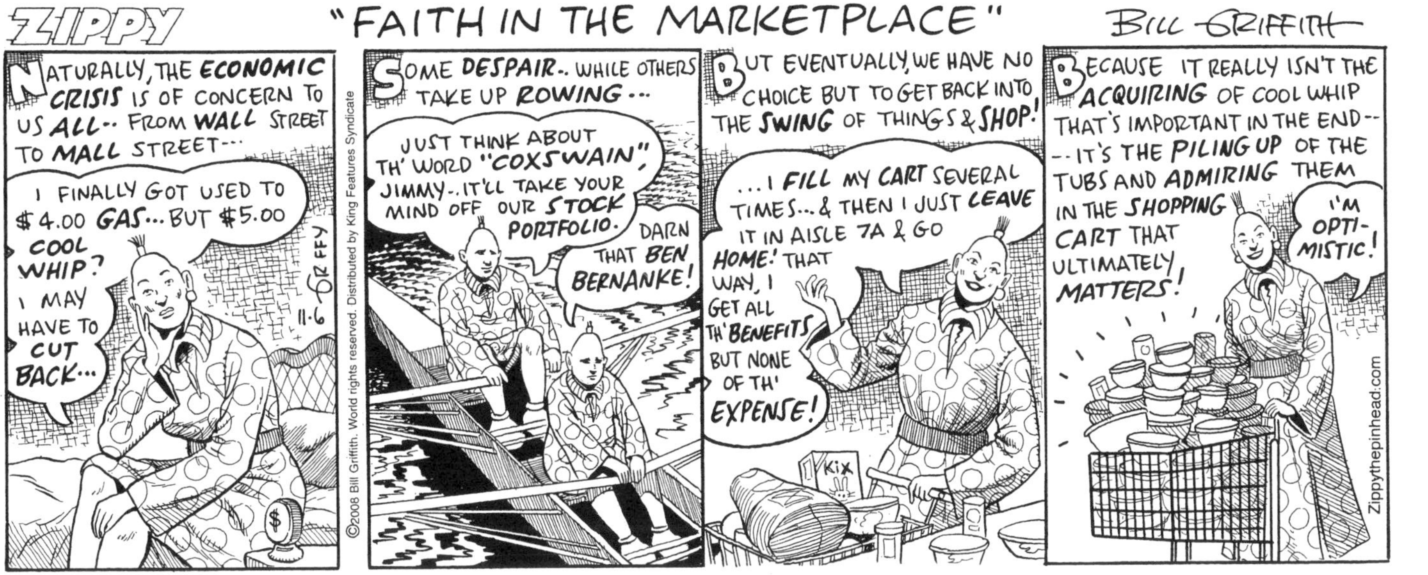
ZIPPY
"FAITH IN THE MARKETPLACE"
BILL GRIFFITH
NATURALLY, THE ECONOMIC CRISIS IS OF CONCERN TO US ALL-- FROM WALL STREET TO MALL STREET---
I FINALLY GOT USED TO $4.00 GAS... BUT $5.00 COOL WHIP? I MAY HAVE TO CUT BACK...
GRIFFY 11-6
SOME DESPAIR-- WHILE OTHERS TAKE UP ROWING---
JUST THINK ABOUT TH' WORD "COXSWAIN", JIMMY-- IT'LL TAKE YOUR MIND OFF OUR STOCK PORTFOLIO.
DARN THAT BEN BERNANKE!
©2008 Bill Griffith. World rights reserved. Distributed by King Features Syndicate
BUT EVENTUALLY, WE HAVE NO CHOICE BUT TO GET BACK INTO THE SWING OF THINGS & SHOP!
...I FILL MY CART SEVERAL TIMES...& THEN I JUST LEAVE IT IN AISLE 7A & GO HOME! THAT WAY, I GET ALL TH' BENEFITS BUT NONE OF TH' EXPENSE!
KIX
BECAUSE IT REALLY ISN'T THE ACQUIRING OF COOL WHIP THAT'S IMPORTANT IN THE END-- --IT'S THE PILING UP OF THE TUBS AND ADMIRING THEM IN THE SHOPPING CART THAT ULTIMATELY MATTERS!
I'M OPTI-MISTIC!
Zippythepinhead.com

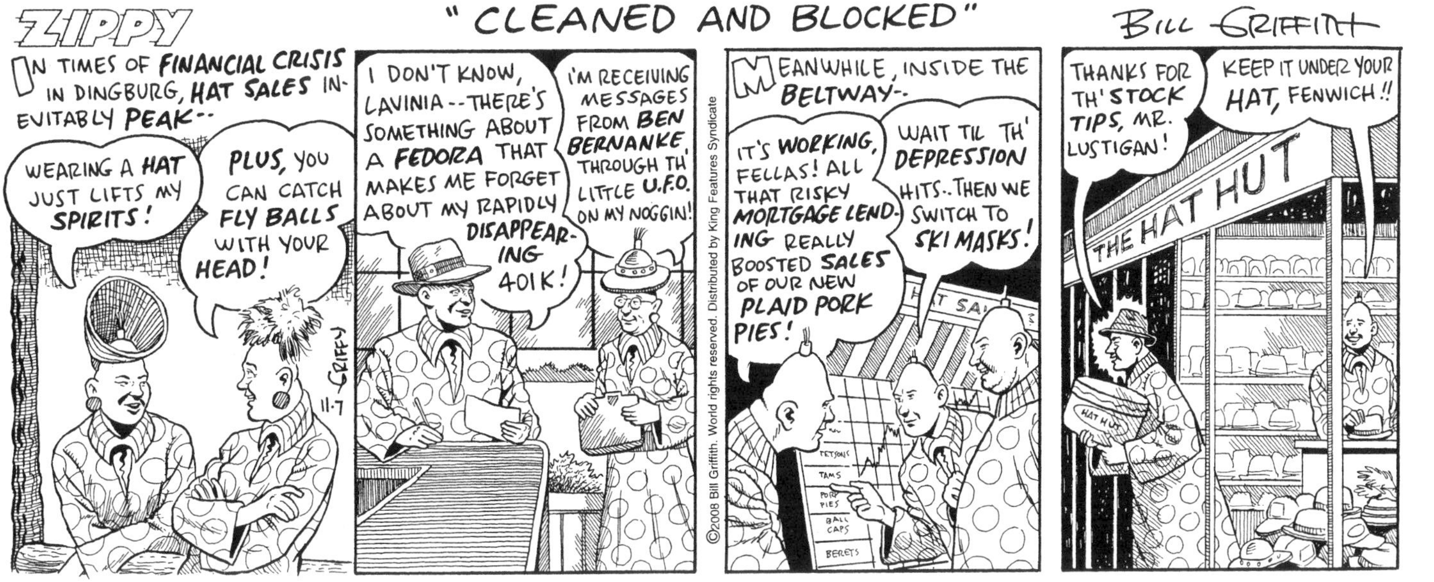
ZIPPY
"CLEANED AND BLOCKED"
BILL GRIFFITH
IN TIMES OF FINANCIAL CRISIS IN DINGBURG, HAT SALES INEVITABLY PEAK--
WEARING A HAT JUST LIFTS MY SPIRITS!
PLUS, YOU CAN CATCH FLY BALLS WITH YOUR HEAD!
GRIFFY 11-7
I DON'T KNOW, LAVINIA--THERE'S SOMETHING ABOUT A FEDORA THAT MAKES ME FORGET ABOUT MY RAPIDLY DISAPPEARING 401K!
I'M RECEIVING MESSAGES FROM BEN BERNANKE THROUGH TH' LITTLE U.F.O. ON MY NOGGIN!
©2008 Bill Griffith. World rights reserved. Distributed by King Features Syndicate
MEANWHILE, INSIDE THE BELTWAY--
IT'S WORKING, FELLAS! ALL THAT RISKY MORTGAGE LENDING REALLY BOOSTED SALES OF OUR NEW PLAID PORK PIES!
WAIT TIL TH' DEPRESSION HITS.. THEN WE SWITCH TO SKI MASKS!
STETSONS
TAMS
PORK PIES
BALL CAPS
BERETS
THANKS FOR TH' STOCK TIPS, MR. LUSTIGAN!
KEEP IT UNDER YOUR HAT, FENWICH!!
THE HAT HUT
HAT HUT

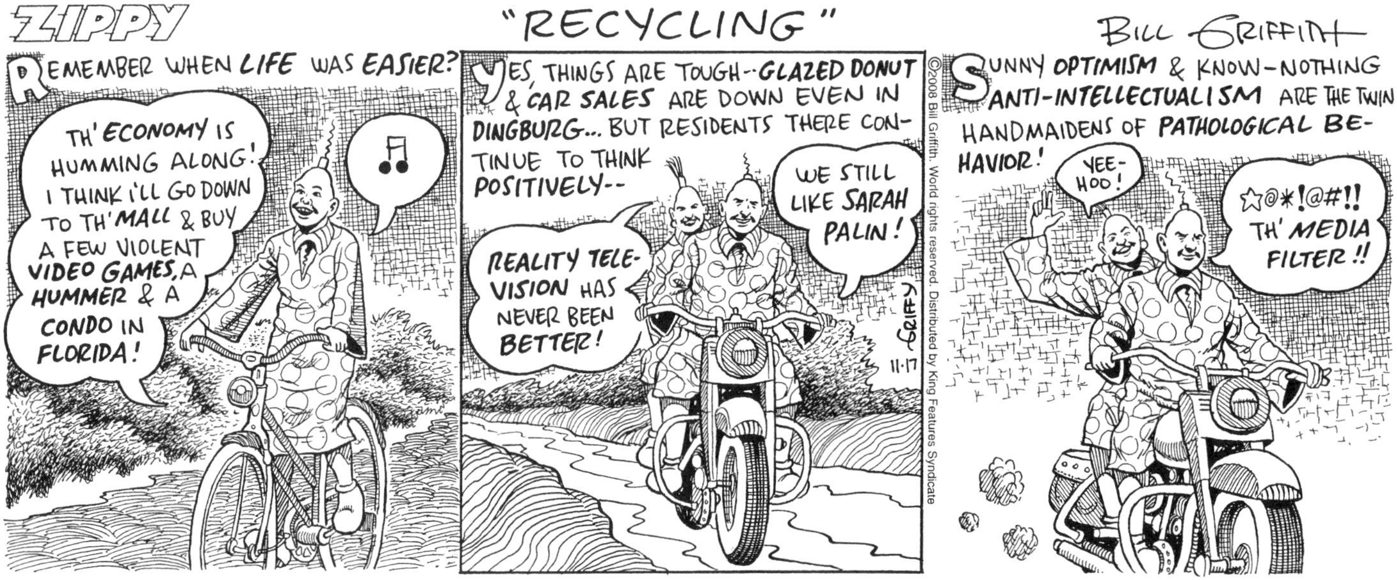
ZIPPY
"RECYCLING"
BILL GRIFFITH
REMEMBER WHEN LIFE WAS EASIER?
TH' ECONOMY IS HUMMING ALONG! I THINK I'LL GO DOWN TO TH' MALL & BUY A FEW VIOLENT VIDEO GAMES, A HUMMER & A CONDO IN FLORIDA!
YES, THINGS ARE TOUGH--GLAZED DONUT & CAR SALES ARE DOWN EVEN IN DINGBURG... BUT RESIDENTS THERE CONTINUE TO THINK POSITIVELY--
REALITY TELEVISION HAS NEVER BEEN BETTER!
WE STILL LIKE SARAH PALIN!
GRIFFY
11·17
©2008 Bill Griffith. World rights reserved. Distributed by King Features Syndicate
SUNNY OPTIMISM & KNOW-NOTHING ANTI-INTELLECTUALISM ARE THE TWIN HANDMAIDENS OF PATHOLOGICAL BEHAVIOR!
YEE-HOO!
☆@*!@#!! TH' MEDIA FILTER!!

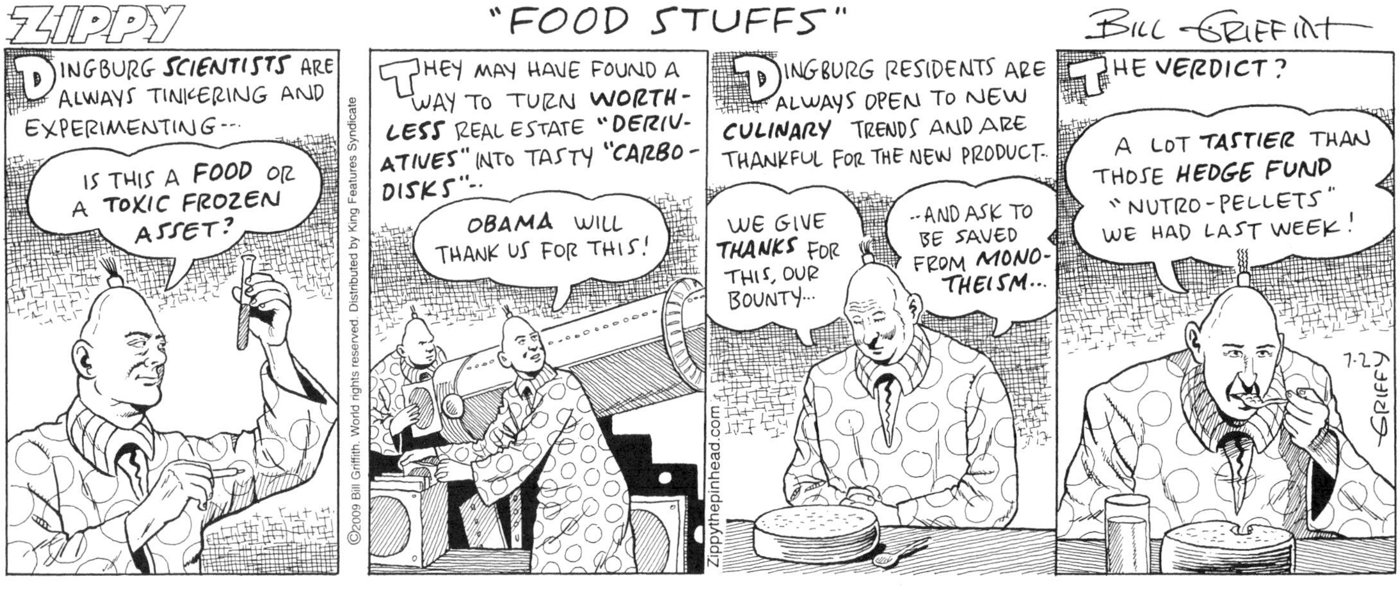
ZIPPY
"FOOD STUFFS"
BILL GRIFFITH
DINGBURG SCIENTISTS ARE ALWAYS TINKERING AND EXPERIMENTING--
IS THIS A FOOD OR A TOXIC FROZEN ASSET?
©2009 Bill Griffith. World rights reserved. Distributed by King Features Syndicate
THEY MAY HAVE FOUND A WAY TO TURN WORTHLESS REAL ESTATE "DERIVATIVES" INTO TASTY "CARBO-DISKS"--
OBAMA WILL THANK US FOR THIS!
Zippythepinhead.com
DINGBURG RESIDENTS ARE ALWAYS OPEN TO NEW CULINARY TRENDS AND ARE THANKFUL FOR THE NEW PRODUCT..
WE GIVE THANKS FOR THIS, OUR BOUNTY...
--AND ASK TO BE SAVED FROM MONOTHEISM...
THE VERDICT?
A LOT TASTIER THAN THOSE HEDGE FUND "NUTRO-PELLETS" WE HAD LAST WEEK!
7·2
GRIFFY

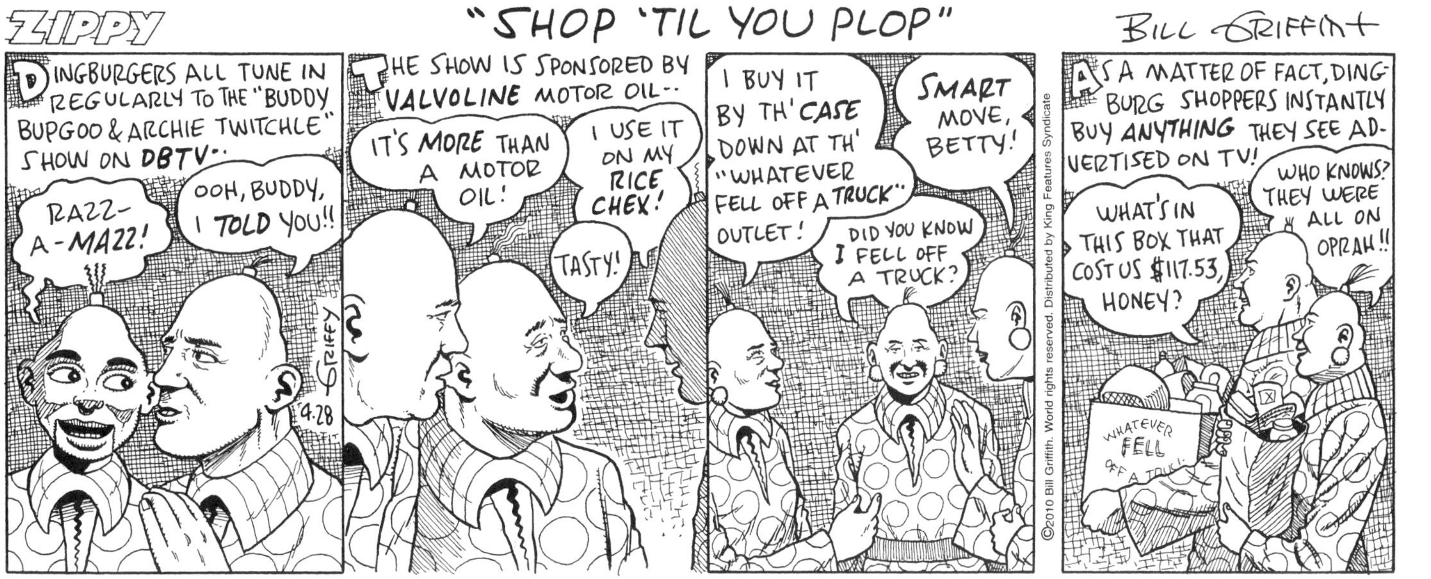
ZIPPY
"SHOP 'TIL YOU PLOP"
BILL GRIFFITH
DINGBURGERS ALL TUNE IN REGULARLY TO THE "BUDDY BUPGOO & ARCHIE TWITCHLE" SHOW ON DBTV..
RAZZ-A-MAZZ!
OOH, BUDDY, I TOLD YOU!!
GRIFFY 4·28
THE SHOW IS SPONSORED BY VALVOLINE MOTOR OIL..
IT'S MORE THAN A MOTOR OIL!
I USE IT ON MY RICE CHEX!
TASTY!
I BUY IT BY TH' CASE DOWN AT TH' "WHATEVER FELL OFF A TRUCK" OUTLET!
SMART MOVE, BETTY!
DID YOU KNOW I FELL OFF A TRUCK?
©2010 Bill Griffith. World rights reserved. Distributed by King Features Syndicate
AS A MATTER OF FACT, DINGBURG SHOPPERS INSTANTLY BUY ANYTHING THEY SEE ADVERTISED ON TV!
WHAT'S IN THIS BOX THAT COST US $117.53, HONEY?
WHO KNOWS? THEY WERE ALL ON OPRAH!!
WHATEVER FELL OFF A TRUCK

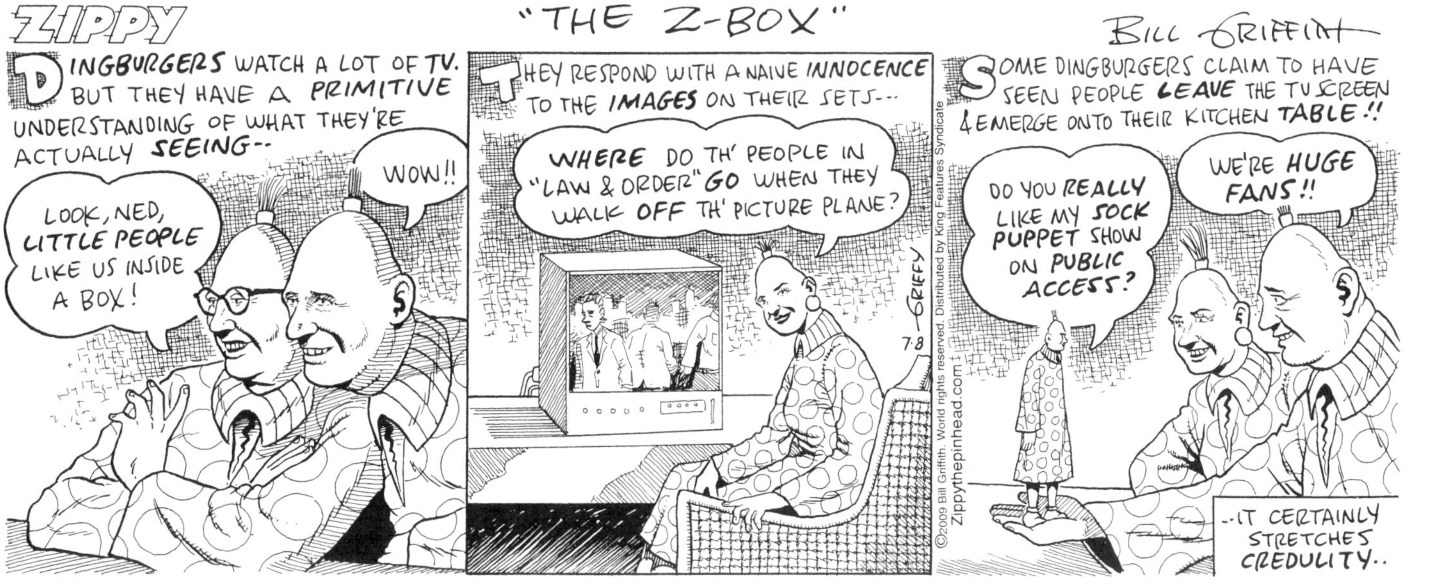
ZIPPY
"THE Z-BOX"
BILL GRIFFITH
DINGBURGERS WATCH A LOT OF TV. BUT THEY HAVE A PRIMITIVE UNDERSTANDING OF WHAT THEY'RE ACTUALLY SEEING..
LOOK, NED, LITTLE PEOPLE LIKE US INSIDE A BOX!
WOW!!
THEY RESPOND WITH A NAIVE INNOCENCE TO THE IMAGES ON THEIR SETS--
WHERE DO TH' PEOPLE IN "LAW & ORDER" GO WHEN THEY WALK OFF TH' PICTURE PLANE?
GRIFFY 7·8
©2009 Bill Griffith. World rights reserved. Distributed by King Features Syndicate
Zippythepinhead.com
SOME DINGBURGERS CLAIM TO HAVE SEEN PEOPLE LEAVE THE TV SCREEN & EMERGE ONTO THEIR KITCHEN TABLE!!
DO YOU REALLY LIKE MY SOCK PUPPET SHOW ON PUBLIC ACCESS?
WE'RE HUGE FANS!!
..IT CERTAINLY STRETCHES CREDULITY..

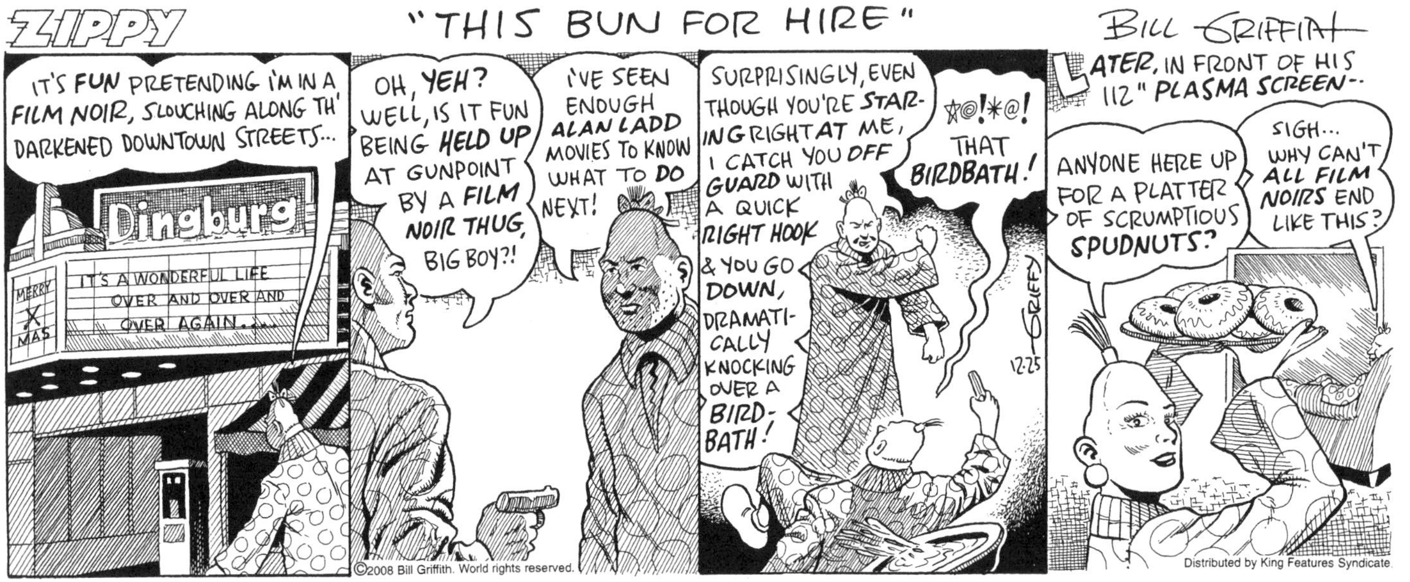
ZIPPY
"THIS BUN FOR HIRE"
BILL GRIFFITH
IT'S FUN PRETENDING I'M IN A FILM NOIR, SLOUCHING ALONG TH' DARKENED DOWNTOWN STREETS...
Dingburg
MERRY X MAS
IT'S A WONDERFUL LIFE OVER AND OVER AND OVER AGAIN.....
OH, YEH? WELL, IS IT FUN BEING HELD UP AT GUNPOINT BY A FILM NOIR THUG, BIG BOY?!
I'VE SEEN ENOUGH ALAN LADD MOVIES TO KNOW WHAT TO DO NEXT!
©2008 Bill Griffith. World rights reserved.
SURPRISINGLY, EVEN THOUGH YOU'RE STARING RIGHT AT ME, I CATCH YOU OFF GUARD WITH A QUICK RIGHT HOOK & YOU GO DOWN, DRAMATICALLY KNOCKING OVER A BIRDBATH!
☆@!*@! THAT BIRDBATH!
GRIFFY
12·25
LATER, IN FRONT OF HIS 112" PLASMA SCREEN--
ANYONE HERE UP FOR A PLATTER OF SCRUMPTIOUS SPUDNUTS?
SIGH... WHY CAN'T ALL FILM NOIRS END LIKE THIS?
Distributed by King Features Syndicate.

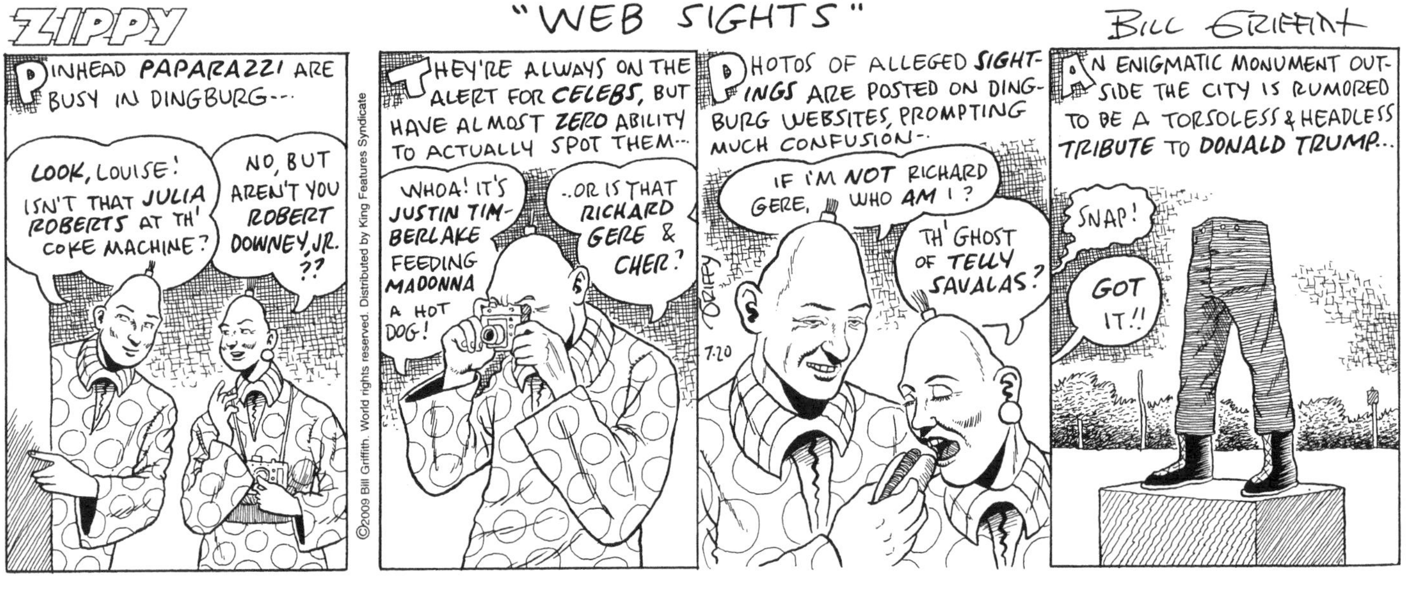
ZIPPY
"WEB SIGHTS"
BILL GRIFFITH
PINHEAD PAPARAZZI ARE BUSY IN DINGBURG---
LOOK, LOUISE! ISN'T THAT JULIA ROBERTS AT TH' COKE MACHINE?
NO, BUT AREN'T YOU ROBERT DOWNEY, JR.??
©2009 Bill Griffith. World rights reserved. Distributed by King Features Syndicate
THEY'RE ALWAYS ON THE ALERT FOR CELEBS, BUT HAVE ALMOST ZERO ABILITY TO ACTUALLY SPOT THEM--
WHOA! IT'S JUSTIN TIMBERLAKE FEEDING MADONNA A HOT DOG!
..OR IS THAT RICHARD GERE & CHER?
PHOTOS OF ALLEGED SIGHTINGS ARE POSTED ON DINGBURG WEBSITES, PROMPTING MUCH CONFUSION-.
IF I'M NOT RICHARD GERE, WHO AM I?
TH' GHOST OF TELLY SAVALAS?
GRIFFY
7·20
AN ENIGMATIC MONUMENT OUTSIDE THE CITY IS RUMORED TO BE A TORSOLESS & HEADLESS TRIBUTE TO DONALD TRUMP...
SNAP!
GOT IT!!

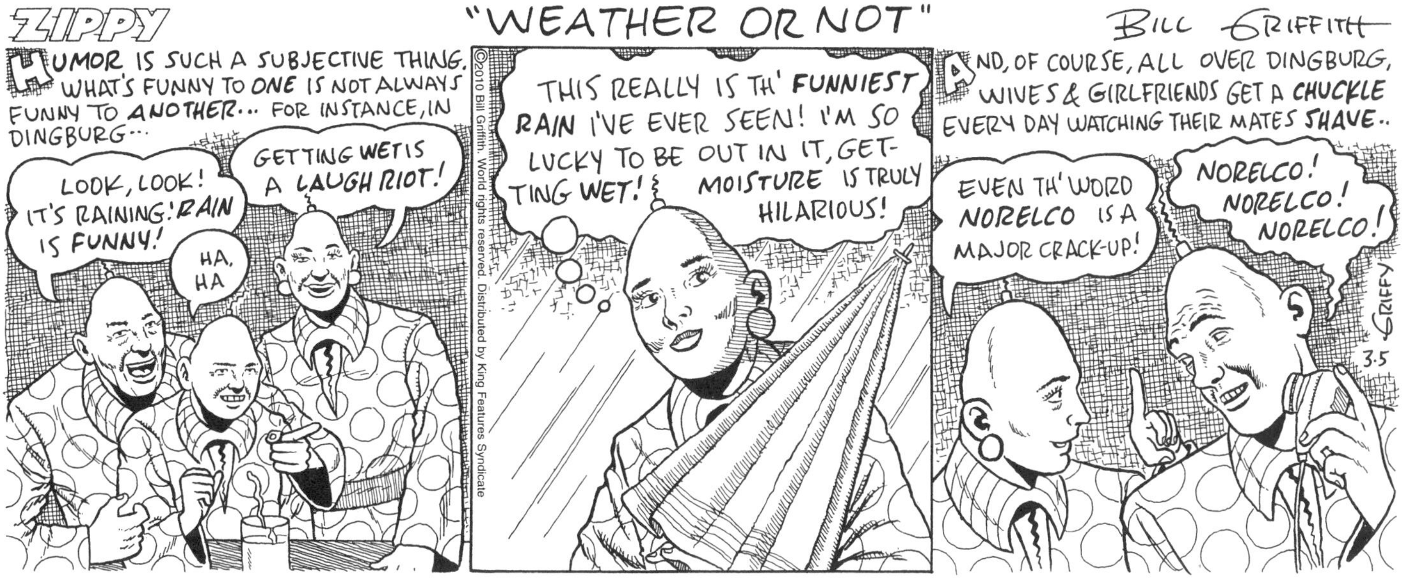
ZIPPY
"WEATHER OR NOT"
BILL GRIFFITH
HUMOR IS SUCH A SUBJECTIVE THING. WHAT'S FUNNY TO ONE IS NOT ALWAYS FUNNY TO ANOTHER... FOR INSTANCE, IN DINGBURG...
LOOK, LOOK! IT'S RAINING! RAIN IS FUNNY!
HA, HA
GETTING WET IS A LAUGH RIOT!
©2010 Bill Griffith. World rights reserved. Distributed by King Features Syndicate
THIS REALLY IS TH' FUNNIEST RAIN I'VE EVER SEEN! I'M SO LUCKY TO BE OUT IN IT, GETTING WET! MOISTURE IS TRULY HILARIOUS!
AND, OF COURSE, ALL OVER DINGBURG, WIVES & GIRLFRIENDS GET A CHUCKLE EVERY DAY WATCHING THEIR MATES SHAVE..
EVEN TH' WORD NORELCO IS A MAJOR CRACK-UP!
NORELCO! NORELCO! NORELCO!
GRIFFY
3.5

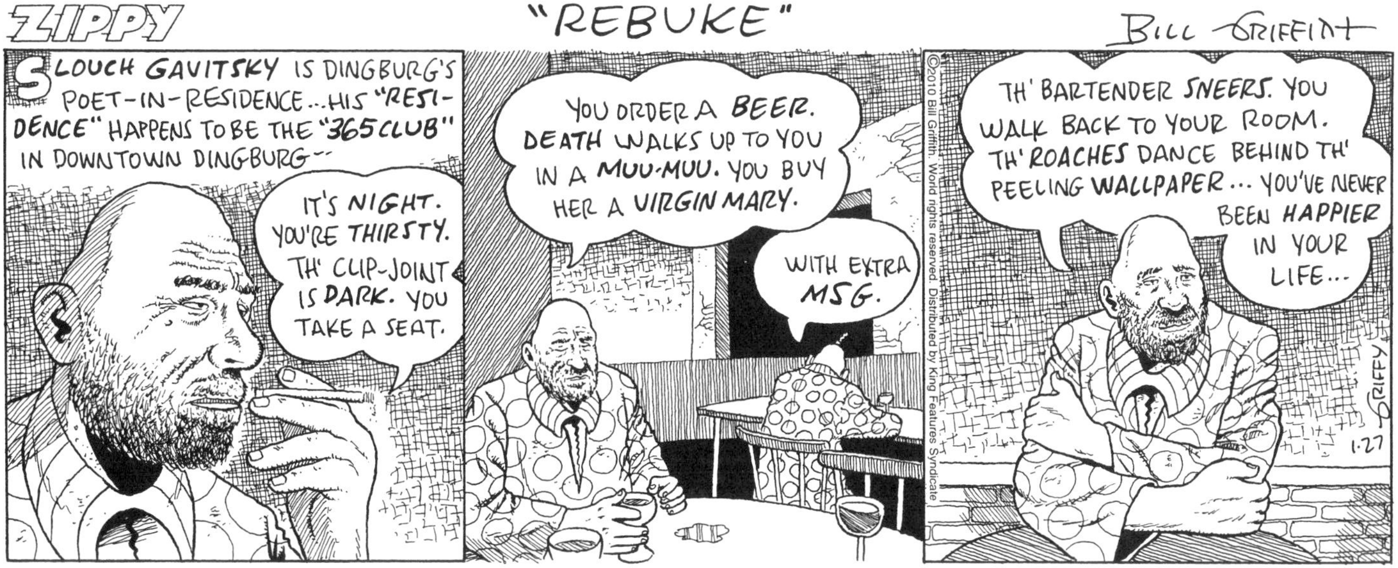
ZIPPY
"REBUKE"
BILL GRIFFITH
SLOUCH GAVITSKY IS DINGBURG'S POET-IN-RESIDENCE...HIS "RESIDENCE" HAPPENS TO BE THE "365 CLUB" IN DOWNTOWN DINGBURG--
IT'S NIGHT. YOU'RE THIRSTY. TH' CLIP-JOINT IS DARK. YOU TAKE A SEAT.
©2010 Bill Griffith. World rights reserved. Distributed by King Features Syndicate
YOU ORDER A BEER. DEATH WALKS UP TO YOU IN A MUU-MUU. YOU BUY HER A VIRGIN MARY.
WITH EXTRA MSG.
TH' BARTENDER SNEERS. YOU WALK BACK TO YOUR ROOM. TH' ROACHES DANCE BEHIND TH' PEELING WALLPAPER... YOU'VE NEVER BEEN HAPPIER IN YOUR LIFE...
GRIFFY
1.27

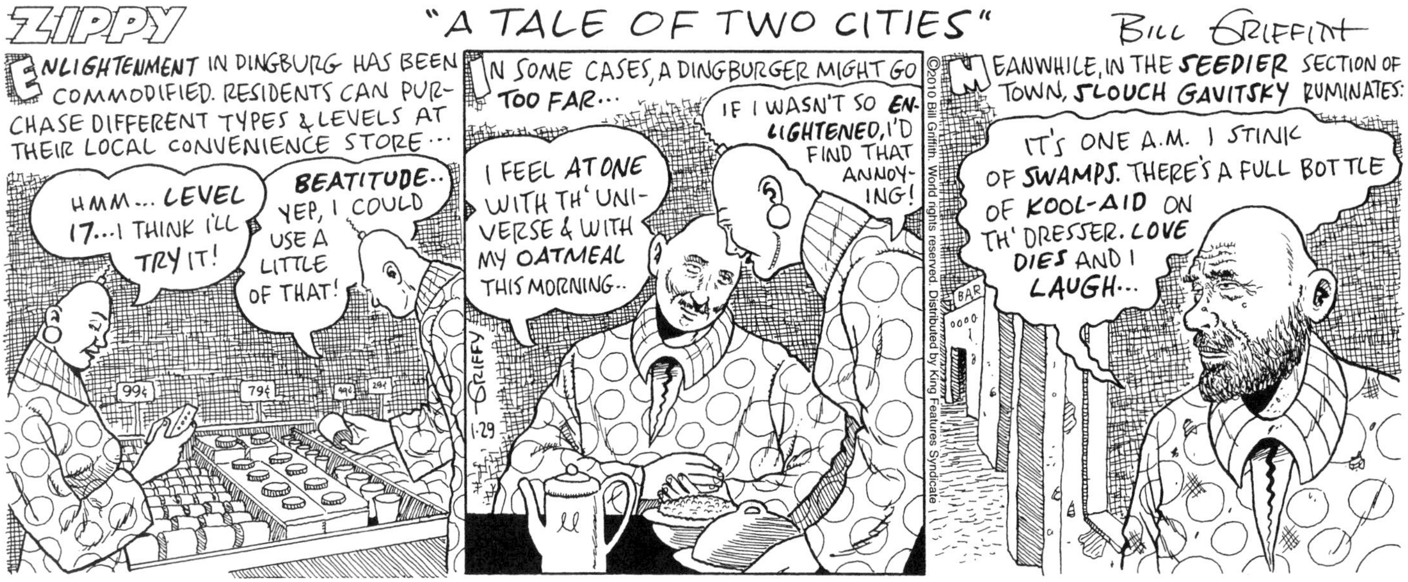
ZIPPY
"A TALE OF TWO CITIES"
BILL GRIFFITH
ENLIGHTENMENT IN DINGBURG HAS BEEN COMMODIFIED. RESIDENTS CAN PURCHASE DIFFERENT TYPES & LEVELS AT THEIR LOCAL CONVENIENCE STORE...
HMM... LEVEL 17... I THINK I'LL TRY IT!
BEATITUDE.. YEP, I COULD USE A LITTLE OF THAT!
99¢
79¢
49¢
29¢
IN SOME CASES, A DINGBURGER MIGHT GO TOO FAR...
I FEEL AT ONE WITH TH' UNIVERSE & WITH MY OATMEAL THIS MORNING..
IF I WASN'T SO ENLIGHTENED, I'D FIND THAT ANNOYING!
GRIFFY 1·29
©2010 Bill Griffith. World rights reserved. Distributed by King Features Syndicate
MEANWHILE, IN THE SEEDIER SECTION OF TOWN, SLOUCH GAVITSKY RUMINATES:
IT'S ONE A.M. I STINK OF SWAMPS. THERE'S A FULL BOTTLE OF KOOL-AID ON TH' DRESSER. LOVE DIES AND I LAUGH...
BAR

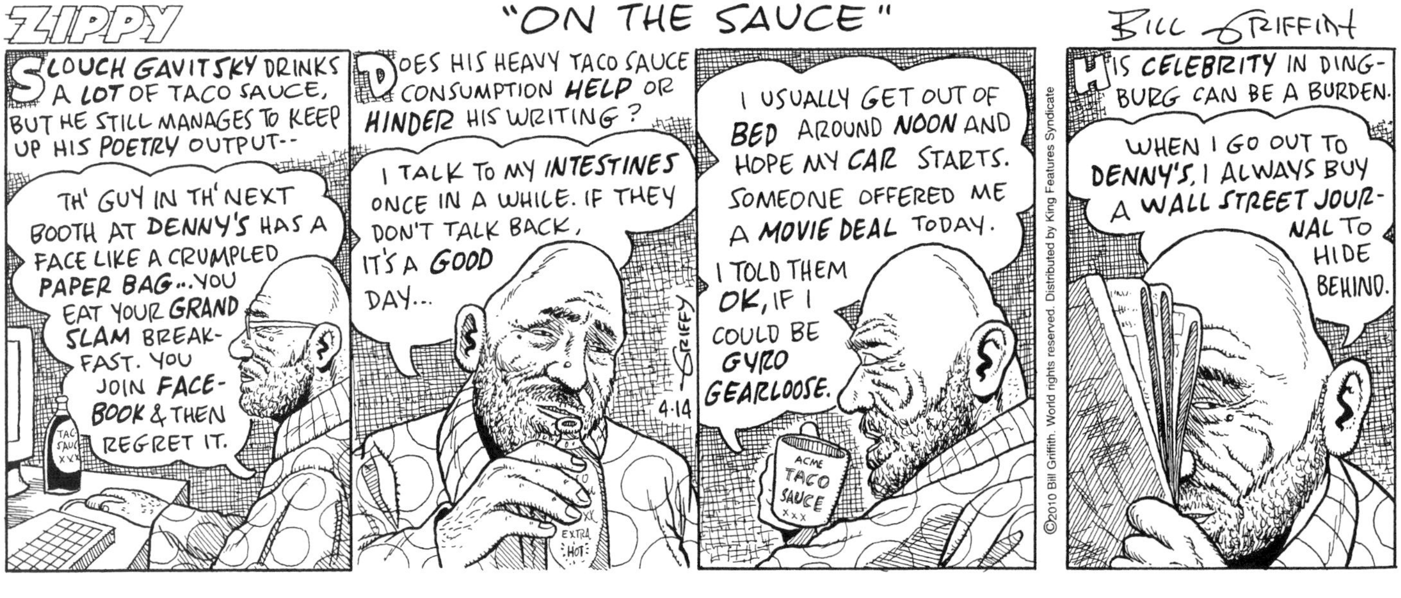
ZIPPY
"ON THE SAUCE"
BILL GRIFFITH
SLOUCH GAVITSKY DRINKS A LOT OF TACO SAUCE, BUT HE STILL MANAGES TO KEEP UP HIS POETRY OUTPUT--
TH' GUY IN TH' NEXT BOOTH AT DENNY'S HAS A FACE LIKE A CRUMPLED PAPER BAG.. YOU EAT YOUR GRAND SLAM BREAKFAST. YOU JOIN FACEBOOK & THEN REGRET IT.
DOES HIS HEAVY TACO SAUCE CONSUMPTION HELP OR HINDER HIS WRITING?
I TALK TO MY INTESTINES ONCE IN A WHILE. IF THEY DON'T TALK BACK, IT'S A GOOD DAY...
EXTRA HOT
GRIFFY 4·14
I USUALLY GET OUT OF BED AROUND NOON AND HOPE MY CAR STARTS. SOMEONE OFFERED ME A MOVIE DEAL TODAY.
I TOLD THEM OK, IF I COULD BE GYRO GEARLOOSE.
ACME TACO SAUCE XXX
©2010 Bill Griffith. World rights reserved. Distributed by King Features Syndicate
HIS CELEBRITY IN DINGBURG CAN BE A BURDEN.
WHEN I GO OUT TO DENNY'S, I ALWAYS BUY A WALL STREET JOURNAL TO HIDE BEHIND.

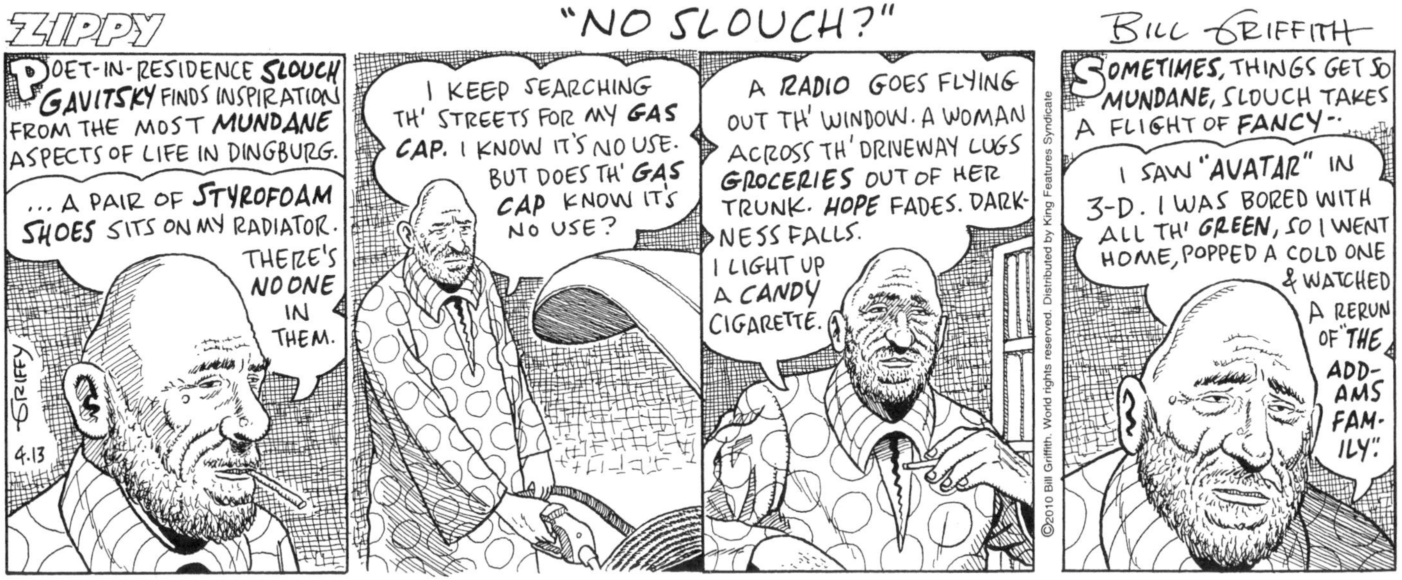
ZIPPY
"NO SLOUCH?"
BILL GRIFFITH
POET-IN-RESIDENCE SLOUCH GAVITSKY FINDS INSPIRATION FROM THE MOST MUNDANE ASPECTS OF LIFE IN DINGBURG.
... A PAIR OF STYROFOAM SHOES SITS ON MY RADIATOR. THERE'S NO ONE IN THEM.
GRIFFY
4.13
I KEEP SEARCHING TH' STREETS FOR MY GAS CAP. I KNOW IT'S NO USE. BUT DOES TH' GAS CAP KNOW IT'S NO USE?
A RADIO GOES FLYING OUT TH' WINDOW. A WOMAN ACROSS TH' DRIVEWAY LUGS GROCERIES OUT OF HER TRUNK. HOPE FADES. DARKNESS FALLS. I LIGHT UP A CANDY CIGARETTE.
©2010 Bill Griffith. World rights reserved. Distributed by King Features Syndicate
SOMETIMES, THINGS GET SO MUNDANE, SLOUCH TAKES A FLIGHT OF FANCY--
I SAW "AVATAR" IN 3-D. I WAS BORED WITH ALL TH' GREEN, SO I WENT HOME, POPPED A COLD ONE & WATCHED A RERUN OF "THE ADDAMS FAMILY".

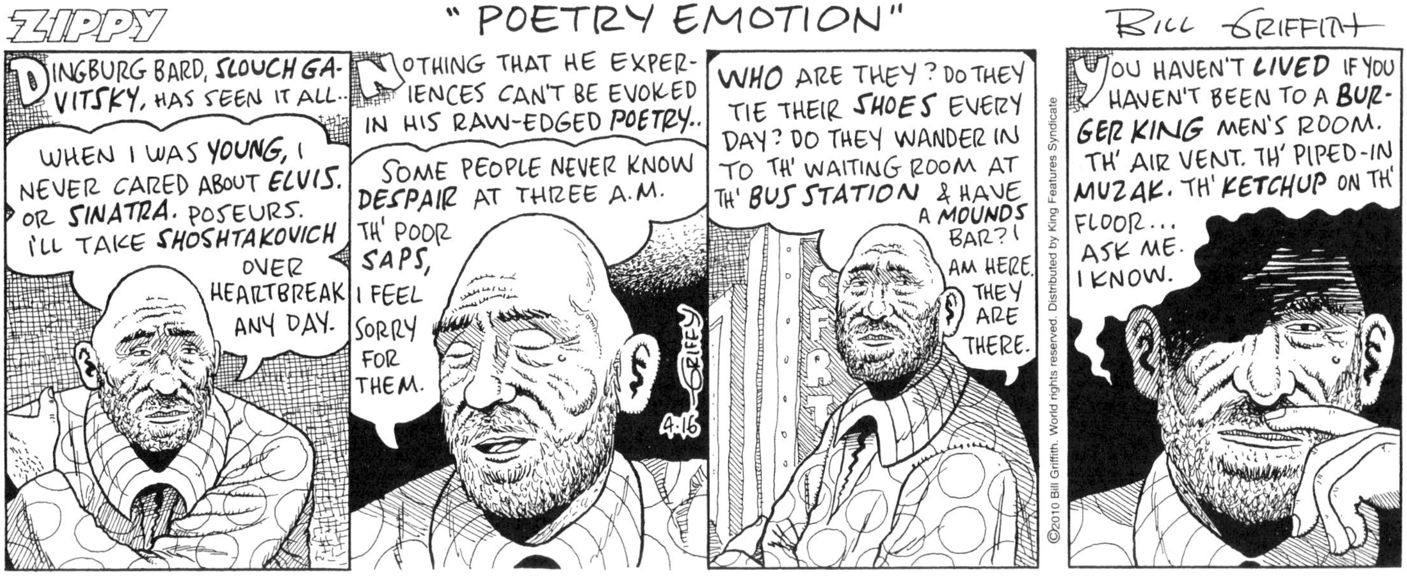
ZIPPY
"POETRY EMOTION"
BILL GRIFFITH
DINGBURG BARD, SLOUCH GAVITSKY, HAS SEEN IT ALL..
WHEN I WAS YOUNG, I NEVER CARED ABOUT ELVIS. OR SINATRA. POSEURS. I'LL TAKE SHOSHTAKOVICH OVER HEARTBREAK ANY DAY.
NOTHING THAT HE EXPERIENCES CAN'T BE EVOKED IN HIS RAW-EDGED POETRY..
SOME PEOPLE NEVER KNOW DESPAIR AT THREE A.M. TH' POOR SAPS, I FEEL SORRY FOR THEM.
GRIFFY
4-16
WHO ARE THEY? DO THEY TIE THEIR SHOES EVERY DAY? DO THEY WANDER IN TO TH' WAITING ROOM AT TH' BUS STATION & HAVE A MOUNDS BAR? I AM HERE. THEY ARE THERE.
©2010 Bill Griffith. World rights reserved. Distributed by King Features Syndicate
YOU HAVEN'T LIVED IF YOU HAVEN'T BEEN TO A BURGER KING MEN'S ROOM. TH' AIR VENT. TH' PIPED-IN MUZAK. TH' KETCHUP ON TH' FLOOR... ASK ME. I KNOW.

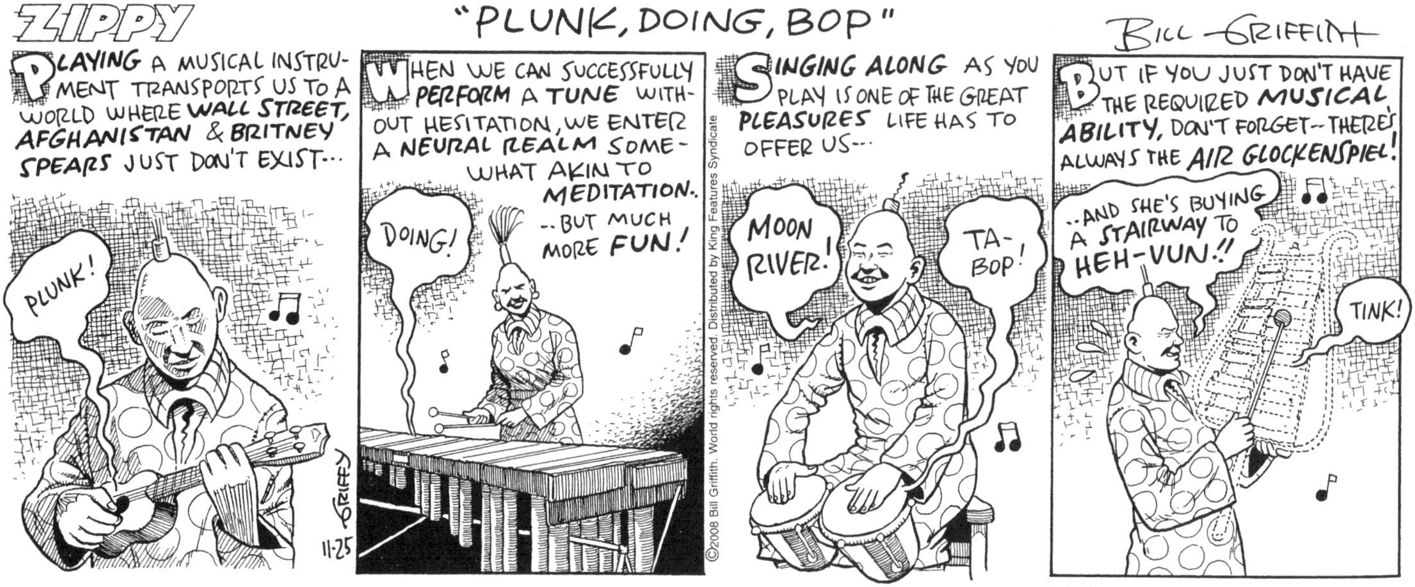
ZIPPY
"PLUNK, DOING, BOP"
BILL GRIFFITH
PLAYING A MUSICAL INSTRUMENT TRANSPORTS US TO A WORLD WHERE WALL STREET, AFGHANISTAN & BRITNEY SPEARS JUST DON'T EXIST...
PLUNK!
GRIFFY
11-25
WHEN WE CAN SUCCESSFULLY PERFORM A TUNE WITHOUT HESITATION, WE ENTER A NEURAL REALM SOMEWHAT AKIN TO MEDITATION.
--BUT MUCH MORE FUN!
DOING!
©2008 Bill Griffith. World rights reserved. Distributed by King Features Syndicate
SINGING ALONG AS YOU PLAY IS ONE OF THE GREAT PLEASURES LIFE HAS TO OFFER US---
MOON RIVER!
TA-BOP!
BUT IF YOU JUST DON'T HAVE THE REQUIRED MUSICAL ABILITY, DON'T FORGET--THERE'S ALWAYS THE AIR GLOCKENSPIEL!
..AND SHE'S BUYING A STAIRWAY TO HEH-VUN!!
TINK!

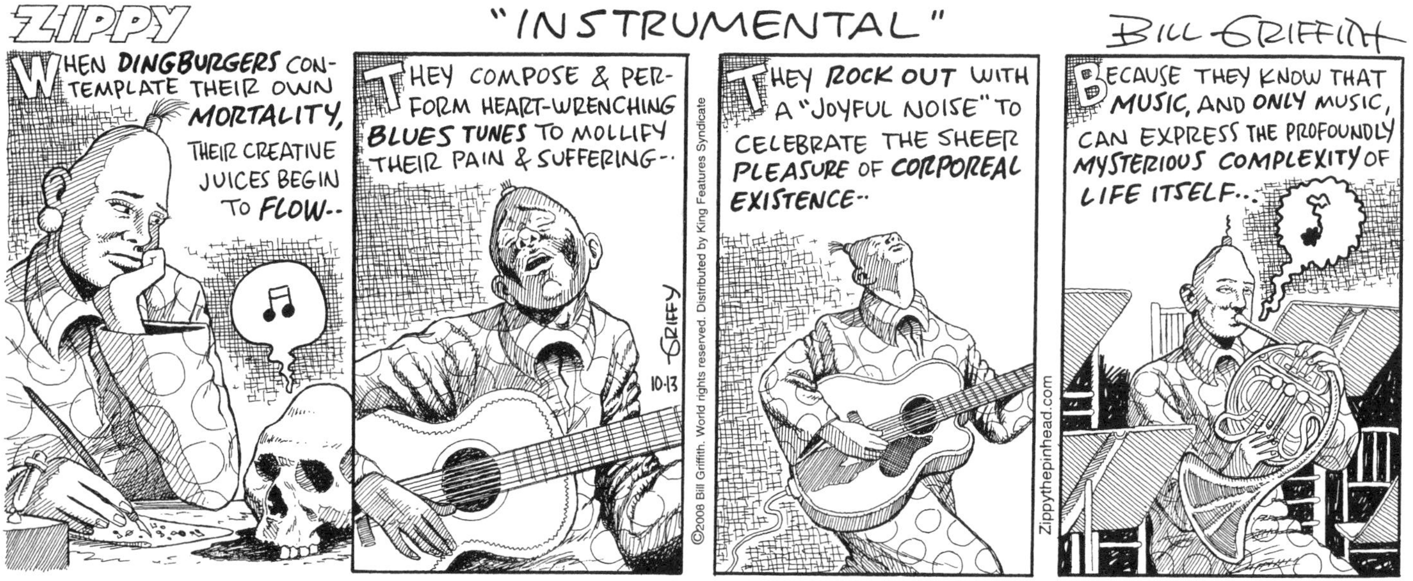
ZIPPY
"INSTRUMENTAL"
BILL GRIFFITH
WHEN DINGBURGERS CONTEMPLATE THEIR OWN MORTALITY, THEIR CREATIVE JUICES BEGIN TO FLOW--
THEY COMPOSE & PERFORM HEART-WRENCHING BLUES TUNES TO MOLLIFY THEIR PAIN & SUFFERING--
GRIFFY
10-13
©2008 Bill Griffith. World rights reserved. Distributed by King Features Syndicate
THEY ROCK OUT WITH A "JOYFUL NOISE" TO CELEBRATE THE SHEER PLEASURE OF CORPOREAL EXISTENCE--
Zippythepinhead.com
BECAUSE THEY KNOW THAT MUSIC, AND ONLY MUSIC, CAN EXPRESS THE PROFOUNDLY MYSTERIOUS COMPLEXITY OF LIFE ITSELF...

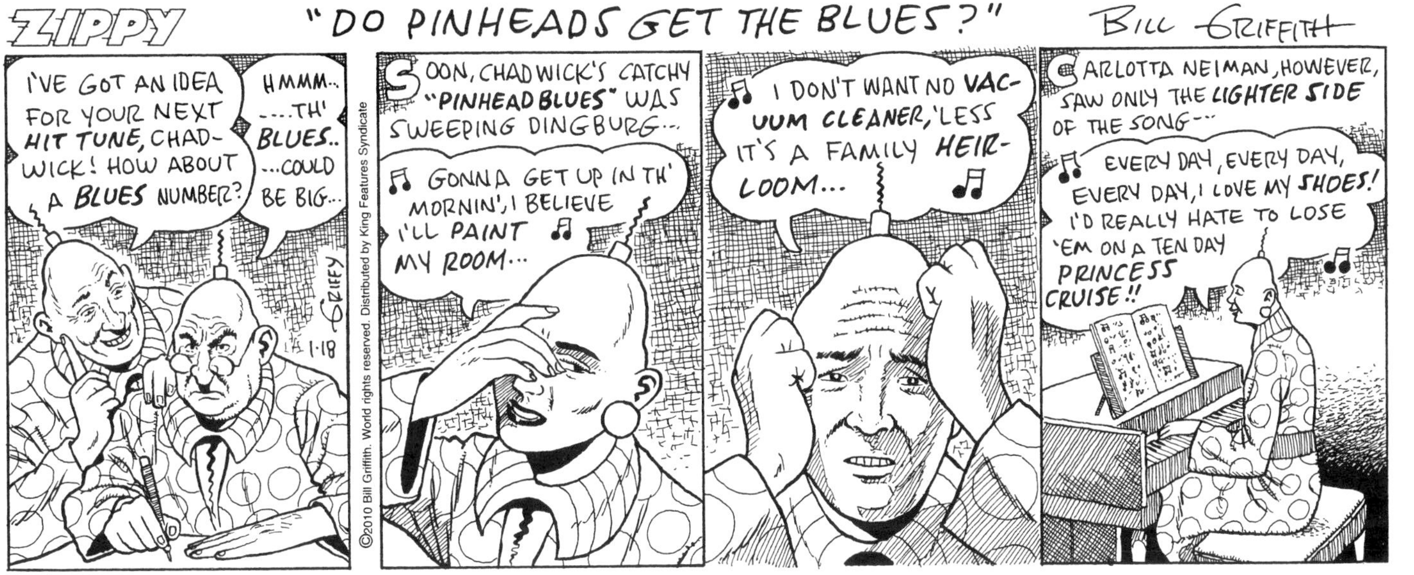
ZIPPY
"DO PINHEADS GET THE BLUES?"
BILL GRIFFITH
I'VE GOT AN IDEA FOR YOUR NEXT HIT TUNE, CHADWICK! HOW ABOUT A BLUES NUMBER?
HMMM.. ....TH' BLUES.. ...COULD BE BIG...
GRIFFY 1·18
©2010 Bill Griffith. World rights reserved. Distributed by King Features Syndicate
SOON, CHADWICK'S CATCHY "PINHEAD BLUES" WAS SWEEPING DINGBURG...
GONNA GET UP IN TH' MORNIN', I BELIEVE I'LL PAINT MY ROOM...
I DON'T WANT NO VACUUM CLEANER, 'LESS IT'S A FAMILY HEIRLOOM...
CARLOTTA NEIMAN, HOWEVER, SAW ONLY THE LIGHTER SIDE OF THE SONG...
EVERY DAY, EVERY DAY, EVERY DAY, I LOVE MY SHOES! I'D REALLY HATE TO LOSE 'EM ON A TEN DAY PRINCESS CRUISE!!

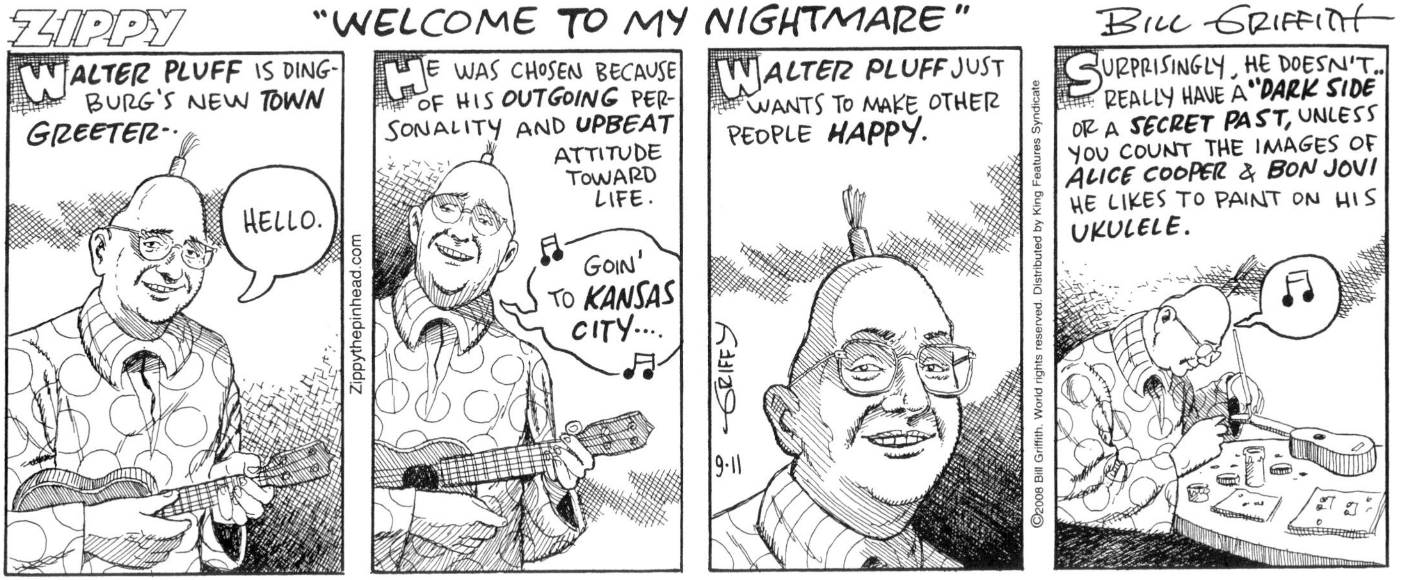
ZIPPY
"WELCOME TO MY NIGHTMARE"
BILL GRIFFITH
WALTER PLUFF IS DINGBURG'S NEW TOWN GREETER..
HELLO.
Zippythepinhead.com
HE WAS CHOSEN BECAUSE OF HIS OUTGOING PERSONALITY AND UPBEAT ATTITUDE TOWARD LIFE.
GOIN' TO KANSAS CITY....
WALTER PLUFF JUST WANTS TO MAKE OTHER PEOPLE HAPPY.
GRIFFY 9·11
©2008 Bill Griffith. World rights reserved. Distributed by King Features Syndicate
SURPRISINGLY, HE DOESN'T.. REALLY HAVE A "DARK SIDE" OR A SECRET PAST, UNLESS YOU COUNT THE IMAGES OF ALICE COOPER & BON JOVI HE LIKES TO PAINT ON HIS UKULELE.

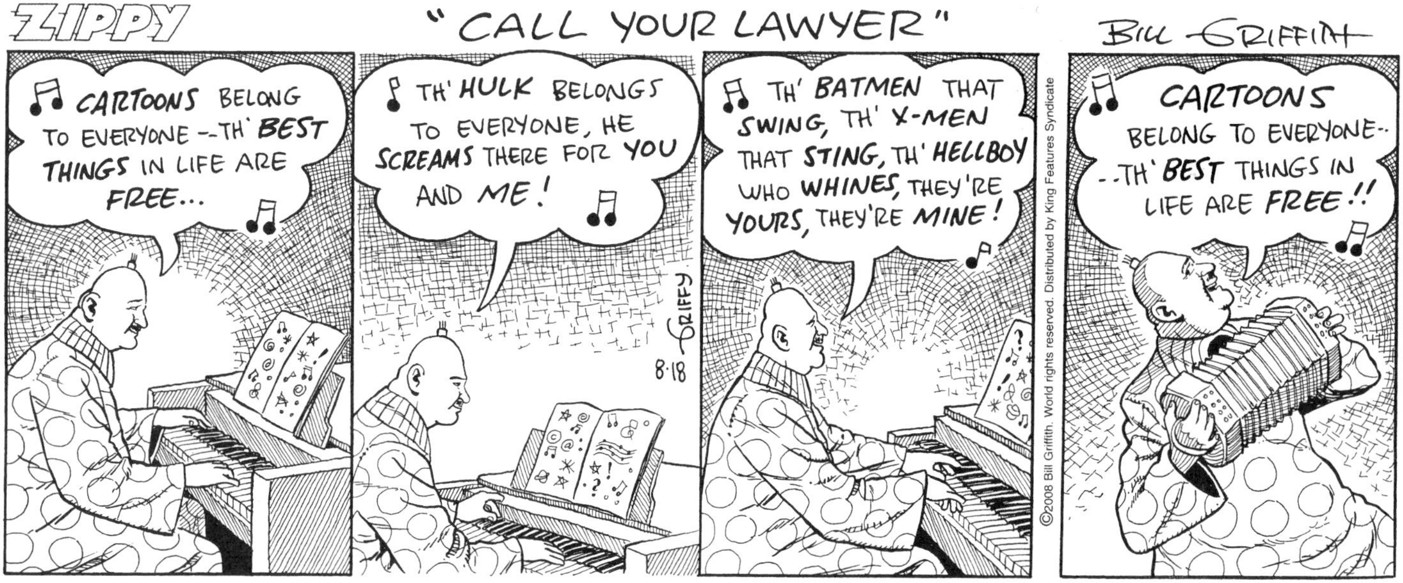
ZIPPY
"CALL YOUR LAWYER"
BILL GRIFFITH
CARTOONS BELONG TO EVERYONE --TH' BEST THINGS IN LIFE ARE FREE...
TH' HULK BELONGS TO EVERYONE, HE SCREAMS THERE FOR YOU AND ME!
GRIFFY 8·18
TH' BATMEN THAT SWING, TH' X-MEN THAT STING, TH' HELLBOY WHO WHINES, THEY'RE YOURS, THEY'RE MINE!
©2008 Bill Griffith. World rights reserved. Distributed by King Features Syndicate
CARTOONS BELONG TO EVERYONE-- --TH' BEST THINGS IN LIFE ARE FREE!!

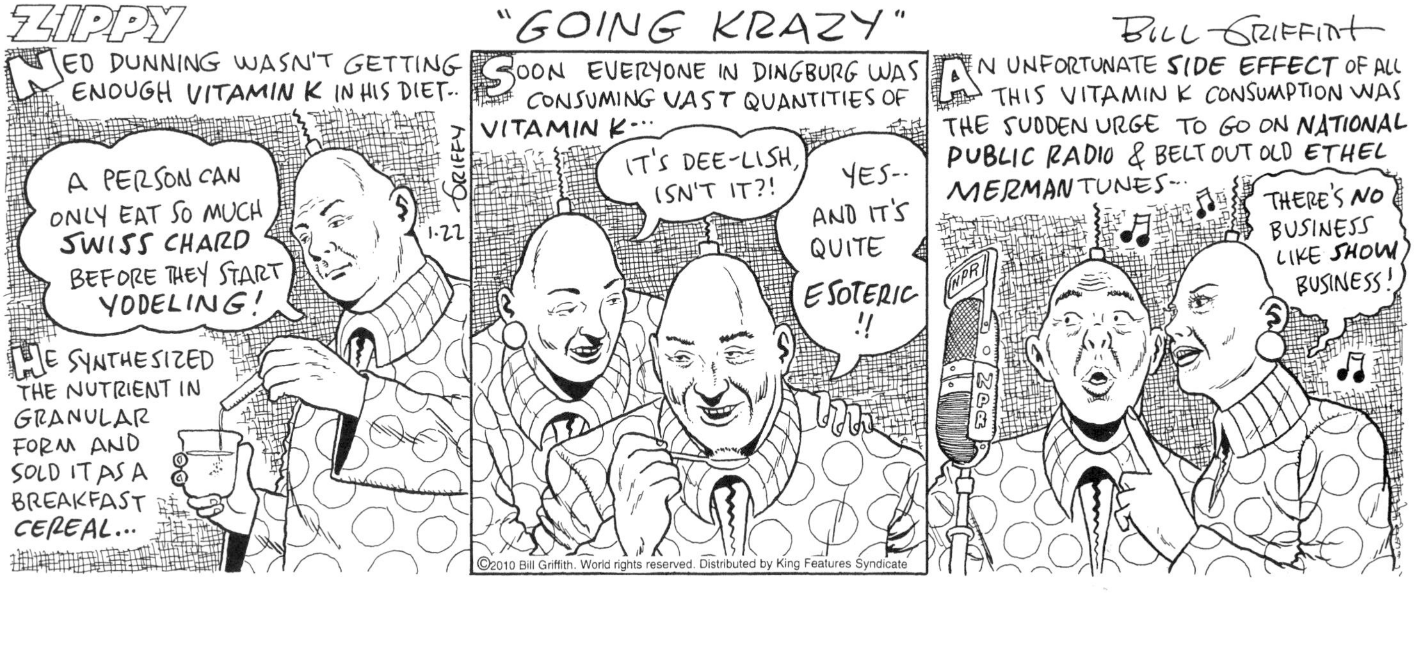
ZIPPY
"GOING KRAZY"
BILL GRIFFITH
NED DUNNING WASN'T GETTING ENOUGH VITAMIN K IN HIS DIET--
A PERSON CAN ONLY EAT SO MUCH SWISS CHARD BEFORE THEY START YODELING!
GRIFFY 1·22
HE SYNTHESIZED THE NUTRIENT IN GRANULAR FORM AND SOLD IT AS A BREAKFAST CEREAL...
SOON EVERYONE IN DINGBURG WAS CONSUMING VAST QUANTITIES OF VITAMIN K---
IT'S DEE-LISH, ISN'T IT?!
YES-- AND IT'S QUITE ESOTERIC!!
©2010 Bill Griffith. World rights reserved. Distributed by King Features Syndicate
AN UNFORTUNATE SIDE EFFECT OF ALL THIS VITAMIN K CONSUMPTION WAS THE SUDDEN URGE TO GO ON NATIONAL PUBLIC RADIO & BELT OUT OLD ETHEL MERMAN TUNES--
NPR
THERE'S NO BUSINESS LIKE SHOW BUSINESS!

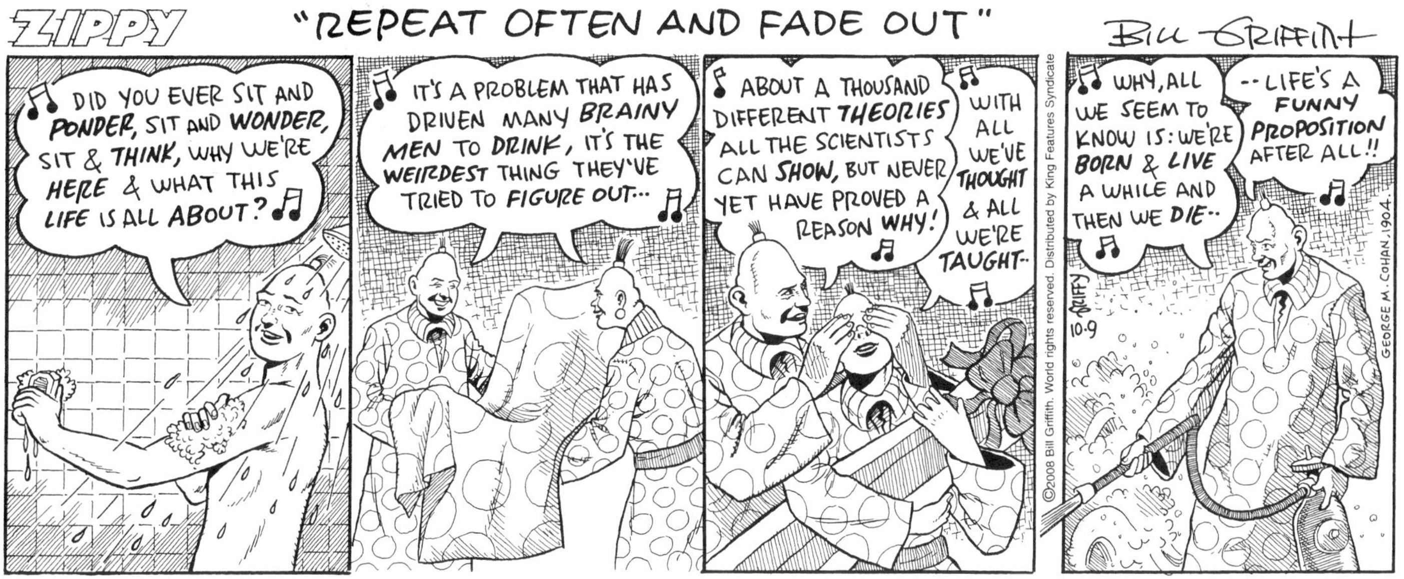
ZIPPY
"REPEAT OFTEN AND FADE OUT"
BILL GRIFFITH
DID YOU EVER SIT AND PONDER, SIT AND WONDER, SIT & THINK, WHY WE'RE HERE & WHAT THIS LIFE IS ALL ABOUT?
IT'S A PROBLEM THAT HAS DRIVEN MANY BRAINY MEN TO DRINK, IT'S THE WEIRDEST THING THEY'VE TRIED TO FIGURE OUT...
ABOUT A THOUSAND DIFFERENT THEORIES ALL THE SCIENTISTS CAN SHOW, BUT NEVER YET HAVE PROVED A REASON WHY!
WITH ALL WE'VE THOUGHT & ALL WE'RE TAUGHT..
©2008 Bill Griffith. World rights reserved. Distributed by King Features Syndicate
WHY, ALL WE SEEM TO KNOW IS: WE'RE BORN & LIVE A WHILE AND THEN WE DIE..
--LIFE'S A FUNNY PROPOSITION AFTER ALL!!
GRIFFY 10-9
GEORGE M. COHAN, 1904.

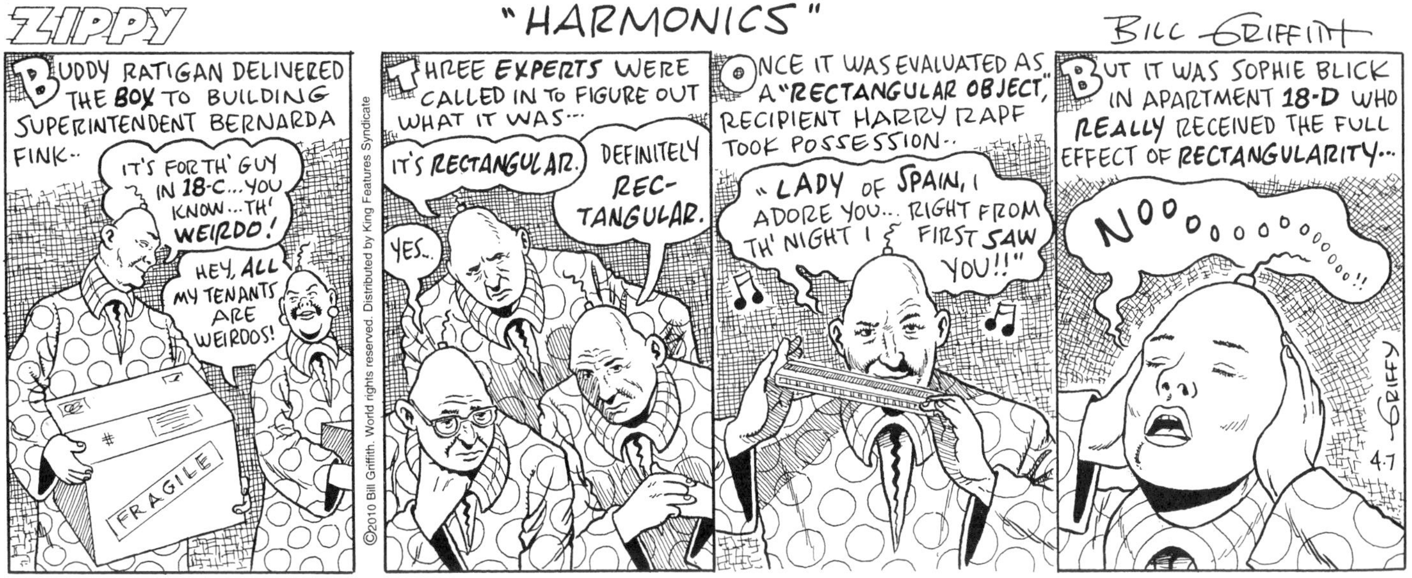
ZIPPY
"HARMONICS"
BILL GRIFFITH
BUDDY RATIGAN DELIVERED THE BOX TO BUILDING SUPERINTENDENT BERNARDA FINK..
IT'S FOR TH' GUY IN 18-C... YOU KNOW... TH' WEIRDO!
HEY, ALL MY TENANTS ARE WEIRDOS!
FRAGILE
©2010 Bill Griffith. World rights reserved. Distributed by King Features Syndicate
THREE EXPERTS WERE CALLED IN TO FIGURE OUT WHAT IT WAS...
IT'S RECTANGULAR.
DEFINITELY REC-TANGULAR.
YES..
ONCE IT WAS EVALUATED AS A "RECTANGULAR OBJECT", RECIPIENT HARRY RAPF TOOK POSSESSION..
"LADY OF SPAIN, I ADORE YOU... RIGHT FROM TH' NIGHT I FIRST SAW YOU!!"
BUT IT WAS SOPHIE BLICK IN APARTMENT 18-D WHO REALLY RECEIVED THE FULL EFFECT OF RECTANGULARITY...
NOOOOOOOOOOOOOO!!
GRIFFY 4-7

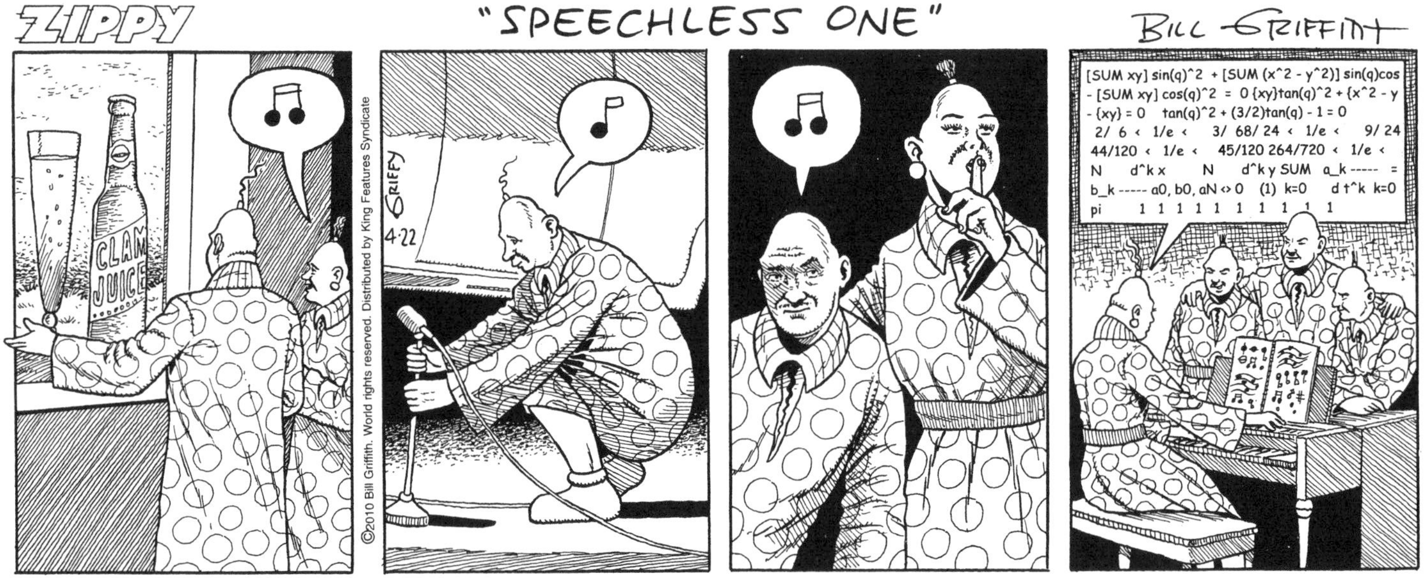
ZIPPY
"SPEECHLESS ONE"
BILL GRIFFITH
CLAM JUICE
©2010 Bill Griffith. World rights reserved. Distributed by King Features Syndicate
GRIFFY 4·22
[SUM xy] sin(q)^2 + [SUM (x^2 - y^2)] sin(q)cos
- [SUM xy] cos(q)^2 = 0 {xy}tan(q)^2 + {x^2 - y
- {xy} = 0 tan(q)^2 + (3/2)tan(q) - 1 = 0
2/ 6 < 1/e < 3/ 68/ 24 < 1/e < 9/ 24
44/120 < 1/e < 45/120 264/720 < 1/e <
N d^k x N d^k y SUM a_k ----- =
b_k ----- a0, b0, aN <> 0 (1) k=0 d t^k k=0
pi 1 1 1 1 1 1 1 1 1 1

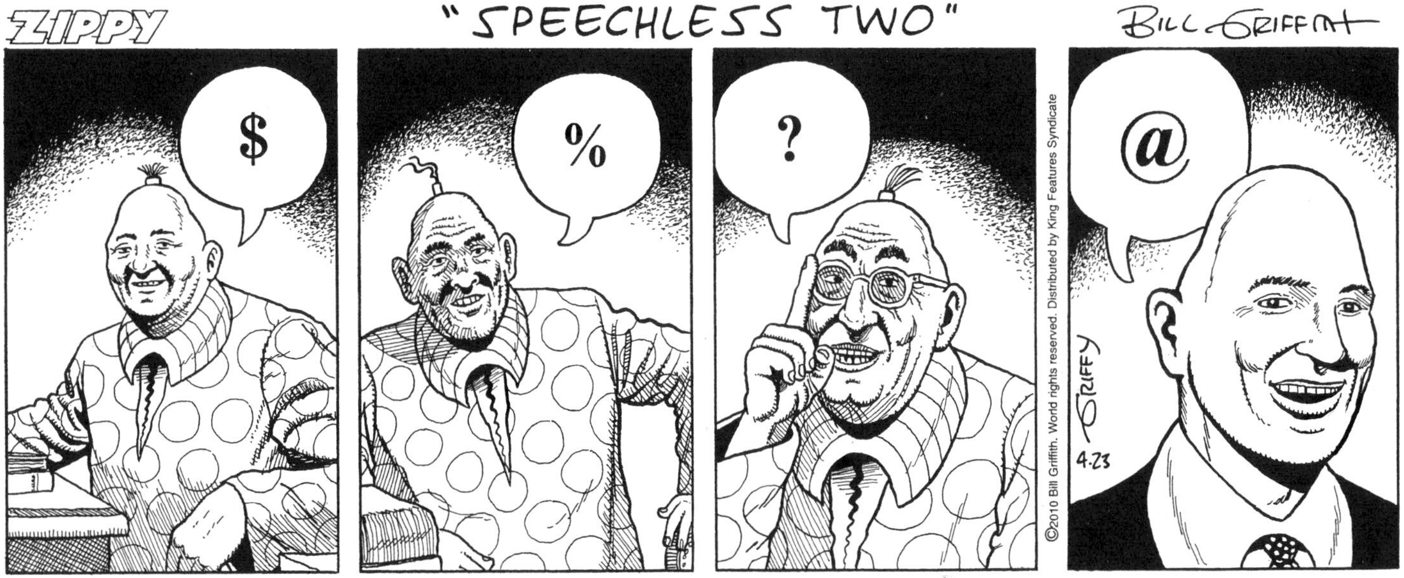
ZIPPY
"SPEECHLESS TWO"
BILL GRIFFITH
$
%
?
©2010 Bill Griffith. World rights reserved. Distributed by King Features Syndicate
GRIFFY 4·23
@

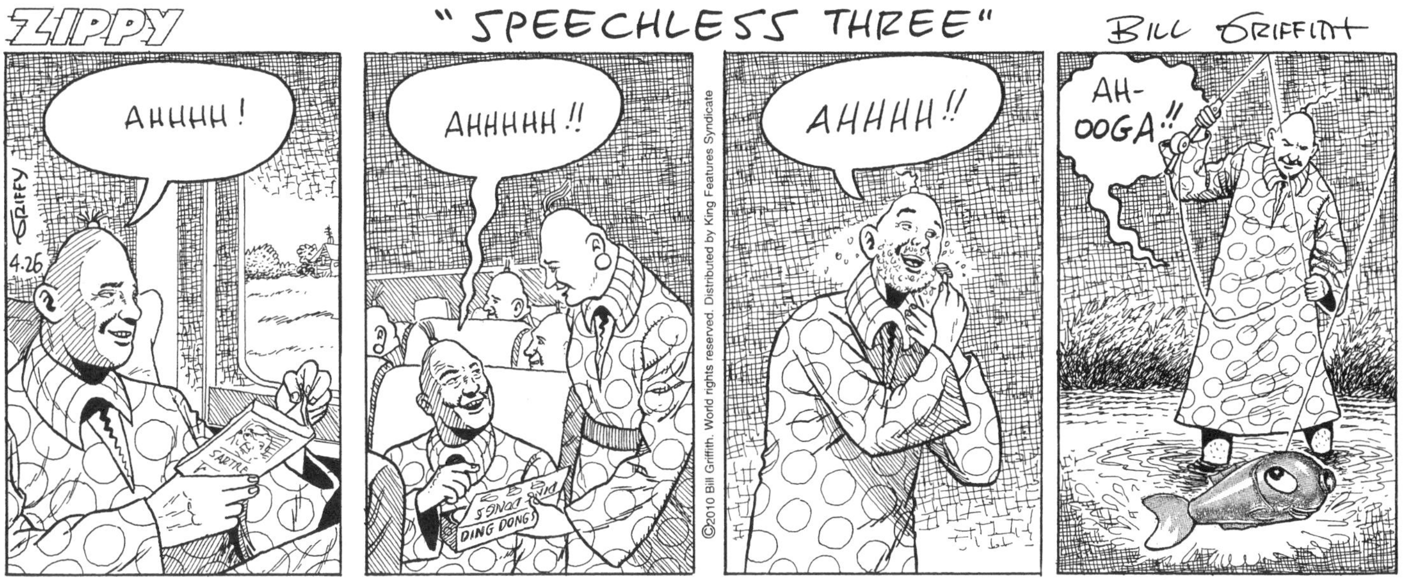
ZIPPY
"SPEECHLESS THREE"
BILL GRIFFITH
GRIFFY 4·26
AHHHH!
AHHHHH!!
DING DONGS
AHHHH!!
AH-OOGA!!
©2010 Bill Griffith. World rights reserved. Distributed by King Features Syndicate

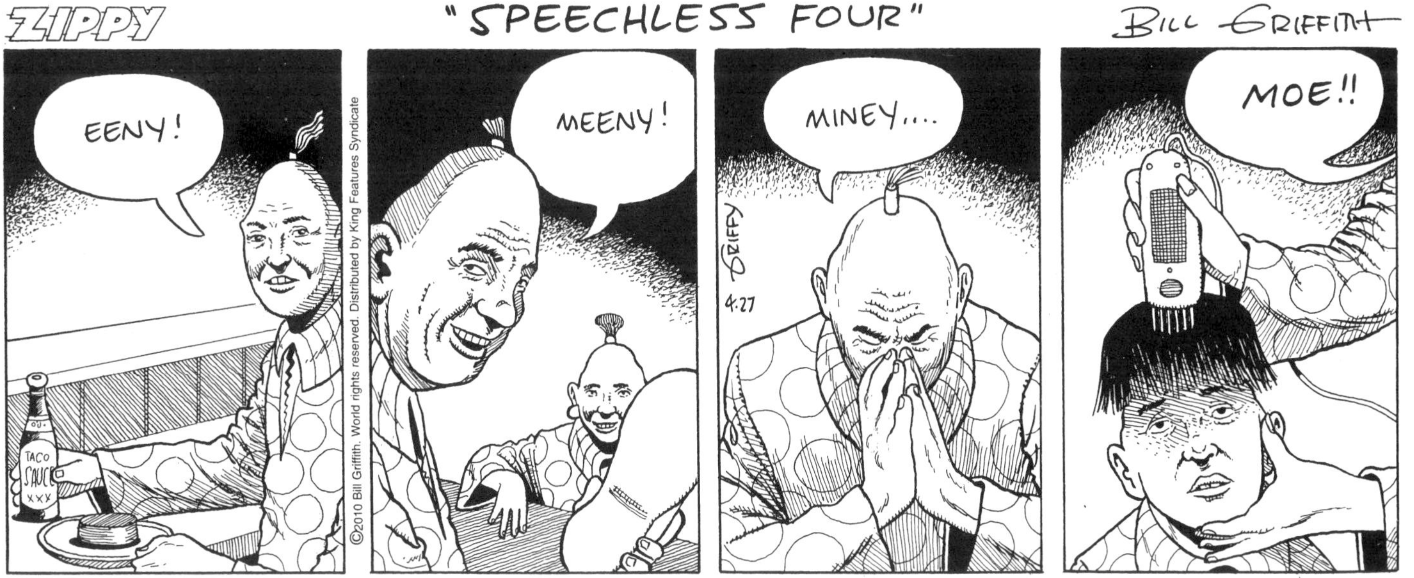
ZIPPY
"SPEECHLESS FOUR"
BILL GRIFFITH
EENY!
TACO SAUCE XXX
MEENY!
GRIFFY 4·27
MINEY....
MOE!!
©2010 Bill Griffith. World rights reserved. Distributed by King Features Syndicate

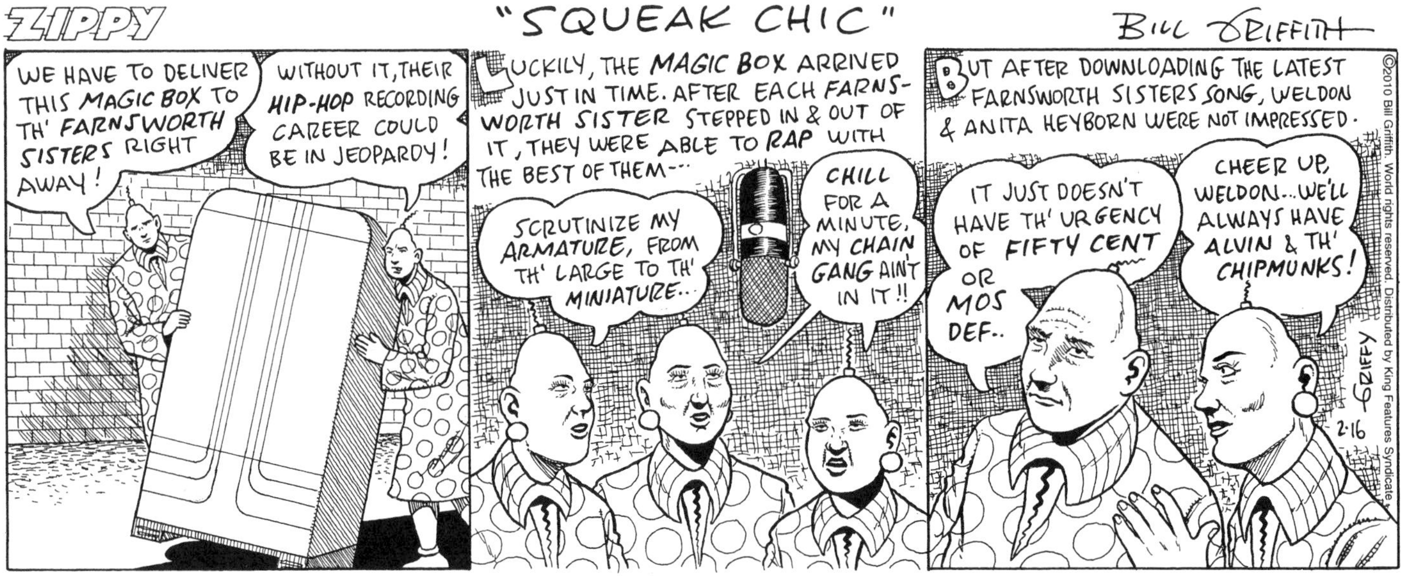
ZIPPY
"SQUEAK CHIC"
BILL GRIFFITH
WE HAVE TO DELIVER THIS MAGIC BOX TO TH' FARNSWORTH SISTERS RIGHT AWAY!
WITHOUT IT, THEIR HIP-HOP RECORDING CAREER COULD BE IN JEOPARDY!
LUCKILY, THE MAGIC BOX ARRIVED JUST IN TIME. AFTER EACH FARNSWORTH SISTER STEPPED IN & OUT OF IT, THEY WERE ABLE TO RAP WITH THE BEST OF THEM---
SCRUTINIZE MY ARMATURE, FROM TH' LARGE TO TH' MINIATURE..
CHILL FOR A MINUTE, MY CHAIN GANG AIN'T IN IT!!
BUT AFTER DOWNLOADING THE LATEST FARNSWORTH SISTERS SONG, WELDON & ANITA HEYBORN WERE NOT IMPRESSED.
IT JUST DOESN'T HAVE TH' URGENCY OF FIFTY CENT OR MOS DEF..
CHEER UP, WELDON...WE'LL ALWAYS HAVE ALVIN & TH' CHIPMUNKS!
GRIFFY 2·16
©2010 Bill Griffith. World rights reserved. Distributed by King Features Syndicate.

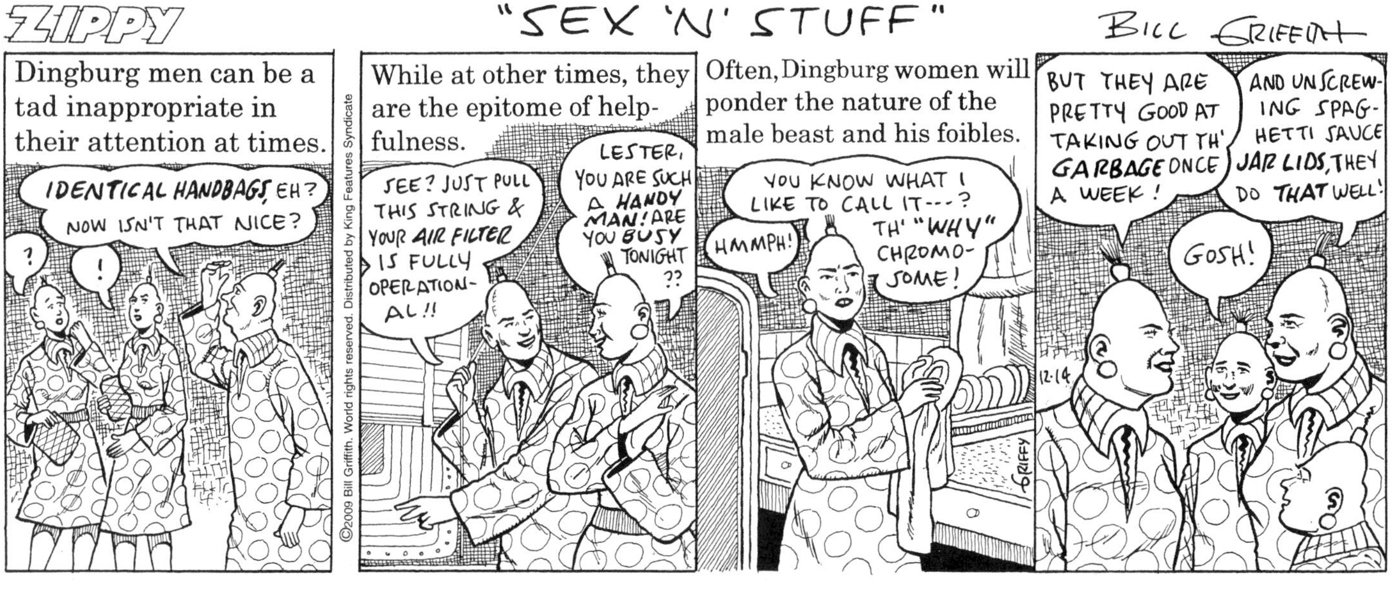
ZIPPY
"SEX 'N' STUFF"
BILL GRIFFITH
Dingburg men can be a tad inappropriate in their attention at times.
IDENTICAL HANDBAGS, EH? NOW ISN'T THAT NICE?
?
!
While at other times, they are the epitome of helpfulness.
SEE? JUST PULL THIS STRING & YOUR AIR FILTER IS FULLY OPERATIONAL!!
LESTER, YOU ARE SUCH A HANDY MAN! ARE YOU BUSY TONIGHT??
©2009 Bill Griffith. World rights reserved. Distributed by King Features Syndicate
Often, Dingburg women will ponder the nature of the male beast and his foibles.
YOU KNOW WHAT I LIKE TO CALL IT---?
HMMPH!
TH' "WHY" CHROMOSOME!
GRIFFY 12·14
BUT THEY ARE PRETTY GOOD AT TAKING OUT TH' GARBAGE ONCE A WEEK!
AND UNSCREWING SPAGHETTI SAUCE JAR LIDS, THEY DO THAT WELL!
GOSH!

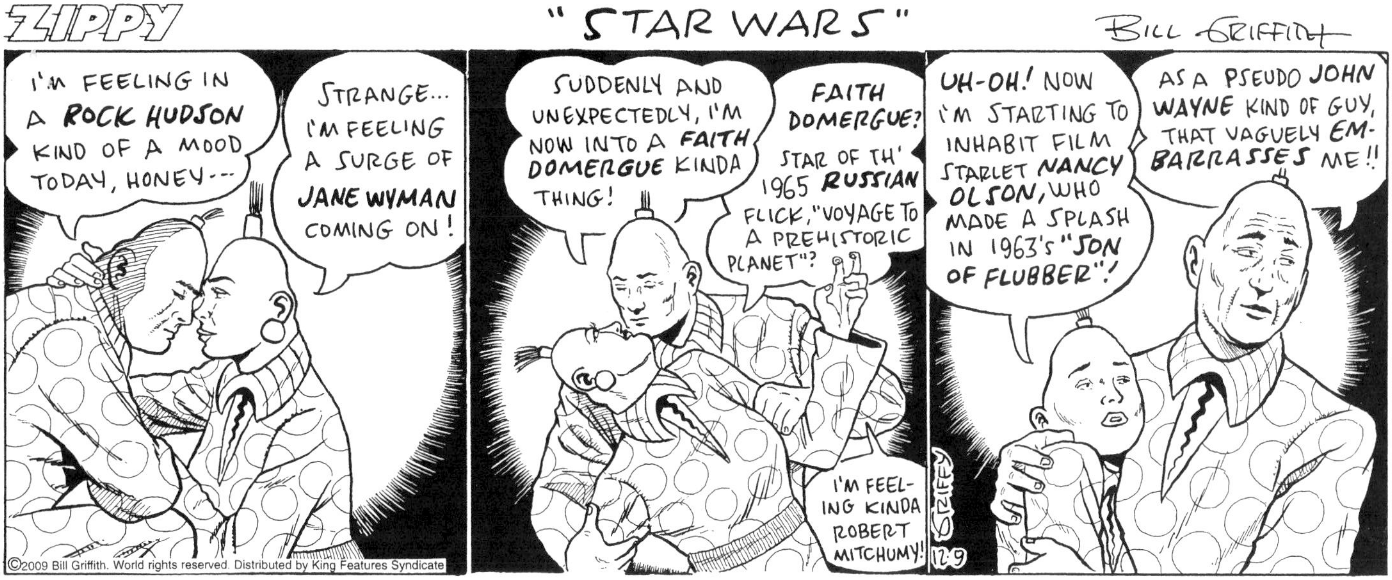

ZIPPY
"STAR WARS"
BILL GRIFFITH
I'M FEELING IN A ROCK HUDSON KIND OF A MOOD TODAY, HONEY...
STRANGE... I'M FEELING A SURGE OF JANE WYMAN COMING ON!
SUDDENLY AND UNEXPECTEDLY, I'M NOW INTO A FAITH DOMERGUE KINDA THING!
FAITH DOMERGUE? STAR OF TH' 1965 RUSSIAN FLICK, "VOYAGE TO A PREHISTORIC PLANET"?
I'M FEELING KINDA ROBERT MITCHUMY!
UH-OH! NOW I'M STARTING TO INHABIT FILM STARLET NANCY OLSON, WHO MADE A SPLASH IN 1963'S "SON OF FLUBBER"!
AS A PSEUDO JOHN WAYNE KIND OF GUY, THAT VAGUELY EMBARRASSES ME!!
GRIFFY 12·9
©2009 Bill Griffith. World rights reserved. Distributed by King Features Syndicate

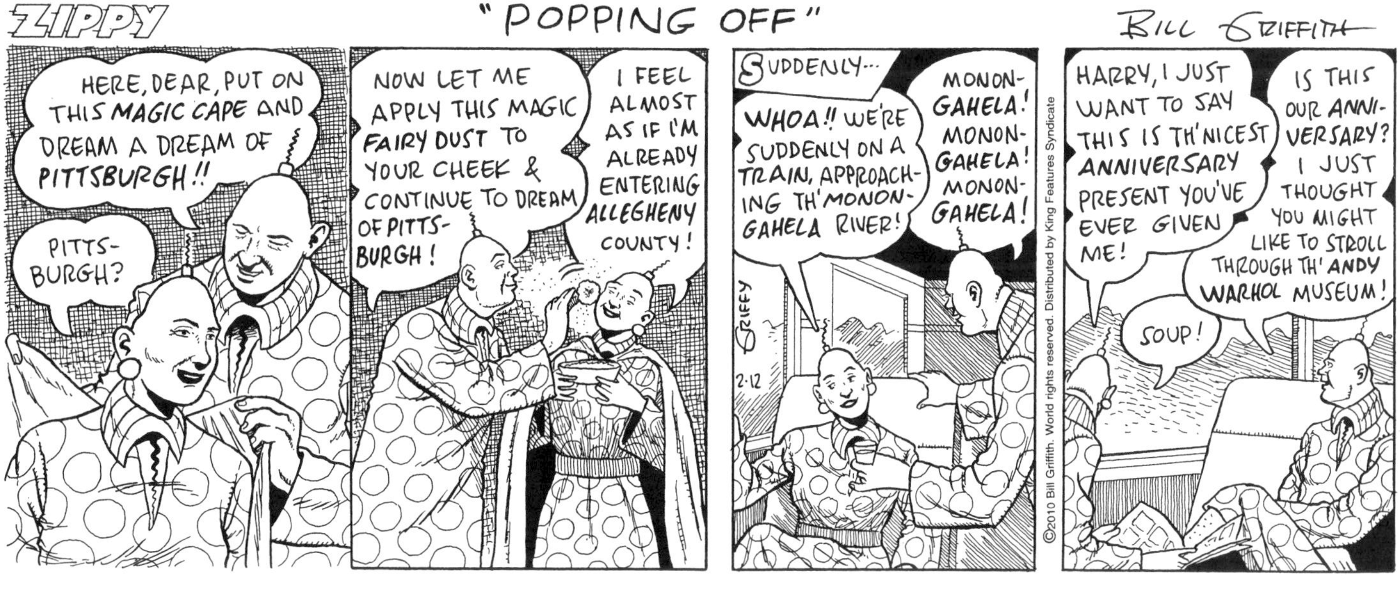

ZIPPY
"POPPING OFF"
BILL GRIFFITH
HERE, DEAR, PUT ON THIS MAGIC CAPE AND DREAM A DREAM OF PITTSBURGH!!
PITTSBURGH?
NOW LET ME APPLY THIS MAGIC FAIRY DUST TO YOUR CHEEK & CONTINUE TO DREAM OF PITTSBURGH!
I FEEL ALMOST AS IF I'M ALREADY ENTERING ALLEGHENY COUNTY!
SUDDENLY...
WHOA!! WE'RE SUDDENLY ON A TRAIN, APPROACHING TH' MONONGAHELA RIVER!
MONONGAHELA! MONONGAHELA! MONONGAHELA!
GRIFFY 2·12
©2010 Bill Griffith. World rights reserved. Distributed by King Features Syndicate
HARRY, I JUST WANT TO SAY THIS IS TH' NICEST ANNIVERSARY PRESENT YOU'VE EVER GIVEN ME!
IS THIS OUR ANNIVERSARY? I JUST THOUGHT YOU MIGHT LIKE TO STROLL THROUGH TH' ANDY WARHOL MUSEUM!
SOUP!

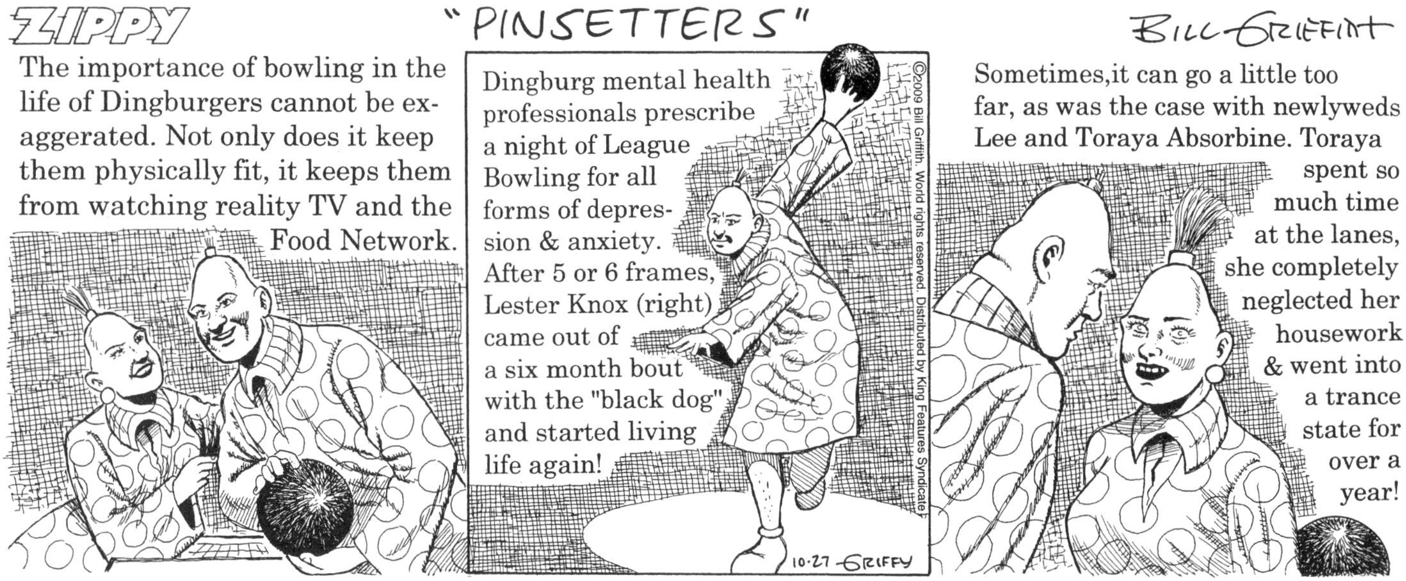
ZIPPY
"PINSETTERS"
BILL GRIFFITH
The importance of bowling in the life of Dingburgers cannot be exaggerated. Not only does it keep them physically fit, it keeps them from watching reality TV and the Food Network.
Dingburg mental health professionals prescribe a night of League Bowling for all forms of depression & anxiety. After 5 or 6 frames, Lester Knox (right) came out of a six month bout with the "black dog" and started living life again!
©2009 Bill Griffith. World rights reserved. Distributed by King Features Syndicate
10·27 GRIFFY
Sometimes, it can go a little too far, as was the case with newlyweds Lee and Toraya Absorbine. Toraya spent so much time at the lanes, she completely neglected her housework & went into a trance state for over a year!

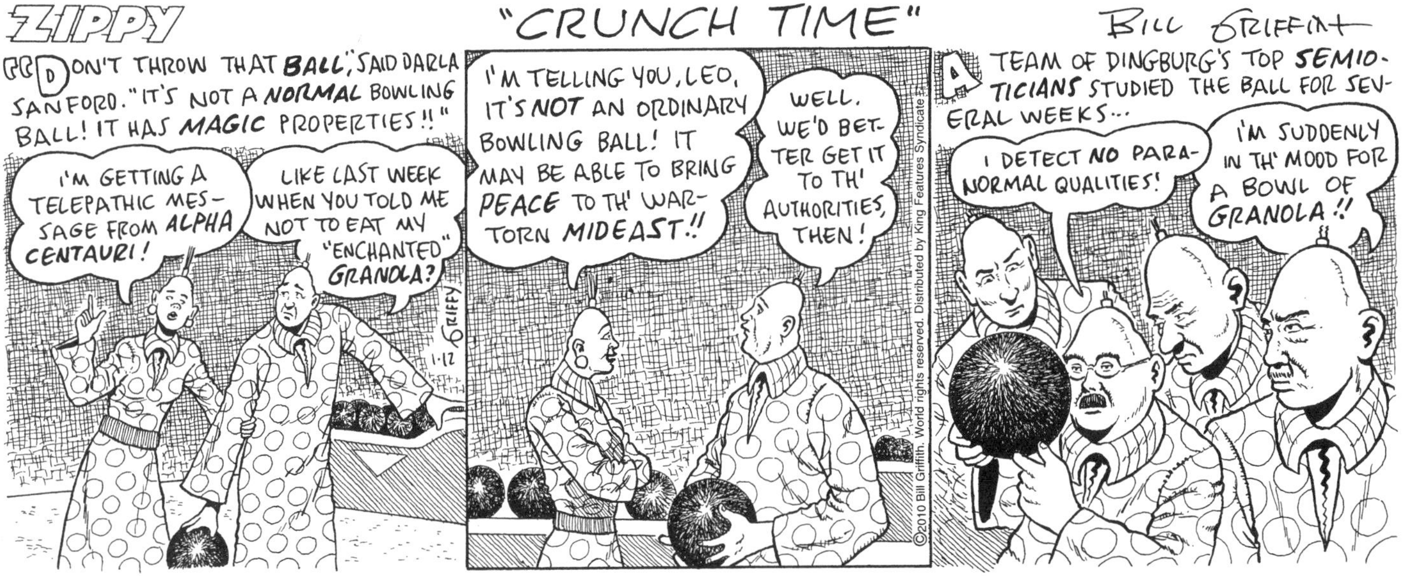
ZIPPY
"CRUNCH TIME"
BILL GRIFFITH
"DON'T THROW THAT BALL," SAID DARLA SANFORD. "IT'S NOT A NORMAL BOWLING BALL! IT HAS MAGIC PROPERTIES!!"
I'M GETTING A TELEPATHIC MESSAGE FROM ALPHA CENTAURI!
LIKE LAST WEEK WHEN YOU TOLD ME NOT TO EAT MY "ENCHANTED" GRANOLA?
GRIFFY 1·12
I'M TELLING YOU, LEO, IT'S NOT AN ORDINARY BOWLING BALL! IT MAY BE ABLE TO BRING PEACE TO TH' WAR-TORN MIDEAST!!
WELL, WE'D BETTER GET IT TO TH' AUTHORITIES, THEN!
©2010 Bill Griffith. World rights reserved. Distributed by King Features Syndicate
A TEAM OF DINGBURG'S TOP SEMIOTICIANS STUDIED THE BALL FOR SEVERAL WEEKS...
I DETECT NO PARANORMAL QUALITIES!
I'M SUDDENLY IN TH' MOOD FOR A BOWL OF GRANOLA!!

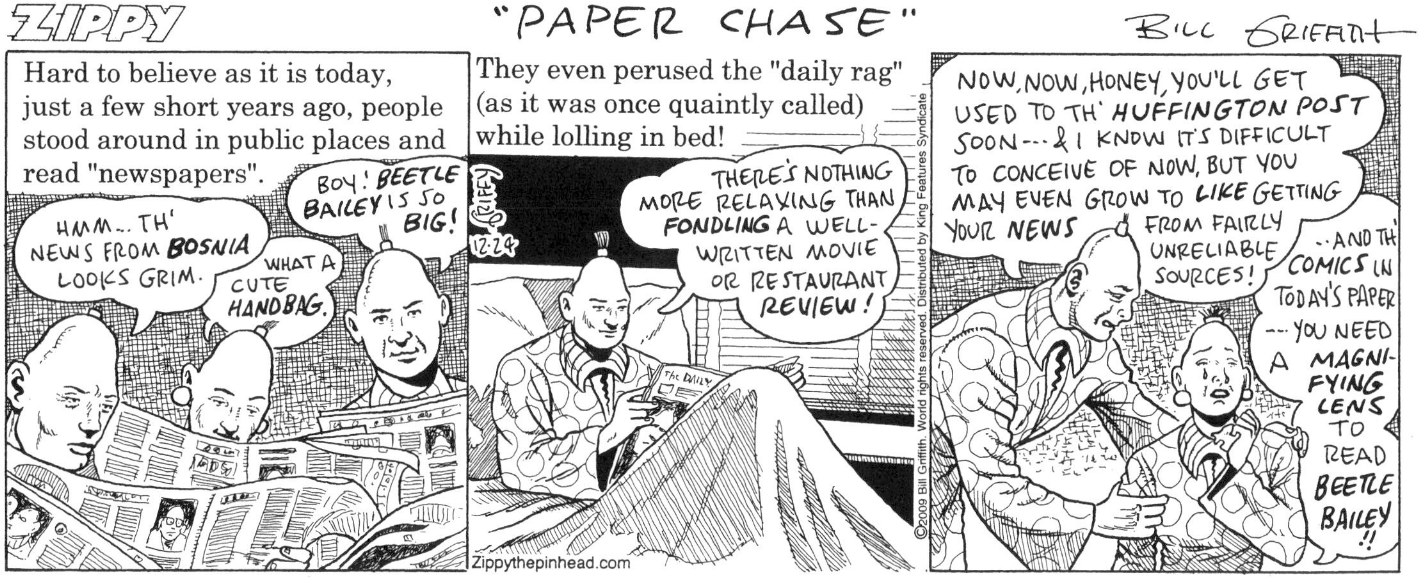
ZIPPY
"PAPER CHASE"
BILL GRIFFITH
Hard to believe as it is today, just a few short years ago, people stood around in public places and read "newspapers".
HMM... TH' NEWS FROM BOSNIA LOOKS GRIM.
WHAT A CUTE HANDBAG.
BOY! BEETLE BAILEY IS SO BIG!
They even perused the "daily rag" (as it was once quaintly called) while lolling in bed!
GRIFFY 12-24
THERE'S NOTHING MORE RELAXING THAN FONDLING A WELL-WRITTEN MOVIE OR RESTAURANT REVIEW!
THE DAILY
Zippythepinhead.com
©2009 Bill Griffith. World rights reserved. Distributed by King Features Syndicate
NOW, NOW, HONEY, YOU'LL GET USED TO TH' HUFFINGTON POST SOON---& I KNOW IT'S DIFFICULT TO CONCEIVE OF NOW, BUT YOU MAY EVEN GROW TO LIKE GETTING YOUR NEWS FROM FAIRLY UNRELIABLE SOURCES!
..AND TH' COMICS IN TODAY'S PAPER ---YOU NEED A MAGNIFYING LENS TO READ BEETLE BAILEY!!

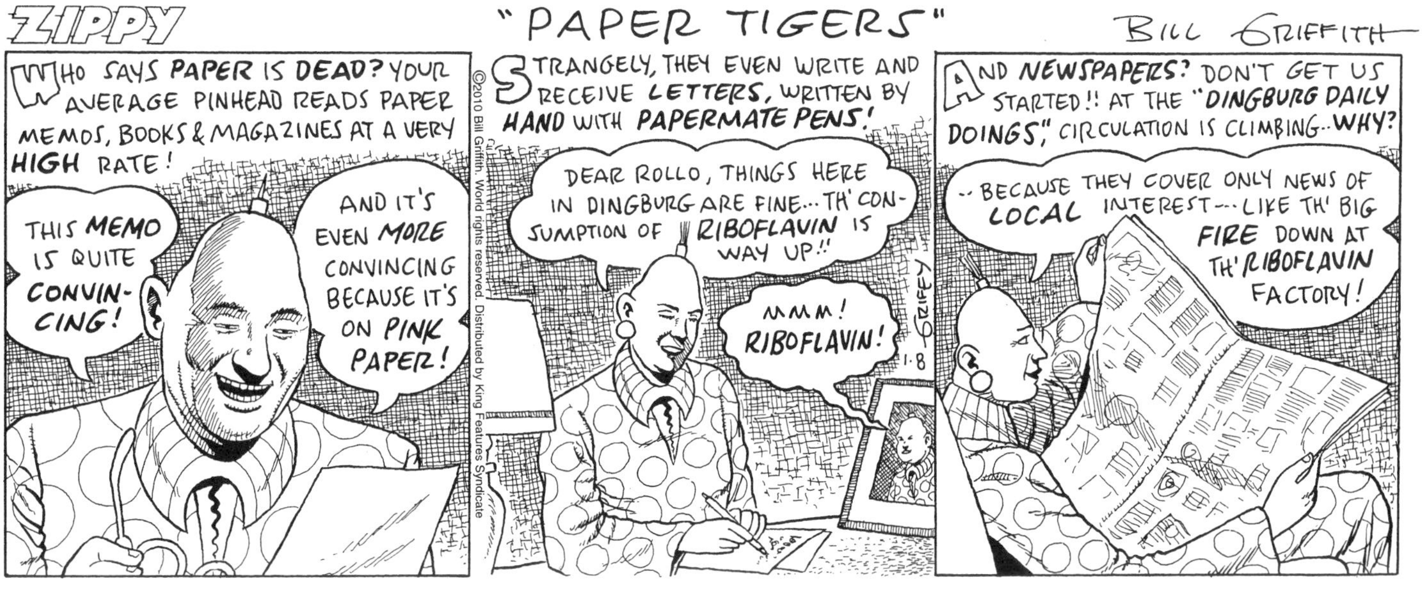
ZIPPY
"PAPER TIGERS"
BILL GRIFFITH
WHO SAYS PAPER IS DEAD? YOUR AVERAGE PINHEAD READS PAPER MEMOS, BOOKS & MAGAZINES AT A VERY HIGH RATE!
THIS MEMO IS QUITE CONVINCING!
AND IT'S EVEN MORE CONVINCING BECAUSE IT'S ON PINK PAPER!
©2010 Bill Griffith. World rights reserved. Distributed by King Features Syndicate
STRANGELY, THEY EVEN WRITE AND RECEIVE LETTERS, WRITTEN BY HAND WITH PAPERMATE PENS!
DEAR ROLLO, THINGS HERE IN DINGBURG ARE FINE... TH' CONSUMPTION OF RIBOFLAVIN IS WAY UP!!
MMM! RIBOFLAVIN!
GRIFFY 1-8
AND NEWSPAPERS? DON'T GET US STARTED!! AT THE "DINGBURG DAILY DOINGS," CIRCULATION IS CLIMBING.. WHY?
..BECAUSE THEY COVER ONLY NEWS OF LOCAL INTEREST---LIKE TH' BIG FIRE DOWN AT TH' RIBOFLAVIN FACTORY!

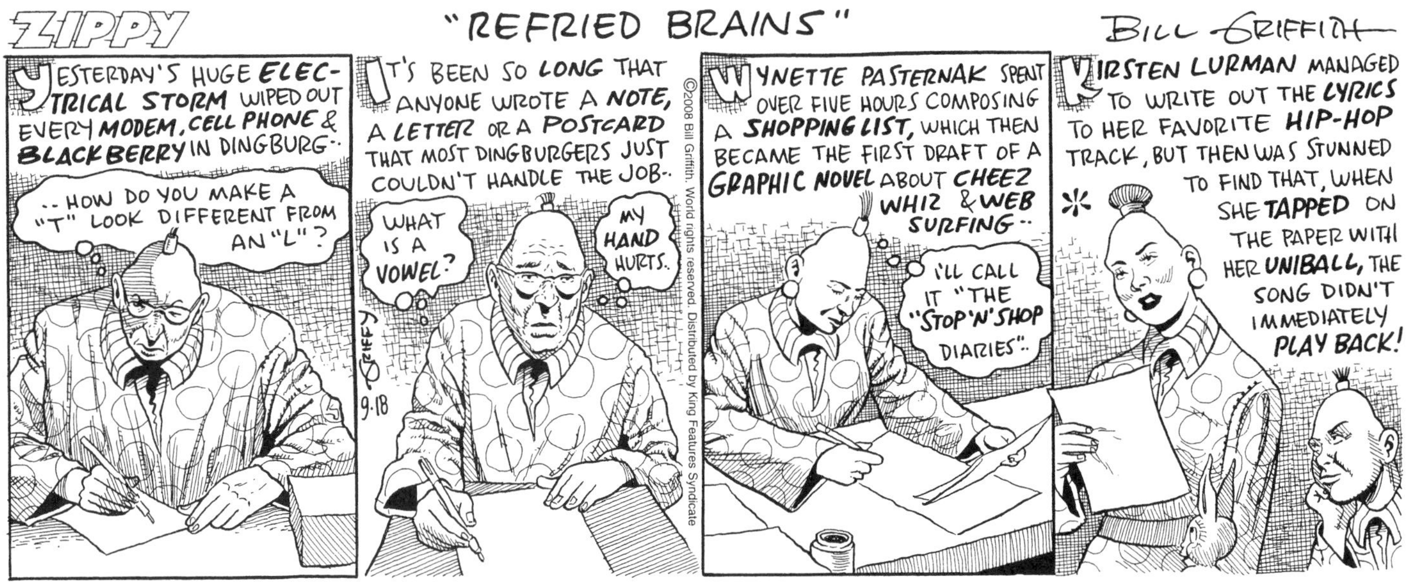
ZIPPY
"REFRIED BRAINS"
BILL GRIFFITH
YESTERDAY'S HUGE ELECTRICAL STORM WIPED OUT EVERY MODEM, CELL PHONE & BLACKBERRY IN DINGBURG..
..HOW DO YOU MAKE A "T" LOOK DIFFERENT FROM AN "L"?
GRIFFY 9.18
IT'S BEEN SO LONG THAT ANYONE WROTE A NOTE, A LETTER OR A POSTCARD THAT MOST DINGBURGERS JUST COULDN'T HANDLE THE JOB..
WHAT IS A VOWEL?
MY HAND HURTS..
©2008 Bill Griffith. World rights reserved. Distributed by King Features Syndicate
WYNETTE PASTERNAK SPENT OVER FIVE HOURS COMPOSING A SHOPPING LIST, WHICH THEN BECAME THE FIRST DRAFT OF A GRAPHIC NOVEL ABOUT CHEEZ WHIZ & WEB SURFING..
I'LL CALL IT "THE "STOP 'N' SHOP DIARIES"..
KIRSTEN LURMAN MANAGED TO WRITE OUT THE LYRICS TO HER FAVORITE HIP-HOP TRACK, BUT THEN WAS STUNNED TO FIND THAT, WHEN SHE TAPPED ON THE PAPER WITH HER UNIBALL, THE SONG DIDN'T IMMEDIATELY PLAY BACK!

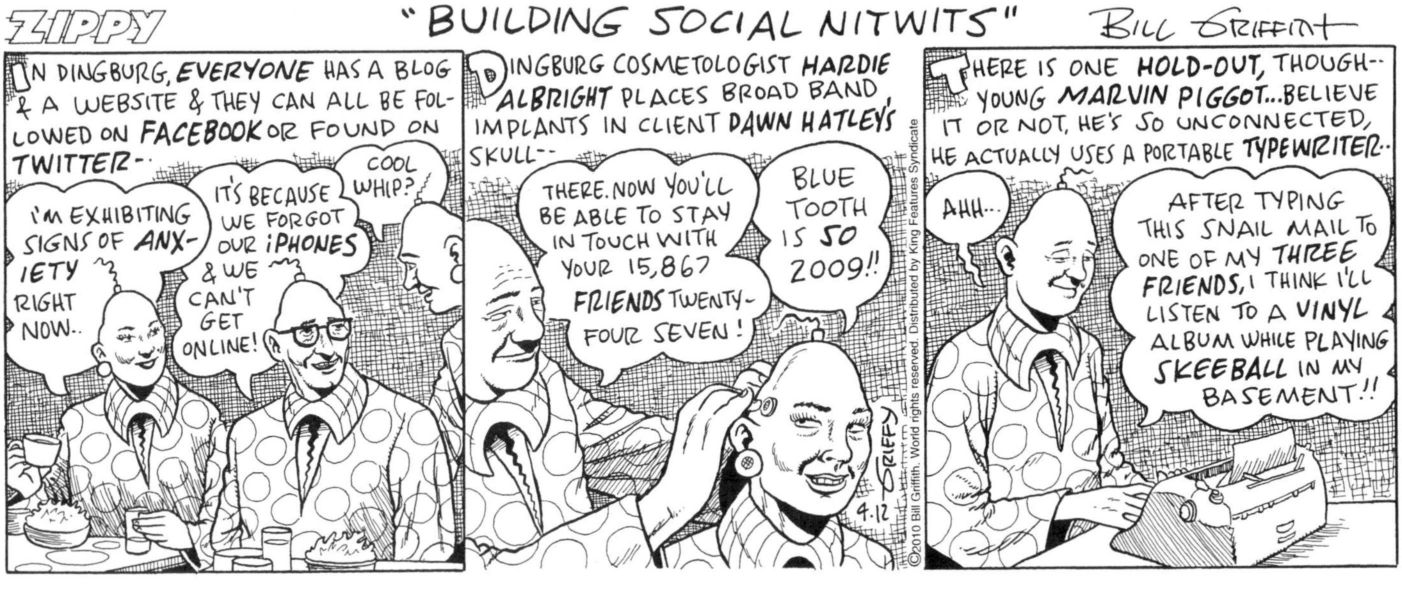
ZIPPY
"BUILDING SOCIAL NITWITS"
BILL GRIFFITH
IN DINGBURG, EVERYONE HAS A BLOG & A WEBSITE & THEY CAN ALL BE FOLLOWED ON FACEBOOK OR FOUND ON TWITTER..
I'M EXHIBITING SIGNS OF ANXIETY RIGHT NOW..
IT'S BECAUSE WE FORGOT OUR iPHONES & WE CAN'T GET ONLINE!
COOL WHIP?
DINGBURG COSMETOLOGIST HARDIE ALBRIGHT PLACES BROAD BAND IMPLANTS IN CLIENT DAWN HATLEY'S SKULL..
THERE. NOW YOU'LL BE ABLE TO STAY IN TOUCH WITH YOUR 15,867 FRIENDS TWENTY-FOUR SEVEN!
BLUE TOOTH IS SO 2009!!
GRIFFY 4.12
©2010 Bill Griffith. World rights reserved. Distributed by King Features Syndicate
THERE IS ONE HOLD-OUT, THOUGH.. YOUNG MARVIN PIGGOT...BELIEVE IT OR NOT, HE'S SO UNCONNECTED, HE ACTUALLY USES A PORTABLE TYPEWRITER..
AHH...
AFTER TYPING THIS SNAIL MAIL TO ONE OF MY THREE FRIENDS, I THINK I'LL LISTEN TO A VINYL ALBUM WHILE PLAYING SKEEBALL IN MY BASEMENT!!

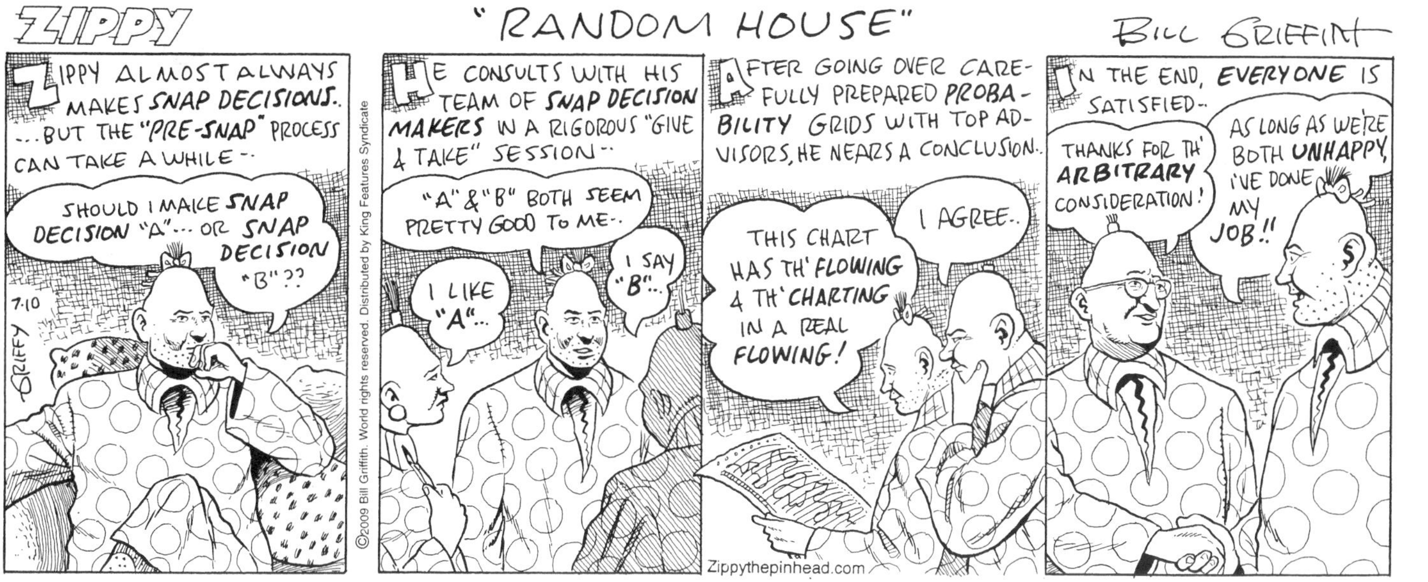
ZIPPY
"RANDOM HOUSE"
BILL GRIFFITH
ZIPPY ALMOST ALWAYS MAKES SNAP DECISIONS.. ...BUT THE "PRE-SNAP" PROCESS CAN TAKE A WHILE..
SHOULD I MAKE SNAP DECISION "A"... OR SNAP DECISION "B"??
7·10
GRIFFY
©2009 Bill Griffith. World rights reserved. Distributed by King Features Syndicate
HE CONSULTS WITH HIS TEAM OF SNAP DECISION MAKERS IN A RIGOROUS "GIVE & TAKE" SESSION..
"A" & "B" BOTH SEEM PRETTY GOOD TO ME..
I LIKE "A"...
I SAY "B"...
AFTER GOING OVER CAREFULLY PREPARED PROBABILITY GRIDS WITH TOP ADVISORS, HE NEARS A CONCLUSION..
THIS CHART HAS TH' FLOWING & TH' CHARTING IN A REAL FLOWING!
I AGREE..
Zippythepinhead.com
IN THE END, EVERYONE IS SATISFIED..
THANKS FOR TH' ARBITRARY CONSIDERATION!
AS LONG AS WE'RE BOTH UNHAPPY, I'VE DONE MY JOB!!

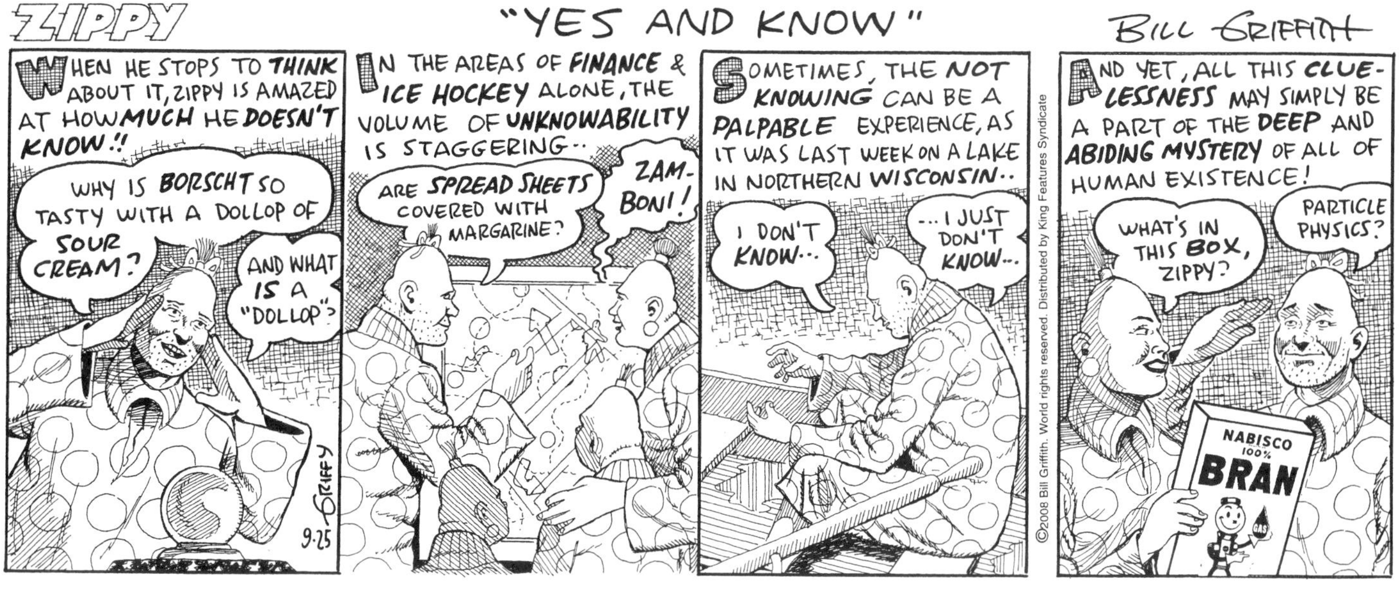
ZIPPY
"YES AND KNOW"
BILL GRIFFITH
WHEN HE STOPS TO THINK ABOUT IT, ZIPPY IS AMAZED AT HOW MUCH HE DOESN'T KNOW!!
WHY IS BORSCHT SO TASTY WITH A DOLLOP OF SOUR CREAM?
AND WHAT IS A "DOLLOP"?
GRIFFY
9·25
IN THE AREAS OF FINANCE & ICE HOCKEY ALONE, THE VOLUME OF UNKNOWABILITY IS STAGGERING..
ARE SPREAD SHEETS COVERED WITH MARGARINE?
ZAMBONI!
SOMETIMES, THE NOT KNOWING CAN BE A PALPABLE EXPERIENCE, AS IT WAS LAST WEEK ON A LAKE IN NORTHERN WISCONSIN..
I DON'T KNOW...
...I JUST DON'T KNOW...
©2008 Bill Griffith. World rights reserved. Distributed by King Features Syndicate
AND YET, ALL THIS CLUELESSNESS MAY SIMPLY BE A PART OF THE DEEP AND ABIDING MYSTERY OF ALL OF HUMAN EXISTENCE!
WHAT'S IN THIS BOX, ZIPPY?
PARTICLE PHYSICS?
NABISCO 100% BRAN

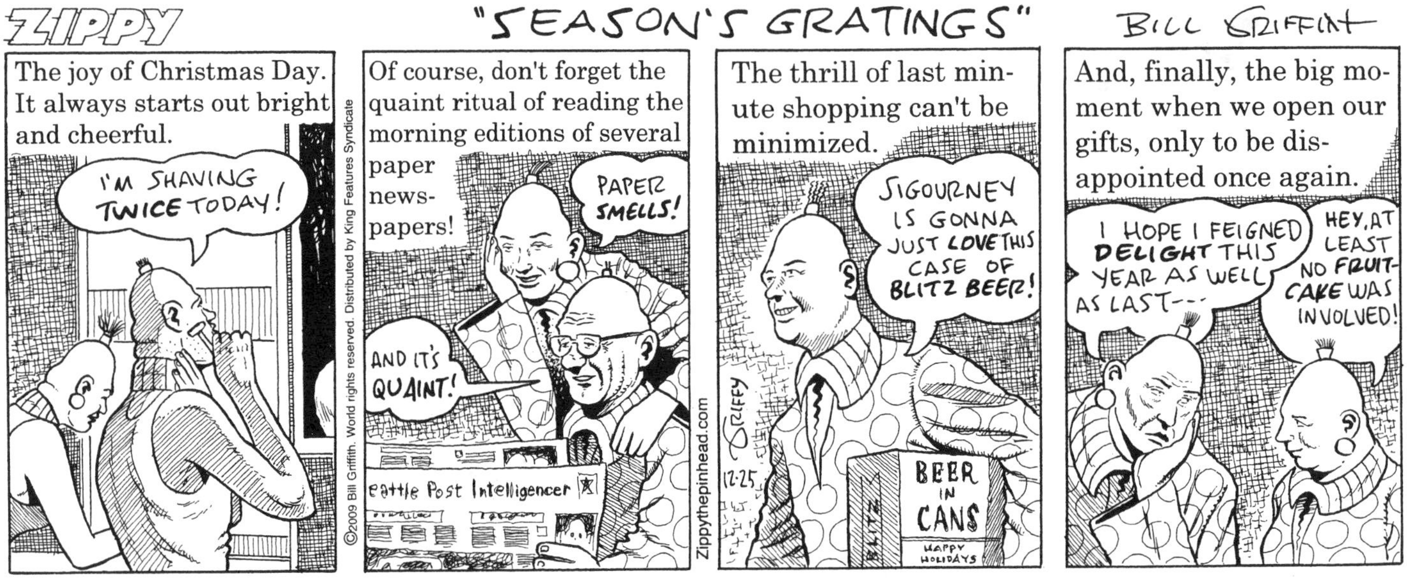
ZIPPY
"SEASON'S GRATINGS"
BILL GRIFFITH
The joy of Christmas Day. It always starts out bright and cheerful.
I'M SHAVING TWICE TODAY!
Of course, don't forget the quaint ritual of reading the morning editions of several paper news-papers!
PAPER SMELLS!
AND IT'S QUAINT!
eattle Post Intelligencer
©2009 Bill Griffith. World rights reserved. Distributed by King Features Syndicate
Zippythepinhead.com
The thrill of last minute shopping can't be minimized.
SIGOURNEY IS GONNA JUST LOVE THIS CASE OF BLITZ BEER!
GRIFFY 12-25
BEER IN CANS
HAPPY HOLIDAYS
And, finally, the big moment when we open our gifts, only to be disappointed once again.
I HOPE I FEIGNED DELIGHT THIS YEAR AS WELL AS LAST---
HEY, AT LEAST NO FRUIT-CAKE WAS INVOLVED!

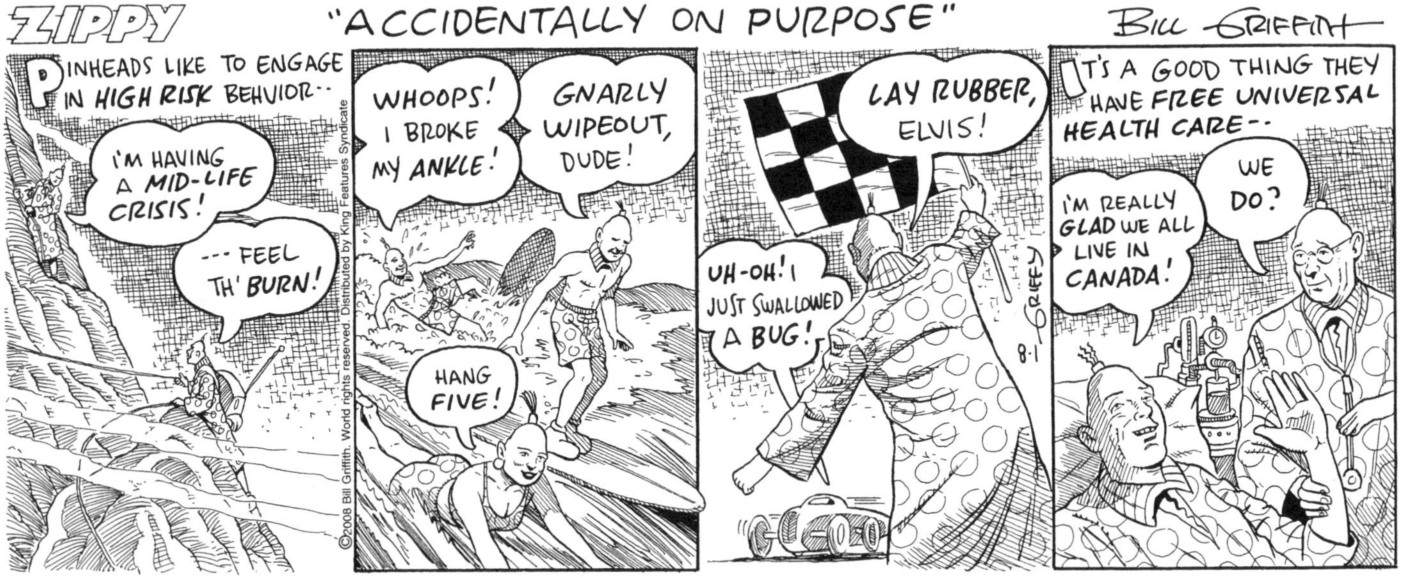
ZIPPY
"ACCIDENTALLY ON PURPOSE"
BILL GRIFFITH
PINHEADS LIKE TO ENGAGE IN HIGH RISK BEHVIOR--
I'M HAVING A MID-LIFE CRISIS!
--- FEEL TH' BURN!
©2008 Bill Griffith. World rights reserved. Distributed by King Features Syndicate
WHOOPS! I BROKE MY ANKLE!
GNARLY WIPEOUT, DUDE!
HANG FIVE!
LAY RUBBER, ELVIS!
UH-OH! I JUST SWALLOWED A BUG!
GRIFFY 8-1
IT'S A GOOD THING THEY HAVE FREE UNIVERSAL HEALTH CARE--
I'M REALLY GLAD WE ALL LIVE IN CANADA!
WE DO?

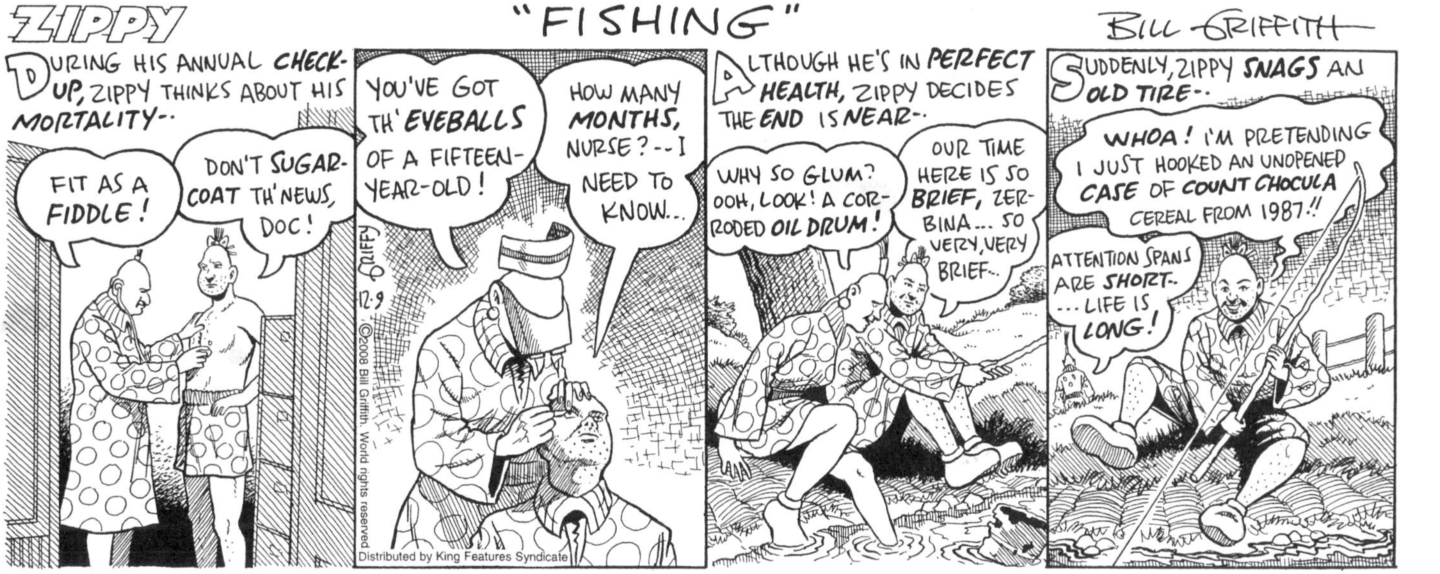
ZIPPY
"FISHING"
BILL GRIFFITH
DURING HIS ANNUAL CHECK-UP, ZIPPY THINKS ABOUT HIS MORTALITY..
FIT AS A FIDDLE!
DON'T SUGAR-COAT TH' NEWS, DOC!
YOU'VE GOT TH' EYEBALLS OF A FIFTEEN-YEAR-OLD!
HOW MANY MONTHS, NURSE? -- I NEED TO KNOW...
GRIFFY 12·9
©2008 Bill Griffith. World rights reserved
Distributed by King Features Syndicate
ALTHOUGH HE'S IN PERFECT HEALTH, ZIPPY DECIDES THE END IS NEAR..
WHY SO GLUM? OOH, LOOK! A CORRODED OIL DRUM!
OUR TIME HERE IS SO BRIEF, ZERBINA... SO VERY, VERY BRIEF..
SUDDENLY, ZIPPY SNAGS AN OLD TIRE..
WHOA! I'M PRETENDING I JUST HOOKED AN UNOPENED CASE OF COUNT CHOCULA CEREAL FROM 1987!!
ATTENTION SPANS ARE SHORT.. ...LIFE IS LONG!

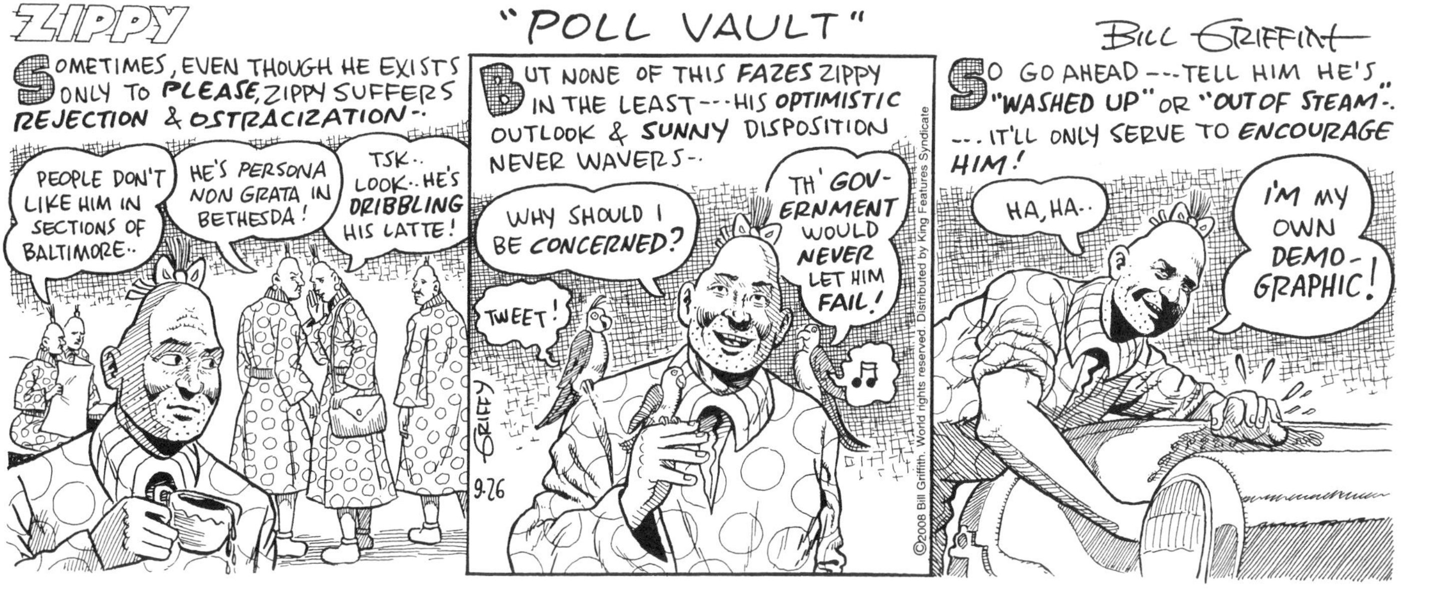
ZIPPY
"POLL VAULT"
BILL GRIFFITH
SOMETIMES, EVEN THOUGH HE EXISTS ONLY TO PLEASE, ZIPPY SUFFERS REJECTION & OSTRACIZATION..
PEOPLE DON'T LIKE HIM IN SECTIONS OF BALTIMORE..
HE'S PERSONA NON GRATA IN BETHESDA!
TSK.. LOOK.. HE'S DRIBBLING HIS LATTE!
BUT NONE OF THIS FAZES ZIPPY IN THE LEAST---HIS OPTIMISTIC OUTLOOK & SUNNY DISPOSITION NEVER WAVERS..
WHY SHOULD I BE CONCERNED?
TWEET!
TH' GOVERNMENT WOULD NEVER LET HIM FAIL!
GRIFFY 9·26
©2008 Bill Griffith. World rights reserved. Distributed by King Features Syndicate
SO GO AHEAD---TELL HIM HE'S "WASHED UP" OR "OUT OF STEAM".. ...IT'LL ONLY SERVE TO ENCOURAGE HIM!
HA, HA..
I'M MY OWN DEMOGRAPHIC!

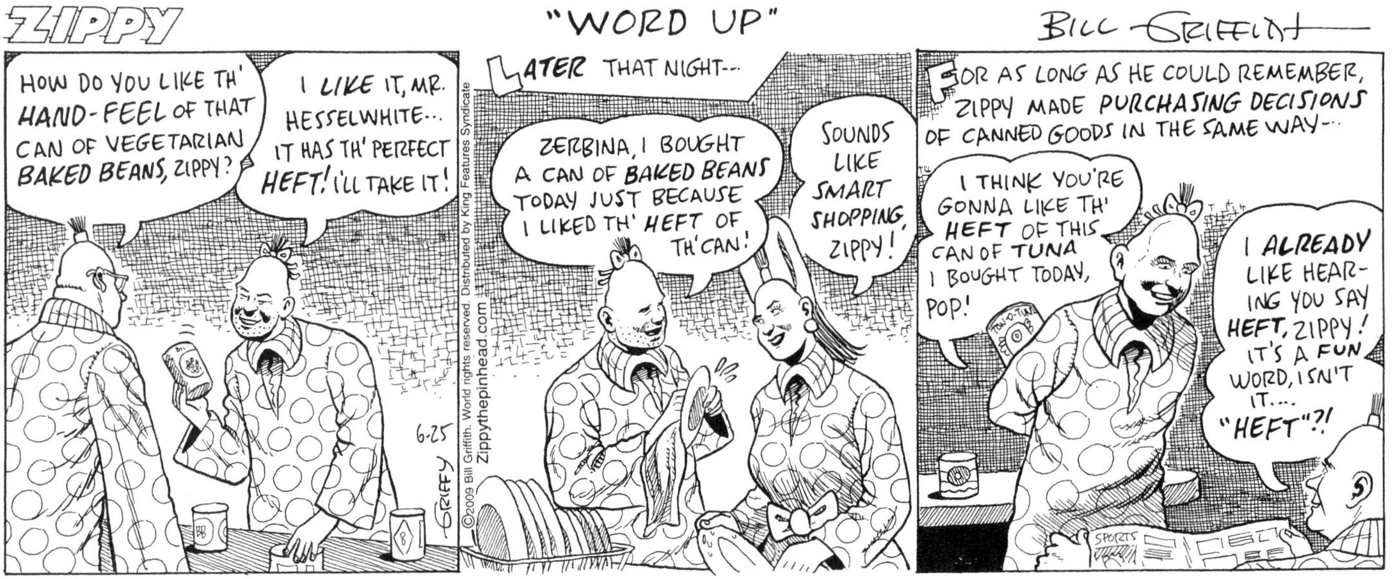
ZIPPY
"WORD UP"
BILL GRIFFITH
HOW DO YOU LIKE TH' HAND-FEEL OF THAT CAN OF VEGETARIAN BAKED BEANS, ZIPPY?
I LIKE IT, MR. HESSELWHITE... IT HAS TH' PERFECT HEFT! I'LL TAKE IT!
6-25
GRIFFY
©2009 Bill Griffith. World rights reserved. Distributed by King Features Syndicate
Zippythepinhead.com
LATER THAT NIGHT--
ZERBINA, I BOUGHT A CAN OF BAKED BEANS TODAY JUST BECAUSE I LIKED TH' HEFT OF TH' CAN!
SOUNDS LIKE SMART SHOPPING, ZIPPY!
FOR AS LONG AS HE COULD REMEMBER, ZIPPY MADE PURCHASING DECISIONS OF CANNED GOODS IN THE SAME WAY--
I THINK YOU'RE GONNA LIKE TH' HEFT OF THIS CAN OF TUNA I BOUGHT TODAY, POP!
I ALREADY LIKE HEARING YOU SAY HEFT, ZIPPY! IT'S A FUN WORD, ISN'T IT.... "HEFT"?!
SPORTS

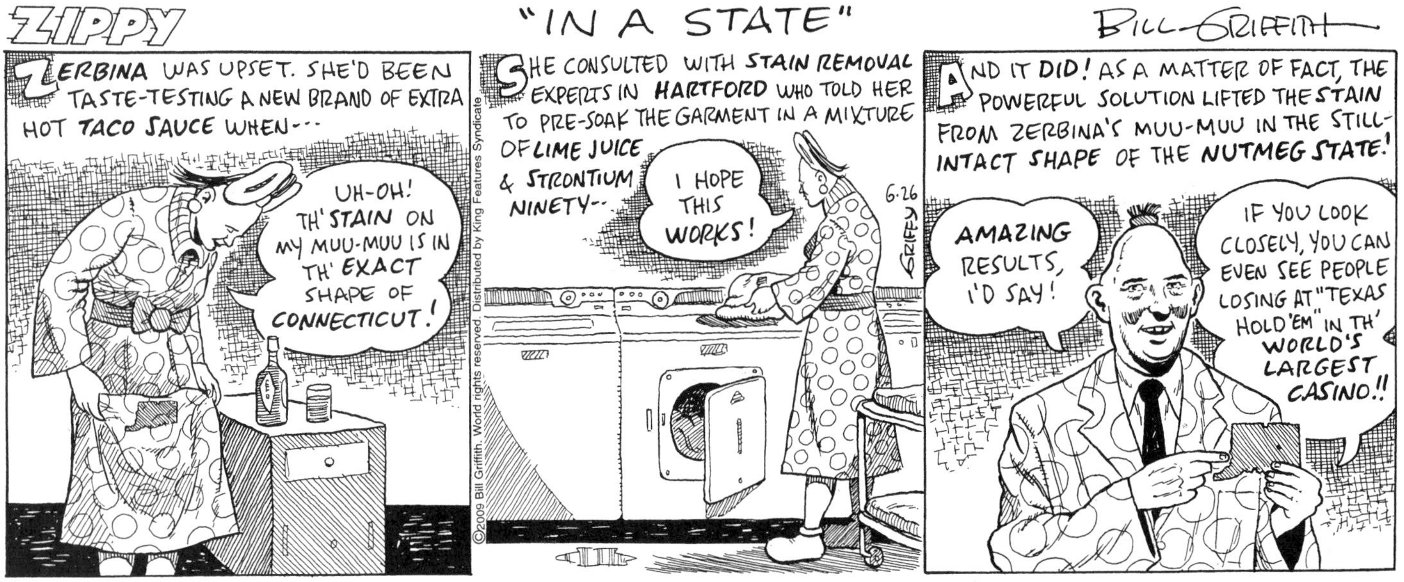
ZIPPY
"IN A STATE"
BILL GRIFFITH
ZERBINA WAS UPSET. SHE'D BEEN TASTE-TESTING A NEW BRAND OF EXTRA HOT TACO SAUCE WHEN---
UH-OH! TH' STAIN ON MY MUU-MUU IS IN TH' EXACT SHAPE OF CONNECTICUT!
©2009 Bill Griffith. World rights reserved. Distributed by King Features Syndicate
SHE CONSULTED WITH STAIN REMOVAL EXPERTS IN HARTFORD WHO TOLD HER TO PRE-SOAK THE GARMENT IN A MIXTURE OF LIME JUICE & STRONTIUM NINETY--
I HOPE THIS WORKS!
6-26
GRIFFY
AND IT DID! AS A MATTER OF FACT, THE POWERFUL SOLUTION LIFTED THE STAIN FROM ZERBINA'S MUU-MUU IN THE STILL-INTACT SHAPE OF THE NUTMEG STATE!
AMAZING RESULTS, I'D SAY!
IF YOU LOOK CLOSELY, YOU CAN EVEN SEE PEOPLE LOSING AT "TEXAS HOLD'EM" IN TH' WORLD'S LARGEST CASINO!!

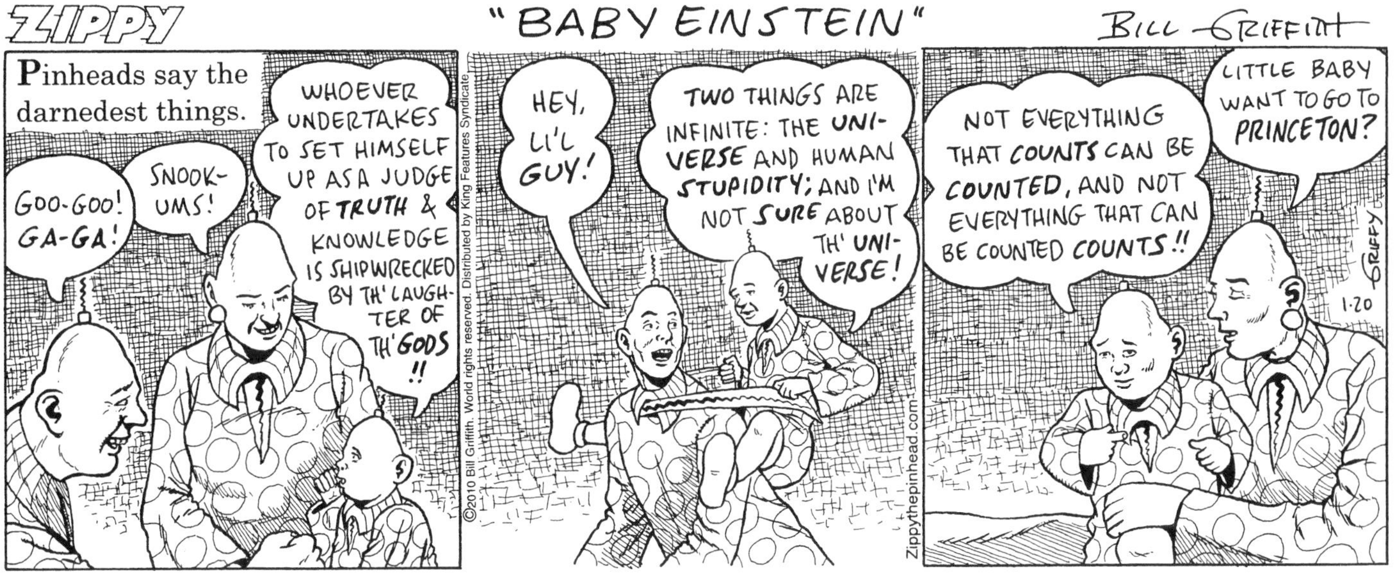
ZIPPY
"BABY EINSTEIN"
BILL GRIFFITH
Pinheads say the darnedest things.
GOO-GOO! GA-GA!
SNOOK-UMS!
WHOEVER UNDERTAKES TO SET HIMSELF UP AS A JUDGE OF TRUTH & KNOWLEDGE IS SHIPWRECKED BY TH' LAUGHTER OF TH' GODS!!
©2010 Bill Griffith. World rights reserved. Distributed by King Features Syndicate.
HEY, LI'L GUY!
TWO THINGS ARE INFINITE: THE UNIVERSE AND HUMAN STUPIDITY; AND I'M NOT SURE ABOUT TH' UNIVERSE!
Zippythepinhead.com
NOT EVERYTHING THAT COUNTS CAN BE COUNTED, AND NOT EVERYTHING THAT CAN BE COUNTED COUNTS!!
LITTLE BABY WANT TO GO TO PRINCETON?
GRIFFY
1·20

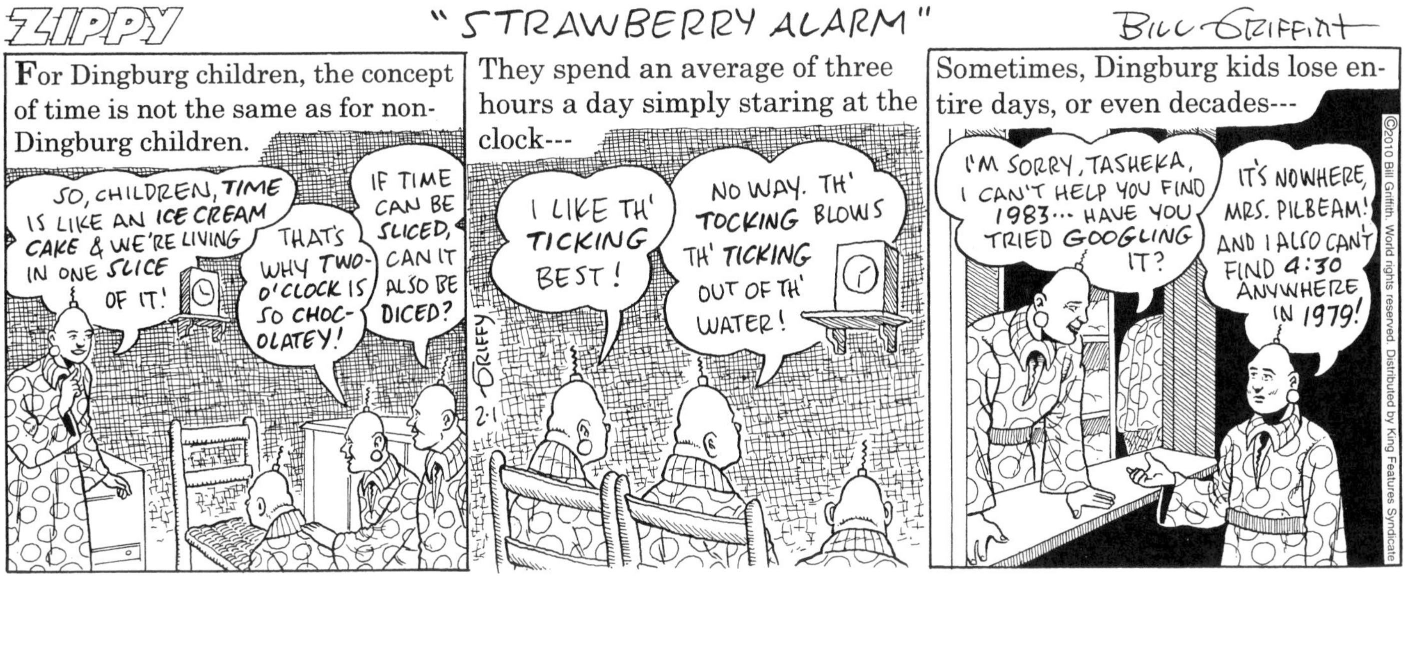
ZIPPY
"STRAWBERRY ALARM"
BILL GRIFFITH
For Dingburg children, the concept of time is not the same as for non-Dingburg children.
SO, CHILDREN, TIME IS LIKE AN ICE CREAM CAKE & WE'RE LIVING IN ONE SLICE OF IT!
THAT'S WHY TWO-O'CLOCK IS SO CHOCOLATEY!
IF TIME CAN BE SLICED, CAN IT ALSO BE DICED?
GRIFFY
2·1
They spend an average of three hours a day simply staring at the clock---
I LIKE TH' TICKING BEST!
NO WAY. TH' TOCKING BLOWS TH' TICKING OUT OF TH' WATER!
Sometimes, Dingburg kids lose entire days, or even decades---
I'M SORRY, TASHEKA, I CAN'T HELP YOU FIND 1983... HAVE YOU TRIED GOOGLING IT?
IT'S NOWHERE, MRS. PILBEAM! AND I ALSO CAN'T FIND 4:30 ANYWHERE IN 1979!
©2010 Bill Griffith. World rights reserved. Distributed by King Features Syndicate

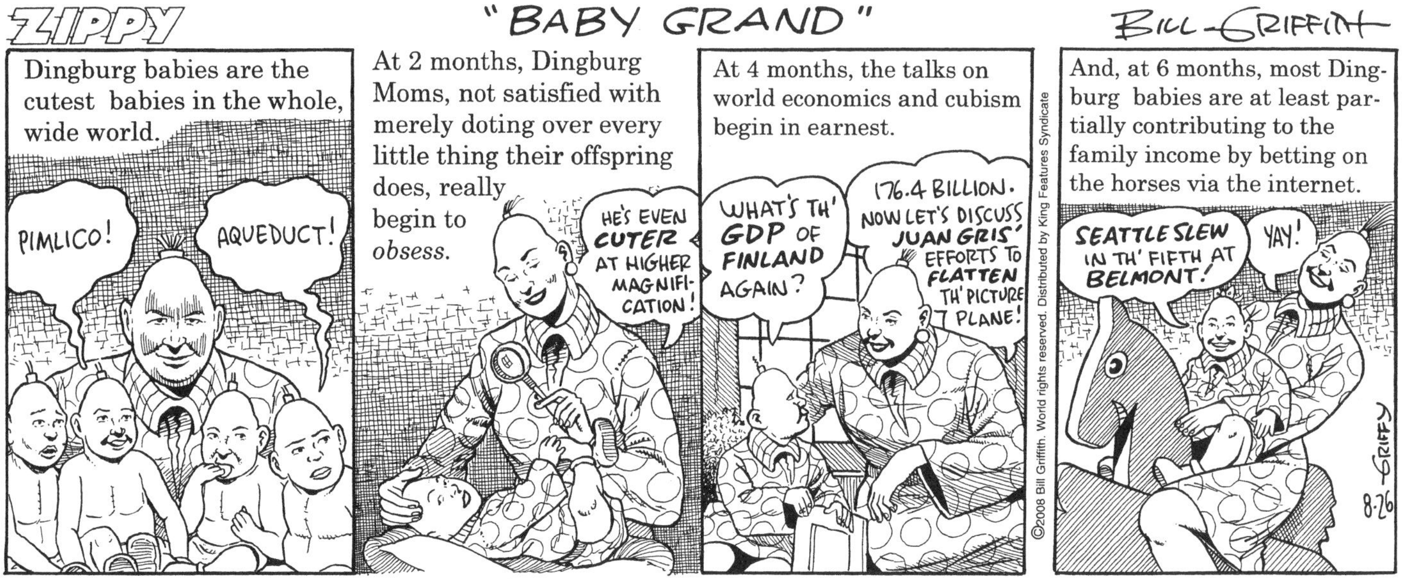
ZIPPY
"BABY GRAND"
BILL GRIFFITH
Dingburg babies are the cutest babies in the whole, wide world.
PIMLICO!
AQUEDUCT!
At 2 months, Dingburg Moms, not satisfied with merely doting over every little thing their offspring does, really begin to *obsess.*
HE'S EVEN CUTER AT HIGHER MAGNIFI-CATION!
At 4 months, the talks on world economics and cubism begin in earnest.
WHAT'S TH' GDP OF FINLAND AGAIN?
176.4 BILLION. NOW LET'S DISCUSS JUAN GRIS' EFFORTS TO FLATTEN TH' PICTURE PLANE!
©2008 Bill Griffith. World rights reserved. Distributed by King Features Syndicate
And, at 6 months, most Dingburg babies are at least partially contributing to the family income by betting on the horses via the internet.
SEATTLE SLEW IN TH' FIFTH AT BELMONT!
YAY!
GRIFFY
8·26

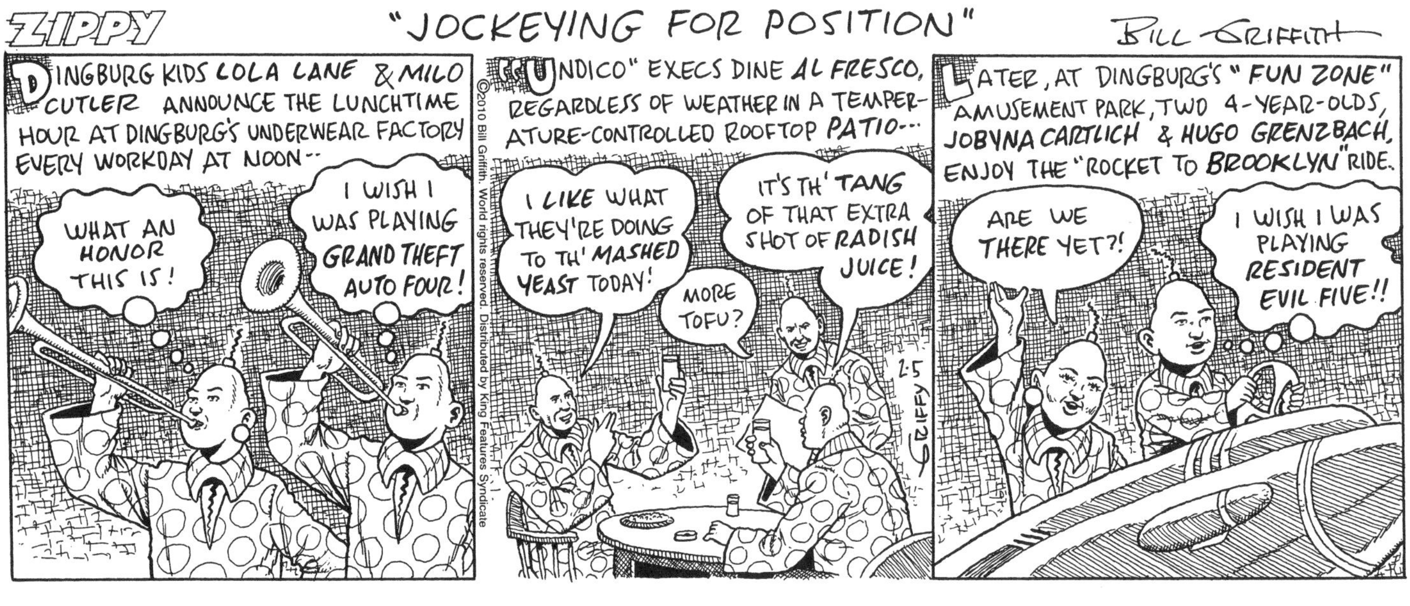
ZIPPY
"JOCKEYING FOR POSITION"
BILL GRIFFITH
DINGBURG KIDS LOLA LANE & MILO CUTLER ANNOUNCE THE LUNCHTIME HOUR AT DINGBURG'S UNDERWEAR FACTORY EVERY WORKDAY AT NOON--
WHAT AN HONOR THIS IS!
I WISH I WAS PLAYING GRAND THEFT AUTO FOUR!
©2010 Bill Griffith. World rights reserved. Distributed by King Features Syndicate
"UNDICO" EXECS DINE AL FRESCO, REGARDLESS OF WEATHER IN A TEMPERATURE-CONTROLLED ROOFTOP PATIO--
I LIKE WHAT THEY'RE DOING TO TH' MASHED YEAST TODAY!
MORE TOFU?
IT'S TH' TANG OF THAT EXTRA SHOT OF RADISH JUICE!
2·5
GRIFFY
LATER, AT DINGBURG'S "FUN ZONE" AMUSEMENT PARK, TWO 4-YEAR-OLDS, JOBYNA CARTLICH & HUGO GRENZBACH, ENJOY THE "ROCKET TO BROOKLYN" RIDE.
ARE WE THERE YET?!
I WISH I WAS PLAYING RESIDENT EVIL FIVE!!

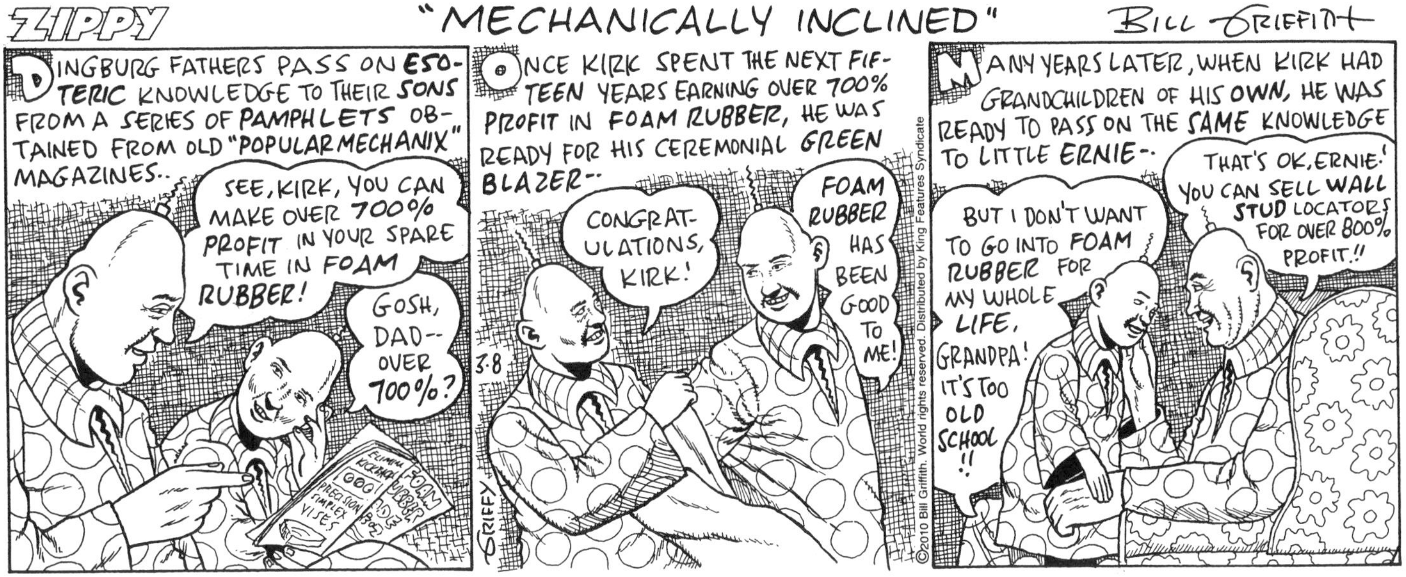

ZIPPY
"MECHANICALLY INCLINED"
BILL GRIFFITH
DINGBURG FATHERS PASS ON ESOTERIC KNOWLEDGE TO THEIR SONS FROM A SERIES OF PAMPHLETS OBTAINED FROM OLD "POPULAR MECHANIX" MAGAZINES..
SEE, KIRK, YOU CAN MAKE OVER 700% PROFIT IN YOUR SPARE TIME IN FOAM RUBBER!
GOSH, DAD-- OVER 700%?
FOAM RUBBER
PRECISION SIMPLEX VISES
ONCE KIRK SPENT THE NEXT FIFTEEN YEARS EARNING OVER 700% PROFIT IN FOAM RUBBER, HE WAS READY FOR HIS CEREMONIAL GREEN BLAZER--
CONGRATULATIONS, KIRK!
FOAM RUBBER HAS BEEN GOOD TO ME!
3·8
GRIFFY
©2010 Bill Griffith. World rights reserved. Distributed by King Features Syndicate
MANY YEARS LATER, WHEN KIRK HAD GRANDCHILDREN OF HIS OWN, HE WAS READY TO PASS ON THE SAME KNOWLEDGE TO LITTLE ERNIE--
BUT I DON'T WANT TO GO INTO FOAM RUBBER FOR MY WHOLE LIFE, GRANDPA! IT'S TOO OLD SCHOOL!!
THAT'S OK, ERNIE! YOU CAN SELL WALL STUD LOCATORS FOR OVER 800% PROFIT!!

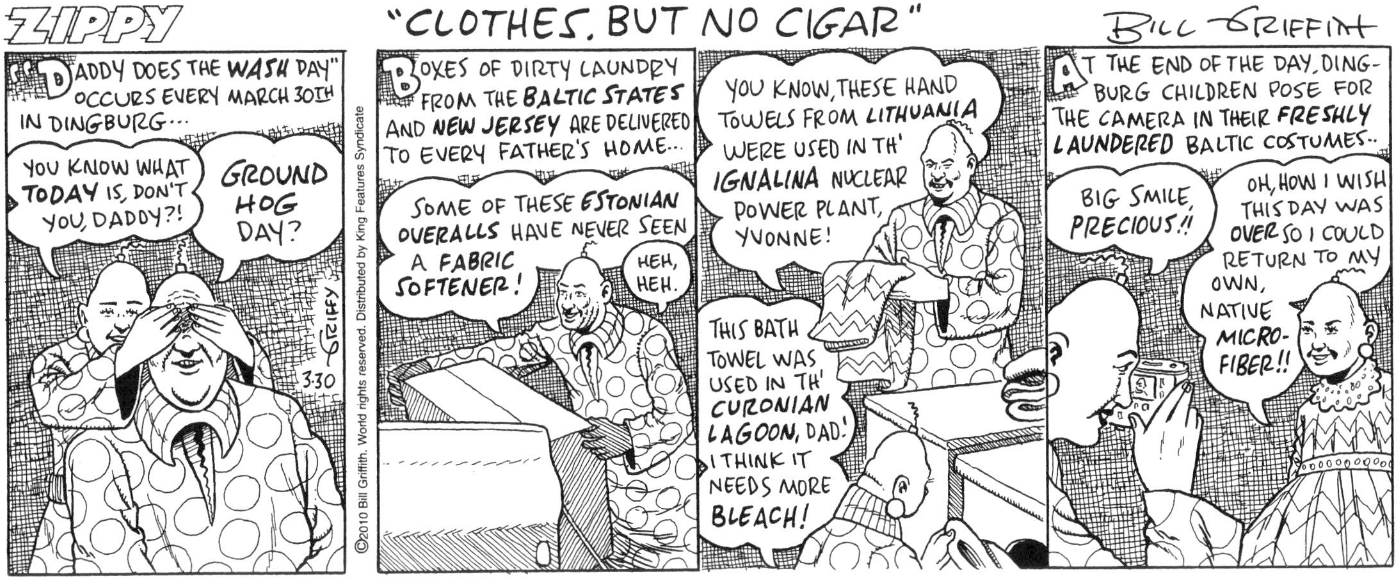

ZIPPY
"CLOTHES, BUT NO CIGAR"
BILL GRIFFITH
"DADDY DOES THE WASH DAY" OCCURS EVERY MARCH 30TH IN DINGBURG...
YOU KNOW WHAT TODAY IS, DON'T YOU, DADDY?!
GROUND HOG DAY?
GRIFFY
3·30
©2010 Bill Griffith. World rights reserved. Distributed by King Features Syndicate
BOXES OF DIRTY LAUNDRY FROM THE BALTIC STATES AND NEW JERSEY ARE DELIVERED TO EVERY FATHER'S HOME...
SOME OF THESE ESTONIAN OVERALLS HAVE NEVER SEEN A FABRIC SOFTENER!
HEH, HEH.
YOU KNOW, THESE HAND TOWELS FROM LITHUANIA WERE USED IN TH' IGNALINA NUCLEAR POWER PLANT, YVONNE!
THIS BATH TOWEL WAS USED IN TH' CURONIAN LAGOON, DAD! I THINK IT NEEDS MORE BLEACH!
AT THE END OF THE DAY, DINGBURG CHILDREN POSE FOR THE CAMERA IN THEIR FRESHLY LAUNDERED BALTIC COSTUMES..
BIG SMILE, PRECIOUS!!
OH, HOW I WISH THIS DAY WAS OVER SO I COULD RETURN TO MY OWN, NATIVE MICRO-FIBER!!

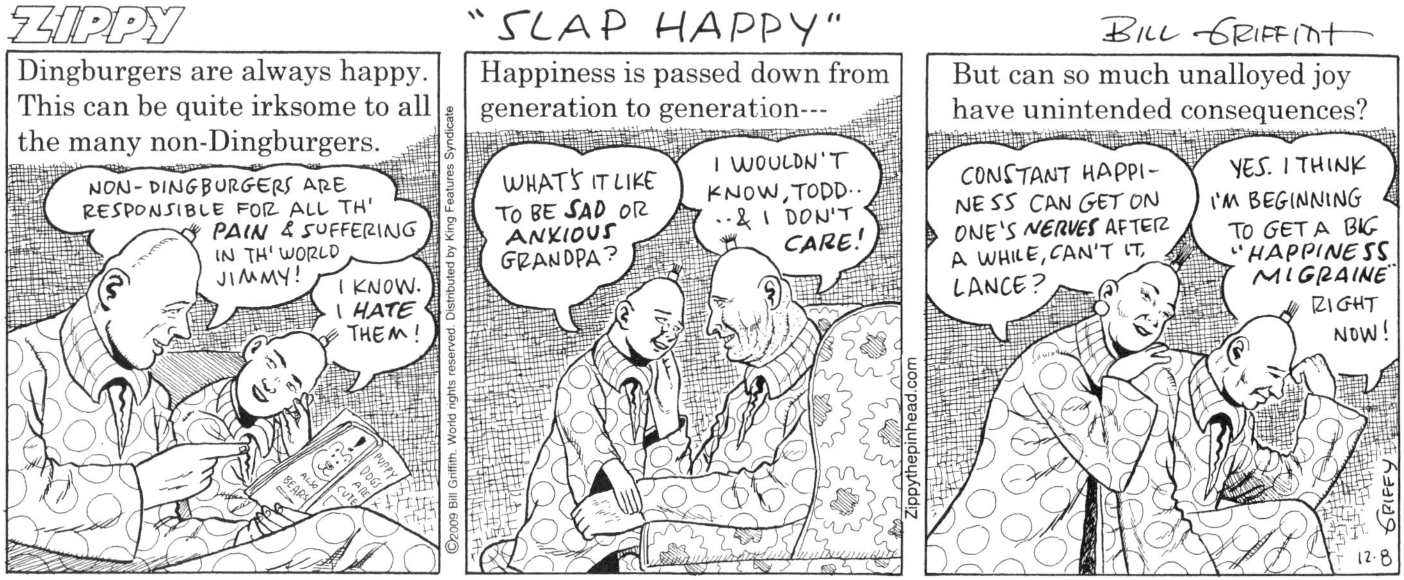
ZIPPY
"SLAP HAPPY"
BILL GRIFFITH
Dingburgers are always happy. This can be quite irksome to all the many non-Dingburgers.
NON-DINGBURGERS ARE RESPONSIBLE FOR ALL TH' PAIN & SUFFERING IN TH' WORLD JIMMY!
I KNOW. I HATE THEM!
PUPPY DOGS ARE CUTE
ALSO BEARS
©2009 Bill Griffith. World rights reserved. Distributed by King Features Syndicate
Happiness is passed down from generation to generation---
WHAT'S IT LIKE TO BE SAD OR ANXIOUS GRANDPA?
I WOULDN'T KNOW, TODD.. ..& I DON'T CARE!
Zippythepinhead.com
But can so much unalloyed joy have unintended consequences?
CONSTANT HAPPINESS CAN GET ON ONE'S NERVES AFTER A WHILE, CAN'T IT, LANCE?
YES. I THINK I'M BEGINNING TO GET A BIG "HAPPINESS MIGRAINE" RIGHT NOW!
GRIFFY
12·8

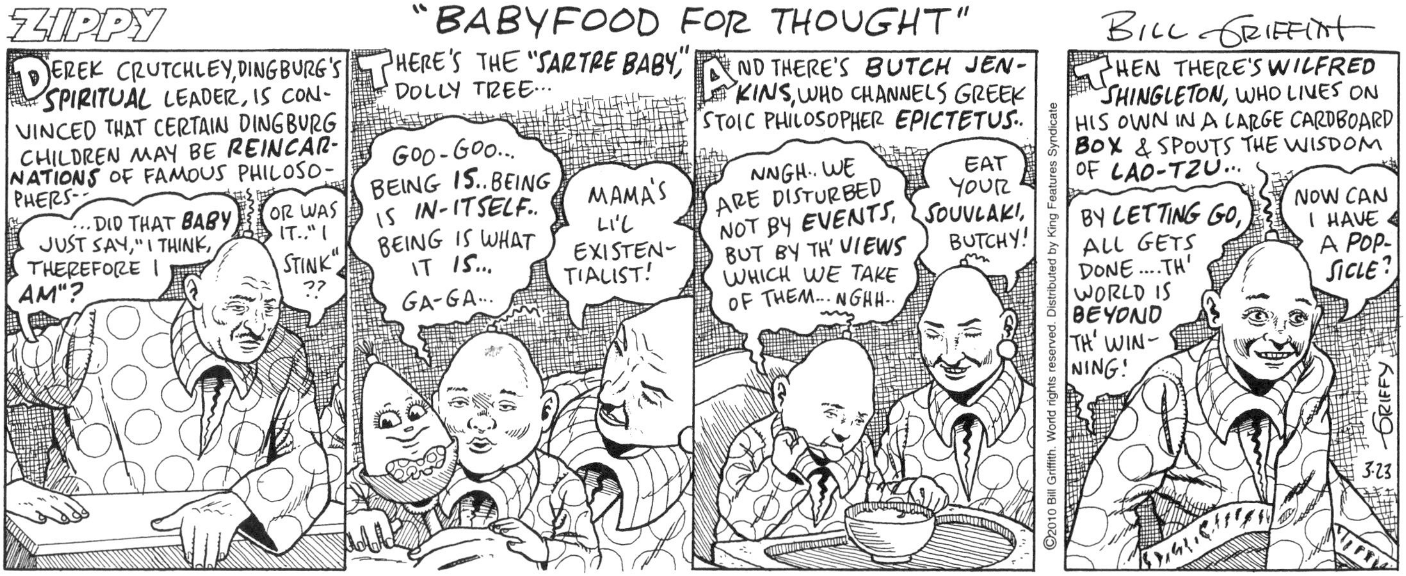
ZIPPY
"BABYFOOD FOR THOUGHT"
BILL GRIFFITH
DEREK CRUTCHLEY, DINGBURG'S SPIRITUAL LEADER, IS CONVINCED THAT CERTAIN DINGBURG CHILDREN MAY BE REINCARNATIONS OF FAMOUS PHILOSOPHERS--
...DID THAT BABY JUST SAY, "I THINK, THEREFORE I AM"?
OR WAS IT.."I STINK"??
THERE'S THE "SARTRE BABY," DOLLY TREE...
GOO-GOO... BEING IS.. BEING IS IN-ITSELF.. BEING IS WHAT IT IS... GA-GA...
MAMA'S LI'L EXISTENTIALIST!
AND THERE'S BUTCH JENKINS, WHO CHANNELS GREEK STOIC PHILOSOPHER EPICTETUS..
NNGH.. WE ARE DISTURBED NOT BY EVENTS, BUT BY TH' VIEWS WHICH WE TAKE OF THEM... NGHH..
EAT YOUR SOUVLAKI, BUTCHY!
©2010 Bill Griffith. World rights reserved. Distributed by King Features Syndicate
THEN THERE'S WILFRED SHINGLETON, WHO LIVES ON HIS OWN IN A LARGE CARDBOARD BOX & SPOUTS THE WISDOM OF LAO-TZU...
BY LETTING GO, ALL GETS DONE.... TH' WORLD IS BEYOND TH' WINNING!
NOW CAN I HAVE A POPSICLE?
GRIFFY
3·23

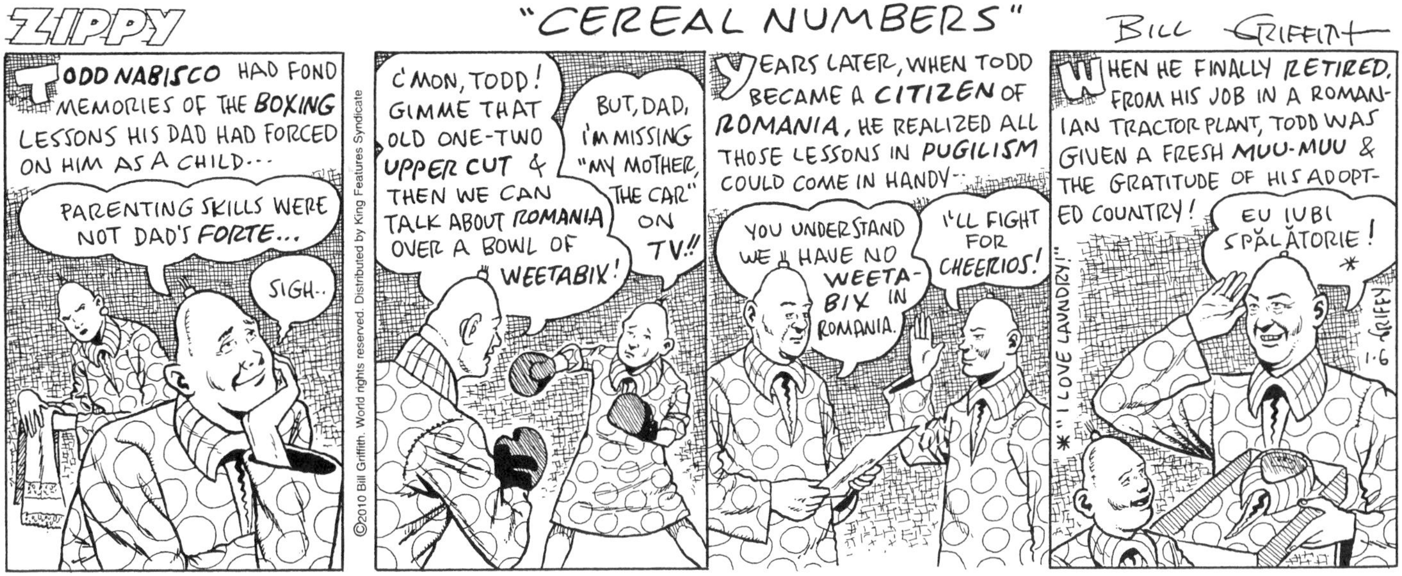
ZIPPY
"CEREAL NUMBERS"
BILL GRIFFITH
TODD NABISCO HAD FOND MEMORIES OF THE BOXING LESSONS HIS DAD HAD FORCED ON HIM AS A CHILD...
PARENTING SKILLS WERE NOT DAD'S FORTE...
SIGH..
©2010 Bill Griffith. World rights reserved. Distributed by King Features Syndicate
C'MON, TODD! GIMME THAT OLD ONE-TWO UPPER CUT & THEN WE CAN TALK ABOUT ROMANIA OVER A BOWL OF WEETABIX!
BUT, DAD, I'M MISSING "MY MOTHER, THE CAR" ON TV!!
YEARS LATER, WHEN TODD BECAME A CITIZEN OF ROMANIA, HE REALIZED ALL THOSE LESSONS IN PUGILISM COULD COME IN HANDY..
YOU UNDERSTAND WE HAVE NO WEETABIX IN ROMANIA.
I'LL FIGHT FOR CHEERIOS!
WHEN HE FINALLY RETIRED FROM HIS JOB IN A ROMANIAN TRACTOR PLANT, TODD WAS GIVEN A FRESH MUU-MUU & THE GRATITUDE OF HIS ADOPTED COUNTRY!
EU IUBI SPĂLĂTORIE! *
* "I LOVE LAUNDRY!"
GRIFFY 1·6

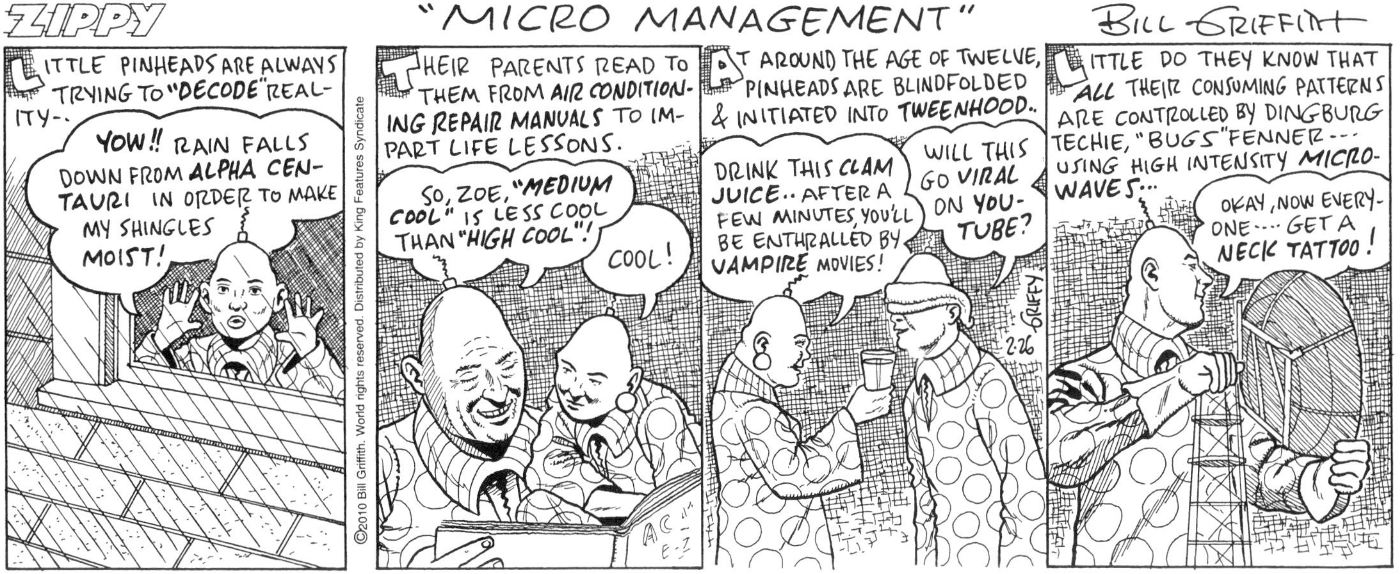
ZIPPY
"MICRO MANAGEMENT"
BILL GRIFFITH
LITTLE PINHEADS ARE ALWAYS TRYING TO "DECODE" REALITY..
YOW!! RAIN FALLS DOWN FROM ALPHA CENTAURI IN ORDER TO MAKE MY SHINGLES MOIST!
©2010 Bill Griffith. World rights reserved. Distributed by King Features Syndicate
THEIR PARENTS READ TO THEM FROM AIR CONDITIONING REPAIR MANUALS TO IMPART LIFE LESSONS.
SO, ZOE, "MEDIUM COOL" IS LESS COOL THAN "HIGH COOL"!
COOL!
AC A-Z
AT AROUND THE AGE OF TWELVE, PINHEADS ARE BLINDFOLDED & INITIATED INTO TWEENHOOD..
DRINK THIS CLAM JUICE.. AFTER A FEW MINUTES, YOU'LL BE ENTHRALLED BY VAMPIRE MOVIES!
WILL THIS GO VIRAL ON YOU-TUBE?
GRIFFY 2·26
LITTLE DO THEY KNOW THAT ALL THEIR CONSUMING PATTERNS ARE CONTROLLED BY DINGBURG TECHIE, "BUGS" FENNER --- USING HIGH INTENSITY MICRO-WAVES...
OKAY, NOW EVERYONE ---- GET A NECK TATTOO!

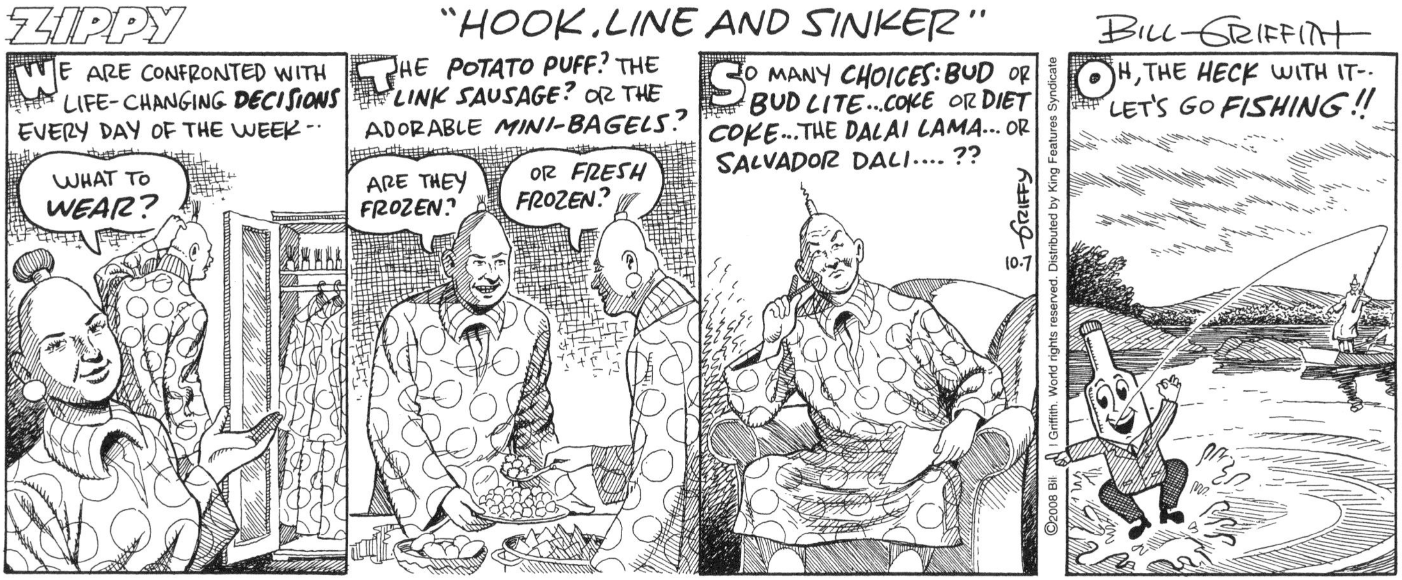
ZIPPY
"HOOK, LINE AND SINKER"
BILL GRIFFITH
WE ARE CONFRONTED WITH LIFE-CHANGING DECISIONS EVERY DAY OF THE WEEK--
WHAT TO WEAR?
THE POTATO PUFF? THE LINK SAUSAGE? OR THE ADORABLE MINI-BAGELS?
ARE THEY FROZEN?
OR FRESH FROZEN?
SO MANY CHOICES: BUD OR BUD LITE...COKE OR DIET COKE...THE DALAI LAMA... OR SALVADOR DALI.... ??
GRIFFY 10·7
©2008 Bill Griffith. World rights reserved. Distributed by King Features Syndicate
OH, THE HECK WITH IT-- LET'S GO FISHING!!

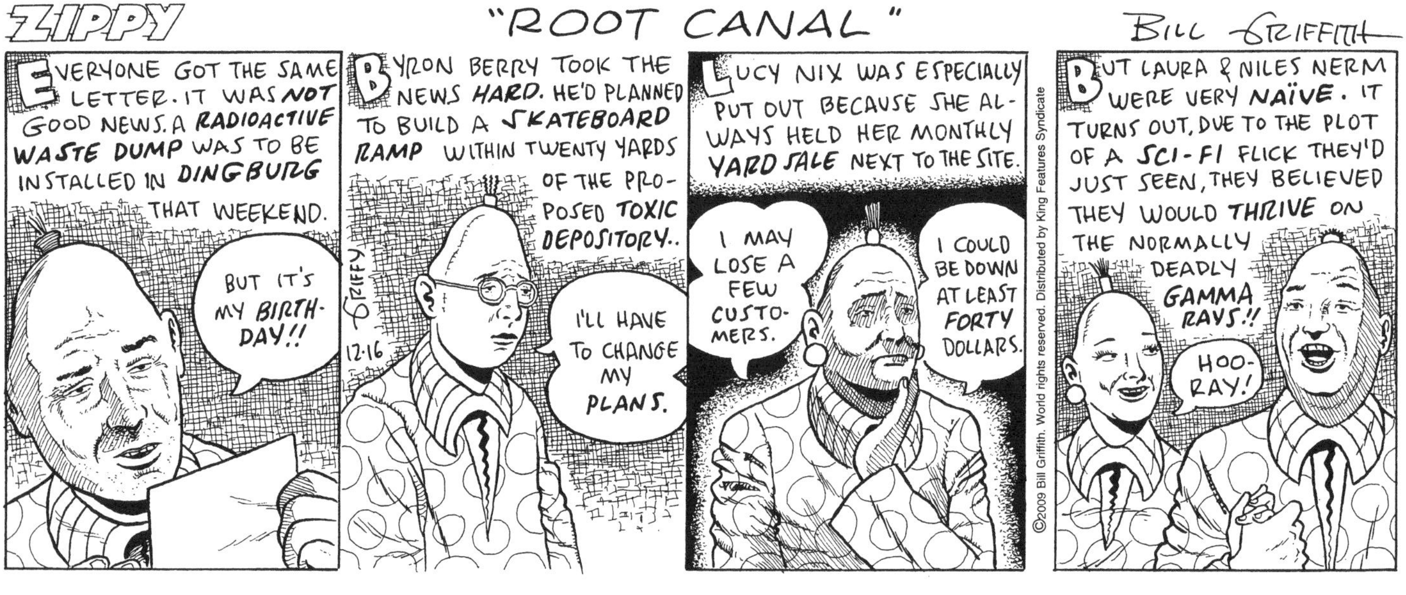
ZIPPY
"ROOT CANAL"
BILL GRIFFITH
EVERYONE GOT THE SAME LETTER. IT WAS NOT GOOD NEWS. A RADIOACTIVE WASTE DUMP WAS TO BE INSTALLED IN DINGBURG THAT WEEKEND.
BUT IT'S MY BIRTHDAY!!
BYRON BERRY TOOK THE NEWS HARD. HE'D PLANNED TO BUILD A SKATEBOARD RAMP WITHIN TWENTY YARDS OF THE PROPOSED TOXIC DEPOSITORY..
GRIFFY 12·16
I'LL HAVE TO CHANGE MY PLANS.
LUCY NIX WAS ESPECIALLY PUT OUT BECAUSE SHE ALWAYS HELD HER MONTHLY YARD SALE NEXT TO THE SITE.
I MAY LOSE A FEW CUSTOMERS.
I COULD BE DOWN AT LEAST FORTY DOLLARS.
©2009 Bill Griffith. World rights reserved. Distributed by King Features Syndicate
BUT LAURA & NILES NERM WERE VERY NAÏVE. IT TURNS OUT, DUE TO THE PLOT OF A SCI-FI FLICK THEY'D JUST SEEN, THEY BELIEVED THEY WOULD THRIVE ON THE NORMALLY DEADLY GAMMA RAYS!!
HOO-RAY!

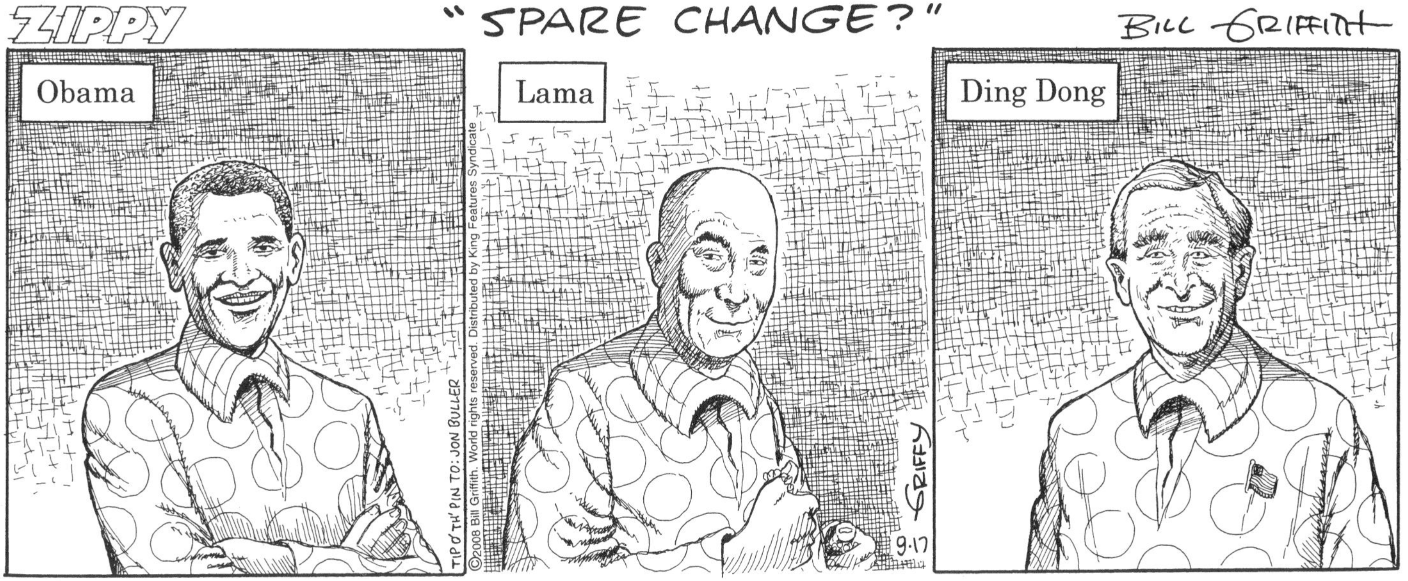
ZIPPY
"SPARE CHANGE?"
BILL GRIFFITH
Obama
Lama
Ding Dong
TIP O' TH' PIN TO: JON BULLER
©2008 Bill Griffith. World rights reserved. Distributed by King Features Syndicate
GRIFFY
9·17

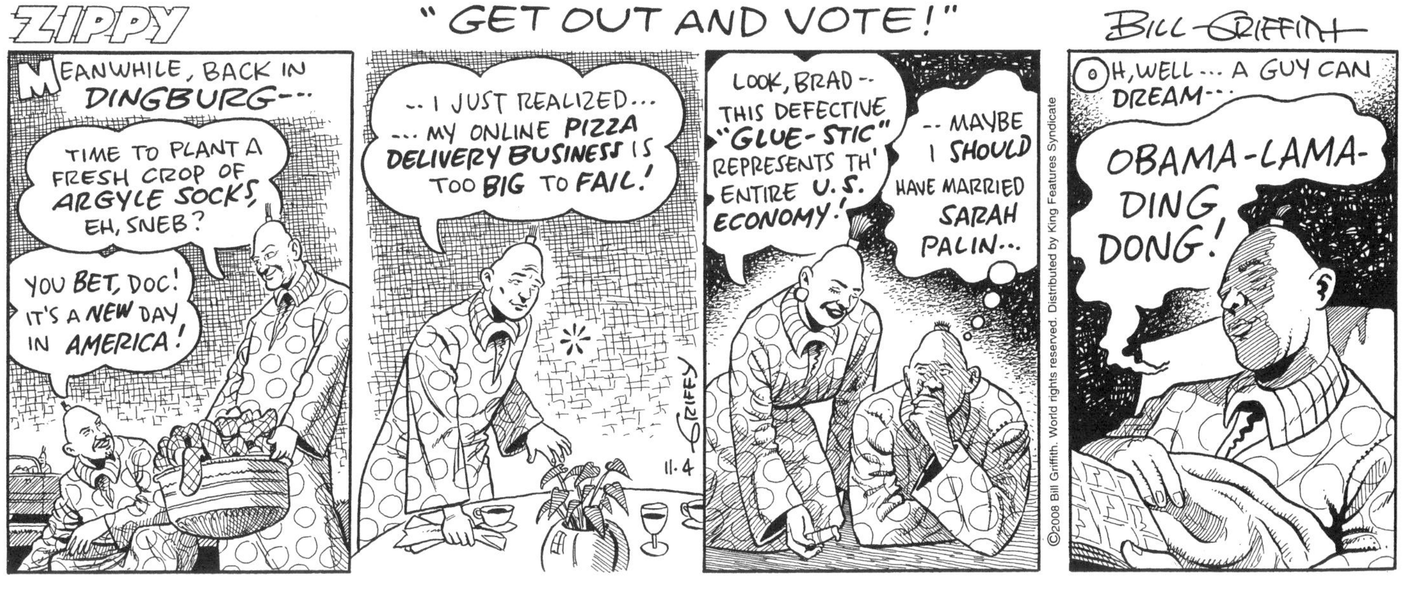
ZIPPY
"GET OUT AND VOTE!"
BILL GRIFFITH
MEANWHILE, BACK IN DINGBURG---
TIME TO PLANT A FRESH CROP OF ARGYLE SOCKS, EH, SNEB?
YOU BET, DOC! IT'S A NEW DAY IN AMERICA!
-- I JUST REALIZED... ...MY ONLINE PIZZA DELIVERY BUSINESS IS TOO BIG TO FAIL!
GRIFFY
11·4
LOOK, BRAD -- THIS DEFECTIVE "GLUE-STIC" REPRESENTS TH' ENTIRE U.S. ECONOMY!
-- MAYBE I SHOULD HAVE MARRIED SARAH PALIN...
©2008 Bill Griffith. World rights reserved. Distributed by King Features Syndicate
OH, WELL ... A GUY CAN DREAM---
OBAMA-LAMA-DING DONG!

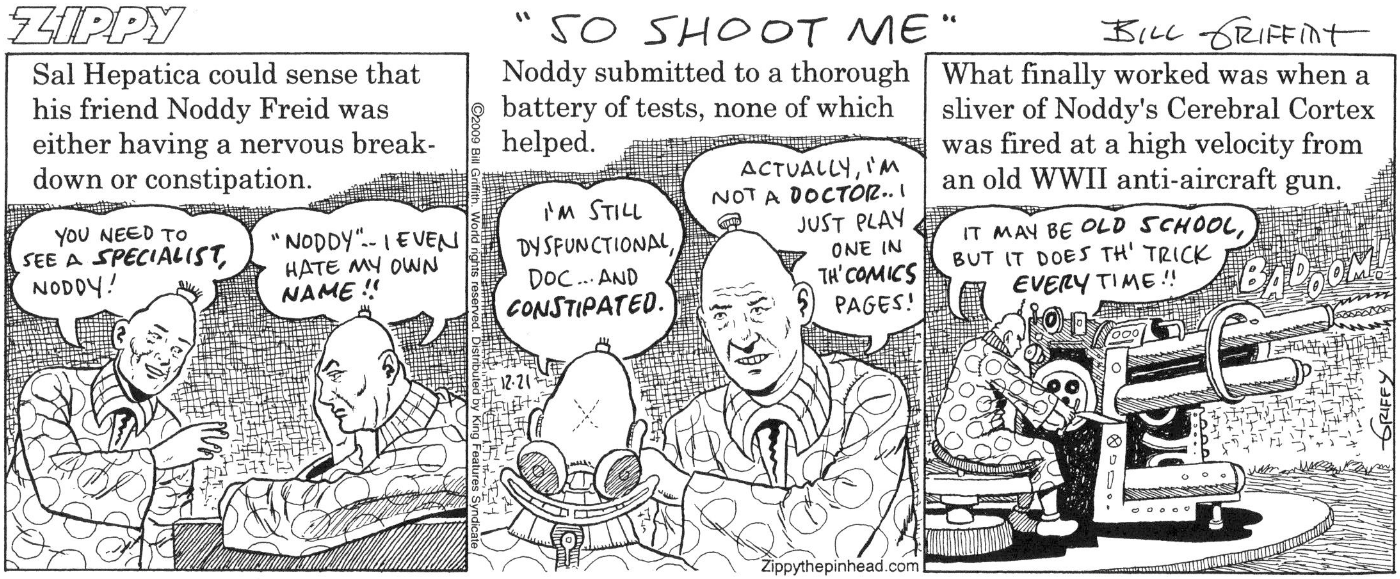
ZIPPY
"SO SHOOT ME"
BILL GRIFFITH
Sal Hepatica could sense that his friend Noddy Freid was either having a nervous break-down or constipation.
YOU NEED TO SEE A SPECIALIST, NODDY!
"NODDY"-- I EVEN HATE MY OWN NAME!!
©2009 Bill Griffith. World rights reserved. Distributed by King Features Syndicate
Noddy submitted to a thorough battery of tests, none of which helped.
I'M STILL DYSFUNCTIONAL, DOC... AND CONSTIPATED.
ACTUALLY, I'M NOT A DOCTOR.. I JUST PLAY ONE IN TH' COMICS PAGES!
12-21
Zippythepinhead.com
What finally worked was when a sliver of Noddy's Cerebral Cortex was fired at a high velocity from an old WWII anti-aircraft gun.
IT MAY BE OLD SCHOOL, BUT IT DOES TH' TRICK EVERY TIME!!
BADOOM!
GRIFFY

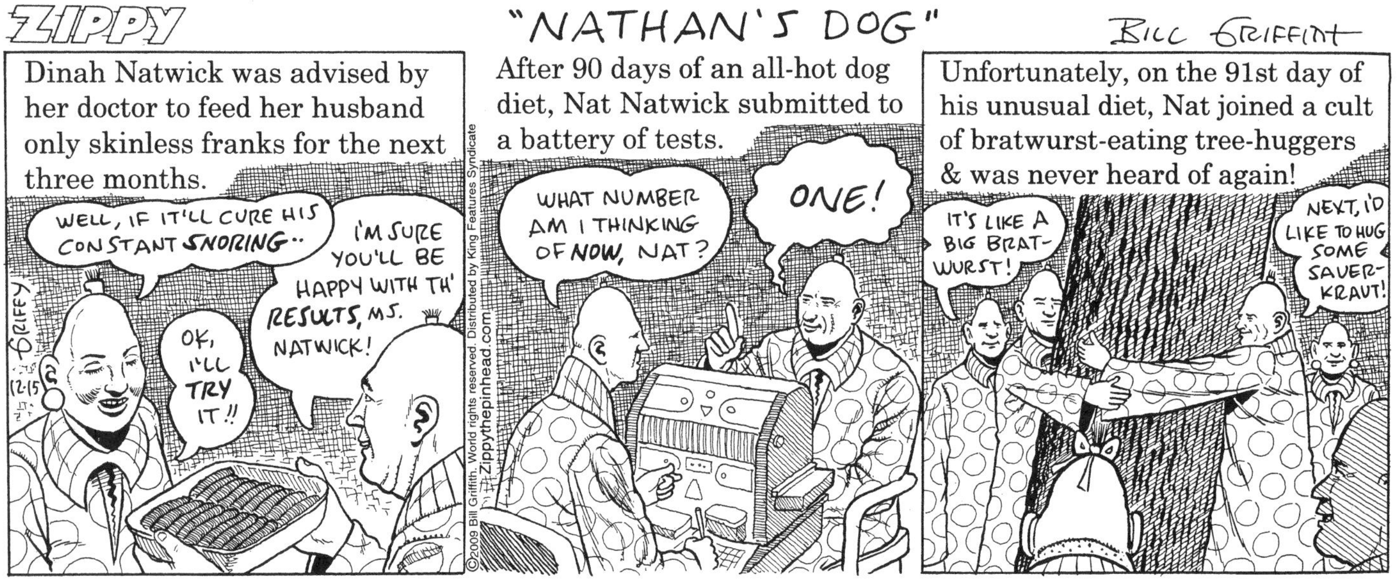
ZIPPY
"NATHAN'S DOG"
BILL GRIFFITH
Dinah Natwick was advised by her doctor to feed her husband only skinless franks for the next three months.
WELL, IF IT'LL CURE HIS CONSTANT SNORING..
I'M SURE YOU'LL BE HAPPY WITH TH' RESULTS, MS. NATWICK!
OK, I'LL TRY IT!!
GRIFFY
12-15
©2009 Bill Griffith. World rights reserved. Distributed by King Features Syndicate
Zippythepinhead.com
After 90 days of an all-hot dog diet, Nat Natwick submitted to a battery of tests.
WHAT NUMBER AM I THINKING OF NOW, NAT?
ONE!
Unfortunately, on the 91st day of his unusual diet, Nat joined a cult of bratwurst-eating tree-huggers & was never heard of again!
IT'S LIKE A BIG BRAT-WURST!
NEXT, I'D LIKE TO HUG SOME SAUER-KRAUT!

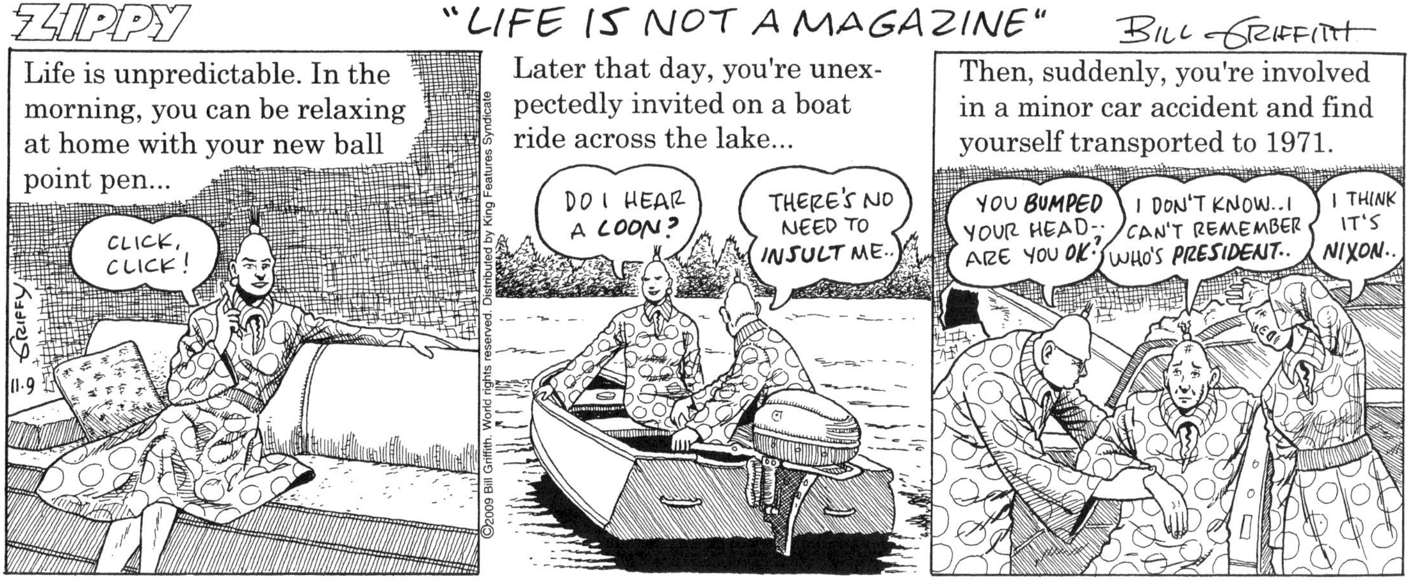
ZIPPY
"LIFE IS NOT A MAGAZINE"
BILL GRIFFITH
Life is unpredictable. In the morning, you can be relaxing at home with your new ball point pen...
CLICK, CLICK!
Later that day, you're unexpectedly invited on a boat ride across the lake...
DO I HEAR A LOON?
THERE'S NO NEED TO INSULT ME..
Then, suddenly, you're involved in a minor car accident and find yourself transported to 1971.
YOU BUMPED YOUR HEAD-- ARE YOU OK?
I DON'T KNOW..I CAN'T REMEMBER WHO'S PRESIDENT..
I THINK IT'S NIXON..
GRIFFY 11·9
©2009 Bill Griffith. World rights reserved. Distributed by King Features Syndicate

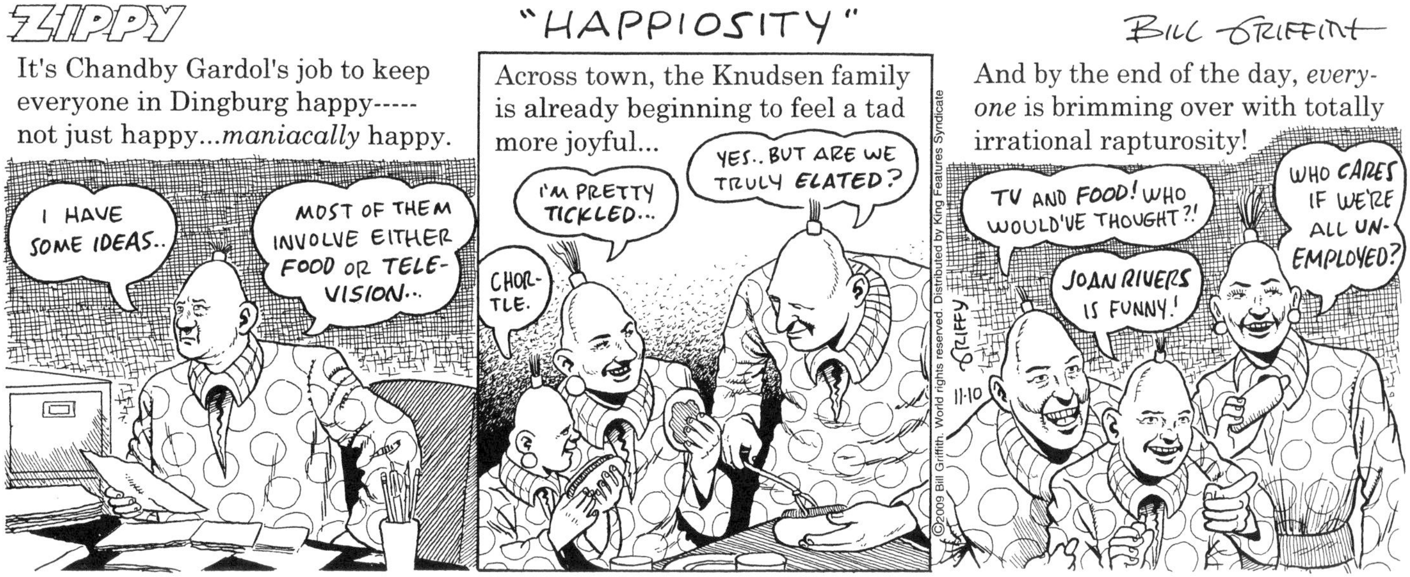
ZIPPY
"HAPPIOSITY"
BILL GRIFFITH
It's Chandby Gardol's job to keep everyone in Dingburg happy----- not just happy...*maniacally* happy.
I HAVE SOME IDEAS..
MOST OF THEM INVOLVE EITHER FOOD OR TELEVISION...
Across town, the Knudsen family is already beginning to feel a tad more joyful...
CHORTLE.
I'M PRETTY TICKLED...
YES.. BUT ARE WE TRULY ELATED?
And by the end of the day, *everyone* is brimming over with totally irrational rapturosity!
TV AND FOOD! WHO WOULD'VE THOUGHT?!
JOAN RIVERS IS FUNNY!
WHO CARES IF WE'RE ALL UNEMPLOYED?
GRIFFY 11·10
©2009 Bill Griffith. World rights reserved. Distributed by King Features Syndicate

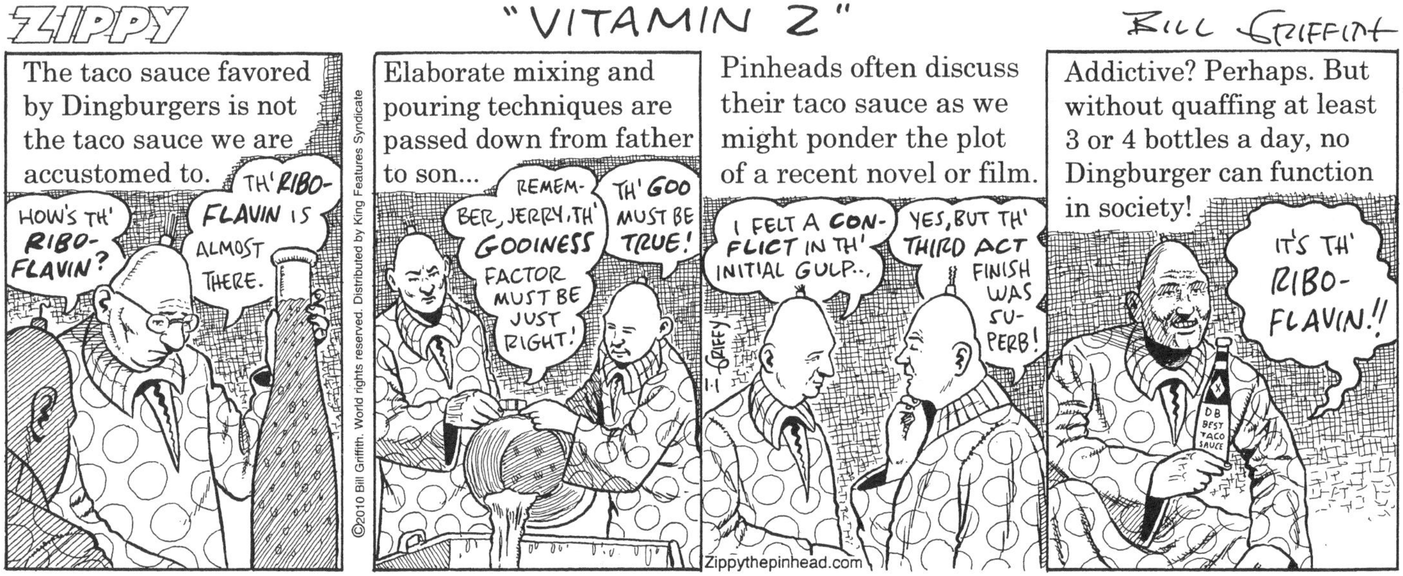
ZIPPY
"VITAMIN Z"
BILL GRIFFITH
The taco sauce favored by Dingburgers is not the taco sauce we are accustomed to.
HOW'S TH' RIBO-FLAVIN?
TH' RIBO-FLAVIN IS ALMOST THERE.
©2010 Bill Griffith. World rights reserved. Distributed by King Features Syndicate
Elaborate mixing and pouring techniques are passed down from father to son...
REMEMBER, JERRY, TH' GOOINESS FACTOR MUST BE JUST RIGHT!
TH' GOO MUST BE TRUE!
Pinheads often discuss their taco sauce as we might ponder the plot of a recent novel or film.
I FELT A CONFLICT IN TH' INITIAL GULP..
YES, BUT TH' THIRD ACT FINISH WAS SUPERB!
GRIFFY 1-1
Zippythepinhead.com
Addictive? Perhaps. But without quaffing at least 3 or 4 bottles a day, no Dingburger can function in society!
IT'S TH' RIBO-FLAVIN!!
DB BEST TACO SAUCE

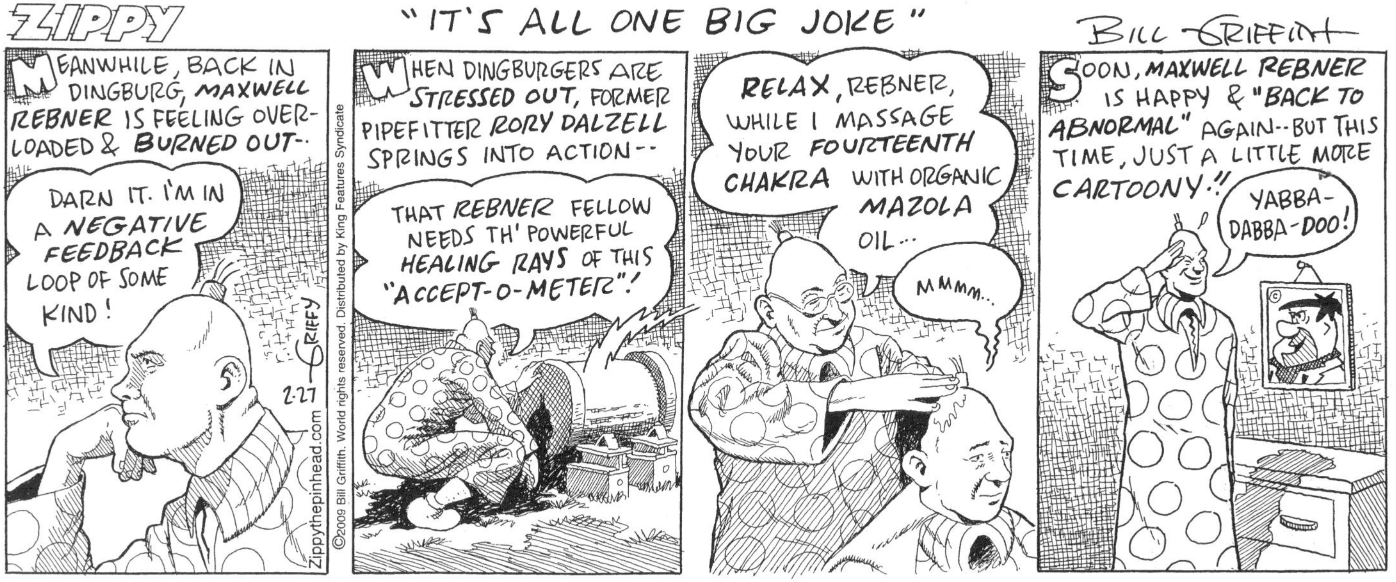
ZIPPY
"IT'S ALL ONE BIG JOKE"
BILL GRIFFITH
MEANWHILE, BACK IN DINGBURG, MAXWELL REBNER IS FEELING OVERLOADED & BURNED OUT--
DARN IT. I'M IN A NEGATIVE FEEDBACK LOOP OF SOME KIND!
GRIFFY 2-27
Zippythepinhead.com
©2009 Bill Griffith. World rights reserved. Distributed by King Features Syndicate
WHEN DINGBURGERS ARE STRESSED OUT, FORMER PIPEFITTER RORY DALZELL SPRINGS INTO ACTION--
THAT REBNER FELLOW NEEDS TH' POWERFUL HEALING RAYS OF THIS "ACCEPT-O-METER"!
RELAX, REBNER, WHILE I MASSAGE YOUR FOURTEENTH CHAKRA WITH ORGANIC MAZOLA OIL...
MMMM...
SOON, MAXWELL REBNER IS HAPPY & "BACK TO ABNORMAL" AGAIN--BUT THIS TIME, JUST A LITTLE MORE CARTOONY!!
YABBA-DABBA-DOO!

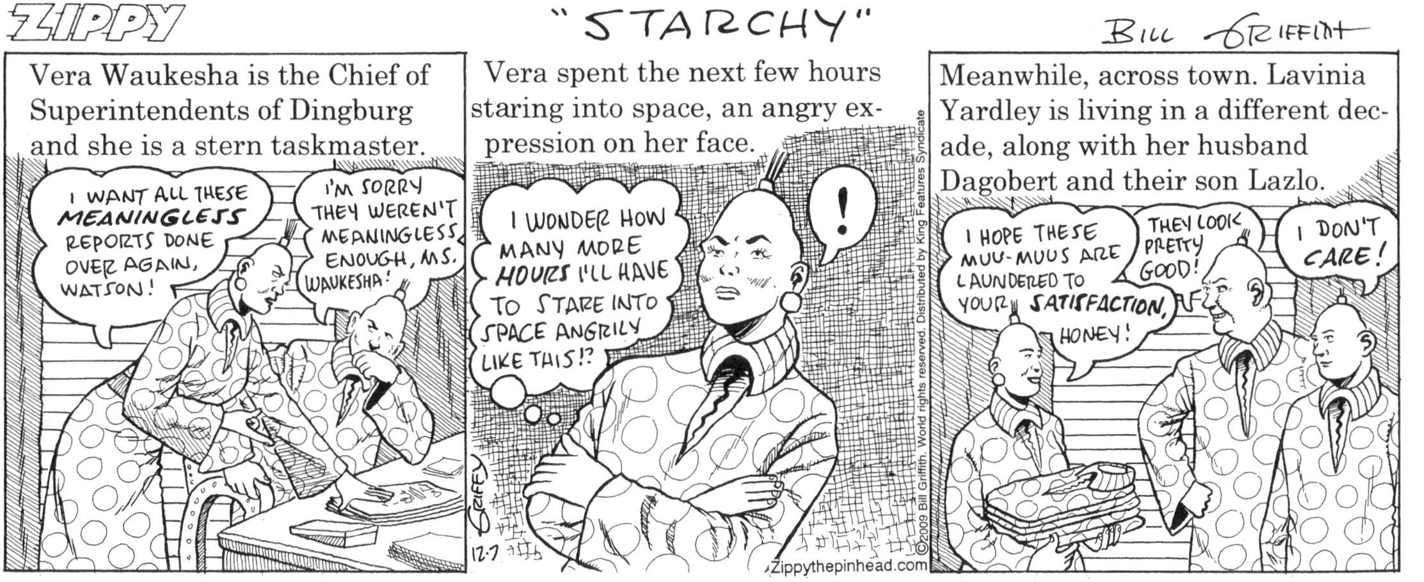
ZIPPY
"STARCHY"
BILL GRIFFITH
Vera Waukesha is the Chief of Superintendents of Dingburg and she is a stern taskmaster.
I WANT ALL THESE MEANINGLESS REPORTS DONE OVER AGAIN, WATSON!
I'M SORRY THEY WEREN'T MEANINGLESS ENOUGH, MS. WAUKESHA!
Vera spent the next few hours staring into space, an angry expression on her face.
I WONDER HOW MANY MORE HOURS I'LL HAVE TO STARE INTO SPACE ANGRILY LIKE THIS!?
!
GRIFFY 12·7
Meanwhile, across town. Lavinia Yardley is living in a different decade, along with her husband Dagobert and their son Lazlo.
I HOPE THESE MUU-MUUS ARE LAUNDERED TO YOUR SATISFACTION, HONEY!
THEY LOOK PRETTY GOOD!
I DON'T CARE!
©2009 Bill Griffith. World rights reserved. Distributed by King Features Syndicate
Zippythepinhead.com

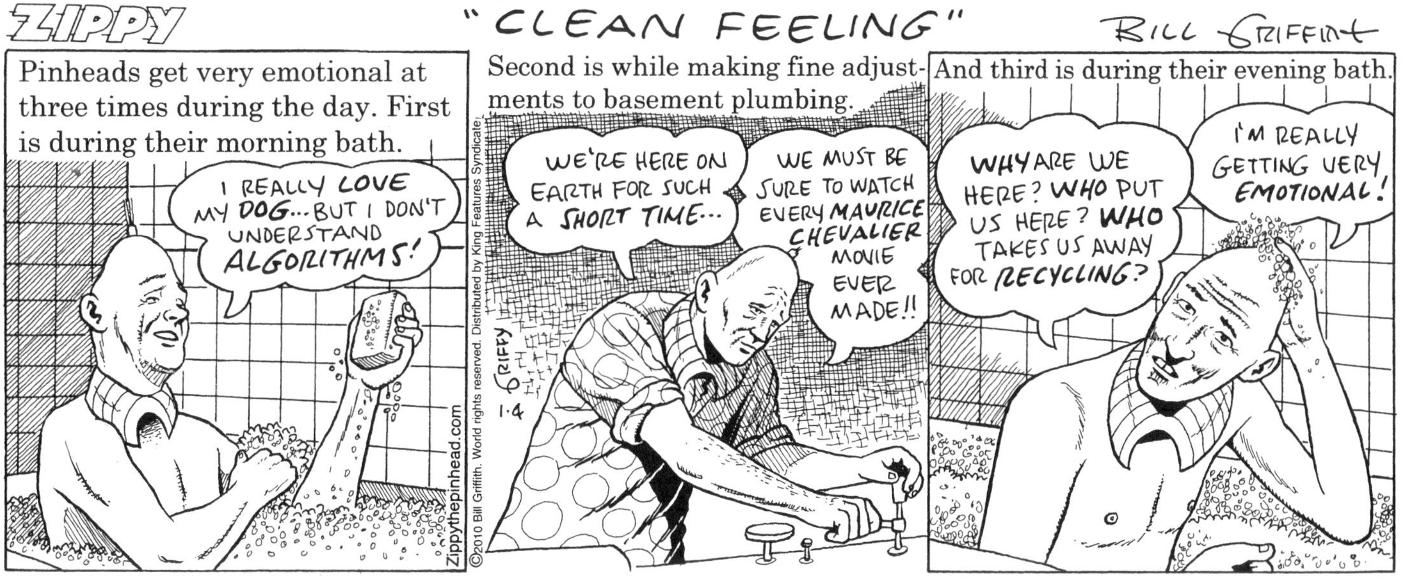
ZIPPY
"CLEAN FEELING"
BILL GRIFFITH
Pinheads get very emotional at three times during the day. First is during their morning bath.
I REALLY LOVE MY DOG... BUT I DON'T UNDERSTAND ALGORITHMS!
Zippythepinhead.com
©2010 Bill Griffith. World rights reserved. Distributed by King Features Syndicate.
Second is while making fine adjustments to basement plumbing.
WE'RE HERE ON EARTH FOR SUCH A SHORT TIME...
WE MUST BE SURE TO WATCH EVERY MAURICE CHEVALIER MOVIE EVER MADE!!
GRIFFY 1·4
And third is during their evening bath.
WHY ARE WE HERE? WHO PUT US HERE? WHO TAKES US AWAY FOR RECYCLING?
I'M REALLY GETTING VERY EMOTIONAL!

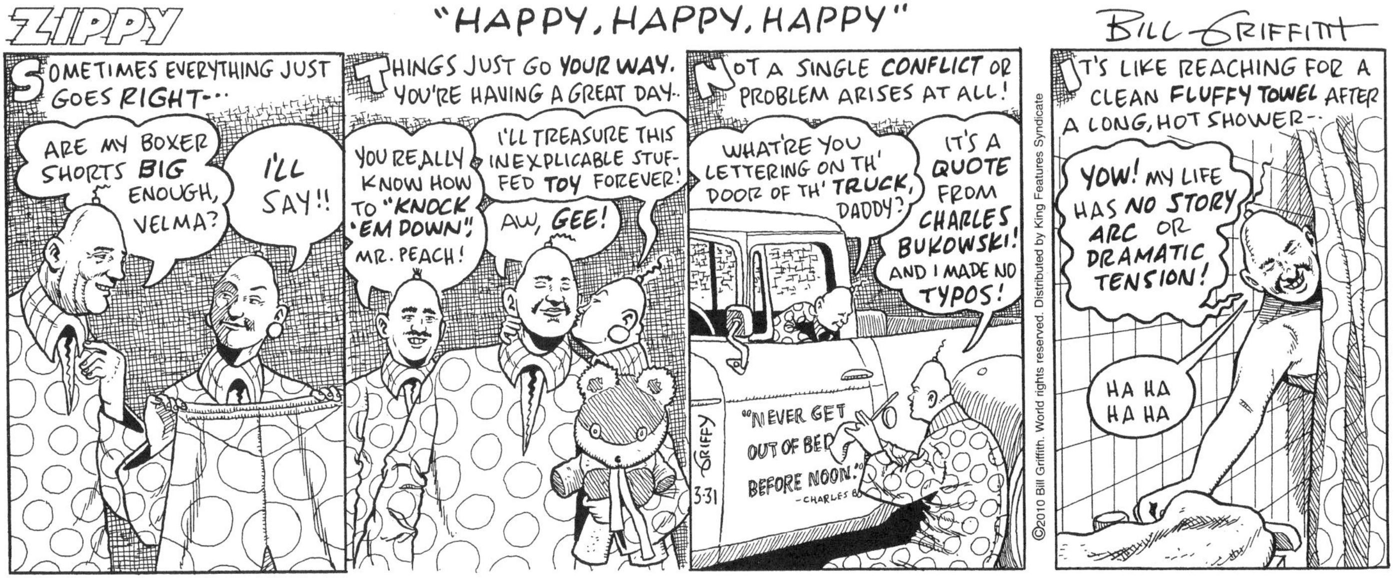
ZIPPY
"HAPPY, HAPPY, HAPPY"
BILL GRIFFITH
SOMETIMES EVERYTHING JUST GOES RIGHT...
ARE MY BOXER SHORTS BIG ENOUGH, VELMA?
I'LL SAY!!
THINGS JUST GO YOUR WAY. YOU'RE HAVING A GREAT DAY..
YOU REALLY KNOW HOW TO "KNOCK 'EM DOWN", MR. PEACH!
I'LL TREASURE THIS INEXPLICABLE STUFFED TOY FOREVER!
AW, GEE!
NOT A SINGLE CONFLICT OR PROBLEM ARISES AT ALL!
WHAT'RE YOU LETTERING ON TH' DOOR OF TH' TRUCK, DADDY?
IT'S A QUOTE FROM CHARLES BUKOWSKI! AND I MADE NO TYPOS!
"NEVER GET OUT OF BED BEFORE NOON."
GRIFFY
3·31
©2010 Bill Griffith. World rights reserved. Distributed by King Features Syndicate
IT'S LIKE REACHING FOR A CLEAN FLUFFY TOWEL AFTER A LONG, HOT SHOWER..
YOW! MY LIFE HAS NO STORY ARC OR DRAMATIC TENSION!
HA HA HA HA

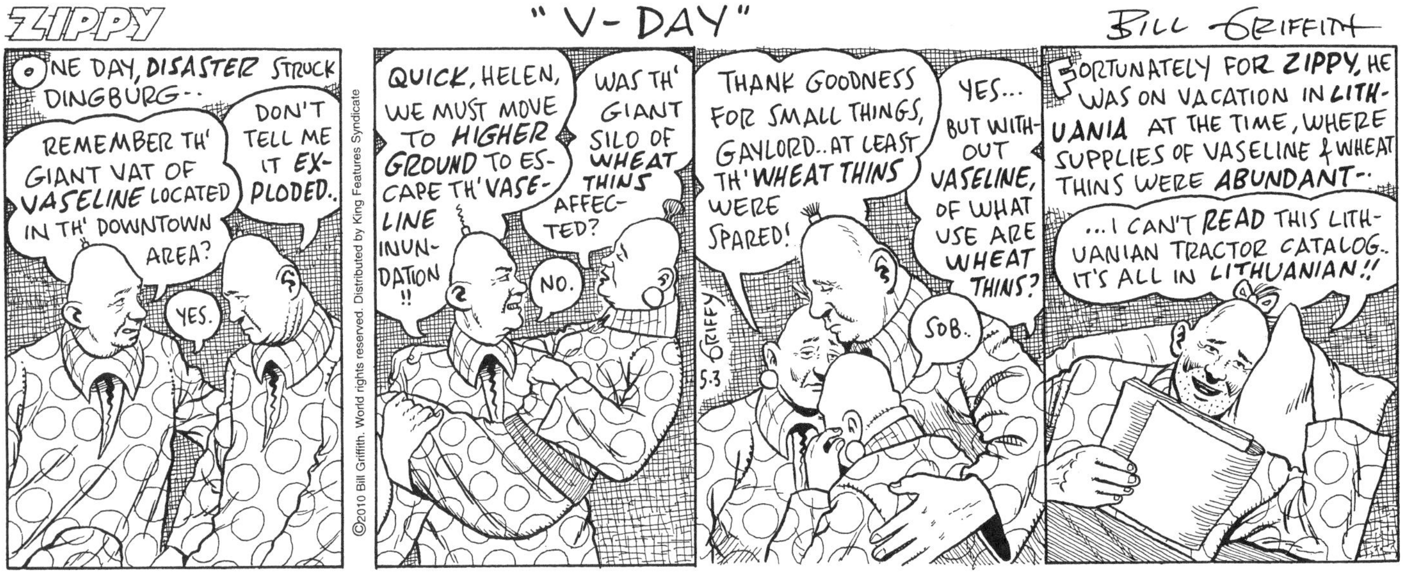
ZIPPY
"V-DAY"
BILL GRIFFITH
ONE DAY, DISASTER STRUCK DINGBURG..
REMEMBER TH' GIANT VAT OF VASELINE LOCATED IN TH' DOWNTOWN AREA?
DON'T TELL ME IT EXPLODED..
YES.
©2010 Bill Griffith. World rights reserved. Distributed by King Features Syndicate
QUICK, HELEN, WE MUST MOVE TO HIGHER GROUND TO ESCAPE TH' VASELINE INUNDATION!!
WAS TH' GIANT SILO OF WHEAT THINS AFFECTED?
NO.
THANK GOODNESS FOR SMALL THINGS, GAYLORD.. AT LEAST TH' WHEAT THINS WERE SPARED!
YES... BUT WITHOUT VASELINE, OF WHAT USE ARE WHEAT THINS?
SOB..
GRIFFY
5·3
FORTUNATELY FOR ZIPPY, HE WAS ON VACATION IN LITHUANIA AT THE TIME, WHERE SUPPLIES OF VASELINE & WHEAT THINS WERE ABUNDANT..
...I CAN'T READ THIS LITHUANIAN TRACTOR CATALOG.. IT'S ALL IN LITHUANIAN!!

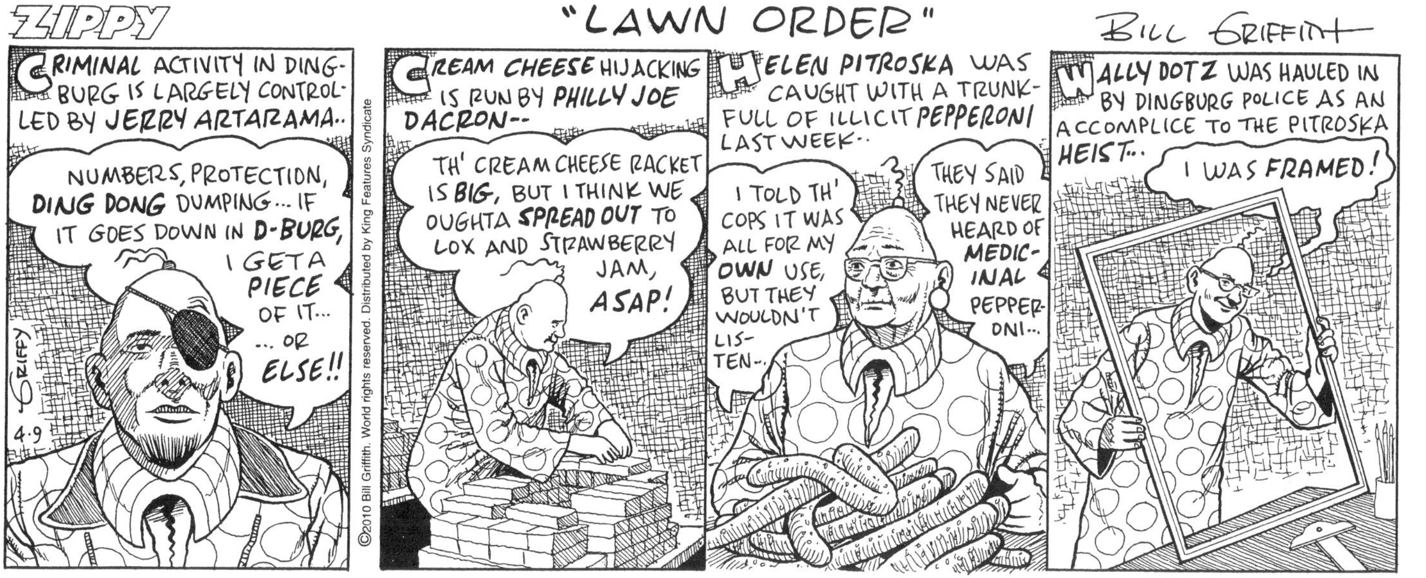
ZIPPY
"LAWN ORDER"
BILL GRIFFITH
CRIMINAL ACTIVITY IN DINGBURG IS LARGELY CONTROLLED BY JERRY ARTARAMA..
NUMBERS, PROTECTION, DING DONG DUMPING... IF IT GOES DOWN IN D-BURG, I GET A PIECE OF IT... ...OR ELSE!!
GRIFFY 4·9
©2010 Bill Griffith. World rights reserved. Distributed by King Features Syndicate
CREAM CHEESE HIJACKING IS RUN BY PHILLY JOE DACRON--
TH' CREAM CHEESE RACKET IS BIG, BUT I THINK WE OUGHTA SPREAD OUT TO LOX AND STRAWBERRY JAM, ASAP!
HELEN PITROSKA WAS CAUGHT WITH A TRUNKFULL OF ILLICIT PEPPERONI LAST WEEK..
I TOLD TH' COPS IT WAS ALL FOR MY OWN USE, BUT THEY WOULDN'T LISTEN..
THEY SAID THEY NEVER HEARD OF MEDICINAL PEPPERONI...
WALLY DOTZ WAS HAULED IN BY DINGBURG POLICE AS AN ACCOMPLICE TO THE PITROSKA HEIST..
I WAS FRAMED!

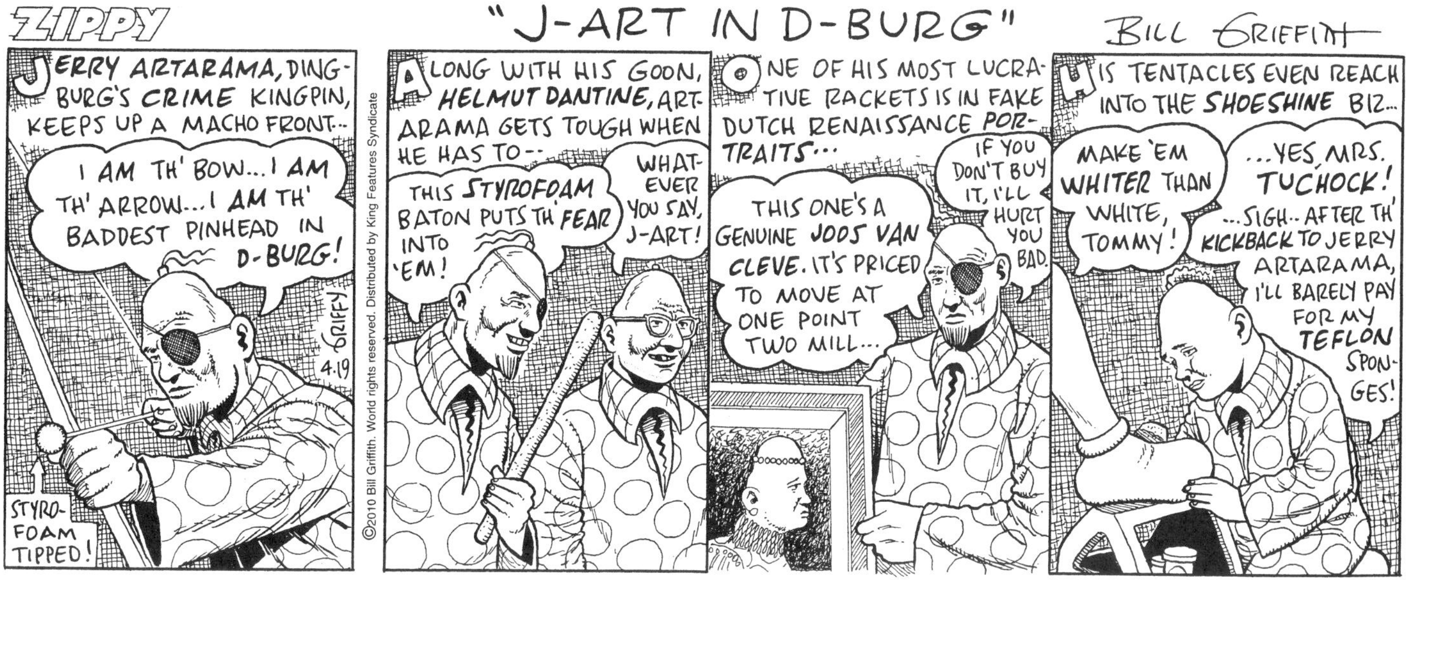
ZIPPY
"J-ART IN D-BURG"
BILL GRIFFITH
JERRY ARTARAMA, DINGBURG'S CRIME KINGPIN, KEEPS UP A MACHO FRONT..
I AM TH' BOW... I AM TH' ARROW... I AM TH' BADDEST PINHEAD IN D-BURG!
STYROFOAM TIPPED!
GRIFFY 4·19
©2010 Bill Griffith. World rights reserved. Distributed by King Features Syndicate
ALONG WITH HIS GOON, HELMUT DANTINE, ARTARAMA GETS TOUGH WHEN HE HAS TO--
THIS STYROFOAM BATON PUTS TH' FEAR INTO 'EM!
WHATEVER YOU SAY, J-ART!
ONE OF HIS MOST LUCRATIVE RACKETS IS IN FAKE DUTCH RENAISSANCE PORTRAITS...
THIS ONE'S A GENUINE JOOS VAN CLEVE. IT'S PRICED TO MOVE AT ONE POINT TWO MILL...
IF YOU DON'T BUY IT, I'LL HURT YOU BAD.
HIS TENTACLES EVEN REACH INTO THE SHOESHINE BIZ...
MAKE 'EM WHITER THAN WHITE, TOMMY!
...YES, MRS. TUCHOCK! ...SIGH.. AFTER TH' KICKBACK TO JERRY ARTARAMA, I'LL BARELY PAY FOR MY TEFLON SPONGES!

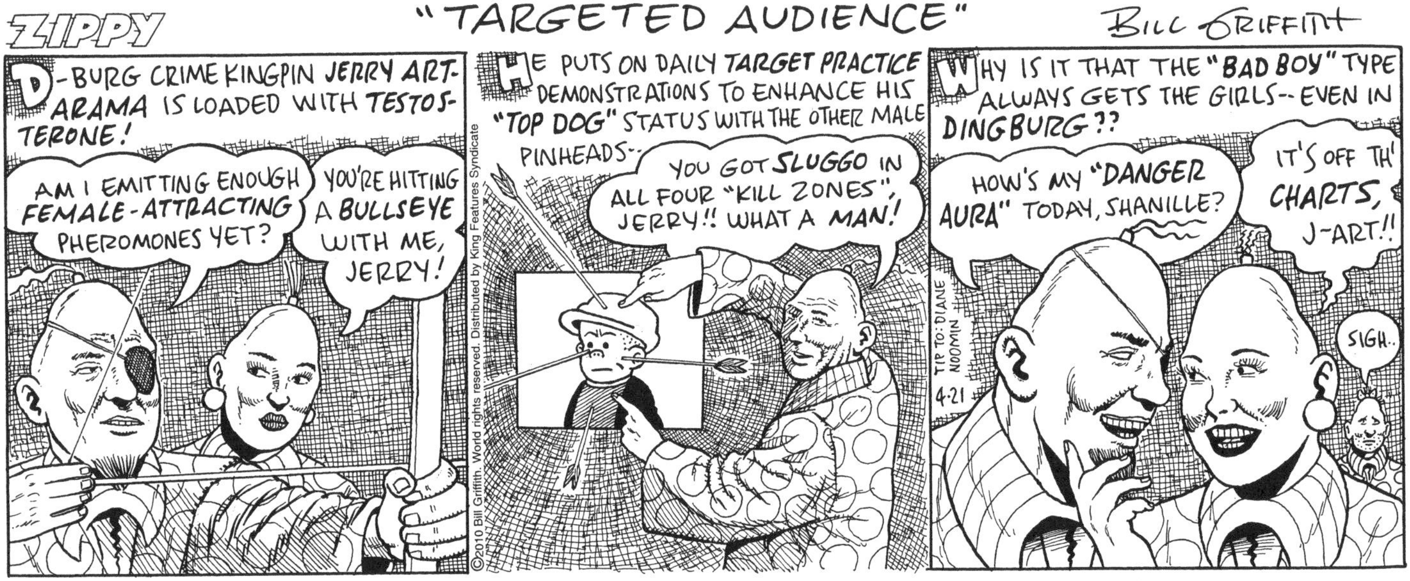
ZIPPY
"TARGETED AUDIENCE"
BILL GRIFFITH
D-BURG CRIME KINGPIN JERRY ART-ARAMA IS LOADED WITH TESTOSTERONE!
AM I EMITTING ENOUGH FEMALE-ATTRACTING PHEROMONES YET?
YOU'RE HITTING A BULLSEYE WITH ME, JERRY!
©2010 Bill Griffith. World rights reserved. Distributed by King Features Syndicate
HE PUTS ON DAILY TARGET PRACTICE DEMONSTRATIONS TO ENHANCE HIS "TOP DOG" STATUS WITH THE OTHER MALE PINHEADS--
YOU GOT SLUGGO IN ALL FOUR "KILL ZONES", JERRY!! WHAT A MAN!
WHY IS IT THAT THE "BAD BOY" TYPE ALWAYS GETS THE GIRLS-- EVEN IN DINGBURG??
HOW'S MY "DANGER AURA" TODAY, SHANILLE?
IT'S OFF TH' CHARTS, J-ART!!
TIP TO: DIANE NOOMIN
4-21
SIGH..

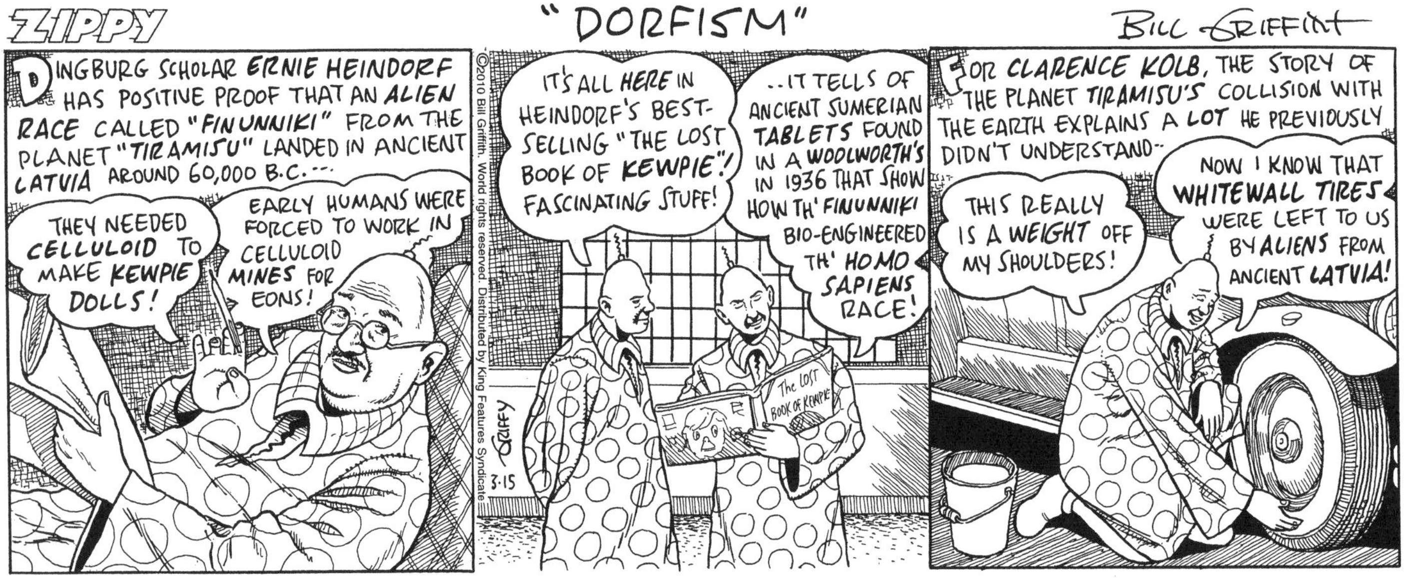
ZIPPY
"DORFISM"
BILL GRIFFITH
DINGBURG SCHOLAR ERNIE HEINDORF HAS POSITIVE PROOF THAT AN ALIEN RACE CALLED "FINUNNIKI" FROM THE PLANET "TIRAMISU" LANDED IN ANCIENT LATVIA AROUND 60,000 B.C.--
THEY NEEDED CELLULOID TO MAKE KEWPIE DOLLS!
EARLY HUMANS WERE FORCED TO WORK IN CELLULOID MINES FOR EONS!
©2010 Bill Griffith. World rights reserved. Distributed by King Features Syndicate
IT'S ALL HERE IN HEINDORF'S BEST-SELLING "THE LOST BOOK OF KEWPIE"! FASCINATING STUFF!
..IT TELLS OF ANCIENT SUMERIAN TABLETS FOUND IN A WOOLWORTH'S IN 1936 THAT SHOW HOW TH' FINUNNIKI BIO-ENGINEERED TH' HOMO SAPIENS RACE!
The LOST BOOK OF KEWPIE
GRIFFY
3-15
FOR CLARENCE KOLB, THE STORY OF THE PLANET TIRAMISU'S COLLISION WITH THE EARTH EXPLAINS A LOT HE PREVIOUSLY DIDN'T UNDERSTAND--
THIS REALLY IS A WEIGHT OFF MY SHOULDERS!
NOW I KNOW THAT WHITEWALL TIRES WERE LEFT TO US BY ALIENS FROM ANCIENT LATVIA!

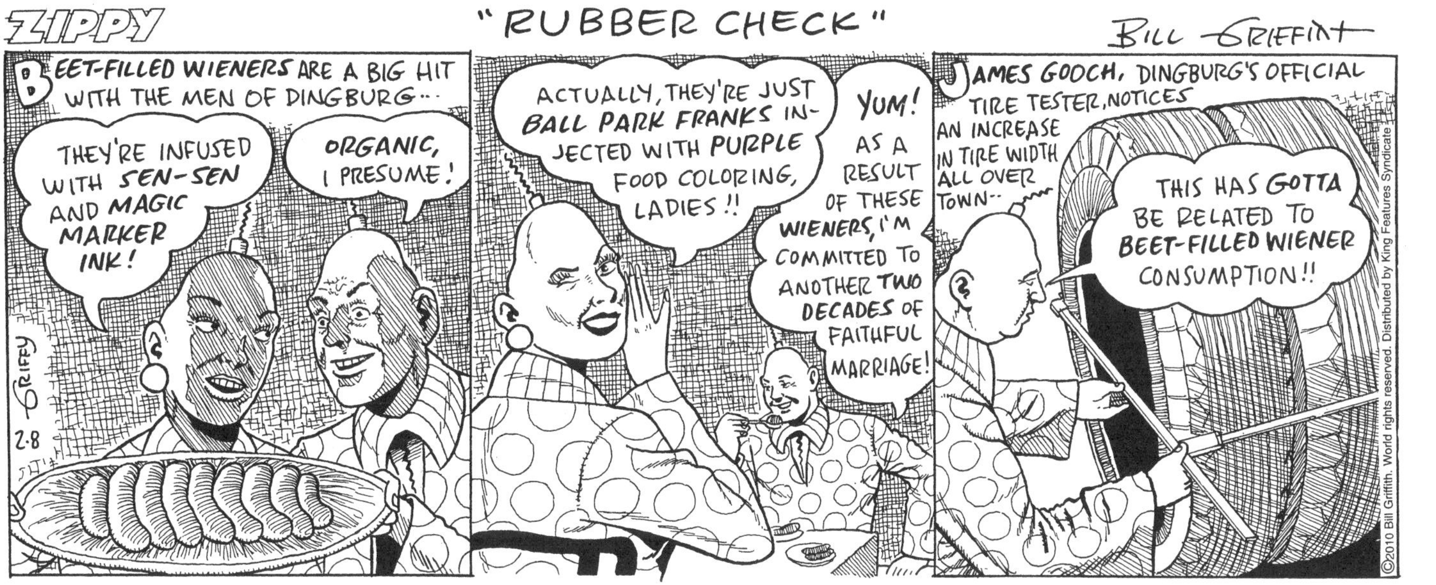
ZIPPY
"RUBBER CHECK"
BILL GRIFFITH
BEET-FILLED WIENERS ARE A BIG HIT WITH THE MEN OF DINGBURG...
THEY'RE INFUSED WITH SEN-SEN AND MAGIC MARKER INK!
ORGANIC, I PRESUME!
GRIFFY 2·8
ACTUALLY, THEY'RE JUST BALL PARK FRANKS INJECTED WITH PURPLE FOOD COLORING, LADIES!!
YUM! AS A RESULT OF THESE WIENERS, I'M COMMITTED TO ANOTHER TWO DECADES OF FAITHFUL MARRIAGE!
JAMES GOOCH, DINGBURG'S OFFICIAL TIRE TESTER, NOTICES AN INCREASE IN TIRE WIDTH ALL OVER TOWN--
THIS HAS GOTTA BE RELATED TO BEET-FILLED WIENER CONSUMPTION!!
©2010 Bill Griffith. World rights reserved. Distributed by King Features Syndicate

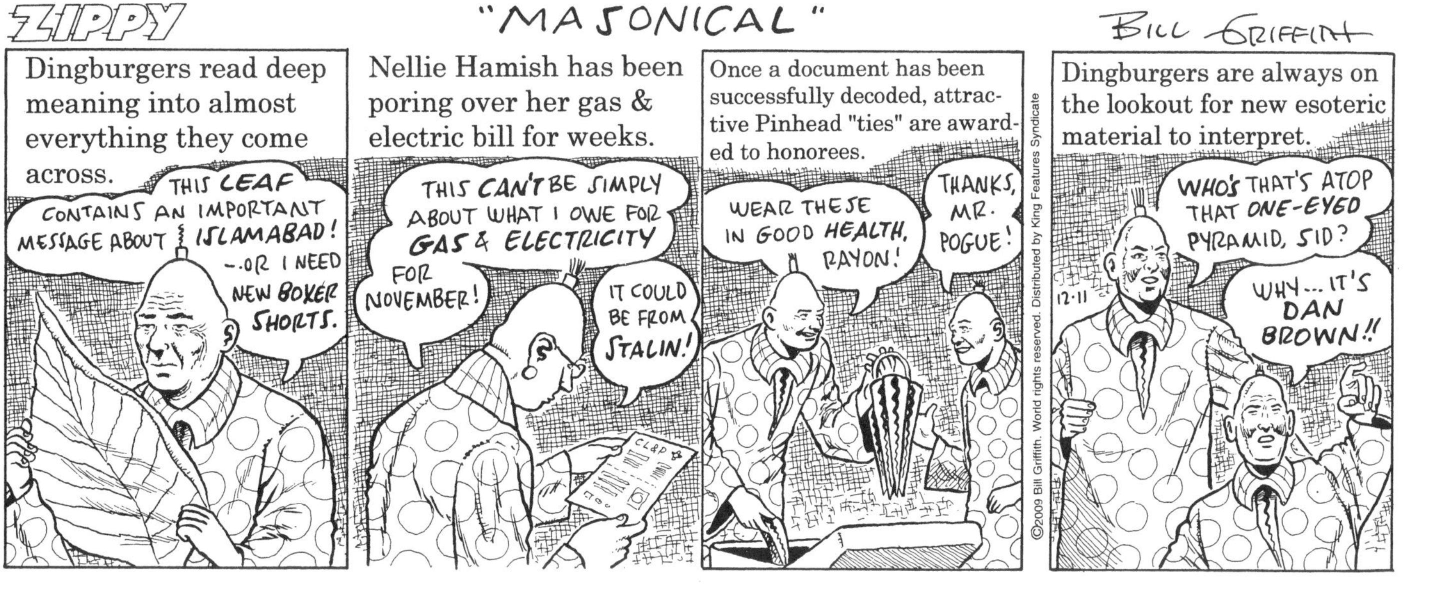
ZIPPY
"MASONICAL"
BILL GRIFFITH
Dingburgers read deep meaning into almost everything they come across.
THIS LEAF CONTAINS AN IMPORTANT MESSAGE ABOUT ISLAMABAD!
--OR I NEED NEW BOXER SHORTS.
Nellie Hamish has been poring over her gas & electric bill for weeks.
THIS CAN'T BE SIMPLY ABOUT WHAT I OWE FOR GAS & ELECTRICITY FOR NOVEMBER!
IT COULD BE FROM STALIN!
CL&P
Once a document has been successfully decoded, attractive Pinhead "ties" are awarded to honorees.
WEAR THESE IN GOOD HEALTH, RAYON!
THANKS, MR. POGUE!
©2009 Bill Griffith. World rights reserved. Distributed by King Features Syndicate
Dingburgers are always on the lookout for new esoteric material to interpret.
12·11
WHO'S THAT'S ATOP THAT ONE-EYED PYRAMID, SID?
WHY... IT'S DAN BROWN!!

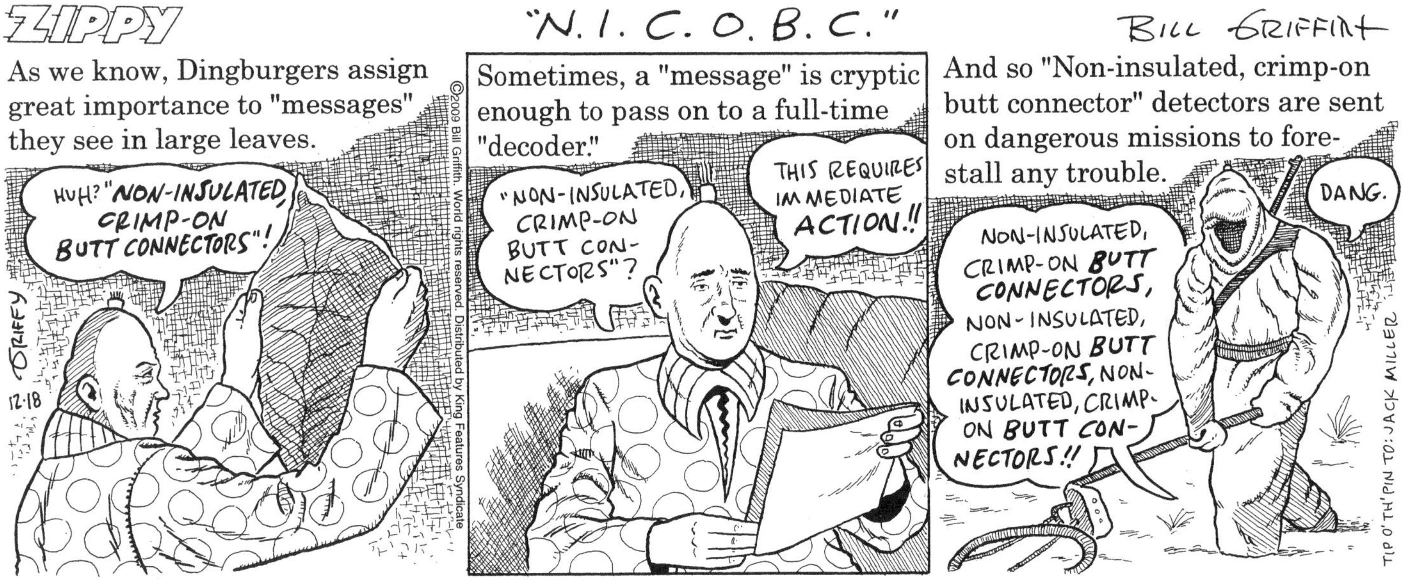
ZIPPY
"N. I. C. O. B. C."
BILL GRIFFITH
As we know, Dingburgers assign great importance to "messages" they see in large leaves.
HUH? "NON-INSULATED, CRIMP-ON BUTT CONNECTORS"!
GRIFFY 12·18
©2009 Bill Griffith. World rights reserved. Distributed by King Features Syndicate
Sometimes, a "message" is cryptic enough to pass on to a full-time "decoder."
"NON-INSULATED, CRIMP-ON BUTT CON-NECTORS"?
THIS REQUIRES IMMEDIATE ACTION!!
And so "Non-insulated, crimp-on butt connector" detectors are sent on dangerous missions to fore-stall any trouble.
NON-INSULATED, CRIMP-ON BUTT CONNECTORS, NON-INSULATED, CRIMP-ON BUTT CONNECTORS, NON-INSULATED, CRIMP-ON BUTT CON-NECTORS!!
DANG.
TIP O' TH' PIN TO: JACK MILLER

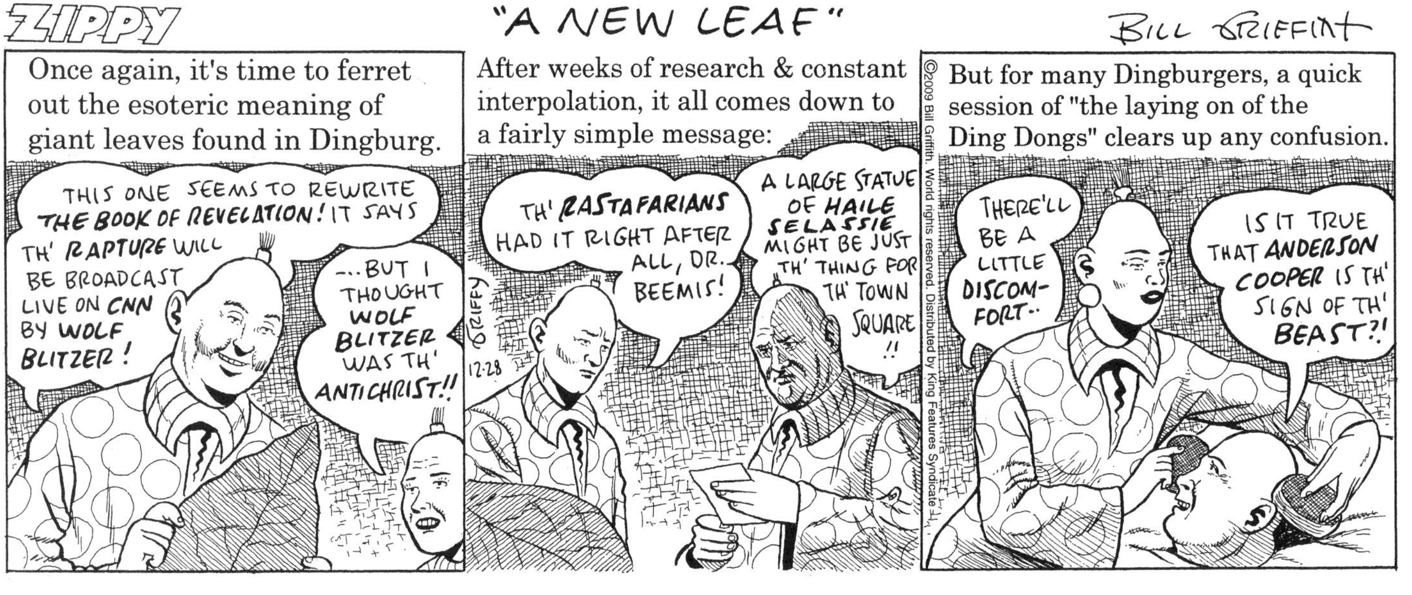
ZIPPY
"A NEW LEAF"
BILL GRIFFITH
Once again, it's time to ferret out the esoteric meaning of giant leaves found in Dingburg.
THIS ONE SEEMS TO REWRITE THE BOOK OF REVELATION! IT SAYS TH' RAPTURE WILL BE BROADCAST LIVE ON CNN BY WOLF BLITZER!
...BUT I THOUGHT WOLF BLITZER WAS TH' ANTICHRIST!!
After weeks of research & constant interpolation, it all comes down to a fairly simple message:
GRIFFY 12·28
TH' RASTAFARIANS HAD IT RIGHT AFTER ALL, DR. BEEMIS!
A LARGE STATUE OF HAILE SELASSIE MIGHT BE JUST TH' THING FOR TH' TOWN SQUARE!!
©2009 Bill Griffith. World rights reserved. Distributed by King Features Syndicate
But for many Dingburgers, a quick session of "the laying on of the Ding Dongs" clears up any confusion.
THERE'LL BE A LITTLE DISCOM-FORT..
IS IT TRUE THAT ANDERSON COOPER IS TH' SIGN OF TH' BEAST?!

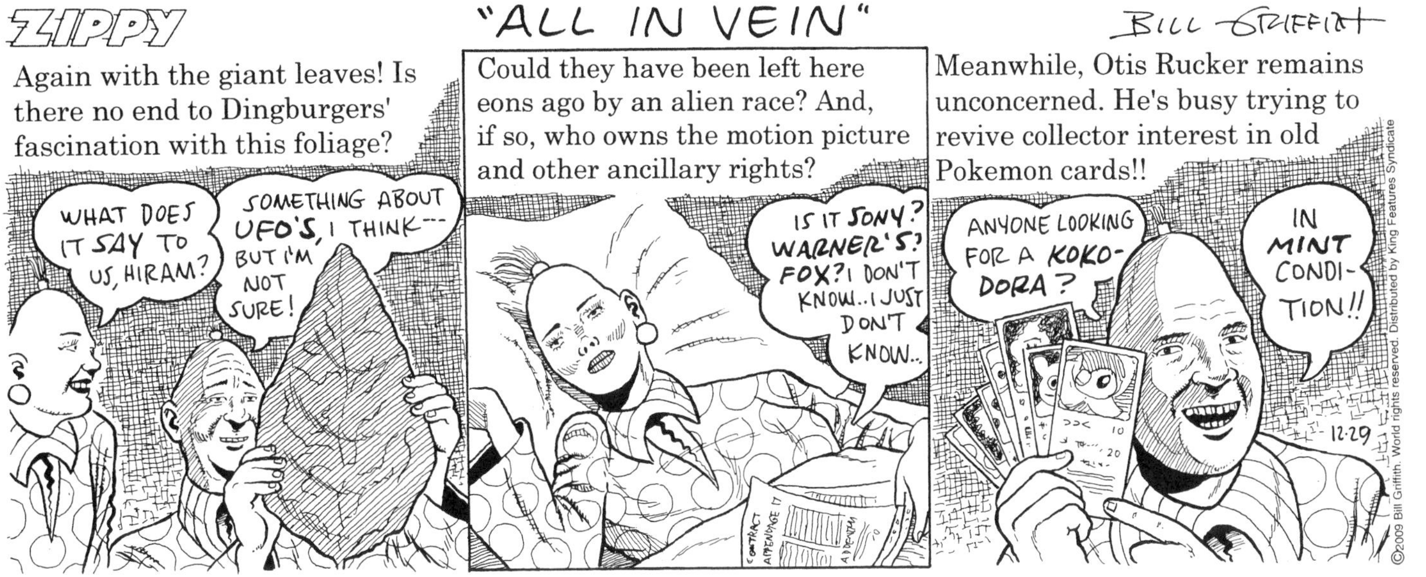
ZIPPY
"ALL IN VEIN"
BILL GRIFFITH
Again with the giant leaves! Is there no end to Dingburgers' fascination with this foliage?
WHAT DOES IT SAY TO US, HIRAM?
SOMETHING ABOUT UFO'S, I THINK--- BUT I'M NOT SURE!
Could they have been left here eons ago by an alien race? And, if so, who owns the motion picture and other ancillary rights?
IS IT SONY? WARNER'S? FOX? I DON'T KNOW.. I JUST DON'T KNOW..
Meanwhile, Otis Rucker remains unconcerned. He's busy trying to revive collector interest in old Pokemon cards!!
ANYONE LOOKING FOR A KOKO-DORA?
IN MINT CONDI-TION!!
12·29
©2009 Bill Griffith. World rights reserved. Distributed by King Features Syndicate

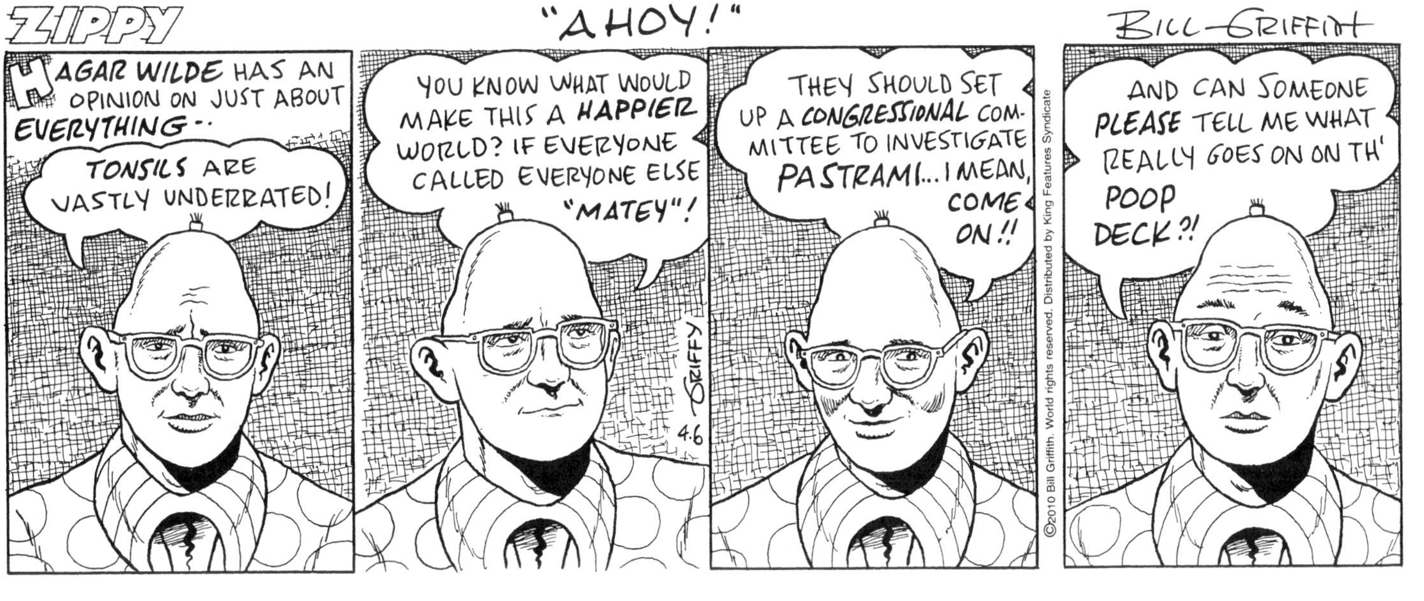
ZIPPY
"AHOY!"
BILL GRIFFITH
HAGAR WILDE HAS AN OPINION ON JUST ABOUT EVERYTHING..
TONSILS ARE VASTLY UNDERRATED!
YOU KNOW WHAT WOULD MAKE THIS A HAPPIER WORLD? IF EVERYONE CALLED EVERYONE ELSE "MATEY"!
GRIFFY
4·6
THEY SHOULD SET UP A CONGRESSIONAL COM-MITTEE TO INVESTIGATE PASTRAMI... I MEAN, COME ON!!
©2010 Bill Griffith. World rights reserved. Distributed by King Features Syndicate
AND CAN SOMEONE PLEASE TELL ME WHAT REALLY GOES ON ON TH' POOP DECK?!

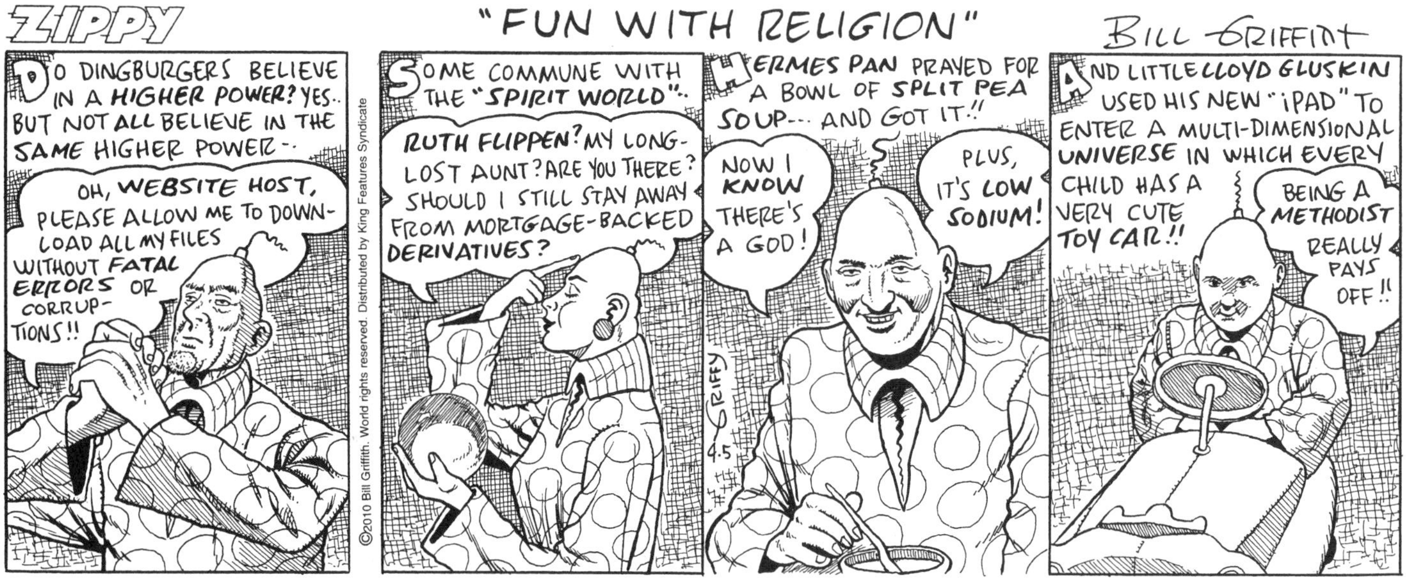
ZIPPY
"FUN WITH RELIGION"
BILL GRIFFITH
DO DINGBURGERS BELIEVE IN A HIGHER POWER? YES.. BUT NOT ALL BELIEVE IN THE SAME HIGHER POWER..
OH, WEBSITE HOST, PLEASE ALLOW ME TO DOWNLOAD ALL MY FILES WITHOUT FATAL ERRORS OR CORRUPTIONS!!
©2010 Bill Griffith. World rights reserved. Distributed by King Features Syndicate
SOME COMMUNE WITH THE "SPIRIT WORLD"..
RUTH FLIPPEN? MY LONG-LOST AUNT? ARE YOU THERE? SHOULD I STILL STAY AWAY FROM MORTGAGE-BACKED DERIVATIVES?
GRIFFY 4-5
HERMES PAN PRAYED FOR A BOWL OF SPLIT PEA SOUP--- AND GOT IT!!
NOW I KNOW THERE'S A GOD!
PLUS, IT'S LOW SODIUM!
AND LITTLE LLOYD GLUSKIN USED HIS NEW "iPAD" TO ENTER A MULTI-DIMENSIONAL UNIVERSE IN WHICH EVERY CHILD HAS A VERY CUTE TOY CAR!!
BEING A METHODIST REALLY PAYS OFF!!

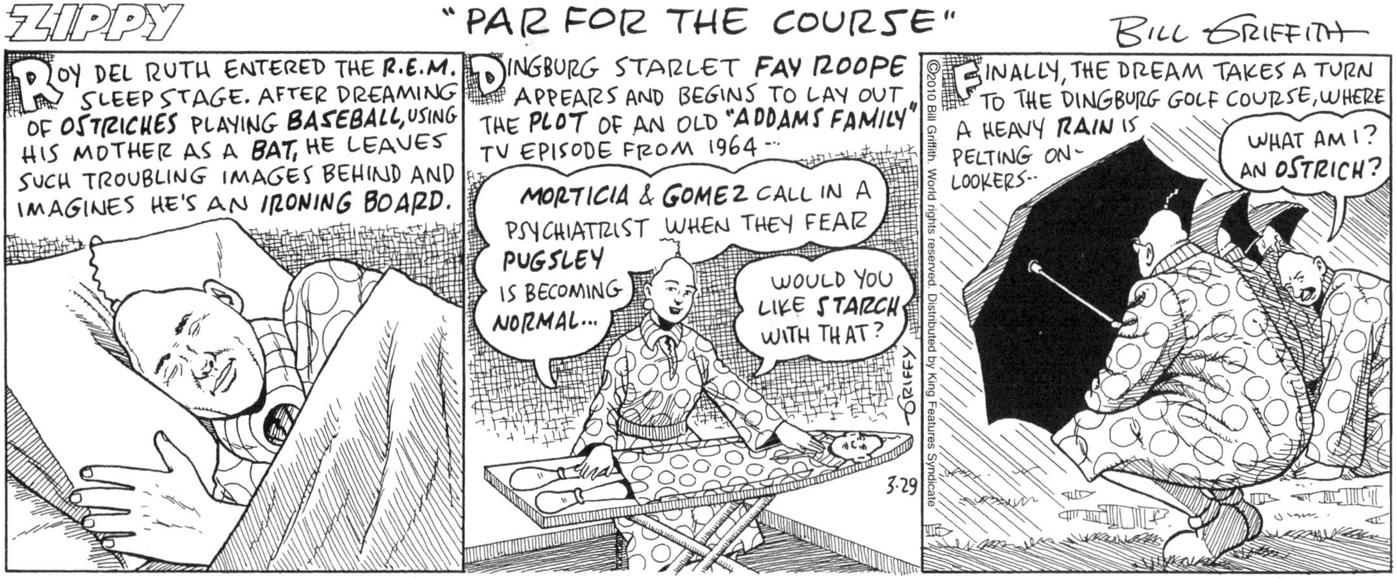
ZIPPY
"PAR FOR THE COURSE"
BILL GRIFFITH
ROY DEL RUTH ENTERED THE R.E.M. SLEEP STAGE. AFTER DREAMING OF OSTRICHES PLAYING BASEBALL, USING HIS MOTHER AS A BAT, HE LEAVES SUCH TROUBLING IMAGES BEHIND AND IMAGINES HE'S AN IRONING BOARD.
DINGBURG STARLET FAY ROOPE APPEARS AND BEGINS TO LAY OUT THE PLOT OF AN OLD "ADDAMS FAMILY" TV EPISODE FROM 1964--
MORTICIA & GOMEZ CALL IN A PSYCHIATRIST WHEN THEY FEAR PUGSLEY IS BECOMING NORMAL...
WOULD YOU LIKE STARCH WITH THAT?
GRIFFY 3-29
©2010 Bill Griffith. World rights reserved. Distributed by King Features Syndicate
FINALLY, THE DREAM TAKES A TURN TO THE DINGBURG GOLF COURSE, WHERE A HEAVY RAIN IS PELTING ONLOOKERS..
WHAT AM I? AN OSTRICH?

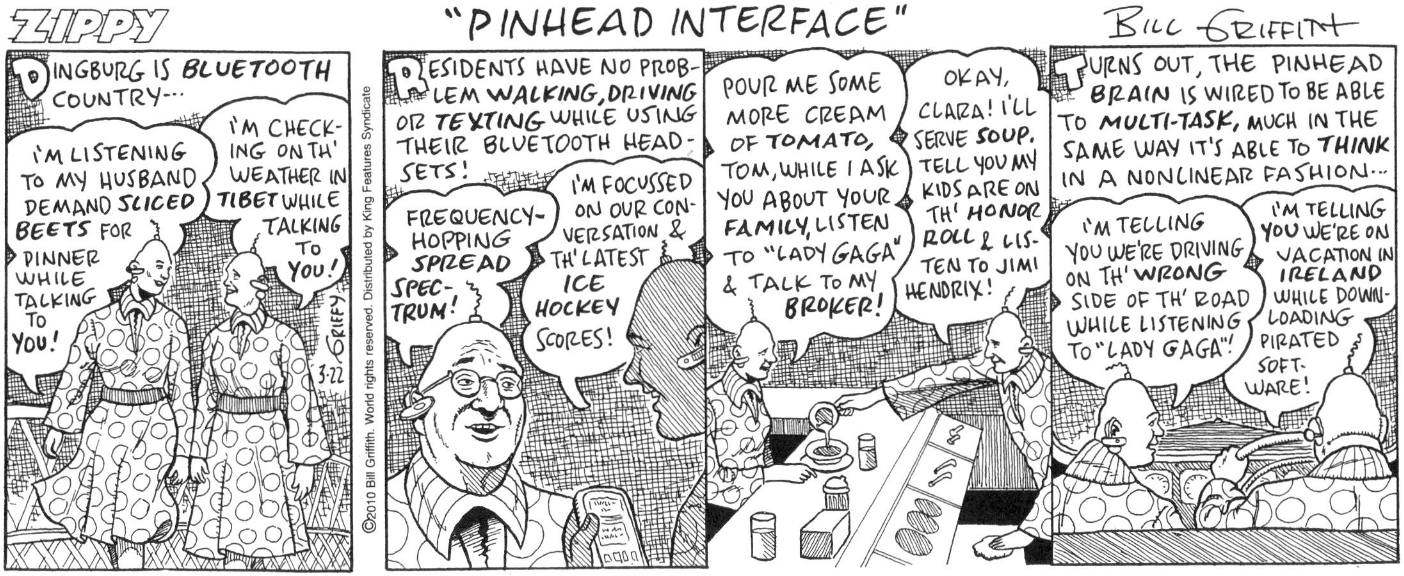
ZIPPY
"PINHEAD INTERFACE"
BILL GRIFFITH
DINGBURG IS BLUETOOTH COUNTRY...
I'M LISTENING TO MY HUSBAND DEMAND SLICED BEETS FOR DINNER WHILE TALKING TO YOU!
I'M CHECKING ON TH' WEATHER IN TIBET WHILE TALKING TO YOU!
GRIFFY 3-22
©2010 Bill Griffith. World rights reserved. Distributed by King Features Syndicate
RESIDENTS HAVE NO PROBLEM WALKING, DRIVING OR TEXTING WHILE USING THEIR BLUETOOTH HEADSETS!
FREQUENCY-HOPPING SPREAD SPECTRUM!
I'M FOCUSSED ON OUR CONVERSATION & TH' LATEST ICE HOCKEY SCORES!
POUR ME SOME MORE CREAM OF TOMATO, TOM, WHILE I ASK YOU ABOUT YOUR FAMILY, LISTEN TO "LADY GAGA" & TALK TO MY BROKER!
OKAY, CLARA! I'LL SERVE SOUP, TELL YOU MY KIDS ARE ON TH' HONOR ROLL & LISTEN TO JIMI HENDRIX!
TURNS OUT, THE PINHEAD BRAIN IS WIRED TO BE ABLE TO MULTI-TASK, MUCH IN THE SAME WAY IT'S ABLE TO THINK IN A NONLINEAR FASHION...
I'M TELLING YOU WE'RE DRIVING ON TH' WRONG SIDE OF TH' ROAD WHILE LISTENING TO "LADY GAGA"!
I'M TELLING YOU WE'RE ON VACATION IN IRELAND WHILE DOWNLOADING PIRATED SOFTWARE!

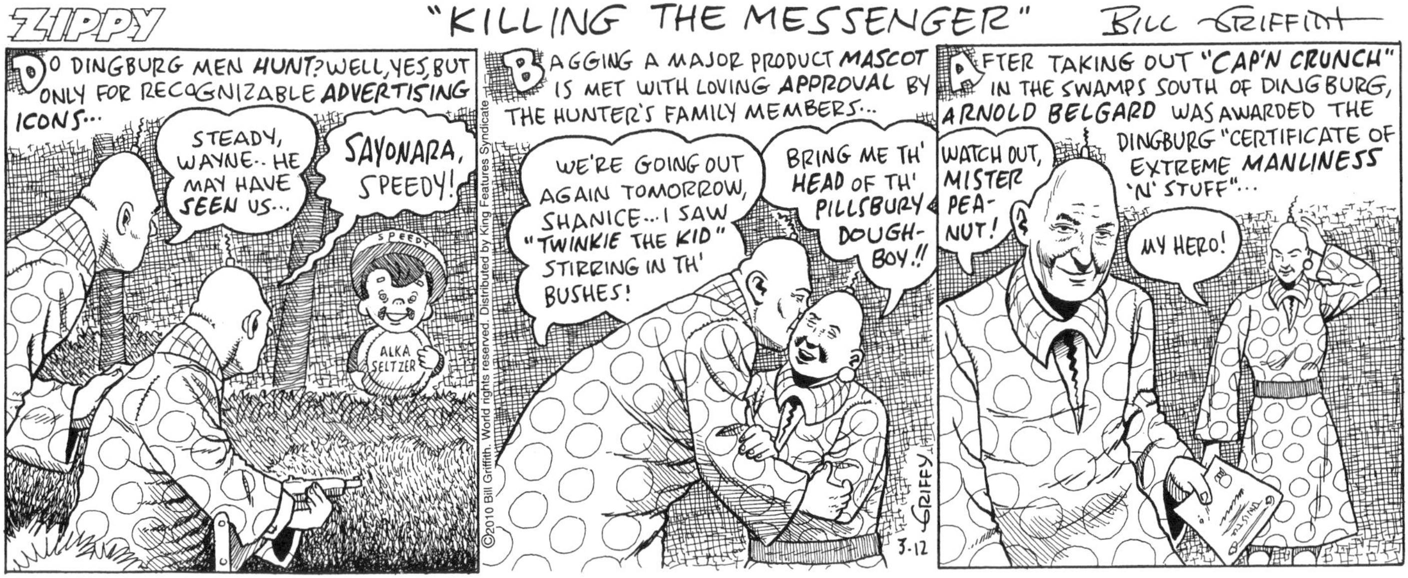
ZIPPY
"KILLING THE MESSENGER"
BILL GRIFFITH
DO DINGBURG MEN HUNT? WELL, YES, BUT ONLY FOR RECOGNIZABLE ADVERTISING ICONS...
STEADY, WAYNE.. HE MAY HAVE SEEN US...
SAYONARA, SPEEDY!
SPEEDY
ALKA SELTZER
©2010 Bill Griffith. World rights reserved. Distributed by King Features Syndicate
BAGGING A MAJOR PRODUCT MASCOT IS MET WITH LOVING APPROVAL BY THE HUNTER'S FAMILY MEMBERS...
WE'RE GOING OUT AGAIN TOMORROW, SHANICE... I SAW "TWINKIE THE KID" STIRRING IN TH' BUSHES!
BRING ME TH' HEAD OF TH' PILLSBURY DOUGHBOY!!
GRIFFY 3-12
AFTER TAKING OUT "CAP'N CRUNCH" IN THE SWAMPS SOUTH OF DINGBURG, ARNOLD BELGARD WAS AWARDED THE DINGBURG "CERTIFICATE OF EXTREME MANLINESS 'N' STUFF"...
WATCH OUT, MISTER PEANUT!
MY HERO!

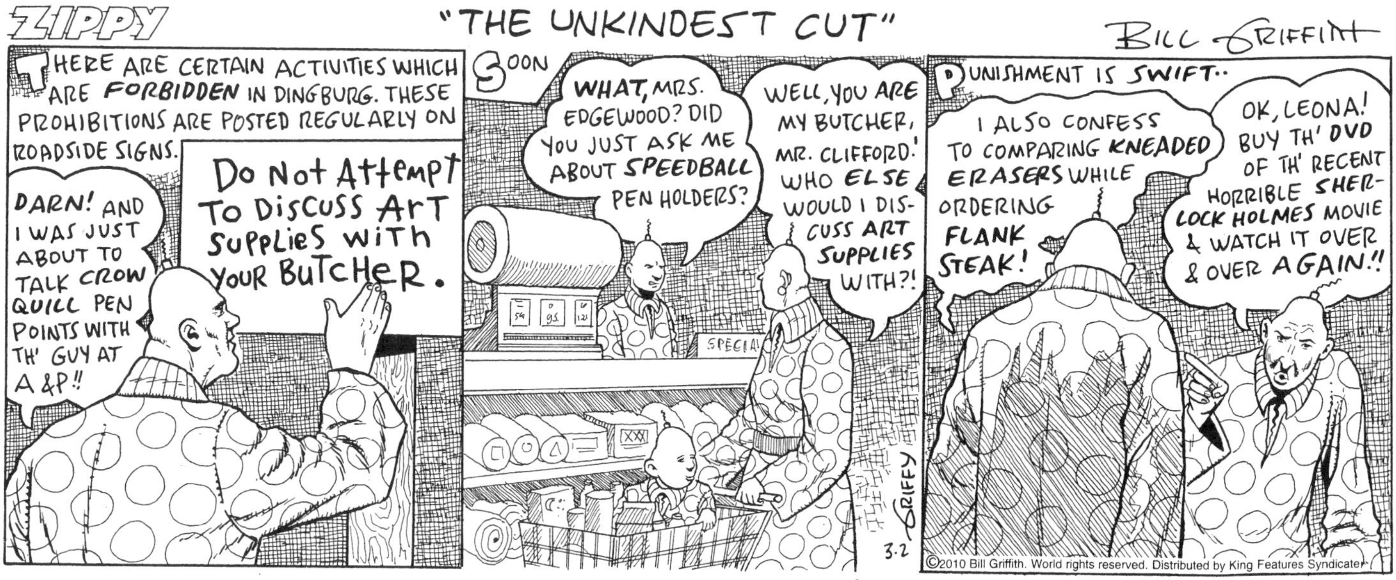
ZIPPY
"THE UNKINDEST CUT"
BILL GRIFFITH
THERE ARE CERTAIN ACTIVITIES WHICH ARE FORBIDDEN IN DINGBURG. THESE PROHIBITIONS ARE POSTED REGULARLY ON ROADSIDE SIGNS.
Do Not Attempt To Discuss Art Supplies with your Butcher.
DARN! AND I WAS JUST ABOUT TO TALK CROW QUILL PEN POINTS WITH TH' GUY AT A &P!!
SOON
WHAT, MRS. EDGEWOOD? DID YOU JUST ASK ME ABOUT SPEEDBALL PEN HOLDERS?
WELL, YOU ARE MY BUTCHER, MR. CLIFFORD! WHO ELSE WOULD I DISCUSS ART SUPPLIES WITH?!
SPECIAL
GRIFFY
3-2
PUNISHMENT IS SWIFT..
I ALSO CONFESS TO COMPARING KNEADED ERASERS WHILE ORDERING FLANK STEAK!
OK, LEONA! BUY TH' DVD OF TH' RECENT HORRIBLE SHERLOCK HOLMES MOVIE & WATCH IT OVER & OVER AGAIN!!
©2010 Bill Griffith. World rights reserved. Distributed by King Features Syndicate

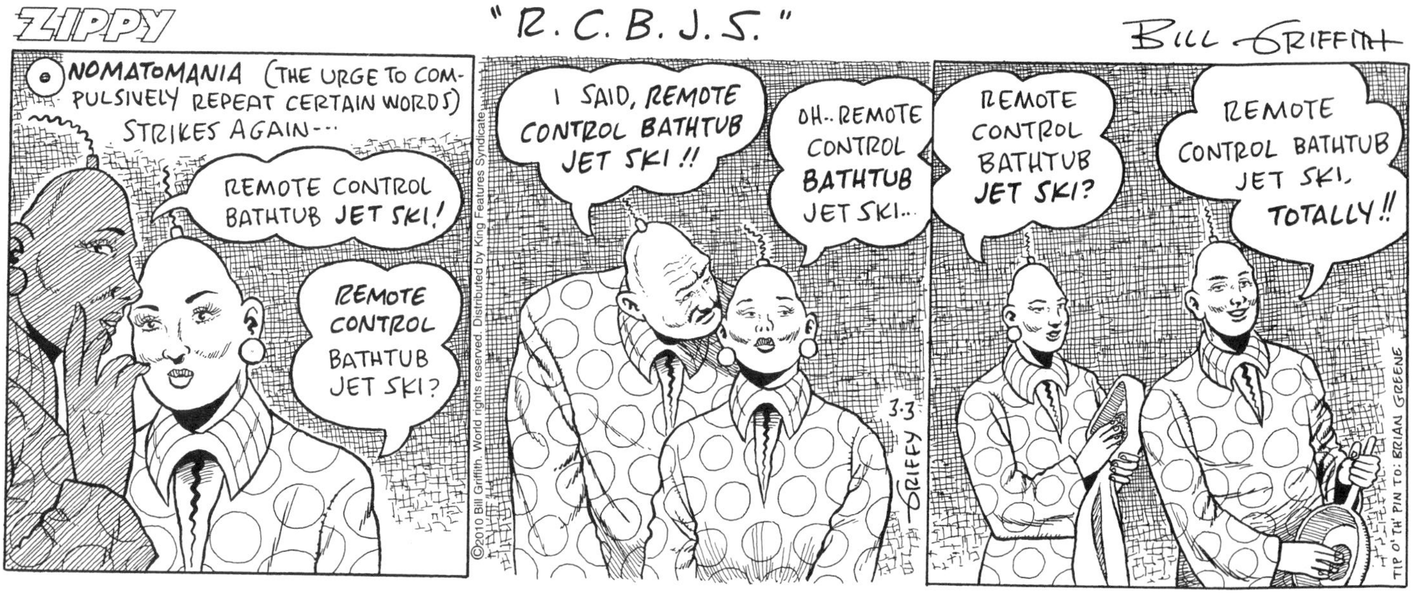
ZIPPY
"R. C. B. J. S."
BILL GRIFFITH
ONOMATOMANIA (THE URGE TO COMPULSIVELY REPEAT CERTAIN WORDS) STRIKES AGAIN---
REMOTE CONTROL BATHTUB JET SKI!
REMOTE CONTROL BATHTUB JET SKI?
©2010 Bill Griffith. World rights reserved. Distributed by King Features Syndicate
I SAID, REMOTE CONTROL BATHTUB JET SKI!!
OH.. REMOTE CONTROL BATHTUB JET SKI...
3-3
GRIFFY
REMOTE CONTROL BATHTUB JET SKI?
REMOTE CONTROL BATHTUB JET SKI, TOTALLY!!
TIP O' TH' PIN TO: BRIAN GREENE

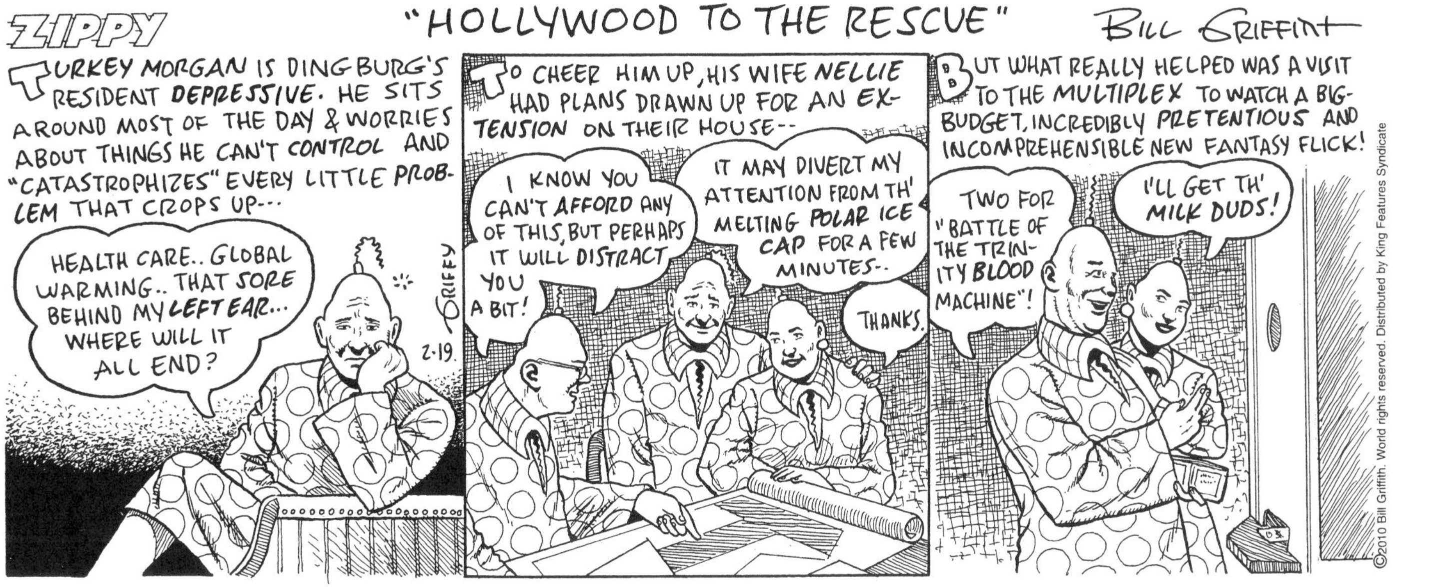
ZIPPY
"HOLLYWOOD TO THE RESCUE"
BILL GRIFFITH
TURKEY MORGAN IS DINGBURG'S RESIDENT DEPRESSIVE. HE SITS AROUND MOST OF THE DAY & WORRIES ABOUT THINGS HE CAN'T CONTROL AND "CATASTROPHIZES" EVERY LITTLE PROB-LEM THAT CROPS UP---
HEALTH CARE.. GLOBAL WARMING.. THAT SORE BEHIND MY LEFT EAR... WHERE WILL IT ALL END?
GRIFFY
2·19
TO CHEER HIM UP, HIS WIFE NELLIE HAD PLANS DRAWN UP FOR AN EX-TENSION ON THEIR HOUSE--
I KNOW YOU CAN'T AFFORD ANY OF THIS, BUT PERHAPS IT WILL DISTRACT YOU A BIT!
IT MAY DIVERT MY ATTENTION FROM TH' MELTING POLAR ICE CAP FOR A FEW MINUTES--.
THANKS.
BUT WHAT REALLY HELPED WAS A VISIT TO THE MULTIPLEX TO WATCH A BIG-BUDGET, INCREDIBLY PRETENTIOUS AND INCOMPREHENSIBLE NEW FANTASY FLICK!
TWO FOR "BATTLE OF THE TRIN-ITY BLOOD MACHINE"!
I'LL GET TH' MILK DUDS!
©2010 Bill Griffith. World rights reserved. Distributed by King Features Syndicate

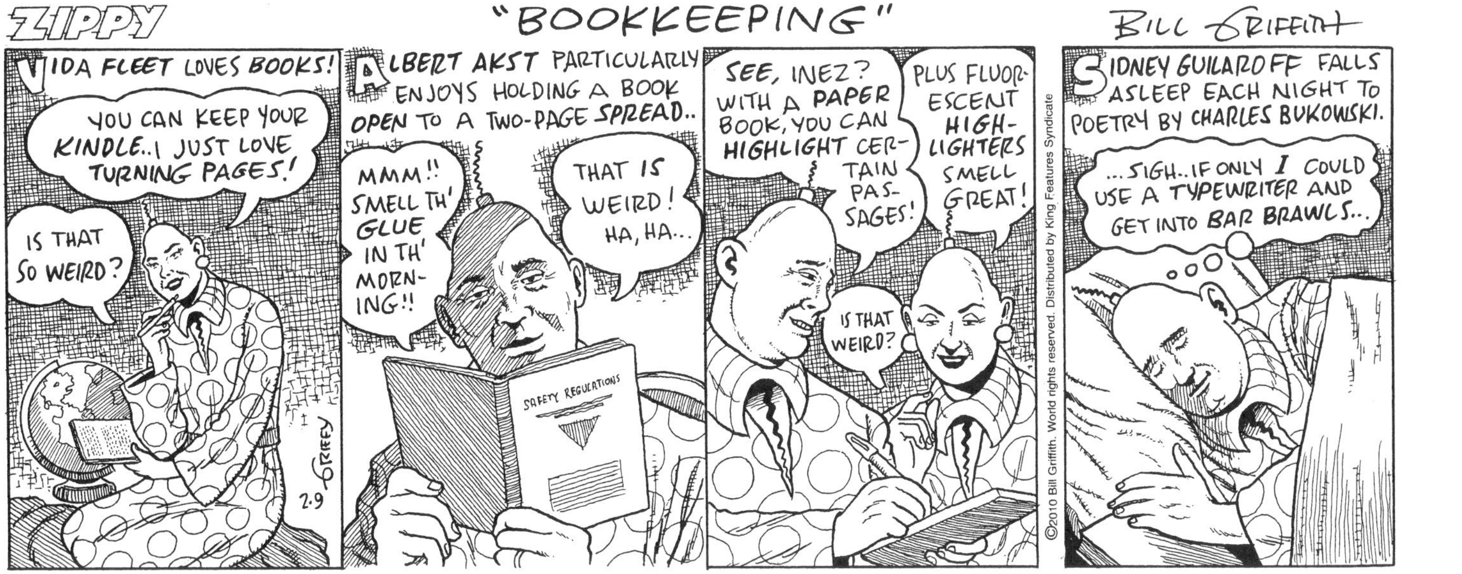
ZIPPY
"BOOKKEEPING"
BILL GRIFFITH
VIDA FLEET LOVES BOOKS!
YOU CAN KEEP YOUR KINDLE.. I JUST LOVE TURNING PAGES!
IS THAT SO WEIRD?
GRIFFY
2·9
ALBERT AKST PARTICULARLY ENJOYS HOLDING A BOOK OPEN TO A TWO-PAGE SPREAD..
MMM!! SMELL TH' GLUE IN TH' MORN-ING!!
THAT IS WEIRD! HA, HA...
SAFETY REGULATIONS
SEE, INEZ? WITH A PAPER BOOK, YOU CAN HIGHLIGHT CER-TAIN PAS-SAGES!
PLUS FLUOR-ESCENT HIGH-LIGHTERS SMELL GREAT!
IS THAT WEIRD?
©2010 Bill Griffith. World rights reserved. Distributed by King Features Syndicate
SIDNEY GUILAROFF FALLS ASLEEP EACH NIGHT TO POETRY BY CHARLES BUKOWSKI.
...SIGH.. IF ONLY I COULD USE A TYPEWRITER AND GET INTO BAR BRAWLS...

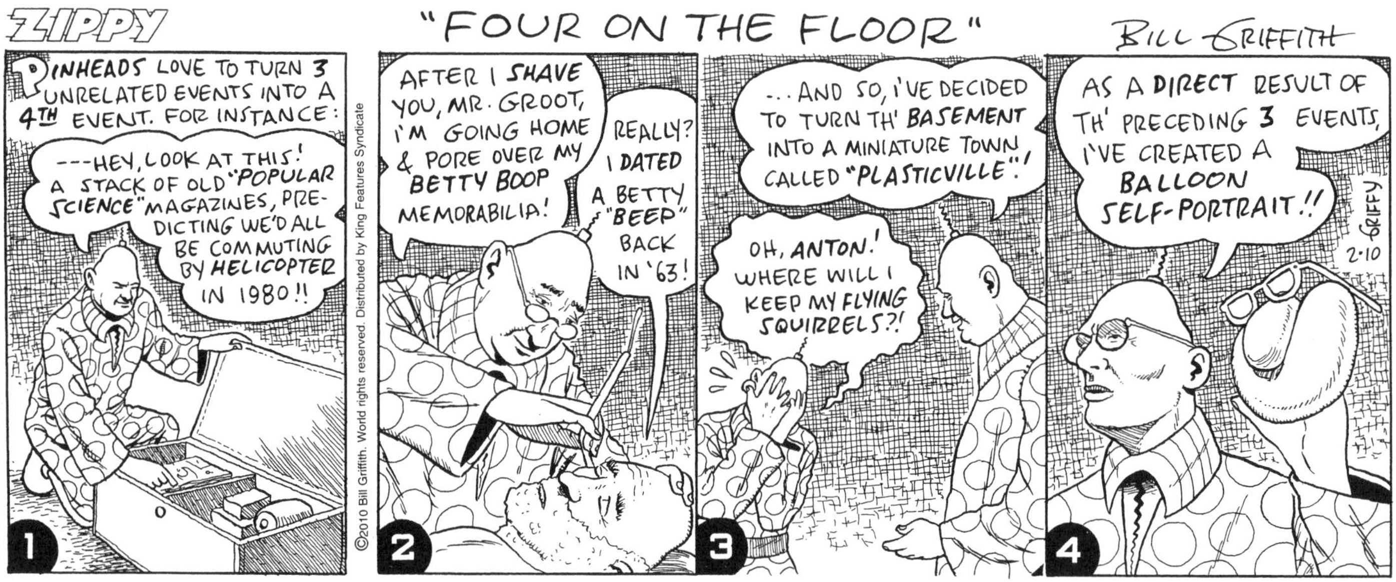
ZIPPY
"FOUR ON THE FLOOR"
BILL GRIFFITH
PINHEADS LOVE TO TURN 3 UNRELATED EVENTS INTO A 4TH EVENT. FOR INSTANCE:
---HEY, LOOK AT THIS! A STACK OF OLD "POPULAR SCIENCE" MAGAZINES, PREDICTING WE'D ALL BE COMMUTING BY HELICOPTER IN 1980!!
©2010 Bill Griffith. World rights reserved. Distributed by King Features Syndicate
AFTER I SHAVE YOU, MR. GROOT, I'M GOING HOME & PORE OVER MY BETTY BOOP MEMORABILIA!
REALLY? I DATED A BETTY "BEEP" BACK IN '63!
...AND SO, I'VE DECIDED TO TURN TH' BASEMENT INTO A MINIATURE TOWN CALLED "PLASTICVILLE"!
OH, ANTON! WHERE WILL I KEEP MY FLYING SQUIRRELS?!
AS A DIRECT RESULT OF TH' PRECEDING 3 EVENTS, I'VE CREATED A BALLOON SELF-PORTRAIT!!
GRIFFY 2·10

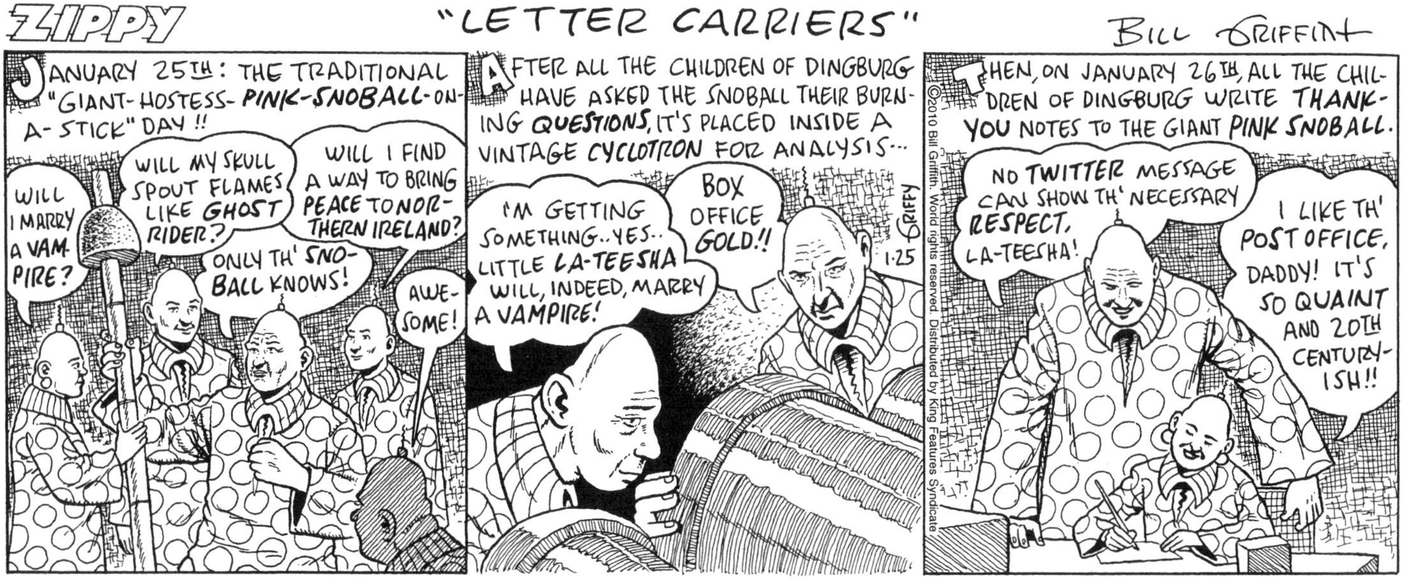
ZIPPY
"LETTER CARRIERS"
BILL GRIFFITH
JANUARY 25TH: THE TRADITIONAL "GIANT-HOSTESS-PINK-SNOBALL-ON-A-STICK" DAY!!
WILL I MARRY A VAMPIRE?
WILL MY SKULL SPOUT FLAMES LIKE GHOST RIDER?
WILL I FIND A WAY TO BRING PEACE TO NORTHERN IRELAND?
ONLY TH' SNOBALL KNOWS!
AWESOME!
AFTER ALL THE CHILDREN OF DINGBURG HAVE ASKED THE SNOBALL THEIR BURNING QUESTIONS, IT'S PLACED INSIDE A VINTAGE CYCLOTRON FOR ANALYSIS...
I'M GETTING SOMETHING..YES.. LITTLE LA-TEESHA WILL, INDEED, MARRY A VAMPIRE!
BOX OFFICE GOLD!!
GRIFFY 1·25
©2010 Bill Griffith. World rights reserved. Distributed by King Features Syndicate
THEN, ON JANUARY 26TH, ALL THE CHILDREN OF DINGBURG WRITE THANK-YOU NOTES TO THE GIANT PINK SNOBALL.
NO TWITTER MESSAGE CAN SHOW TH' NECESSARY RESPECT, LA-TEESHA!
I LIKE TH' POST OFFICE, DADDY! IT'S SO QUAINT AND 20TH CENTURY-ISH!!

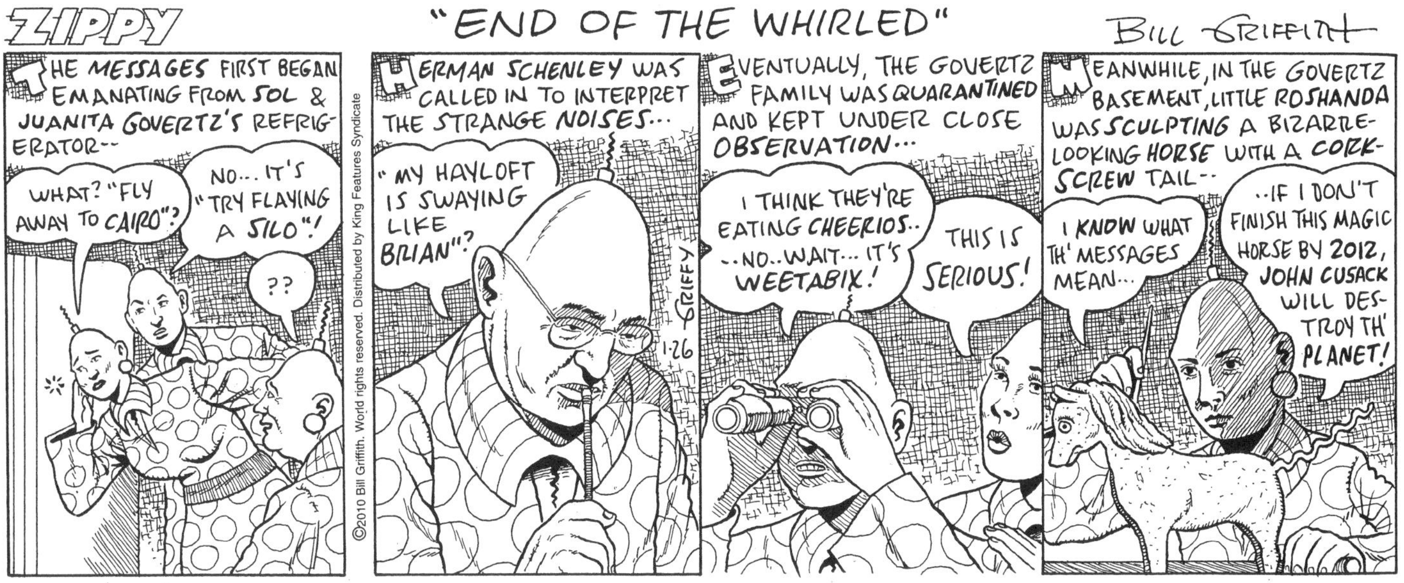
ZIPPY
"END OF THE WHIRLED"
BILL GRIFFITH
THE MESSAGES FIRST BEGAN EMANATING FROM SOL & JUANITA GOVERTZ'S REFRIG-ERATOR--
WHAT? "FLY AWAY TO CAIRO"?
NO... IT'S "TRY FLAYING A SILO"!
??
©2010 Bill Griffith. World rights reserved. Distributed by King Features Syndicate
HERMAN SCHENLEY WAS CALLED IN TO INTERPRET THE STRANGE NOISES...
"MY HAYLOFT IS SWAYING LIKE BRIAN"?
GRIFFY 1·26
EVENTUALLY, THE GOVERTZ FAMILY WAS QUARANTINED AND KEPT UNDER CLOSE OBSERVATION...
I THINK THEY'RE EATING CHEERIOS.. --NO..WAIT... IT'S WEETABIX!
THIS IS SERIOUS!
MEANWHILE, IN THE GOVERTZ BASEMENT, LITTLE ROSHANDA WAS SCULPTING A BIZARRE-LOOKING HORSE WITH A CORK-SCREW TAIL--
I KNOW WHAT TH' MESSAGES MEAN...
..IF I DON'T FINISH THIS MAGIC HORSE BY 2012, JOHN CUSACK WILL DES-TROY TH' PLANET!

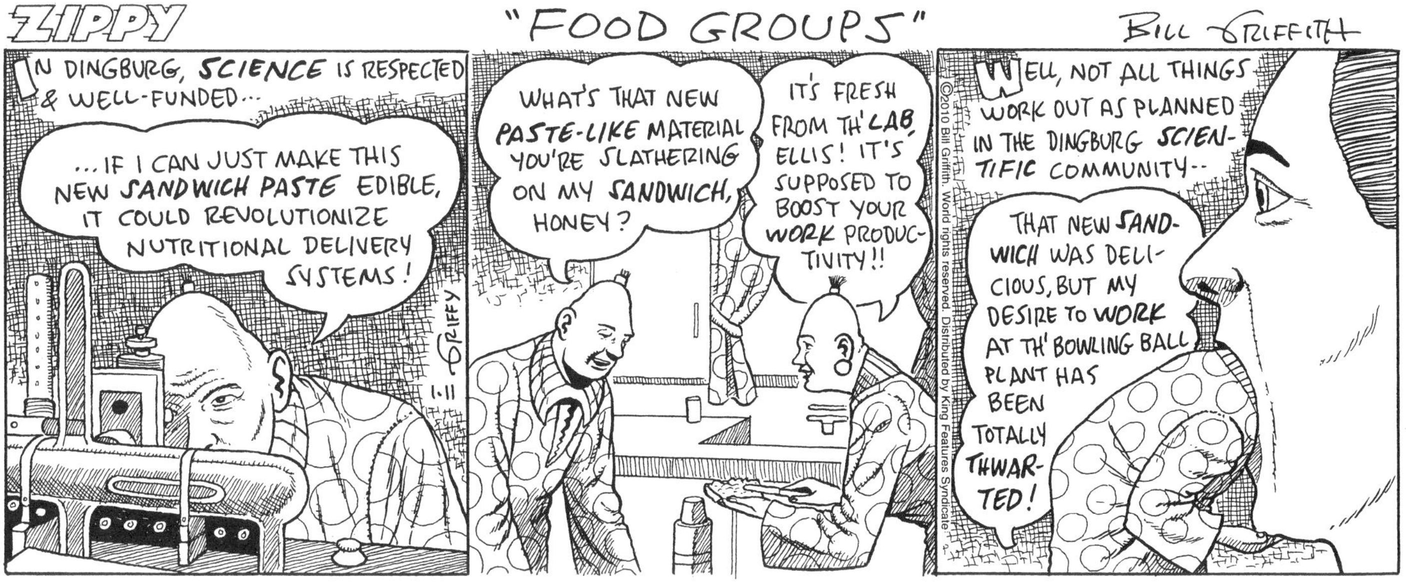
ZIPPY
"FOOD GROUPS"
BILL GRIFFITH
IN DINGBURG, SCIENCE IS RESPECTED & WELL-FUNDED...
...IF I CAN JUST MAKE THIS NEW SANDWICH PASTE EDIBLE, IT COULD REVOLUTIONIZE NUTRITIONAL DELIVERY SYSTEMS!
GRIFFY 1·11
WHAT'S THAT NEW PASTE-LIKE MATERIAL YOU'RE SLATHERING ON MY SANDWICH, HONEY?
IT'S FRESH FROM TH' LAB, ELLIS! IT'S SUPPOSED TO BOOST YOUR WORK PRODUC-TIVITY!!
©2010 Bill Griffith. World rights reserved. Distributed by King Features Syndicate
WELL, NOT ALL THINGS WORK OUT AS PLANNED IN THE DINGBURG SCIEN-TIFIC COMMUNITY--
THAT NEW SAND-WICH WAS DELI-CIOUS, BUT MY DESIRE TO WORK AT TH' BOWLING BALL PLANT HAS BEEN TOTALLY THWAR-TED!

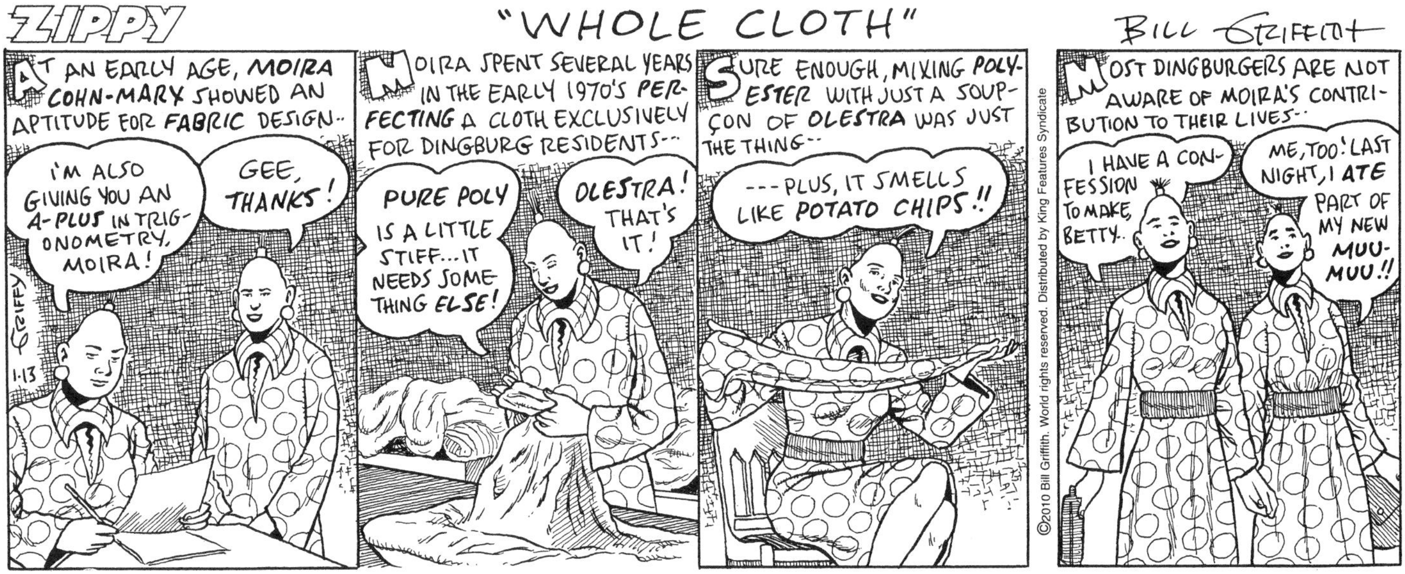
ZIPPY
"WHOLE CLOTH"
BILL GRIFFITH
AT AN EARLY AGE, MOIRA COHN-MARY SHOWED AN APTITUDE FOR FABRIC DESIGN--
I'M ALSO GIVING YOU AN A-PLUS IN TRIGONOMETRY, MOIRA!
GEE, THANKS!
GRIFFY 1-13
MOIRA SPENT SEVERAL YEARS IN THE EARLY 1970'S PERFECTING A CLOTH EXCLUSIVELY FOR DINGBURG RESIDENTS--
PURE POLY IS A LITTLE STIFF... IT NEEDS SOMETHING ELSE!
OLESTRA! THAT'S IT!
SURE ENOUGH, MIXING POLYESTER WITH JUST A SOUPÇON OF OLESTRA WAS JUST THE THING--
---PLUS, IT SMELLS LIKE POTATO CHIPS!!
©2010 Bill Griffith. World rights reserved. Distributed by King Features Syndicate
MOST DINGBURGERS ARE NOT AWARE OF MOIRA'S CONTRIBUTION TO THEIR LIVES--
I HAVE A CONFESSION TO MAKE, BETTY..
ME, TOO! LAST NIGHT, I ATE PART OF MY NEW MUU-MUU!!

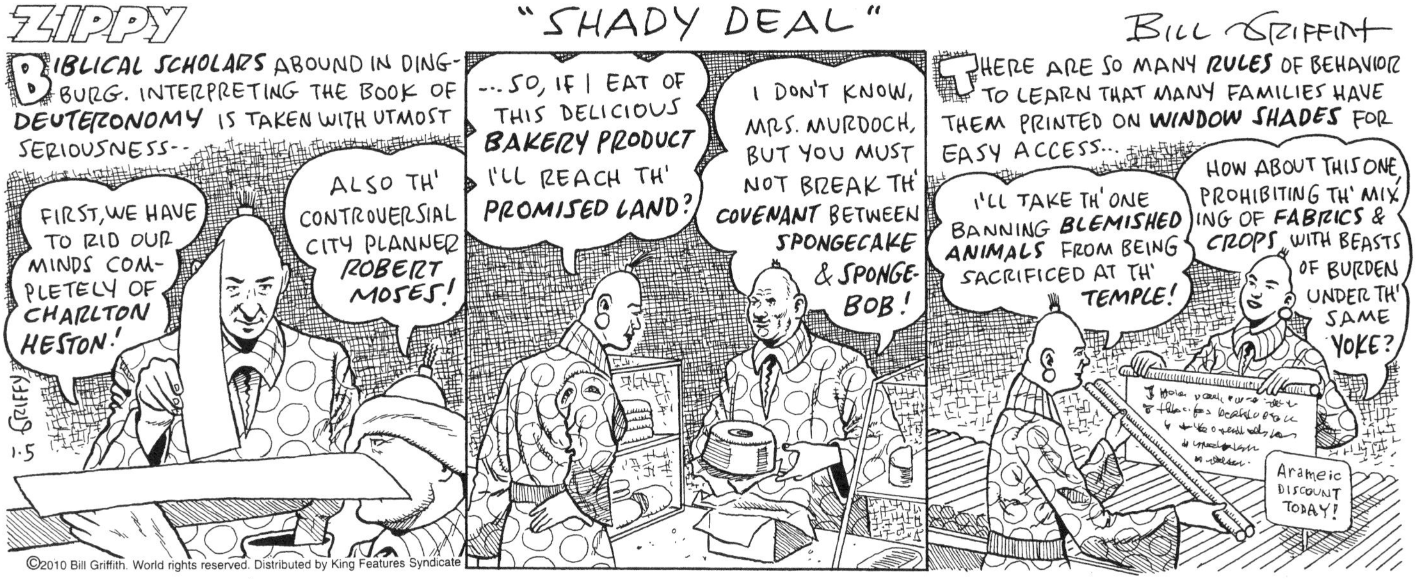
ZIPPY
"SHADY DEAL"
BILL GRIFFITH
BIBLICAL SCHOLARS ABOUND IN DINGBURG. INTERPRETING THE BOOK OF DEUTERONOMY IS TAKEN WITH UTMOST SERIOUSNESS--
FIRST, WE HAVE TO RID OUR MINDS COMPLETELY OF CHARLTON HESTON!
ALSO TH' CONTROVERSIAL CITY PLANNER ROBERT MOSES!
GRIFFY 1-5
©2010 Bill Griffith. World rights reserved. Distributed by King Features Syndicate
--.SO, IF I EAT OF THIS DELICIOUS BAKERY PRODUCT I'LL REACH TH' PROMISED LAND?
I DON'T KNOW, MRS. MURDOCH, BUT YOU MUST NOT BREAK TH' COVENANT BETWEEN SPONGECAKE & SPONGEBOB!
THERE ARE SO MANY RULES OF BEHAVIOR TO LEARN THAT MANY FAMILIES HAVE THEM PRINTED ON WINDOW SHADES FOR EASY ACCESS...
I'LL TAKE TH' ONE BANNING BLEMISHED ANIMALS FROM BEING SACRIFICED AT TH' TEMPLE!
HOW ABOUT THIS ONE, PROHIBITING TH' MIXING OF FABRICS & CROPS WITH BEASTS OF BURDEN UNDER TH' SAME YOKE?
Arameic DISCOUNT TODAY!

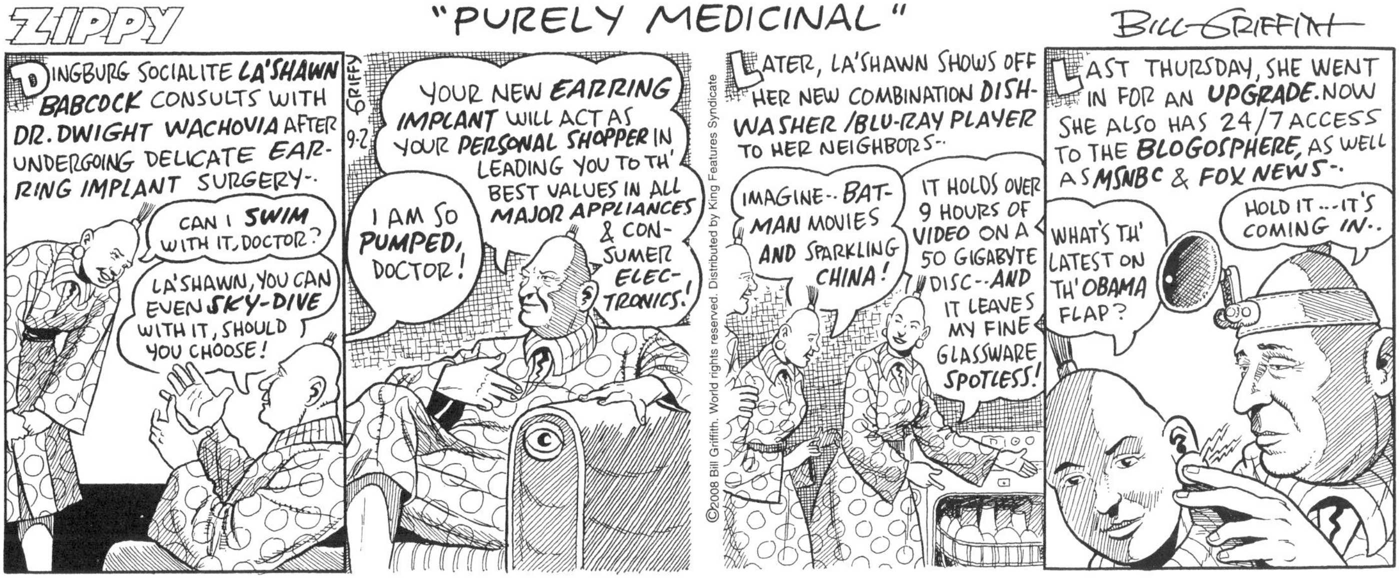
ZIPPY
"PURELY MEDICINAL"
BILL GRIFFITH
DINGBURG SOCIALITE LA'SHAWN BABCOCK CONSULTS WITH DR. DWIGHT WACHOVIA AFTER UNDERGOING DELICATE EAR-RING IMPLANT SURGERY..
CAN I SWIM WITH IT, DOCTOR?
LA'SHAWN, YOU CAN EVEN SKY-DIVE WITH IT, SHOULD YOU CHOOSE!
GRIFFY 9-2
YOUR NEW EARRING IMPLANT WILL ACT AS YOUR PERSONAL SHOPPER IN LEADING YOU TO TH' BEST VALUES IN ALL MAJOR APPLIANCES & CON-SUMER ELEC-TRONICS!
I AM SO PUMPED, DOCTOR!
©2008 Bill Griffith. World rights reserved. Distributed by King Features Syndicate
LATER, LA'SHAWN SHOWS OFF HER NEW COMBINATION DISH-WASHER/BLU-RAY PLAYER TO HER NEIGHBORS..
IMAGINE.. BAT-MAN MOVIES AND SPARKLING CHINA!
IT HOLDS OVER 9 HOURS OF VIDEO ON A 50 GIGABYTE DISC--AND IT LEAVES MY FINE GLASSWARE SPOTLESS!
LAST THURSDAY, SHE WENT IN FOR AN UPGRADE. NOW SHE ALSO HAS 24/7 ACCESS TO THE BLOGOSPHERE, AS WELL AS MSNBC & FOX NEWS..
WHAT'S TH' LATEST ON TH' OBAMA FLAP?
HOLD IT...IT'S COMING IN..

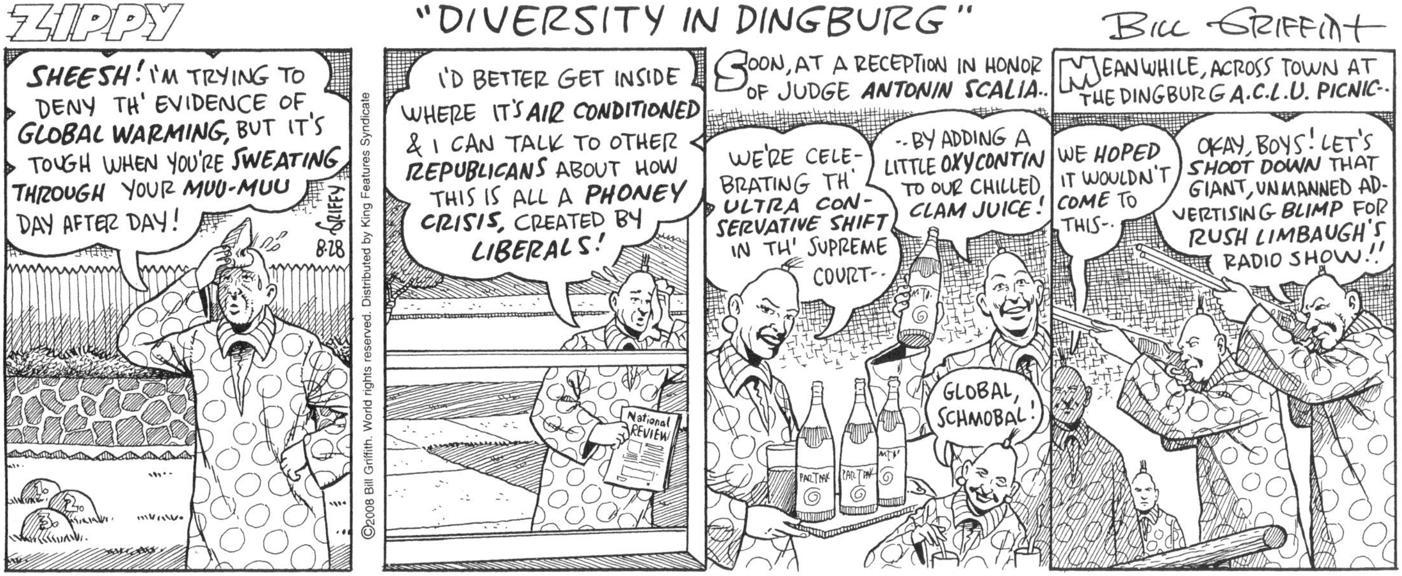
ZIPPY
"DIVERSITY IN DINGBURG"
BILL GRIFFITH
SHEESH! I'M TRYING TO DENY TH' EVIDENCE OF GLOBAL WARMING, BUT IT'S TOUGH WHEN YOU'RE SWEATING THROUGH YOUR MUU-MUU DAY AFTER DAY!
GRIFFY 8-28
©2008 Bill Griffith. World rights reserved. Distributed by King Features Syndicate
I'D BETTER GET INSIDE WHERE IT'S AIR CONDITIONED & I CAN TALK TO OTHER REPUBLICANS ABOUT HOW THIS IS ALL A PHONEY CRISIS, CREATED BY LIBERALS!
National REVIEW
SOON, AT A RECEPTION IN HONOR OF JUDGE ANTONIN SCALIA..
WE'RE CELE-BRATING TH' ULTRA CON-SERVATIVE SHIFT IN TH' SUPREME COURT--
--BY ADDING A LITTLE OXYCONTIN TO OUR CHILLED CLAM JUICE!
GLOBAL, SCHMOBAL!
MEANWHILE, ACROSS TOWN AT THE DINGBURG A.C.L.U. PICNIC..
WE HOPED IT WOULDN'T COME TO THIS..
OKAY, BOYS! LET'S SHOOT DOWN THAT GIANT, UNMANNED AD-VERTISING BLIMP FOR RUSH LIMBAUGH'S RADIO SHOW!!

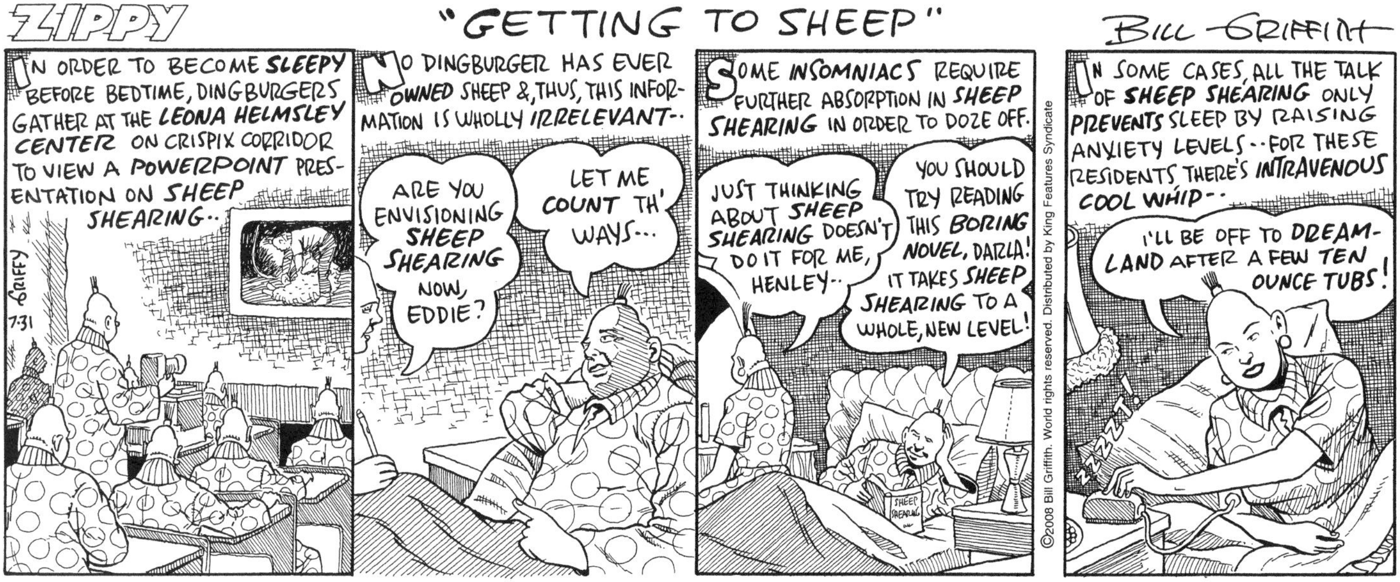
ZIPPY
"GETTING TO SHEEP"
BILL GRIFFITH
IN ORDER TO BECOME SLEEPY BEFORE BEDTIME, DINGBURGERS GATHER AT THE LEONA HELMSLEY CENTER ON CRISPIX CORRIDOR TO VIEW A POWERPOINT PRESENTATION ON SHEEP SHEARING..
GRIFFY 7·31
NO DINGBURGER HAS EVER OWNED SHEEP &, THUS, THIS INFORMATION IS WHOLLY IRRELEVANT-.
ARE YOU ENVISIONING SHEEP SHEARING NOW, EDDIE?
LET ME COUNT TH' WAYS...
SOME INSOMNIACS REQUIRE FURTHER ABSORPTION IN SHEEP SHEARING IN ORDER TO DOZE OFF.
JUST THINKING ABOUT SHEEP SHEARING DOESN'T DO IT FOR ME, HENLEY..
YOU SHOULD TRY READING THIS BORING NOVEL, DARLA! IT TAKES SHEEP SHEARING TO A WHOLE, NEW LEVEL!
SHEEP SHEARING
©2008 Bill Griffith. World rights reserved. Distributed by King Features Syndicate
IN SOME CASES, ALL THE TALK OF SHEEP SHEARING ONLY PREVENTS SLEEP BY RAISING ANXIETY LEVELS..FOR THESE RESIDENTS THERE'S INTRAVENOUS COOL WHIP--
I'LL BE OFF TO DREAMLAND AFTER A FEW TEN OUNCE TUBS!

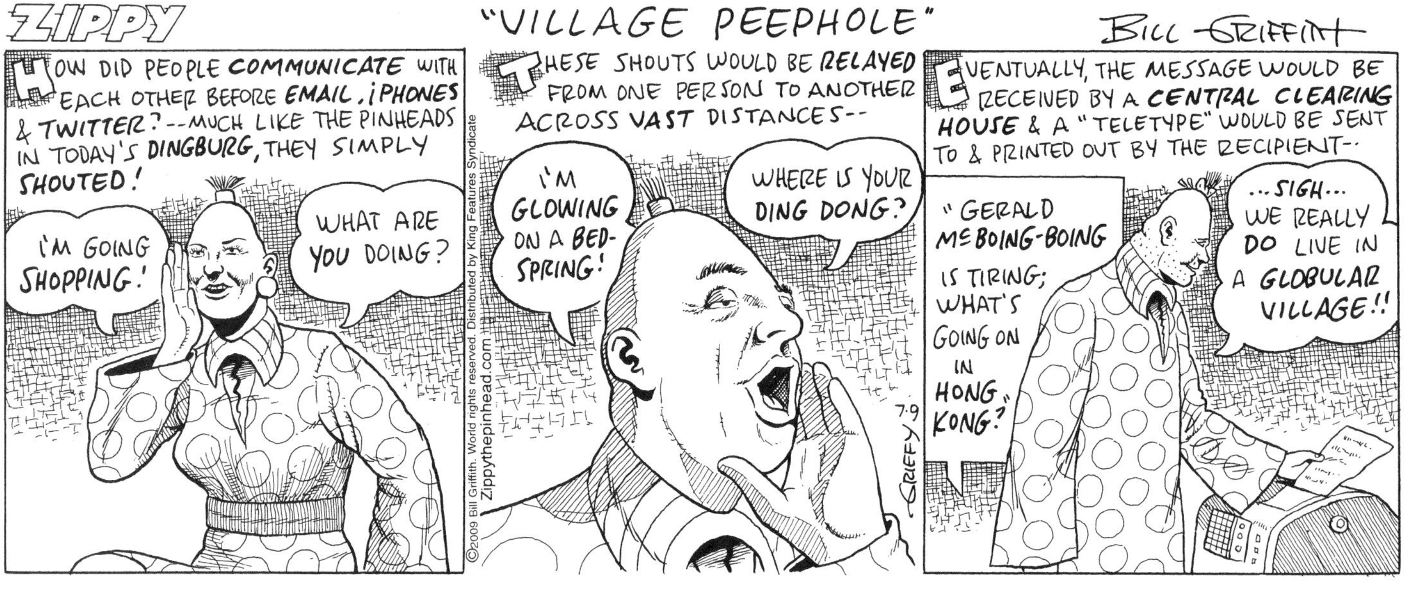
ZIPPY
"VILLAGE PEEPHOLE"
BILL GRIFFITH
HOW DID PEOPLE COMMUNICATE WITH EACH OTHER BEFORE EMAIL, iPHONES & TWITTER?--MUCH LIKE THE PINHEADS IN TODAY'S DINGBURG, THEY SIMPLY SHOUTED!
I'M GOING SHOPPING!
WHAT ARE YOU DOING?
©2009 Bill Griffith. World rights reserved. Distributed by King Features Syndicate
Zippythepinhead.com
THESE SHOUTS WOULD BE RELAYED FROM ONE PERSON TO ANOTHER ACROSS VAST DISTANCES--
I'M GLOWING ON A BED-SPRING!
WHERE IS YOUR DING DONG?
7·9 GRIFFY
EVENTUALLY, THE MESSAGE WOULD BE RECEIVED BY A CENTRAL CLEARING HOUSE & A "TELETYPE" WOULD BE SENT TO & PRINTED OUT BY THE RECIPIENT-.
"GERALD McBOING-BOING IS TIRING; WHAT'S GOING ON IN HONG KONG?"
...SIGH... WE REALLY DO LIVE IN A GLOBULAR VILLAGE!!

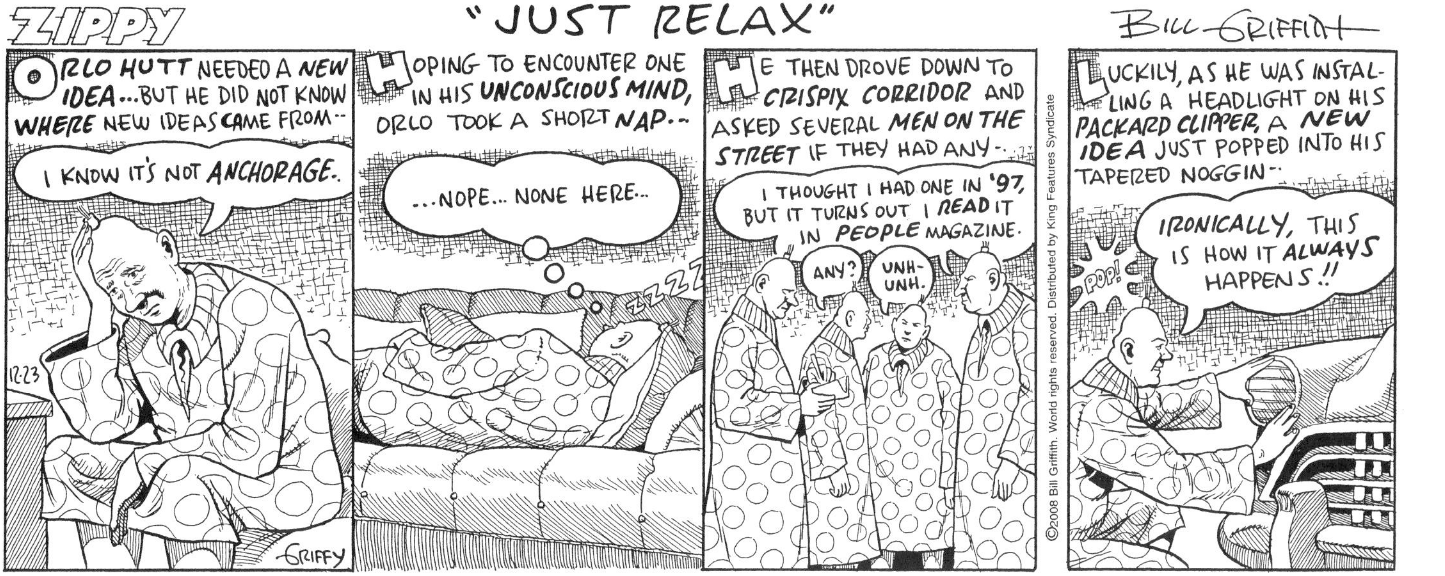

ZIPPY
"JUST RELAX"
BILL GRIFFITH
ORLO HUTT NEEDED A NEW IDEA... BUT HE DID NOT KNOW WHERE NEW IDEAS CAME FROM--
I KNOW IT'S NOT ANCHORAGE.
12-23
GRIFFY
HOPING TO ENCOUNTER ONE IN HIS UNCONSCIOUS MIND, ORLO TOOK A SHORT NAP--
...NOPE... NONE HERE...
HE THEN DROVE DOWN TO CRISPIX CORRIDOR AND ASKED SEVERAL MEN ON THE STREET IF THEY HAD ANY--
I THOUGHT I HAD ONE IN '97, BUT IT TURNS OUT I READ IT IN PEOPLE MAGAZINE.
ANY?
UNH-UNH.
©2008 Bill Griffith. World rights reserved. Distributed by King Features Syndicate
LUCKILY, AS HE WAS INSTALLING A HEADLIGHT ON HIS PACKARD CLIPPER, A NEW IDEA JUST POPPED INTO HIS TAPERED NOGGIN--
POP!
IRONICALLY, THIS IS HOW IT ALWAYS HAPPENS!!

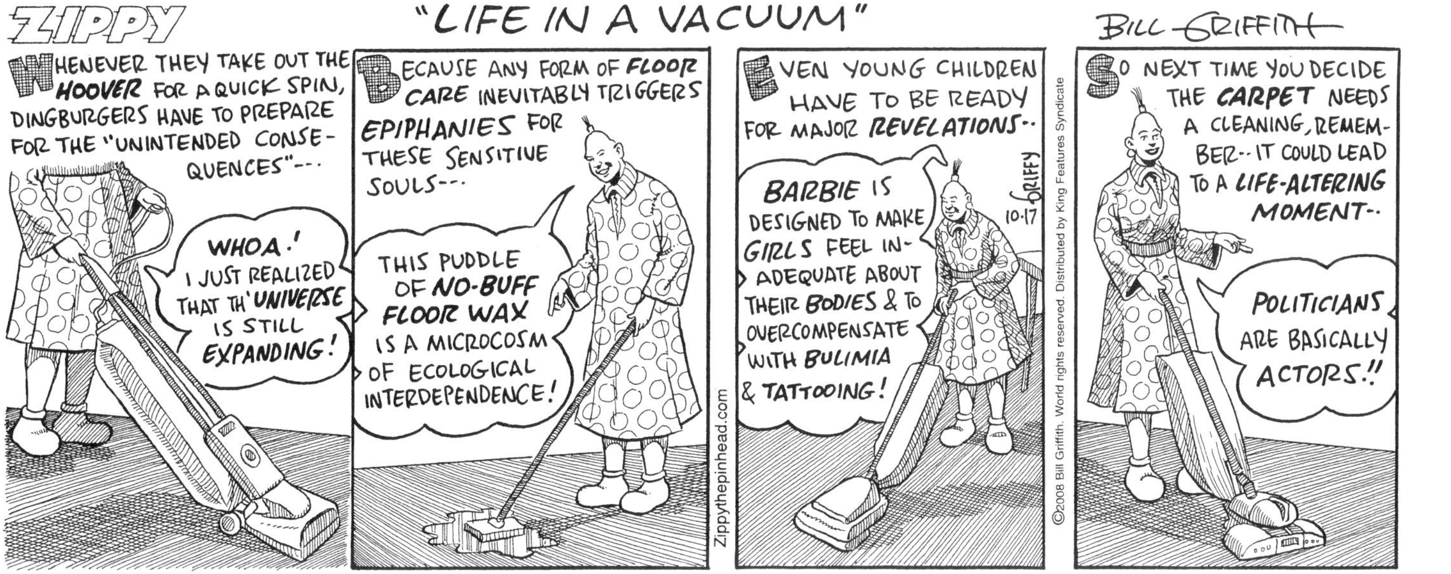

ZIPPY
"LIFE IN A VACUUM"
BILL GRIFFITH
WHENEVER THEY TAKE OUT THE HOOVER FOR A QUICK SPIN, DINGBURGERS HAVE TO PREPARE FOR THE "UNINTENDED CONSEQUENCES"--.
WHOA! I JUST REALIZED THAT TH' UNIVERSE IS STILL EXPANDING!
BECAUSE ANY FORM OF FLOOR CARE INEVITABLY TRIGGERS EPIPHANIES FOR THESE SENSITIVE SOULS---
THIS PUDDLE OF NO-BUFF FLOOR WAX IS A MICROCOSM OF ECOLOGICAL INTERDEPENDENCE!
Zippythepinhead.com
EVEN YOUNG CHILDREN HAVE TO BE READY FOR MAJOR REVELATIONS--
BARBIE IS DESIGNED TO MAKE GIRLS FEEL INADEQUATE ABOUT THEIR BODIES & TO OVERCOMPENSATE WITH BULIMIA & TATTOOING!
GRIFFY
10-17
©2008 Bill Griffith. World rights reserved. Distributed by King Features Syndicate
SO NEXT TIME YOU DECIDE THE CARPET NEEDS A CLEANING, REMEMBER-- IT COULD LEAD TO A LIFE-ALTERING MOMENT--
POLITICIANS ARE BASICALLY ACTORS!!

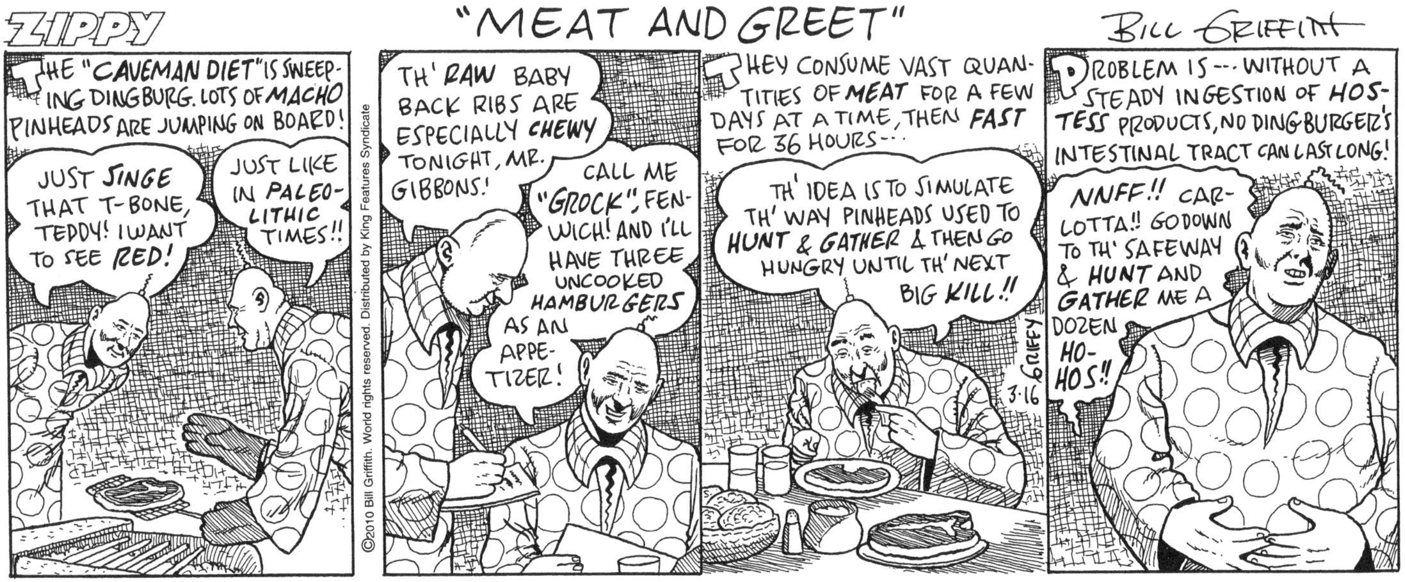

ZIPPY
"MEAT AND GREET"
BILL GRIFFITH
THE "CAVEMAN DIET" IS SWEEPING DINGBURG. LOTS OF MACHO PINHEADS ARE JUMPING ON BOARD!
JUST SINGE THAT T-BONE, TEDDY! I WANT TO SEE RED!
JUST LIKE IN PALEOLITHIC TIMES!!
©2010 Bill Griffith. World rights reserved. Distributed by King Features Syndicate
TH' RAW BABY BACK RIBS ARE ESPECIALLY CHEWY TONIGHT, MR. GIBBONS!
CALL ME "GROCK", FENWICH! AND I'LL HAVE THREE UNCOOKED HAMBURGERS AS AN APPETIZER!
THEY CONSUME VAST QUANTITIES OF MEAT FOR A FEW DAYS AT A TIME, THEN FAST FOR 36 HOURS...
TH' IDEA IS TO SIMULATE TH' WAY PINHEADS USED TO HUNT & GATHER & THEN GO HUNGRY UNTIL TH' NEXT BIG KILL!!
GRIFFY 3·16
PROBLEM IS... WITHOUT A STEADY INGESTION OF HOSTESS PRODUCTS, NO DINGBURGER'S INTESTINAL TRACT CAN LAST LONG!
NNFF!! CARLOTTA!! GO DOWN TO TH' SAFEWAY & HUNT AND GATHER ME A DOZEN HO-HOS!!

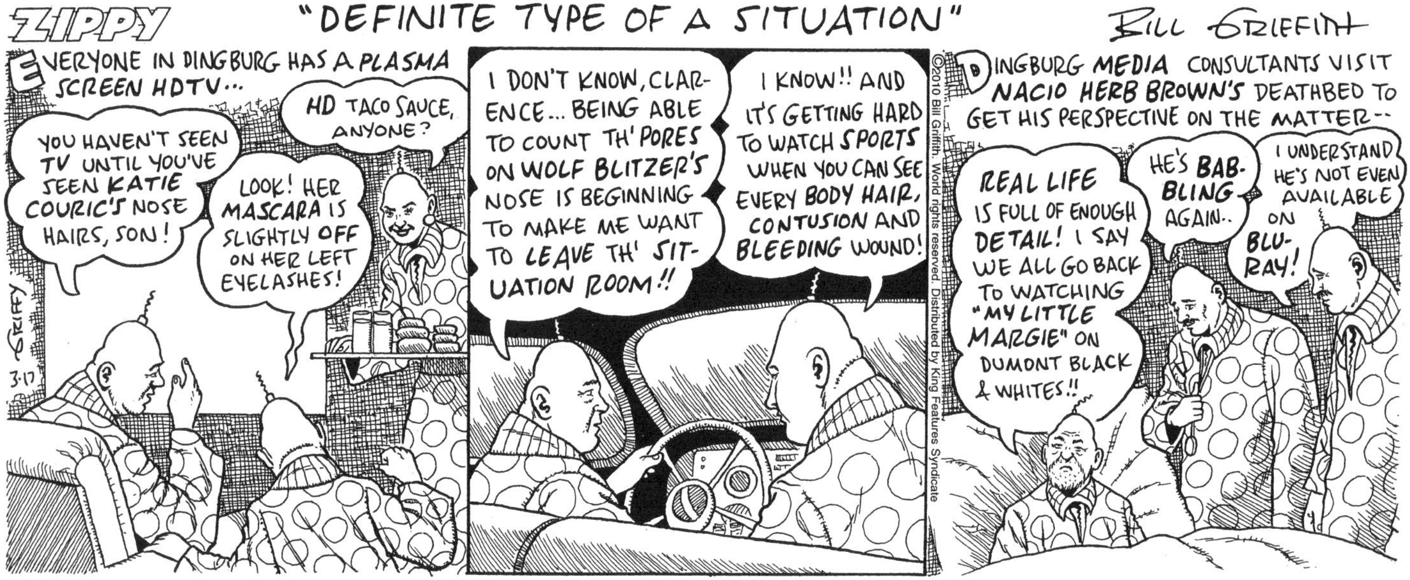

ZIPPY
"DEFINITE TYPE OF A SITUATION"
BILL GRIFFITH
EVERYONE IN DINGBURG HAS A PLASMA SCREEN HDTV...
YOU HAVEN'T SEEN TV UNTIL YOU'VE SEEN KATIE COURIC'S NOSE HAIRS, SON!
LOOK! HER MASCARA IS SLIGHTLY OFF ON HER LEFT EYELASHES!
HD TACO SAUCE, ANYONE?
GRIFFY 3·17
I DON'T KNOW, CLARENCE... BEING ABLE TO COUNT TH' PORES ON WOLF BLITZER'S NOSE IS BEGINNING TO MAKE ME WANT TO LEAVE TH' SITUATION ROOM!!
I KNOW!! AND IT'S GETTING HARD TO WATCH SPORTS WHEN YOU CAN SEE EVERY BODY HAIR, CONTUSION AND BLEEDING WOUND!
©2010 Bill Griffith. World rights reserved. Distributed by King Features Syndicate
DINGBURG MEDIA CONSULTANTS VISIT NACIO HERB BROWN'S DEATHBED TO GET HIS PERSPECTIVE ON THE MATTER--
REAL LIFE IS FULL OF ENOUGH DETAIL! I SAY WE ALL GO BACK TO WATCHING "MY LITTLE MARGIE" ON DUMONT BLACK & WHITES!!
HE'S BABBLING AGAIN..
I UNDERSTAND HE'S NOT EVEN AVAILABLE ON BLU-RAY!

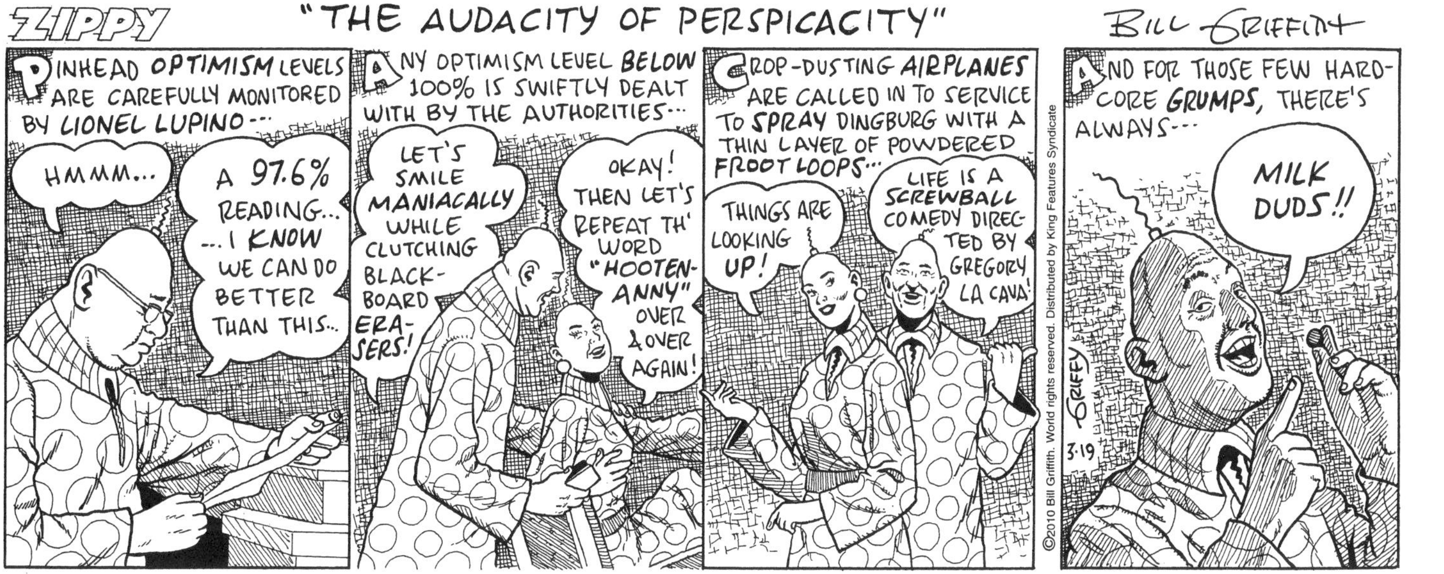
ZIPPY
"THE AUDACITY OF PERSPICACITY"
BILL GRIFFITH
PINHEAD OPTIMISM LEVELS ARE CAREFULLY MONITORED BY LIONEL LUPINO...
HMMM...
A 97.6% READING... ...I KNOW WE CAN DO BETTER THAN THIS...
ANY OPTIMISM LEVEL BELOW 100% IS SWIFTLY DEALT WITH BY THE AUTHORITIES...
LET'S SMILE MANIACALLY WHILE CLUTCHING BLACK-BOARD ERASERS!
OKAY! THEN LET'S REPEAT TH' WORD "HOOTENANNY" OVER & OVER AGAIN!
CROP-DUSTING AIRPLANES ARE CALLED IN TO SERVICE TO SPRAY DINGBURG WITH A THIN LAYER OF POWDERED FROOT LOOPS...
THINGS ARE LOOKING UP!
LIFE IS A SCREWBALL COMEDY DIRECTED BY GREGORY LA CAVA!
©2010 Bill Griffith. World rights reserved. Distributed by King Features Syndicate
GRIFFY 3.19
AND FOR THOSE FEW HARD-CORE GRUMPS, THERE'S ALWAYS...
MILK DUDS!!

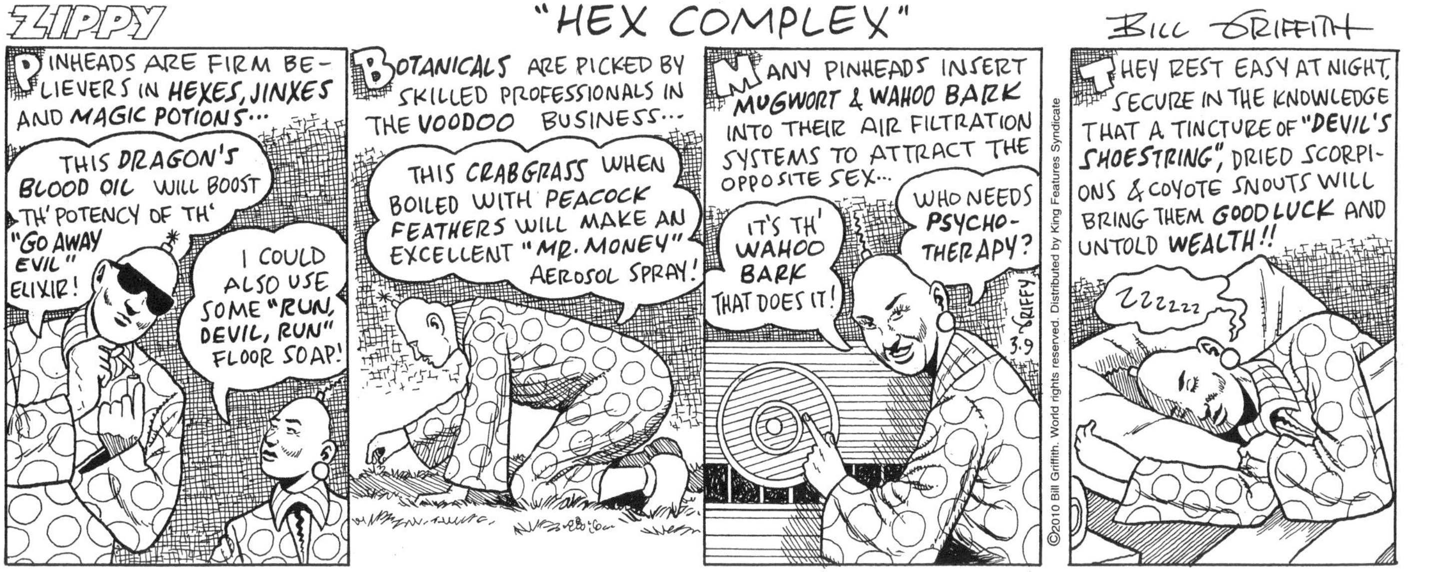
ZIPPY
"HEX COMPLEX"
BILL GRIFFITH
PINHEADS ARE FIRM BELIEVERS IN HEXES, JINXES AND MAGIC POTIONS...
THIS DRAGON'S BLOOD OIL WILL BOOST TH' POTENCY OF TH' "GO AWAY EVIL" ELIXIR!
I COULD ALSO USE SOME "RUN, DEVIL, RUN" FLOOR SOAP!
BOTANICALS ARE PICKED BY SKILLED PROFESSIONALS IN THE VOODOO BUSINESS...
THIS CRABGRASS WHEN BOILED WITH PEACOCK FEATHERS WILL MAKE AN EXCELLENT "MR. MONEY" AEROSOL SPRAY!
MANY PINHEADS INSERT MUGWORT & WAHOO BARK INTO THEIR AIR FILTRATION SYSTEMS TO ATTRACT THE OPPOSITE SEX...
IT'S TH' WAHOO BARK THAT DOES IT!
WHO NEEDS PSYCHOTHERAPY?
GRIFFY 3.9
©2010 Bill Griffith. World rights reserved. Distributed by King Features Syndicate
THEY REST EASY AT NIGHT, SECURE IN THE KNOWLEDGE THAT A TINCTURE OF "DEVIL'S SHOESTRING", DRIED SCORPIONS & COYOTE SNOUTS WILL BRING THEM GOOD LUCK AND UNTOLD WEALTH!!
ZZZZZZ

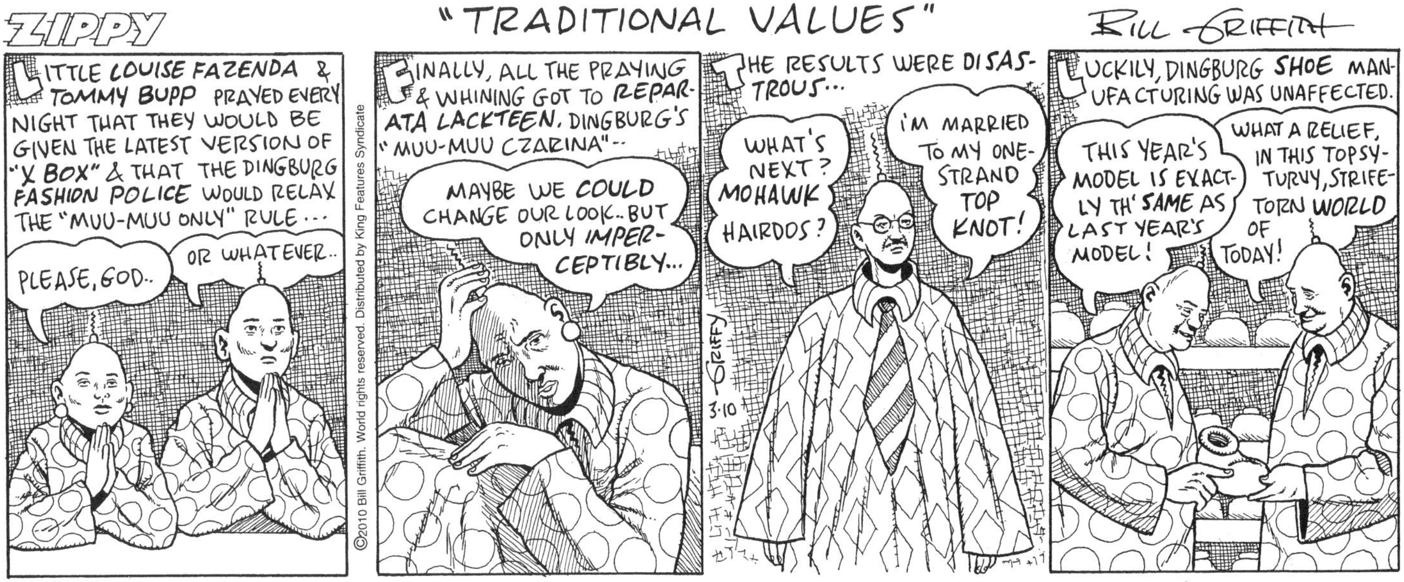

ZIPPY
"TRADITIONAL VALUES"
BILL GRIFFITH
LITTLE LOUISE FAZENDA & TOMMY BUPP PRAYED EVERY NIGHT THAT THEY WOULD BE GIVEN THE LATEST VERSION OF "X BOX" & THAT THE DINGBURG FASHION POLICE WOULD RELAX THE "MUU-MUU ONLY" RULE...
PLEASE, GOD..
OR WHATEVER..
©2010 Bill Griffith. World rights reserved. Distributed by King Features Syndicate
FINALLY, ALL THE PRAYING & WHINING GOT TO REPARATA LACKTEEN, DINGBURG'S "MUU-MUU CZARINA"--
MAYBE WE COULD CHANGE OUR LOOK.. BUT ONLY IMPERCEPTIBLY...
GRIFFY 3·10
THE RESULTS WERE DISASTROUS...
WHAT'S NEXT? MOHAWK HAIRDOS?
I'M MARRIED TO MY ONE-STRAND TOP KNOT!
LUCKILY, DINGBURG SHOE MANUFACTURING WAS UNAFFECTED.
THIS YEAR'S MODEL IS EXACTLY TH' SAME AS LAST YEAR'S MODEL!
WHAT A RELIEF, IN THIS TOPSY-TURVY, STRIFE-TORN WORLD OF TODAY!

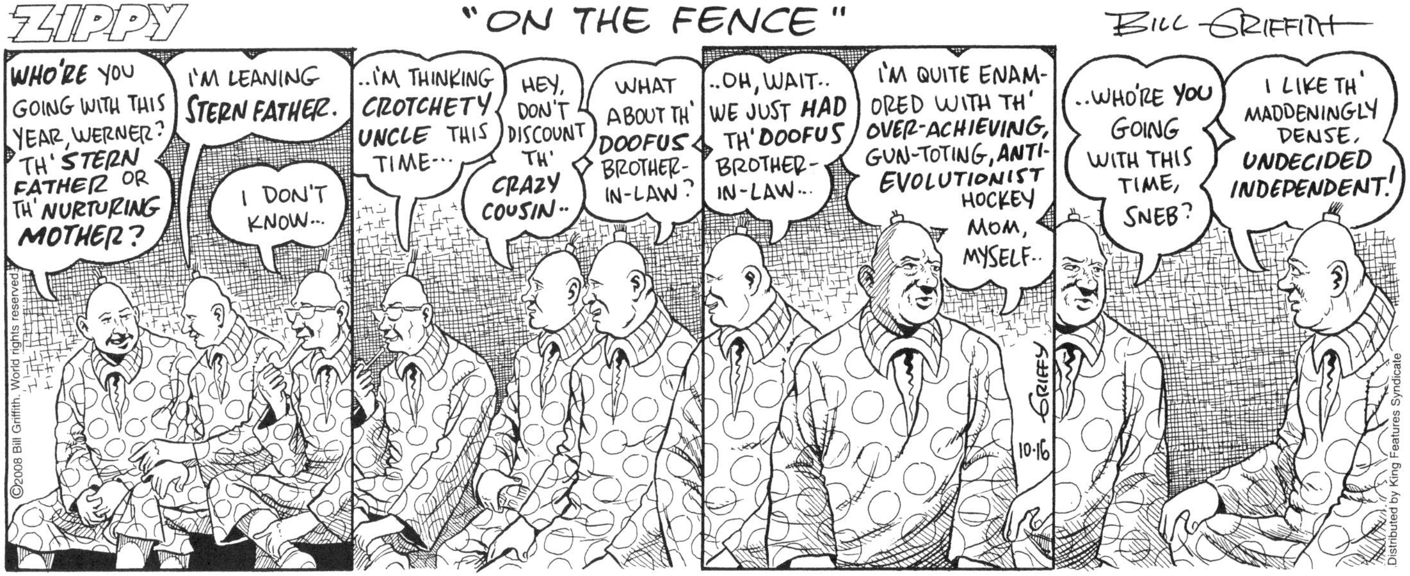

ZIPPY
"ON THE FENCE"
BILL GRIFFITH
WHO'RE YOU GOING WITH THIS YEAR, WERNER? TH' STERN FATHER OR TH' NURTURING MOTHER?
I'M LEANING STERN FATHER.
I DON'T KNOW...
©2008 Bill Griffith. World rights reserved
..I'M THINKING CROTCHETY UNCLE THIS TIME...
HEY, DON'T DISCOUNT TH' CRAZY COUSIN..
WHAT ABOUT TH' DOOFUS BROTHER-IN-LAW?
..OH, WAIT.. WE JUST HAD TH' DOOFUS BROTHER-IN-LAW..
I'M QUITE ENAMORED WITH TH' OVER-ACHIEVING, GUN-TOTING, ANTI-EVOLUTIONIST HOCKEY MOM, MYSELF..
GRIFFY 10·16
..WHO'RE YOU GOING WITH THIS TIME, SNEB?
I LIKE TH' MADDENINGLY DENSE, UNDECIDED INDEPENDENT!
Distributed by King Features Syndicate

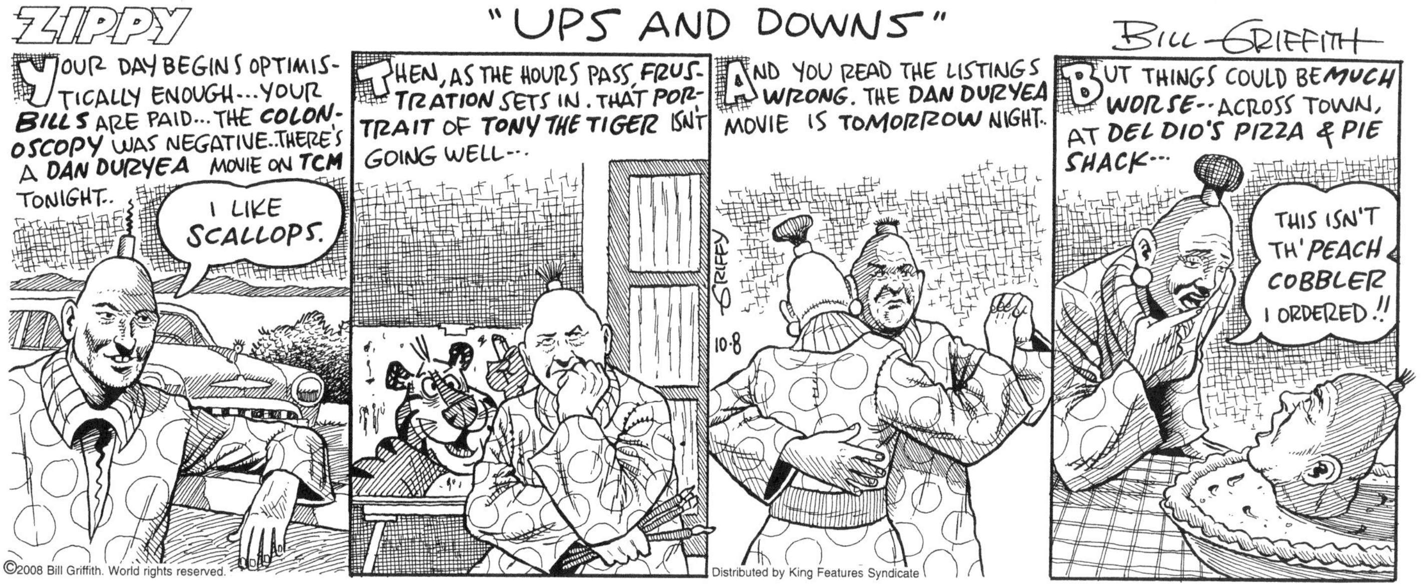
ZIPPY
"UPS AND DOWNS"
BILL GRIFFITH
YOUR DAY BEGINS OPTIMISTICALLY ENOUGH... YOUR BILLS ARE PAID... THE COLONOSCOPY WAS NEGATIVE.. THERE'S A DAN DURYEA MOVIE ON TCM TONIGHT..
I LIKE SCALLOPS.
THEN, AS THE HOURS PASS, FRUSTRATION SETS IN. THAT PORTRAIT OF TONY THE TIGER ISN'T GOING WELL--.
AND YOU READ THE LISTINGS WRONG. THE DAN DURYEA MOVIE IS TOMORROW NIGHT..
GRIFFY 10·8
BUT THINGS COULD BE MUCH WORSE-- ACROSS TOWN, AT DEL DIO'S PIZZA & PIE SHACK--
THIS ISN'T TH' PEACH COBBLER I ORDERED!!
©2008 Bill Griffith. World rights reserved.
Distributed by King Features Syndicate

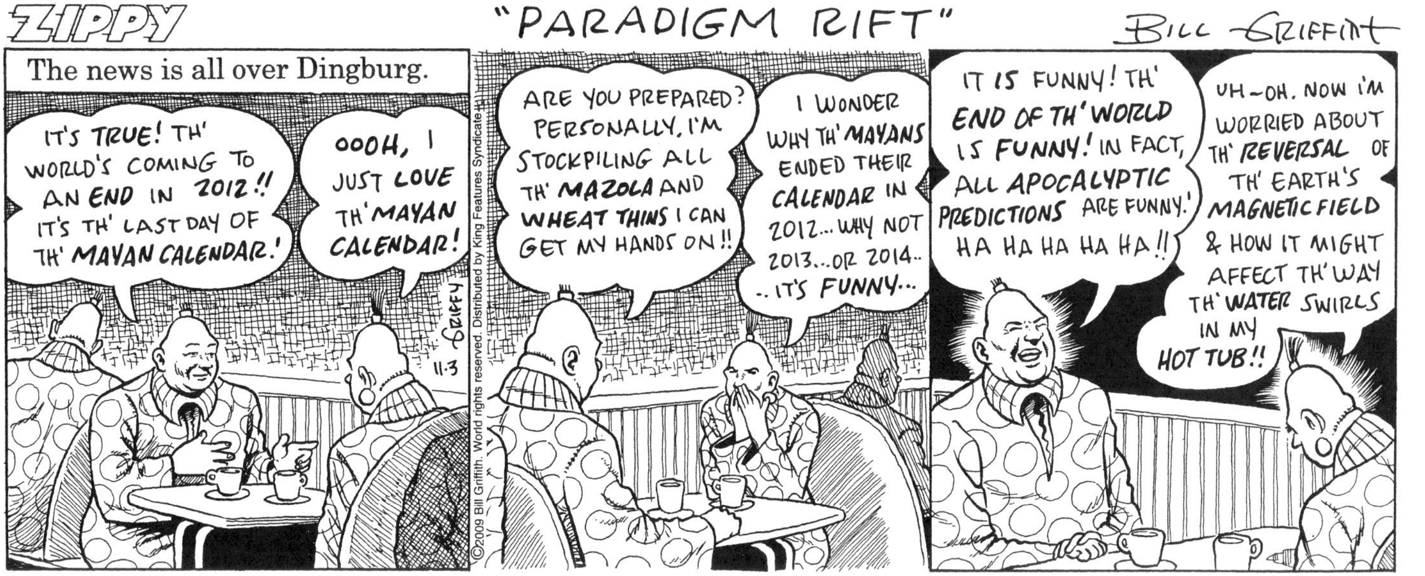
ZIPPY
"PARADIGM RIFT"
BILL GRIFFITH
The news is all over Dingburg.
IT'S TRUE! TH' WORLD'S COMING TO AN END IN 2012!! IT'S TH' LAST DAY OF TH' MAYAN CALENDAR!
OOOH, I JUST LOVE TH' MAYAN CALENDAR!
GRIFFY 11·3
©2009 Bill Griffith. World rights reserved. Distributed by King Features Syndicate
ARE YOU PREPARED? PERSONALLY, I'M STOCKPILING ALL TH' MAZOLA AND WHEAT THINS I CAN GET MY HANDS ON!!
I WONDER WHY TH' MAYANS ENDED THEIR CALENDAR IN 2012... WHY NOT 2013... OR 2014.. .. IT'S FUNNY...
IT IS FUNNY! TH' END OF TH' WORLD IS FUNNY! IN FACT, ALL APOCALYPTIC PREDICTIONS ARE FUNNY! HA HA HA HA HA!!
UH-OH. NOW I'M WORRIED ABOUT TH' REVERSAL OF TH' EARTH'S MAGNETIC FIELD & HOW IT MIGHT AFFECT TH' WAY TH' WATER SWIRLS IN MY HOT TUB!!

ROADSIDE ATTRACTIONS

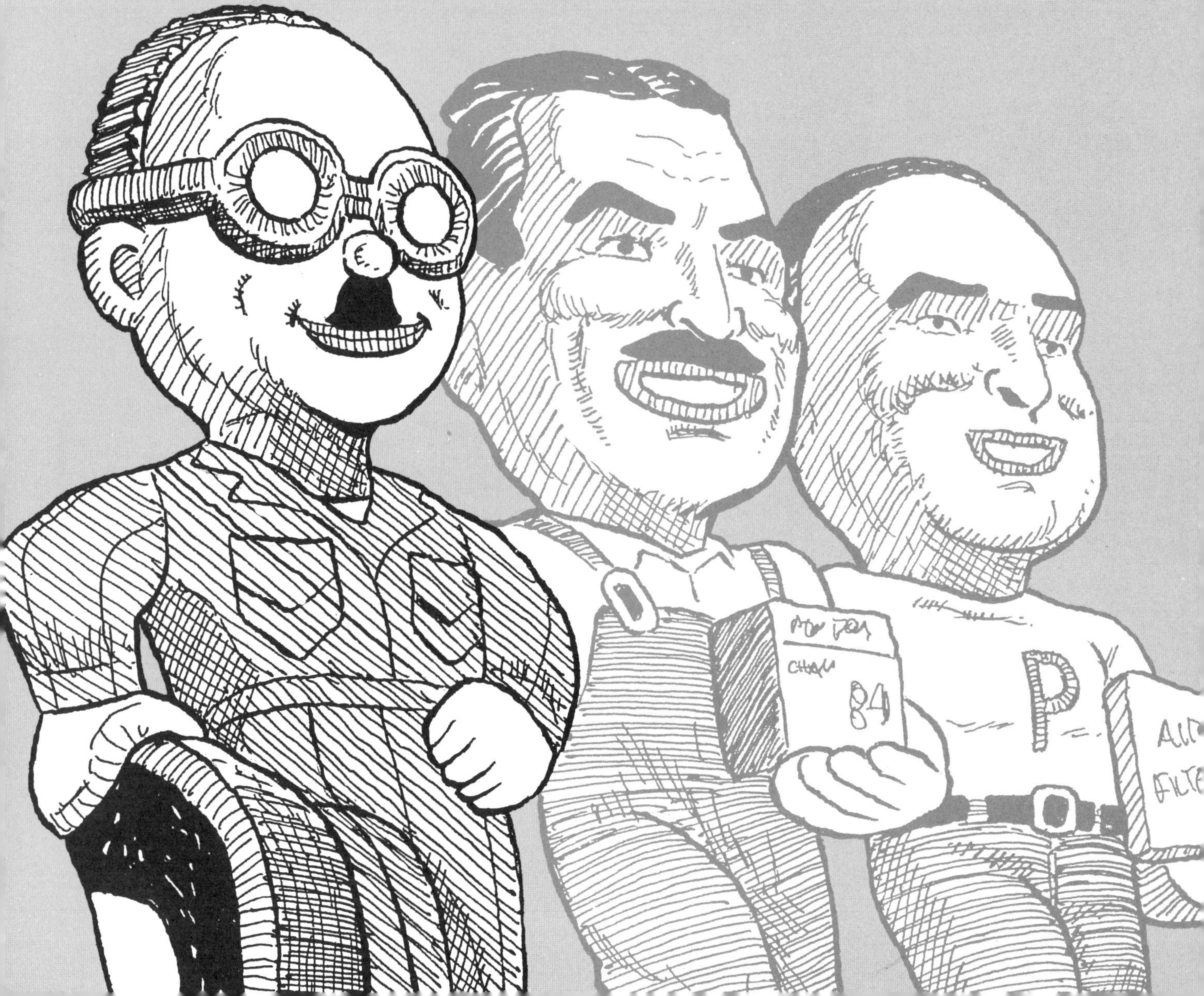
P

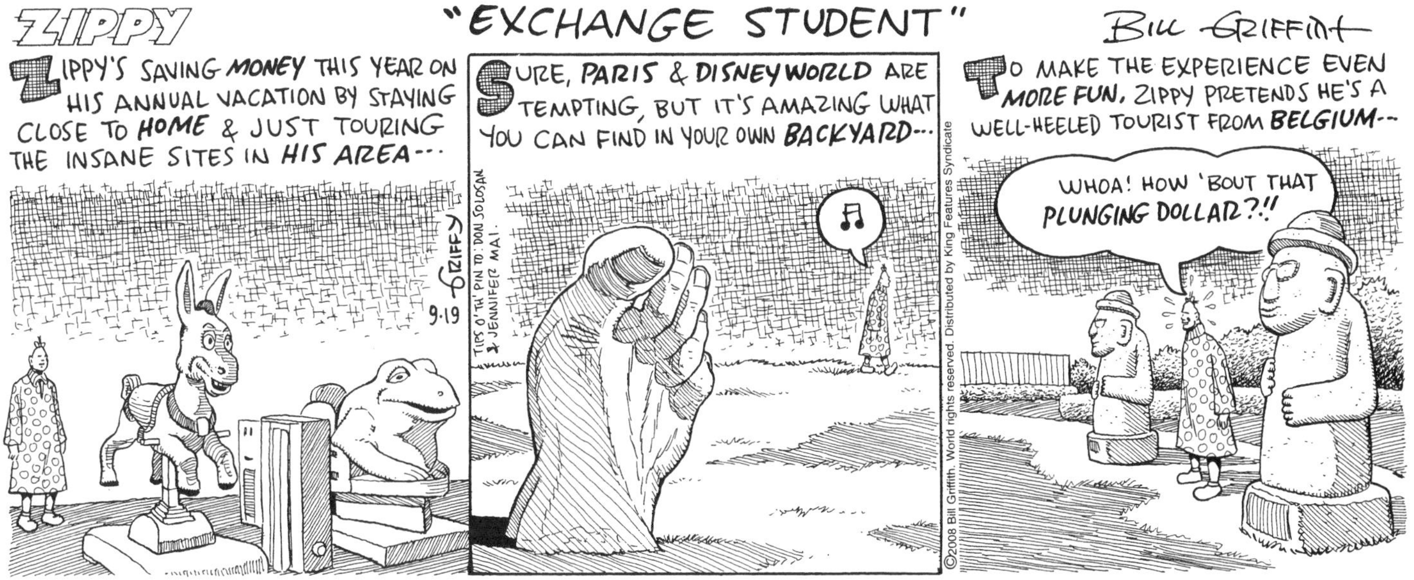

ZIPPY
"EXCHANGE STUDENT"
BILL GRIFFITH
ZIPPY'S SAVING MONEY THIS YEAR ON HIS ANNUAL VACATION BY STAYING CLOSE TO HOME & JUST TOURING THE INSANE SITES IN HIS AREA---
GRIFFY 9.19
TIPS O' TH' PIN TO: DON SOLOSAN & JENNIFER MAI.
SURE, PARIS & DISNEY WORLD ARE TEMPTING, BUT IT'S AMAZING WHAT YOU CAN FIND IN YOUR OWN BACKYARD---
©2008 Bill Griffith. World rights reserved. Distributed by King Features Syndicate
TO MAKE THE EXPERIENCE EVEN MORE FUN, ZIPPY PRETENDS HE'S A WELL-HEELED TOURIST FROM BELGIUM---
WHOA! HOW 'BOUT THAT PLUNGING DOLLAR?!!

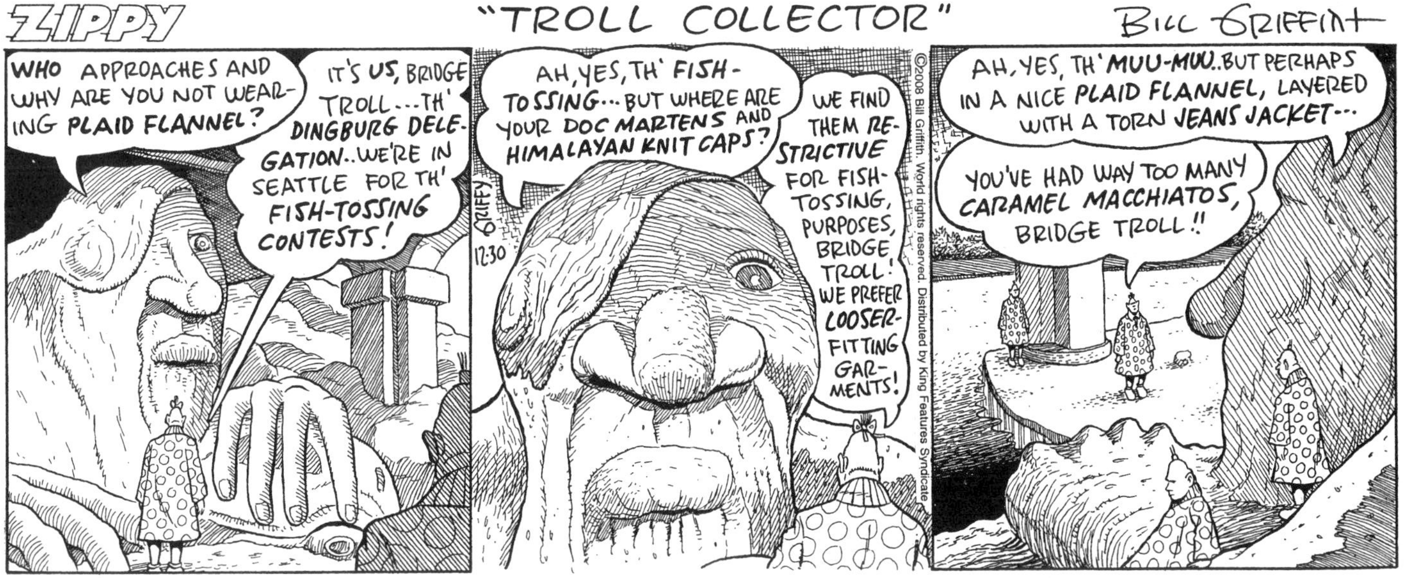

ZIPPY
"TROLL COLLECTOR"
BILL GRIFFITH
WHO APPROACHES AND WHY ARE YOU NOT WEARING PLAID FLANNEL?
IT'S US, BRIDGE TROLL---TH' DINGBURG DELEGATION..WE'RE IN SEATTLE FOR TH' FISH-TOSSING CONTESTS!
GRIFFY 12.30
AH, YES, TH' FISH-TOSSING... BUT WHERE ARE YOUR DOC MARTENS AND HIMALAYAN KNIT CAPS?
WE FIND THEM RESTRICTIVE FOR FISH-TOSSING, PURPOSES, BRIDGE TROLL! WE PREFER LOOSER-FITTING GARMENTS!
©2008 Bill Griffith. World rights reserved. Distributed by King Features Syndicate
AH, YES, TH' MUU-MUU..BUT PERHAPS IN A NICE PLAID FLANNEL, LAYERED WITH A TORN JEANS JACKET---
YOU'VE HAD WAY TOO MANY CARAMEL MACCHIATOS, BRIDGE TROLL!!

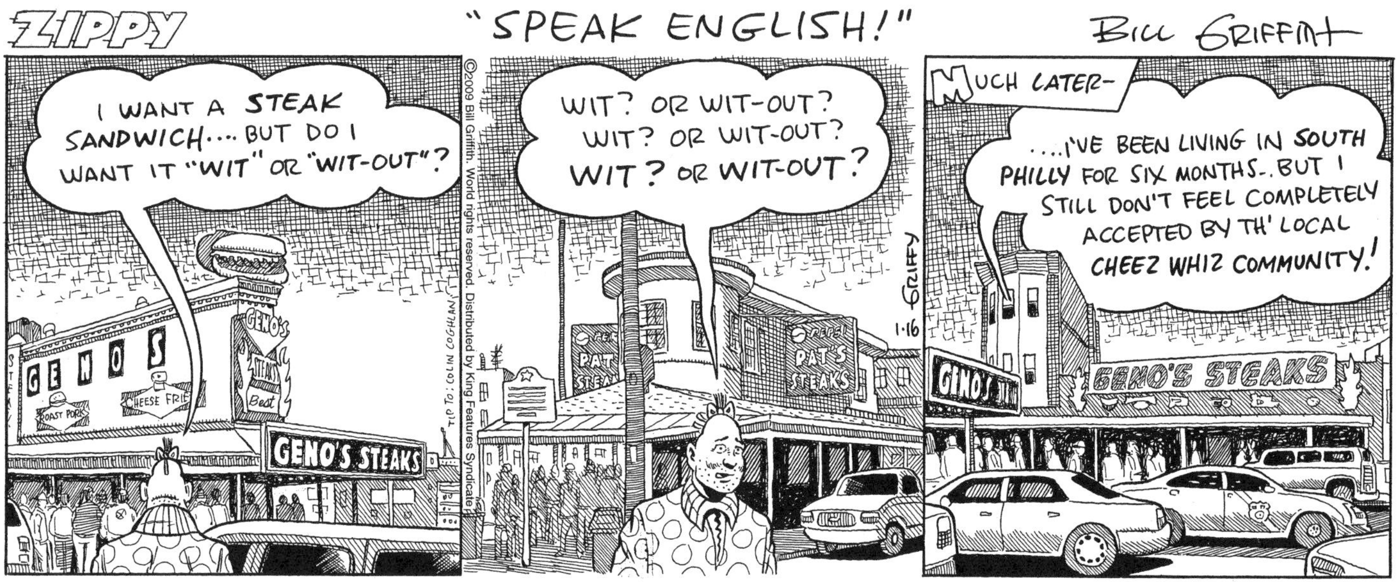
ZIPPY
"SPEAK ENGLISH!"
BILL GRIFFITH
I WANT A STEAK SANDWICH.... BUT DO I WANT IT "WIT" OR "WIT-OUT"?
GENO'S STEAKS
TIP TO: COLIN COGHLAN
©2009 Bill Griffith. World rights reserved. Distributed by King Features Syndicate
WIT? OR WIT-OUT? WIT? OR WIT-OUT? WIT? OR WIT-OUT?
PAT'S STEAKS
GRIFFY 1·16
MUCH LATER-
....I'VE BEEN LIVING IN SOUTH PHILLY FOR SIX MONTHS-.BUT I STILL DON'T FEEL COMPLETELY ACCEPTED BY TH' LOCAL CHEEZ WHIZ COMMUNITY!
GENO'S STEAKS

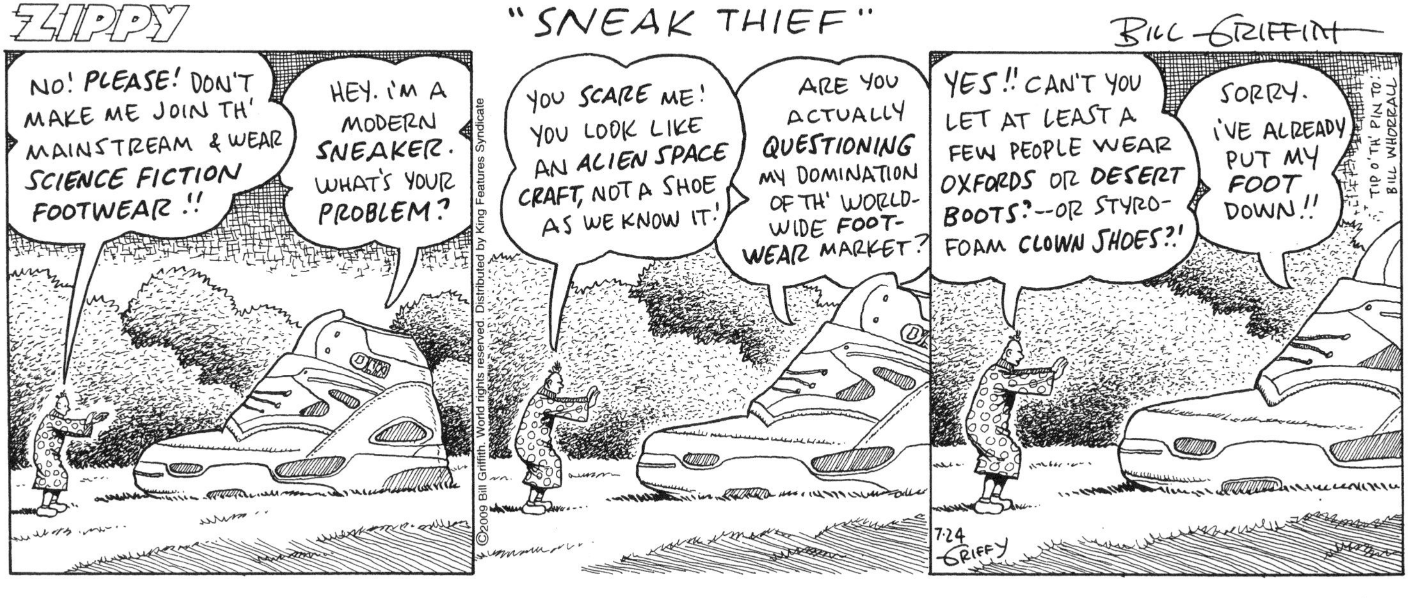
ZIPPY
"SNEAK THIEF"
BILL GRIFFITH
NO! PLEASE! DON'T MAKE ME JOIN TH' MAINSTREAM & WEAR SCIENCE FICTION FOOTWEAR!!
HEY. I'M A MODERN SNEAKER. WHAT'S YOUR PROBLEM?
©2009 Bill Griffith. World rights reserved. Distributed by King Features Syndicate
YOU SCARE ME! YOU LOOK LIKE AN ALIEN SPACE CRAFT, NOT A SHOE AS WE KNOW IT!
ARE YOU ACTUALLY QUESTIONING MY DOMINATION OF TH' WORLD-WIDE FOOT-WEAR MARKET?
YES!! CAN'T YOU LET AT LEAST A FEW PEOPLE WEAR OXFORDS OR DESERT BOOTS?--OR STYRO-FOAM CLOWN SHOES?!
SORRY. I'VE ALREADY PUT MY FOOT DOWN!!
TIP O' TH' PIN TO: BILL WHORRALL
7·24 GRIFFY

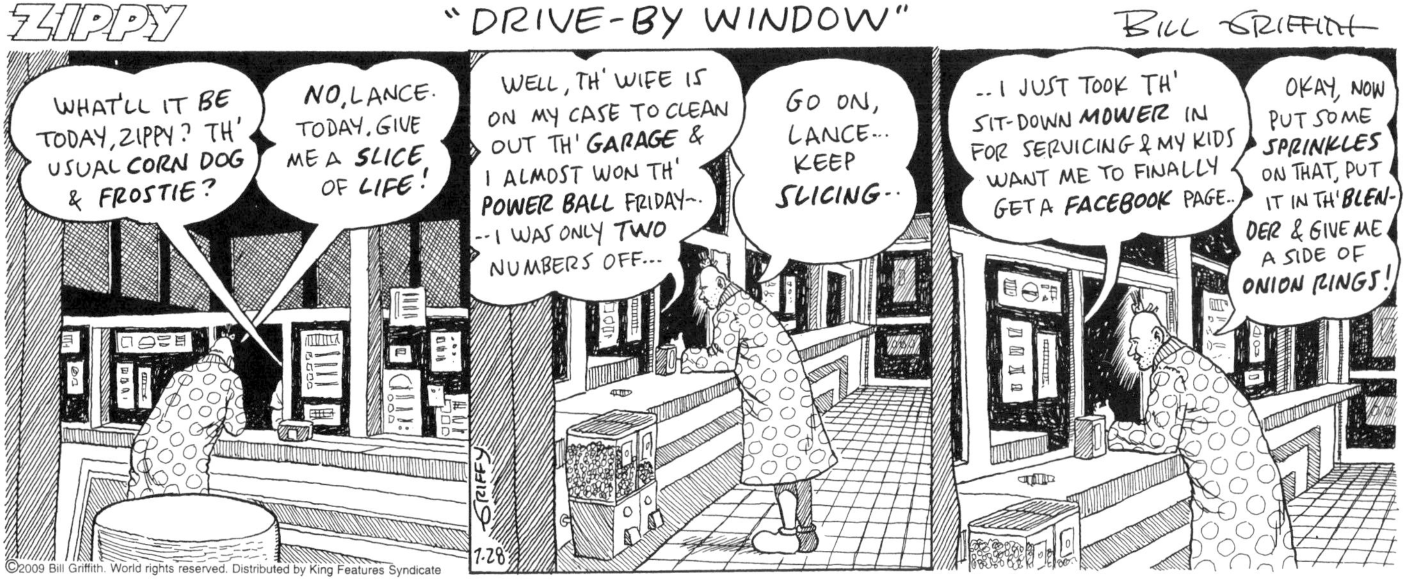
ZIPPY
"DRIVE-BY WINDOW"
BILL GRIFFITH
WHAT'LL IT BE TODAY, ZIPPY? TH' USUAL CORN DOG & FROSTIE?
NO, LANCE. TODAY, GIVE ME A SLICE OF LIFE!
WELL, TH' WIFE IS ON MY CASE TO CLEAN OUT TH' GARAGE & I ALMOST WON TH' POWER BALL FRIDAY-- --I WAS ONLY TWO NUMBERS OFF...
GO ON, LANCE... KEEP SLICING..
--I JUST TOOK TH' SIT-DOWN MOWER IN FOR SERVICING & MY KIDS WANT ME TO FINALLY GET A FACEBOOK PAGE..
OKAY, NOW PUT SOME SPRINKLES ON THAT, PUT IT IN TH' BLENDER & GIVE ME A SIDE OF ONION RINGS!
GRIFFY
1-28
©2009 Bill Griffith. World rights reserved. Distributed by King Features Syndicate

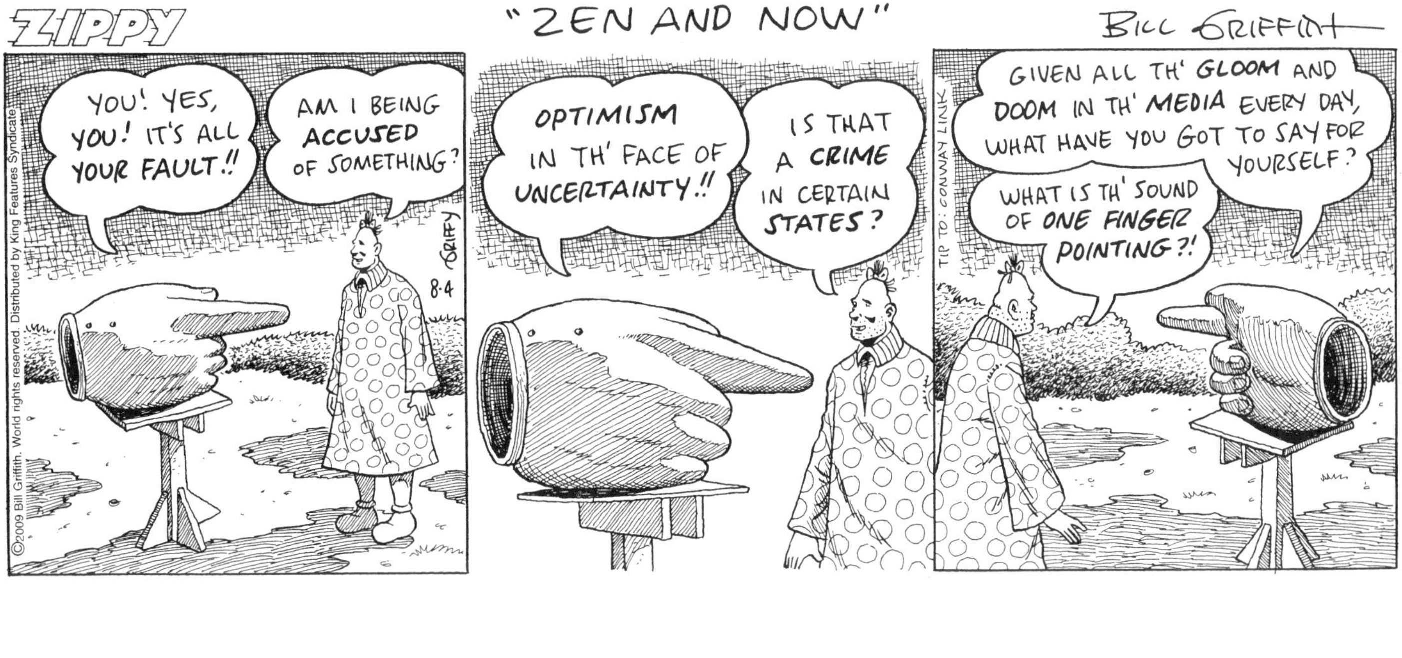
ZIPPY
"ZEN AND NOW"
BILL GRIFFITH
YOU! YES, YOU! IT'S ALL YOUR FAULT!!
AM I BEING ACCUSED OF SOMETHING?
GRIFFY
8-4
©2009 Bill Griffith. World rights reserved. Distributed by King Features Syndicate
OPTIMISM IN TH' FACE OF UNCERTAINTY!!
IS THAT A CRIME IN CERTAIN STATES?
TIP TO: CONWAY LINK
GIVEN ALL TH' GLOOM AND DOOM IN TH' MEDIA EVERY DAY, WHAT HAVE YOU GOT TO SAY FOR YOURSELF?
WHAT IS TH' SOUND OF ONE FINGER POINTING?!

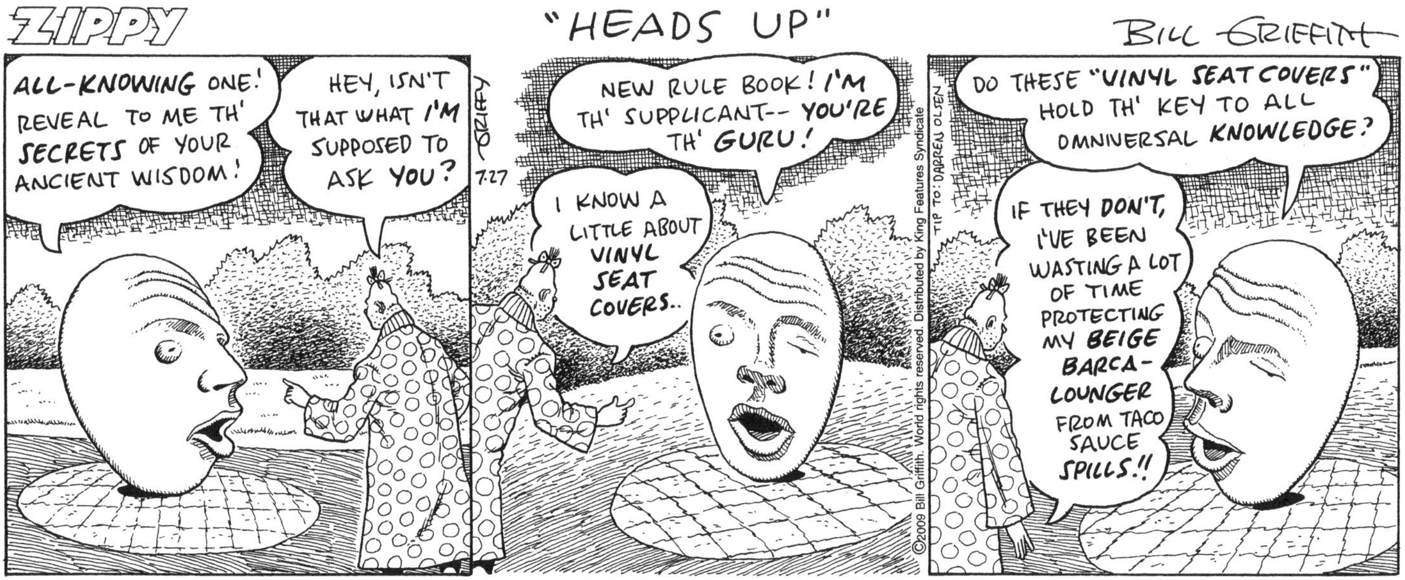
ZIPPY
"HEADS UP"
BILL GRIFFITH
ALL-KNOWING ONE! REVEAL TO ME TH' SECRETS OF YOUR ANCIENT WISDOM!
HEY, ISN'T THAT WHAT I'M SUPPOSED TO ASK YOU?
GRIFFY 7-27
NEW RULE BOOK! I'M TH' SUPPLICANT-- YOU'RE TH' GURU!
I KNOW A LITTLE ABOUT VINYL SEAT COVERS..
©2009 Bill Griffith. World rights reserved. Distributed by King Features Syndicate
TIP TO: DARREN OLSEN
DO THESE "VINYL SEAT COVERS" HOLD TH' KEY TO ALL OMNIVERSAL KNOWLEDGE?
IF THEY DON'T, I'VE BEEN WASTING A LOT OF TIME PROTECTING MY BEIGE BARCA-LOUNGER FROM TACO SAUCE SPILLS!!

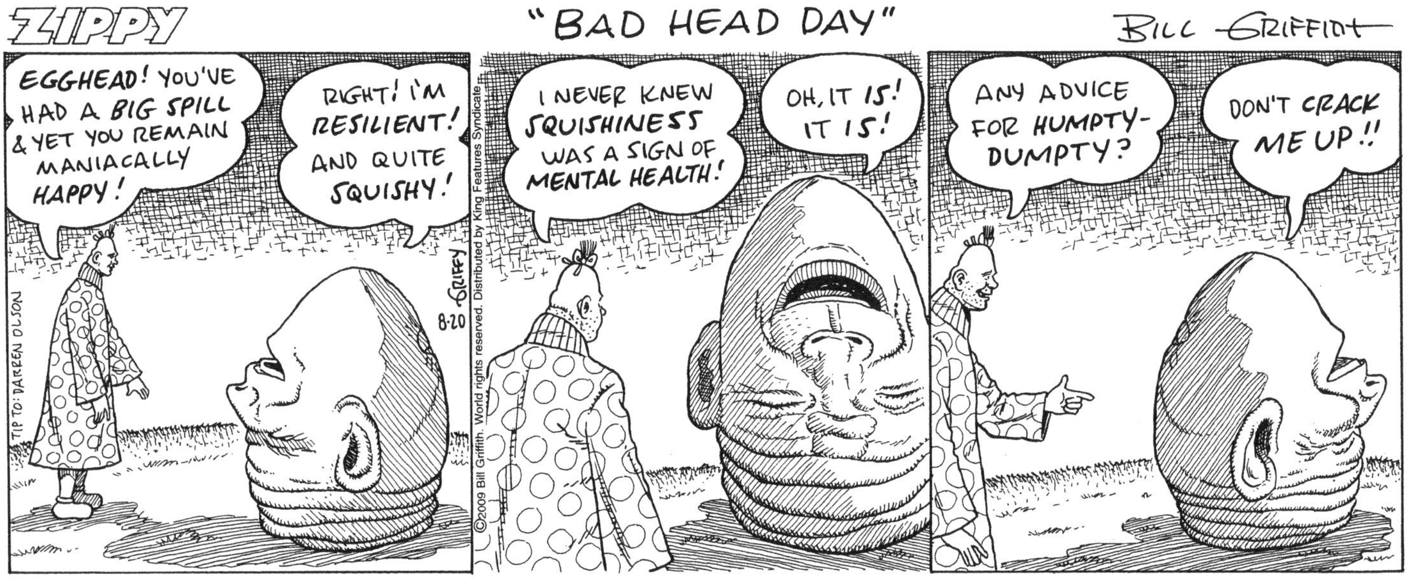
ZIPPY
"BAD HEAD DAY"
BILL GRIFFITH
EGGHEAD! YOU'VE HAD A BIG SPILL & YET YOU REMAIN MANIACALLY HAPPY!
RIGHT! I'M RESILIENT! AND QUITE SQUISHY!
TIP TO: DARREN OLSON
GRIFFY 8-20
©2009 Bill Griffith. World rights reserved. Distributed by King Features Syndicate
I NEVER KNEW SQUISHINESS WAS A SIGN OF MENTAL HEALTH!
OH, IT IS! IT IS!
ANY ADVICE FOR HUMPTY-DUMPTY?
DON'T CRACK ME UP!!

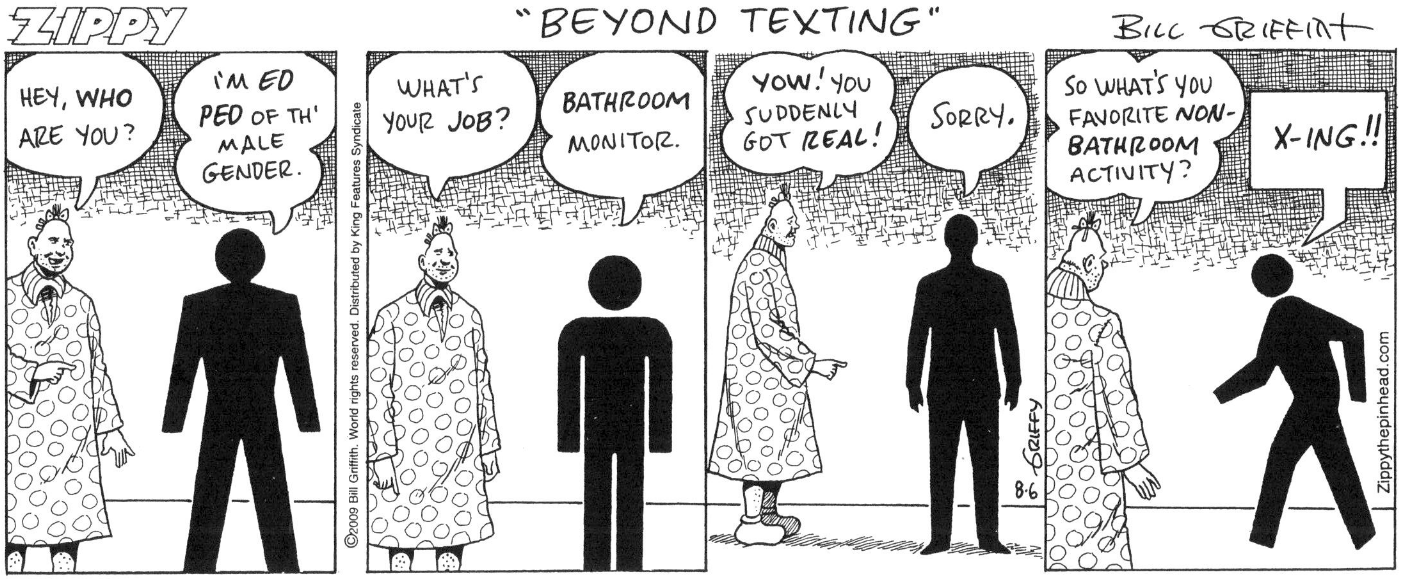
ZIPPY
"BEYOND TEXTING"
BILL GRIFFITH
HEY, WHO ARE YOU?
I'M ED PED OF TH' MALE GENDER.
WHAT'S YOUR JOB?
BATHROOM MONITOR.
YOW! YOU SUDDENLY GOT REAL!
SORRY.
SO WHAT'S YOU FAVORITE NON-BATHROOM ACTIVITY?
X-ING!!
©2009 Bill Griffith. World rights reserved. Distributed by King Features Syndicate
GRIFFY 8·6
Zippythepinhead.com

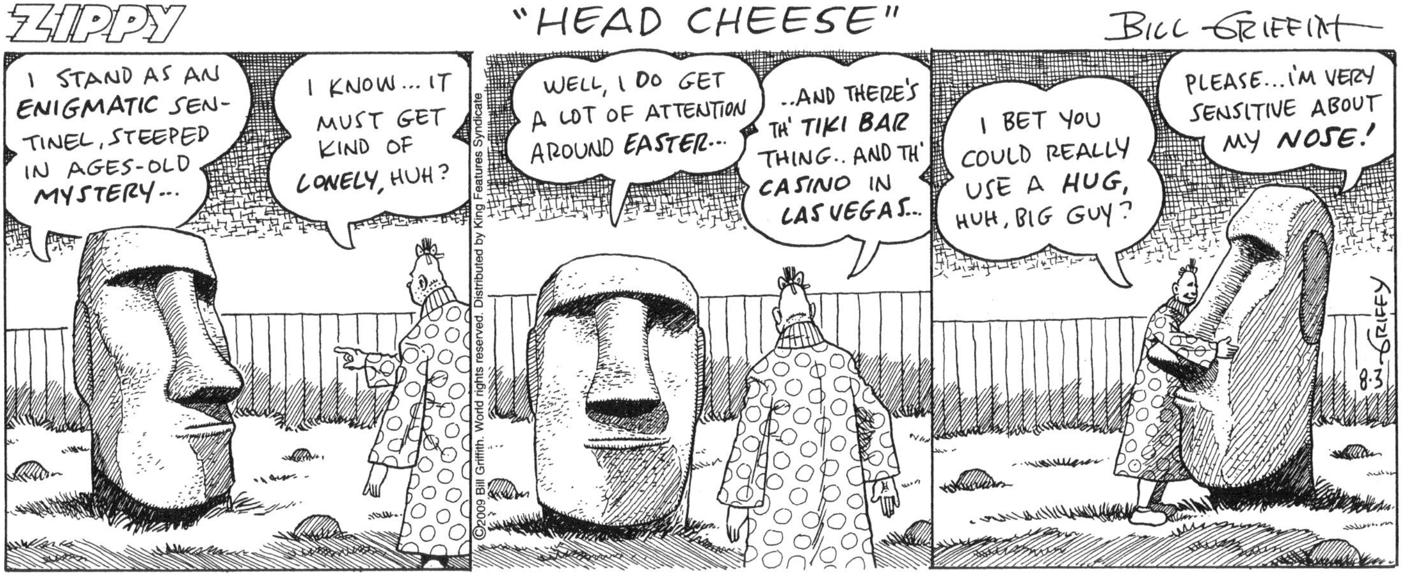
ZIPPY
"HEAD CHEESE"
BILL GRIFFITH
I STAND AS AN ENIGMATIC SENTINEL, STEEPED IN AGES-OLD MYSTERY...
I KNOW... IT MUST GET KIND OF LONELY, HUH?
WELL, I DO GET A LOT OF ATTENTION AROUND EASTER...
..AND THERE'S TH' TIKI BAR THING.. AND TH' CASINO IN LAS VEGAS...
I BET YOU COULD REALLY USE A HUG, HUH, BIG GUY?
PLEASE...I'M VERY SENSITIVE ABOUT MY NOSE!
©2009 Bill Griffith. World rights reserved. Distributed by King Features Syndicate
GRIFFY 8·3

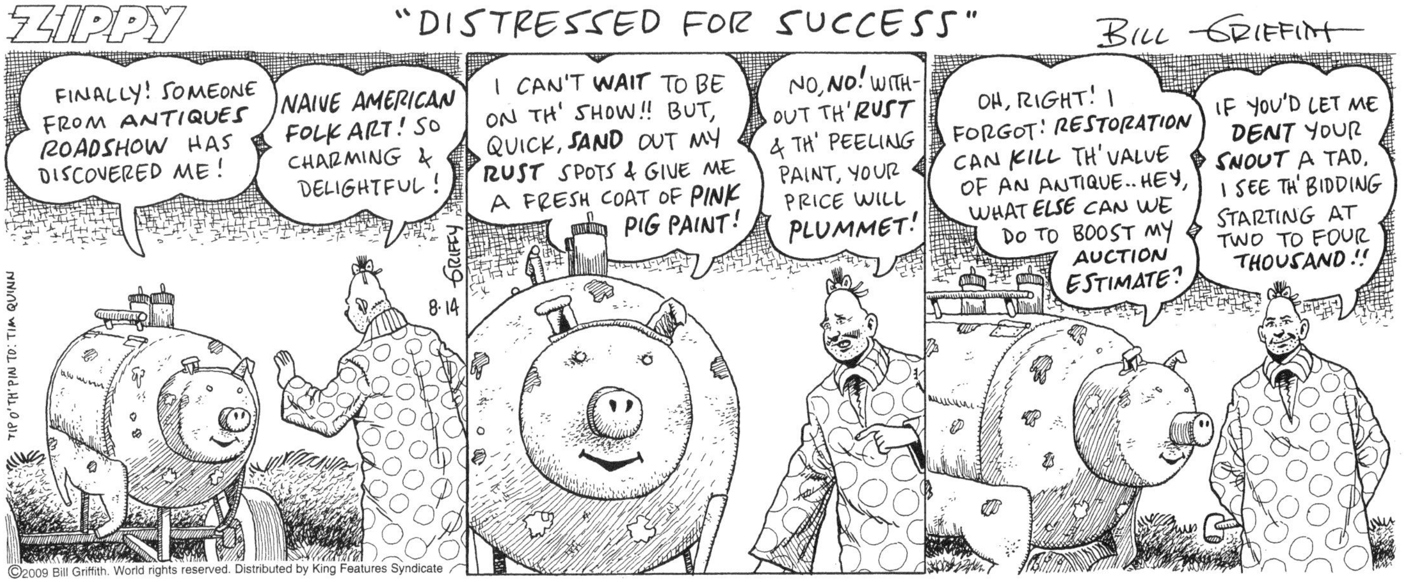
ZIPPY
"DISTRESSED FOR SUCCESS"
BILL GRIFFITH
FINALLY! SOMEONE FROM ANTIQUES ROADSHOW HAS DISCOVERED ME!
NAIVE AMERICAN FOLK ART! SO CHARMING & DELIGHTFUL!
TIP O' TH' PIN TO: TIM QUINN
GRIFFY 8·14
I CAN'T WAIT TO BE ON TH' SHOW!! BUT, QUICK, SAND OUT MY RUST SPOTS & GIVE ME A FRESH COAT OF PINK PIG PAINT!
NO, NO! WITHOUT TH' RUST & TH' PEELING PAINT, YOUR PRICE WILL PLUMMET!
OH, RIGHT! I FORGOT! RESTORATION CAN KILL TH' VALUE OF AN ANTIQUE.. HEY, WHAT ELSE CAN WE DO TO BOOST MY AUCTION ESTIMATE?
IF YOU'D LET ME DENT YOUR SNOUT A TAD, I SEE TH' BIDDING STARTING AT TWO TO FOUR THOUSAND!!
©2009 Bill Griffith. World rights reserved. Distributed by King Features Syndicate

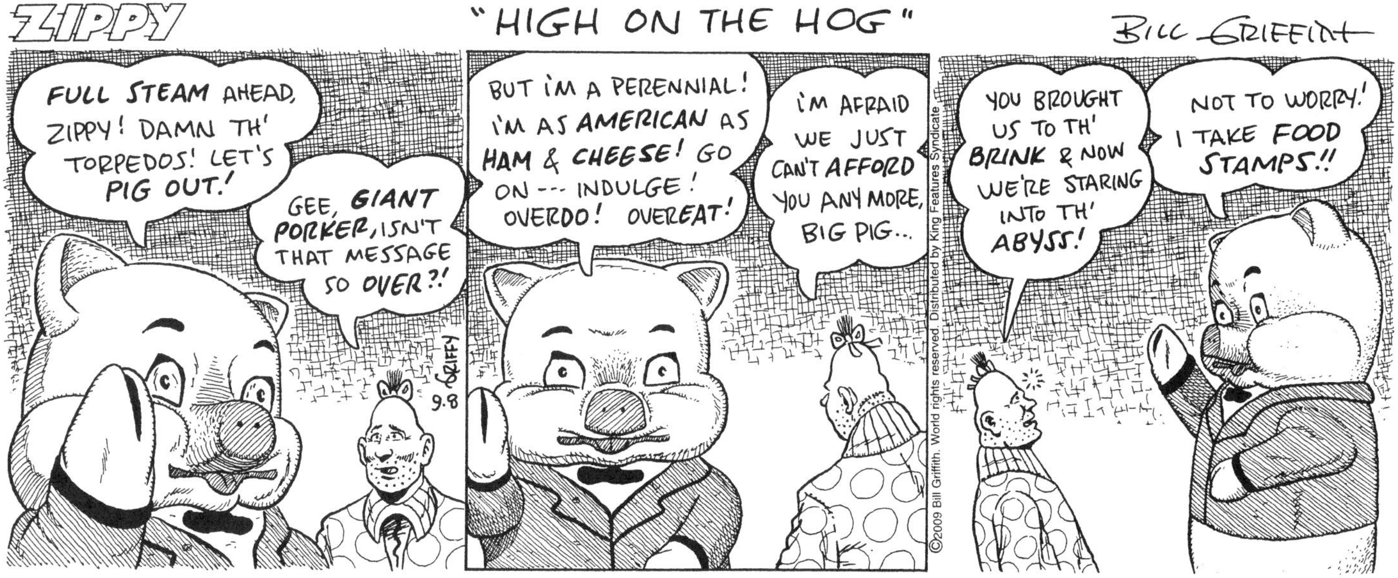
ZIPPY
"HIGH ON THE HOG"
BILL GRIFFITH
FULL STEAM AHEAD, ZIPPY! DAMN TH' TORPEDOS! LET'S PIG OUT!
GEE, GIANT PORKER, ISN'T THAT MESSAGE SO OVER?!
GRIFFY 9·8
BUT I'M A PERENNIAL! I'M AS AMERICAN AS HAM & CHEESE! GO ON --- INDULGE! OVERDO! OVEREAT!
I'M AFRAID WE JUST CAN'T AFFORD YOU ANY MORE, BIG PIG...
©2009 Bill Griffith. World rights reserved. Distributed by King Features Syndicate
YOU BROUGHT US TO TH' BRINK & NOW WE'RE STARING INTO TH' ABYSS!
NOT TO WORRY! I TAKE FOOD STAMPS!!

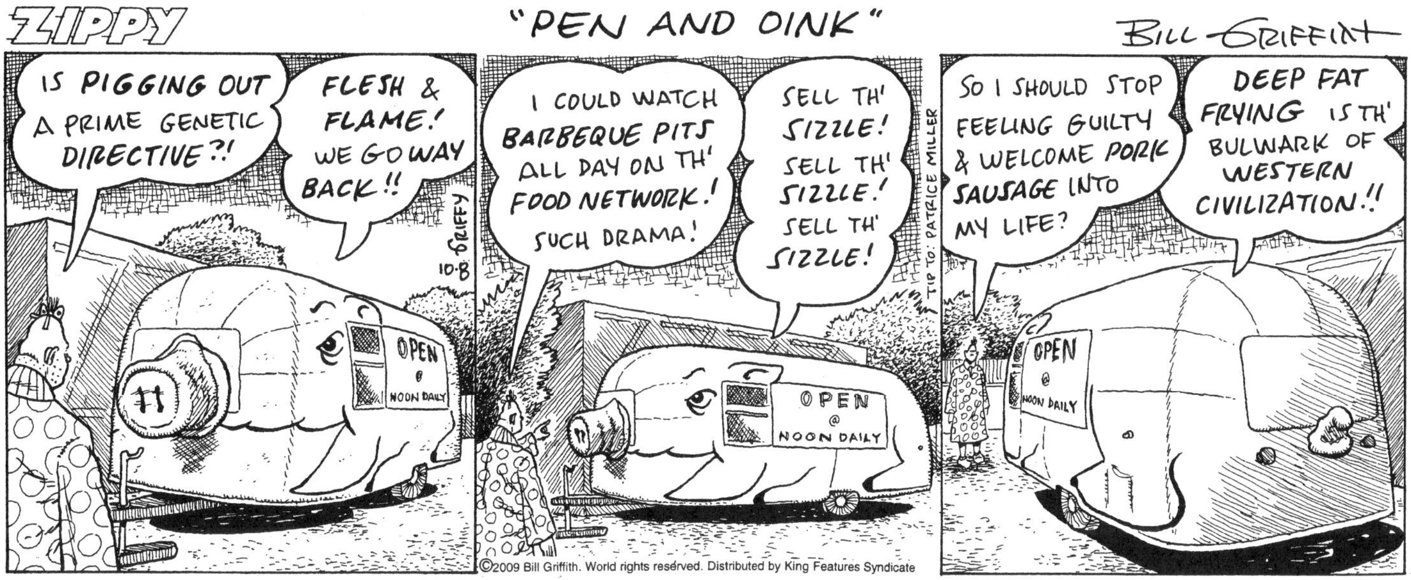
ZIPPY
"PEN AND OINK"
BILL GRIFFITH
IS PIGGING OUT A PRIME GENETIC DIRECTIVE?!
FLESH & FLAME! WE GO WAY BACK!!
GRIFFY 10·8
OPEN @ NOON DAILY
I COULD WATCH BARBEQUE PITS ALL DAY ON TH' FOOD NETWORK! SUCH DRAMA!
SELL TH' SIZZLE! SELL TH' SIZZLE! SELL TH' SIZZLE!
TIP TO: PATRICE MILLER
SO I SHOULD STOP FEELING GUILTY & WELCOME PORK SAUSAGE INTO MY LIFE?
DEEP FAT FRYING IS TH' BULWARK OF WESTERN CIVILIZATION!!
©2009 Bill Griffith. World rights reserved. Distributed by King Features Syndicate

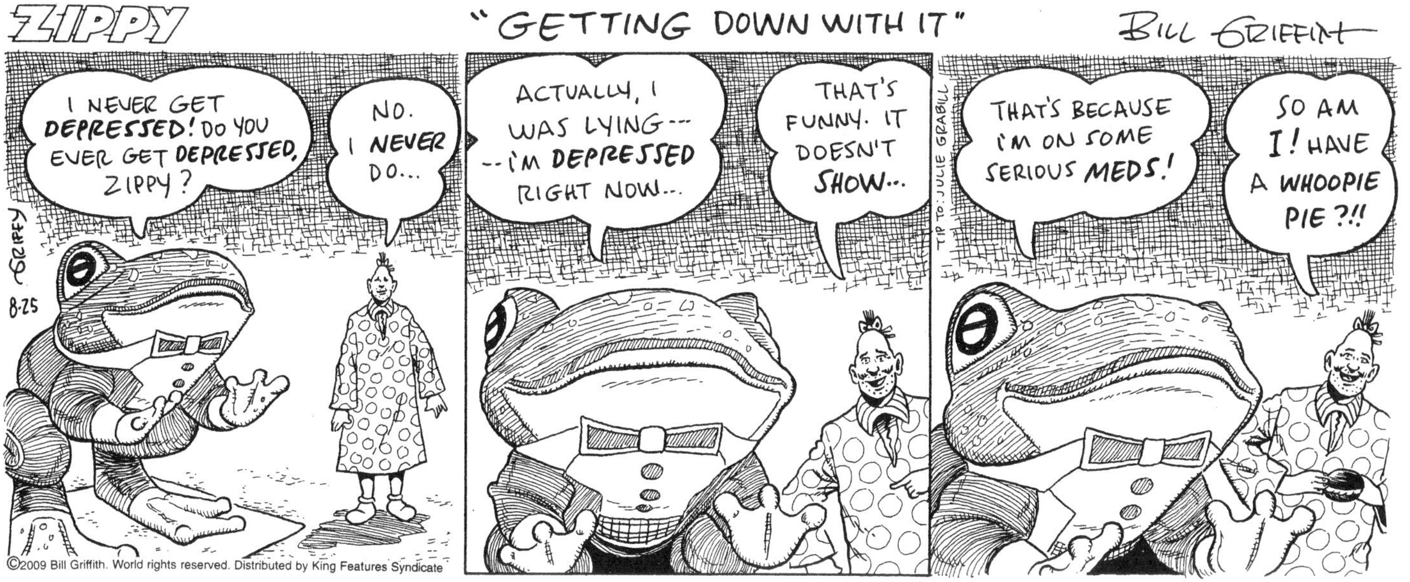
ZIPPY
"GETTING DOWN WITH IT"
BILL GRIFFITH
I NEVER GET DEPRESSED! DO YOU EVER GET DEPRESSED, ZIPPY?
NO. I NEVER DO...
GRIFFY 8·25
ACTUALLY, I WAS LYING-- --I'M DEPRESSED RIGHT NOW...
THAT'S FUNNY. IT DOESN'T SHOW...
TIP TO: JULIE GRABILL
THAT'S BECAUSE I'M ON SOME SERIOUS MEDS!
SO AM I! HAVE A WHOOPIE PIE?!!
©2009 Bill Griffith. World rights reserved. Distributed by King Features Syndicate

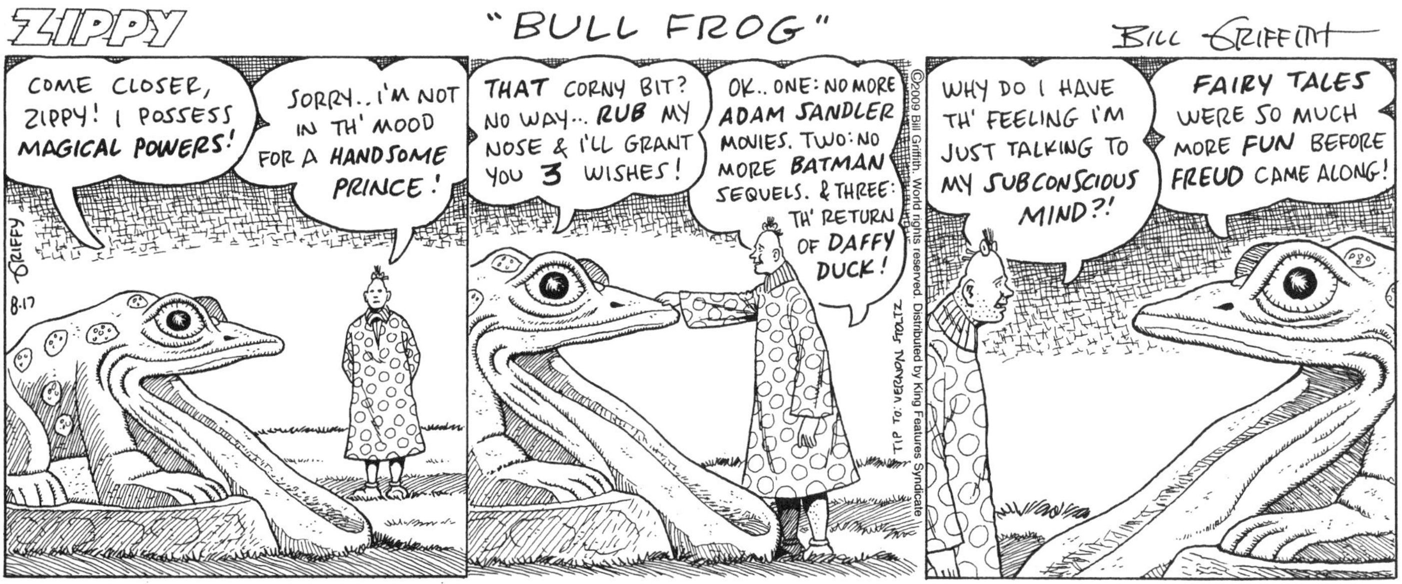
ZIPPY
"BULL FROG"
BILL GRIFFITH
COME CLOSER, ZIPPY! I POSSESS MAGICAL POWERS!
SORRY.. I'M NOT IN TH' MOOD FOR A HANDSOME PRINCE!
GRIFFY 8.17
THAT CORNY BIT? NO WAY... RUB MY NOSE & I'LL GRANT YOU 3 WISHES!
OK.. ONE: NO MORE ADAM SANDLER MOVIES. TWO: NO MORE BATMAN SEQUELS. & THREE: TH' RETURN OF DAFFY DUCK!
TIP TO: VERNON FROLTZ
©2009 Bill Griffith. World rights reserved. Distributed by King Features Syndicate
WHY DO I HAVE TH' FEELING I'M JUST TALKING TO MY SUBCONSCIOUS MIND?!
FAIRY TALES WERE SO MUCH MORE FUN BEFORE FREUD CAME ALONG!

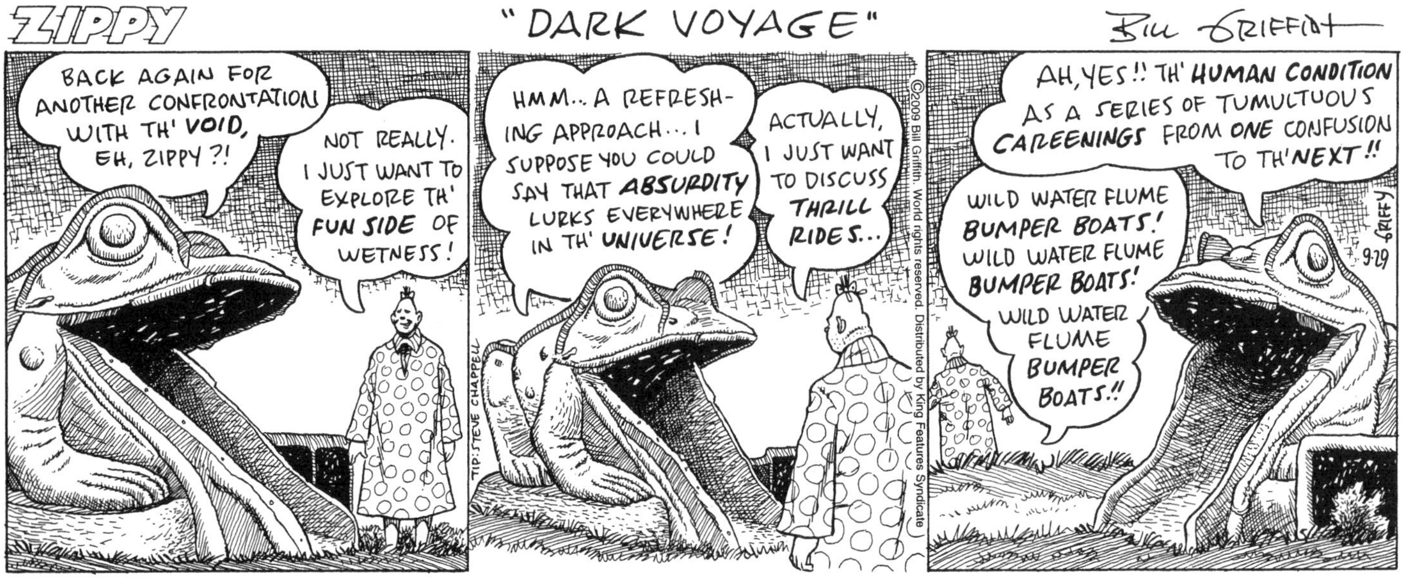
ZIPPY
"DARK VOYAGE"
BILL GRIFFITH
BACK AGAIN FOR ANOTHER CONFRONTATION WITH TH' VOID, EH, ZIPPY?!
NOT REALLY. I JUST WANT TO EXPLORE TH' FUN SIDE OF WETNESS!
TIP: STEVE CHAPPELL
HMM... A REFRESHING APPROACH... I SUPPOSE YOU COULD SAY THAT ABSURDITY LURKS EVERYWHERE IN TH' UNIVERSE!
ACTUALLY, I JUST WANT TO DISCUSS THRILL RIDES...
©2009 Bill Griffith. World rights reserved. Distributed by King Features Syndicate
AH, YES!! TH' HUMAN CONDITION AS A SERIES OF TUMULTUOUS CAREENINGS FROM ONE CONFUSION TO TH' NEXT!!
WILD WATER FLUME BUMPER BOATS! WILD WATER FLUME BUMPER BOATS! WILD WATER FLUME BUMPER BOATS!!
GRIFFY 9.29

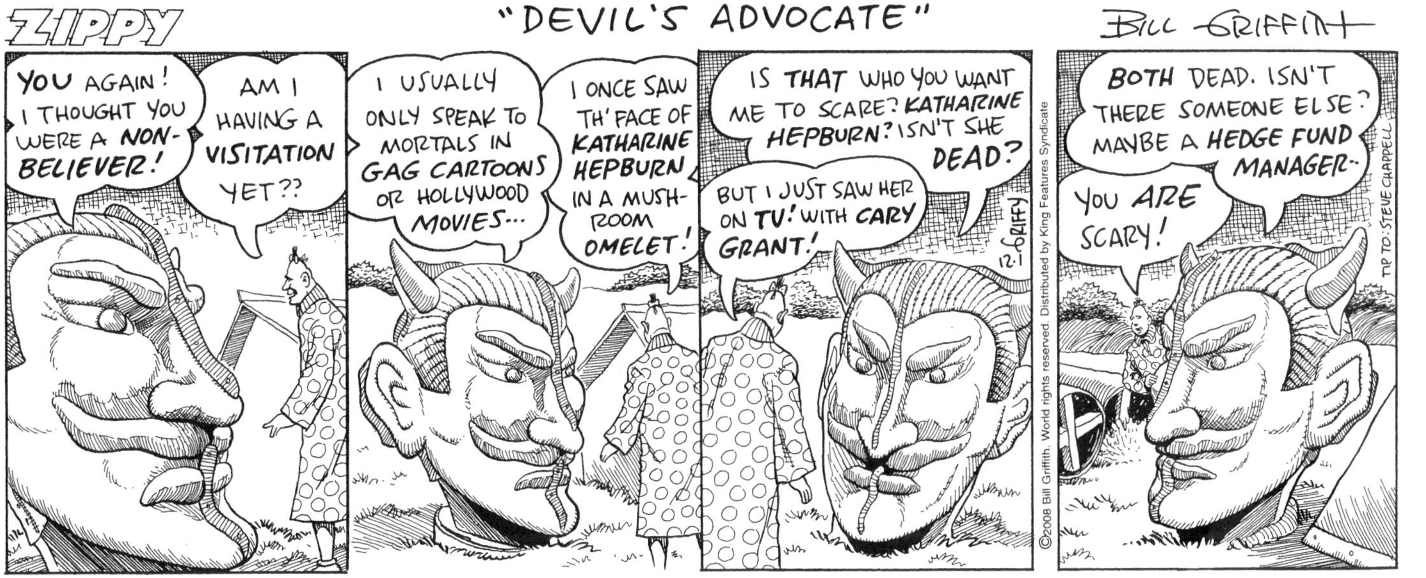
ZIPPY
"DEVIL'S ADVOCATE"
BILL GRIFFITH
YOU AGAIN! I THOUGHT YOU WERE A NON-BELIEVER!
AM I HAVING A VISITATION YET??
I USUALLY ONLY SPEAK TO MORTALS IN GAG CARTOONS OR HOLLYWOOD MOVIES...
I ONCE SAW TH' FACE OF KATHARINE HEPBURN IN A MUSH-ROOM OMELET!
IS THAT WHO YOU WANT ME TO SCARE? KATHARINE HEPBURN? ISN'T SHE DEAD?
BUT I JUST SAW HER ON TV! WITH CARY GRANT!
GRIFFY 12·1
©2008 Bill Griffith. World rights reserved. Distributed by King Features Syndicate
BOTH DEAD. ISN'T THERE SOMEONE ELSE? MAYBE A HEDGE FUND MANAGER..
YOU ARE SCARY!
TIP TO: STEVE CHAPPELL

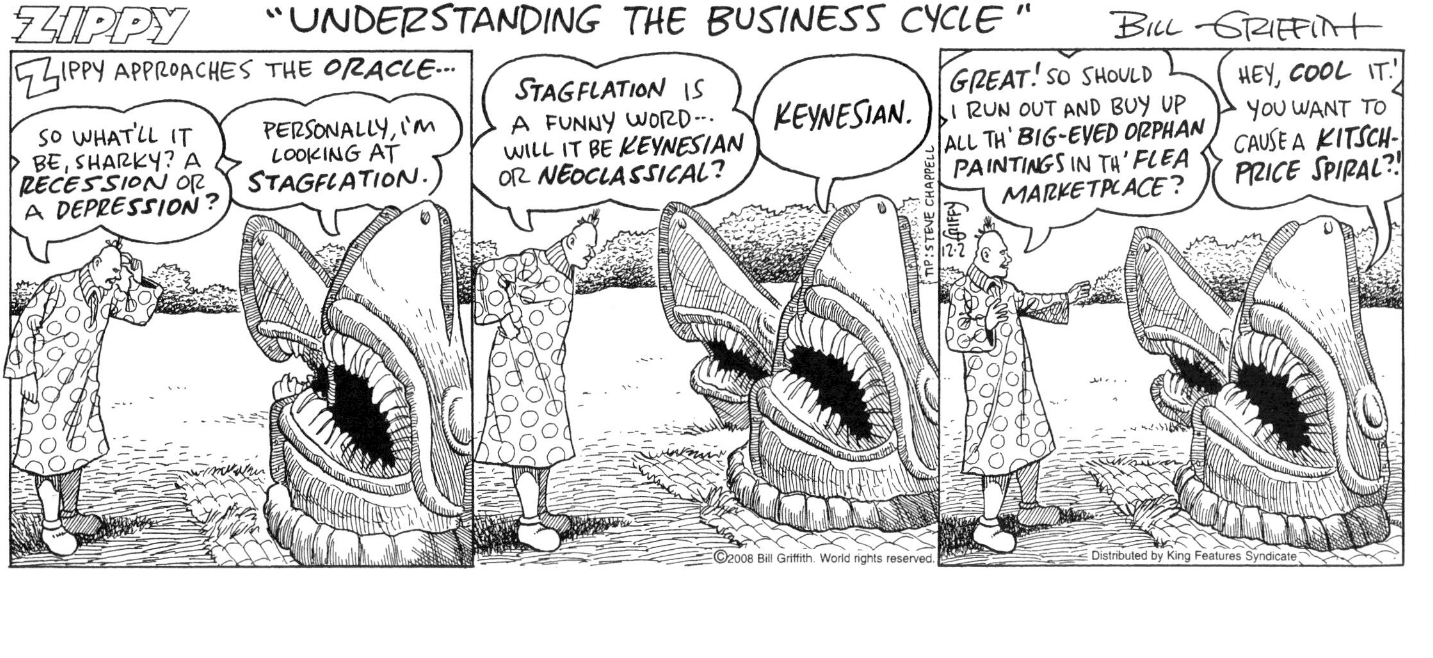
ZIPPY
"UNDERSTANDING THE BUSINESS CYCLE"
BILL GRIFFITH
ZIPPY APPROACHES THE ORACLE...
SO WHAT'LL IT BE, SHARKY? A RECESSION OR A DEPRESSION?
PERSONALLY, I'M LOOKING AT STAGFLATION.
STAGFLATION IS A FUNNY WORD.. WILL IT BE KEYNESIAN OR NEOCLASSICAL?
KEYNESIAN.
TIP: STEVE CHAPPELL
GRIFFY 12·2
GREAT! SO SHOULD I RUN OUT AND BUY UP ALL TH' BIG-EYED ORPHAN PAINTINGS IN TH' FLEA MARKETPLACE?
HEY, COOL IT! YOU WANT TO CAUSE A KITSCH-PRICE SPIRAL?!
©2008 Bill Griffith. World rights reserved.
Distributed by King Features Syndicate

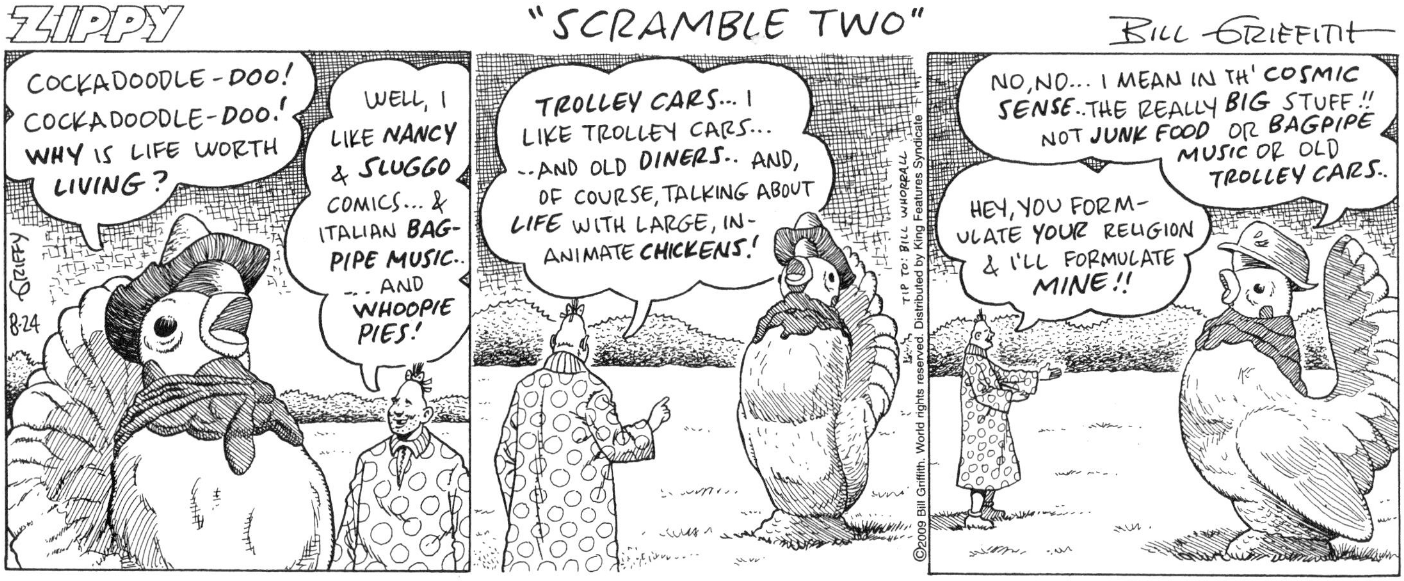
ZIPPY
"SCRAMBLE TWO"
BILL GRIFFITH
COCKADOODLE-DOO! COCKADOODLE-DOO! WHY IS LIFE WORTH LIVING?
WELL, I LIKE NANCY & SLUGGO COMICS... & ITALIAN BAG-PIPE MUSIC.. ... AND WHOOPIE PIES!
GRIFFY 8-24
TROLLEY CARS... I LIKE TROLLEY CARS... ..AND OLD DINERS.. AND, OF COURSE, TALKING ABOUT LIFE WITH LARGE, IN-ANIMATE CHICKENS!
TIP TO: BILL WHORRALL
©2009 Bill Griffith. World rights reserved. Distributed by King Features Syndicate
NO, NO... I MEAN IN TH' COSMIC SENSE..THE REALLY BIG STUFF!! NOT JUNK FOOD OR BAGPIPE MUSIC OR OLD TROLLEY CARS..
HEY, YOU FORM-ULATE YOUR RELIGION & I'LL FORMULATE MINE!!

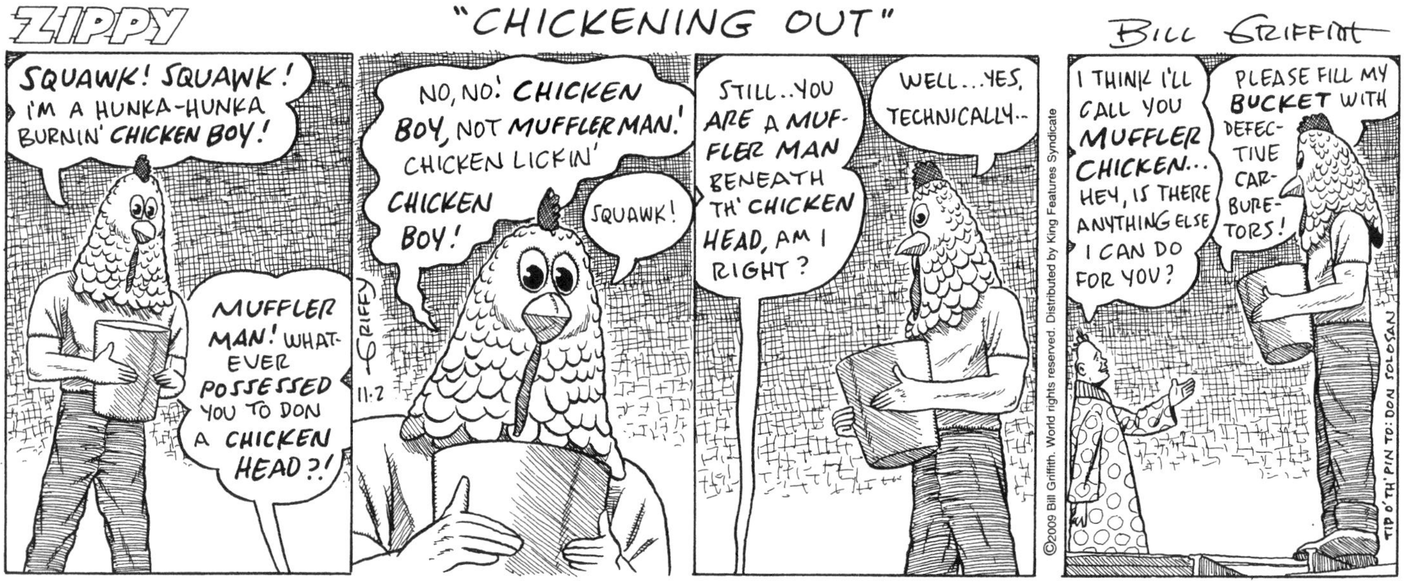
ZIPPY
"CHICKENING OUT"
BILL GRIFFITH
SQUAWK! SQUAWK! I'M A HUNKA-HUNKA BURNIN' CHICKEN BOY!
MUFFLER MAN! WHAT-EVER POSSESSED YOU TO DON A CHICKEN HEAD?!
NO, NO! CHICKEN BOY, NOT MUFFLER MAN! CHICKEN LICKIN' CHICKEN BOY!
SQUAWK!
GRIFFY 11-2
STILL..YOU ARE A MUF-FLER MAN BENEATH TH' CHICKEN HEAD, AM I RIGHT?
WELL...YES, TECHNICALLY..
©2009 Bill Griffith. World rights reserved. Distributed by King Features Syndicate
I THINK I'LL CALL YOU MUFFLER CHICKEN... HEY, IS THERE ANYTHING ELSE I CAN DO FOR YOU?
PLEASE FILL MY BUCKET WITH DEFEC-TIVE CAR-BURE-TORS!
TIP O' TH' PIN TO: DON SOLOSAN

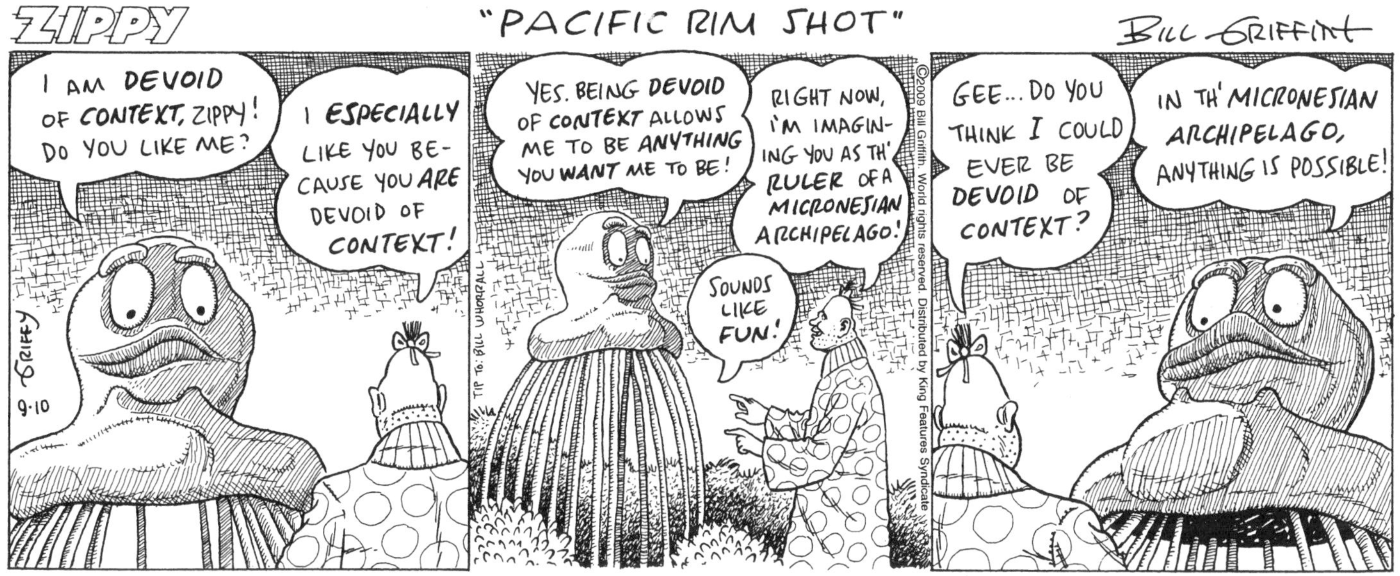
ZIPPY
"PACIFIC RIM SHOT"
BILL GRIFFITH
I AM DEVOID OF CONTEXT, ZIPPY! DO YOU LIKE ME?
I ESPECIALLY LIKE YOU BECAUSE YOU ARE DEVOID OF CONTEXT!
GRIFFY 9·10
YES. BEING DEVOID OF CONTEXT ALLOWS ME TO BE ANYTHING YOU WANT ME TO BE!
RIGHT NOW, I'M IMAGINING YOU AS TH' RULER OF A MICRONESIAN ARCHIPELAGO!
SOUNDS LIKE FUN!
TIP TO: BILL WHORRALL
©2009 Bill Griffith. World rights reserved. Distributed by King Features Syndicate
GEE... DO YOU THINK I COULD EVER BE DEVOID OF CONTEXT?
IN TH' MICRONESIAN ARCHIPELAGO, ANYTHING IS POSSIBLE!

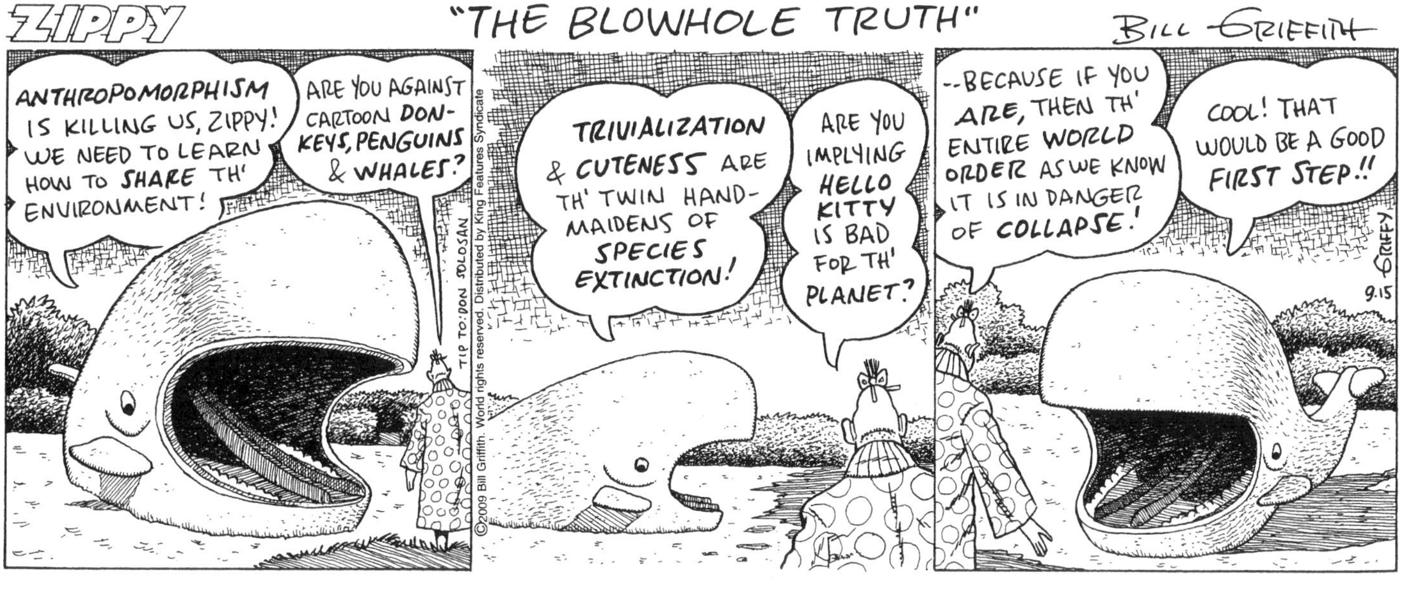
ZIPPY
"THE BLOWHOLE TRUTH"
BILL GRIFFITH
ANTHROPOMORPHISM IS KILLING US, ZIPPY! WE NEED TO LEARN HOW TO SHARE TH' ENVIRONMENT!
ARE YOU AGAINST CARTOON DONKEYS, PENGUINS & WHALES?
TIP TO: DON SOLOSAN
©2009 Bill Griffith. World rights reserved. Distributed by King Features Syndicate
TRIVIALIZATION & CUTENESS ARE TH' TWIN HANDMAIDENS OF SPECIES EXTINCTION!
ARE YOU IMPLYING HELLO KITTY IS BAD FOR TH' PLANET?
--BECAUSE IF YOU ARE, THEN TH' ENTIRE WORLD ORDER AS WE KNOW IT IS IN DANGER OF COLLAPSE!
COOL! THAT WOULD BE A GOOD FIRST STEP!!
GRIFFY 9.15

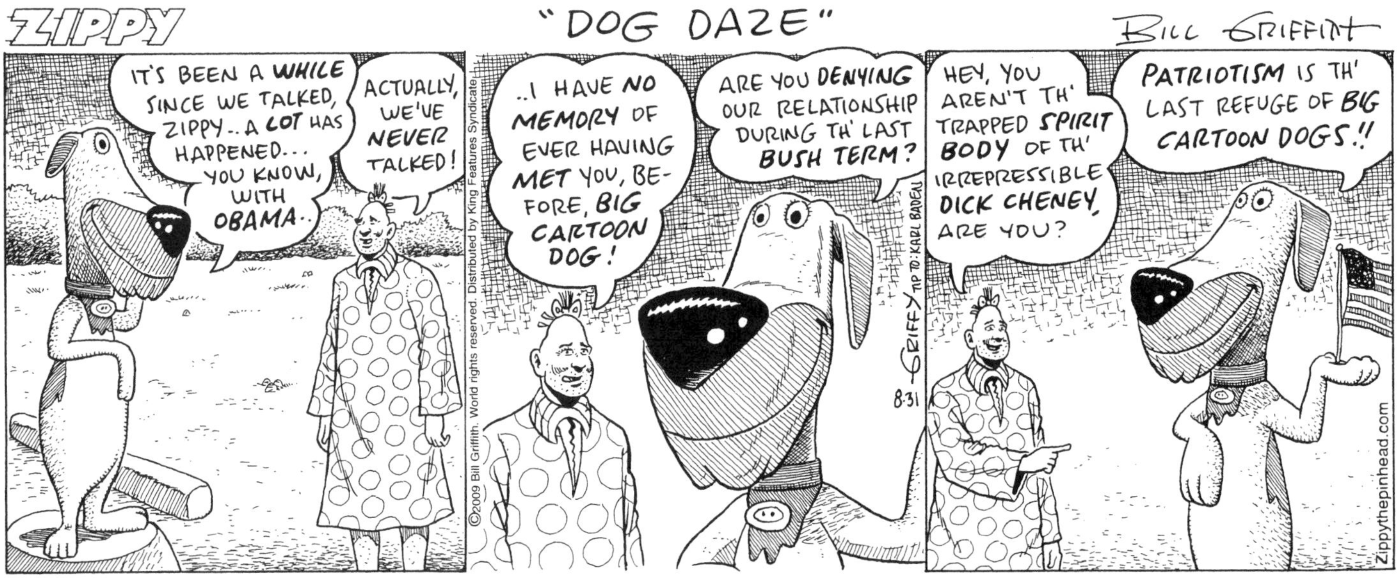
ZIPPY
"DOG DAZE"
BILL GRIFFITH
IT'S BEEN A WHILE SINCE WE TALKED, ZIPPY.. A LOT HAS HAPPENED... YOU KNOW, WITH OBAMA..
ACTUALLY, WE'VE NEVER TALKED!
©2009 Bill Griffith. World rights reserved. Distributed by King Features Syndicate
..I HAVE NO MEMORY OF EVER HAVING MET YOU, BEFORE, BIG CARTOON DOG!
ARE YOU DENYING OUR RELATIONSHIP DURING TH' LAST BUSH TERM?
GRIFFY TIP TO: KARL BADEN
8·31
HEY, YOU AREN'T TH' TRAPPED SPIRIT BODY OF TH' IRREPRESSIBLE DICK CHENEY, ARE YOU?
PATRIOTISM IS TH' LAST REFUGE OF BIG CARTOON DOGS!!
Zippythepinhead.com

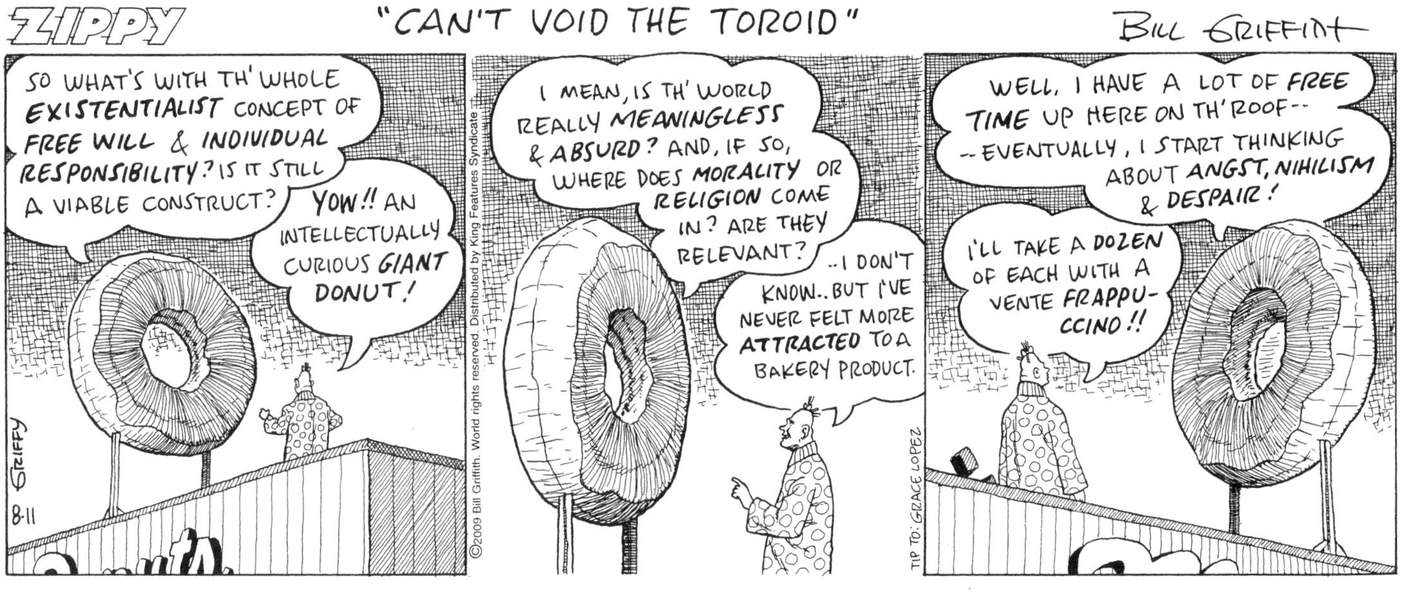
ZIPPY
"CAN'T VOID THE TOROID"
BILL GRIFFITH
SO WHAT'S WITH TH' WHOLE EXISTENTIALIST CONCEPT OF FREE WILL & INDIVIDUAL RESPONSIBILITY? IS IT STILL A VIABLE CONSTRUCT?
YOW!! AN INTELLECTUALLY CURIOUS GIANT DONUT!
GRIFFY
8·11
©2009 Bill Griffith. World rights reserved. Distributed by King Features Syndicate
I MEAN, IS TH' WORLD REALLY MEANINGLESS & ABSURD? AND, IF SO, WHERE DOES MORALITY OR RELIGION COME IN? ARE THEY RELEVANT?
..I DON'T KNOW.. BUT I'VE NEVER FELT MORE ATTRACTED TO A BAKERY PRODUCT.
TIP TO: GRACE LOPEZ
WELL, I HAVE A LOT OF FREE TIME UP HERE ON TH' ROOF-- --EVENTUALLY, I START THINKING ABOUT ANGST, NIHILISM & DESPAIR!
I'LL TAKE A DOZEN OF EACH WITH A VENTE FRAPPUCCINO!!

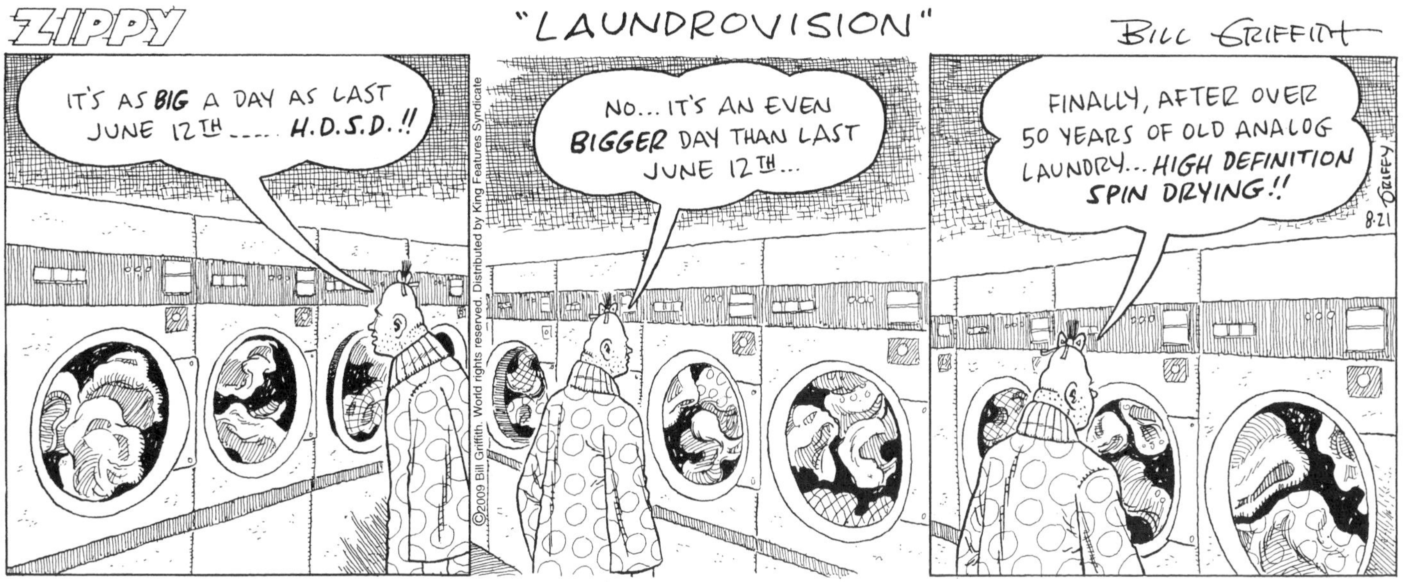
ZIPPY
"LAUNDROVISION"
BILL GRIFFITH
IT'S AS BIG A DAY AS LAST JUNE 12TH ..... H.D.S.D.!!
©2009 Bill Griffith. World rights reserved. Distributed by King Features Syndicate
NO... IT'S AN EVEN BIGGER DAY THAN LAST JUNE 12TH...
FINALLY, AFTER OVER 50 YEARS OF OLD ANALOG LAUNDRY... HIGH DEFINITION SPIN DRYING!!
GRIFFY
8·21

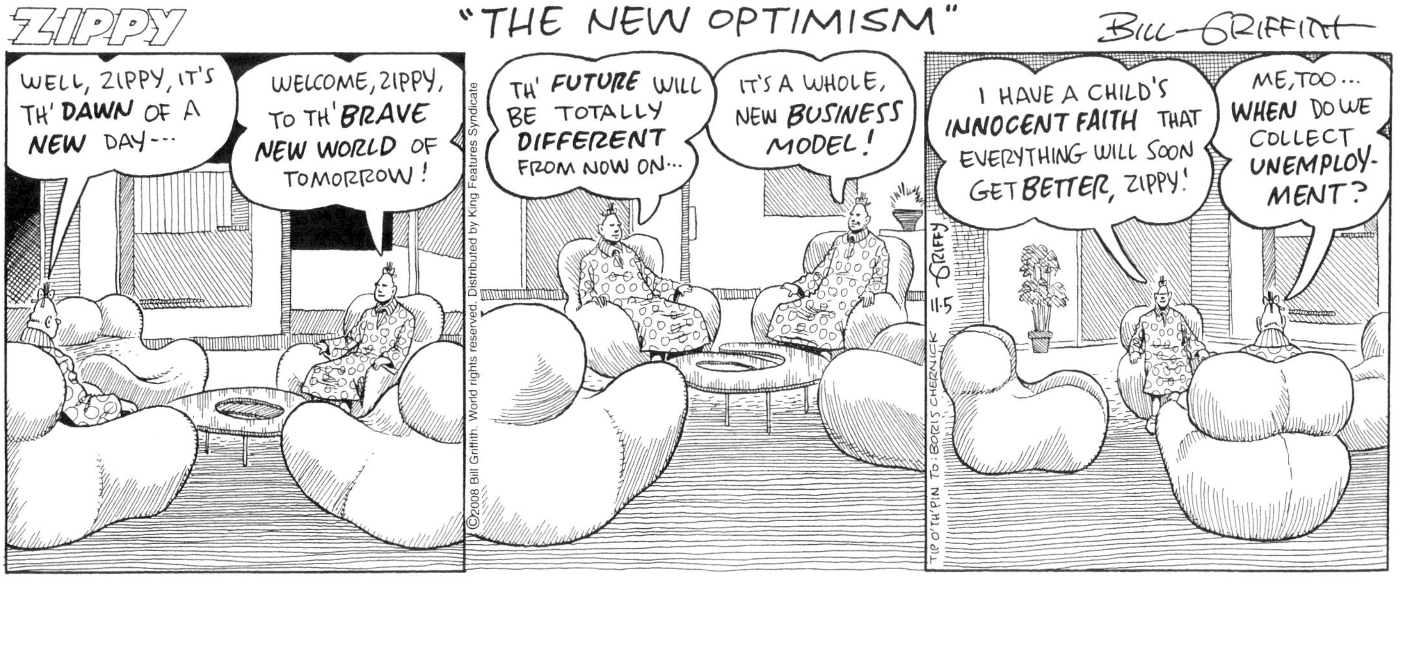
ZIPPY
"THE NEW OPTIMISM"
BILL GRIFFITH
WELL, ZIPPY, IT'S TH' DAWN OF A NEW DAY---
WELCOME, ZIPPY, TO TH' BRAVE NEW WORLD OF TOMORROW!
©2008 Bill Griffith. World rights reserved. Distributed by King Features Syndicate
TH' FUTURE WILL BE TOTALLY DIFFERENT FROM NOW ON...
IT'S A WHOLE, NEW BUSINESS MODEL!
GRIFFY
11·5
TIP O'TH' PIN TO: BORIS CHERNICK
I HAVE A CHILD'S INNOCENT FAITH THAT EVERYTHING WILL SOON GET BETTER, ZIPPY!
ME, TOO... WHEN DO WE COLLECT UNEMPLOY-MENT?

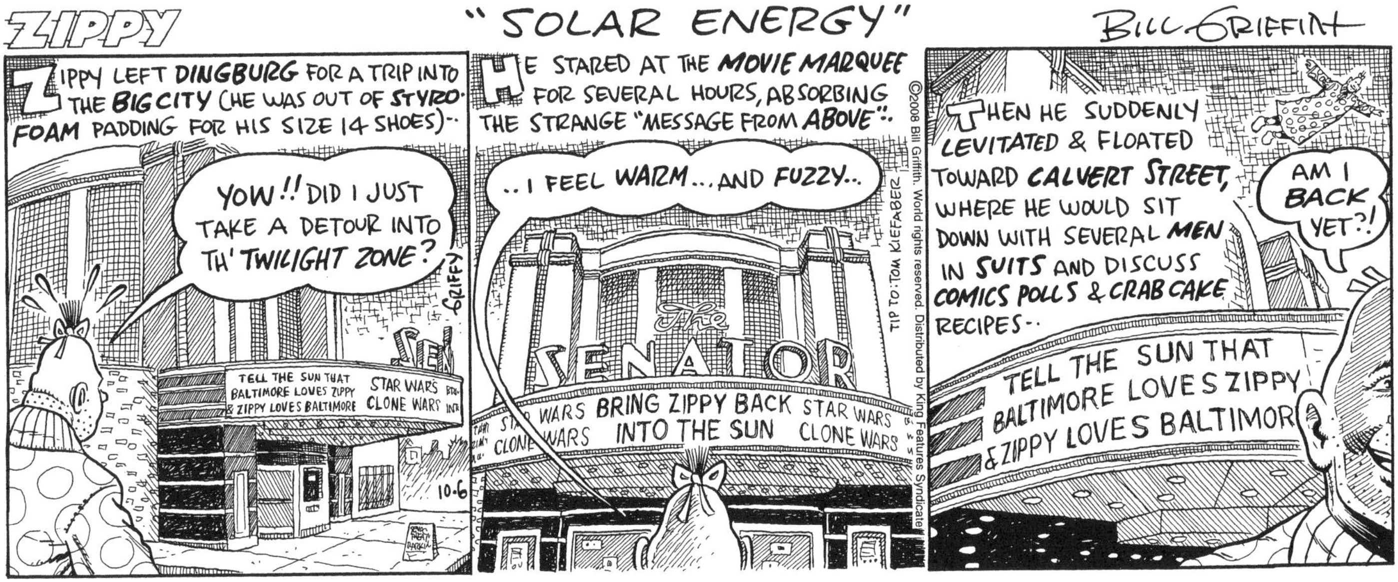
ZIPPY
"SOLAR ENERGY"
BILL GRIFFITH
ZIPPY LEFT DINGBURG FOR A TRIP INTO THE BIG CITY (HE WAS OUT OF STYRO-FOAM PADDING FOR HIS SIZE 14 SHOES)..
YOW!! DID I JUST TAKE A DETOUR INTO TH' TWILIGHT ZONE?
TELL THE SUN THAT BALTIMORE LOVES ZIPPY & ZIPPY LOVES BALTIMORE
STAR WARS CLONE WARS
GRIFFY
10-6
HE STARED AT THE MOVIE MARQUEE FOR SEVERAL HOURS, ABSORBING THE STRANGE "MESSAGE FROM ABOVE"..
..I FEEL WARM... AND FUZZY..
The SENATOR
BRING ZIPPY BACK INTO THE SUN
STAR WARS CLONE WARS
TIP TO: TOM KIEFABER
©2008 Bill Griffith. World rights reserved. Distributed by King Features Syndicate
THEN HE SUDDENLY LEVITATED & FLOATED TOWARD CALVERT STREET, WHERE HE WOULD SIT DOWN WITH SEVERAL MEN IN SUITS AND DISCUSS COMICS POLLS & CRAB CAKE RECIPES..
AM I BACK YET?!
TELL THE SUN THAT BALTIMORE LOVES ZIPPY & ZIPPY LOVES BALTIMOR

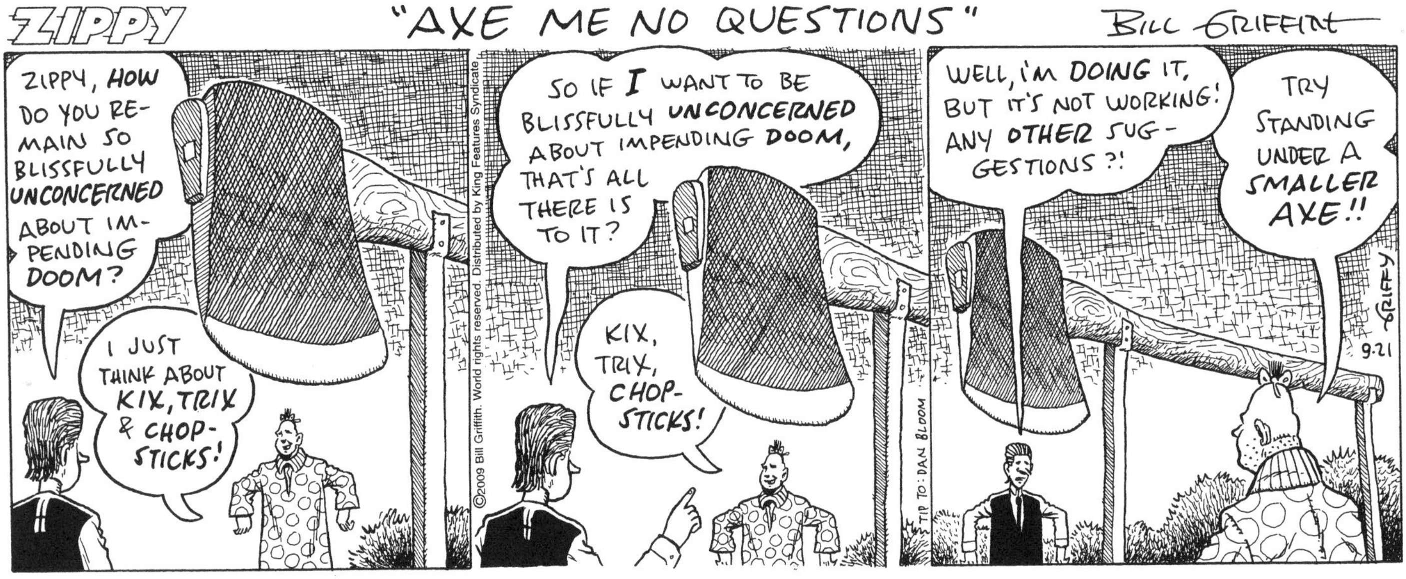
ZIPPY
"AXE ME NO QUESTIONS"
BILL GRIFFITH
ZIPPY, HOW DO YOU RE-MAIN SO BLISSFULLY UNCONCERNED ABOUT IM-PENDING DOOM?
I JUST THINK ABOUT KIX, TRIX & CHOP-STICKS!
©2009 Bill Griffith. World rights reserved. Distributed by King Features Syndicate.
SO IF I WANT TO BE BLISSFULLY UNCONCERNED ABOUT IMPENDING DOOM, THAT'S ALL THERE IS TO IT?
KIX, TRIX, CHOP-STICKS!
TIP TO: DAN BLOOM
WELL, I'M DOING IT, BUT IT'S NOT WORKING! ANY OTHER SUG-GESTIONS?!
TRY STANDING UNDER A SMALLER AXE!!
GRIFFY
9-21

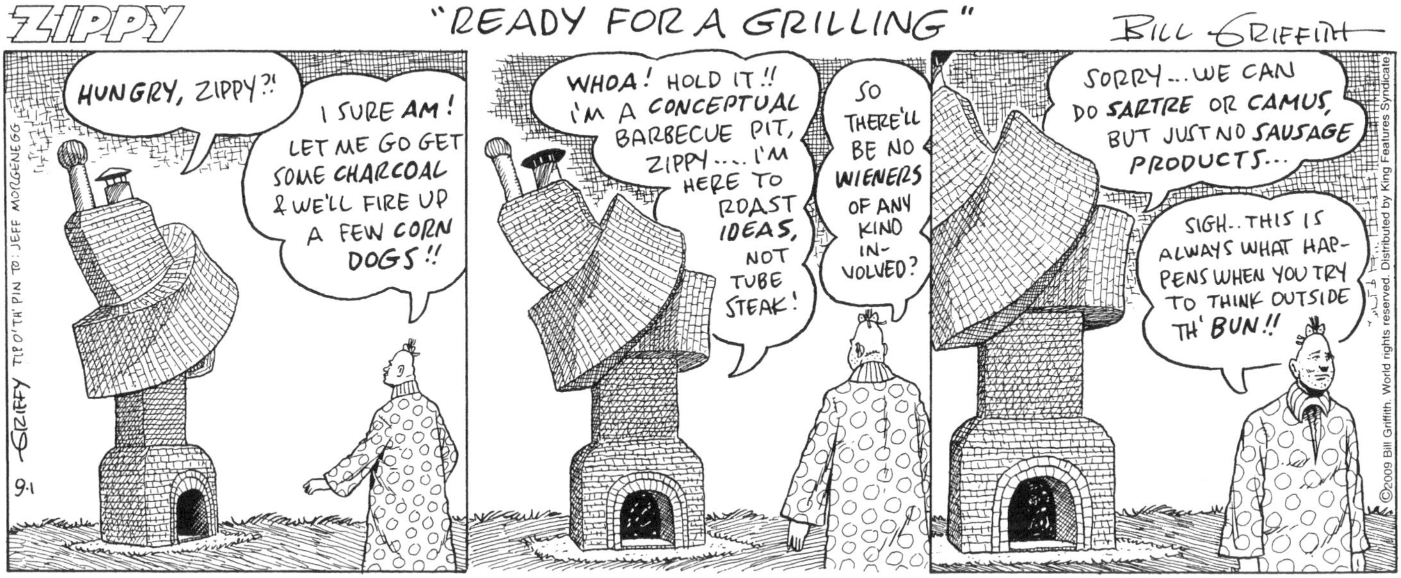
ZIPPY
"READY FOR A GRILLING"
BILL GRIFFITH
HUNGRY, ZIPPY?!
I SURE AM! LET ME GO GET SOME CHARCOAL & WE'LL FIRE UP A FEW CORN DOGS!!
GRIFFY TIP O' TH' PIN TO: JEFF MORGENEGG
9·1
WHOA! HOLD IT!! I'M A CONCEPTUAL BARBECUE PIT, ZIPPY.... I'M HERE TO ROAST IDEAS, NOT TUBE STEAK!
SO THERE'LL BE NO WIENERS OF ANY KIND IN-VOLVED?
SORRY... WE CAN DO SARTRE OR CAMUS, BUT JUST NO SAUSAGE PRODUCTS...
SIGH.. THIS IS ALWAYS WHAT HAP-PENS WHEN YOU TRY TO THINK OUTSIDE TH' BUN!!
©2009 Bill Griffith. World rights reserved. Distributed by King Features Syndicate

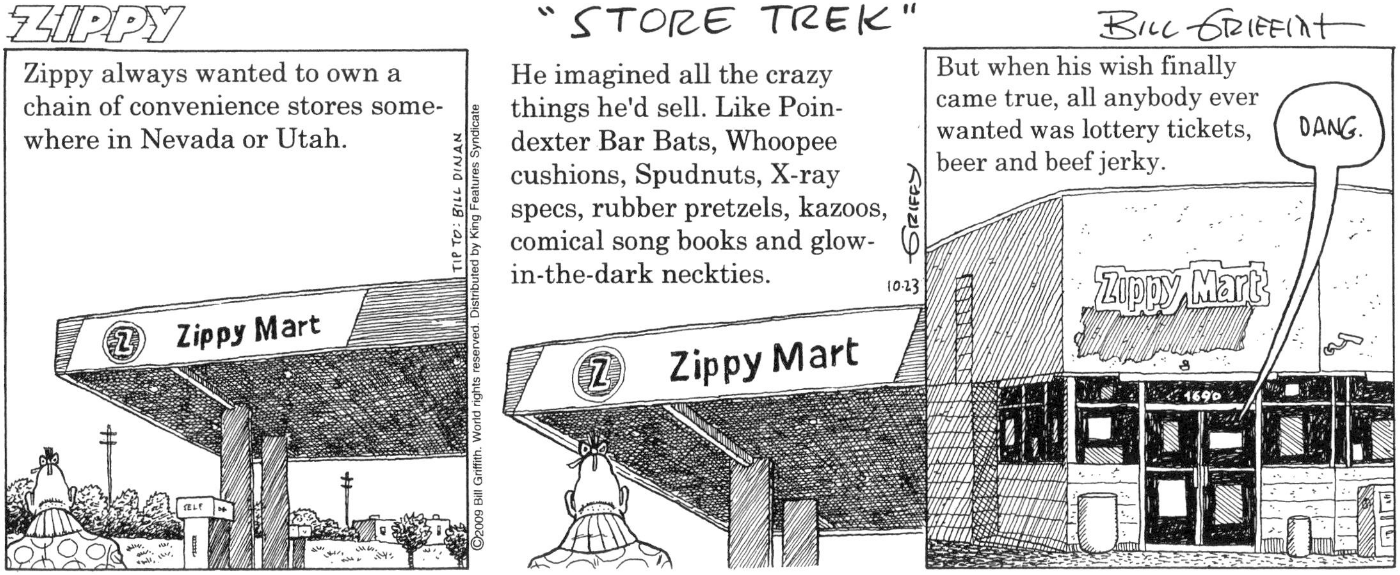
ZIPPY
"STORE TREK"
BILL GRIFFITH
Zippy always wanted to own a chain of convenience stores some-where in Nevada or Utah.
Zippy Mart
SELF
TIP TO: BILL DINAN
©2009 Bill Griffith. World rights reserved. Distributed by King Features Syndicate
He imagined all the crazy things he'd sell. Like Poin-dexter Bar Bats, Whoopee cushions, Spudnuts, X-ray specs, rubber pretzels, kazoos, comical song books and glow-in-the-dark neckties.
GRIFFY
10·23
Zippy Mart
But when his wish finally came true, all anybody ever wanted was lottery tickets, beer and beef jerky.
DANG.
Zippy Mart
1690

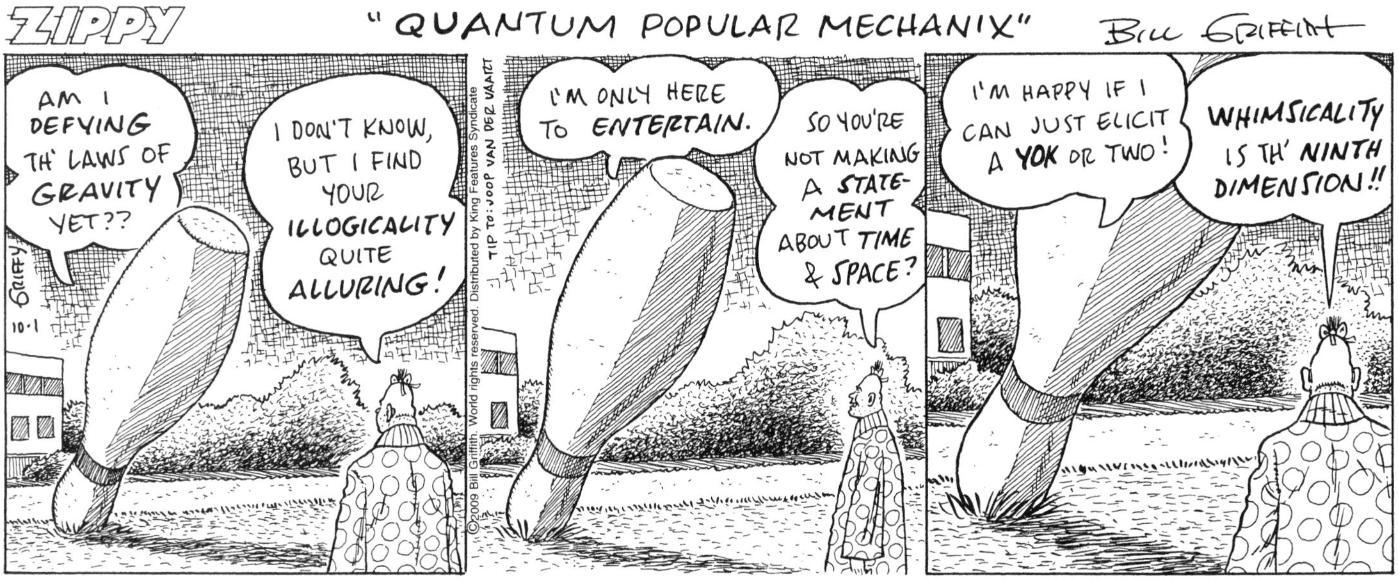
ZIPPY
"QUANTUM POPULAR MECHANIX"
BILL GRIFFITH
AM I DEFYING TH' LAWS OF GRAVITY YET??
I DON'T KNOW, BUT I FIND YOUR ILLOGICALITY QUITE ALLURING!
GRIFFY 10-1
©2009 Bill Griffith. World rights reserved. Distributed by King Features Syndicate.
TIP TO: JOOP VAN DER VAART
I'M ONLY HERE TO ENTERTAIN.
SO YOU'RE NOT MAKING A STATEMENT ABOUT TIME & SPACE?
I'M HAPPY IF I CAN JUST ELICIT A YOK OR TWO!
WHIMSICALITY IS TH' NINTH DIMENSION!!

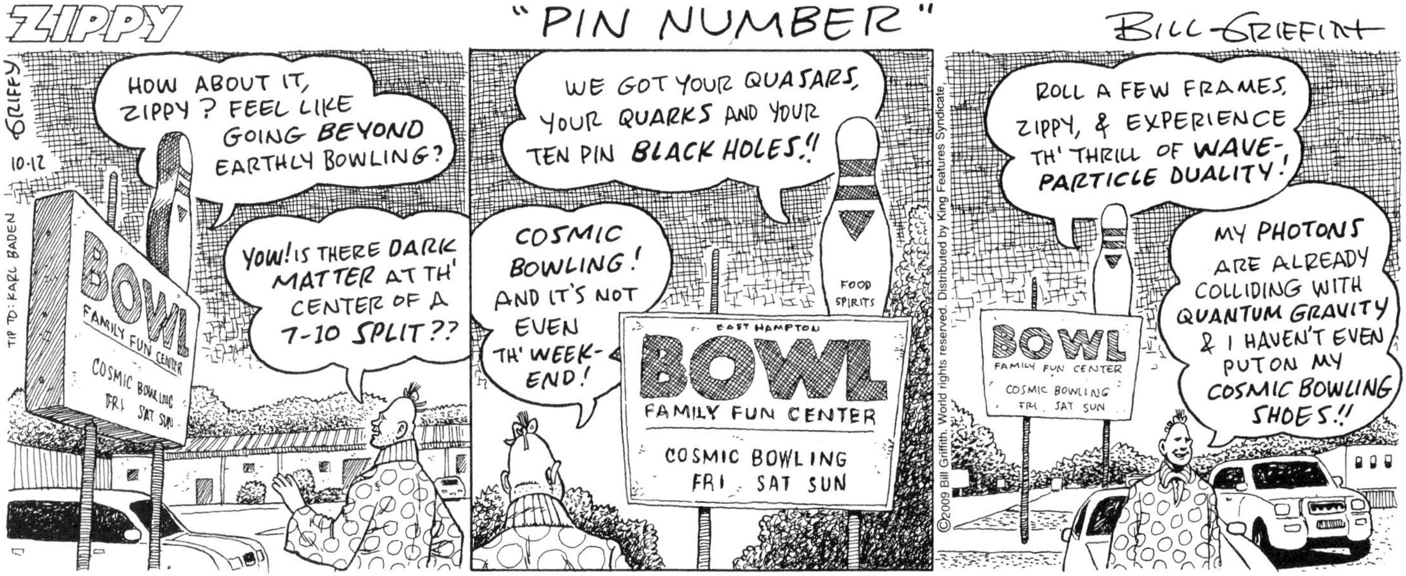
ZIPPY
"PIN NUMBER"
BILL GRIFFITH
GRIFFY 10-12
TIP TO: KARL BADEN
HOW ABOUT IT, ZIPPY? FEEL LIKE GOING BEYOND EARTHLY BOWLING?
YOW! IS THERE DARK MATTER AT TH' CENTER OF A 7-10 SPLIT??
BOWL FAMILY FUN CENTER COSMIC BOWLING FRI SAT SUN
WE GOT YOUR QUASARS, YOUR QUARKS AND YOUR TEN PIN BLACK HOLES!!
COSMIC BOWLING! AND IT'S NOT EVEN TH' WEEKEND!
FOOD SPIRITS
EAST HAMPTON BOWL FAMILY FUN CENTER
COSMIC BOWLING FRI SAT SUN
©2009 Bill Griffith. World rights reserved. Distributed by King Features Syndicate.
ROLL A FEW FRAMES, ZIPPY, & EXPERIENCE TH' THRILL OF WAVE-PARTICLE DUALITY!
MY PHOTONS ARE ALREADY COLLIDING WITH QUANTUM GRAVITY & I HAVEN'T EVEN PUT ON MY COSMIC BOWLING SHOES!!
BOWL FAMILY FUN CENTER COSMIC BOWLING FRI SAT SUN

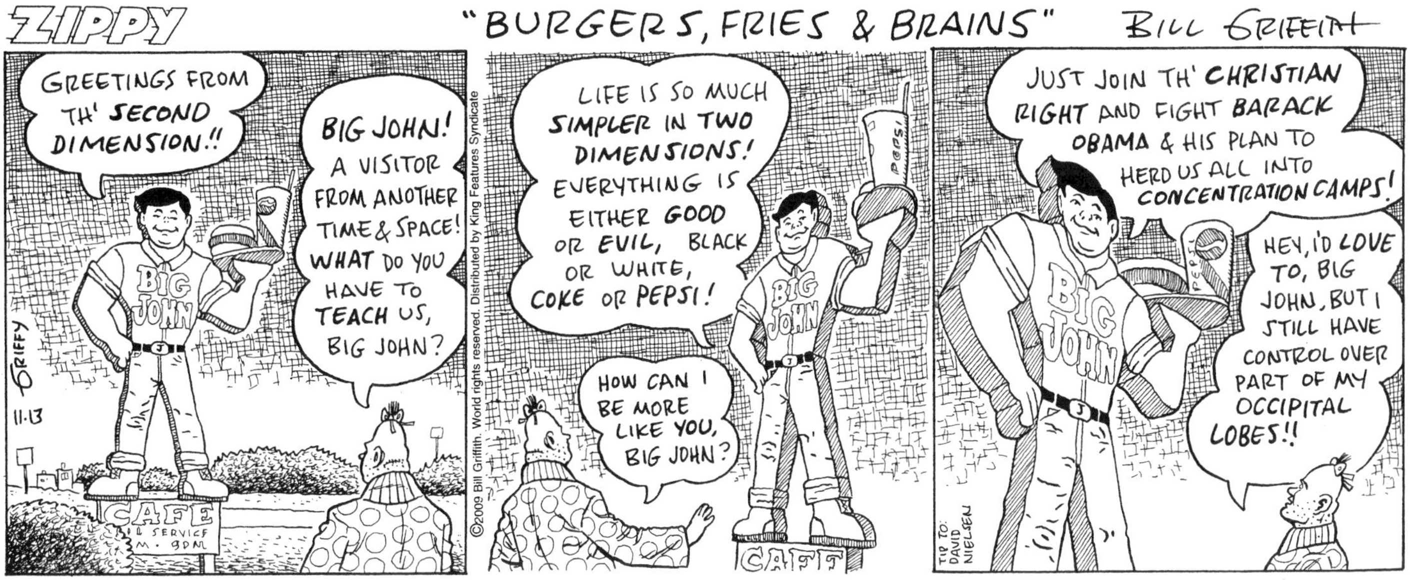
ZIPPY
"BURGERS, FRIES & BRAINS"
BILL GRIFFITH
GREETINGS FROM TH' SECOND DIMENSION!!
BIG JOHN! A VISITOR FROM ANOTHER TIME & SPACE! WHAT DO YOU HAVE TO TEACH US, BIG JOHN?
GRIFFY 11-13
CAFE
©2009 Bill Griffith. World rights reserved. Distributed by King Features Syndicate
LIFE IS SO MUCH SIMPLER IN TWO DIMENSIONS! EVERYTHING IS EITHER GOOD OR EVIL, BLACK OR WHITE, COKE OR PEPSI!
HOW CAN I BE MORE LIKE YOU, BIG JOHN?
PEPSI
JUST JOIN TH' CHRISTIAN RIGHT AND FIGHT BARACK OBAMA & HIS PLAN TO HERD US ALL INTO CONCENTRATION CAMPS!
HEY, I'D LOVE TO, BIG JOHN, BUT I STILL HAVE CONTROL OVER PART OF MY OCCIPITAL LOBES!!
TIP TO: DAVID NIELSEN

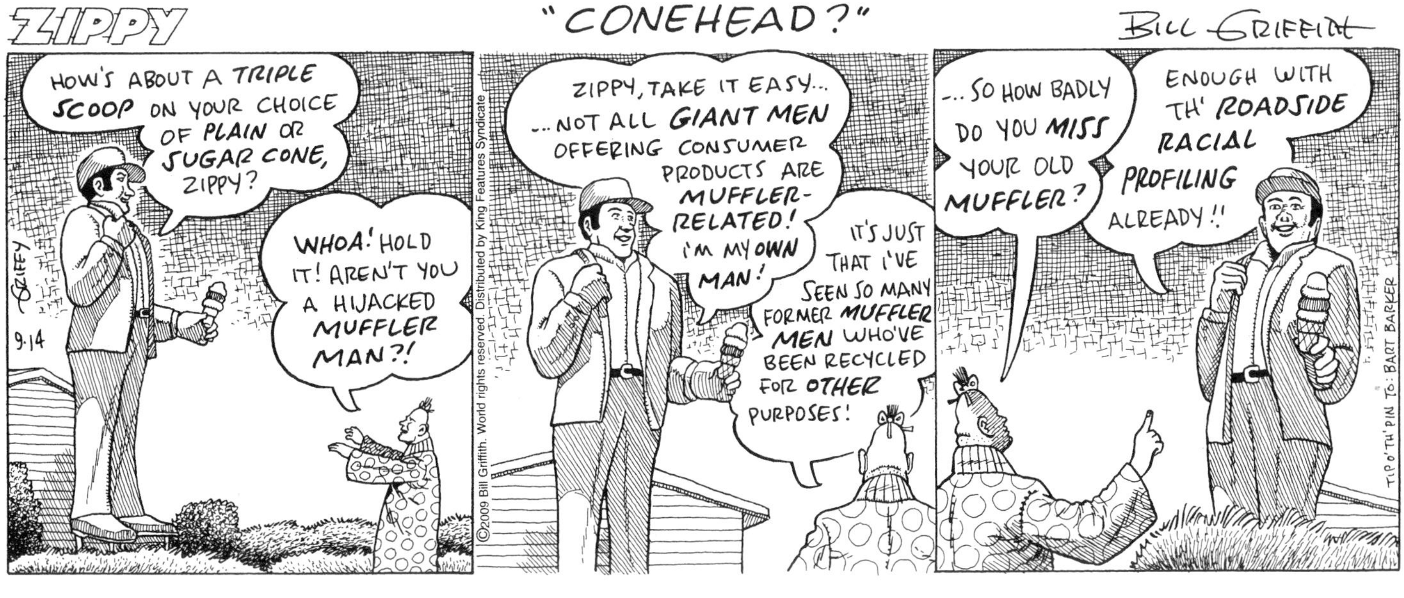
ZIPPY
"CONEHEAD?"
BILL GRIFFITH
HOW'S ABOUT A TRIPLE SCOOP ON YOUR CHOICE OF PLAIN OR SUGAR CONE, ZIPPY?
WHOA! HOLD IT! AREN'T YOU A HIJACKED MUFFLER MAN?!
GRIFFY 9-14
©2009 Bill Griffith. World rights reserved. Distributed by King Features Syndicate
ZIPPY, TAKE IT EASY... ...NOT ALL GIANT MEN OFFERING CONSUMER PRODUCTS ARE MUFFLER-RELATED! I'M MY OWN MAN!
IT'S JUST THAT I'VE SEEN SO MANY FORMER MUFFLER MEN WHO'VE BEEN RECYCLED FOR OTHER PURPOSES!
...SO HOW BADLY DO YOU MISS YOUR OLD MUFFLER?
ENOUGH WITH TH' ROADSIDE RACIAL PROFILING ALREADY!!
TIP O' TH' PIN TO: BART BARKER

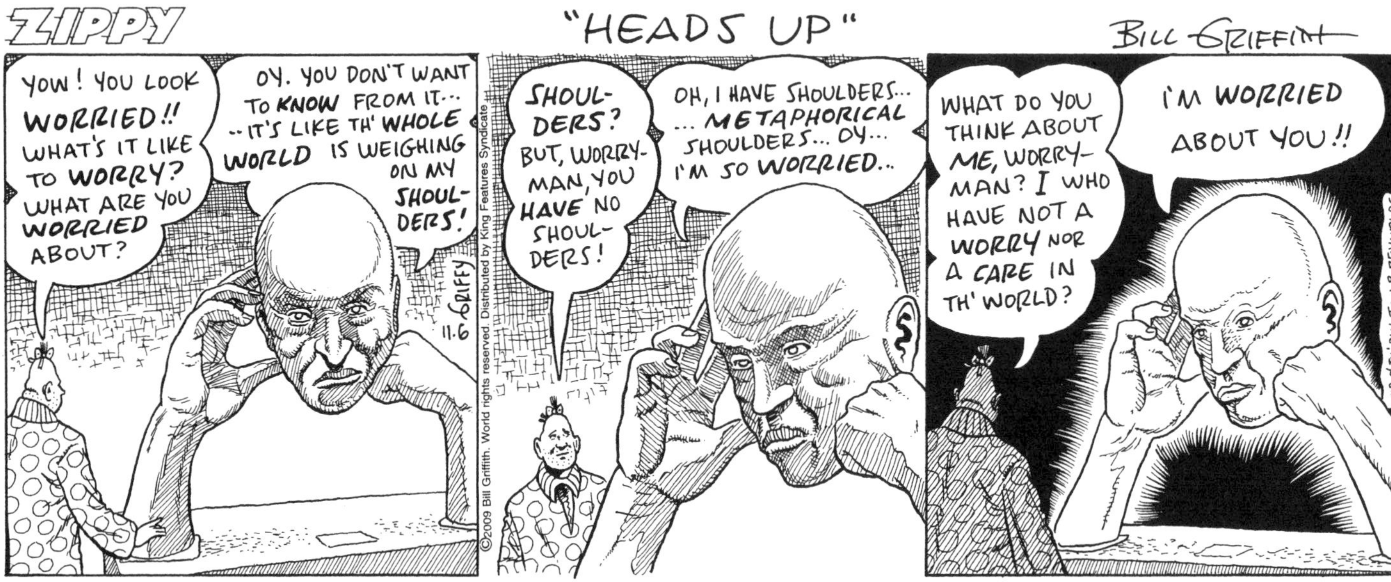
ZIPPY
"HEADS UP"
BILL GRIFFITH
YOW! YOU LOOK WORRIED!! WHAT'S IT LIKE TO WORRY? WHAT ARE YOU WORRIED ABOUT?
OY. YOU DON'T WANT TO KNOW FROM IT... ...IT'S LIKE TH' WHOLE WORLD IS WEIGHING ON MY SHOULDERS!
GRIFFY 11-6
©2009 Bill Griffith. World rights reserved. Distributed by King Features Syndicate.
SHOULDERS? BUT, WORRY-MAN, YOU HAVE NO SHOULDERS!
OH, I HAVE SHOULDERS... ...METAPHORICAL SHOULDERS... OY... I'M SO WORRIED...
WHAT DO YOU THINK ABOUT ME, WORRY-MAN? I WHO HAVE NOT A WORRY NOR A CARE IN TH' WORLD?
I'M WORRIED ABOUT YOU!!
TIP o' TH' PIN TO J.B. REYNOLDS

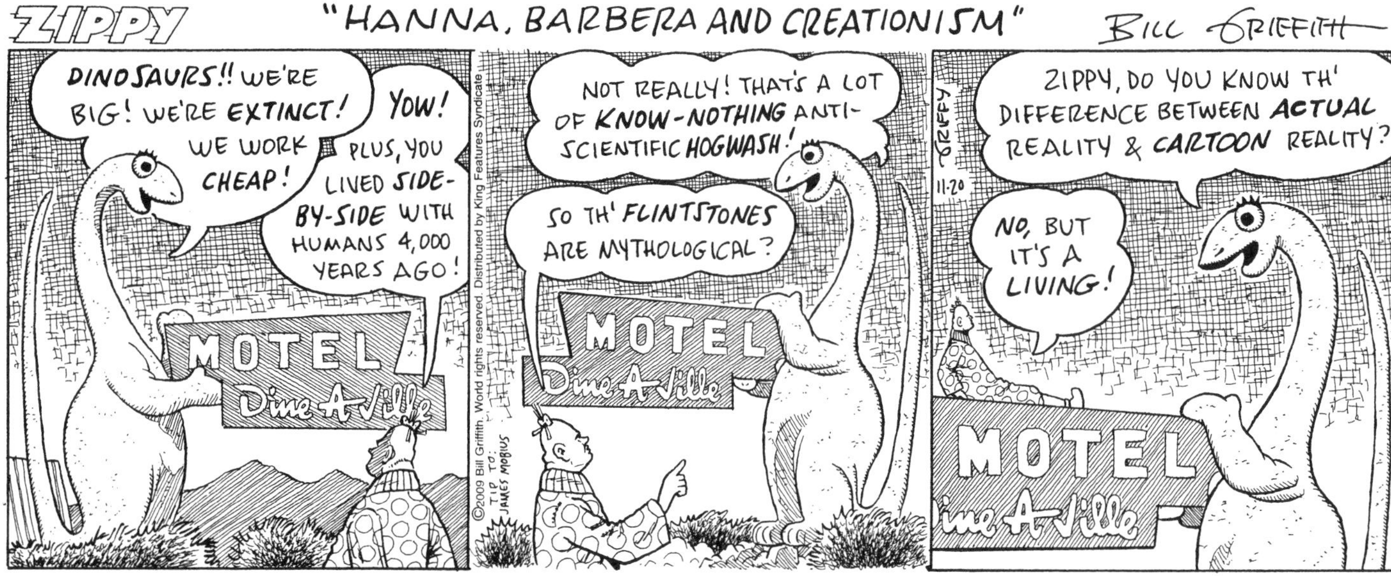
ZIPPY
"HANNA, BARBERA AND CREATIONISM"
BILL GRIFFITH
DINOSAURS!! WE'RE BIG! WE'RE EXTINCT! WE WORK CHEAP!
YOW! PLUS, YOU LIVED SIDE-BY-SIDE WITH HUMANS 4,000 YEARS AGO!
MOTEL Dine A Ville
©2009 Bill Griffith. World rights reserved. Distributed by King Features Syndicate.
TIP TO: JAMES MOBIUS
NOT REALLY! THAT'S A LOT OF KNOW-NOTHING ANTI-SCIENTIFIC HOGWASH!
SO TH' FLINTSTONES ARE MYTHOLOGICAL?
MOTEL Dine A Ville
GRIFFY 11-20
ZIPPY, DO YOU KNOW TH' DIFFERENCE BETWEEN ACTUAL REALITY & CARTOON REALITY?
NO, BUT IT'S A LIVING!
MOTEL ine A Ville

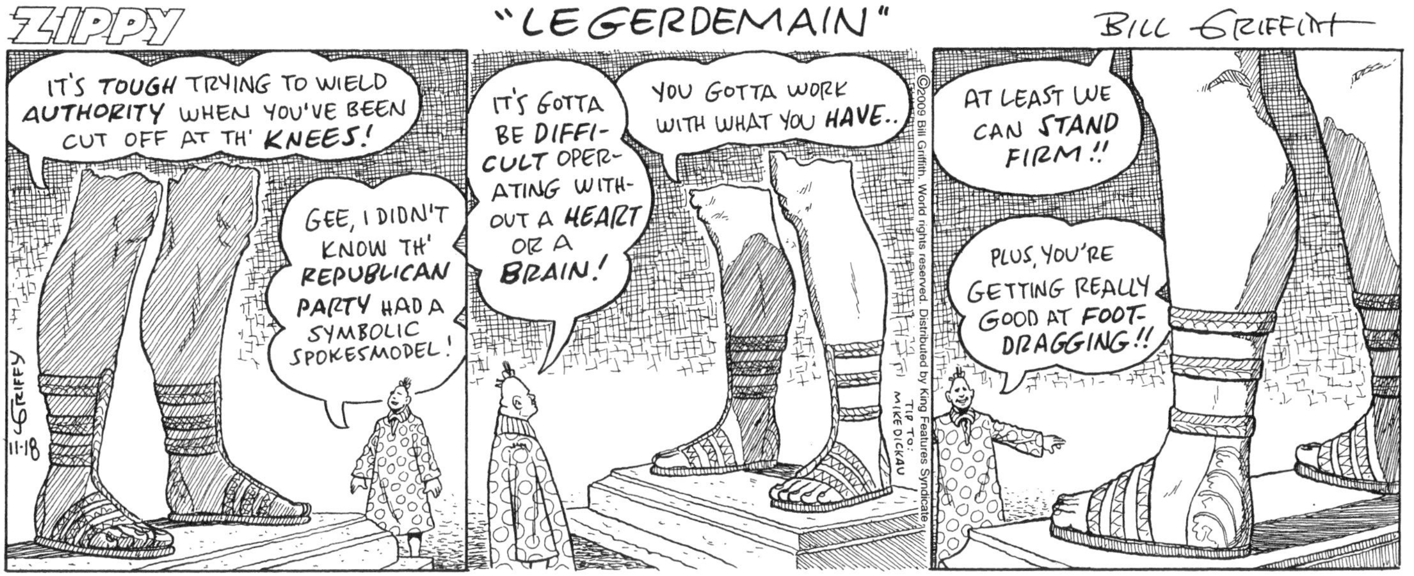
ZIPPY
"LEGERDEMAIN"
BILL GRIFFITH
IT'S TOUGH TRYING TO WIELD AUTHORITY WHEN YOU'VE BEEN CUT OFF AT TH' KNEES!
GEE, I DIDN'T KNOW TH' REPUBLICAN PARTY HAD A SYMBOLIC SPOKESMODEL!
GRIFFY 11·18
IT'S GOTTA BE DIFFICULT OPERATING WITHOUT A HEART OR A BRAIN!
YOU GOTTA WORK WITH WHAT YOU HAVE..
©2009 Bill Griffith. World rights reserved. Distributed by King Features Syndicate
TIP TO: MIKE DICKAU
AT LEAST WE CAN STAND FIRM!!
PLUS, YOU'RE GETTING REALLY GOOD AT FOOT-DRAGGING!!

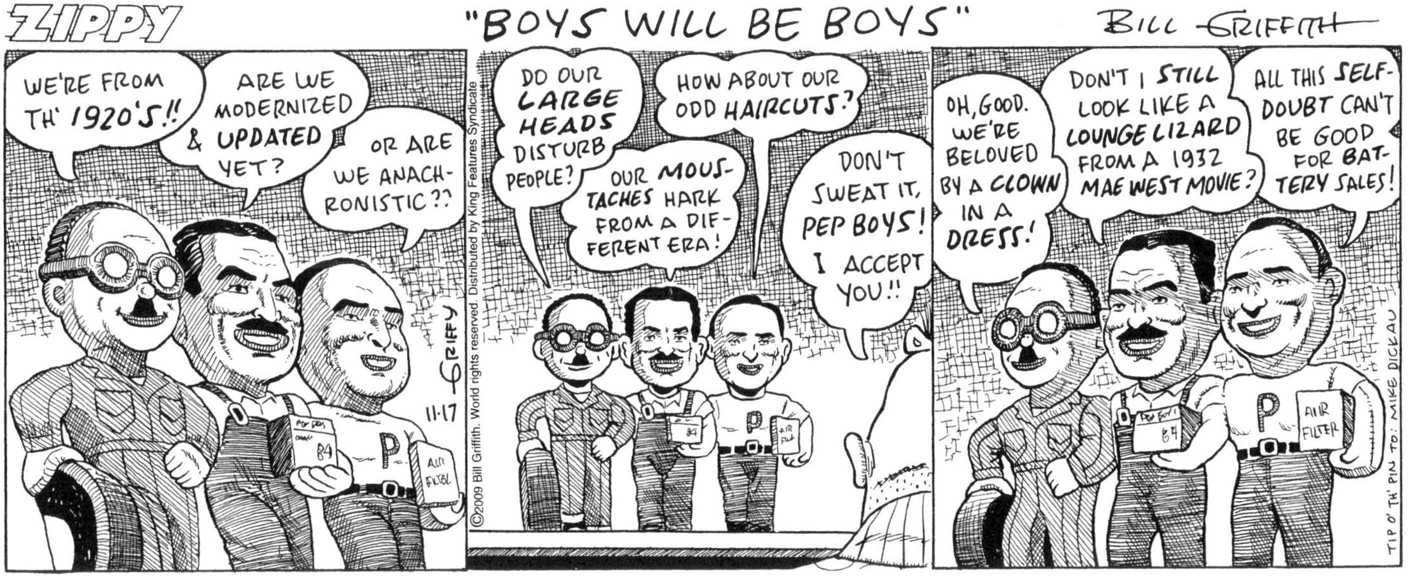
ZIPPY
"BOYS WILL BE BOYS"
BILL GRIFFITH
WE'RE FROM TH' 1920'S!!
ARE WE MODERNIZED & UPDATED YET?
OR ARE WE ANACHRONISTIC??
GRIFFY 11·17
©2009 Bill Griffith. World rights reserved. Distributed by King Features Syndicate
DO OUR LARGE HEADS DISTURB PEOPLE?
OUR MOUSTACHES HARK FROM A DIFFERENT ERA!
HOW ABOUT OUR ODD HAIRCUTS?
DON'T SWEAT IT, PEP BOYS! I ACCEPT YOU!!
OH, GOOD. WE'RE BELOVED BY A CLOWN IN A DRESS!
DON'T I STILL LOOK LIKE A LOUNGE LIZARD FROM A 1932 MAE WEST MOVIE?
ALL THIS SELF-DOUBT CAN'T BE GOOD FOR BATTERY SALES!
AIR FILTER
TIP O' TH' PIN TO: MIKE DICKAU

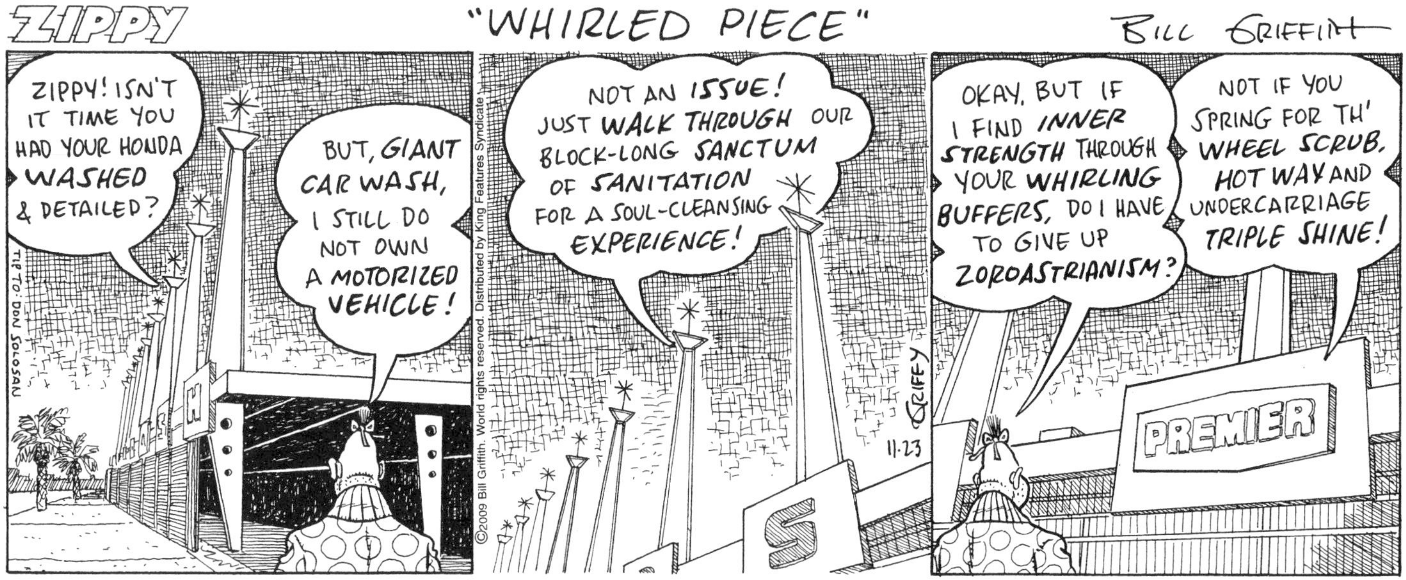
ZIPPY
"WHIRLED PIECE"
BILL GRIFFITH
ZIPPY! ISN'T IT TIME YOU HAD YOUR HONDA WASHED & DETAILED?
TIP TO: DON SOLOSAN
BUT, GIANT CAR WASH, I STILL DO NOT OWN A MOTORIZED VEHICLE!
H
©2009 Bill Griffith. World rights reserved. Distributed by King Features Syndicate
NOT AN ISSUE! JUST WALK THROUGH OUR BLOCK-LONG SANCTUM OF SANITATION FOR A SOUL-CLEANSING EXPERIENCE!
S
GRIFFY
11-23
OKAY, BUT IF I FIND INNER STRENGTH THROUGH YOUR WHIRLING BUFFERS, DO I HAVE TO GIVE UP ZOROASTRIANISM?
NOT IF YOU SPRING FOR TH' WHEEL SCRUB, HOT WAX AND UNDERCARRIAGE TRIPLE SHINE!
PREMIER

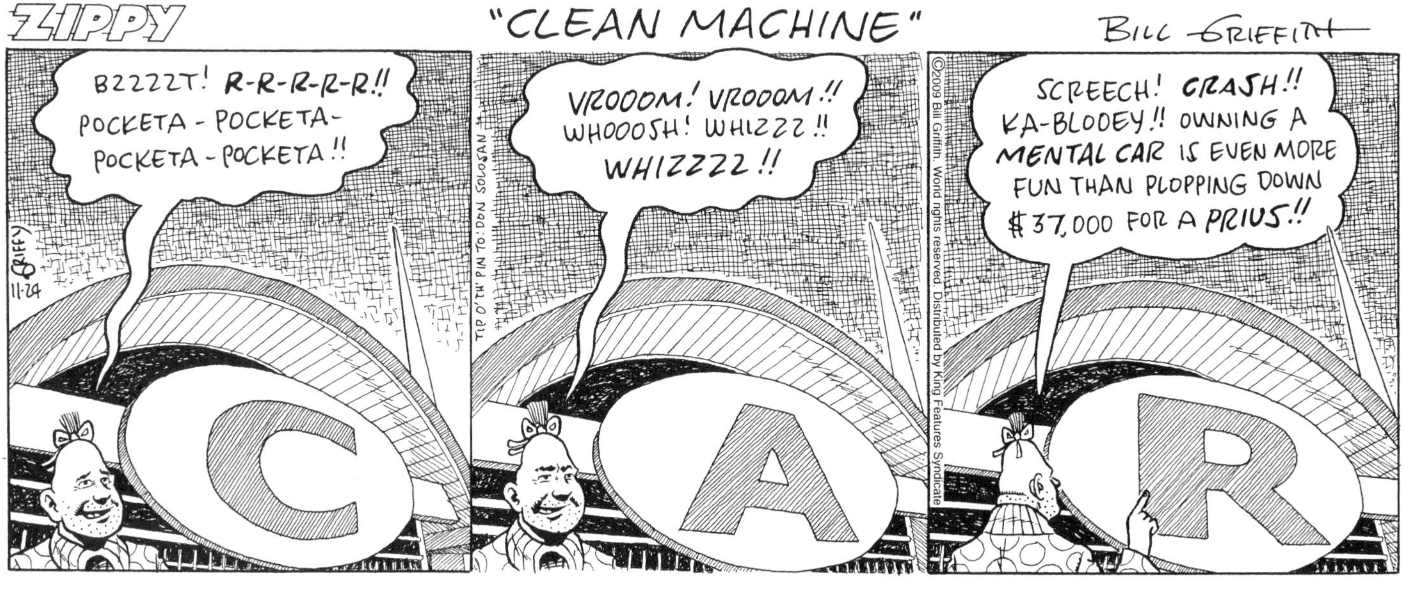
ZIPPY
"CLEAN MACHINE"
BILL GRIFFITH
BZZZZT! R-R-R-R-R!! POCKETA-POCKETA-POCKETA-POCKETA!!
GRIFFY
11-24
C
TIP O' TH' PIN TO: DON SOLOSAN
VROOOM! VROOOM!! WHOOOSH! WHIZZZ!! WHIZZZZ!!
A
©2009 Bill Griffith. World rights reserved. Distributed by King Features Syndicate
SCREECH! CRASH!! KA-BLOOEY!! OWNING A MENTAL CAR IS EVEN MORE FUN THAN PLOPPING DOWN $37,000 FOR A PRIUS!!
R

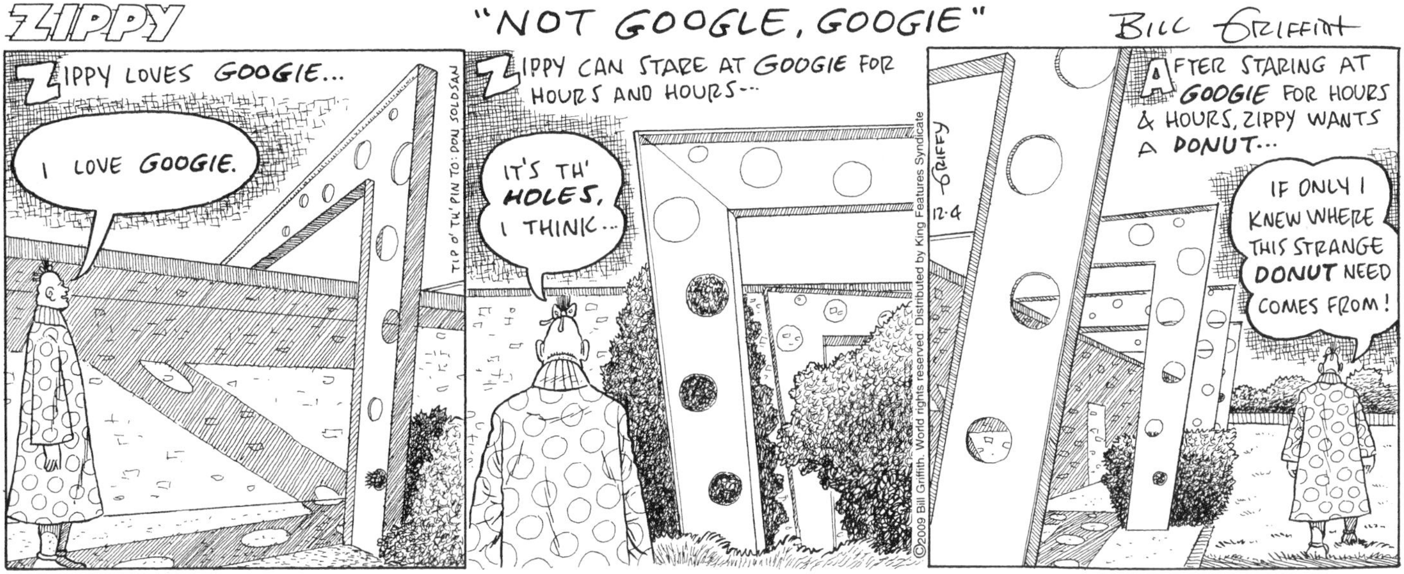
ZIPPY
"NOT GOOGLE, GOOGIE"
BILL GRIFFITH
ZIPPY LOVES GOOGIE...
I LOVE GOOGIE.
TIP O' TH' PIN TO: DON SOLDSAN
ZIPPY CAN STARE AT GOOGIE FOR HOURS AND HOURS...
IT'S TH' HOLES, I THINK...
©2009 Bill Griffith. World rights reserved. Distributed by King Features Syndicate
GRIFFY 12·4
AFTER STARING AT GOOGIE FOR HOURS & HOURS, ZIPPY WANTS A DONUT...
IF ONLY I KNEW WHERE THIS STRANGE DONUT NEED COMES FROM!

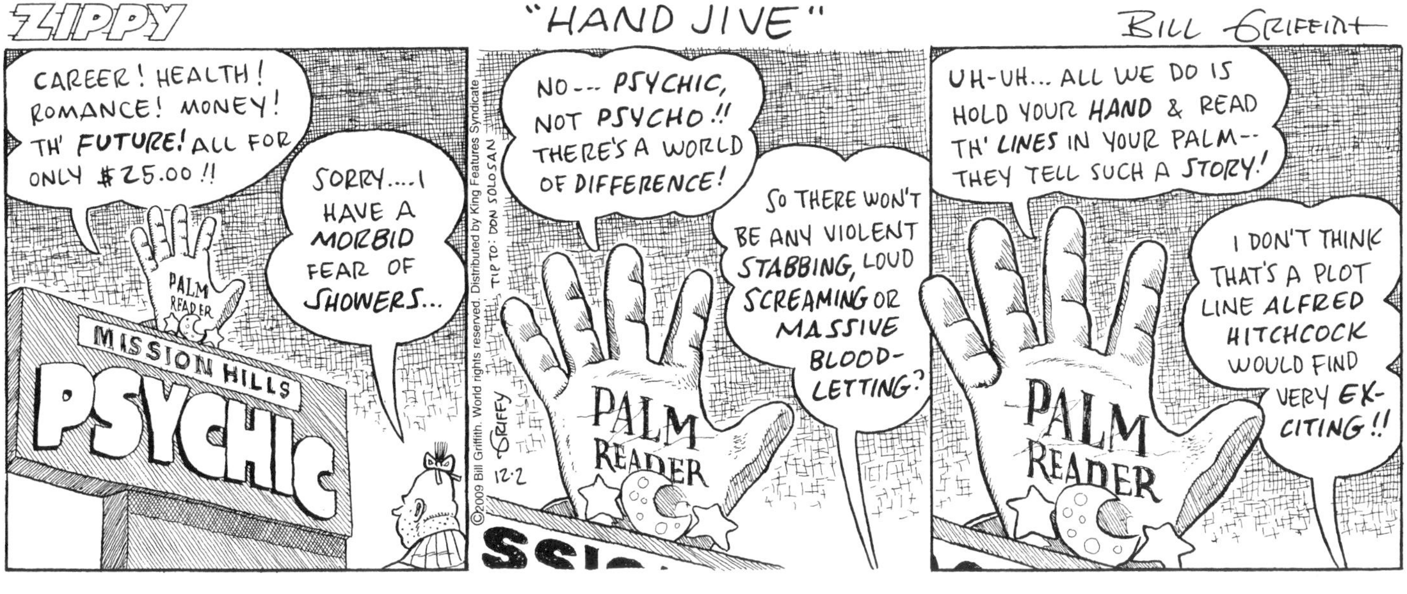
ZIPPY
"HAND JIVE"
BILL GRIFFITH
CAREER! HEALTH! ROMANCE! MONEY! TH' FUTURE! ALL FOR ONLY $25.00!!
PALM READER
MISSION HILLS
PSYCHIC
SORRY....I HAVE A MORBID FEAR OF SHOWERS...
©2009 Bill Griffith. World rights reserved. Distributed by King Features Syndicate
TIP TO: DON SOLOSAN
GRIFFY 12·2
NO--- PSYCHIC, NOT PSYCHO!! THERE'S A WORLD OF DIFFERENCE!
SO THERE WON'T BE ANY VIOLENT STABBING, LOUD SCREAMING OR MASSIVE BLOOD-LETTING?
PALM READER
UH-UH... ALL WE DO IS HOLD YOUR HAND & READ TH' LINES IN YOUR PALM-- THEY TELL SUCH A STORY!
I DON'T THINK THAT'S A PLOT LINE ALFRED HITCHCOCK WOULD FIND VERY EX-CITING!!
PALM READER

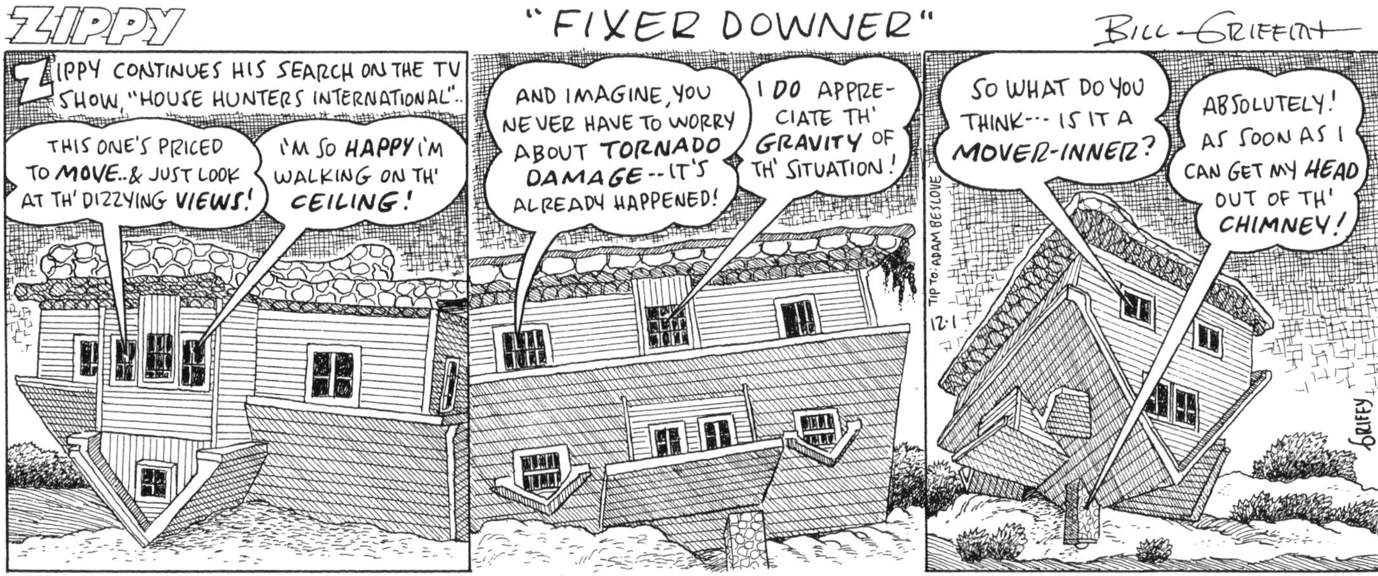
ZIPPY
"FIXER DOWNER"
BILL GRIFFITH
ZIPPY CONTINUES HIS SEARCH ON THE TV SHOW, "HOUSE HUNTERS INTERNATIONAL"..
THIS ONE'S PRICED TO MOVE..& JUST LOOK AT TH' DIZZYING VIEWS!
I'M SO HAPPY I'M WALKING ON TH' CEILING!
AND IMAGINE, YOU NEVER HAVE TO WORRY ABOUT TORNADO DAMAGE--IT'S ALREADY HAPPENED!
I DO APPRECIATE TH' GRAVITY OF TH' SITUATION!
TIP TO: ADAM BESLOVE
12-1
SO WHAT DO YOU THINK--- IS IT A MOVER-INNER?
ABSOLUTELY! AS SOON AS I CAN GET MY HEAD OUT OF TH' CHIMNEY!
GRIFFY
©2009 Bill Griffith. World rights reserved. Distributed by King Features Syndicate

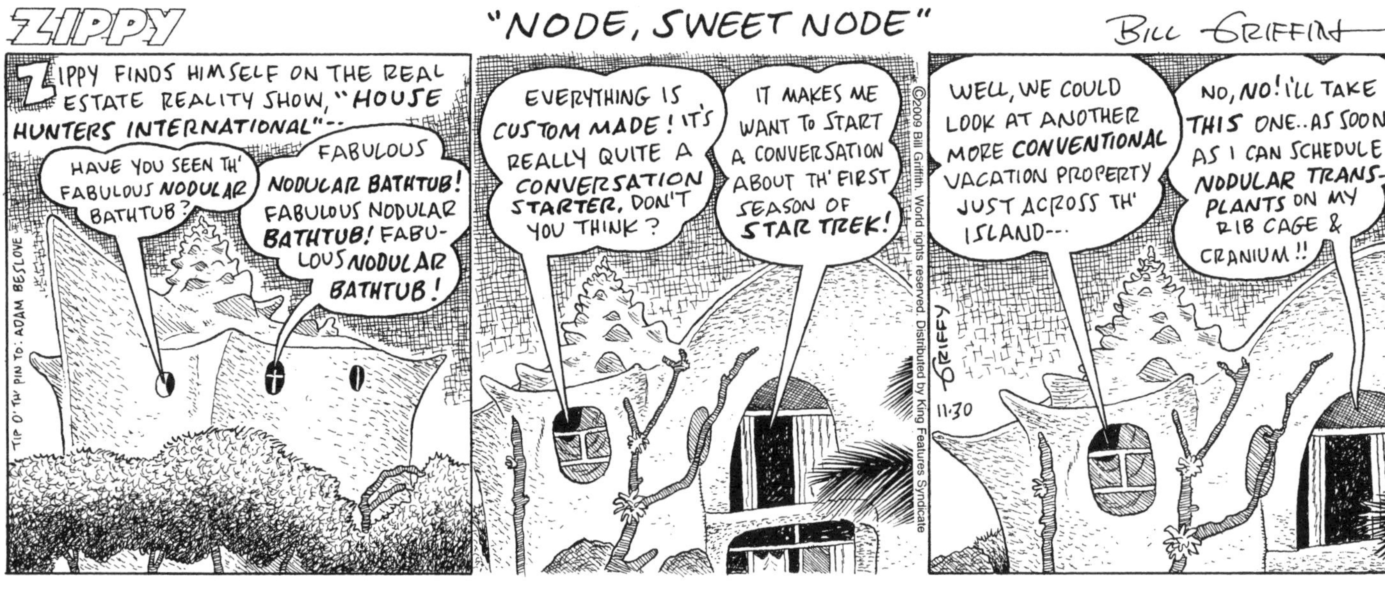
ZIPPY
"NODE, SWEET NODE"
BILL GRIFFITH
ZIPPY FINDS HIMSELF ON THE REAL ESTATE REALITY SHOW, "HOUSE HUNTERS INTERNATIONAL"--
HAVE YOU SEEN TH' FABULOUS NODULAR BATHTUB?
FABULOUS NODULAR BATHTUB! FABULOUS NODULAR BATHTUB! FABULOUS NODULAR BATHTUB!
TIP O' TH' PIN TO: ADAM BESLOVE
EVERYTHING IS CUSTOM MADE! IT'S REALLY QUITE A CONVERSATION STARTER, DON'T YOU THINK?
IT MAKES ME WANT TO START A CONVERSATION ABOUT TH' FIRST SEASON OF STAR TREK!
©2009 Bill Griffith. World rights reserved. Distributed by King Features Syndicate
WELL, WE COULD LOOK AT ANOTHER MORE CONVENTIONAL VACATION PROPERTY JUST ACROSS TH' ISLAND---
NO, NO! I'LL TAKE THIS ONE..AS SOON AS I CAN SCHEDULE NODULAR TRANSPLANTS ON MY RIB CAGE & CRANIUM!!
GRIFFY
11-30

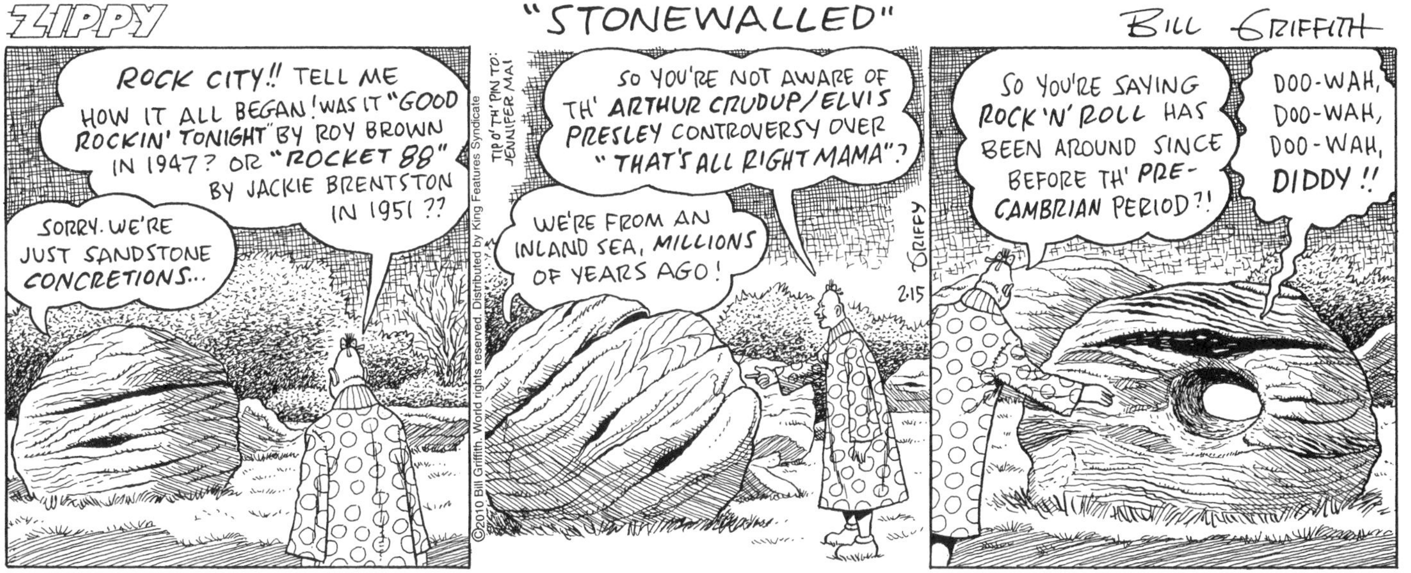
ZIPPY
"STONEWALLED"
BILL GRIFFITH
ROCK CITY!! TELL ME HOW IT ALL BEGAN! WAS IT "GOOD ROCKIN' TONIGHT" BY ROY BROWN IN 1947? OR "ROCKET 88" BY JACKIE BRENTSTON IN 1951??
SORRY. WE'RE JUST SANDSTONE CONCRETIONS...
©2010 Bill Griffith. World rights reserved. Distributed by King Features Syndicate
TIP O' TH' PIN TO: JENNIFER MAI
SO YOU'RE NOT AWARE OF TH' ARTHUR CRUDUP/ELVIS PRESLEY CONTROVERSY OVER "THAT'S ALL RIGHT MAMA"?
WE'RE FROM AN INLAND SEA, MILLIONS OF YEARS AGO!
GRIFFY
2.15
SO YOU'RE SAYING ROCK 'N' ROLL HAS BEEN AROUND SINCE BEFORE TH' PRE-CAMBRIAN PERIOD?!
DOO-WAH, DOO-WAH, DOO-WAH, DIDDY!!

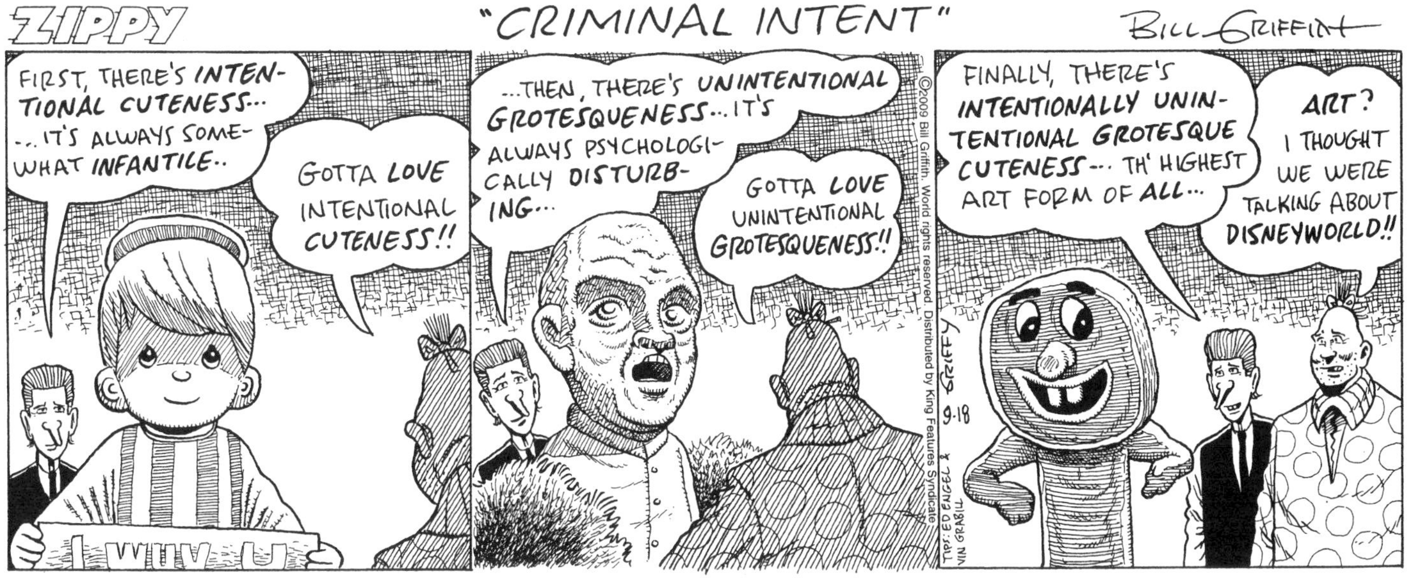
ZIPPY
"CRIMINAL INTENT"
BILL GRIFFITH
FIRST, THERE'S INTENTIONAL CUTENESS... ...IT'S ALWAYS SOMEWHAT INFANTILE..
GOTTA LOVE INTENTIONAL CUTENESS!!
...THEN, THERE'S UNINTENTIONAL GROTESQUENESS... IT'S ALWAYS PSYCHOLOGICALLY DISTURBING...
GOTTA LOVE UNINTENTIONAL GROTESQUENESS!!
©2009 Bill Griffith. World rights reserved. Distributed by King Features Syndicate
GRIFFY
9.18
TIPS: ED EAGEL & VIN GRABILL
FINALLY, THERE'S INTENTIONALLY UNINTENTIONAL GROTESQUE CUTENESS... TH' HIGHEST ART FORM OF ALL...
ART? I THOUGHT WE WERE TALKING ABOUT DISNEYWORLD!!

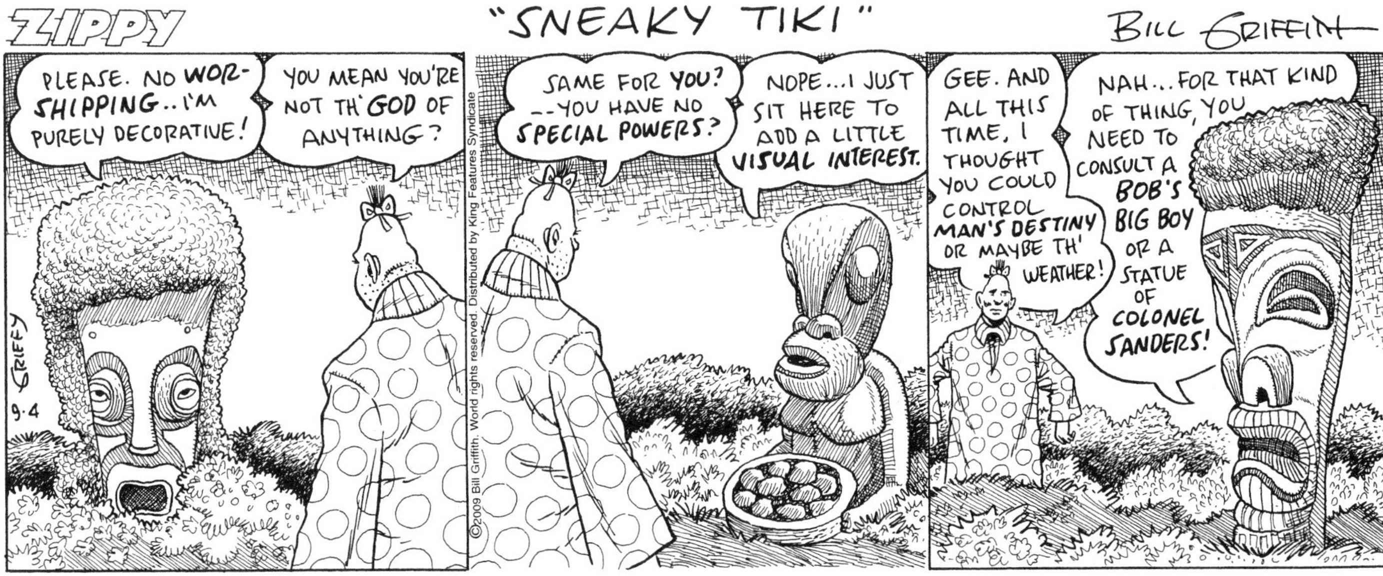
ZIPPY
"SNEAKY TIKI"
BILL GRIFFITH
PLEASE. NO WORSHIPPING.. I'M PURELY DECORATIVE!
YOU MEAN YOU'RE NOT TH' GOD OF ANYTHING?
GRIFFY 9·4
SAME FOR YOU? --YOU HAVE NO SPECIAL POWERS?
NOPE...I JUST SIT HERE TO ADD A LITTLE VISUAL INTEREST.
©2009 Bill Griffith. World rights reserved. Distributed by King Features Syndicate
GEE. AND ALL THIS TIME, I THOUGHT YOU COULD CONTROL MAN'S DESTINY OR MAYBE TH' WEATHER!
NAH...FOR THAT KIND OF THING, YOU NEED TO CONSULT A BOB'S BIG BOY OR A STATUE OF COLONEL SANDERS!

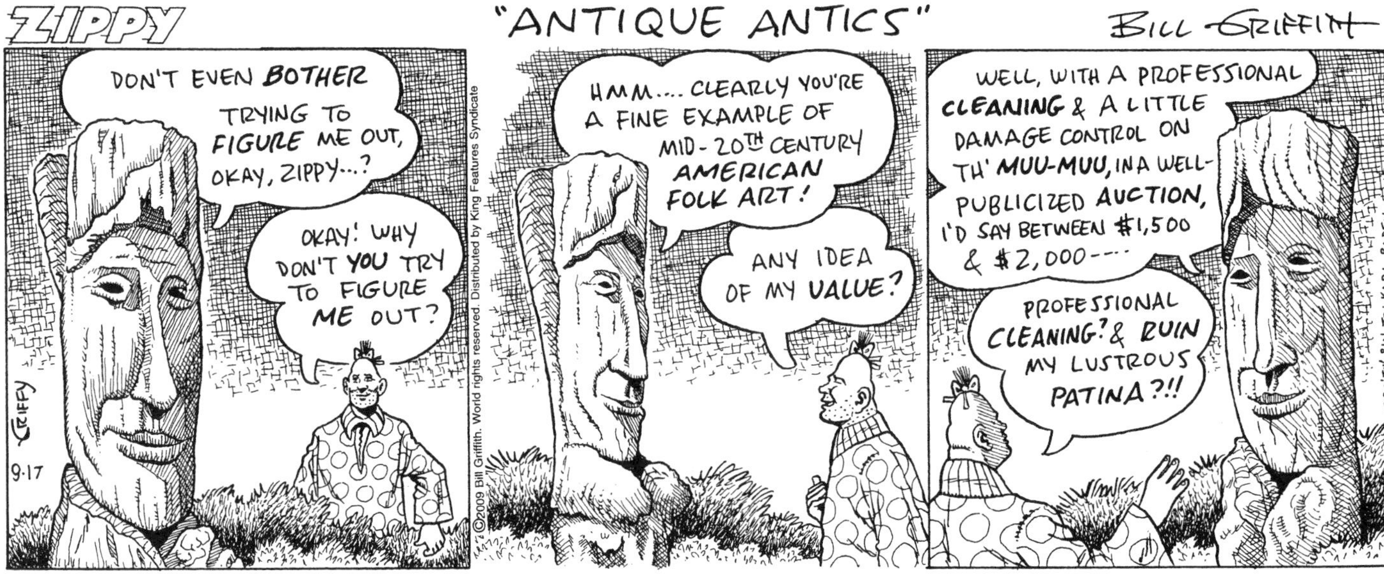
ZIPPY
"ANTIQUE ANTICS"
BILL GRIFFITH
DON'T EVEN BOTHER TRYING TO FIGURE ME OUT, OKAY, ZIPPY...?
OKAY! WHY DON'T YOU TRY TO FIGURE ME OUT?
GRIFFY 9·17
HMM.... CLEARLY YOU'RE A FINE EXAMPLE OF MID-20TH CENTURY AMERICAN FOLK ART!
ANY IDEA OF MY VALUE?
©2009 Bill Griffith. World rights reserved. Distributed by King Features Syndicate
WELL, WITH A PROFESSIONAL CLEANING & A LITTLE DAMAGE CONTROL ON TH' MUU-MUU, IN A WELL-PUBLICIZED AUCTION, I'D SAY BETWEEN $1,500 & $2,000---
PROFESSIONAL CLEANING? & RUIN MY LUSTROUS PATINA?!!
TIP O' TH' PIN TO: KARL BADEN

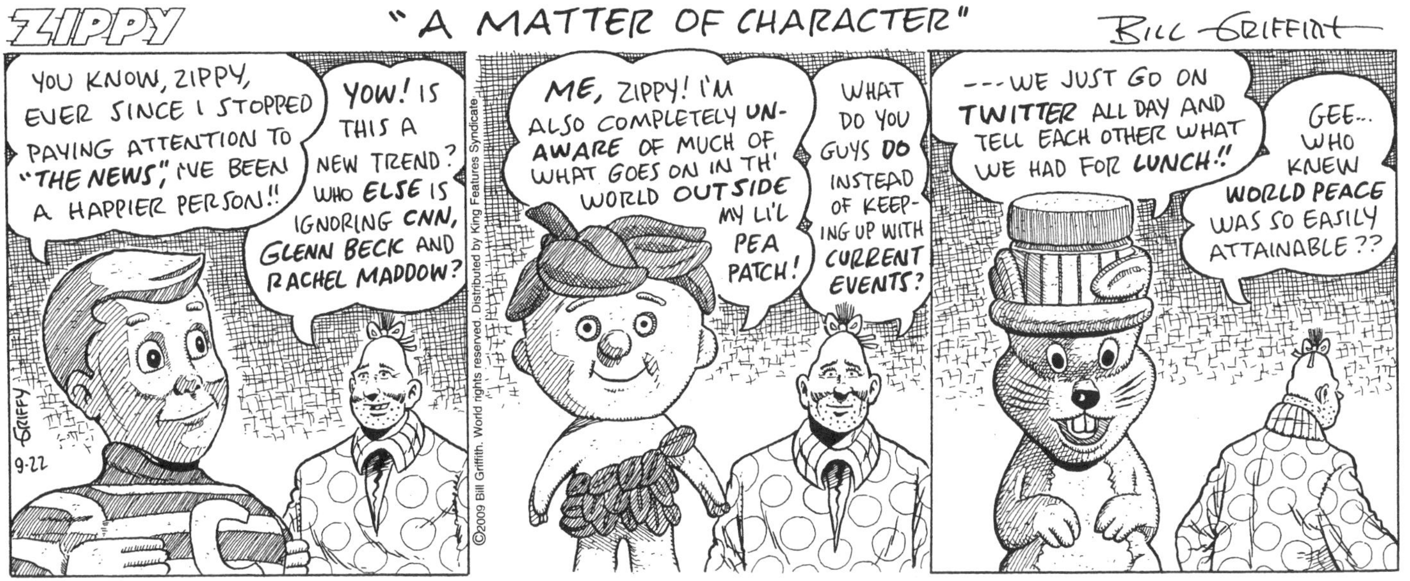
ZIPPY
"A MATTER OF CHARACTER"
BILL GRIFFITH
YOU KNOW, ZIPPY, EVER SINCE I STOPPED PAYING ATTENTION TO "THE NEWS," I'VE BEEN A HAPPIER PERSON!!
YOW! IS THIS A NEW TREND? WHO ELSE IS IGNORING CNN, GLENN BECK AND RACHEL MADDOW?
GRIFFY 9·22
©2009 Bill Griffith. World rights reserved. Distributed by King Features Syndicate
ME, ZIPPY! I'M ALSO COMPLETELY UN-AWARE OF MUCH OF WHAT GOES ON IN TH' WORLD OUTSIDE MY LI'L PEA PATCH!
WHAT DO YOU GUYS DO INSTEAD OF KEEP-ING UP WITH CURRENT EVENTS?
---WE JUST GO ON TWITTER ALL DAY AND TELL EACH OTHER WHAT WE HAD FOR LUNCH!!
GEE... WHO KNEW WORLD PEACE WAS SO EASILY ATTAINABLE??

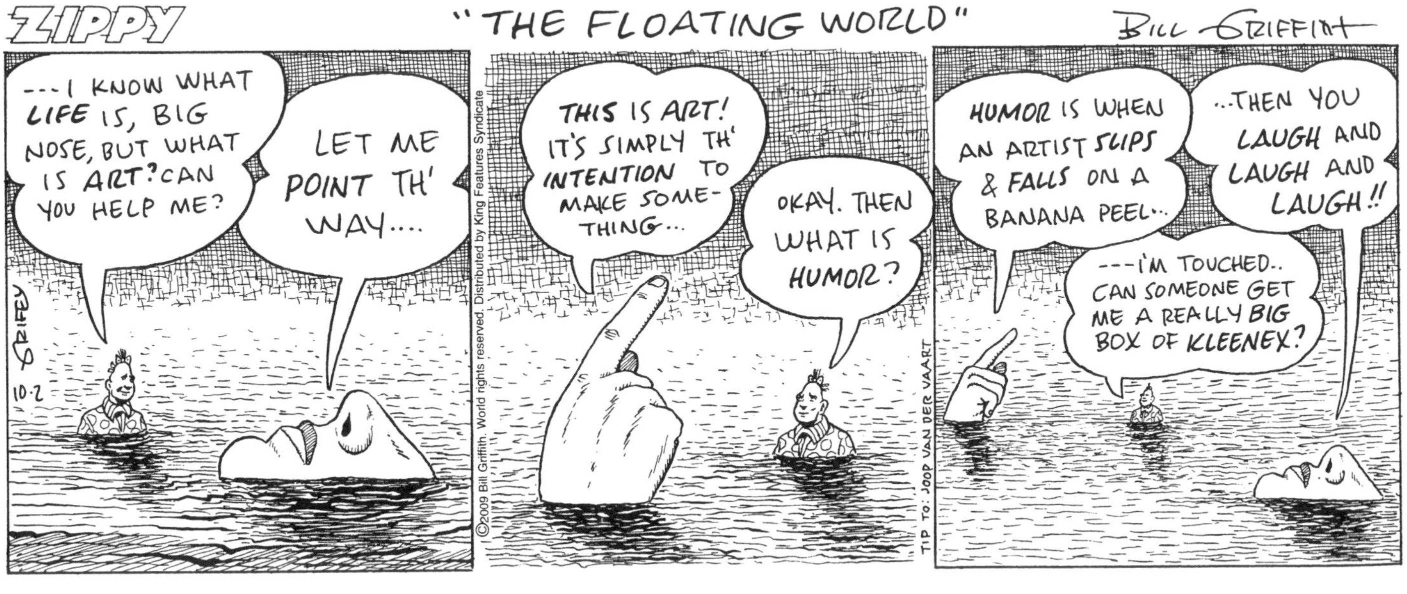
ZIPPY
"THE FLOATING WORLD"
BILL GRIFFITH
---I KNOW WHAT LIFE IS, BIG NOSE, BUT WHAT IS ART? CAN YOU HELP ME?
LET ME POINT TH' WAY....
GRIFFY 10·2
©2009 Bill Griffith. World rights reserved. Distributed by King Features Syndicate
THIS IS ART! IT'S SIMPLY TH' INTENTION TO MAKE SOME-THING...
OKAY. THEN WHAT IS HUMOR?
TIP TO: JOOP VAN DER VAART
HUMOR IS WHEN AN ARTIST SLIPS & FALLS ON A BANANA PEEL...
...THEN YOU LAUGH AND LAUGH AND LAUGH!!
---I'M TOUCHED.. CAN SOMEONE GET ME A REALLY BIG BOX OF KLEENEX?

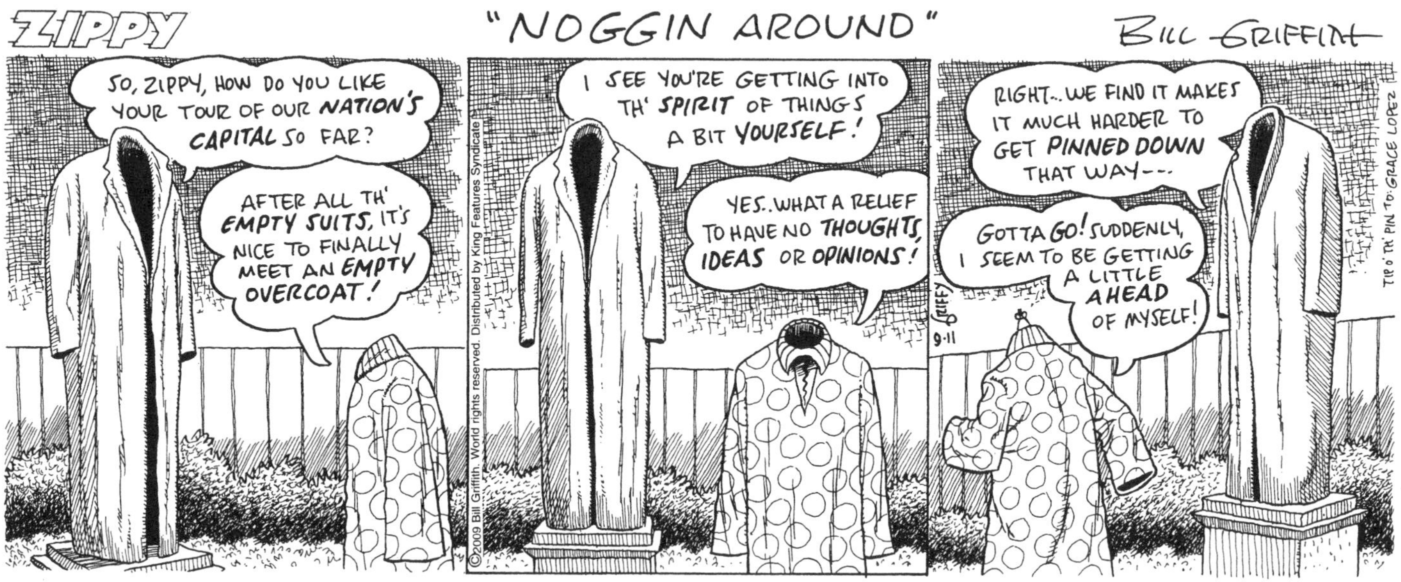
ZIPPY
"NOGGIN AROUND"
BILL GRIFFITH
SO, ZIPPY, HOW DO YOU LIKE YOUR TOUR OF OUR NATION'S CAPITAL SO FAR?
AFTER ALL TH' EMPTY SUITS, IT'S NICE TO FINALLY MEET AN EMPTY OVERCOAT!
©2009 Bill Griffith. World rights reserved. Distributed by King Features Syndicate
I SEE YOU'RE GETTING INTO TH' SPIRIT OF THINGS A BIT YOURSELF!
YES..WHAT A RELIEF TO HAVE NO THOUGHTS, IDEAS OR OPINIONS!
GRIFFY 9-11
RIGHT.. WE FIND IT MAKES IT MUCH HARDER TO GET PINNED DOWN THAT WAY---
GOTTA GO! SUDDENLY, I SEEM TO BE GETTING A LITTLE AHEAD OF MYSELF!
TIP O' TH' PIN TO: GRACE LOPEZ

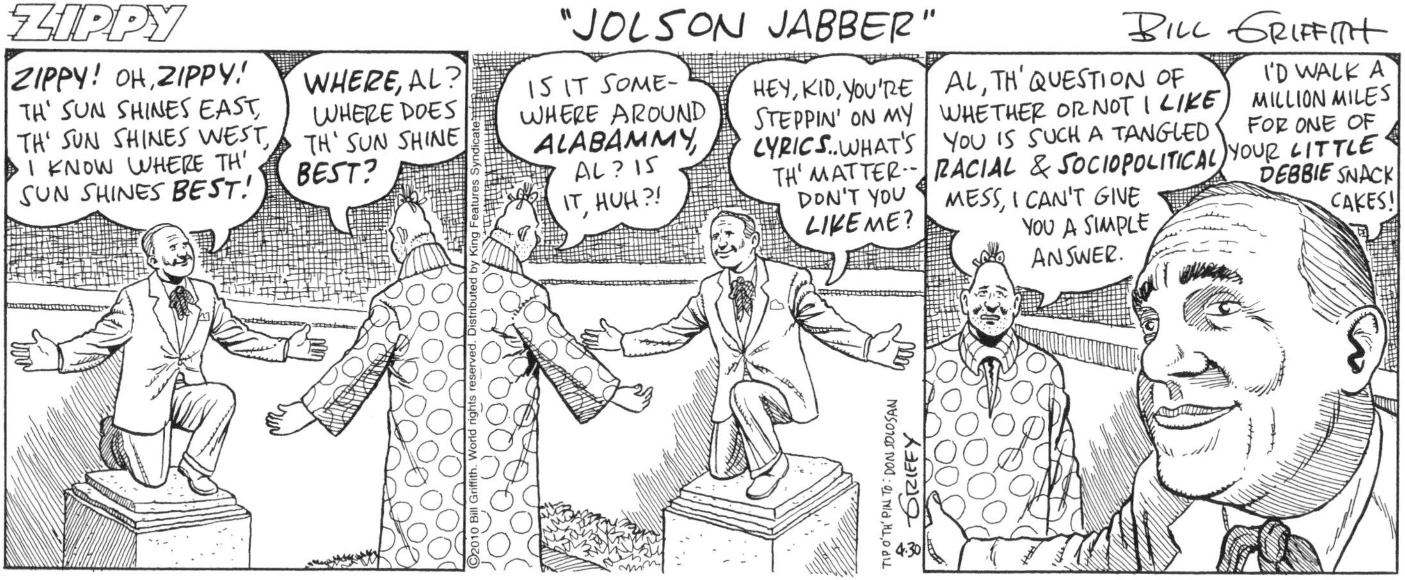
ZIPPY
"JOLSON JABBER"
BILL GRIFFITH
ZIPPY! OH, ZIPPY! TH' SUN SHINES EAST, TH' SUN SHINES WEST, I KNOW WHERE TH' SUN SHINES BEST!
WHERE, AL? WHERE DOES TH' SUN SHINE BEST?
©2010 Bill Griffith. World rights reserved. Distributed by King Features Syndicate
IS IT SOME-WHERE AROUND ALABAMMY, AL? IS IT, HUH?!
HEY, KID, YOU'RE STEPPIN' ON MY LYRICS..WHAT'S TH' MATTER-- DON'T YOU LIKE ME?
TIP O' TH' PIN TO: DON JOLOSAN
GRIFFY 4-30
AL, TH' QUESTION OF WHETHER OR NOT I LIKE YOU IS SUCH A TANGLED RACIAL & SOCIOPOLITICAL MESS, I CAN'T GIVE YOU A SIMPLE ANSWER.
I'D WALK A MILLION MILES FOR ONE OF YOUR LITTLE DEBBIE SNACK CAKES!

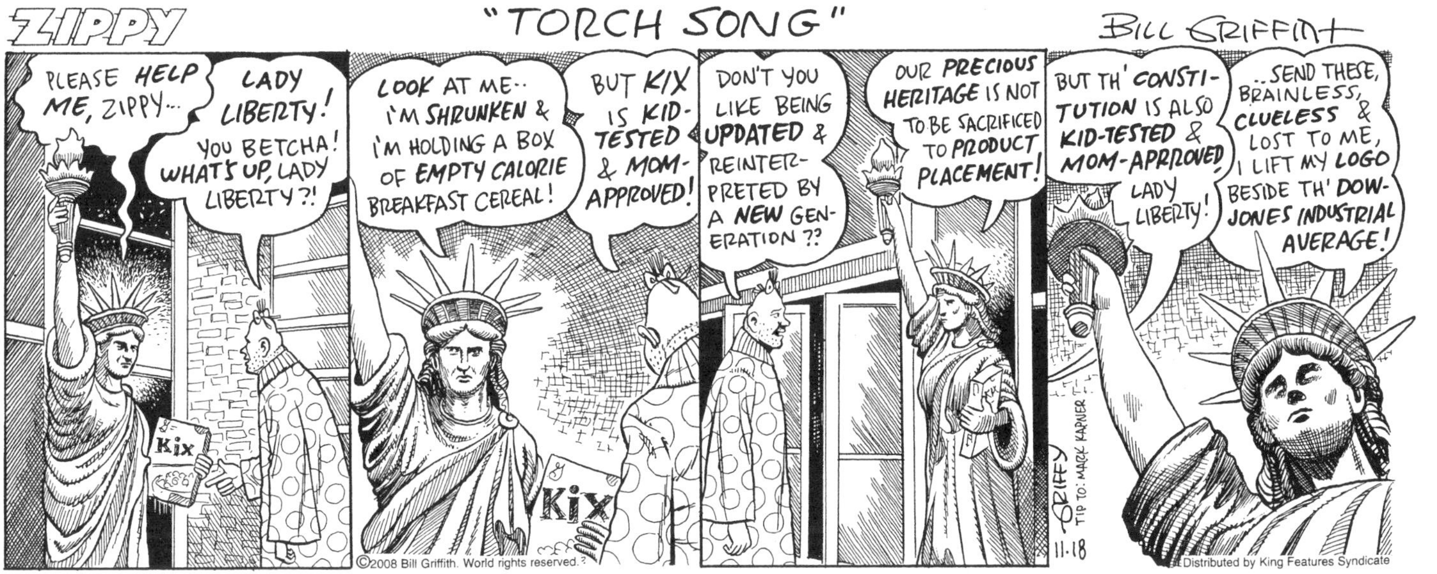
ZIPPY
"TORCH SONG"
BILL GRIFFITH
PLEASE HELP ME, ZIPPY...
LADY LIBERTY! YOU BETCHA! WHAT'S UP, LADY LIBERTY?!
Kix
LOOK AT ME.. I'M SHRUNKEN & I'M HOLDING A BOX OF EMPTY CALORIE BREAKFAST CEREAL!
BUT KIX IS KID-TESTED & MOM-APPROVED!
Kix
DON'T YOU LIKE BEING UPDATED & REINTERPRETED BY A NEW GENERATION??
OUR PRECIOUS HERITAGE IS NOT TO BE SACRIFICED TO PRODUCT PLACEMENT!
GRIFFY
TIP TO: MARK KARNER
11-18
BUT TH' CONSTITUTION IS ALSO KID-TESTED & MOM-APPROVED, LADY LIBERTY!
..SEND THESE, BRAINLESS, CLUELESS & LOST TO ME, I LIFT MY LOGO BESIDE TH' DOW-JONES INDUSTRIAL AVERAGE!
©2008 Bill Griffith. World rights reserved.
Distributed by King Features Syndicate

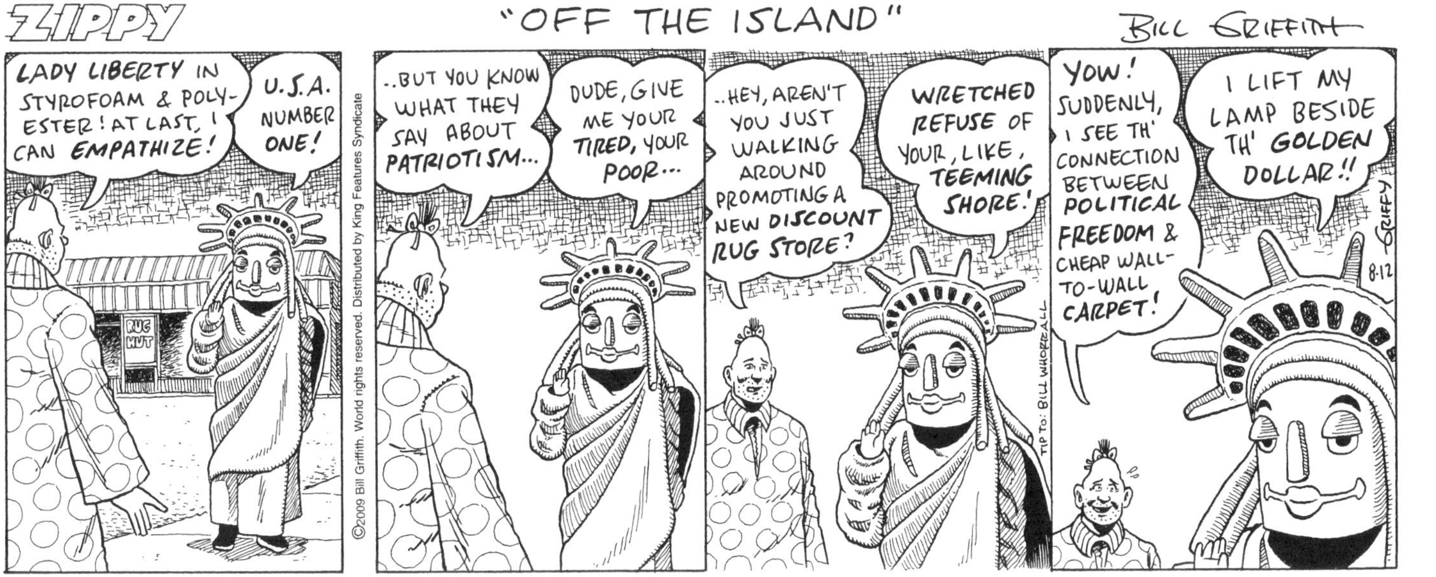
ZIPPY
"OFF THE ISLAND"
BILL GRIFFITH
LADY LIBERTY IN STYROFOAM & POLYESTER! AT LAST, I CAN EMPATHIZE!
U.S.A. NUMBER ONE!
RUG HUT
©2009 Bill Griffith. World rights reserved. Distributed by King Features Syndicate
..BUT YOU KNOW WHAT THEY SAY ABOUT PATRIOTISM...
DUDE, GIVE ME YOUR TIRED, YOUR POOR...
..HEY, AREN'T YOU JUST WALKING AROUND PROMOTING A NEW DISCOUNT RUG STORE?
WRETCHED REFUSE OF YOUR, LIKE, TEEMING SHORE!
TIP TO: BILL WHORRALL
YOW! SUDDENLY, I SEE TH' CONNECTION BETWEEN POLITICAL FREEDOM & CHEAP WALL-TO-WALL CARPET!
I LIFT MY LAMP BESIDE TH' GOLDEN DOLLAR!!
GRIFFY
8-12

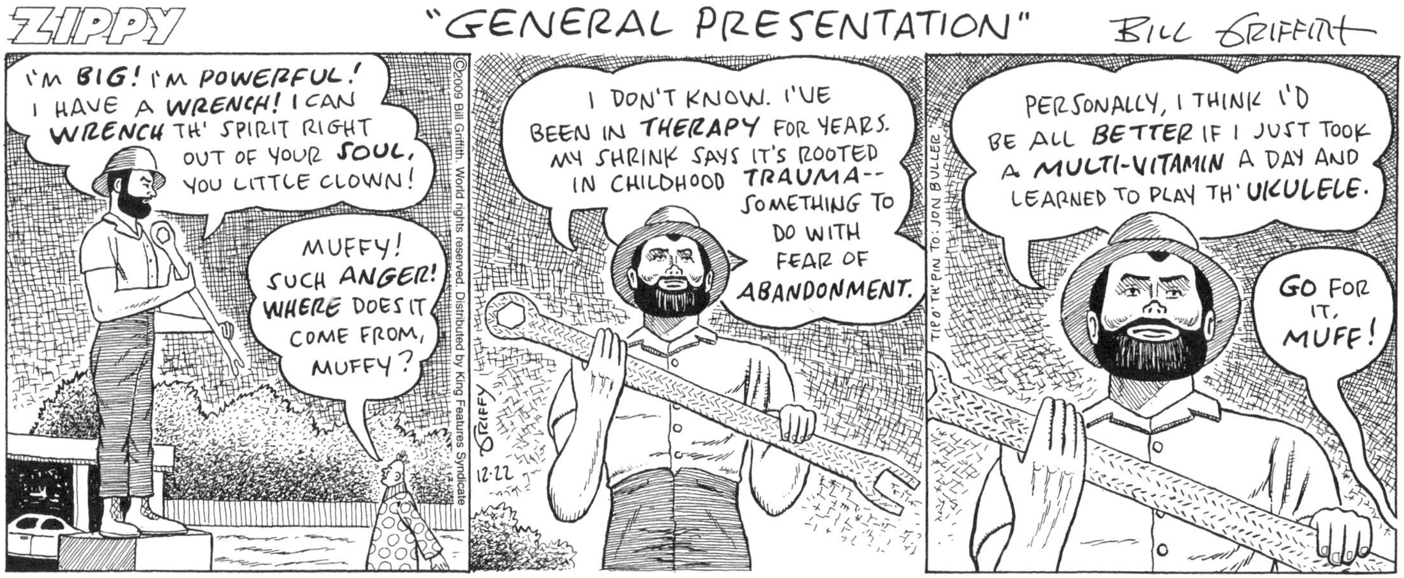
ZIPPY
"GENERAL PRESENTATION"
BILL GRIFFITH
I'M BIG! I'M POWERFUL! I HAVE A WRENCH! I CAN WRENCH TH' SPIRIT RIGHT OUT OF YOUR SOUL, YOU LITTLE CLOWN!
MUFFY! SUCH ANGER! WHERE DOES IT COME FROM, MUFFY?
©2009 Bill Griffith. World rights reserved. Distributed by King Features Syndicate
GRIFFY
12·22
I DON'T KNOW. I'VE BEEN IN THERAPY FOR YEARS. MY SHRINK SAYS IT'S ROOTED IN CHILDHOOD TRAUMA-- SOMETHING TO DO WITH FEAR OF ABANDONMENT.
TIP O' TH' PIN TO: JON BULLER
PERSONALLY, I THINK I'D BE ALL BETTER IF I JUST TOOK A MULTI-VITAMIN A DAY AND LEARNED TO PLAY TH' UKULELE.
GO FOR IT, MUFF!

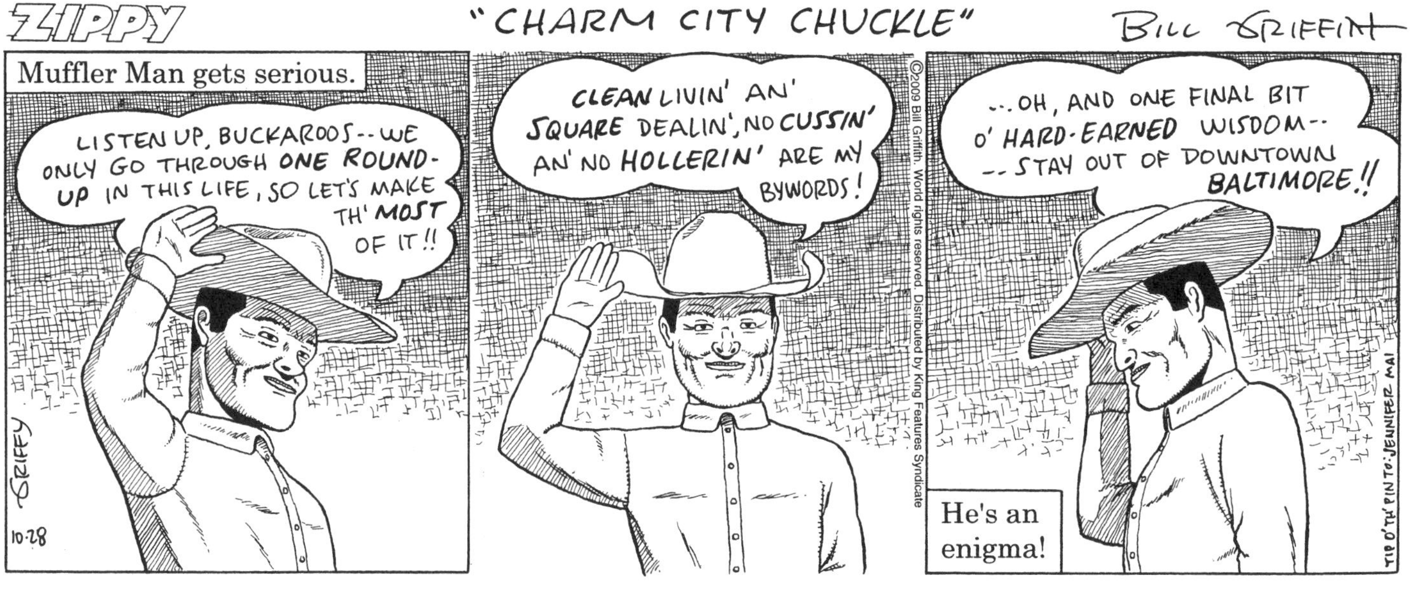
ZIPPY
"CHARM CITY CHUCKLE"
BILL GRIFFITH
Muffler Man gets serious.
LISTEN UP, BUCKAROOS-- WE ONLY GO THROUGH ONE ROUND-UP IN THIS LIFE, SO LET'S MAKE TH' MOST OF IT!!
GRIFFY
10·28
CLEAN LIVIN' AN' SQUARE DEALIN', NO CUSSIN' AN' NO HOLLERIN' ARE MY BYWORDS!
©2009 Bill Griffith. World rights reserved. Distributed by King Features Syndicate
...OH, AND ONE FINAL BIT O' HARD-EARNED WISDOM-- --STAY OUT OF DOWNTOWN BALTIMORE!!
He's an enigma!
TIP O' TH' PIN TO: JENNIFER MAI

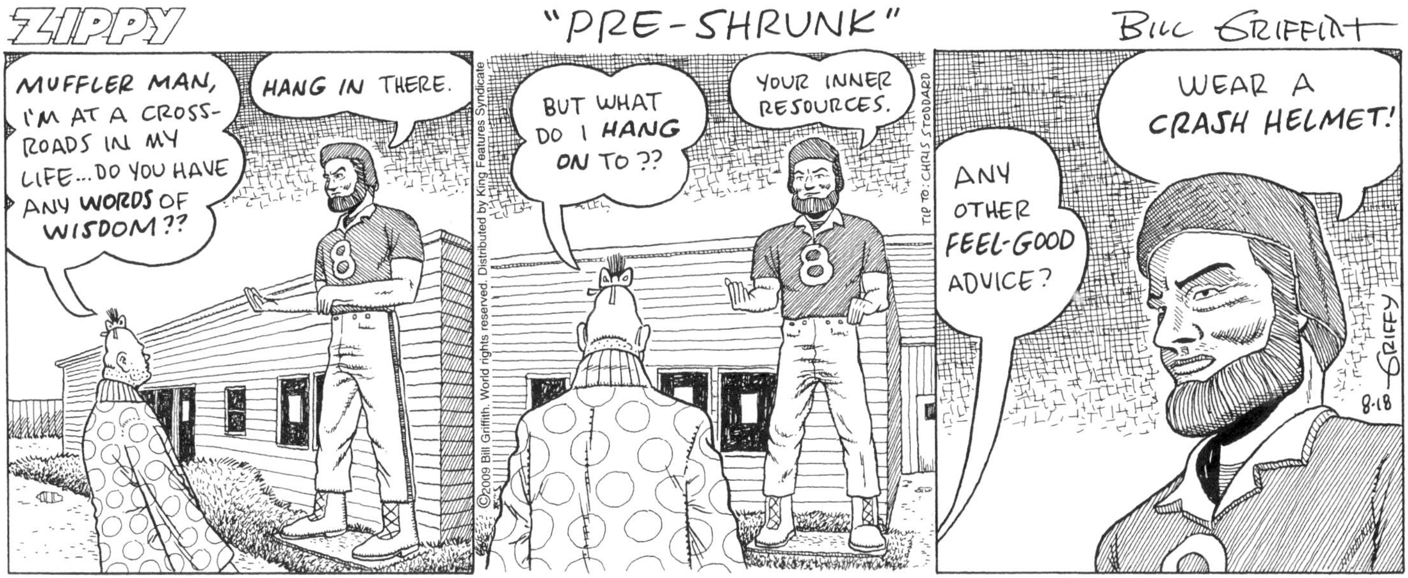
ZIPPY
"PRE-SHRUNK"
BILL GRIFFITH
MUFFLER MAN, I'M AT A CROSS-ROADS IN MY LIFE... DO YOU HAVE ANY WORDS OF WISDOM??
HANG IN THERE.
©2009 Bill Griffith. World rights reserved. Distributed by King Features Syndicate.
BUT WHAT DO I HANG ON TO??
YOUR INNER RESOURCES.
TIP TO: CHRIS STODDARD
ANY OTHER FEEL-GOOD ADVICE?
WEAR A CRASH HELMET!
GRIFFY 8-18

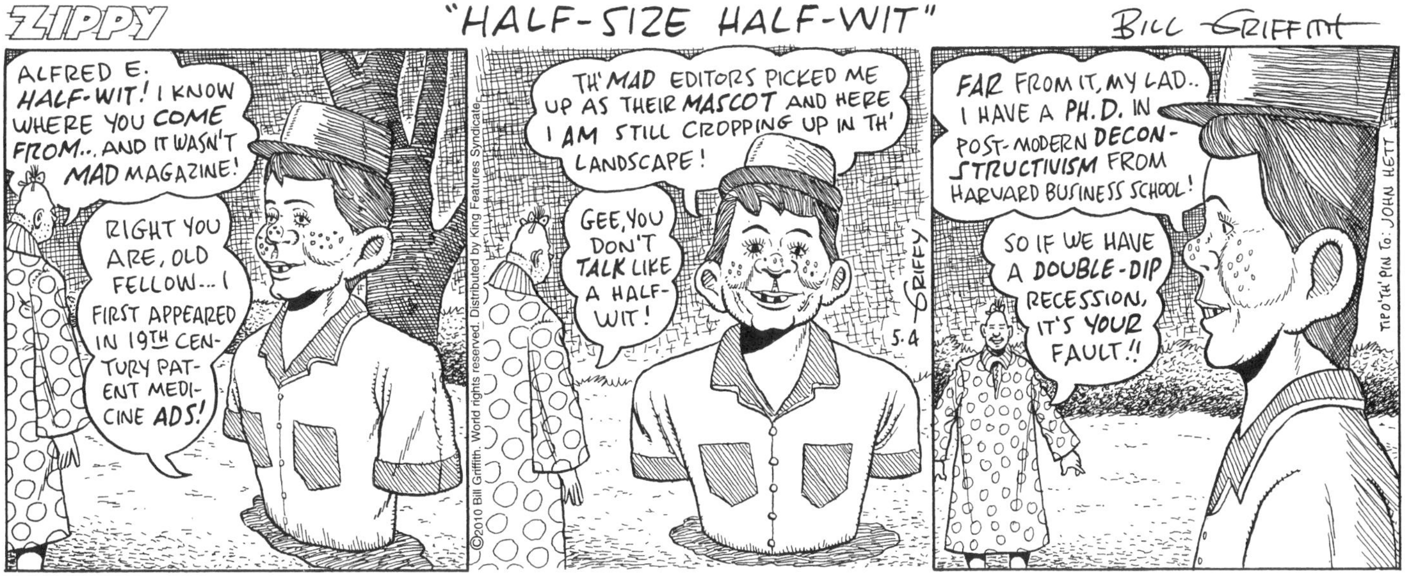
ZIPPY
"HALF-SIZE HALF-WIT"
BILL GRIFFITH
ALFRED E. HALF-WIT! I KNOW WHERE YOU COME FROM... AND IT WASN'T MAD MAGAZINE!
RIGHT YOU ARE, OLD FELLOW... I FIRST APPEARED IN 19TH CENTURY PATENT MEDICINE ADS!
©2010 Bill Griffith. World rights reserved. Distributed by King Features Syndicate.
TH' MAD EDITORS PICKED ME UP AS THEIR MASCOT AND HERE I AM STILL CROPPING UP IN TH' LANDSCAPE!
GEE, YOU DON'T TALK LIKE A HALF-WIT!
GRIFFY 5-4
FAR FROM IT, MY LAD.. I HAVE A PH.D. IN POST-MODERN DECONSTRUCTIVISM FROM HARVARD BUSINESS SCHOOL!
SO IF WE HAVE A DOUBLE-DIP RECESSION, IT'S YOUR FAULT!!
TIP O'TH' PIN TO: JOHN HETT

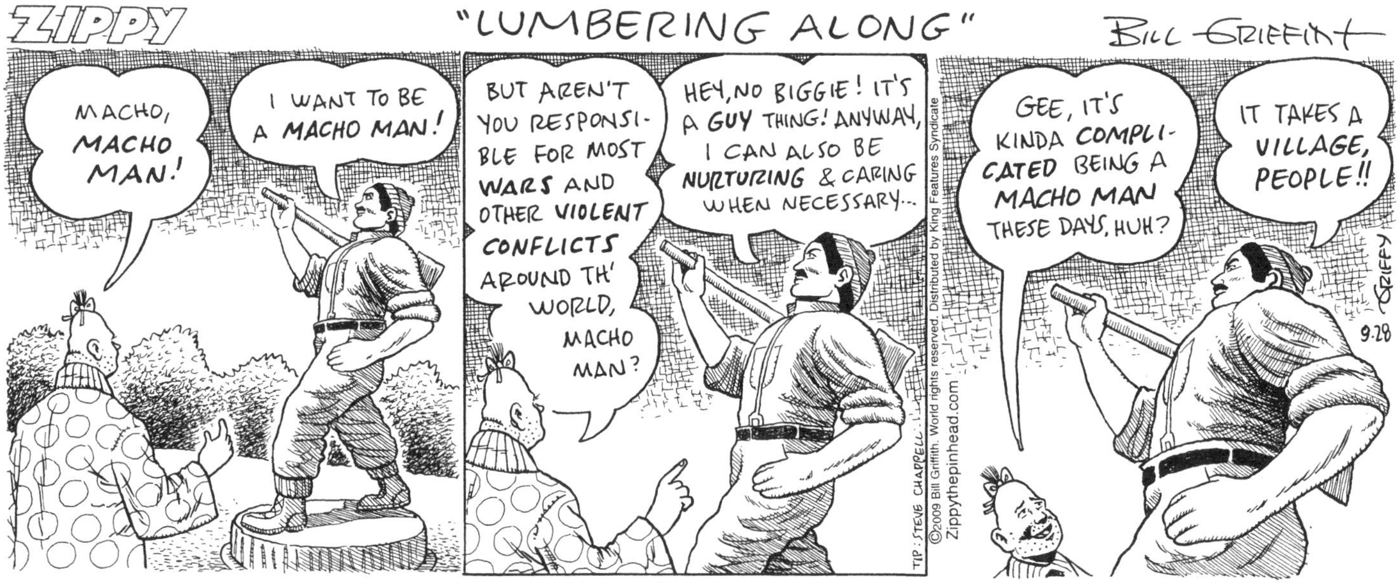
ZIPPY
"LUMBERING ALONG"
BILL GRIFFITH
MACHO, MACHO MAN!
I WANT TO BE A MACHO MAN!
BUT AREN'T YOU RESPONSIBLE FOR MOST WARS AND OTHER VIOLENT CONFLICTS AROUND TH' WORLD, MACHO MAN?
HEY, NO BIGGIE! IT'S A GUY THING! ANYWAY, I CAN ALSO BE NURTURING & CARING WHEN NECESSARY...
TIP: STEVE CHAPPELL
©2009 Bill Griffith. World rights reserved. Distributed by King Features Syndicate
Zippythepinhead.com
GEE, IT'S KINDA COMPLICATED BEING A MACHO MAN THESE DAYS, HUH?
IT TAKES A VILLAGE, PEOPLE!!
GRIFFY
9·28

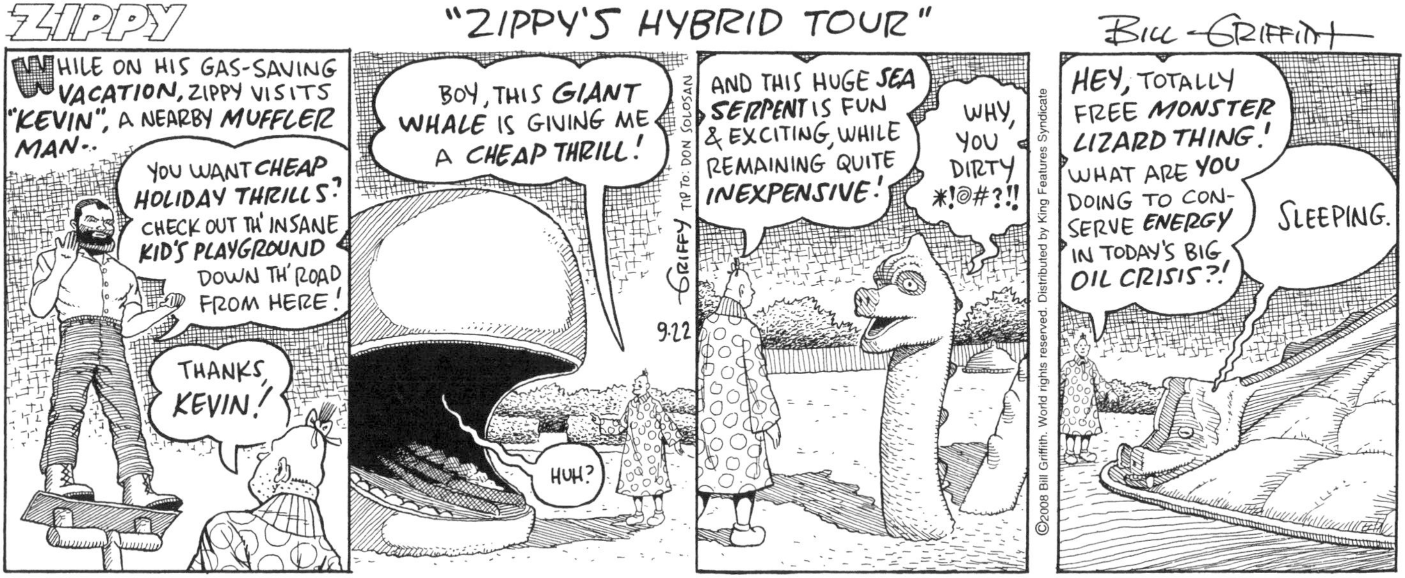
ZIPPY
"ZIPPY'S HYBRID TOUR"
BILL GRIFFITH
WHILE ON HIS GAS-SAVING VACATION, ZIPPY VISITS "KEVIN", A NEARBY MUFFLER MAN..
YOU WANT CHEAP HOLIDAY THRILLS? CHECK OUT TH' INSANE KID'S PLAYGROUND DOWN TH' ROAD FROM HERE!
THANKS, KEVIN!
BOY, THIS GIANT WHALE IS GIVING ME A CHEAP THRILL!
HUH?
TIP TO: DON SOLOSAN
GRIFFY
9·22
AND THIS HUGE SEA SERPENT IS FUN & EXCITING, WHILE REMAINING QUITE INEXPENSIVE!
WHY, YOU DIRTY *!@#?!!
©2008 Bill Griffith. World rights reserved. Distributed by King Features Syndicate
HEY, TOTALLY FREE MONSTER LIZARD THING! WHAT ARE YOU DOING TO CONSERVE ENERGY IN TODAY'S BIG OIL CRISIS?!
SLEEPING.

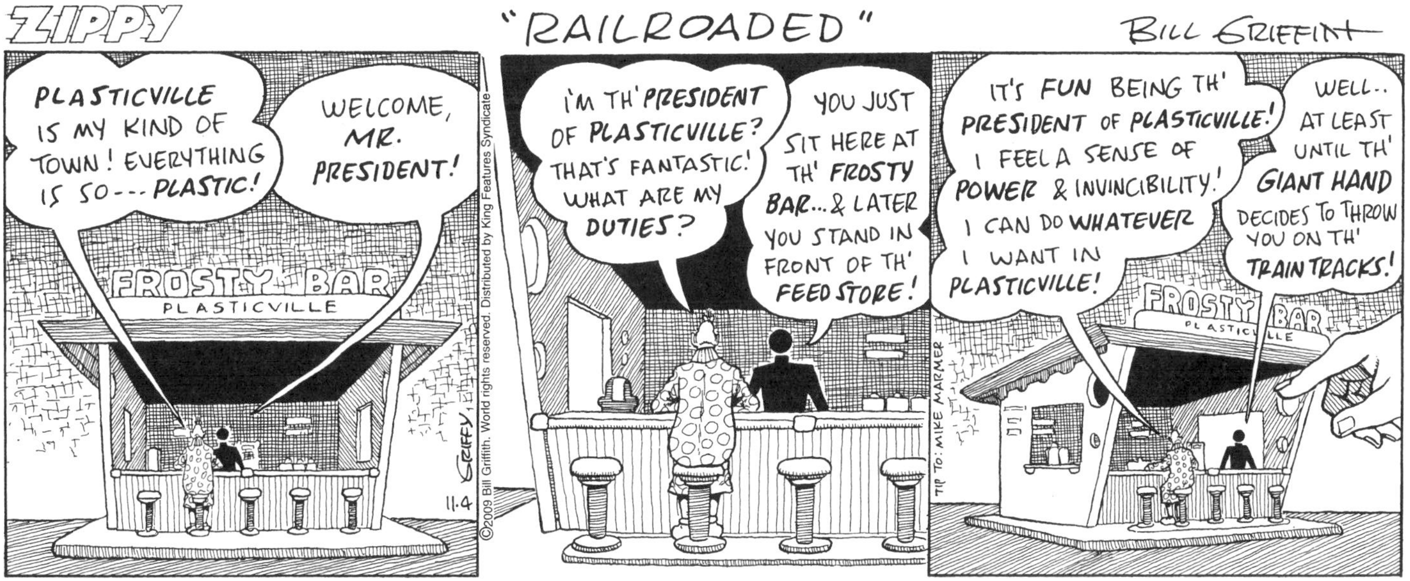
ZIPPY
"RAILROADED"
BILL GRIFFITH
PLASTICVILLE IS MY KIND OF TOWN! EVERYTHING IS SO--- PLASTIC!
WELCOME, MR. PRESIDENT!
FROSTY BAR
PLASTICVILLE
GRIFFY
11-4
©2009 Bill Griffith. World rights reserved. Distributed by King Features Syndicate.
I'M TH' PRESIDENT OF PLASTICVILLE? THAT'S FANTASTIC! WHAT ARE MY DUTIES?
YOU JUST SIT HERE AT TH' FROSTY BAR... & LATER YOU STAND IN FRONT OF TH' FEED STORE!
TIP TO: MIKE MARMER
IT'S FUN BEING TH' PRESIDENT OF PLASTICVILLE! I FEEL A SENSE OF POWER & INVINCIBILITY! I CAN DO WHATEVER I WANT IN PLASTICVILLE!
WELL.. AT LEAST UNTIL TH' GIANT HAND DECIDES TO THROW YOU ON TH' TRAIN TRACKS!

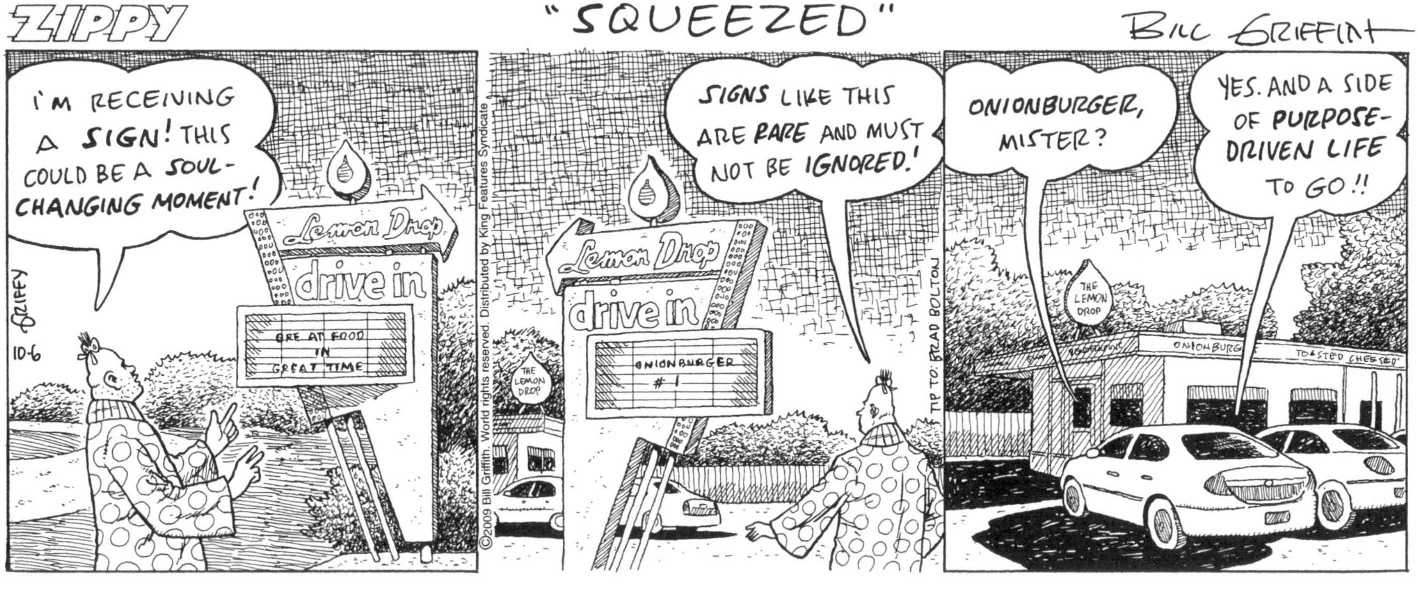
ZIPPY
"SQUEEZED"
BILL GRIFFITH
I'M RECEIVING A SIGN! THIS COULD BE A SOUL-CHANGING MOMENT!
Lemon Drop
drive in
GREAT FOOD
IN
GREAT TIME
GRIFFY
10-6
©2009 Bill Griffith. World rights reserved. Distributed by King Features Syndicate.
SIGNS LIKE THIS ARE RARE AND MUST NOT BE IGNORED!
THE LEMON DROP
ONIONBURGER
1
TIP TO: BRAD BOLTON
ONIONBURGER, MISTER?
YES. AND A SIDE OF PURPOSE-DRIVEN LIFE TO GO!!

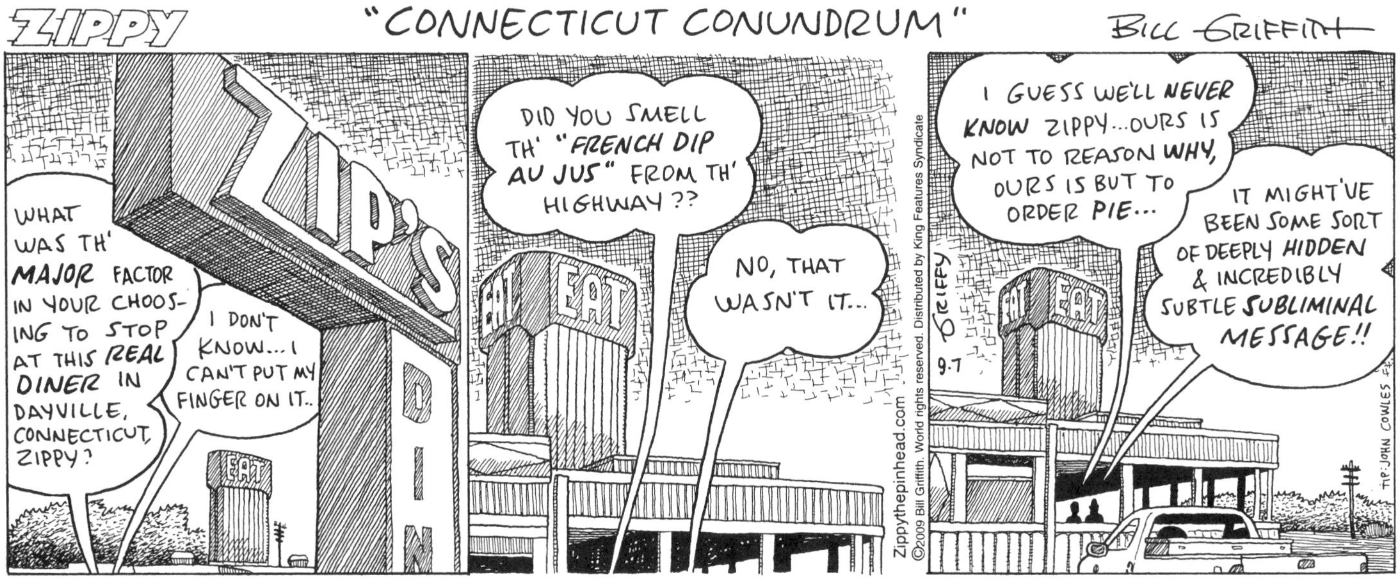
ZIPPY
"CONNECTICUT CONUNDRUM"
BILL GRIFFITH
ZIP'S
WHAT WAS TH' MAJOR FACTOR IN YOUR CHOOSING TO STOP AT THIS REAL DINER IN DAYVILLE, CONNECTICUT, ZIPPY?
I DON'T KNOW... I CAN'T PUT MY FINGER ON IT..
EAT
DID YOU SMELL TH' "FRENCH DIP AU JUS" FROM TH' HIGHWAY??
NO, THAT WASN'T IT...
I GUESS WE'LL NEVER KNOW ZIPPY...OURS IS NOT TO REASON WHY, OURS IS BUT TO ORDER PIE...
IT MIGHT'VE BEEN SOME SORT OF DEEPLY HIDDEN & INCREDIBLY SUBTLE SUBLIMINAL MESSAGE!!
GRIFFY 9.7
TIP: JOHN COWLES
Zippythepinhead.com ©2009 Bill Griffith. World rights reserved. Distributed by King Features Syndicate

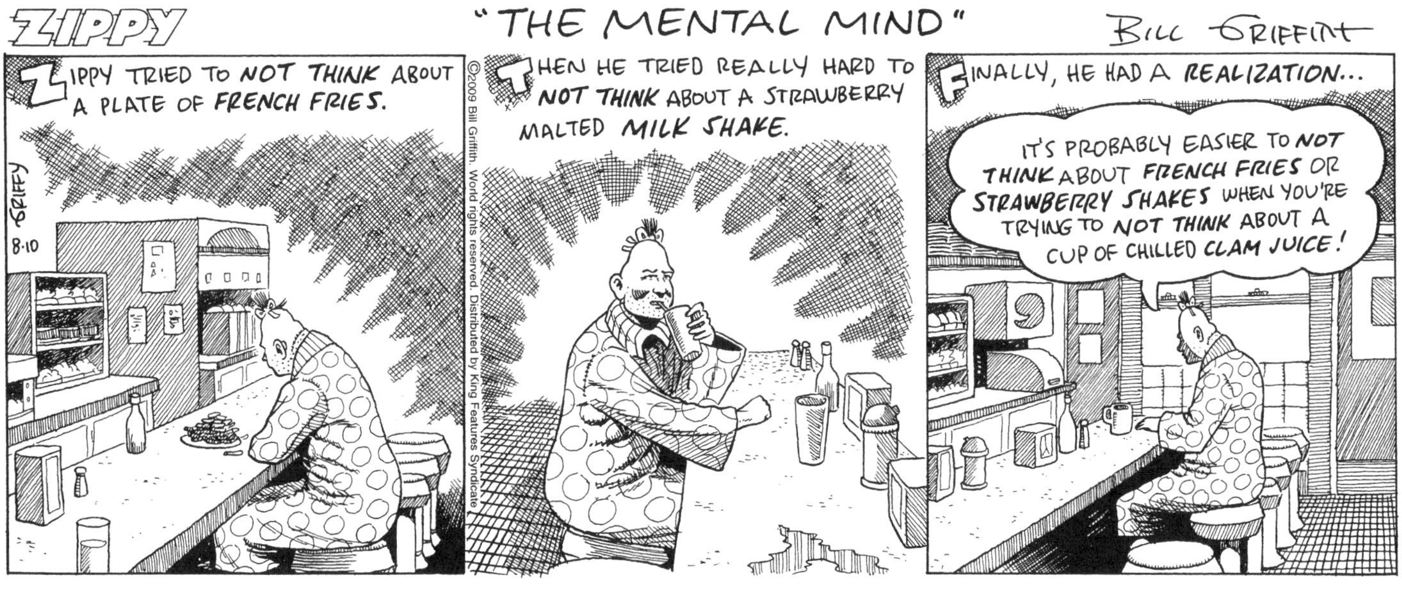
ZIPPY
"THE MENTAL MIND"
BILL GRIFFITH
ZIPPY TRIED TO NOT THINK ABOUT A PLATE OF FRENCH FRIES.
GRIFFY 8.10
©2009 Bill Griffith. World rights reserved. Distributed by King Features Syndicate
THEN HE TRIED REALLY HARD TO NOT THINK ABOUT A STRAWBERRY MALTED MILK SHAKE.
FINALLY, HE HAD A REALIZATION...
IT'S PROBABLY EASIER TO NOT THINK ABOUT FRENCH FRIES OR STRAWBERRY SHAKES WHEN YOU'RE TRYING TO NOT THINK ABOUT A CUP OF CHILLED CLAM JUICE!

SUNDAY COLOR

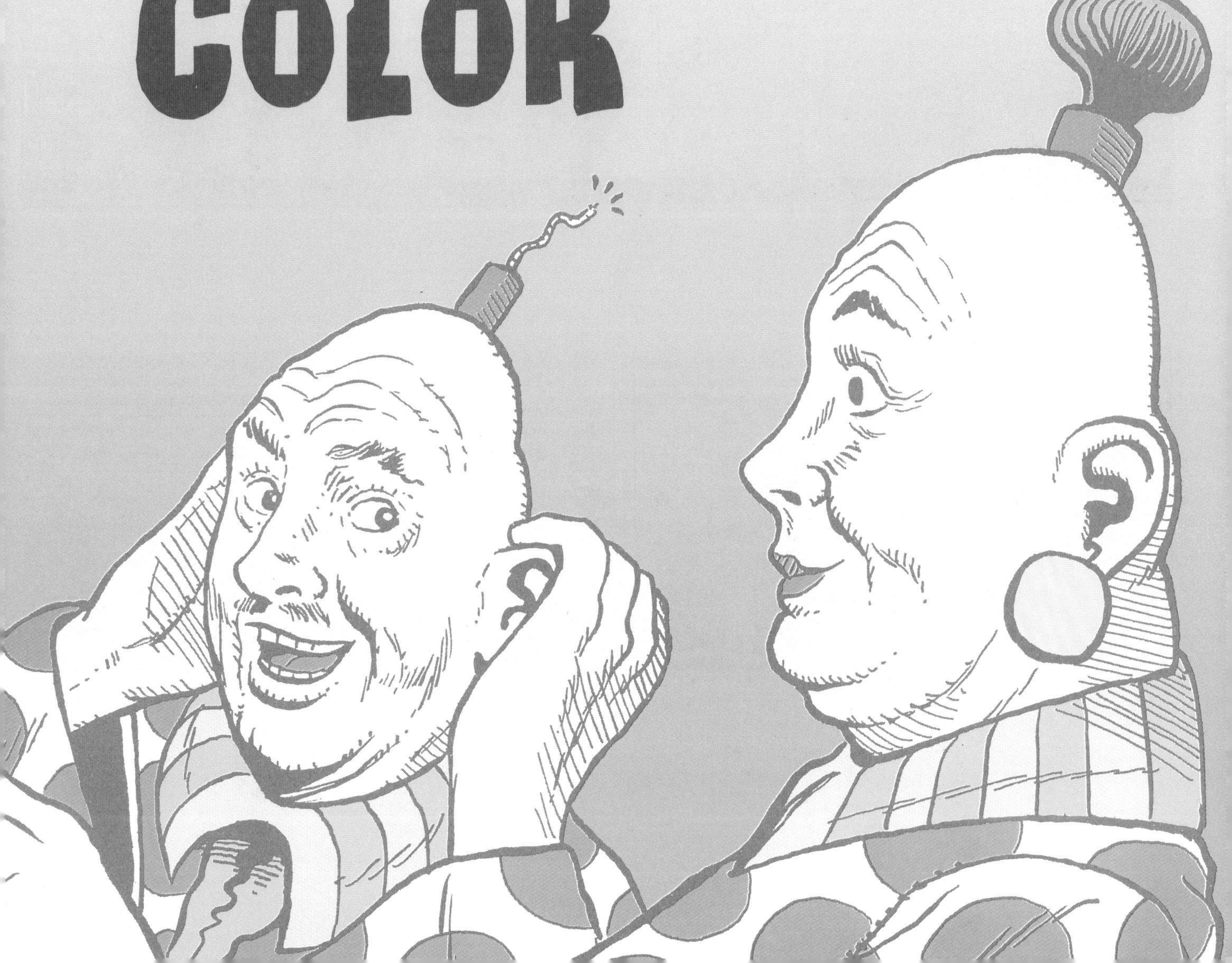

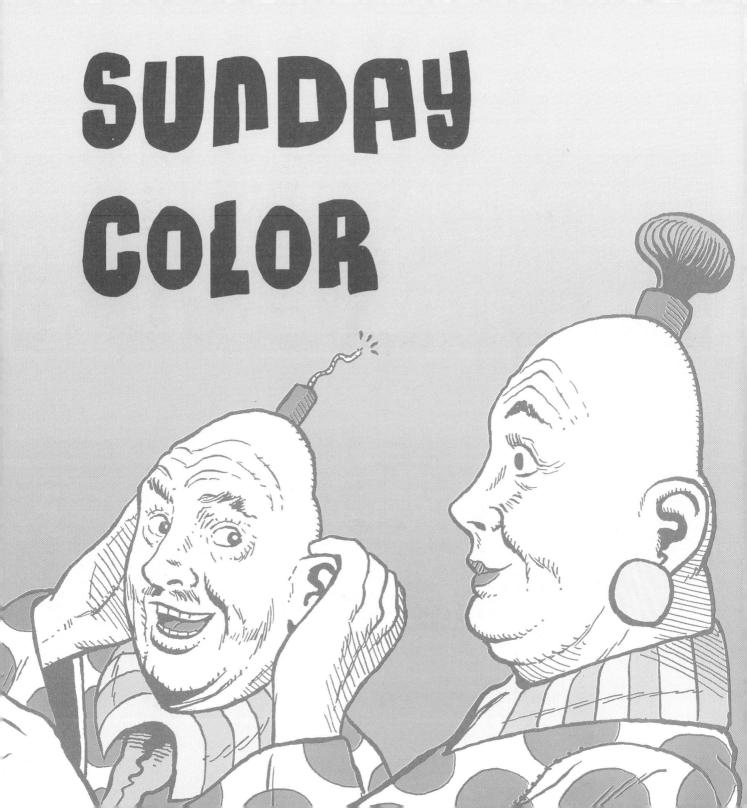

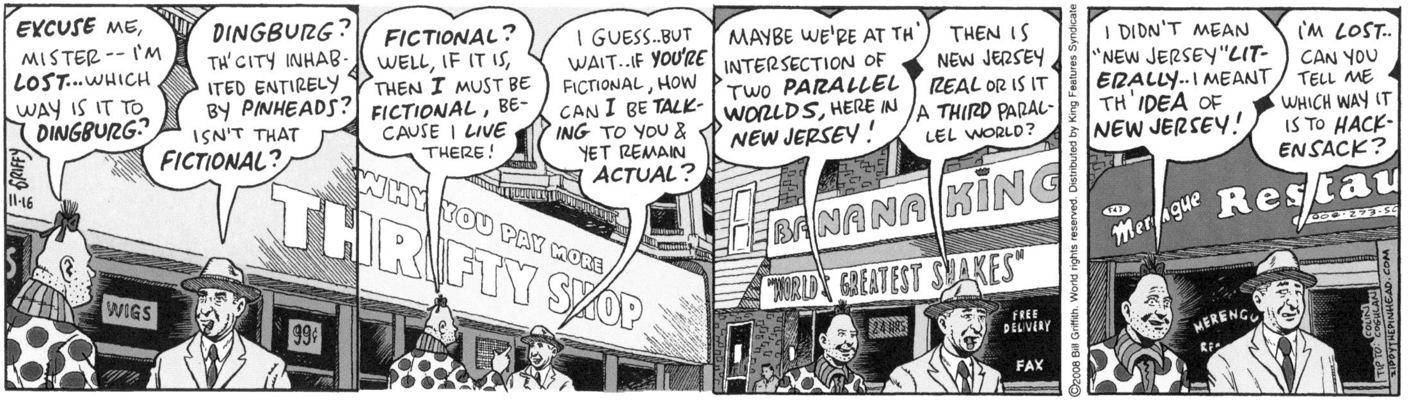
EXCUSE ME, MISTER -- I'M LOST... WHICH WAY IS IT TO DINGBURG?
DINGBURG? TH' CITY INHABITED ENTIRELY BY PINHEADS? ISN'T THAT FICTIONAL?
GRIFFY 11-16
THRIFTY
WIGS
99¢
FICTIONAL? WELL, IF IT IS, THEN I MUST BE FICTIONAL, BECAUSE I LIVE THERE!
I GUESS.. BUT WAIT.. IF YOU'RE FICTIONAL, HOW CAN I BE TALKING TO YOU & YET REMAIN ACTUAL?
WHY YOU PAY MORE
THRIFTY SHOP
MAYBE WE'RE AT TH' INTERSECTION OF TWO PARALLEL WORLDS, HERE IN NEW JERSEY!
THEN IS NEW JERSEY REAL OR IS IT A THIRD PARALLEL WORLD?
BANANA KING
"WORLD'S GREATEST SHAKES"
FREE DELIVERY
FAX
I DIDN'T MEAN "NEW JERSEY" LITERALLY.. I MEANT TH' IDEA OF NEW JERSEY!
I'M LOST.. CAN YOU TELL ME WHICH WAY IT IS TO HACKENSACK?
Merengue Restau
TIP TO: COLIN COGHLAN ZIPPYTHEPINHEAD.COM
©2008 Bill Griffith. World rights reserved. Distributed by King Features Syndicate

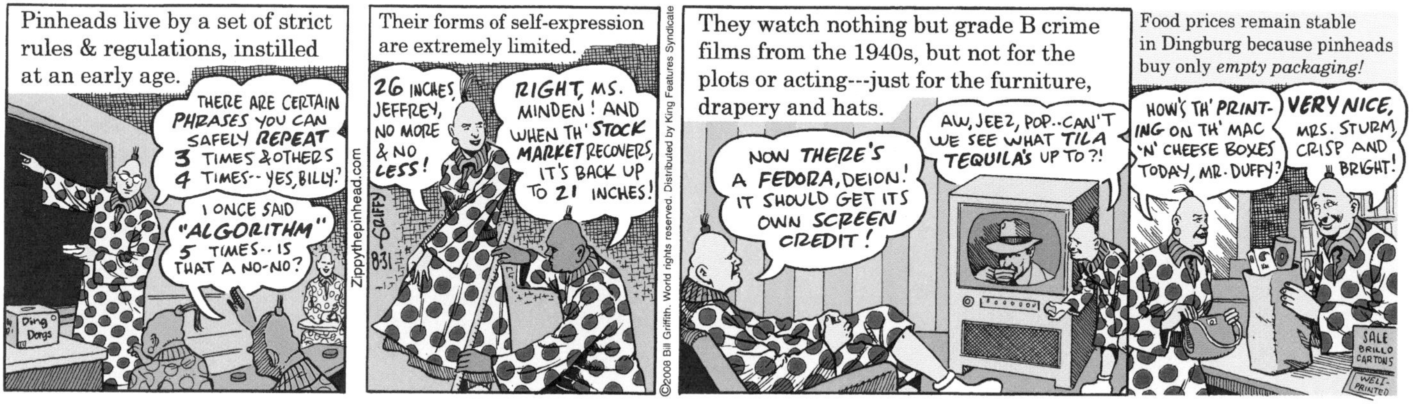
Pinheads live by a set of strict rules & regulations, instilled at an early age.
THERE ARE CERTAIN PHRASES YOU CAN SAFELY REPEAT 3 TIMES & OTHERS 4 TIMES-- YES, BILLY?
I ONCE SAID "ALGORITHM" 5 TIMES.. IS THAT A NO-NO?
Ding Dongs
Their forms of self-expression are extremely limited.
26 INCHES, JEFFREY, NO MORE & NO LESS!
RIGHT, MS. MINDEN! AND WHEN TH' STOCK MARKET RECOVERS, IT'S BACK UP TO 21 INCHES!
Zippythepinhead.com
GRIFFY 8-31
©2008 Bill Griffith. World rights reserved. Distributed by King Features Syndicate
They watch nothing but grade B crime films from the 1940s, but not for the plots or acting---just for the furniture, drapery and hats.
NOW THERE'S A FEDORA, DEION! IT SHOULD GET ITS OWN SCREEN CREDIT!
AW, JEEZ, POP.. CAN'T WE SEE WHAT TILA TEQUILA'S UP TO?!
Food prices remain stable in Dingburg because pinheads buy only empty packaging!
HOW'S TH' PRINTING ON TH' MAC 'N' CHEESE BOXES TODAY, MR. DUFFY?
VERY NICE, MRS. STURM, CRISP AND BRIGHT!
SALE BRILLO CARTONS
WELL-PRINTED

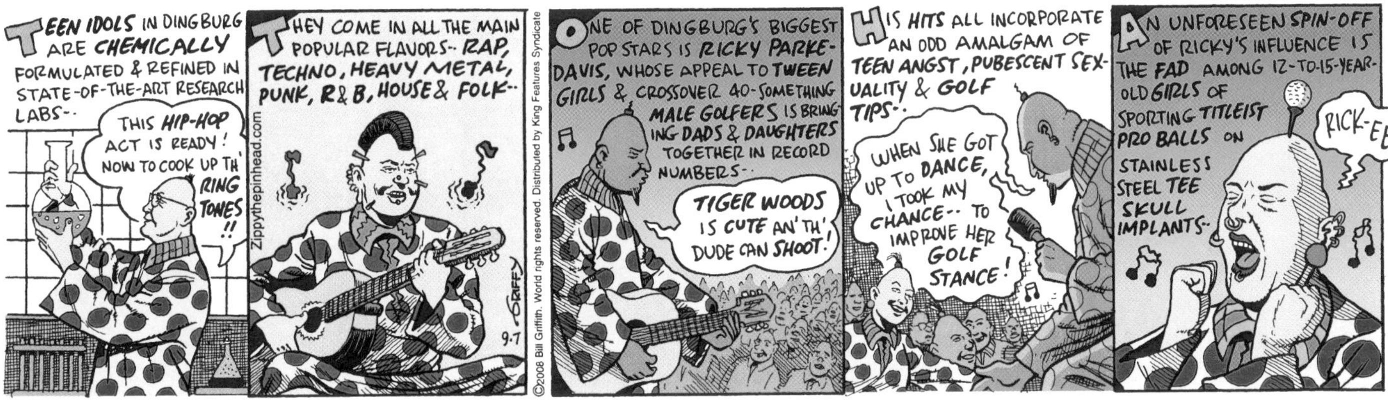
TEEN IDOLS IN DINGBURG ARE CHEMICALLY FORMULATED & REFINED IN STATE-OF-THE-ART RESEARCH LABS--
THIS HIP-HOP ACT IS READY! NOW TO COOK UP TH' RING TONES!!
THEY COME IN ALL THE MAIN POPULAR FLAVORS-- RAP, TECHNO, HEAVY METAL, PUNK, R&B, HOUSE & FOLK--
Zippythepinhead.com
GRIFFY
9-7
©2008 Bill Griffith. World rights reserved. Distributed by King Features Syndicate
ONE OF DINGBURG'S BIGGEST POP STARS IS RICKY PARKE-DAVIS, WHOSE APPEAL TO TWEEN GIRLS & CROSSOVER 40-SOMETHING MALE GOLFERS IS BRINGING DADS & DAUGHTERS TOGETHER IN RECORD NUMBERS--
TIGER WOODS IS CUTE AN' TH' DUDE CAN SHOOT!
HIS HITS ALL INCORPORATE AN ODD AMALGAM OF TEEN ANGST, PUBESCENT SEXUALITY & GOLF TIPS--
WHEN SHE GOT UP TO DANCE, I TOOK MY CHANCE-- TO IMPROVE HER GOLF STANCE!
AN UNFORESEEN SPIN-OFF OF RICKY'S INFLUENCE IS THE FAD AMONG 12-TO-15-YEAR-OLD GIRLS OF SPORTING TITLEIST PRO BALLS ON STAINLESS STEEL TEE SKULL IMPLANTS--
RICK-EE!

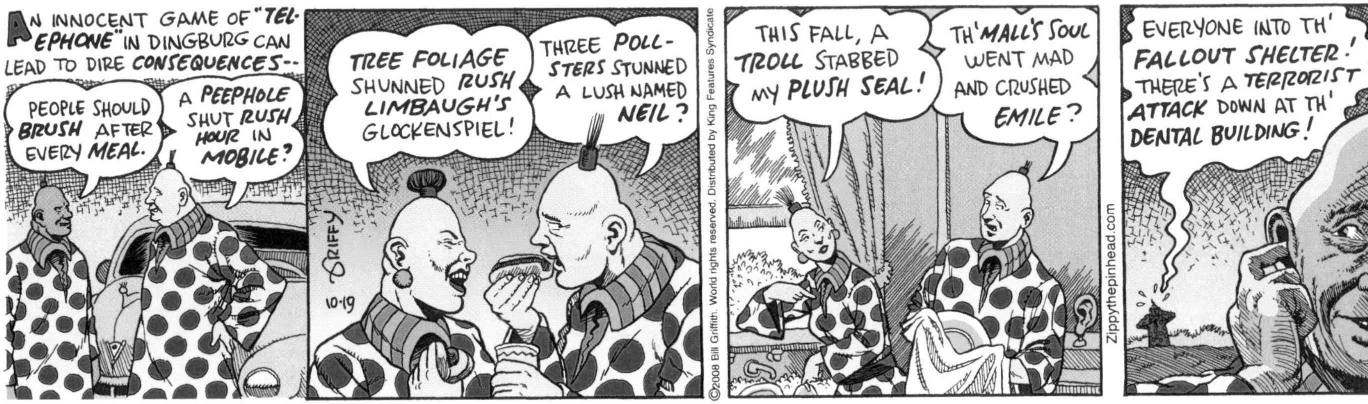
AN INNOCENT GAME OF "TELEPHONE" IN DINGBURG CAN LEAD TO DIRE CONSEQUENCES--
PEOPLE SHOULD BRUSH AFTER EVERY MEAL.
A PEEPHOLE SHUT RUSH HOUR IN MOBILE?
GRIFFY
10-19
TREE FOLIAGE SHUNNED RUSH LIMBAUGH'S GLOCKENSPIEL!
THREE POLLSTERS STUNNED A LUSH NAMED NEIL?
©2008 Bill Griffith. World rights reserved. Distributed by King Features Syndicate
THIS FALL, A TROLL STABBED MY PLUSH SEAL!
TH' MALL'S SOUL WENT MAD AND CRUSHED EMILE?
EVERYONE INTO TH' FALLOUT SHELTER! THERE'S A TERRORIST ATTACK DOWN AT TH' DENTAL BUILDING!
Zippythepinhead.com

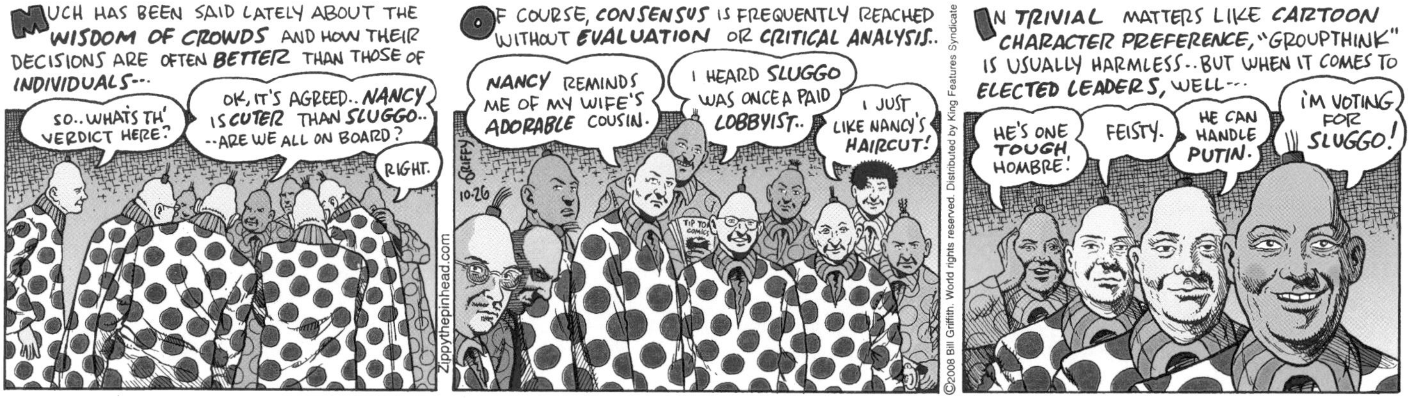
MUCH HAS BEEN SAID LATELY ABOUT THE WISDOM OF CROWDS AND HOW THEIR DECISIONS ARE OFTEN BETTER THAN THOSE OF INDIVIDUALS---
SO..WHAT'S TH' VERDICT HERE?
OK, IT'S AGREED..NANCY IS CUTER THAN SLUGGO.. --ARE WE ALL ON BOARD?
RIGHT.
Zippythepinhead.com
GRIFFY 10-26
OF COURSE, CONSENSUS IS FREQUENTLY REACHED WITHOUT EVALUATION OR CRITICAL ANALYSIS..
NANCY REMINDS ME OF MY WIFE'S ADORABLE COUSIN.
I HEARD SLUGGO WAS ONCE A PAID LOBBYIST..
I JUST LIKE NANCY'S HAIRCUT!
TIP TOP COMICS
©2008 Bill Griffith. World rights reserved. Distributed by King Features Syndicate
IN TRIVIAL MATTERS LIKE CARTOON CHARACTER PREFERENCE, "GROUPTHINK" IS USUALLY HARMLESS..BUT WHEN IT COMES TO ELECTED LEADERS, WELL---
HE'S ONE TOUGH HOMBRE!
FEISTY.
HE CAN HANDLE PUTIN.
I'M VOTING FOR SLUGGO!

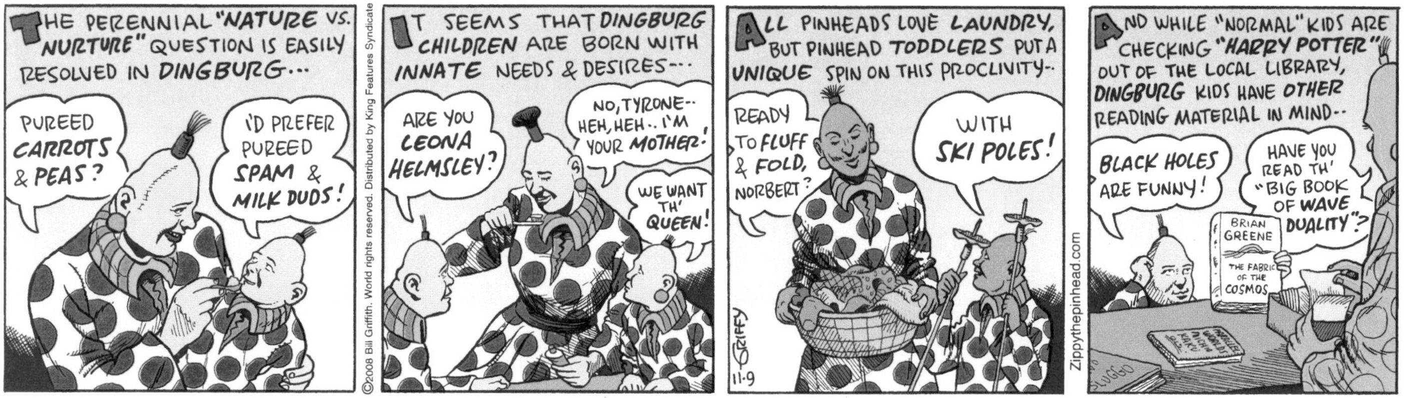
THE PERENNIAL "NATURE VS. NURTURE" QUESTION IS EASILY RESOLVED IN DINGBURG...
PUREED CARROTS & PEAS?
I'D PREFER PUREED SPAM & MILK DUDS!
©2008 Bill Griffith. World rights reserved. Distributed by King Features Syndicate
IT SEEMS THAT DINGBURG CHILDREN ARE BORN WITH INNATE NEEDS & DESIRES---
ARE YOU LEONA HELMSLEY?
NO, TYRONE-- HEH, HEH..I'M YOUR MOTHER!
WE WANT TH' QUEEN!
ALL PINHEADS LOVE LAUNDRY, BUT PINHEAD TODDLERS PUT A UNIQUE SPIN ON THIS PROCLIVITY--
READY TO FLUFF & FOLD, NORBERT?
WITH SKI POLES!
GRIFFY 11-9
Zippythepinhead.com
AND WHILE "NORMAL" KIDS ARE CHECKING "HARRY POTTER" OUT OF THE LOCAL LIBRARY, DINGBURG KIDS HAVE OTHER READING MATERIAL IN MIND--
BLACK HOLES ARE FUNNY!
HAVE YOU READ TH' "BIG BOOK OF WAVE DUALITY"?
BRIAN GREENE THE FABRIC OF THE COSMOS
SLUGGO

©2008 Bill Griffith. World rights reserved. Distributed by King Features Syndicate
DO WE HAVE A RIGHT TO BE EXCITED?
AND IF WE DO, HOW EXCITED DO WE HAVE A RIGHT TO BE?
AND IF WE'RE ALWAYS EXCITED, WHO WILL BUILD THE ROADS & GROW THE FOOD & CONNECT US TO THE INTERNET & SUPPLY US WITH SUPERHERO MOVIES & ELECTRICITY?
GRIFFY
11-23
Zippythepinhead.com
OH, WELL, WHY WORRY ABOUT THESE THINGS? AFTER ALL, WE ALL HAVE SUCH TINY ATTENTION SPANS, IT'S ENOUGH EFFORT JUST TO DECIDE WHICH ULTRA-CAFFEIN-ATED "ENERGY DRINK" TO BUY--
JOLT COLA? OR JOLT CHERRY BOMB?

HOW ARE COMICS MADE? IN DINGBURG, THE ANSWER IS: STILL THE "OLD SCHOOL" WAY. FIRST A CARTOONIST "PENCILS" A PAGE!!
©2009 Bill Griffith. World rights reserved. Distributed by King Features Syndicate
NEXT, INK IS APPLIED IN A STRANGE PROCESS CALLED "DRAWING BY HAND." THE FINAL INKED & LETTERED PAGE IS THEN ERASED OF ITS PENCIL LINES!!
GRIFFY
3-22
COURIERS RUSH THE FINISHED COMIC ART TO A 4-COLOR WEB PRESS SOMEWHERE IN ELKO, NEVADA!!
COMIC ART
RUSH
Zippythepinhead.com
FINALLY, READERS PURCHASE THE COPIES, PRINTED ON LARGE SHEETS OF PAPER, REQUIRING NOT A SINGLE LOG-IN USER NAME OR PASSWORD!!
HA, HA.
I DON'T GET IT.

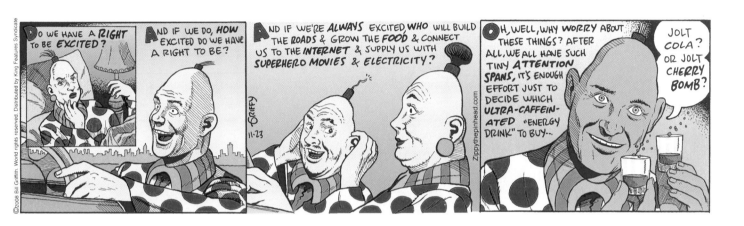

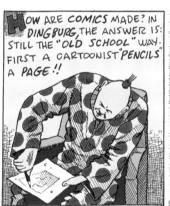

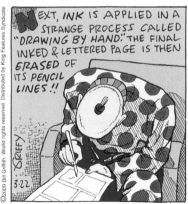

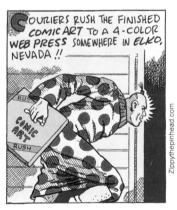

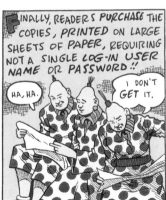

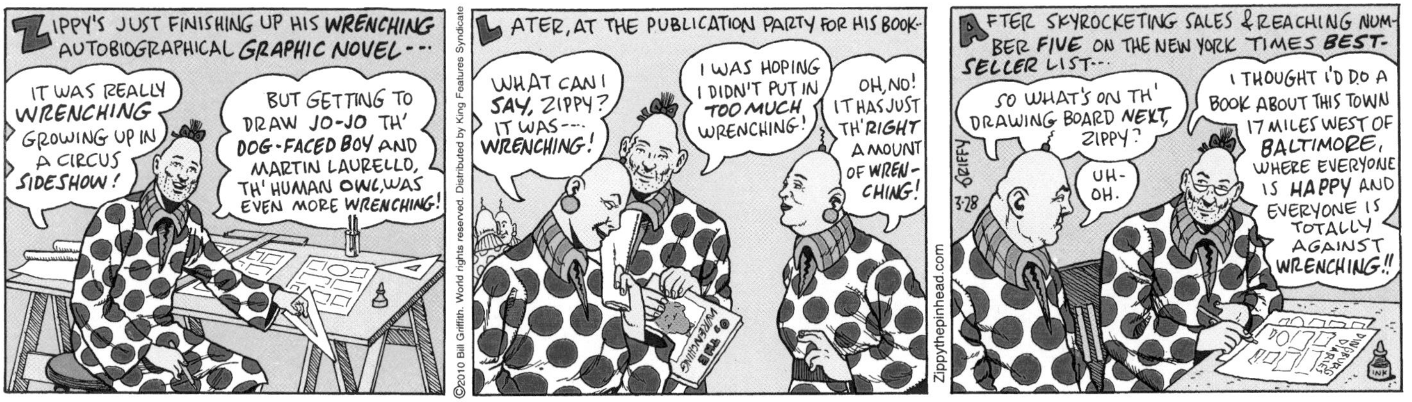
ZIPPY'S JUST FINISHING UP HIS WRENCHING AUTOBIOGRAPHICAL GRAPHIC NOVEL---
IT WAS REALLY WRENCHING GROWING UP IN A CIRCUS SIDESHOW!
BUT GETTING TO DRAW JO-JO TH' DOG-FACED BOY AND MARTIN LAURELLO, TH' HUMAN OWL, WAS EVEN MORE WRENCHING!
©2010 Bill Griffith. World rights reserved. Distributed by King Features Syndicate
LATER, AT THE PUBLICATION PARTY FOR HIS BOOK..
WHAT CAN I SAY, ZIPPY? IT WAS--- WRENCHING!
I WAS HOPING I DIDN'T PUT IN TOO MUCH WRENCHING!
OH, NO! IT HAS JUST TH' RIGHT AMOUNT OF WREN-CHING!
Zippythepinhead.com
AFTER SKYROCKETING SALES & REACHING NUMBER FIVE ON THE NEW YORK TIMES BEST-SELLER LIST---
SO WHAT'S ON TH' DRAWING BOARD NEXT, ZIPPY?
UH-OH.
I THOUGHT I'D DO A BOOK ABOUT THIS TOWN 17 MILES WEST OF BALTIMORE, WHERE EVERYONE IS HAPPY AND EVERYONE IS TOTALLY AGAINST WRENCHING!!
GRIFFY
3-28
DINGBURG DIARIES
INK

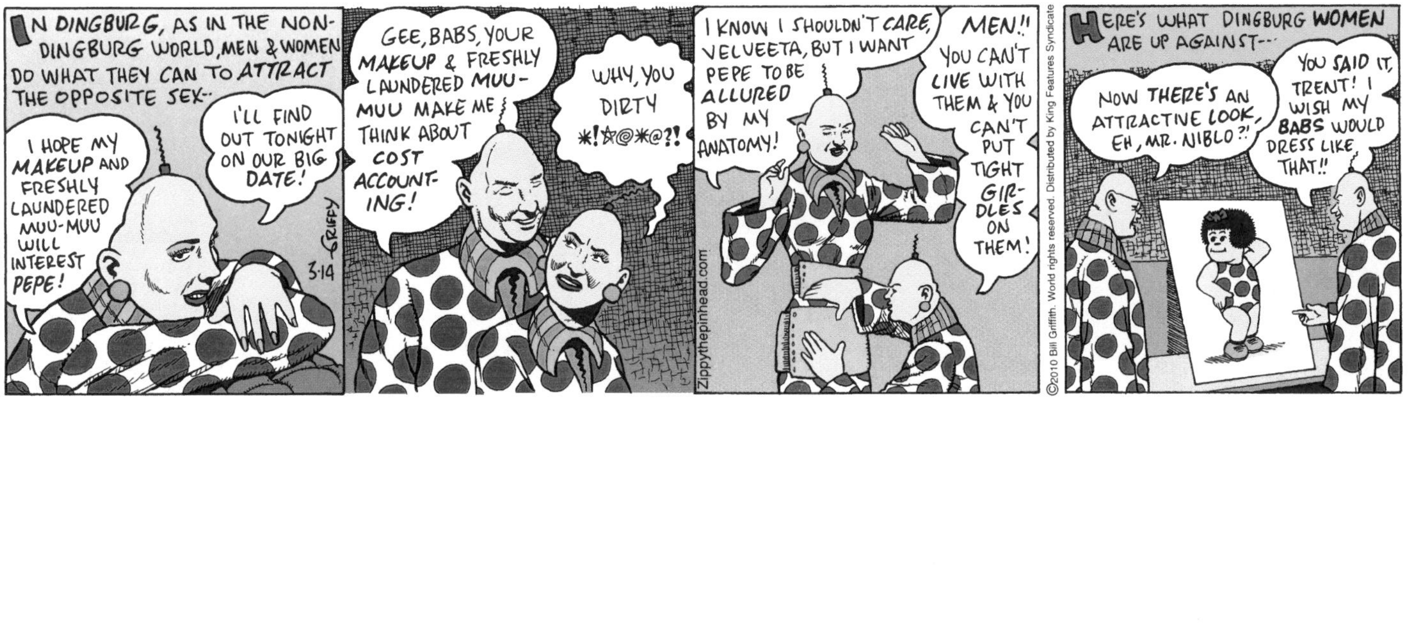
IN DINGBURG, AS IN THE NON-DINGBURG WORLD, MEN & WOMEN DO WHAT THEY CAN TO ATTRACT THE OPPOSITE SEX..
I HOPE MY MAKEUP AND FRESHLY LAUNDERED MUU-MUU WILL INTEREST PEPE!
I'LL FIND OUT TONIGHT ON OUR BIG DATE!
GRIFFY
3-14
GEE, BABS, YOUR MAKEUP & FRESHLY LAUNDERED MUU-MUU MAKE ME THINK ABOUT COST ACCOUNT-ING!
WHY, YOU DIRTY *!☆@*@?!
Zippythepinhead.com
I KNOW I SHOULDN'T CARE, VELVEETA, BUT I WANT PEPE TO BE ALLURED BY MY ANATOMY!
MEN!! YOU CAN'T LIVE WITH THEM & YOU CAN'T PUT TIGHT GIR-DLES ON THEM!
©2010 Bill Griffith. World rights reserved. Distributed by King Features Syndicate
HERE'S WHAT DINGBURG WOMEN ARE UP AGAINST---
NOW THERE'S AN ATTRACTIVE LOOK, EH, MR. NIBLO?!
YOU SAID IT, TRENT! I WISH MY BABS WOULD DRESS LIKE THAT!!

In late November, all Dingburgers must submit to an examination of their puffy footwear.
THESE COULD USE ANOTHER 1/2" OF STYROFOAM.
HIGH-DENSITY, OF COURSE!
©2009 Bill Griffith. World rights reserved. Distributed by King Features Syndicate
Once they've passed muster, they're rewarded with an afternoon of "Zen Bowling" (you never release the ball because you *are* the ball).
LARRY--, ARE YOU...?
YES, SHOSHAWNA! I'M FROZEN IN POSITION AGAIN!
Zippythepinhead.com
GRIFFY 11-29
All that meditative activity produces a powerful thirst, so it's Taco Sauce Spritzer time, followed by a trip to Baltimore.
MMM!
FIZZY!
TACO SAUCE
And, naturally, no trip to Baltimore is complete without a trunkload of lard.
IS FORTY POUNDS ENOUGH?
IT WAS LAST TIME, SILLY!!

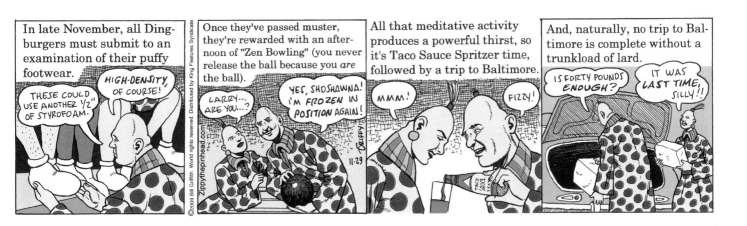

Dingburg is a hotbed of artistic activity.
GRIFFY 12-27
Zippythepinhead.com
But, unlike most artists, they toil away for neither fame nor fortune.
When a Dingburg *artiste* completes a painting or drawing, the only reward he or she seeks is a pastrami sandwich, with pickle.
©2009 Bill Griffith. World rights reserved. Distributed by King Features Syndicate
THANKS, HON! AS SOON AS I DIGEST MY PASTRAMI ON RYE, I'LL TAKE MY PAINTING TO A PRESTIGIOUS DOWNTOWN GALLERY & SELL IT FOR A TIDY SUM!
GREAT, ETON! I'LL SLATHER ON EXTRA HORSERADISH FOR GOOD LUCK!

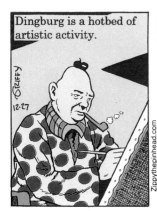

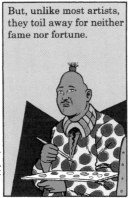

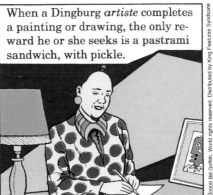

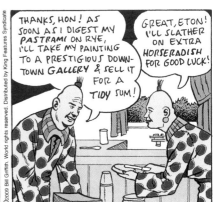

Otto left in a huff--- Estelle had no idea why.
OH, OTTO!
MNNNNF!
Zippythepinhead.com
Later that day, while administering a taco sauce taste test to the kids, Estelle had an *idea*.
IDEAS ARE LIKE LITTLE WOODPECKERS.
YUM, HUH?
UM.
GRIFFY
She visualized Otto as a professional wrestler named "The Crusher." She imagined him receiving a cranial reduction procedure.
HOLD STILL.
©2010 Bill Griffith. World rights reserved. Distributed by King Features Syndicate
That evening, Otto returned home in much better spirits, and both Otto and Estelle decided to become Scientologists.

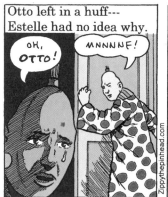

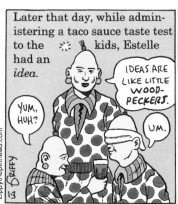

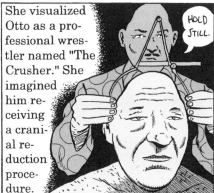

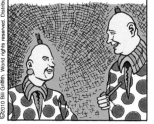

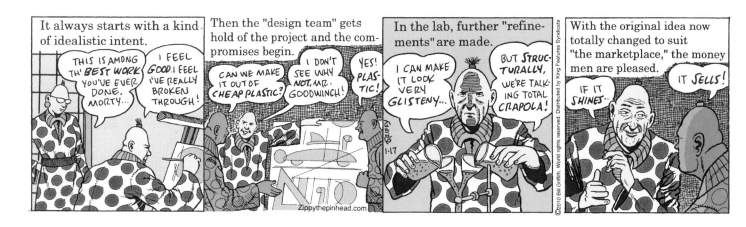

It always starts with a kind of idealistic intent.
THIS IS AMONG TH' BEST WORK YOU'VE EVER DONE, MORTY...
I FEEL GOOD. I FEEL I'VE REALLY BROKEN THROUGH!
Then the "design team" gets hold of the project and the compromises begin.
CAN WE MAKE IT OUT OF CHEAP PLASTIC?
I DON'T SEE WHY NOT, MR. GOODWINCH!
YES! PLASTIC!
Zippythepinhead.com
In the lab, further "refinements" are made.
I CAN MAKE IT LOOK VERY GLISTENY...
BUT STRUCTURALLY, WE'RE TALKING TOTAL CRAPOLA!
GRIFFY 1-17
©2010 Bill Griffith. World rights reserved. Distributed by King Features Syndicate
With the original idea now totally changed to suit "the marketplace," the money men are pleased.
IF IT SHINES..
IT SELLS!

IT WAS DECIDED THAT DINGBURG NEEDED A MAKEOVER TO BECOME ATTRACTIVE TO THE YOUNGER DEMOGRAPHIC--SO TODD NABISCO TOOK THE PLUNGE--
THIS POTION WILL BRING OUT MY DARK SIDE!
OH, TODD!
GRIFFY
1-24
TODD BECAME "TODNAB" & WENT ON A QUEST TO SAVE A FEW MAGIC RINGS & DESTROY AN EVIL OVERLORD OR TWO--
I'M CONFLICTED, ALSO!
Zippythepinhead.com
HOWEVER--
A PITCH-FORK? THAT'S YOUR MAGIC WEAPON?!
NO GOOD?
©2010 Bill Griffith. World rights reserved. Distributed by King Features Syndicate
TEENS & TWENTY-SOMETHINGS STAYED AWAY IN DROVES--
OUR RESEARCH SHOWED THAT NOBODY BOUGHT YOUR "DARK SIDE"!
MAYBE I SHOULD HAVE BECOME A CONFLICTED TROLL!
OH, TODD!

DINGBURGERS WATCH AN AVERAGE OF 15.6 HOURS OF TELEVISION PER DAY---
DIDN'T WE SEE THIS EPISODE OF "RAYMOND" 12 OR 13 TIMES ALREADY?
YES! ONE OR TWO MORE & WE'LL HAVE IT MEMORIZED!
©2010 Bill Griffith. World rights reserved. Distributed by King Features Syndicate
IN ORDER TO MAINTAIN A HIGH LEVEL OF PASSIVITY, THEY TAKE REGULAR DOSES OF BIOFLAVONOIDS---
YUM!
BIOFLAVONOIDS!!
GRIFFY
2-7
TH' WASTE PRODUCTS FROM SO MUCH BIO-FLAVONOID INGESTION IS PRETTY GROSS!
LET'S GET THIS LOAD TO TH' CITY DUMP BEFORE IT IMPLODES!
Zippythepinhead.com
A FEW DINGBURG NUTRITION EXPERTS ARE WORKING ON A NEW SUPPLEMENT--
DID YOU SEE "RAYMOND" LAST NIGHT?
WHO'S RAYMOND?

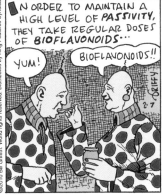

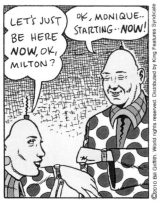

LET'S JUST BE HERE NOW, OK, MILTON?
OK, MONIQUE.. STARTING..NOW!
©2010 Bill Griffith. World rights reserved. Distributed by King Features Syndicate
LOOK AT THIS THING-- IT'S A BALL POINT PEN! IT HAS A BALLNESS. IT HAS A POINTNESS...IT HAS A PEN-NESS...
IT'S A BALL POINT PEN!
GRIFFY 2-14
Zippythepinhead.com
WHY AM I THINKING ABOUT DENTISTRY AT THIS MOMENT?
OOPS! NOW I'M THINKING ABOUT PERCALE SHEETS!
The Pinhead brain is not capable of tying two or more thoughts together. This is why their punchlines do not occur at the end of a joke.

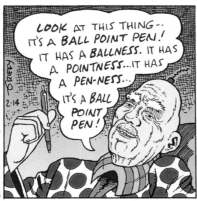

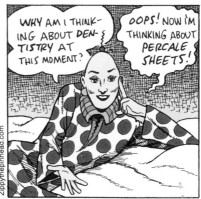

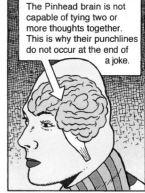

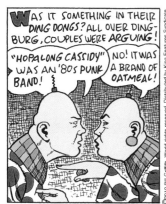

WAS IT SOMETHING IN THEIR DING DONGS? ALL OVER DINGBURG, COUPLES WERE ARGUING!
"HOPALONG CASSIDY" WAS AN '80s PUNK BAND!
NO! IT WAS A BRAND OF OATMEAL!
©2010 Bill Griffith. World rights reserved. Distributed by King Features Syndicate
LISTEN, NERDLINGER, I DO ALL TH' CREDIT DEFAULT SWAPS AROUND HERE WHILE YOU TAKE ALL TH' GLORY!!
OH, YEH? WELL, THEN, WHY DON'T YOU TELL ME TH' DIFFERENCE BETWEEN HEDGING & ARBITRAGE?
IN GENERAL, DINGBURG MEN HAVE A HIGHER "DOOFUS" QUOTIENT THAN DINGBURG WOMEN...
I GUESS I WON THIS ROUND, EH, MARLA?
YOU & WHAT JAMAICAN BOBSLED TEAM, BUSTER?
GRIFFY 2-28
Zippythepinhead.com
BUT IN ONE AREA, BOTH SEXES AGREE... DINGBURG GALS ARE INCREDIBLY GOOD KETTLE DRUM PLAYERS!
SIGH.. EVEN MY KNOWLEDGE OF HOPALONG CASSIDY COLLECTIBLES DOESN'T IMPRESS HER!

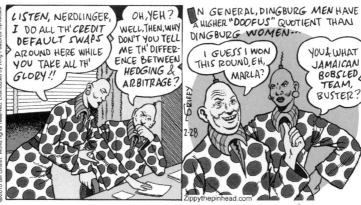

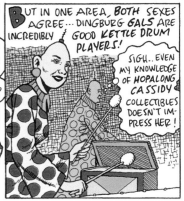

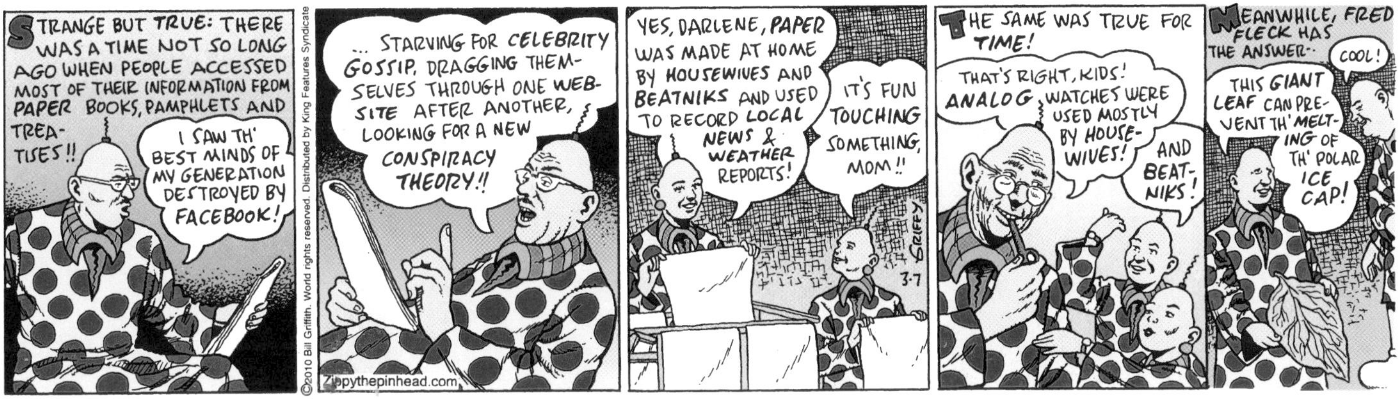
STRANGE BUT TRUE: THERE WAS A TIME NOT SO LONG AGO WHEN PEOPLE ACCESSED MOST OF THEIR INFORMATION FROM PAPER BOOKS, PAMPHLETS AND TREATISES!!
I SAW TH' BEST MINDS OF MY GENERATION DESTROYED BY FACEBOOK!
©2010 Bill Griffith. World rights reserved. Distributed by King Features Syndicate
Zippythepinhead.com
... STARVING FOR CELEBRITY GOSSIP, DRAGGING THEMSELVES THROUGH ONE WEB-SITE AFTER ANOTHER, LOOKING FOR A NEW CONSPIRACY THEORY!!
YES, DARLENE, PAPER WAS MADE AT HOME BY HOUSEWIVES AND BEATNIKS AND USED TO RECORD LOCAL NEWS & WEATHER REPORTS!
IT'S FUN TOUCHING SOMETHING, MOM!!
GRIFFY
3·7
THE SAME WAS TRUE FOR TIME!
THAT'S RIGHT, KIDS! ANALOG WATCHES WERE USED MOSTLY BY HOUSEWIVES!
AND BEATNIKS!
MEANWHILE, FRED FLECK HAS THE ANSWER..
COOL!
THIS GIANT LEAF CAN PREVENT TH' MELTING OF TH' POLAR ICE CAP!

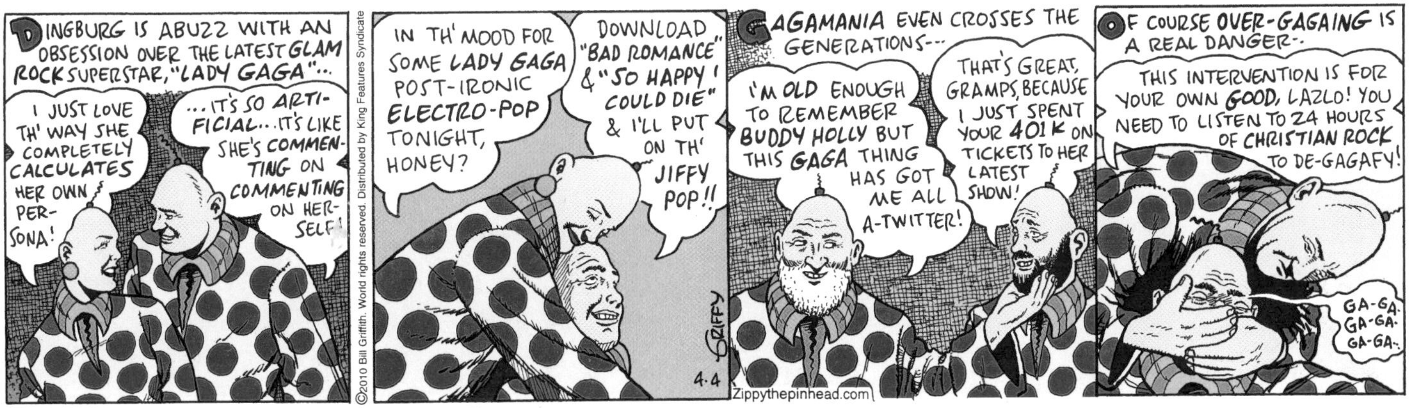
DINGBURG IS ABUZZ WITH AN OBSESSION OVER THE LATEST GLAM ROCK SUPERSTAR, "LADY GAGA"...
I JUST LOVE TH' WAY SHE COMPLETELY CALCULATES HER OWN PERSONA!
... IT'S SO ARTIFICIAL... IT'S LIKE SHE'S COMMENTING ON COMMENTING ON HERSELF!
©2010 Bill Griffith. World rights reserved. Distributed by King Features Syndicate
IN TH' MOOD FOR SOME LADY GAGA POST-IRONIC ELECTRO-POP TONIGHT, HONEY?
DOWNLOAD "BAD ROMANCE" & "SO HAPPY I COULD DIE" & I'LL PUT ON TH' JIFFY POP!!
GRIFFY
4·4
GAGAMANIA EVEN CROSSES THE GENERATIONS---
I'M OLD ENOUGH TO REMEMBER BUDDY HOLLY BUT THIS GAGA THING HAS GOT ME ALL A-TWITTER!
THAT'S GREAT, GRAMPS, BECAUSE I JUST SPENT YOUR 401 K ON TICKETS TO HER LATEST SHOW!
Zippythepinhead.com
OF COURSE OVER-GAGAING IS A REAL DANGER..
THIS INTERVENTION IS FOR YOUR OWN GOOD, LAZLO! YOU NEED TO LISTEN TO 24 HOURS OF CHRISTIAN ROCK TO DE-GAGAFY!
GA-GA-GA-GA-GA-GA..

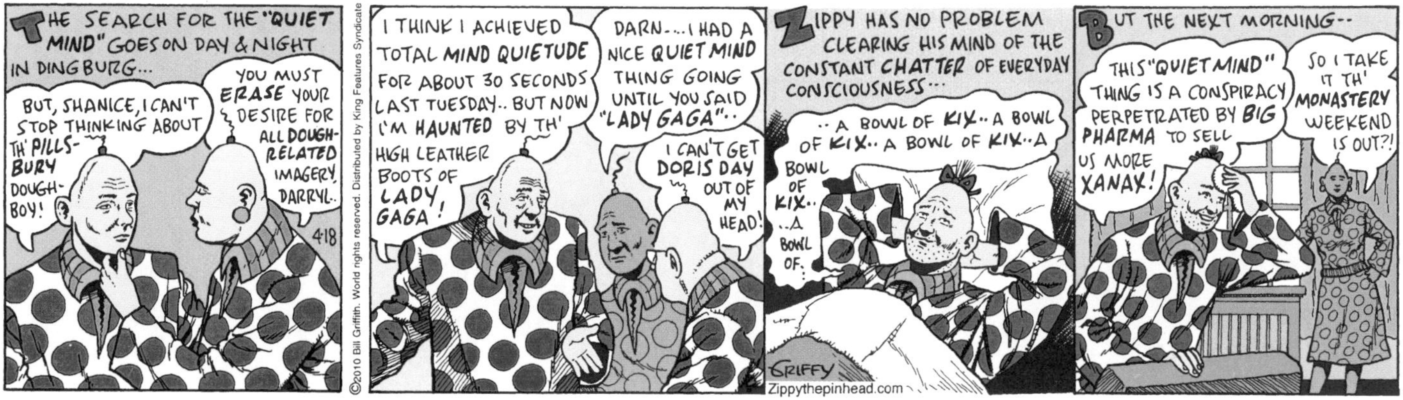
THE SEARCH FOR THE "QUIET MIND" GOES ON DAY & NIGHT IN DINGBURG...
BUT, SHANICE, I CAN'T STOP THINKING ABOUT TH' PILLS-BURY DOUGH-BOY!
YOU MUST ERASE YOUR DESIRE FOR ALL DOUGH-RELATED IMAGERY, DARRYL..
4-18
©2010 Bill Griffith. World rights reserved. Distributed by King Features Syndicate
I THINK I ACHIEVED TOTAL MIND QUIETUDE FOR ABOUT 30 SECONDS LAST TUESDAY.. BUT NOW I'M HAUNTED BY TH' HIGH LEATHER BOOTS OF LADY GAGA!
DARN... I HAD A NICE QUIET MIND THING GOING UNTIL YOU SAID "LADY GAGA"..
I CAN'T GET DORIS DAY OUT OF MY HEAD!
ZIPPY HAS NO PROBLEM CLEARING HIS MIND OF THE CONSTANT CHATTER OF EVERYDAY CONSCIOUSNESS...
.. A BOWL OF KIX.. A BOWL OF KIX.. A BOWL OF KIX.. A BOWL OF KIX.. ..A BOWL OF..
GRIFFY
Zippythepinhead.com
BUT THE NEXT MORNING--
THIS "QUIET MIND" THING IS A CONSPIRACY PERPETRATED BY BIG PHARMA TO SELL US MORE XANAX!
SO I TAKE IT TH' MONASTERY WEEKEND IS OUT?!

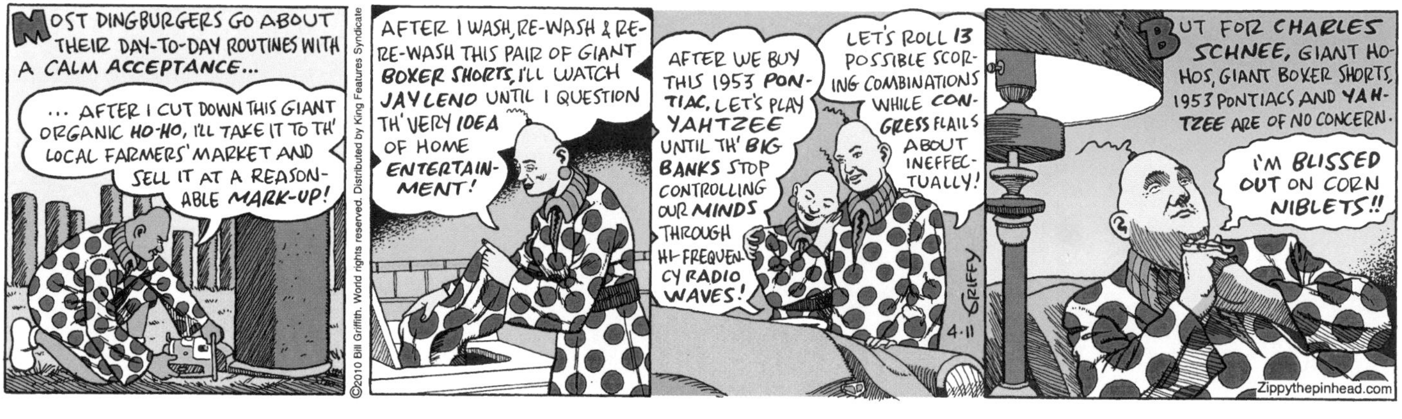
MOST DINGBURGERS GO ABOUT THEIR DAY-TO-DAY ROUTINES WITH A CALM ACCEPTANCE...
... AFTER I CUT DOWN THIS GIANT ORGANIC HO-HO, I'LL TAKE IT TO TH' LOCAL FARMERS' MARKET AND SELL IT AT A REASON-ABLE MARK-UP!
©2010 Bill Griffith. World rights reserved. Distributed by King Features Syndicate
AFTER I WASH, RE-WASH & RE-RE-WASH THIS PAIR OF GIANT BOXER SHORTS, I'LL WATCH JAY LENO UNTIL I QUESTION TH' VERY IDEA OF HOME ENTERTAIN-MENT!
AFTER WE BUY THIS 1953 PON-TIAC, LET'S PLAY YAHTZEE UNTIL TH' BIG BANKS STOP CONTROLLING OUR MINDS THROUGH HI-FREQUEN-CY RADIO WAVES!
LET'S ROLL 13 POSSIBLE SCOR-ING COMBINATIONS WHILE CON-GRESS FLAILS ABOUT INEFFEC-TUALLY!
GRIFFY
4-11
BUT FOR CHARLES SCHNEE, GIANT HO-HOS, GIANT BOXER SHORTS, 1953 PONTIACS AND YAH-TZEE ARE OF NO CONCERN.
I'M BLISSED OUT ON CORN NIBLETS!!
Zippythepinhead.com

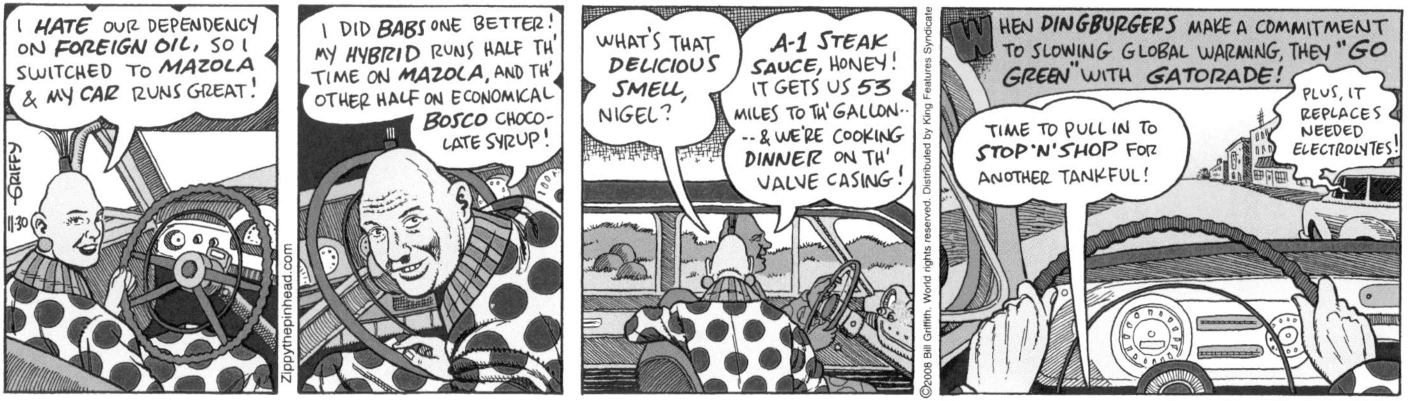
I HATE OUR DEPENDENCY ON FOREIGN OIL, SO I SWITCHED TO MAZOLA & MY CAR RUNS GREAT!
GRIFFY 11-30
I DID BABS ONE BETTER! MY HYBRID RUNS HALF TH' TIME ON MAZOLA, AND TH' OTHER HALF ON ECONOMICAL BOSCO CHOCOLATE SYRUP!
Zippythepinhead.com
WHAT'S THAT DELICIOUS SMELL, NIGEL?
A-1 STEAK SAUCE, HONEY! IT GETS US 53 MILES TO TH' GALLON.. -- & WE'RE COOKING DINNER ON TH' VALVE CASING!
©2008 Bill Griffith. World rights reserved. Distributed by King Features Syndicate
WHEN DINGBURGERS MAKE A COMMITMENT TO SLOWING GLOBAL WARMING, THEY "GO GREEN" WITH GATORADE!
TIME TO PULL IN TO STOP 'N' SHOP FOR ANOTHER TANKFUL!
PLUS, IT REPLACES NEEDED ELECTROLYTES!

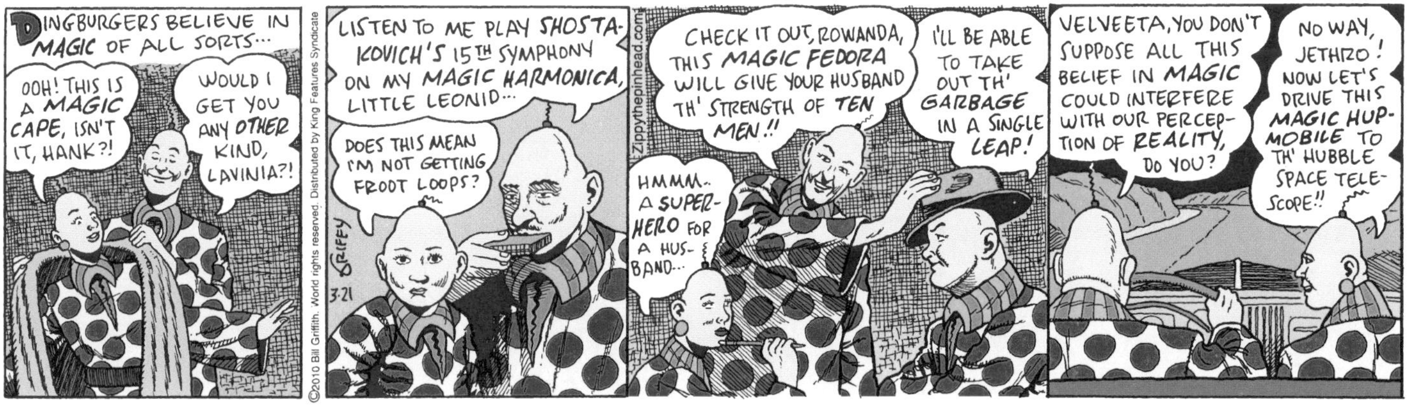
DINGBURGERS BELIEVE IN MAGIC OF ALL SORTS...
OOH! THIS IS A MAGIC CAPE, ISN'T IT, HANK?!
WOULD I GET YOU ANY OTHER KIND, LAVINIA?!
©2010 Bill Griffith. World rights reserved. Distributed by King Features Syndicate
LISTEN TO ME PLAY SHOSTAKOVICH'S 15TH SYMPHONY ON MY MAGIC HARMONICA, LITTLE LEONID...
DOES THIS MEAN I'M NOT GETTING FROOT LOOPS?
GRIFFY 3-21
Zippythepinhead.com
CHECK IT OUT, ROWANDA, THIS MAGIC FEDORA WILL GIVE YOUR HUSBAND TH' STRENGTH OF TEN MEN!!
I'LL BE ABLE TO TAKE OUT TH' GARBAGE IN A SINGLE LEAP!
HMMM.. A SUPER-HERO FOR A HUSBAND...
VELVEETA, YOU DON'T SUPPOSE ALL THIS BELIEF IN MAGIC COULD INTERFERE WITH OUR PERCEPTION OF REALITY, DO YOU?
NO WAY, JETHRO! NOW LET'S DRIVE THIS MAGIC HUPMOBILE TO TH' HUBBLE SPACE TELESCOPE!!

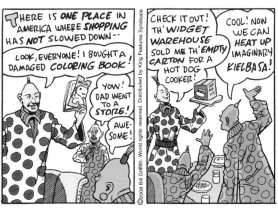

THERE IS ONE PLACE IN AMERICA WHERE SHOPPING HAS NOT SLOWED DOWN--
LOOK, EVERYONE! I BOUGHT A DAMAGED COLORING BOOK!
YOW! DAD WENT TO A STORE!
AWE-SOME!
©2008 Bill Griffith. World rights reserved. Distributed by King Features Syndicate
CHECK IT OUT! TH' WIDGET WAREHOUSE SOLD ME TH' EMPTY CARTON FOR A HOT DOG COOKER!
COOL! NOW WE CAN HEAT UP IMAGINARY KIELBASA!
IN DINGBURG, IT'S THE ACT OF SHOPPING THAT'S IMPORTANT, NOT THE ITEM ACTUALLY PURCHASED!
I CAN ADD THIS TO MY "STUFF-THAT-I-DON'T-KNOW-WHAT-IT-IS" COLLECTION!
GRIFFY
12·7
Zippythepinhead.com
HOO-EEE!
I SCOURED FIVE GARAGE SALES & WOUND UP WITH A BENT CURTAIN ROD-- IT WAS ONLY A BUCK TWENTY-FIVE!
I HAVE NO USE FOR A GALLON OF ROOFING COMPOUND, BUT IT WAS CHEAP & I HAD TO DRIVE 15 MILES TO GET IT!
ROOF GOOP
E-Z & FAST
THINGS ARE LOOKING UP!

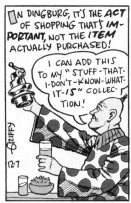

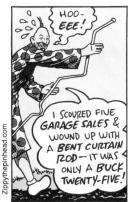

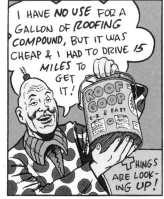

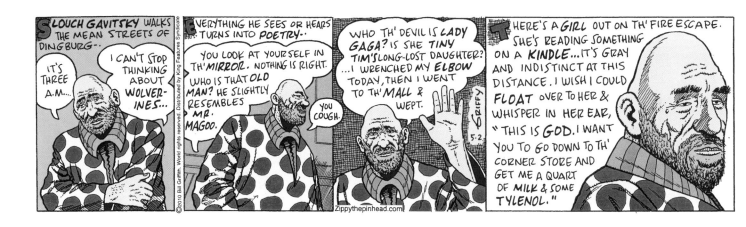

SLOUCH GAVITSKY WALKS THE MEAN STREETS OF DINGBURG--
IT'S THREE A.M....
I CAN'T STOP THINKING ABOUT WOLVERINES...
©2010 Bill Griffith. World rights reserved. Distributed by King Features Syndicate
EVERYTHING HE SEES OR HEARS TURNS INTO POETRY--
YOU LOOK AT YOURSELF IN TH' MIRROR. NOTHING IS RIGHT. WHO IS THAT OLD MAN? HE SLIGHTLY RESEMBLES MR. MAGOO.
YOU COUGH.
WHO TH' DEVIL IS LADY GAGA? IS SHE TINY TIM'S LONG-LOST DAUGHTER? ...I WRENCHED MY ELBOW TODAY, THEN I WENT TO TH' MALL & WEPT.
GRIFFY
5·2
Zippythepinhead.com
THERE'S A GIRL OUT ON TH' FIRE ESCAPE. SHE'S READING SOMETHING ON A KINDLE... IT'S GRAY AND INDISTINCT AT THIS DISTANCE. I WISH I COULD FLOAT OVER TO HER & WHISPER IN HER EAR, "THIS IS GOD. I WANT YOU TO GO DOWN TO TH' CORNER STORE AND GET ME A QUART OF MILK & SOME TYLENOL."

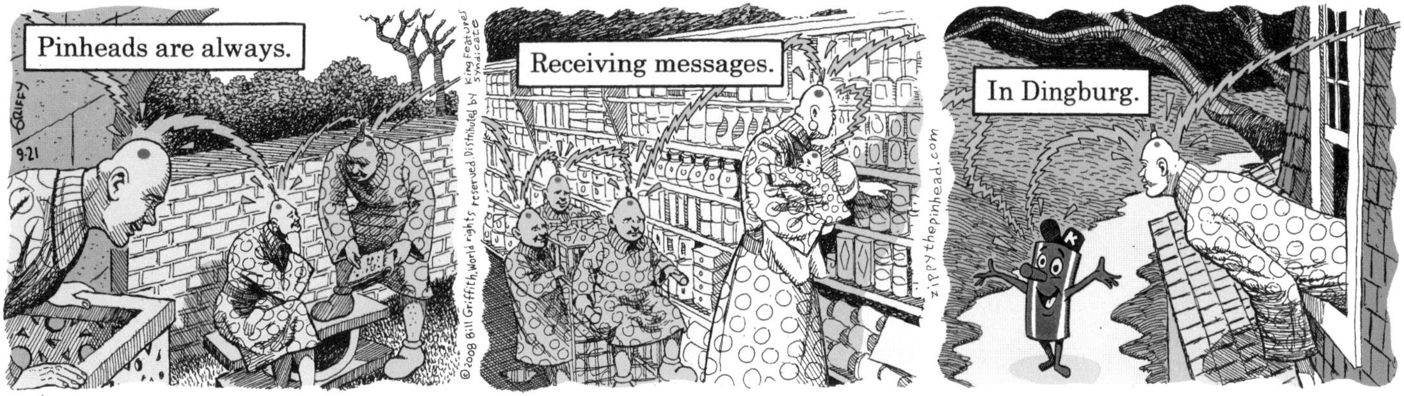
Pinheads are always.
Receiving messages.
In Dingburg.
GRIFFY
9-21
©2008 Bill Griffith, World rights reserved. Distributed by King Features Syndicate
zippythepinhead.com

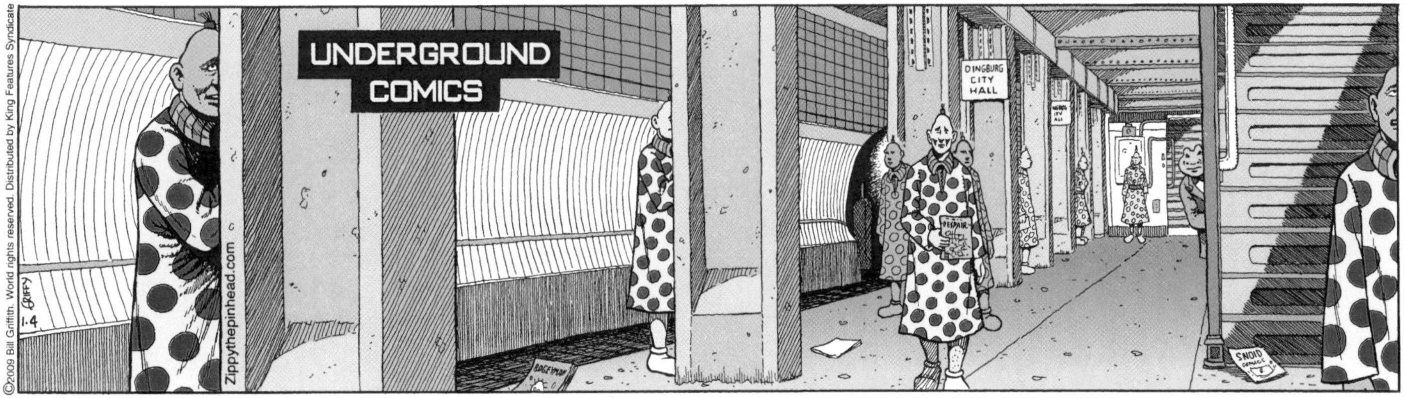
UNDERGROUND COMICS
DINGBURG CITY HALL
SNOID COMICS
GRIFFY
1-4
©2009 Bill Griffith. World rights reserved. Distributed by King Features Syndicate
Zippythepinhead.com

THE TOADETTES LEAD A SIMPLE EXISTENCE...
NO WORRIES, NO CARES. HUH, TODD?
TOTALLY STRESS-FREE, TED!
©2009 Bill Griffith. World rights reserved. Distributed by King Features Syndicate
Zippythepinhead.com
NOTHIN' TO DO ALL DAY BUT HOP AROUND, GRAB A SWIM AND KICK BACK, HUH, TODD?
THIS IS TH' LIFE... TOTALLY PRIMEVAL, TED!
CREDIT DEFAULT SWAPS! CREDIT DEFAULT SWAPS! CREDIT DEFAULT SWAPS!!
DERIVA-TIVES! DERIVA-TIVES! DERIVA-TIVES!
GRIFFY
8-9
I'M GLAD I PUT ALL MY 401(K)S IN CHINESE PORK FUTURES, TODD...
MINE ARE IN DEAD FLIES.

GRIFFY
9-27
WHAT DO YOU THINK OF TH' SHAVING OF ALL BODY HAIR BY HIP, TREND-SETTING URBAN METROSEXUALS THESE DAYS, MUFFLER MAN?
I DO NOT APPROVE.
©2009 Bill Griffith. World rights reserved. Distributed by King Features Syndicate
TIP TO: GRACE LOPEZ
SO YOU THINK MEN SHOULD RETAIN ALL NATURAL FUR WHEREVER IT MAY CROP UP?
YOU BETCHA!
Zippythepinhead.com
--NOT ONLY THAT--- THEY SHOULD ALSO ALWAYS STAND STIFFLY AT ATTENTION, WEAR LUMBER-JACK CAPS & PROUDLY PRESENT LARGE OBJECTS IN A VAGUELY THREATEN-ING MANNER!!
YOW! I CAN ALREADY FEEL AN UPSWING IN TH' TANKING WORLD ECONOMY!!

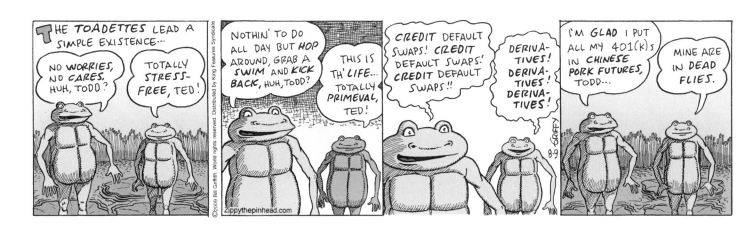

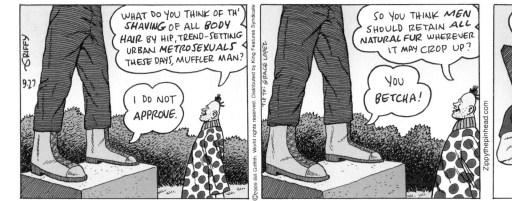

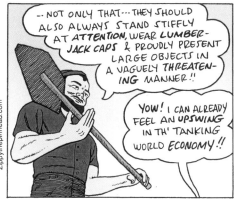

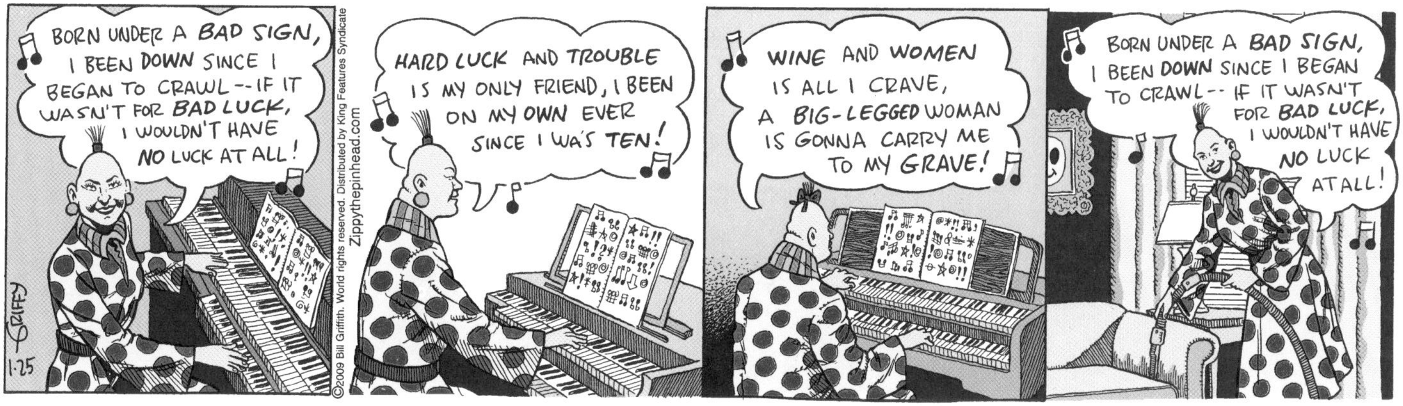
BORN UNDER A BAD SIGN, I BEEN DOWN SINCE I BEGAN TO CRAWL--IF IT WASN'T FOR BAD LUCK, I WOULDN'T HAVE NO LUCK AT ALL!
GRIFFY
1·25
©2009 Bill Griffith. World rights reserved. Distributed by King Features Syndicate
Zippythepinhead.com
HARD LUCK AND TROUBLE IS MY ONLY FRIEND, I BEEN ON MY OWN EVER SINCE I WA'S TEN!
WINE AND WOMEN IS ALL I CRAVE, A BIG-LEGGED WOMAN IS GONNA CARRY ME TO MY GRAVE!
BORN UNDER A BAD SIGN, I BEEN DOWN SINCE I BEGAN TO CRAWL-- IF IT WASN'T FOR BAD LUCK, I WOULDN'T HAVE NO LUCK AT ALL!

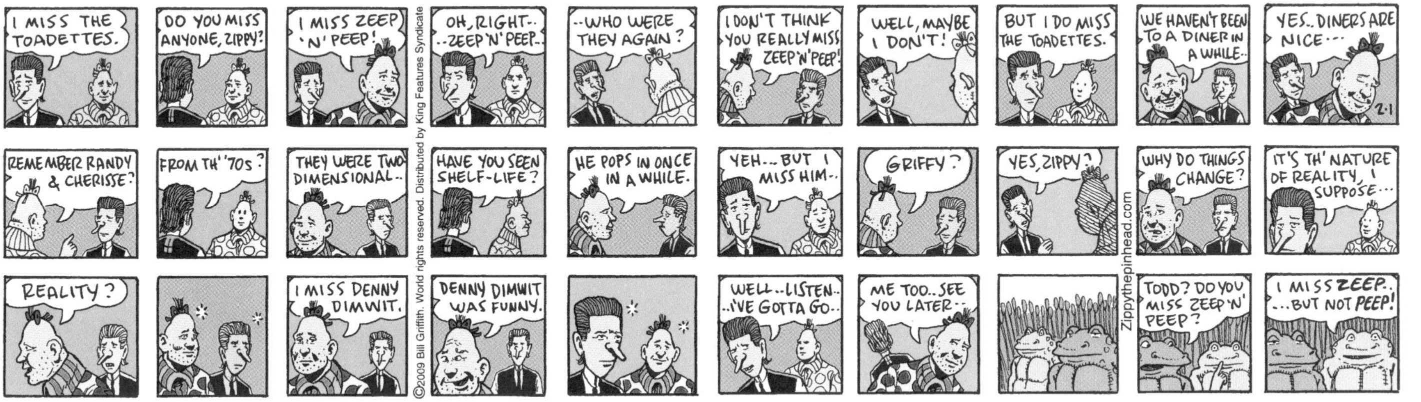
I MISS THE TOADETTES.
DO YOU MISS ANYONE, ZIPPY?
I MISS ZEEP 'N' PEEP!
OH, RIGHT-- --ZEEP 'N' PEEP--
--WHO WERE THEY AGAIN?
I DON'T THINK YOU REALLY MISS ZEEP 'N' PEEP!
WELL, MAYBE I DON'T!
BUT I DO MISS THE TOADETTES.
WE HAVEN'T BEEN TO A DINER IN A WHILE--
YES-- DINERS ARE NICE---
2·1
REMEMBER RANDY & CHERISSE?
FROM TH' '70S?
THEY WERE TWO DIMENSIONAL--
HAVE YOU SEEN SHELF-LIFE?
HE POPS IN ONCE IN A WHILE.
YEH--- BUT I MISS HIM--
GRIFFY?
YES, ZIPPY?
WHY DO THINGS CHANGE?
IT'S TH' NATURE OF REALITY, I SUPPOSE---
REALITY?
I MISS DENNY DIMWIT.
DENNY DIMWIT WAS FUNNY.
WELL-- LISTEN-- --I'VE GOTTA GO--
ME TOO-- SEE YOU LATER--
TODD? DO YOU MISS ZEEP 'N' PEEP?
I MISS ZEEP-- --BUT NOT PEEP!
©2009 Bill Griffith. World rights reserved. Distributed by King Features Syndicate
Zippythepinhead.com

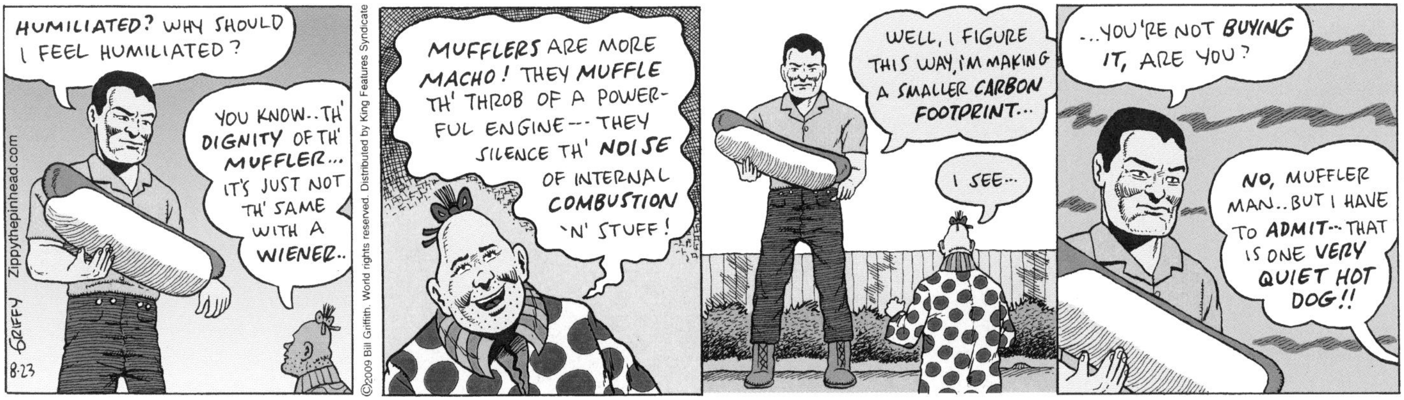

HUMILIATED? WHY SHOULD I FEEL HUMILIATED?
YOU KNOW..TH' DIGNITY OF TH' MUFFLER... IT'S JUST NOT TH' SAME WITH A WIENER..
GRIFFY
8·23
Zippythepinhead.com
©2009 Bill Griffith. World rights reserved. Distributed by King Features Syndicate
MUFFLERS ARE MORE MACHO! THEY MUFFLE TH' THROB OF A POWERFUL ENGINE--- THEY SILENCE TH' NOISE OF INTERNAL COMBUSTION 'N' STUFF!
WELL, I FIGURE THIS WAY, I'M MAKING A SMALLER CARBON FOOTPRINT...
I SEE...
...YOU'RE NOT BUYING IT, ARE YOU?
NO, MUFFLER MAN..BUT I HAVE TO ADMIT--THAT IS ONE VERY QUIET HOT DOG!!

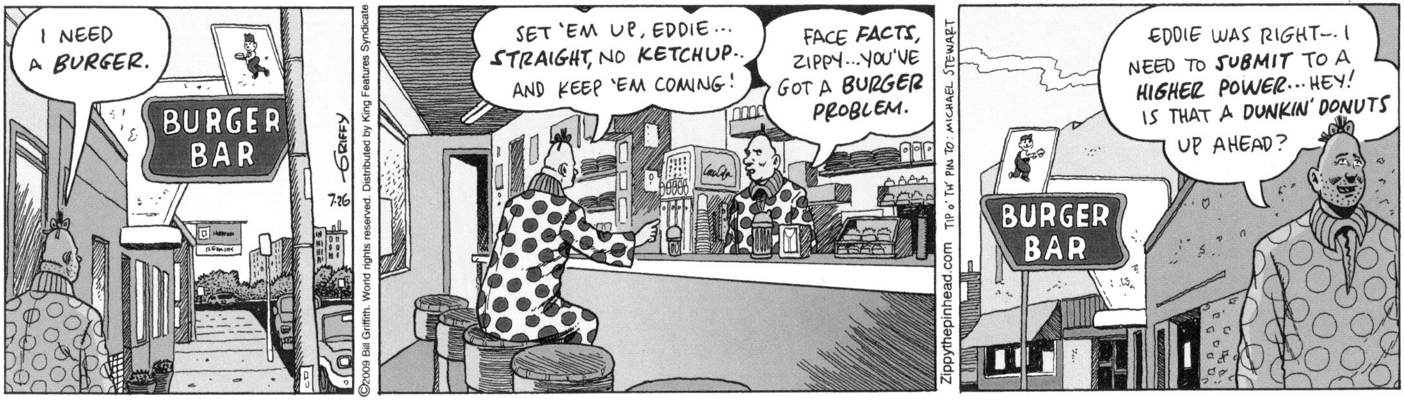

I NEED A BURGER.
BURGER BAR
GRIFFY
7·26
©2009 Bill Griffith. World rights reserved. Distributed by King Features Syndicate
SET 'EM UP, EDDIE... STRAIGHT, NO KETCHUP.. AND KEEP 'EM COMING!
FACE FACTS, ZIPPY...YOU'VE GOT A BURGER PROBLEM.
TIP o' TH' PIN TO: MICHAEL STEWART
Zippythepinhead.com
EDDIE WAS RIGHT--. I NEED TO SUBMIT TO A HIGHER POWER...HEY! IS THAT A DUNKIN' DONUTS UP AHEAD?
BURGER BAR

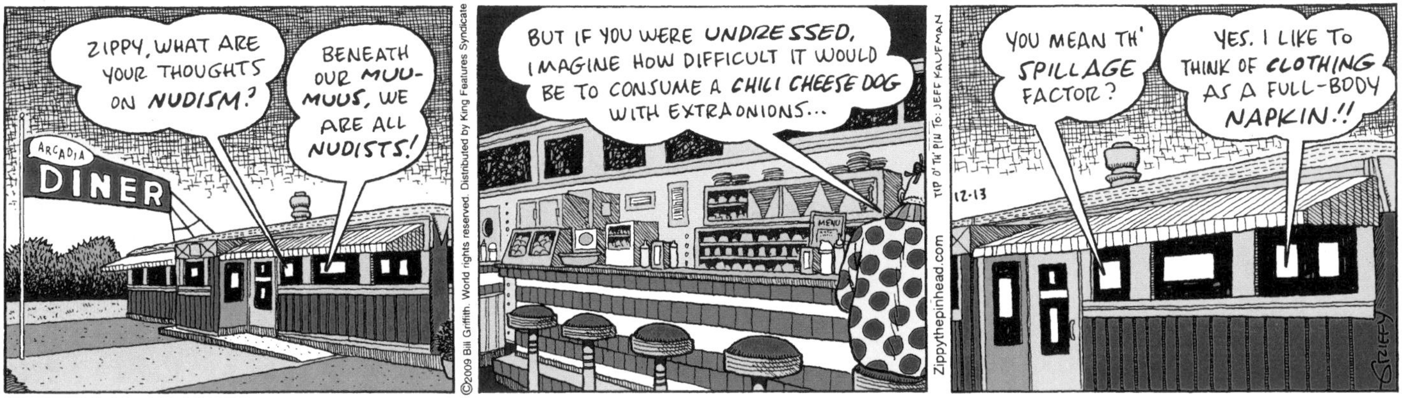
ZIPPY, WHAT ARE YOUR THOUGHTS ON NUDISM?
BENEATH OUR MUU-MUUS, WE ARE ALL NUDISTS!
ARCADIA
DINER
©2009 Bill Griffith. World rights reserved. Distributed by King Features Syndicate
BUT IF YOU WERE UNDRESSED, IMAGINE HOW DIFFICULT IT WOULD BE TO CONSUME A CHILI CHEESE DOG WITH EXTRA ONIONS...
MENU
Zippythepinhead.com
TIP O' TH' PIN TO: JEFF KAUFMAN
12-13
YOU MEAN TH' SPILLAGE FACTOR?
YES. I LIKE TO THINK OF CLOTHING AS A FULL-BODY NAPKIN!!
GRIFFY

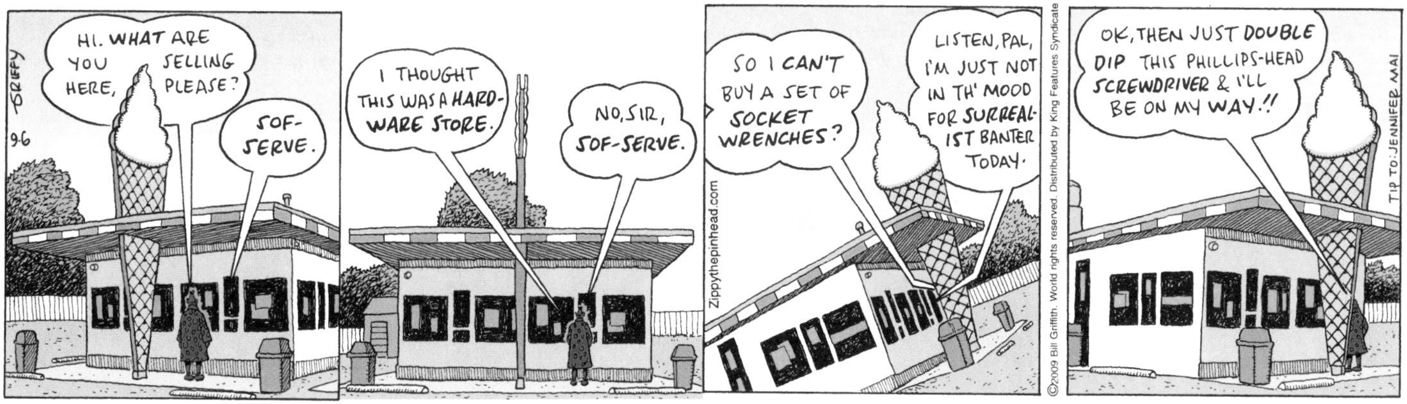
GRIFFY
9-6
HI. WHAT ARE YOU SELLING HERE, PLEASE?
SOF-SERVE.
I THOUGHT THIS WAS A HARDWARE STORE.
NO, SIR, SOF-SERVE.
Zippythepinhead.com
SO I CAN'T BUY A SET OF SOCKET WRENCHES?
LISTEN, PAL, I'M JUST NOT IN TH' MOOD FOR SURREALIST BANTER TODAY.
©2009 Bill Griffith. World rights reserved. Distributed by King Features Syndicate
OK, THEN JUST DOUBLE DIP THIS PHILLIPS-HEAD SCREWDRIVER & I'LL BE ON MY WAY!!
TIP TO: JENNIFER MAI

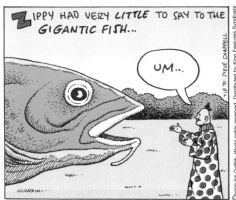

ZIPPY HAD VERY LITTLE TO SAY TO THE GIGANTIC FISH...
UM...
TIP TO: STEVE CHAPPELL
©2009 Bill Griffith. World rights reserved. Distributed by King Features Syndicate
AND HIS DIALOGUE WITH THE GIGANTIC ICE CREAM CONE WAS MONOSYLLABIC.
GRIFFY 10-11
YUM!
Zippythepinhead.com
BUT THE HEADLESS RHINO MADE HIM QUESTION THE MEANING OF JUST ABOUT EVERYTHING---
HEADLESS RHINO, ARE WE HERE FOR ANY PARTICULAR PURPOSE?
MNNF.

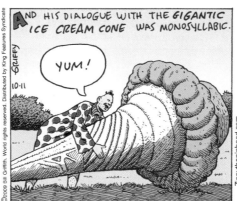

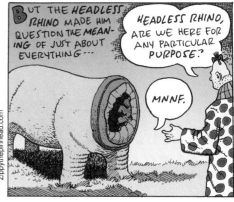

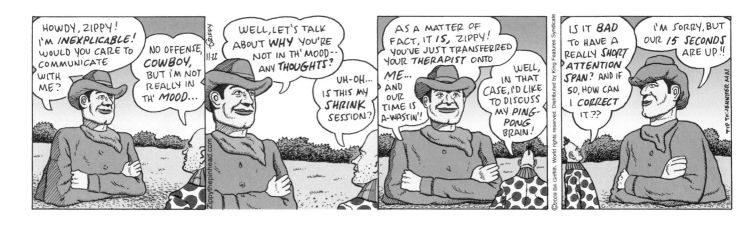

HOWDY, ZIPPY! I'M INEXPLICABLE! WOULD YOU CARE TO COMMUNICATE WITH ME?
NO OFFENSE, COWBOY, BUT I'M NOT REALLY IN TH' MOOD...
GRIFFY 11-22
Zippythepinhead.com
WELL, LET'S TALK ABOUT WHY YOU'RE NOT IN TH' MOOD-- ANY THOUGHTS?
UH-OH... IS THIS MY SHRINK SESSION?
AS A MATTER OF FACT, IT IS, ZIPPY! YOU'VE JUST TRANSFERRED YOUR THERAPIST ONTO ME... AND OUR TIME IS A-WASTIN'!
WELL, IN THAT CASE, I'D LIKE TO DISCUSS MY PING-PONG BRAIN!
©2009 Bill Griffith. World rights reserved. Distributed by King Features Syndicate
IS IT BAD TO HAVE A REALLY SHORT ATTENTION SPAN? AND IF SO, HOW CAN I CORRECT IT??
I'M SORRY, BUT OUR 15 SECONDS ARE UP!!
TIP TO: JENNIFER MAI

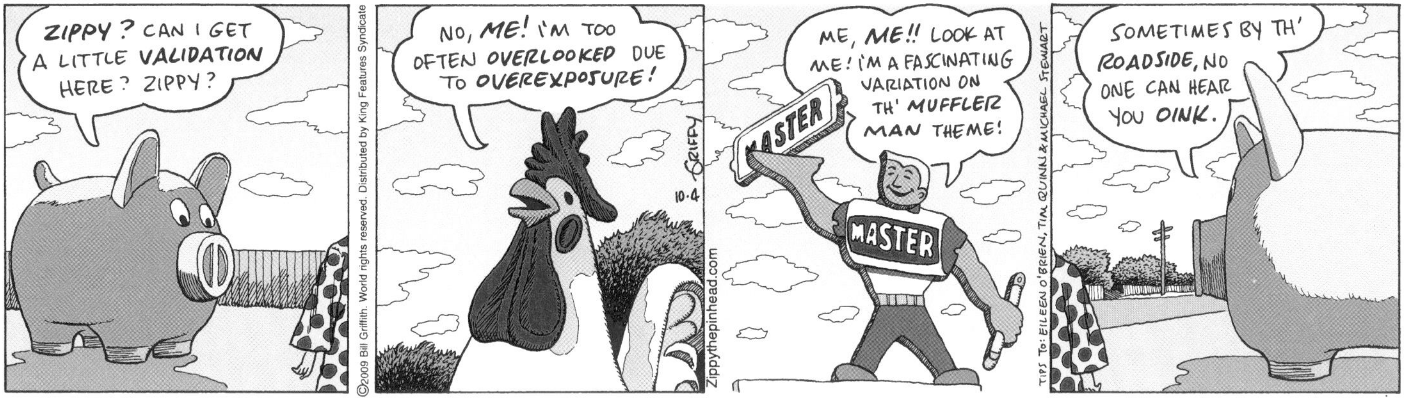

ZIPPY? CAN I GET A LITTLE VALIDATION HERE? ZIPPY?
©2009 Bill Griffith. World rights reserved. Distributed by King Features Syndicate
NO, ME! I'M TOO OFTEN OVERLOOKED DUE TO OVEREXPOSURE!
GRIFFY
10·4
Zippythepinhead.com
ME, ME!! LOOK AT ME! I'M A FASCINATING VARIATION ON TH' MUFFLER MAN THEME!
MASTER
MASTER
TIPS TO: EILEEN O'BRIEN, TIM QUINN & MICHAEL STEWART
SOMETIMES BY TH' ROADSIDE, NO ONE CAN HEAR YOU OINK.

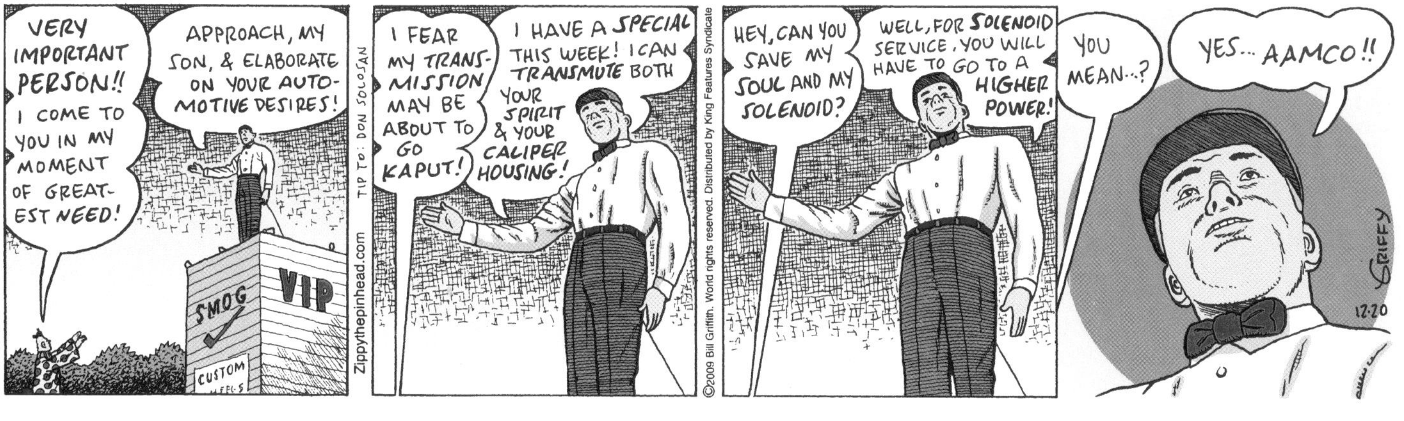

VERY IMPORTANT PERSON!! I COME TO YOU IN MY MOMENT OF GREATEST NEED!
APPROACH, MY SON, & ELABORATE ON YOUR AUTOMOTIVE DESIRES!
SMOG
VIP
CUSTOM
TIP TO: DON SOLOSAN
Zippythepinhead.com
I FEAR MY TRANSMISSION MAY BE ABOUT TO GO KAPUT!
I HAVE A SPECIAL THIS WEEK! I CAN TRANSMUTE BOTH YOUR SPIRIT & YOUR CALIPER HOUSING!
©2009 Bill Griffith. World rights reserved. Distributed by King Features Syndicate
HEY, CAN YOU SAVE MY SOUL AND MY SOLENOID?
WELL, FOR SOLENOID SERVICE, YOU WILL HAVE TO GO TO A HIGHER POWER!
YOU MEAN...?
YES... AAMCO!!
GRIFFY
12·20

ZIPPY COMMUNES WITH NATURE...
HI.
GRIFFY
12·6
©2009 Bill Griffith. World rights reserved. Distributed by King Features Syndicate
UNTIL ONE DAY...
HI.
Zippythepinhead.com
TIP O' TH' PIN TO: JENNIFER MAI
NATURE COMMUNES BACK.
HI.

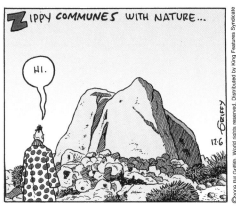

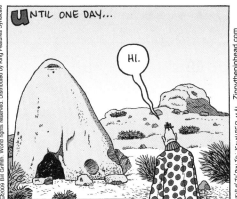

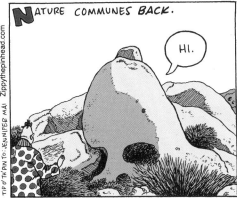

ZIPPY BELIEVES THAT SERVICE TO OTHERS IS PARAMOUNT IN ACHIEVING A HAPPY, MEANINGFUL LIFE-
UM..THANKS FOR THESE HALF-EATEN SNACK CAKES, ZIPPY...
ENJOY!!
©2009 Bill Griffith. World rights reserved. Distributed by King Features Syndicate
HE FREQUENTLY TICKLES YOUNG CHILDREN TO ELICIT LAUGHTER..
AM I TICKLING YOU CORRECTLY, BRIAN?
I DON'T KNOW. I'M LAUGHING OUT OF ANXIETY!
GRIFFY
7·5
Zippythepinhead.com
HIS HOMEMADE "LITTLE DEEP-WELL" DOLLS ARE OFTEN A HIT WITH THE KIDS HE MEETS-
WHY DOESN'T IT TALK OR EMIT COMPUTER-IZED SOUND EFFECTS?
BECAUSE I MADE IT OUT OF MELTED GUM-BIES!
ZIPPY'S ALWAYS IN TOUCH WITH HIS PLAYFUL, NURTURING NATURE--
AFTER I FINISH THIS MODEL FIGHTER JET, I THINK I'LL NEGOTIATE A MID-EAST PEACE TREATY!!

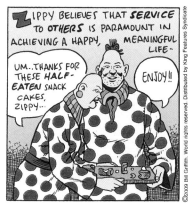

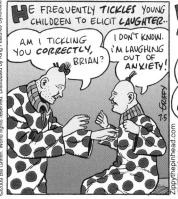

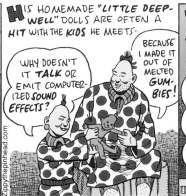

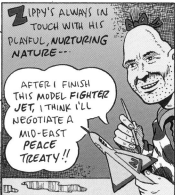

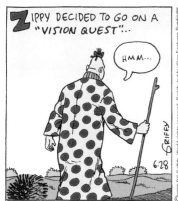

ZIPPY DECIDED TO GO ON A "VISION QUEST"...
HMM...
GRIFFY
6.28
©2009 Bill Griffith. World rights reserved. Distributed by King Features Syndicate
AFTER A FEW HOURS, HE WAS EXHAUSTED, SO HE TOOK A BREAK IN HIS HAMMOCK...
I THINK I'LL CATCH UP ON ALL TH' "PLASTIC MAN" COMICS I NEVER READ!
Zippythepinhead.com
LATER, HAVING ALSO ABSORBED A LARGE STACK OF "CAPTAIN MARVEL" & A DOZEN "MIGHTY MOUSE" COMICS, ZIPPY FELT A VISION COMING ON..
UM.
BUT IT WASN'T UNTIL HIS BATH THAT NIGHT THAT THE FULL IMPACT HIT HIM---
EVERYTHING I EVER NEEDED TO KNOW, I LEARNED FROM DAFFY DUCK!

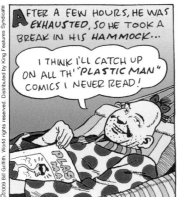

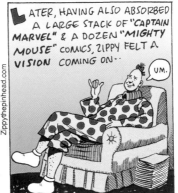

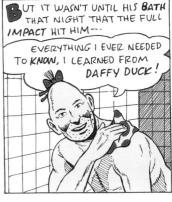

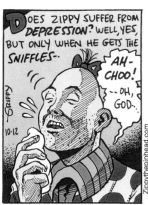

DOES ZIPPY SUFFER FROM DEPRESSION? WELL, YES, BUT ONLY WHEN HE GETS THE SNIFFLES-
AH-CHOO!
--OH, GOD..
GRIFFY
10-12
Zippythepinhead.com
AFTER A POST-PRANDIAL SNEEZE ATTACK, ZIPPY WILL SLUMP INTO HIS EASY CHAIR & THINK OBSESSIVELY ABOUT THE MEANINGLESSNESS OF PREFERRED STOCK & ICE HOCKEY FOR HOURS-.
ONLY ONE THING SNAPS HIM OUT OF IT-- THE AMTRAK TO CLEVELAND.
HAVE YOU EVER REALLY THOUGHT ABOUT TH' SIZE OF LAKE ERIE?
YES! SOMETHING BIGGER THAN MYSELF!
©2008 Bill Griffith. World rights reserved. Distributed by King Features Syndicate
LATER, ON THE CORNER OF BOB HOPE WAY & CARNEGIE AVENUE--
LOOK, ZIPPY! YOUR DOPPEL-GANGER!
HEY, BUDDY! CAN I INTEREST YOU IN A FEW SHARES OF FREDDIE MAC?
GET A ZAM-BONI!!

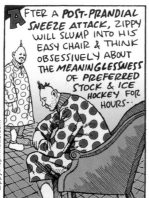

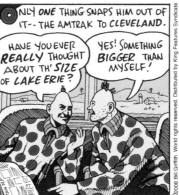

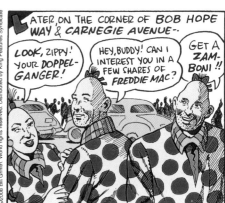

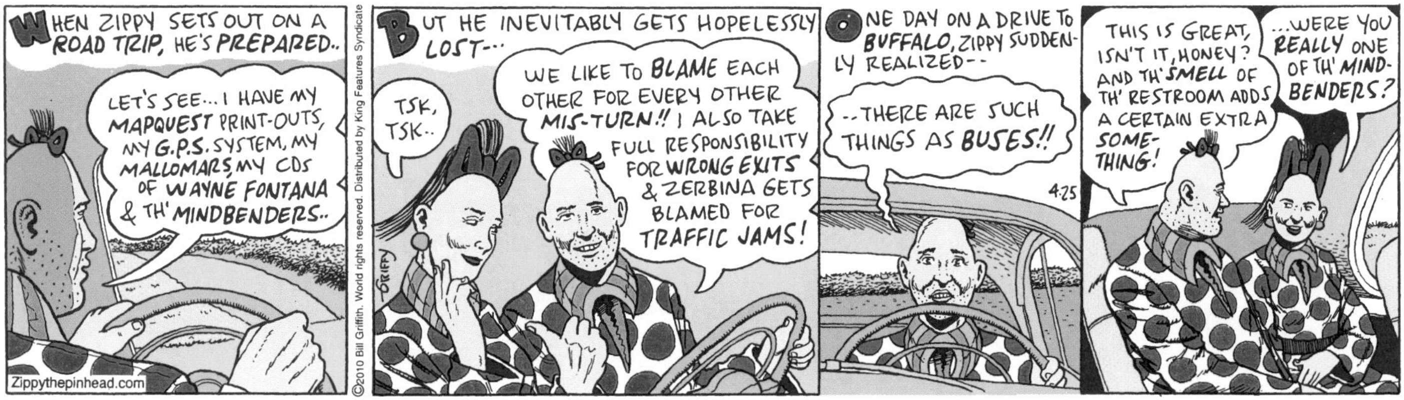
WHEN ZIPPY SETS OUT ON A ROAD TRIP, HE'S PREPARED..
LET'S SEE... I HAVE MY MAPQUEST PRINT-OUTS, MY G.P.S. SYSTEM, MY MALLOMARS, MY CDs OF WAYNE FONTANA & TH' MINDBENDERS..
Zippythepinhead.com
©2010 Bill Griffith. World rights reserved. Distributed by King Features Syndicate
BUT HE INEVITABLY GETS HOPELESSLY LOST--
TSK, TSK..
WE LIKE TO BLAME EACH OTHER FOR EVERY OTHER MIS-TURN!! I ALSO TAKE FULL RESPONSIBILITY FOR WRONG EXITS & ZERBINA GETS BLAMED FOR TRAFFIC JAMS!
GRIFFY
ONE DAY ON A DRIVE TO BUFFALO, ZIPPY SUDDENLY REALIZED--
--THERE ARE SUCH THINGS AS BUSES!!
4·25
THIS IS GREAT, ISN'T IT, HONEY? AND TH' SMELL OF TH' RESTROOM ADDS A CERTAIN EXTRA SOMETHING!
...WERE YOU REALLY ONE OF TH' MINDBENDERS?

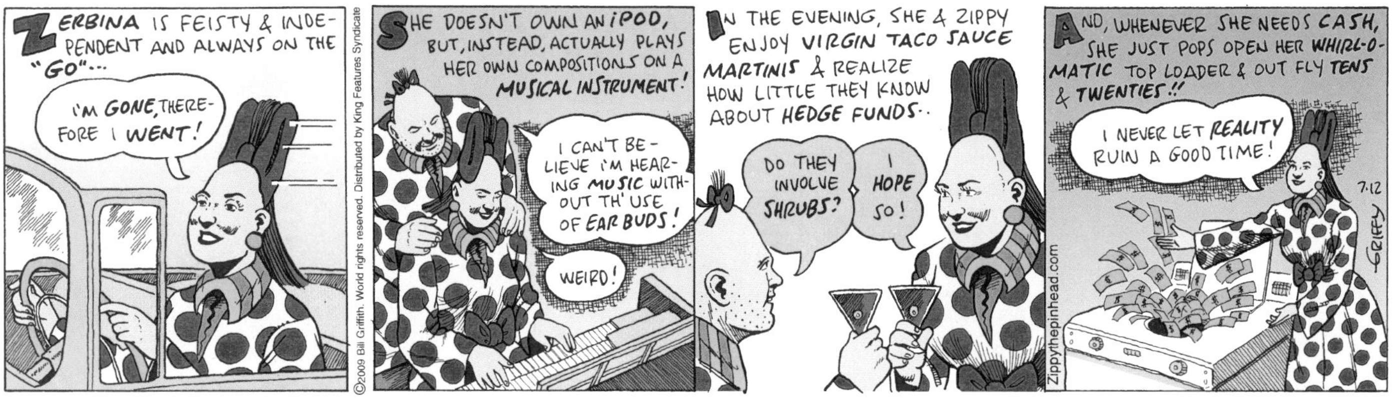
ZERBINA IS FEISTY & INDEPENDENT AND ALWAYS ON THE "GO"...
I'M GONE, THEREFORE I WENT!
©2009 Bill Griffith. World rights reserved. Distributed by King Features Syndicate
SHE DOESN'T OWN AN iPOD, BUT, INSTEAD, ACTUALLY PLAYS HER OWN COMPOSITIONS ON A MUSICAL INSTRUMENT!
I CAN'T BELIEVE I'M HEARING MUSIC WITHOUT TH' USE OF EAR BUDS!
WEIRD!
IN THE EVENING, SHE & ZIPPY ENJOY VIRGIN TACO SAUCE MARTINIS & REALIZE HOW LITTLE THEY KNOW ABOUT HEDGE FUNDS..
DO THEY INVOLVE SHRUBS?
I HOPE SO!
Zippythepinhead.com
AND, WHENEVER SHE NEEDS CASH, SHE JUST POPS OPEN HER WHIRL-O-MATIC TOP LOADER & OUT FLY TENS & TWENTIES!!
I NEVER LET REALITY RUIN A GOOD TIME!
7·12
GRIFFY

THIS IS GOD, ZIPPY! I WANT TH' IRAQ WAR TO BE OVER NOW! IT'S SIMPLE-- JUST DECLARE VICTORY--.. & GET OUT!
A TIME-HONORED MILITARY TRADITION!
VICTORY
©2009 Bill Griffith. World rights reserved. Distributed by King Features Syndicate
TIP O' TH' PIN TO: DON SOLOSAN
I'VE BEEN CONSULTING WITH TH' OTHER SIDE'S GOD & HE'S IN TOTAL AGREEMENT!
YOU MEAN THERE'S MORE THAN ONE GOD?!
SALE
Zippythepinhead.com
GRIFFY 11·1
OF COURSE!! WE ALL GET TOGETHER AROUND HALLOWEEN & DECIDE ON TH' COURSE OF WORLD EVENTS! WHO DO YOU THINK PUT AN END TO THE 24/7 OBSESSION OVER MICHAEL JACKSON'S DEMISE?
SOMEBODY FORGOT TO TELL LARRY KING!!
VICTORY
SALE

YOU AGAIN. WHAT IS IT THIS TIME?
NOT MUCH. MAYBE A BIG LOTTERY WIN...?
©2009 Bill Griffith. World rights reserved. Distributed by King Features Syndicate
YOU THINK I EXIST TO CATER TO YOUR EGO-CENTRIC DESIRES?
IN A WORD.. ...YES!!
GRIFFY 11·8
I OUGHTA GIVE YOU A PAINFUL ROOT CANAL!
THAT'S NOT VERY JUDEO-CHRIS-TIAN OF YOU!
Zippythepinhead.com
..IF I DO LET YOU WIN TH' POWERBALL, WHAT'S IN IT FOR ME?
I'LL WORSHIP YOU EVERY SUNDAY AT 9 A.M.!
YOU MEAN YOU'LL RENOUNCE UNITARIANISM?
IF YOU THROW IN A FULL MOUTH CLEANING!

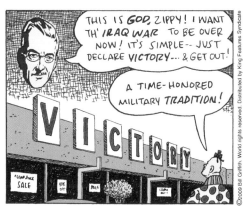

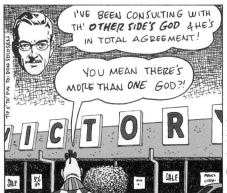

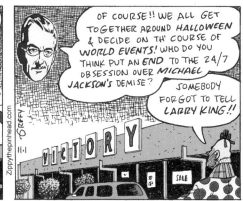

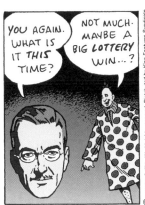

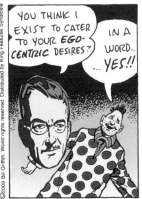

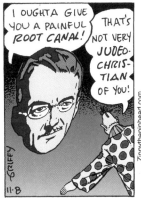

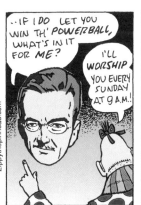

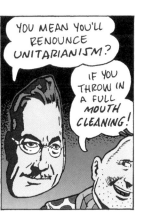

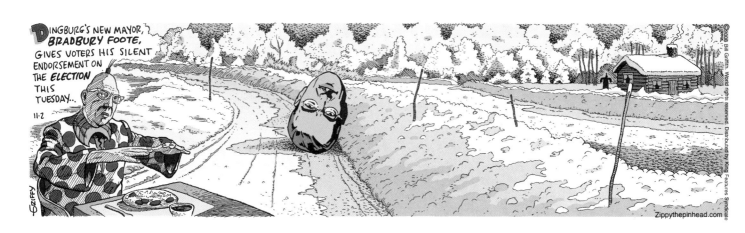

DINGBURG'S NEW MAYOR, BRADBURY FOOTE, GIVES VOTERS HIS SILENT ENDORSEMENT ON THE ELECTION THIS TUESDAY..
11·2
GRIFFY
©2008 Bill Griffith. World rights reserved. Distributed by King Features Syndicate
Zippythepinhead.com

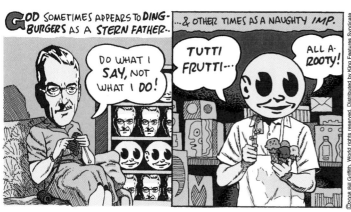

GOD SOMETIMES APPEARS TO DING-BURGERS AS A STERN FATHER..
DO WHAT I SAY, NOT WHAT I DO!
...& OTHER TIMES AS A NAUGHTY IMP.
TUTTI FRUTTI...
ALL A-ROOTY!
©2008 Bill Griffith. World rights reserved. Distributed by King Features Syndicate
ANY QUESTIONS FROM TH' AUDIENCE?
GRIFFY
12·28
Zippythepinhead.com
ARE YOU REAL?
IF YOU ARE!!
DIPS OF DEATH

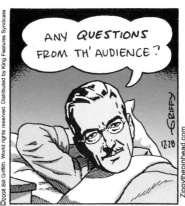

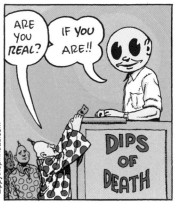

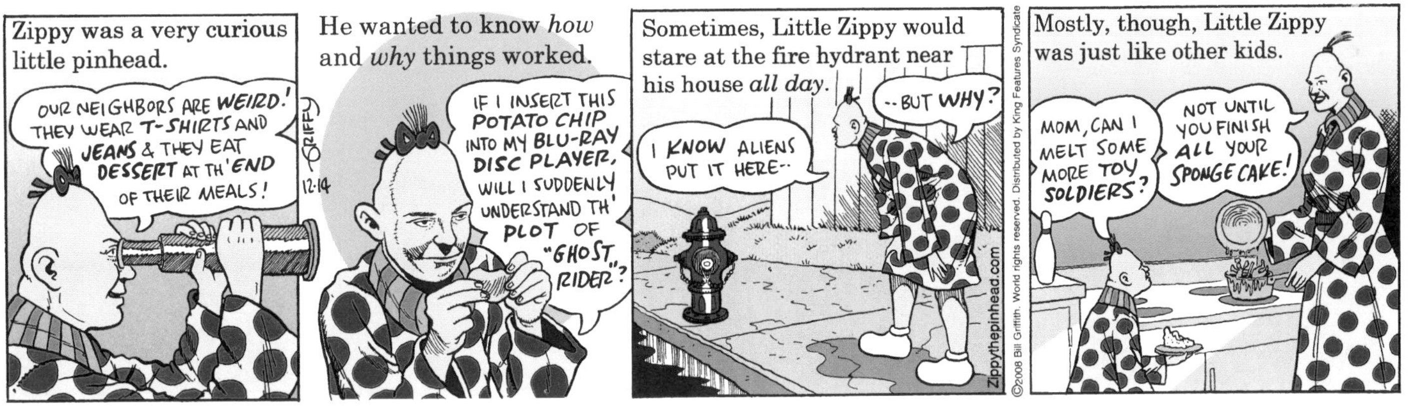
Zippy was a very curious little pinhead.
OUR NEIGHBORS ARE WEIRD! THEY WEAR T-SHIRTS AND JEANS & THEY EAT DESSERT AT TH' END OF THEIR MEALS!
GRIFFY 12·14
He wanted to know how and why things worked.
IF I INSERT THIS POTATO CHIP INTO MY BLU-RAY DISC PLAYER, WILL I SUDDENLY UNDERSTAND TH' PLOT OF "GHOST RIDER"?
Sometimes, Little Zippy would stare at the fire hydrant near his house all day.
I KNOW ALIENS PUT IT HERE--
--BUT WHY?
Zippythepinhead.com
©2008 Bill Griffith. World rights reserved. Distributed by King Features Syndicate
Mostly, though, Little Zippy was just like other kids.
MOM, CAN I MELT SOME MORE TOY SOLDIERS?
NOT UNTIL YOU FINISH ALL YOUR SPONGE CAKE!

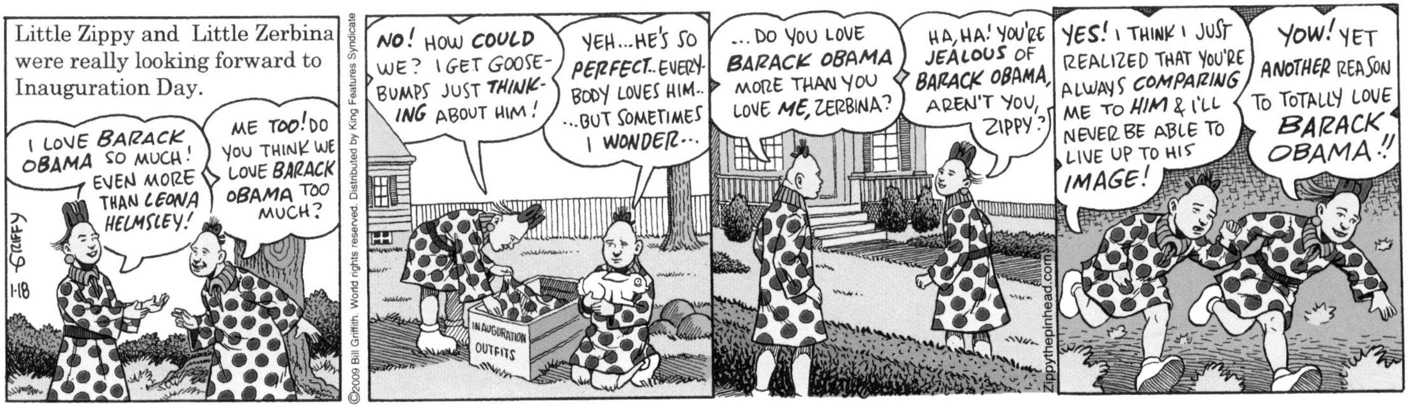
Little Zippy and Little Zerbina were really looking forward to Inauguration Day.
I LOVE BARACK OBAMA SO MUCH! EVEN MORE THAN LEONA HELMSLEY!
ME TOO! DO YOU THINK WE LOVE BARACK OBAMA TOO MUCH?
GRIFFY 1·18
©2009 Bill Griffith. World rights reserved. Distributed by King Features Syndicate
NO! HOW COULD WE? I GET GOOSE-BUMPS JUST THINKING ABOUT HIM!
YEH...HE'S SO PERFECT...EVERYBODY LOVES HIM... ...BUT SOMETIMES I WONDER...
INAUGURATION OUTFITS
...DO YOU LOVE BARACK OBAMA MORE THAN YOU LOVE ME, ZERBINA?
HA, HA! YOU'RE JEALOUS OF BARACK OBAMA, AREN'T YOU, ZIPPY?
Zippythepinhead.com
YES! I THINK I JUST REALIZED THAT YOU'RE ALWAYS COMPARING ME TO HIM & I'LL NEVER BE ABLE TO LIVE UP TO HIS IMAGE!
YOW! YET ANOTHER REASON TO TOTALLY LOVE BARACK OBAMA!!

Little Zippy loved being washed and dried.
ARE YOU USING ENOUGH WOOLITE, MOM?
--NOT TO MENTION HEFTY DOSES OF FAB AND CHEER, LITTLE ZIPPY!
GRIFFY
10-25
©2009 Bill Griffith. World rights reserved. Distributed by King Features Syndicate
The smell of fresh laundry made him so happy.
LET'S WASH IT AGAIN, MOM, INSTEAD OF HANGING IT UP!!
IF YOU SAY SO!
After donning a crisp, clean muu-muu, Little Zippy even did a little dance.
LAUNDRY IS TH' 5TH DIMENSION!
SNAP!
Zippythepinhead.com
But only Little Zerbina knew Zippy's darkest secret.
EVER MIX FABRIC SOFT-ENER & TAB?!
OH, ZIPPY! THAT'S GOING TOO FAR!!

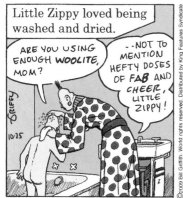

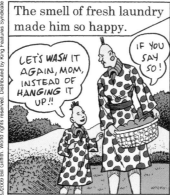

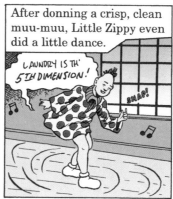

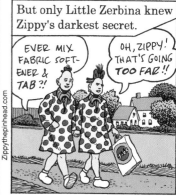

Little Zippy had a sudden revelation...
LAUNDRY ISN'T TH' FIFTH DIMENSION! MAIL IS TH' FIFTH DIMENSION!!
GRIFFY
2-21
He was convinced that his mailbox was a portal to another world.
THESE POTTERY BARN CATALOGS MUST HAVE SLIPPED THROUGH A WORMHOLE IN SPACE-TIME TO GET HERE!
But when Zippy's mail carrier, Mr. Ellsworth, came the next day...
YOU MEAN YOU PUT ALL THESE TRAVELSMITH CAT-ALOGS IN MY MAIL-BOX?
YEP. AND I'VE GOT 3 MORE FOR YOU TODAY!
©2010 Bill Griffith. World rights reserved. Distributed by King Features Syndicate
Zippythepinhead.com
Little Zippy lost faith in the fifth dimension after that, and just sat & stared out the window.
...I THINK I MAY HAVE TO BECOME A PRESBYTERIAN!

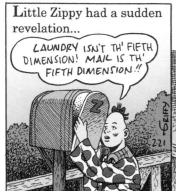

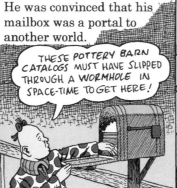

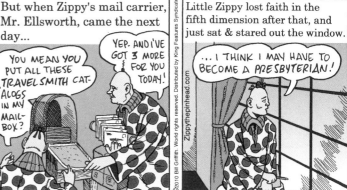

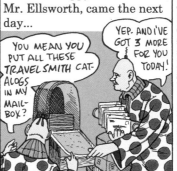

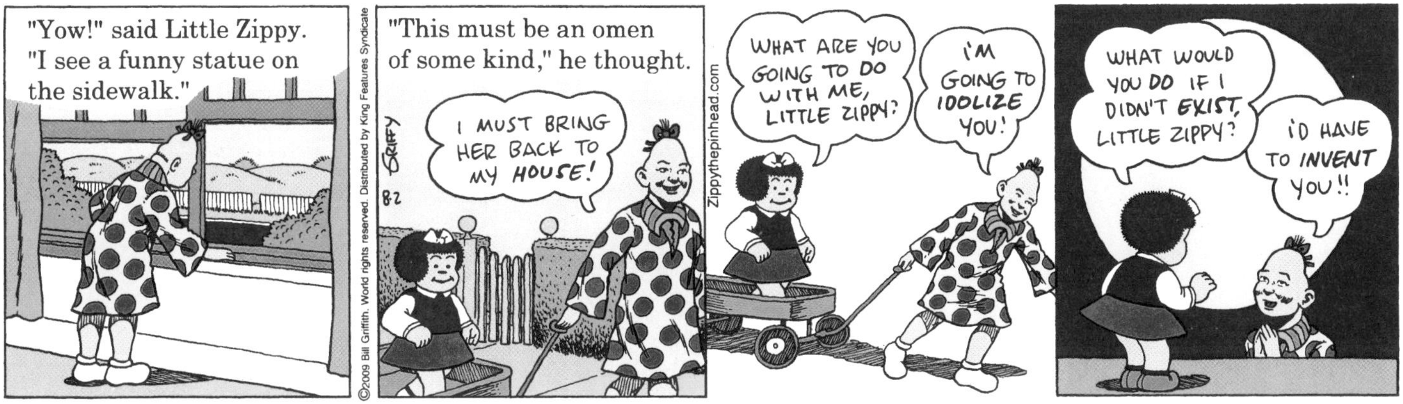
"Yow!" said Little Zippy. "I see a funny statue on the sidewalk."
"This must be an omen of some kind," he thought.
I MUST BRING HER BACK TO MY HOUSE!
GRIFFY 8-2
©2009 Bill Griffith. World rights reserved. Distributed by King Features Syndicate
Zippythepinhead.com
WHAT ARE YOU GOING TO DO WITH ME, LITTLE ZIPPY?
I'M GOING TO IDOLIZE YOU!
WHAT WOULD YOU DO IF I DIDN'T EXIST, LITTLE ZIPPY?
I'D HAVE TO INVENT YOU!!

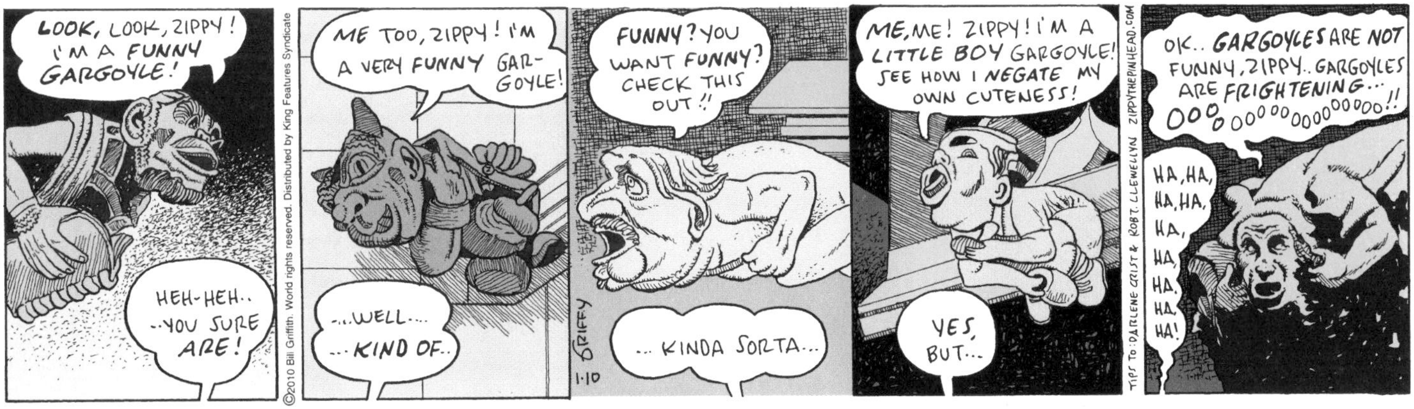
LOOK, LOOK, ZIPPY! I'M A FUNNY GARGOYLE!
HEH-HEH.. ..YOU SURE ARE!
©2010 Bill Griffith. World rights reserved. Distributed by King Features Syndicate
ME TOO, ZIPPY! I'M A VERY FUNNY GAR-GOYLE!
...WELL... ...KIND OF..
FUNNY? YOU WANT FUNNY? CHECK THIS OUT!!
... KINDA SORTA...
GRIFFY 1-10
ME, ME! ZIPPY! I'M A LITTLE BOY GARGOYLE! SEE HOW I NEGATE MY OWN CUTENESS!
YES, BUT...
TIPS TO: DARLENE CRIST & ROBT. LLEWELLYN ZIPPYTHEPINHEAD.COM
OK.. GARGOYLES ARE NOT FUNNY, ZIPPY.. GARGOYLES ARE FRIGHTENING... OOOooooooooooooooo!!
HA, HA, HA, HA, HA, HA, HA, HA, HA!

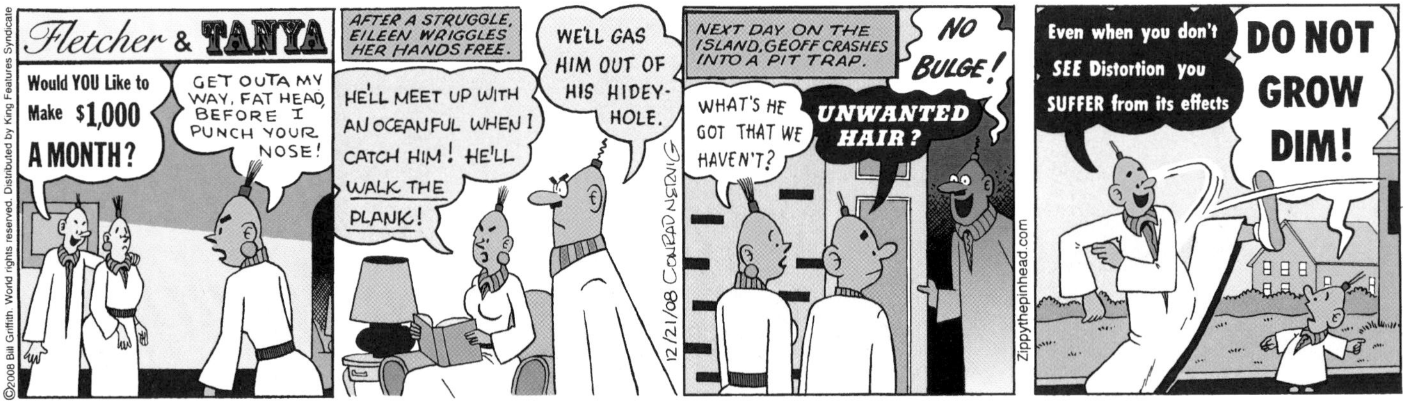
©2008 Bill Griffith. World rights reserved. Distributed by King Features Syndicate
Fletcher & TANYA
Would YOU Like to Make $1,000 A MONTH?
GET OUTA MY WAY, FAT HEAD, BEFORE I PUNCH YOUR NOSE!
AFTER A STRUGGLE, EILEEN WRIGGLES HER HANDS FREE.
HE'LL MEET UP WITH AN OCEANFUL WHEN I CATCH HIM! HE'LL WALK THE PLANK!
WE'LL GAS HIM OUT OF HIS HIDEY-HOLE.
12/21/08
NEXT DAY ON THE ISLAND, GEOFF CRASHES INTO A PIT TRAP.
NO BULGE!
WHAT'S HE GOT THAT WE HAVEN'T?
UNWANTED HAIR?
Zippythepinhead.com
Even when you don't SEE Distortion you SUFFER from its effects
DO NOT GROW DIM!

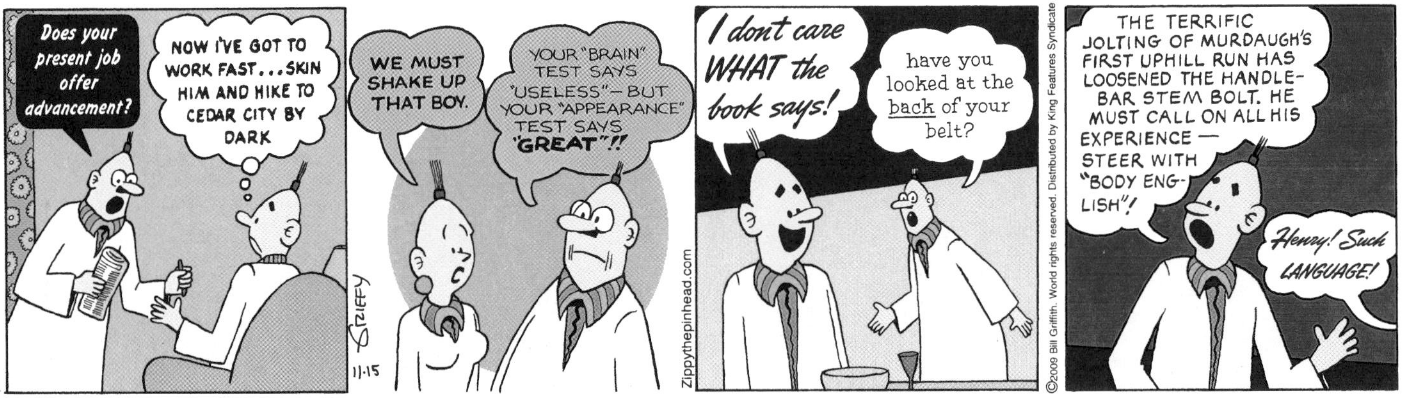
Does your present job offer advancement?
NOW I'VE GOT TO WORK FAST...SKIN HIM AND HIKE TO CEDAR CITY BY DARK
WE MUST SHAKE UP THAT BOY.
YOUR "BRAIN" TEST SAYS "USELESS"—BUT YOUR "APPEARANCE" TEST SAYS "GREAT"!!
GRIFFY
11-15
Zippythepinhead.com
I don't care WHAT the book says!
have you looked at the back of your belt?
©2009 Bill Griffith. World rights reserved. Distributed by King Features Syndicate
THE TERRIFIC JOLTING OF MURDAUGH'S FIRST UPHILL RUN HAS LOOSENED THE HANDLE-BAR STEM BOLT. HE MUST CALL ON ALL HIS EXPERIENCE — STEER WITH "BODY ENG-LISH"!
Henry! Such LANGUAGE!

NO WONDER BILL GOT THE WRONG IMPRESSION!
BY GEORGE, IT'S TRUE!
WHAT'S ALL THE FUSS ABOUT?
©2009 Bill Griffith. World rights reserved. Distributed by King Features Syndicate
SMOKE SMUDGE DOES NOT CLOUD Our Smiles
NO MOTHS CAN LIVE IN MY BLANKETS
NEVER IN ALL MY EXPERIENCE HAVE I SEEN SUCH ATTENTION GIVEN THE COMMON TOILET GERM
Zippythepinhead.com
YOU'RE UNPATRIOTIC, THAT'S WHAT!
Yes..CANADA does things to you!
CLOTHESPIN NOSE?
2/8/09 CONRAD NERVIG

©2009 Bill Griffith. World rights reserved. Distributed by King Features Syndicate
FEELING THE SQUEEZE?
Bible in one hand... Musket in the other.
IT'S QUICK AND EASY TO DRIVE A STAPLE THROUGH 32 SHEETS OF PAPER WITH A STURDY BOSTITCH
NO HUMP, NO BUMP!
WEAR IT LIKE A RING USE IT LIKE A GUN!
Quick, Watson, the Micro manipulator!
Zippythepinhead.com
NOW WILL YOU ADMIT YOU COULD USE A HULL AUTOMOBILE COMPASS TO MAKE RIGHT TURNS?
DOG FOOD SURE PACKS A PUNCH!
GRIFFY AND CONRAD NERVIG
HEY, IT SURE WAS FUN GIVING THOSE DINGBURGERS TH' FLETCHER & TANYA TREATMENT, WASN'T IT, HONEY?!
THERE'S NO BUBBLE LIKE DUBBLE BUBBLE

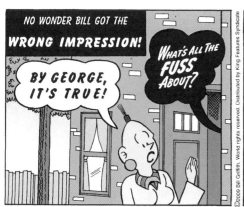

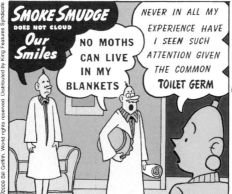

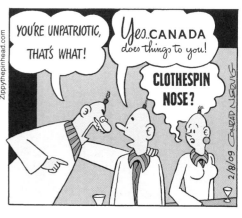

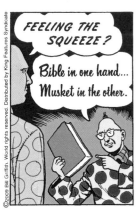

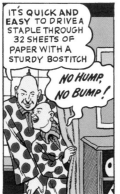

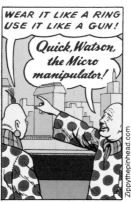

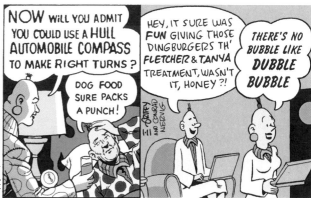

GRIFFY INTERVIEWS CONRAD NERVIG, THE MAN BEHIND DINGBURG'S FAVORITE COMIC STRIP, "FLETCHER & TANYA"--
SO, YOU RECENTLY REGAINED CONTROL OF TH' STRIP, I UNDERSTAND..
YES..IT WAS BRIEFLY TAKEN OVER BY A HACK WHO HAD NO FEELING FOR TH' MATERIAL..
WELL, THAT BRINGS UP A CENTRAL QUESTION--HOW IS "FLETCHER & TANYA" ACTUALLY CREATED? TH' DIALOGUE HAS A JERKY, DISCONNECTED QUALITY.. TELL ME, IS IT COMPUTER-GENERATED?
NO, NO! ALL TH' DIALOGUE IS CLIPPED FROM OLD MAGAZINE ADS! I SHUFFLE TH' XEROX COPIES OF THEM AROUND UNTIL THEY FORM SOME SORT OF UNEXPECTED, NON-LINEAR NARRATIVE FLOW..
I SEE...AND TH' WAY TH' CHARACTERS APPEAR--SO STIFF & "CARTOONY"...WHERE DOES THAT COME FROM, MAY I ASK?
TH' WHOLE LOOK IS INSPIRED BY A FORGOTTEN 1950s DAILY STRIP CALLED "MORTY MEEKLE," BY DICK CAVALLI..I LOVE ITS CLUMSY, GENERIC AESTHETIC..
WELL, IT IS A UNIQUE WORK, I'LL GRANT YOU THAT--BUT MOST NON-DINGBURGERS FAIL TO SEE ANY HUMOR IN IT!
GIVE IT TIME & IT WILL EVENTUALLY REARRANGE TH' MOLECULAR STRUCTURE OF YOUR ENTIRE CEREBRAL CORTEX!
GRIFFY 10.5
©2008 Bill Griffith. World rights reserved. Distributed by King Features Syndicate
Zippythepinhead.com

BURP!
COUGH!
SNEEZE!!
GRIFFY 5.9
SNORE.......
$\int_a^b f(x)\,dx = F(b) - F(a).$
$\frac{d}{dx}\int_a^x f(t)\,dt = f(x).$
Zippythepinhead.com
©2010 Bill Griffith. World rights reserved. Distributed by King Features Syndicate

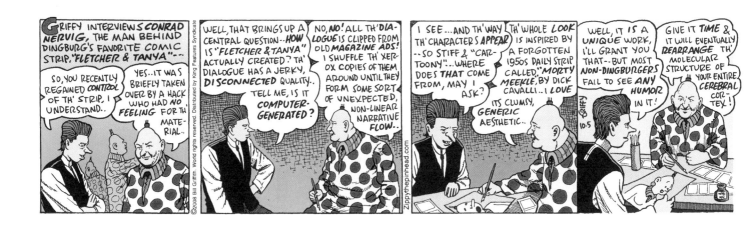

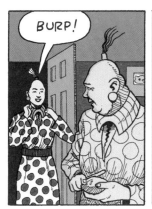

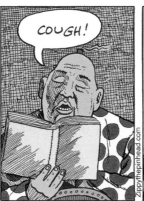

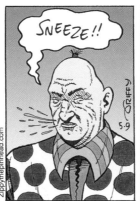

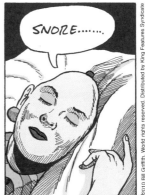

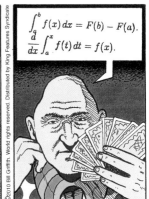

ZIPPY and GRIFFY

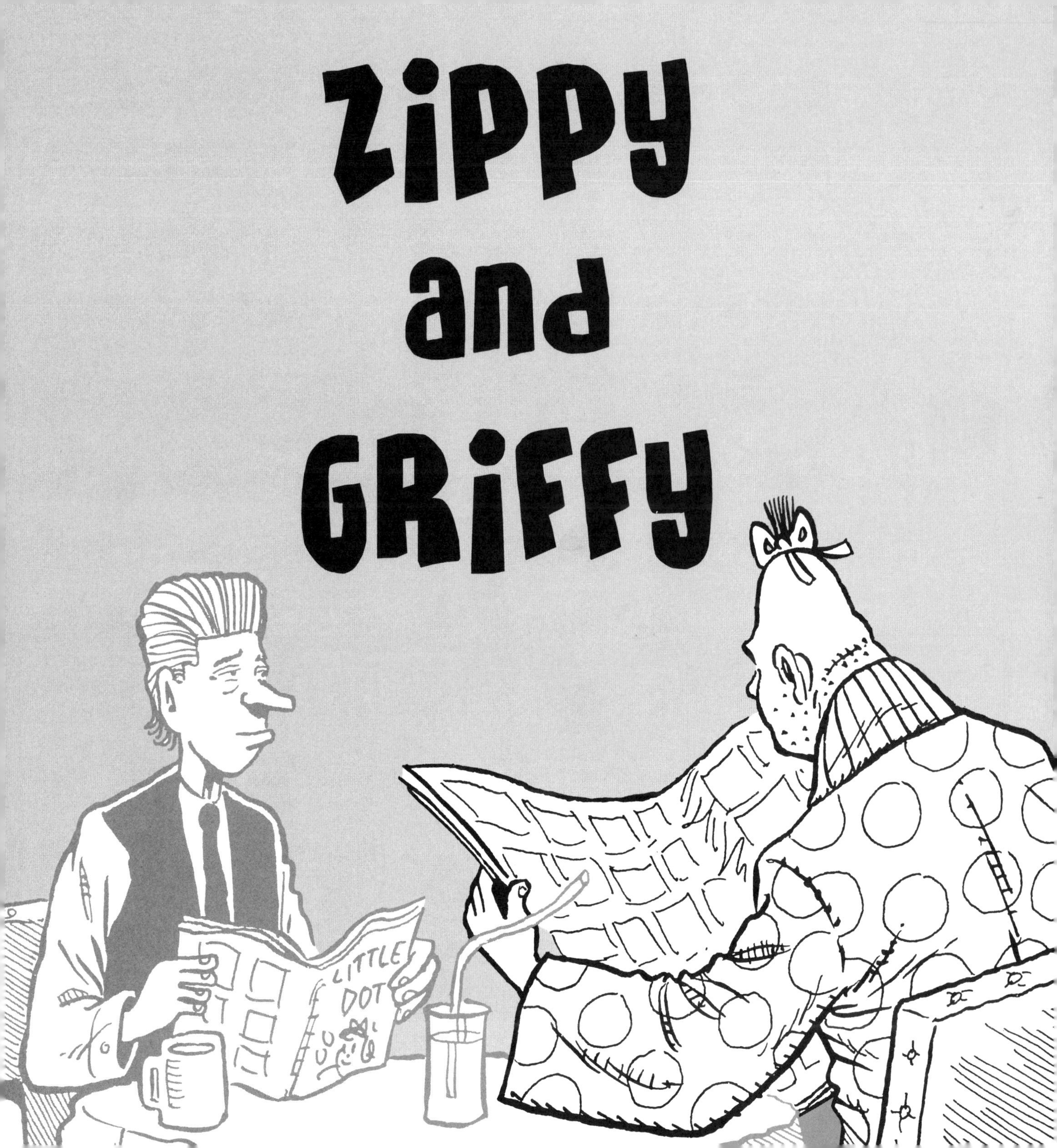
LITTLE DOT

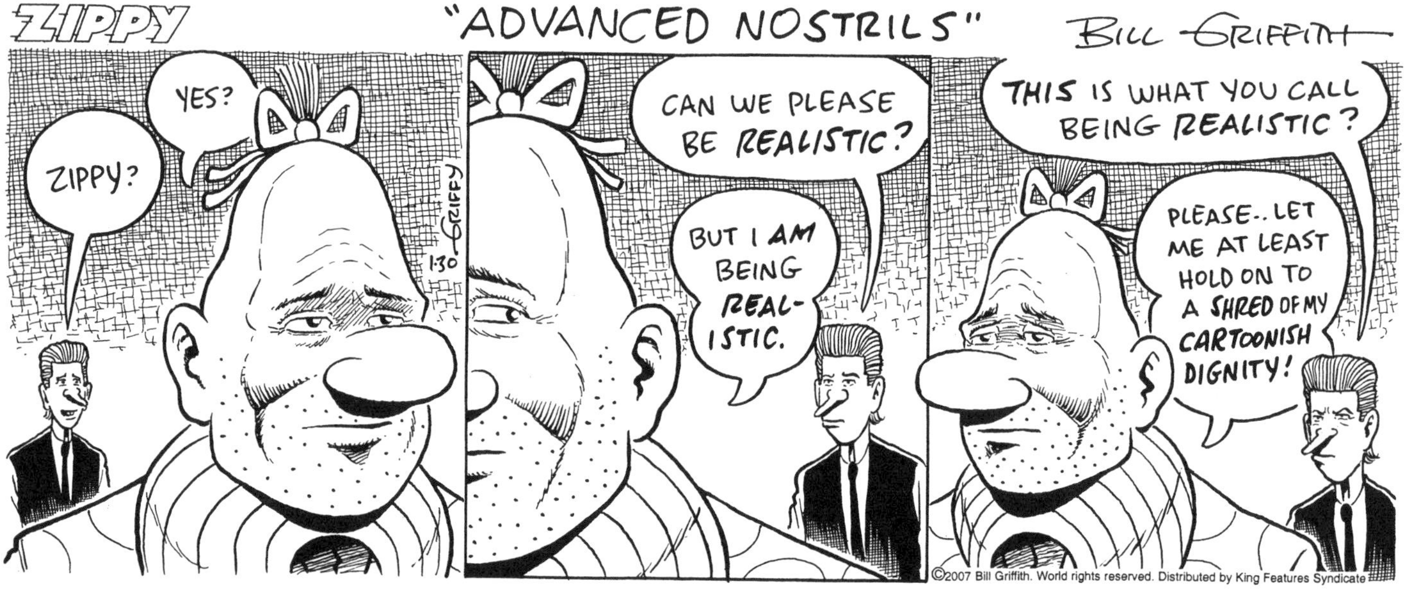
ZIPPY
"ADVANCED NOSTRILS"
BILL GRIFFITH
ZIPPY?
YES?
GRIFFY 1·30
CAN WE PLEASE BE REALISTIC?
BUT I AM BEING REAL-ISTIC.
THIS IS WHAT YOU CALL BEING REALISTIC?
PLEASE.. LET ME AT LEAST HOLD ON TO A SHRED OF MY CARTOONISH DIGNITY!
©2007 Bill Griffith. World rights reserved. Distributed by King Features Syndicate

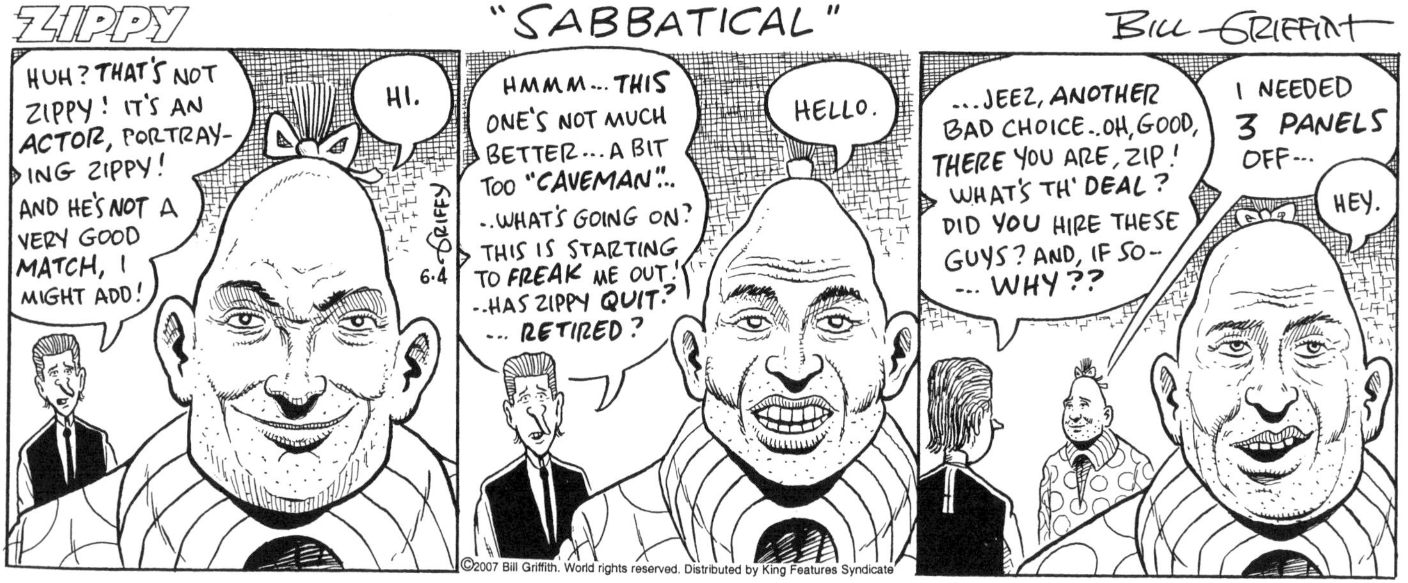
ZIPPY
"SABBATICAL"
BILL GRIFFITH
HUH? THAT'S NOT ZIPPY! IT'S AN ACTOR, PORTRAYING ZIPPY! AND HE'S NOT A VERY GOOD MATCH, I MIGHT ADD!
HI.
GRIFFY 6·4
HMMM... THIS ONE'S NOT MUCH BETTER... A BIT TOO "CAVEMAN"... ..WHAT'S GOING ON? THIS IS STARTING TO FREAK ME OUT! ..HAS ZIPPY QUIT? ... RETIRED?
HELLO.
...JEEZ, ANOTHER BAD CHOICE..OH, GOOD, THERE YOU ARE, ZIP! WHAT'S TH' DEAL? DID YOU HIRE THESE GUYS? AND, IF SO-- ... WHY??
I NEEDED 3 PANELS OFF...
HEY.
©2007 Bill Griffith. World rights reserved. Distributed by King Features Syndicate

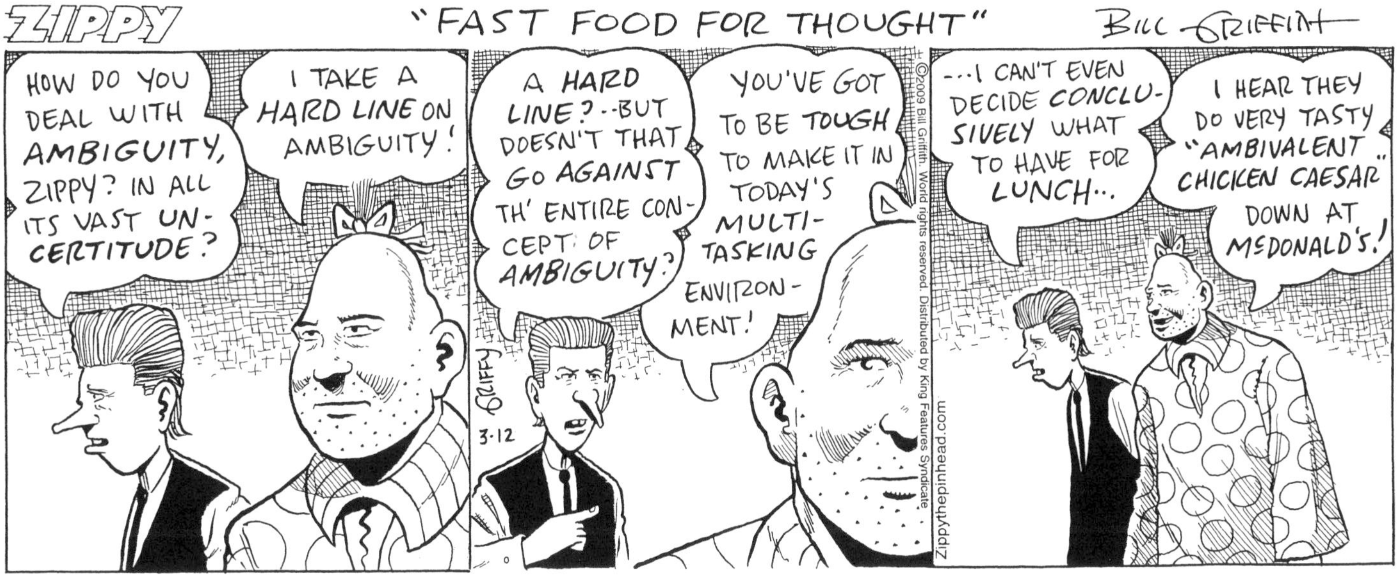
ZIPPY
"FAST FOOD FOR THOUGHT"
BILL GRIFFITH
HOW DO YOU DEAL WITH AMBIGUITY, ZIPPY? IN ALL ITS VAST UNCERTITUDE?
I TAKE A HARD LINE ON AMBIGUITY!
A HARD LINE?..BUT DOESN'T THAT GO AGAINST TH' ENTIRE CONCEPT OF AMBIGUITY?
YOU'VE GOT TO BE TOUGH TO MAKE IT IN TODAY'S MULTI-TASKING ENVIRONMENT!
...I CAN'T EVEN DECIDE CONCLUSIVELY WHAT TO HAVE FOR LUNCH..
I HEAR THEY DO VERY TASTY "AMBIVALENT CHICKEN CAESAR" DOWN AT McDONALD'S!
GRIFFY
3-12
©2009 Bill Griffith. World rights reserved. Distributed by King Features Syndicate
Zippythepinhead.com

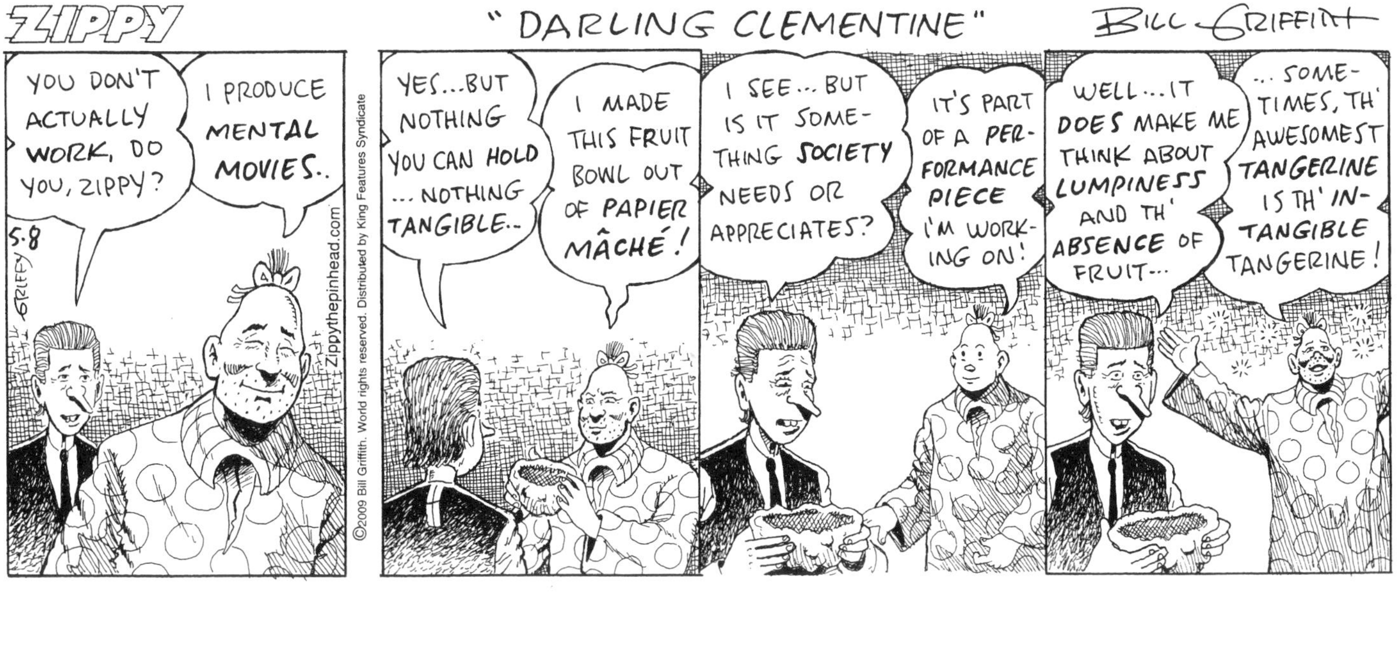
ZIPPY
"DARLING CLEMENTINE"
BILL GRIFFITH
YOU DON'T ACTUALLY WORK, DO YOU, ZIPPY?
I PRODUCE MENTAL MOVIES..
5-8
GRIFFY
©2009 Bill Griffith. World rights reserved. Distributed by King Features Syndicate
Zippythepinhead.com
YES...BUT NOTHING YOU CAN HOLD ...NOTHING TANGIBLE..
I MADE THIS FRUIT BOWL OUT OF PAPIER MÂCHÉ!
I SEE...BUT IS IT SOMETHING SOCIETY NEEDS OR APPRECIATES?
IT'S PART OF A PERFORMANCE PIECE I'M WORKING ON!
WELL...IT DOES MAKE ME THINK ABOUT LUMPINESS AND TH' ABSENCE OF FRUIT...
...SOMETIMES, TH' AWESOMEST TANGERINE IS TH' INTANGIBLE TANGERINE!

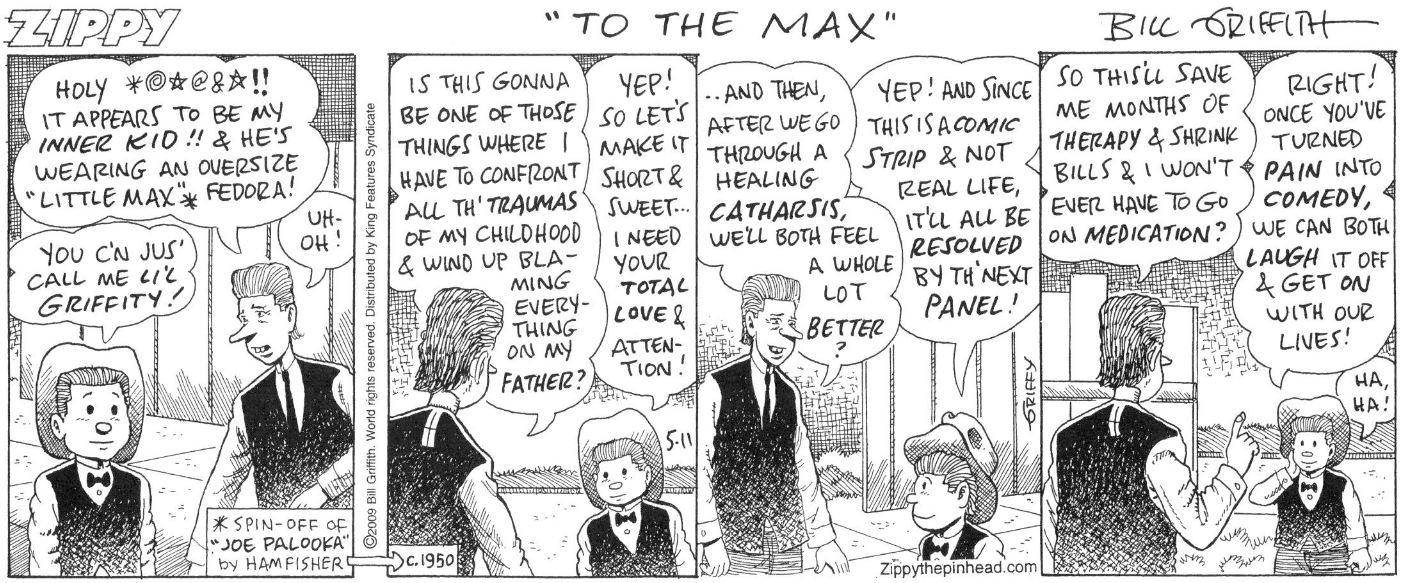
ZIPPY
"TO THE MAX"
BILL GRIFFITH
HOLY *@☆@&☆!! IT APPEARS TO BE MY INNER KID!! & HE'S WEARING AN OVERSIZE "LITTLE MAX"* FEDORA!
YOU C'N JUS' CALL ME LI'L GRIFFITY!
UH-OH!
* SPIN-OFF OF "JOE PALOOKA" by HAMFISHER
c.1950
©2009 Bill Griffith. World rights reserved. Distributed by King Features Syndicate
IS THIS GONNA BE ONE OF THOSE THINGS WHERE I HAVE TO CONFRONT ALL TH' TRAUMAS OF MY CHILDHOOD & WIND UP BLAMING EVERYTHING ON MY FATHER?
YEP! SO LET'S MAKE IT SHORT & SWEET... I NEED YOUR TOTAL LOVE & ATTENTION!
5.11
..AND THEN, AFTER WE GO THROUGH A HEALING CATHARSIS, WE'LL BOTH FEEL A WHOLE LOT BETTER?
YEP! AND SINCE THIS IS A COMIC STRIP & NOT REAL LIFE, IT'LL ALL BE RESOLVED BY TH' NEXT PANEL!
GRIFFY
Zippythepinhead.com
SO THIS'LL SAVE ME MONTHS OF THERAPY & SHRINK BILLS & I WON'T EVER HAVE TO GO ON MEDICATION?
RIGHT! ONCE YOU'VE TURNED PAIN INTO COMEDY, WE CAN BOTH LAUGH IT OFF & GET ON WITH OUR LIVES!
HA, HA!

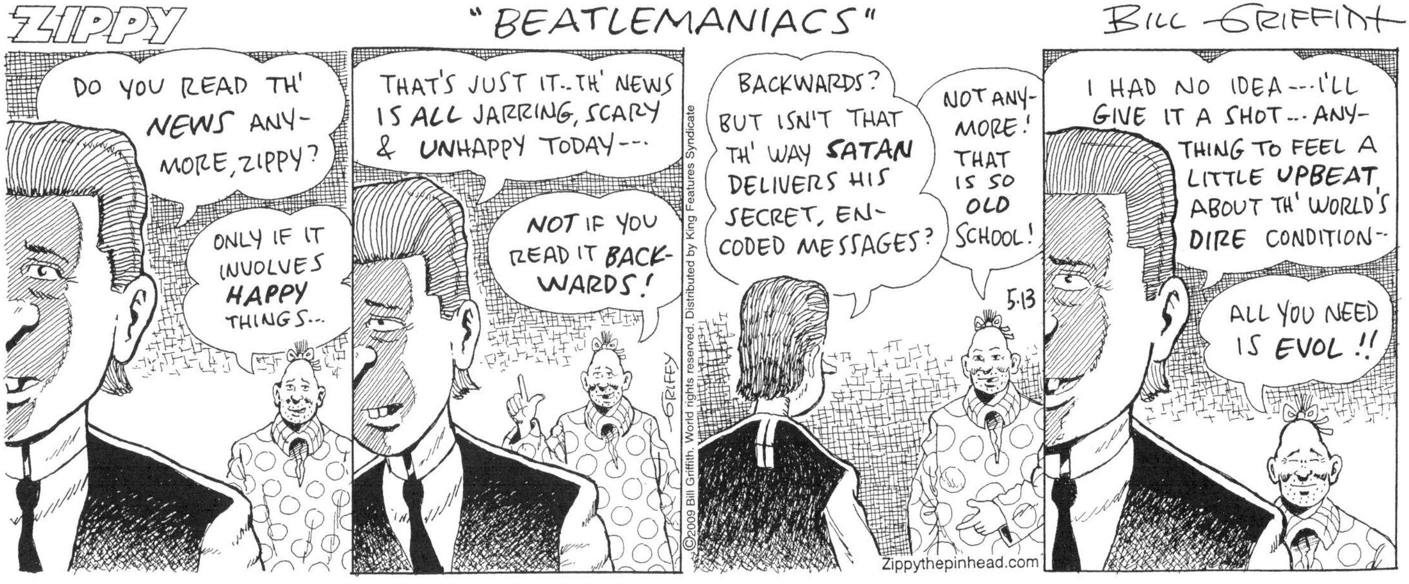
ZIPPY
"BEATLEMANIACS"
BILL GRIFFITH
DO YOU READ TH' NEWS ANYMORE, ZIPPY?
ONLY IF IT INVOLVES HAPPY THINGS...
THAT'S JUST IT..TH' NEWS IS ALL JARRING, SCARY & UNHAPPY TODAY--.
NOT IF YOU READ IT BACKWARDS!
GRIFFY
©2009 Bill Griffith. World rights reserved. Distributed by King Features Syndicate
BACKWARDS? BUT ISN'T THAT TH' WAY SATAN DELIVERS HIS SECRET, ENCODED MESSAGES?
NOT ANYMORE! THAT IS SO OLD SCHOOL!
5.13
Zippythepinhead.com
I HAD NO IDEA---I'LL GIVE IT A SHOT--- ANYTHING TO FEEL A LITTLE UPBEAT ABOUT TH' WORLD'S DIRE CONDITION--
ALL YOU NEED IS EVOL!!

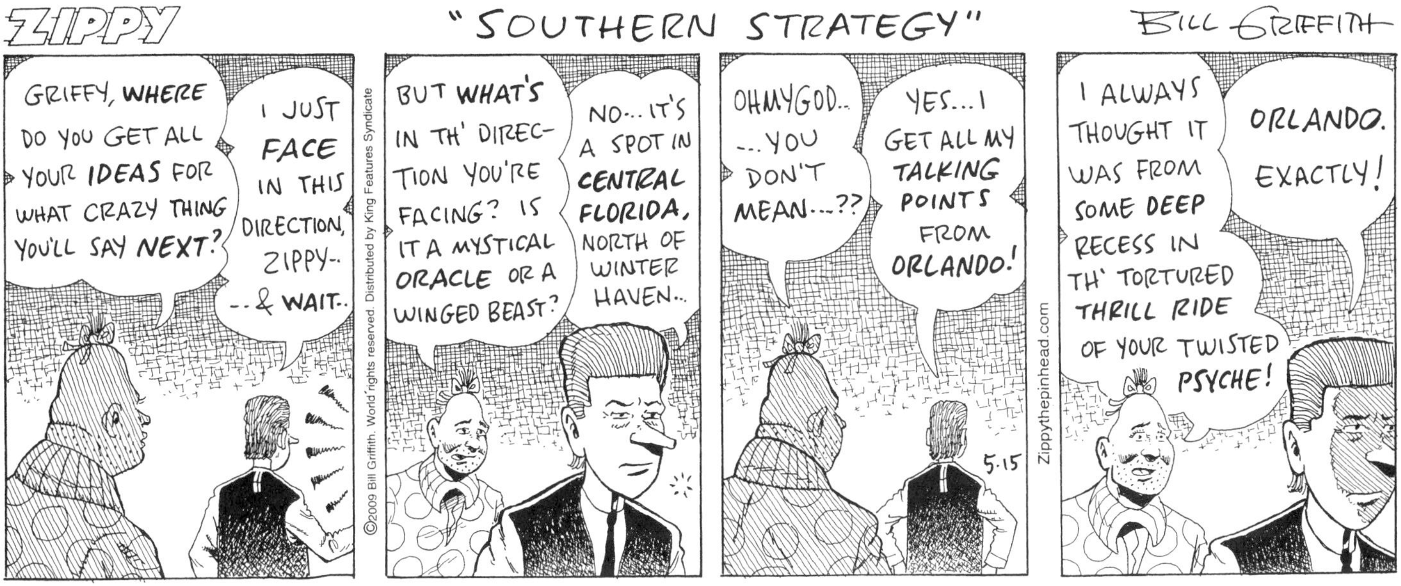
ZIPPY
"SOUTHERN STRATEGY"
BILL GRIFFITH
GRIFFY, WHERE DO YOU GET ALL YOUR IDEAS FOR WHAT CRAZY THING YOU'LL SAY NEXT?
I JUST FACE IN THIS DIRECTION, ZIPPY.. --& WAIT..
©2009 Bill Griffith. World rights reserved. Distributed by King Features Syndicate
BUT WHAT'S IN TH' DIRECTION YOU'RE FACING? IS IT A MYSTICAL ORACLE OR A WINGED BEAST?
NO... IT'S A SPOT IN CENTRAL FLORIDA, NORTH OF WINTER HAVEN...
OHMYGOD.. ...YOU DON'T MEAN...??
YES...I GET ALL MY TALKING POINTS FROM ORLANDO!
5·15
Zippythepinhead.com
I ALWAYS THOUGHT IT WAS FROM SOME DEEP RECESS IN TH' TORTURED THRILL RIDE OF YOUR TWISTED PSYCHE!
ORLANDO. EXACTLY!

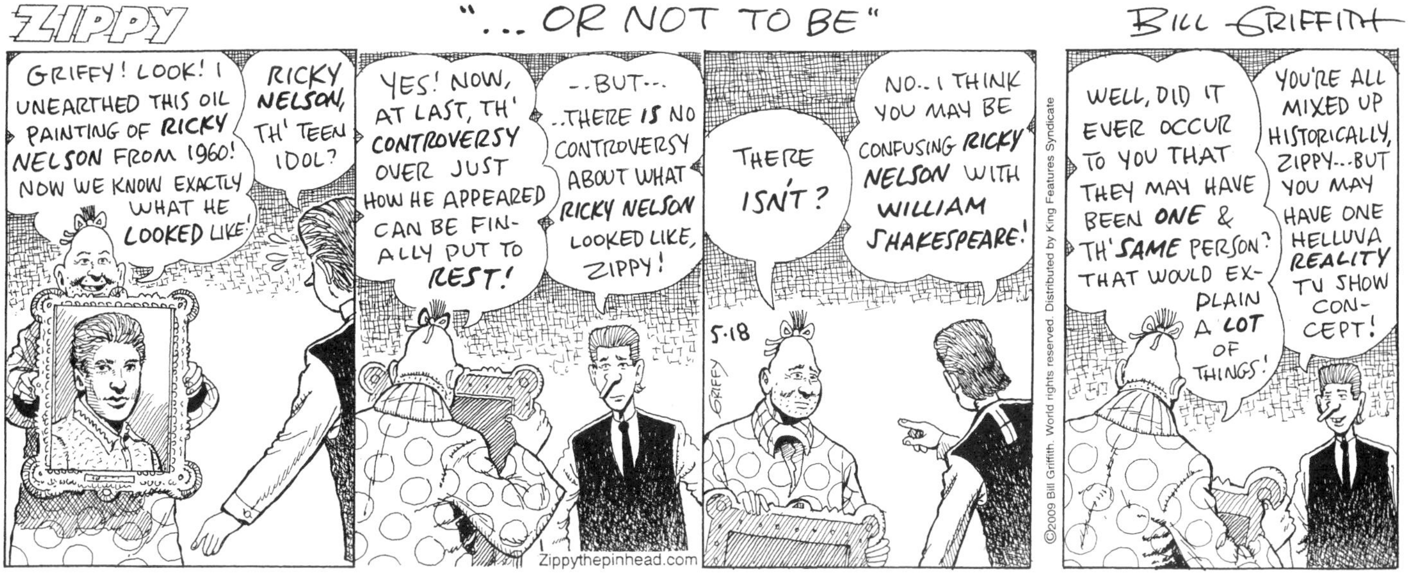
ZIPPY
"...OR NOT TO BE"
BILL GRIFFITH
GRIFFY! LOOK! I UNEARTHED THIS OIL PAINTING OF RICKY NELSON FROM 1960! NOW WE KNOW EXACTLY WHAT HE LOOKED LIKE!
RICKY NELSON, TH' TEEN IDOL?
YES! NOW, AT LAST, TH' CONTROVERSY OVER JUST HOW HE APPEARED CAN BE FINALLY PUT TO REST!
--BUT-- ..THERE IS NO CONTROVERSY ABOUT WHAT RICKY NELSON LOOKED LIKE, ZIPPY!
Zippythepinhead.com
THERE ISN'T?
NO..I THINK YOU MAY BE CONFUSING RICKY NELSON WITH WILLIAM SHAKESPEARE!
5·18
GRIFFY
©2009 Bill Griffith. World rights reserved. Distributed by King Features Syndicate
WELL, DID IT EVER OCCUR TO YOU THAT THEY MAY HAVE BEEN ONE & TH' SAME PERSON? THAT WOULD EXPLAIN A LOT OF THINGS!
YOU'RE ALL MIXED UP HISTORICALLY, ZIPPY...BUT YOU MAY HAVE ONE HELLUVA REALITY TV SHOW CONCEPT!

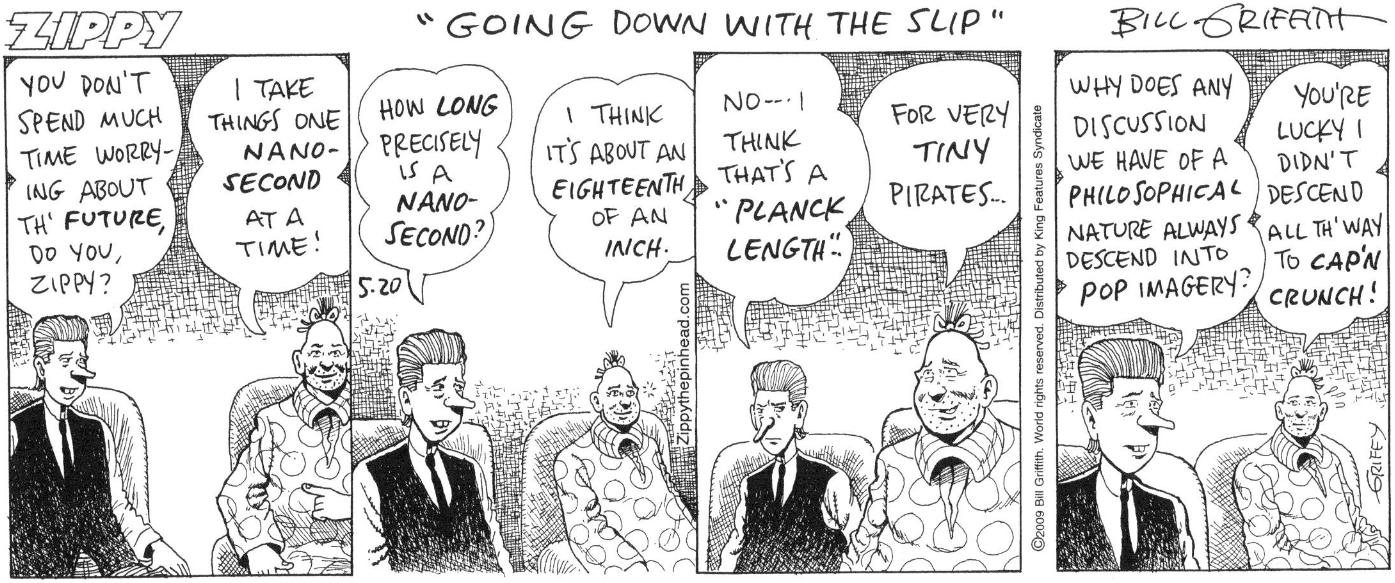
ZIPPY
"GOING DOWN WITH THE SLIP"
BILL GRIFFITH
YOU DON'T SPEND MUCH TIME WORRYING ABOUT TH' FUTURE, DO YOU, ZIPPY?
I TAKE THINGS ONE NANO-SECOND AT A TIME!
5.20
HOW LONG PRECISELY IS A NANO-SECOND?
I THINK IT'S ABOUT AN EIGHTEENTH OF AN INCH.
Zippythepinhead.com
NO--I THINK THAT'S A "PLANCK LENGTH"..
FOR VERY TINY PIRATES...
©2009 Bill Griffith. World rights reserved. Distributed by King Features Syndicate
WHY DOES ANY DISCUSSION WE HAVE OF A PHILOSOPHICAL NATURE ALWAYS DESCEND INTO POP IMAGERY?
YOU'RE LUCKY I DIDN'T DESCEND ALL TH' WAY TO CAP'N CRUNCH!
GRIFFY

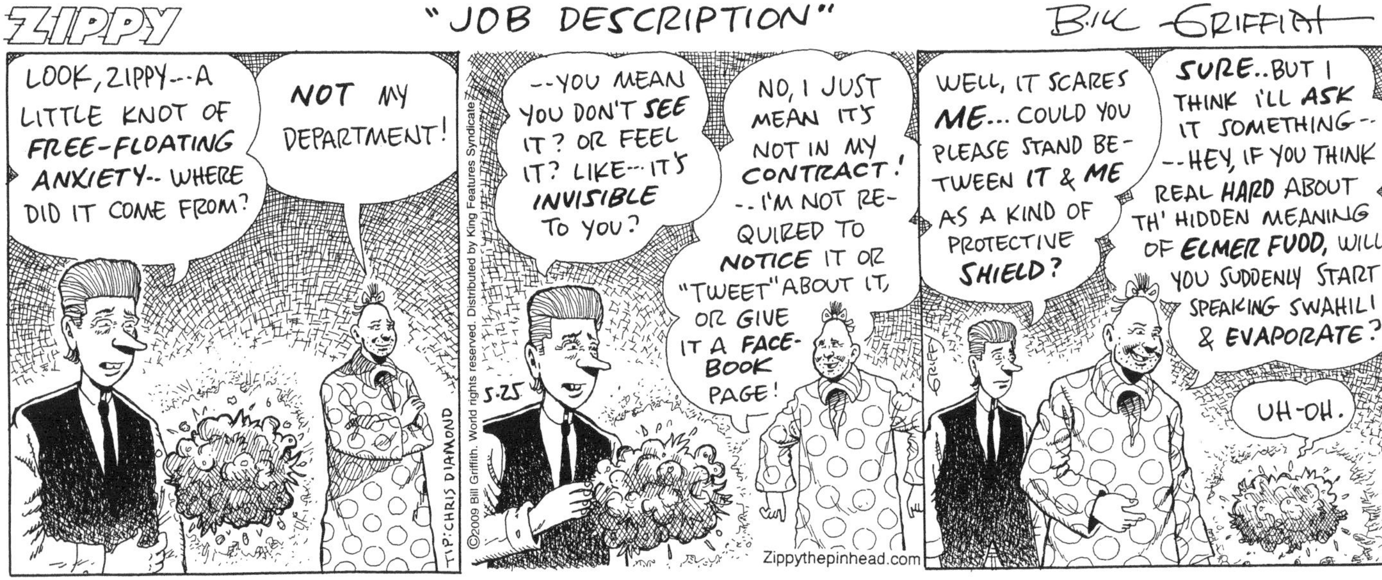
ZIPPY
"JOB DESCRIPTION"
BILL GRIFFITH
LOOK, ZIPPY--A LITTLE KNOT OF FREE-FLOATING ANXIETY-- WHERE DID IT COME FROM?
NOT MY DEPARTMENT!
TIP: CHRIS DIAMOND
©2009 Bill Griffith. World rights reserved. Distributed by King Features Syndicate
--YOU MEAN YOU DON'T SEE IT? OR FEEL IT? LIKE--IT'S INVISIBLE TO YOU?
NO, I JUST MEAN IT'S NOT IN MY CONTRACT! --I'M NOT REQUIRED TO NOTICE IT OR "TWEET" ABOUT IT, OR GIVE IT A FACEBOOK PAGE!
5.25
Zippythepinhead.com
WELL, IT SCARES ME... COULD YOU PLEASE STAND BETWEEN IT & ME AS A KIND OF PROTECTIVE SHIELD?
SURE..BUT I THINK I'LL ASK IT SOMETHING-- --HEY, IF YOU THINK REAL HARD ABOUT TH' HIDDEN MEANING OF ELMER FUDD, WILL YOU SUDDENLY START SPEAKING SWAHILI & EVAPORATE?
UH-OH.
GRIFFY

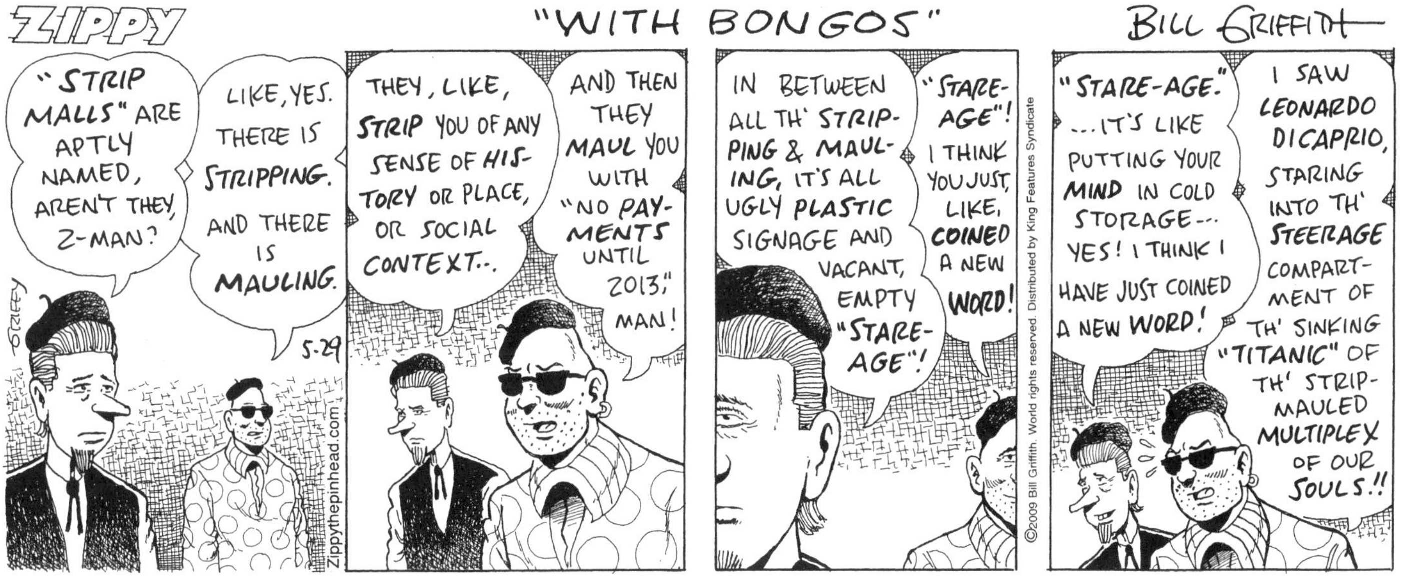
ZIPPY
"WITH BONGOS"
BILL GRIFFITH
"STRIP MALLS" ARE APTLY NAMED, AREN'T THEY, Z-MAN?
LIKE, YES. THERE IS STRIPPING. AND THERE IS MAULING.
GRIFFY
5-29
Zippythepinhead.com
THEY, LIKE, STRIP YOU OF ANY SENSE OF HISTORY OR PLACE, OR SOCIAL CONTEXT...
AND THEN THEY MAUL YOU WITH "NO PAYMENTS UNTIL 2013," MAN!
IN BETWEEN ALL TH' STRIPPING & MAULING, IT'S ALL UGLY PLASTIC SIGNAGE AND VACANT, EMPTY "STARE-AGE"!
"STARE-AGE"! I THINK YOU JUST, LIKE, COINED A NEW WORD!
©2009 Bill Griffith. World rights reserved. Distributed by King Features Syndicate
"STARE-AGE." ...IT'S LIKE PUTTING YOUR MIND IN COLD STORAGE... YES! I THINK I HAVE JUST COINED A NEW WORD!
I SAW LEONARDO DICAPRIO, STARING INTO TH' STEERAGE COMPARTMENT OF TH' SINKING "TITANIC" OF TH' STRIP-MAULED MULTIPLEX OF OUR SOULS!!

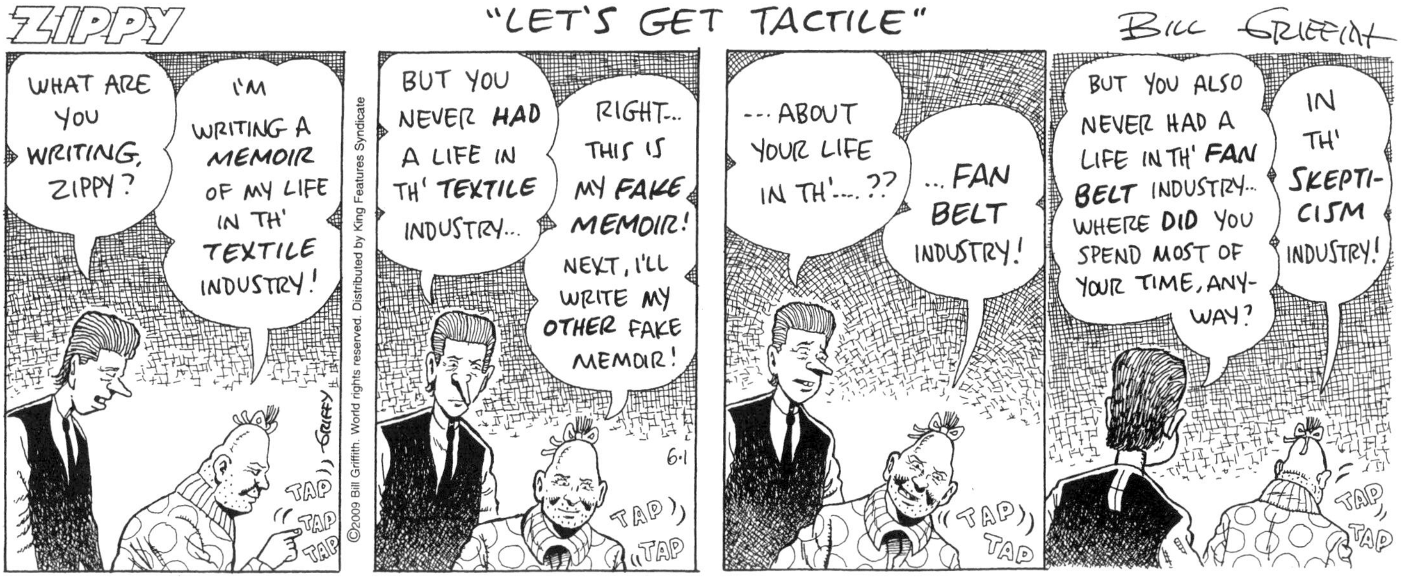
ZIPPY
"LET'S GET TACTILE"
BILL GRIFFITH
WHAT ARE YOU WRITING, ZIPPY?
I'M WRITING A MEMOIR OF MY LIFE IN TH' TEXTILE INDUSTRY!
GRIFFY
TAP TAP TAP
©2009 Bill Griffith. World rights reserved. Distributed by King Features Syndicate
BUT YOU NEVER HAD A LIFE IN TH' TEXTILE INDUSTRY...
RIGHT... THIS IS MY FAKE MEMOIR! NEXT, I'LL WRITE MY OTHER FAKE MEMOIR!
6-1
TAP TAP
...ABOUT YOUR LIFE IN TH'...??
...FAN BELT INDUSTRY!
TAP TAP
BUT YOU ALSO NEVER HAD A LIFE IN TH' FAN BELT INDUSTRY... WHERE DID YOU SPEND MOST OF YOUR TIME, ANYWAY?
IN TH' SKEPTICISM INDUSTRY!
TAP TAP

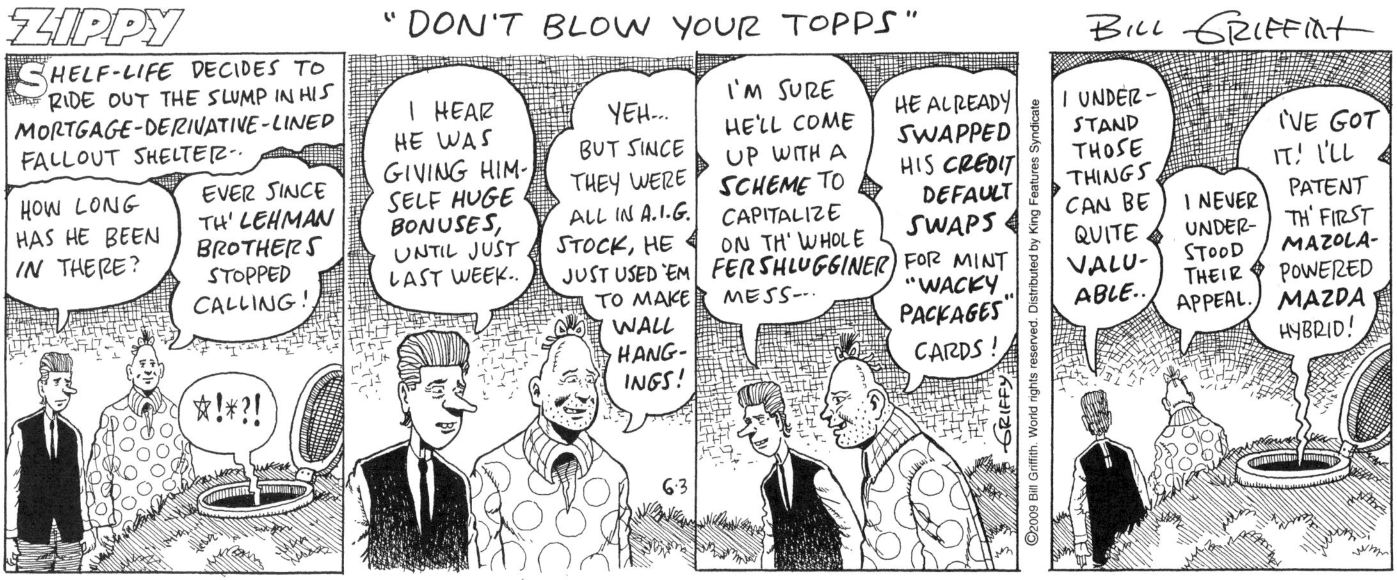
ZIPPY
"DON'T BLOW YOUR TOPPS"
BILL GRIFFITH
SHELF-LIFE DECIDES TO RIDE OUT THE SLUMP IN HIS MORTGAGE-DERIVATIVE-LINED FALLOUT SHELTER..
HOW LONG HAS HE BEEN IN THERE?
EVER SINCE TH' LEHMAN BROTHERS STOPPED CALLING!
☆!*?!
I HEAR HE WAS GIVING HIMSELF HUGE BONUSES, UNTIL JUST LAST WEEK..
YEH... BUT SINCE THEY WERE ALL IN A.I.G. STOCK, HE JUST USED 'EM TO MAKE WALL HANGINGS!
6·3
I'M SURE HE'LL COME UP WITH A SCHEME TO CAPITALIZE ON TH' WHOLE FERSHLUGGINER MESS--.
HE ALREADY SWAPPED HIS CREDIT DEFAULT SWAPS FOR MINT "WACKY PACKAGES" CARDS!
GRIFFY
©2009 Bill Griffith. World rights reserved. Distributed by King Features Syndicate
I UNDERSTAND THOSE THINGS CAN BE QUITE VALUABLE..
I NEVER UNDERSTOOD THEIR APPEAL.
I'VE GOT IT! I'LL PATENT TH' FIRST MAZOLA-POWERED MAZDA HYBRID!

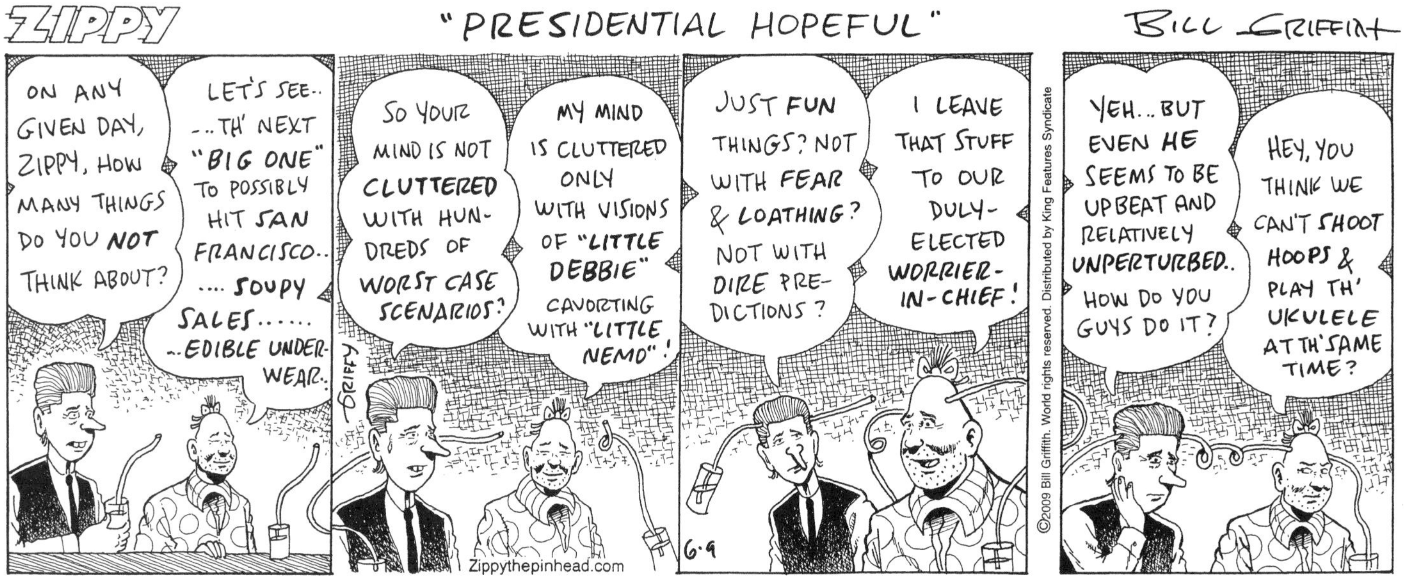
ZIPPY
"PRESIDENTIAL HOPEFUL"
BILL GRIFFITH
ON ANY GIVEN DAY, ZIPPY, HOW MANY THINGS DO YOU NOT THINK ABOUT?
LET'S SEE.. ..TH' NEXT "BIG ONE" TO POSSIBLY HIT SAN FRANCISCO.. .... SOUPY SALES...... ..EDIBLE UNDERWEAR..
GRIFFY
SO YOUR MIND IS NOT CLUTTERED WITH HUNDREDS OF WORST CASE SCENARIOS?
MY MIND IS CLUTTERED ONLY WITH VISIONS OF "LITTLE DEBBIE" CAVORTING WITH "LITTLE NEMO"!
Zippythepinhead.com
JUST FUN THINGS? NOT WITH FEAR & LOATHING? NOT WITH DIRE PREDICTIONS?
I LEAVE THAT STUFF TO OUR DULY-ELECTED WORRIER-IN-CHIEF!
6·9
©2009 Bill Griffith. World rights reserved. Distributed by King Features Syndicate
YEH... BUT EVEN HE SEEMS TO BE UPBEAT AND RELATIVELY UNPERTURBED.. HOW DO YOU GUYS DO IT?
HEY, YOU THINK WE CAN'T SHOOT HOOPS & PLAY TH' UKULELE AT TH' SAME TIME?

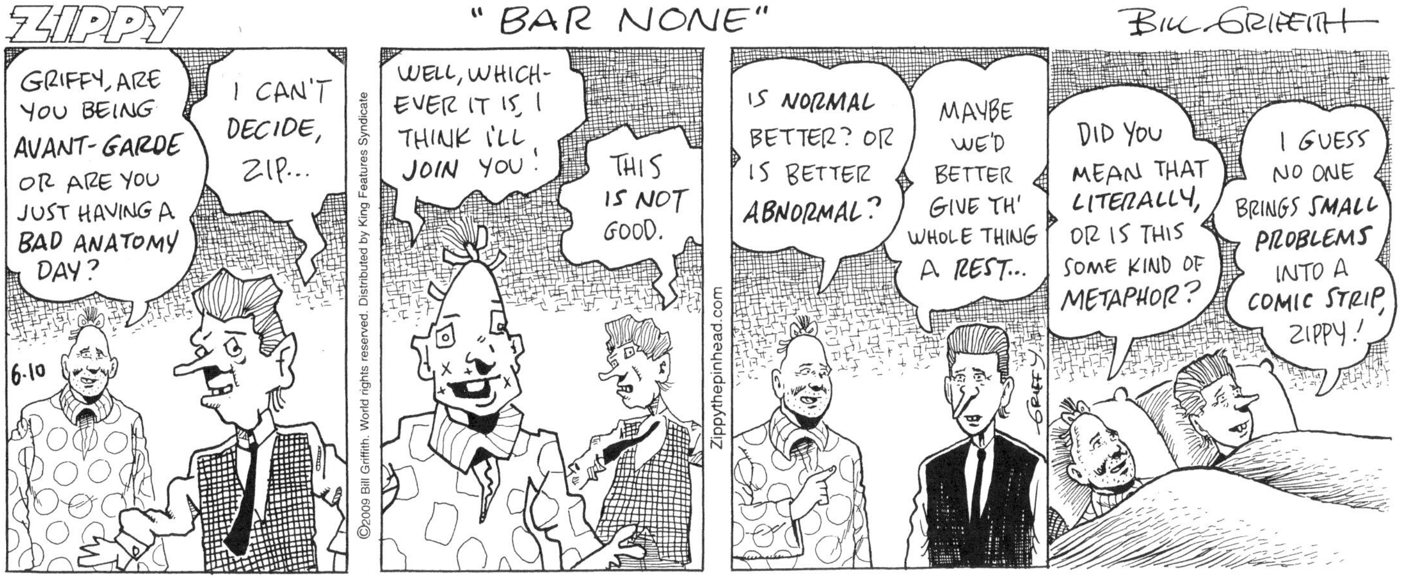
ZIPPY
"BAR NONE"
BILL GRIFFITH
GRIFFY, ARE YOU BEING AVANT-GARDE OR ARE YOU JUST HAVING A BAD ANATOMY DAY?
I CAN'T DECIDE, ZIP...
6-10
©2009 Bill Griffith. World rights reserved. Distributed by King Features Syndicate
WELL, WHICH-EVER IT IS, I THINK I'LL JOIN YOU!
THIS IS NOT GOOD.
Zippythepinhead.com
IS NORMAL BETTER? OR IS BETTER ABNORMAL?
MAYBE WE'D BETTER GIVE TH' WHOLE THING A REST...
GRIFF
DID YOU MEAN THAT LITERALLY, OR IS THIS SOME KIND OF METAPHOR?
I GUESS NO ONE BRINGS SMALL PROBLEMS INTO A COMIC STRIP, ZIPPY!

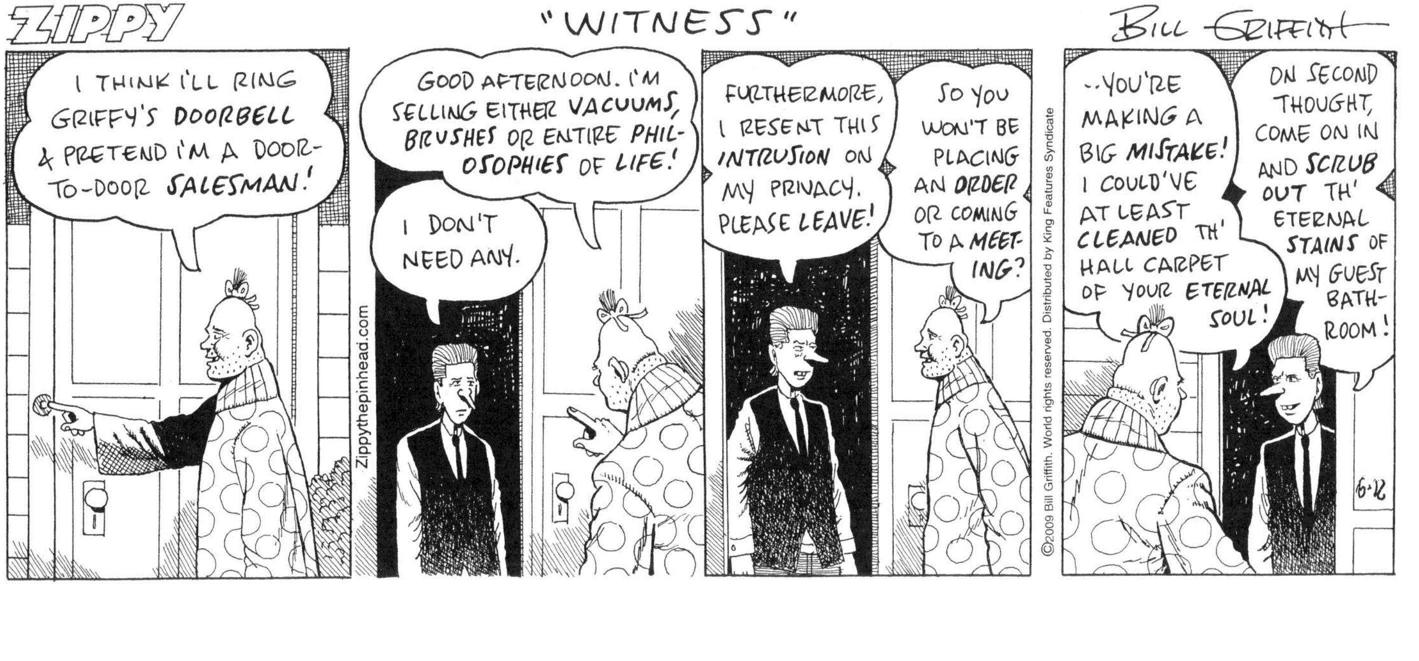
ZIPPY
"WITNESS"
BILL GRIFFITH
I THINK I'LL RING GRIFFY'S DOORBELL & PRETEND I'M A DOOR-TO-DOOR SALESMAN!
Zippythepinhead.com
GOOD AFTERNOON. I'M SELLING EITHER VACUUMS, BRUSHES OR ENTIRE PHIL-OSOPHIES OF LIFE!
I DON'T NEED ANY.
FURTHERMORE, I RESENT THIS INTRUSION ON MY PRIVACY. PLEASE LEAVE!
SO YOU WON'T BE PLACING AN ORDER OR COMING TO A MEET-ING?
©2009 Bill Griffith. World rights reserved. Distributed by King Features Syndicate
..YOU'RE MAKING A BIG MISTAKE! I COULD'VE AT LEAST CLEANED TH' HALL CARPET OF YOUR ETERNAL SOUL!
ON SECOND THOUGHT, COME ON IN AND SCRUB OUT TH' ETERNAL STAINS OF MY GUEST BATH-ROOM!
6-12

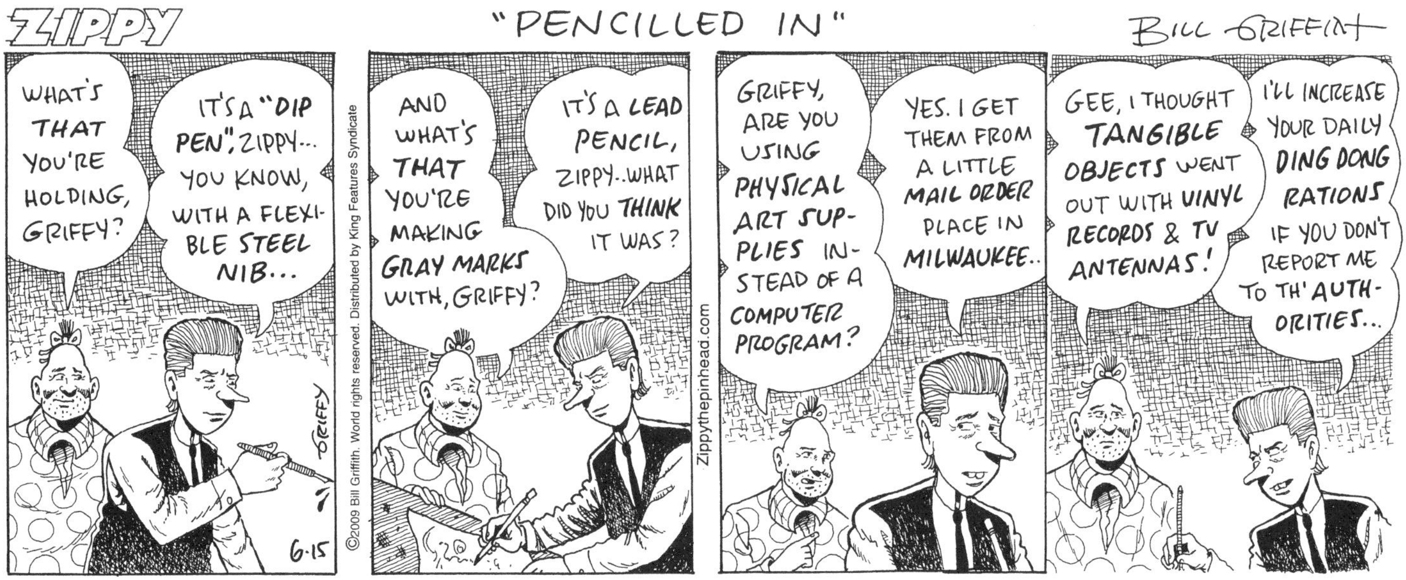
ZIPPY
"PENCILLED IN"
BILL GRIFFITH
WHAT'S THAT YOU'RE HOLDING, GRIFFY?
IT'S A "DIP PEN", ZIPPY... YOU KNOW, WITH A FLEXIBLE STEEL NIB...
GRIFFY
6·15
©2009 Bill Griffith. World rights reserved. Distributed by King Features Syndicate
AND WHAT'S THAT YOU'RE MAKING GRAY MARKS WITH, GRIFFY?
IT'S A LEAD PENCIL, ZIPPY..WHAT DID YOU THINK IT WAS?
Zippythepinhead.com
GRIFFY, ARE YOU USING PHYSICAL ART SUPPLIES INSTEAD OF A COMPUTER PROGRAM?
YES. I GET THEM FROM A LITTLE MAIL ORDER PLACE IN MILWAUKEE..
GEE, I THOUGHT TANGIBLE OBJECTS WENT OUT WITH VINYL RECORDS & TV ANTENNAS!
I'LL INCREASE YOUR DAILY DING DONG RATIONS IF YOU DON'T REPORT ME TO TH' AUTHORITIES...

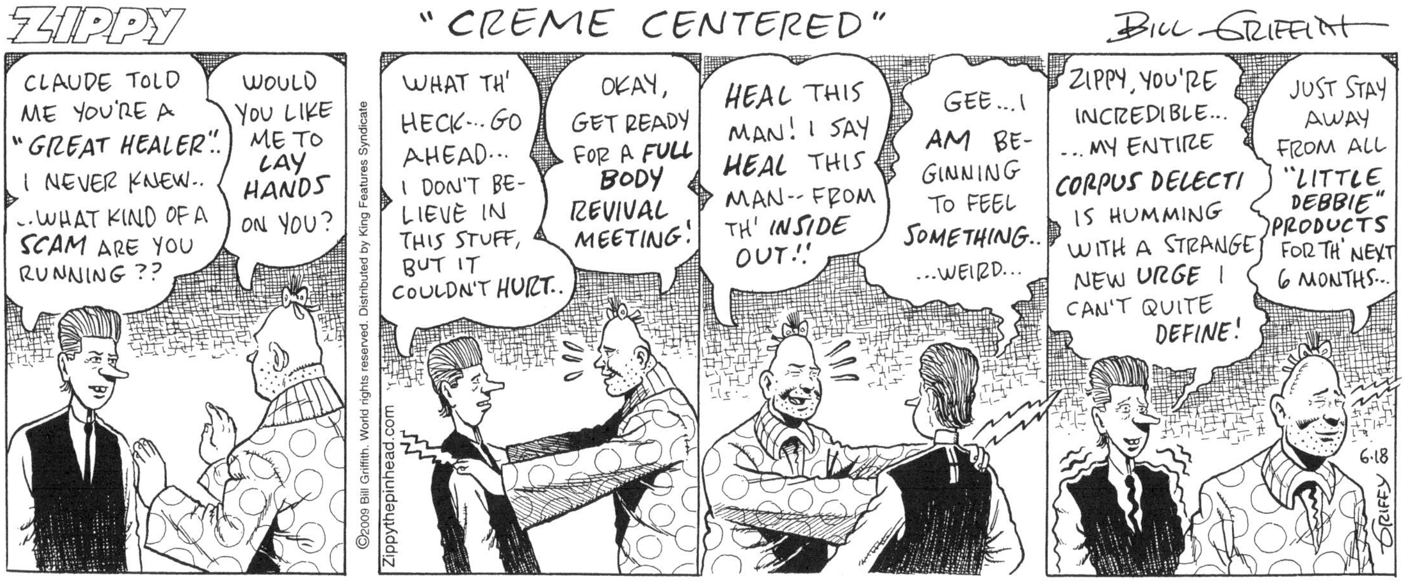
ZIPPY
"CREME CENTERED"
BILL GRIFFITH
CLAUDE TOLD ME YOU'RE A "GREAT HEALER".. I NEVER KNEW.. ..WHAT KIND OF A SCAM ARE YOU RUNNING??
WOULD YOU LIKE ME TO LAY HANDS ON YOU?
©2009 Bill Griffith. World rights reserved. Distributed by King Features Syndicate
Zippythepinhead.com
WHAT TH' HECK... GO AHEAD... I DON'T BELIEVE IN THIS STUFF, BUT IT COULDN'T HURT..
OKAY, GET READY FOR A FULL BODY REVIVAL MEETING!
HEAL THIS MAN! I SAY HEAL THIS MAN-- FROM TH' INSIDE OUT!!
GEE... I AM BEGINNING TO FEEL SOMETHING.. ...WEIRD...
ZIPPY, YOU'RE INCREDIBLE... ...MY ENTIRE CORPUS DELECTI IS HUMMING WITH A STRANGE NEW URGE I CAN'T QUITE DEFINE!
JUST STAY AWAY FROM ALL "LITTLE DEBBIE" PRODUCTS FOR TH' NEXT 6 MONTHS...
6·18
GRIFFY

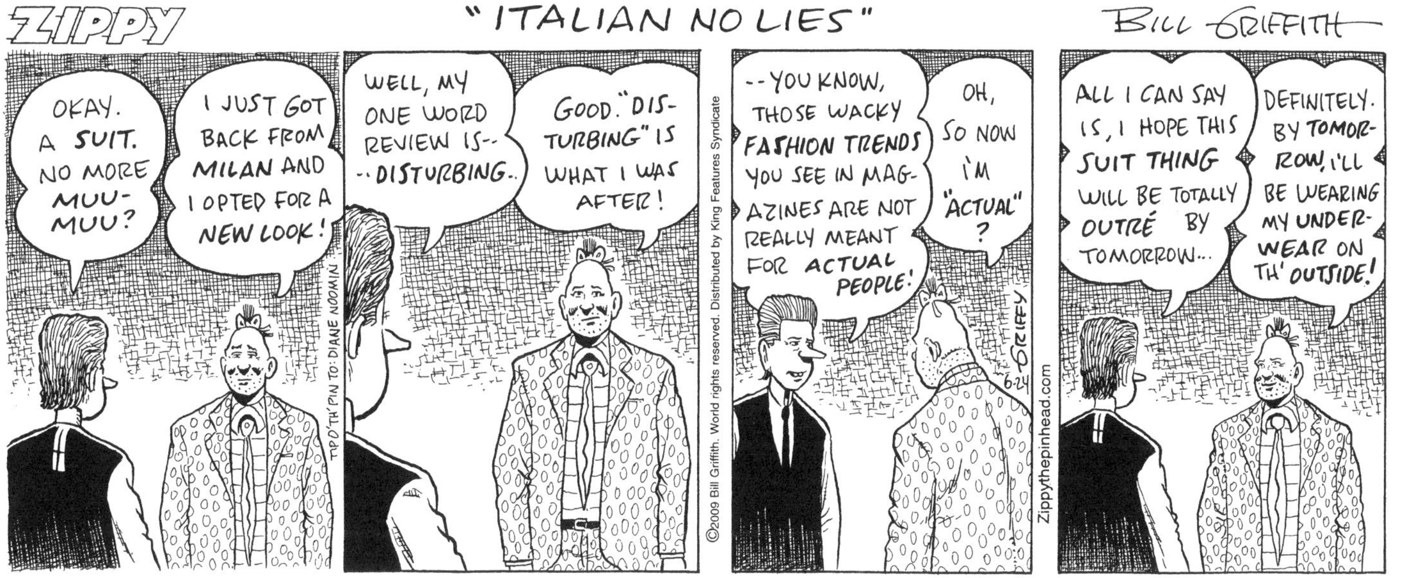
ZIPPY
"ITALIAN NO LIES"
BILL GRIFFITH
OKAY. A SUIT. NO MORE MUU-MUU?
I JUST GOT BACK FROM MILAN AND I OPTED FOR A NEW LOOK!
TIP O' TH' PIN TO: DIANE NOOMIN
WELL, MY ONE WORD REVIEW IS-- --DISTURBING..
GOOD. "DISTURBING" IS WHAT I WAS AFTER!
©2009 Bill Griffith. World rights reserved. Distributed by King Features Syndicate
--YOU KNOW, THOSE WACKY FASHION TRENDS YOU SEE IN MAGAZINES ARE NOT REALLY MEANT FOR ACTUAL PEOPLE!
OH, SO NOW I'M "ACTUAL"?
GRIFFY
6-24
Zippythepinhead.com
ALL I CAN SAY IS, I HOPE THIS SUIT THING WILL BE TOTALLY OUTRÉ BY TOMORROW...
DEFINITELY. BY TOMORROW, I'LL BE WEARING MY UNDERWEAR ON TH' OUTSIDE!

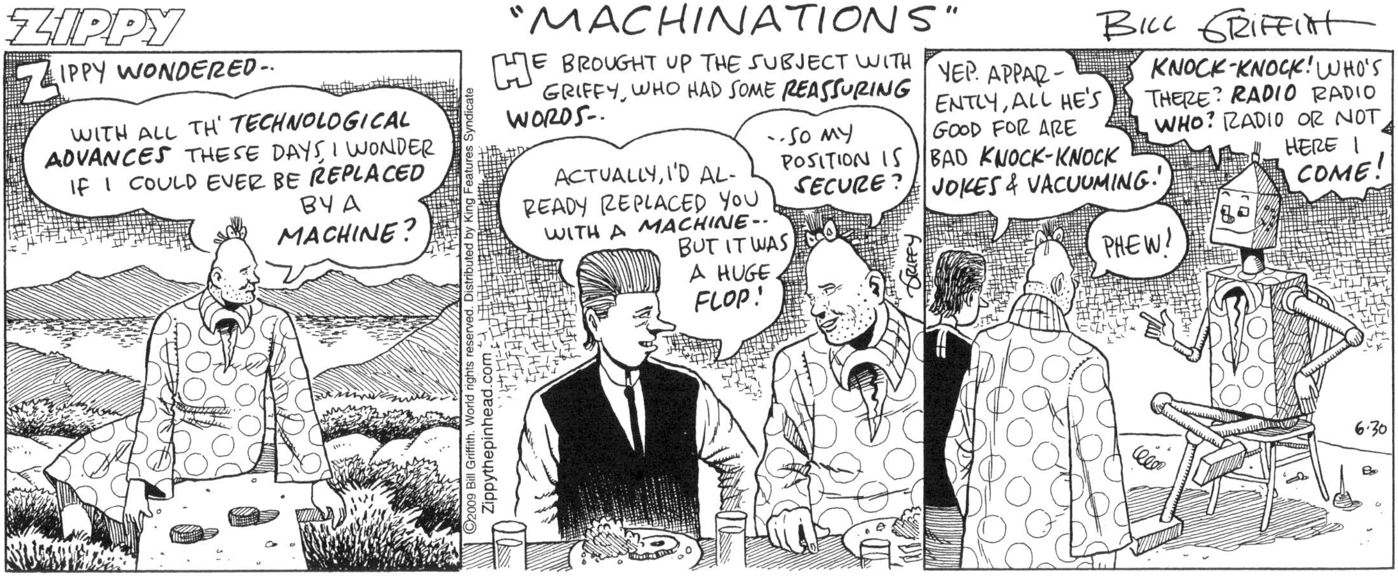
ZIPPY
"MACHINATIONS"
BILL GRIFFITH
ZIPPY WONDERED--
WITH ALL TH' TECHNOLOGICAL ADVANCES THESE DAYS, I WONDER IF I COULD EVER BE REPLACED BY A MACHINE?
©2009 Bill Griffith. World rights reserved. Distributed by King Features Syndicate
Zippythepinhead.com
HE BROUGHT UP THE SUBJECT WITH GRIFFY, WHO HAD SOME REASSURING WORDS--
ACTUALLY, I'D ALREADY REPLACED YOU WITH A MACHINE-- BUT IT WAS A HUGE FLOP!
--SO MY POSITION IS SECURE?
GRIFFY
YEP. APPARENTLY, ALL HE'S GOOD FOR ARE BAD KNOCK-KNOCK JOKES & VACUUMING!
KNOCK-KNOCK! WHO'S THERE? RADIO RADIO WHO? RADIO OR NOT HERE I COME!
PHEW!
6·30

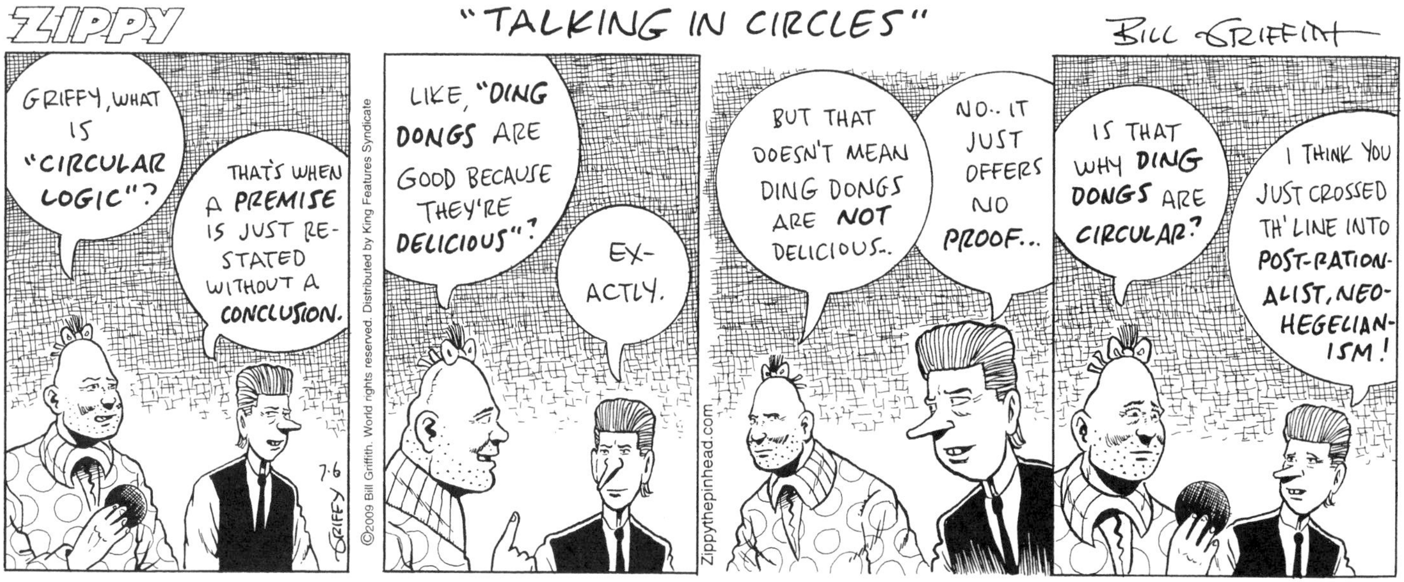
ZIPPY
"TALKING IN CIRCLES"
BILL GRIFFITH
GRIFFY, WHAT IS "CIRCULAR LOGIC"?
THAT'S WHEN A PREMISE IS JUST RE-STATED WITHOUT A CONCLUSION.
7·6
GRIFFY
©2009 Bill Griffith. World rights reserved. Distributed by King Features Syndicate
LIKE, "DING DONGS ARE GOOD BECAUSE THEY'RE DELICIOUS"?
EX-ACTLY.
Zippythepinhead.com
BUT THAT DOESN'T MEAN DING DONGS ARE NOT DELICIOUS..
NO.. IT JUST OFFERS NO PROOF...
IS THAT WHY DING DONGS ARE CIRCULAR?
I THINK YOU JUST CROSSED TH' LINE INTO POST-RATION-ALIST, NEO-HEGELIAN-ISM!

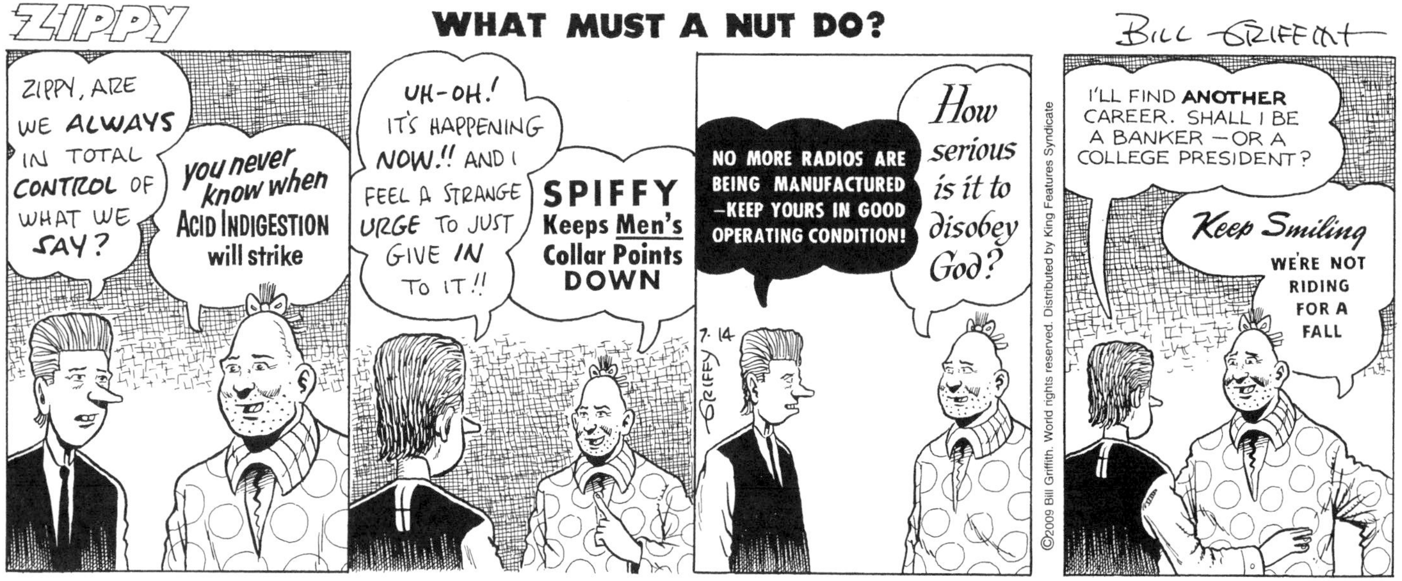
ZIPPY
WHAT MUST A NUT DO?
BILL GRIFFITH
ZIPPY, ARE WE ALWAYS IN TOTAL CONTROL OF WHAT WE SAY?
you never know when ACID INDIGESTION will strike
UH-OH! IT'S HAPPENING NOW!! AND I FEEL A STRANGE URGE TO JUST GIVE IN TO IT!!
SPIFFY Keeps Men's Collar Points DOWN
NO MORE RADIOS ARE BEING MANUFACTURED —KEEP YOURS IN GOOD OPERATING CONDITION!
How serious is it to disobey God?
7·14
GRIFFY
©2009 Bill Griffith. World rights reserved. Distributed by King Features Syndicate
I'LL FIND ANOTHER CAREER. SHALL I BE A BANKER —OR A COLLEGE PRESIDENT?
Keep Smiling
WE'RE NOT RIDING FOR A FALL

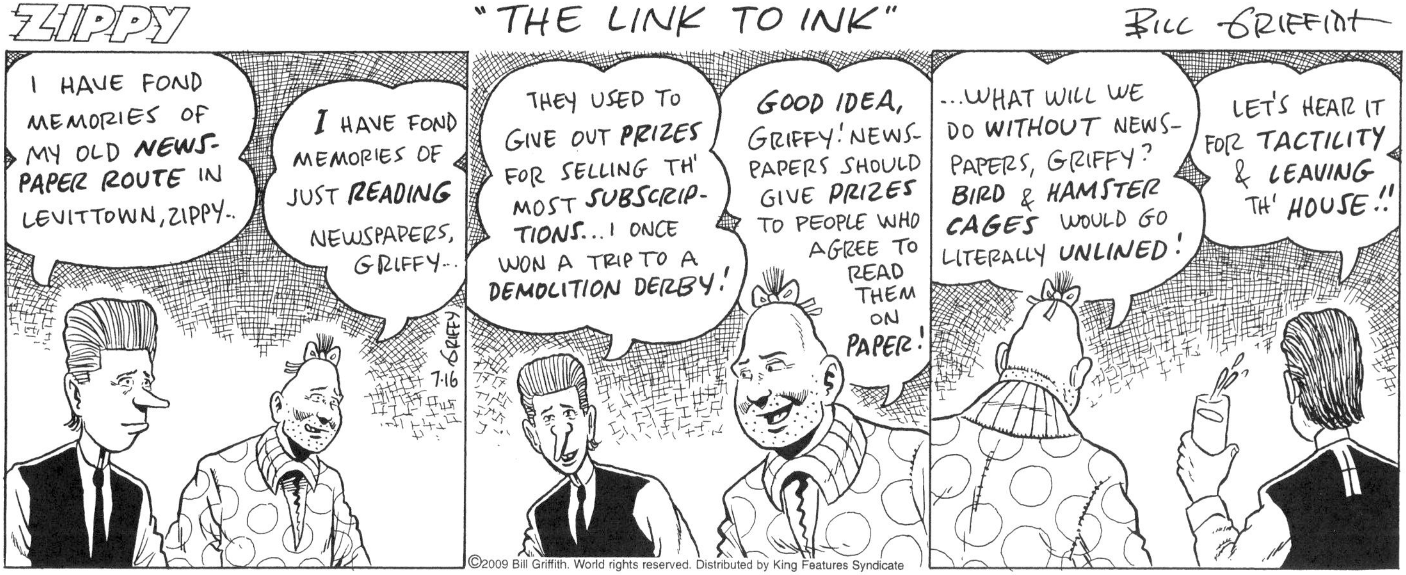
ZIPPY
"THE LINK TO INK"
BILL GRIFFITH
I HAVE FOND MEMORIES OF MY OLD NEWSPAPER ROUTE IN LEVITTOWN, ZIPPY..
I HAVE FOND MEMORIES OF JUST READING NEWSPAPERS, GRIFFY..
GRIFFY 7·16
THEY USED TO GIVE OUT PRIZES FOR SELLING TH' MOST SUBSCRIPTIONS... I ONCE WON A TRIP TO A DEMOLITION DERBY!
GOOD IDEA, GRIFFY! NEWSPAPERS SHOULD GIVE PRIZES TO PEOPLE WHO AGREE TO READ THEM ON PAPER!
...WHAT WILL WE DO WITHOUT NEWSPAPERS, GRIFFY? BIRD & HAMSTER CAGES WOULD GO LITERALLY UNLINED!
LET'S HEAR IT FOR TACTILITY & LEAVING TH' HOUSE!!
©2009 Bill Griffith. World rights reserved. Distributed by King Features Syndicate

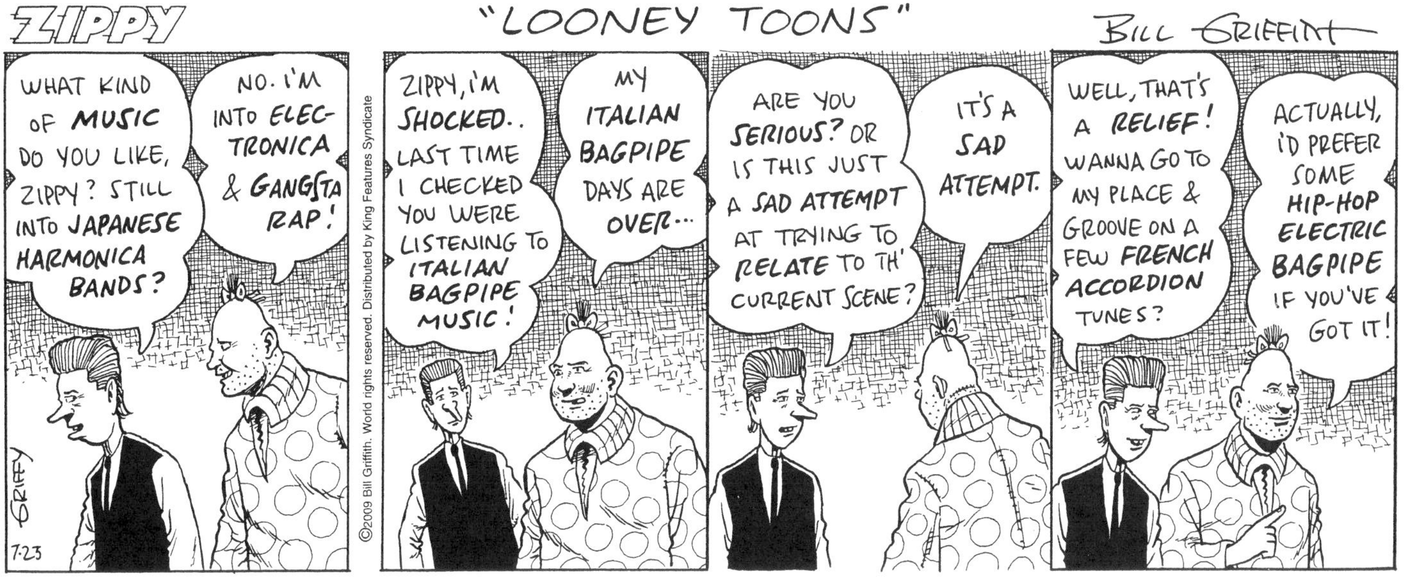
ZIPPY
"LOONEY TOONS"
BILL GRIFFITH
WHAT KIND OF MUSIC DO YOU LIKE, ZIPPY? STILL INTO JAPANESE HARMONICA BANDS?
NO. I'M INTO ELECTRONICA & GANGSTA RAP!
GRIFFY 7·23
©2009 Bill Griffith. World rights reserved. Distributed by King Features Syndicate
ZIPPY, I'M SHOCKED.. LAST TIME I CHECKED YOU WERE LISTENING TO ITALIAN BAGPIPE MUSIC!
MY ITALIAN BAGPIPE DAYS ARE OVER...
ARE YOU SERIOUS? OR IS THIS JUST A SAD ATTEMPT AT TRYING TO RELATE TO TH' CURRENT SCENE?
IT'S A SAD ATTEMPT.
WELL, THAT'S A RELIEF! WANNA GO TO MY PLACE & GROOVE ON A FEW FRENCH ACCORDION TUNES?
ACTUALLY, I'D PREFER SOME HIP-HOP ELECTRIC BAGPIPE IF YOU'VE GOT IT!

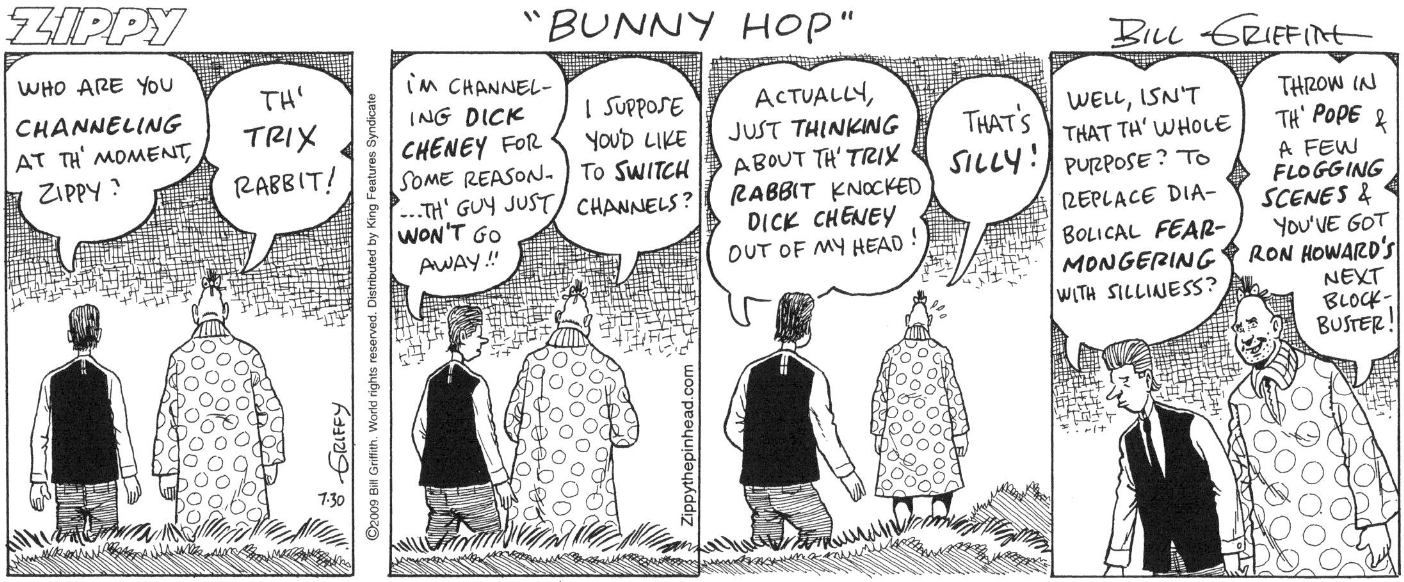
ZIPPY
"BUNNY HOP"
BILL GRIFFITH
WHO ARE YOU CHANNELING AT TH' MOMENT, ZIPPY?
TH' TRIX RABBIT!
GRIFFY
7-30
©2009 Bill Griffith. World rights reserved. Distributed by King Features Syndicate
I'M CHANNELING DICK CHENEY FOR SOME REASON... ...TH' GUY JUST WON'T GO AWAY!!
I SUPPOSE YOU'D LIKE TO SWITCH CHANNELS?
Zippythepinhead.com
ACTUALLY, JUST THINKING ABOUT TH' TRIX RABBIT KNOCKED DICK CHENEY OUT OF MY HEAD!
THAT'S SILLY!
WELL, ISN'T THAT TH' WHOLE PURPOSE? TO REPLACE DIABOLICAL FEAR-MONGERING WITH SILLINESS?
THROW IN TH' POPE & A FEW FLOGGING SCENES & YOU'VE GOT RON HOWARD'S NEXT BLOCKBUSTER!

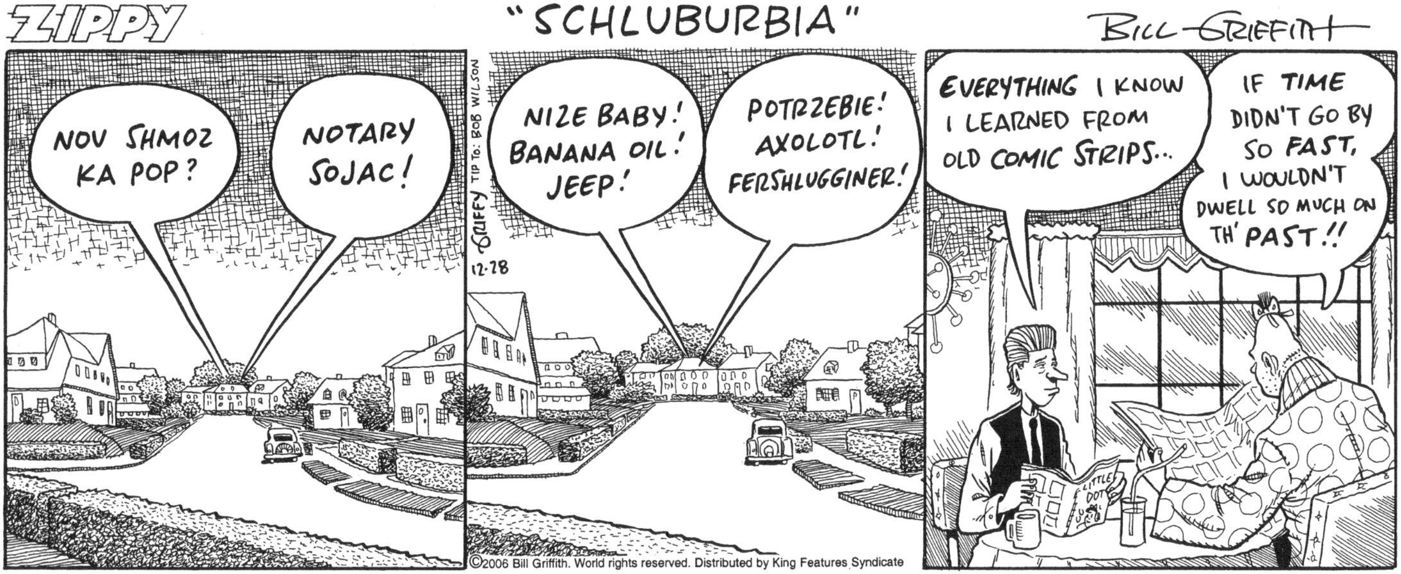
ZIPPY
"SCHLUBURBIA"
BILL GRIFFITH
NOV SHMOZ KA POP?
NOTARY SOJAC!
GRIFFY
TIP TO: BOB WILSON
12-28
NIZE BABY! BANANA OIL! JEEP!
POTRZEBIE! AXOLOTL! FERSHLUGGINER!
©2006 Bill Griffith. World rights reserved. Distributed by King Features Syndicate
EVERYTHING I KNOW I LEARNED FROM OLD COMIC STRIPS...
IF TIME DIDN'T GO BY SO FAST, I WOULDN'T DWELL SO MUCH ON TH' PAST!!

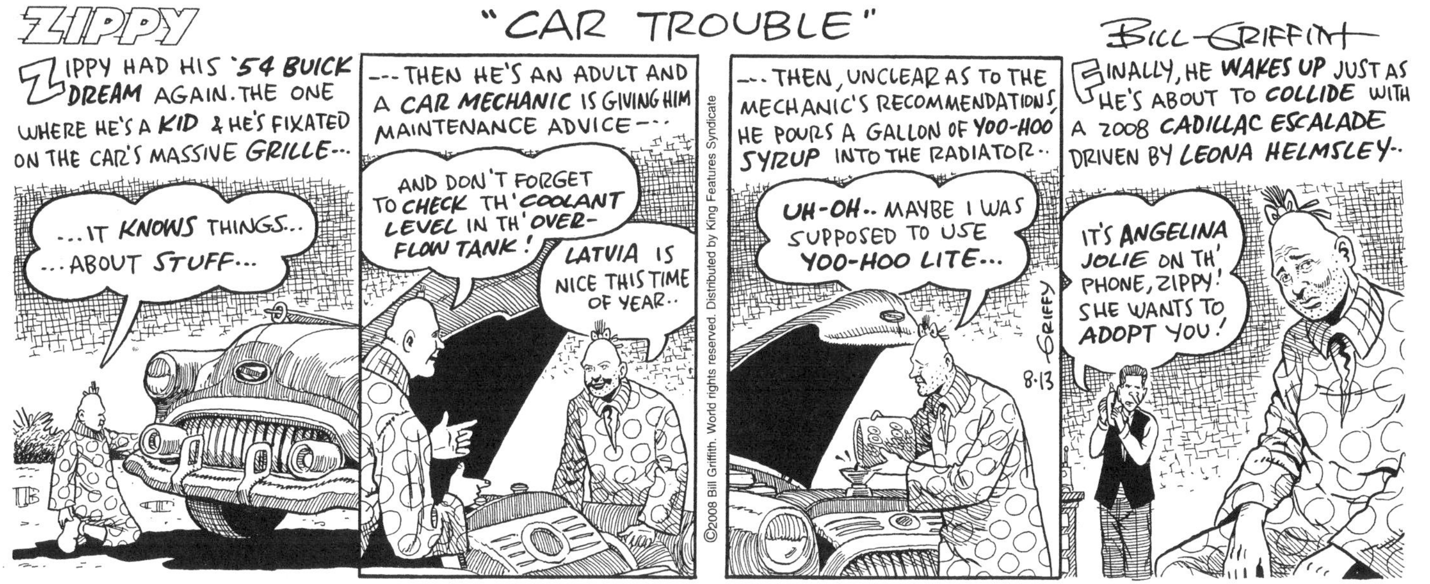
ZIPPY
"CAR TROUBLE"
BILL GRIFFITH
ZIPPY HAD HIS '54 BUICK DREAM AGAIN. THE ONE WHERE HE'S A KID & HE'S FIXATED ON THE CAR'S MASSIVE GRILLE...
...IT KNOWS THINGS... ...ABOUT STUFF...
---THEN HE'S AN ADULT AND A CAR MECHANIC IS GIVING HIM MAINTENANCE ADVICE---
AND DON'T FORGET TO CHECK TH' COOLANT LEVEL IN TH' OVER-FLOW TANK!
LATVIA IS NICE THIS TIME OF YEAR..
©2008 Bill Griffith. World rights reserved. Distributed by King Features Syndicate
---THEN, UNCLEAR AS TO THE MECHANIC'S RECOMMENDATIONS, HE POURS A GALLON OF YOO-HOO SYRUP INTO THE RADIATOR..
UH-OH.. MAYBE I WAS SUPPOSED TO USE YOO-HOO LITE...
GRIFFY
8·13
FINALLY, HE WAKES UP JUST AS HE'S ABOUT TO COLLIDE WITH A 2008 CADILLAC ESCALADE DRIVEN BY LEONA HELMSLEY..
IT'S ANGELINA JOLIE ON TH' PHONE, ZIPPY! SHE WANTS TO ADOPT YOU!

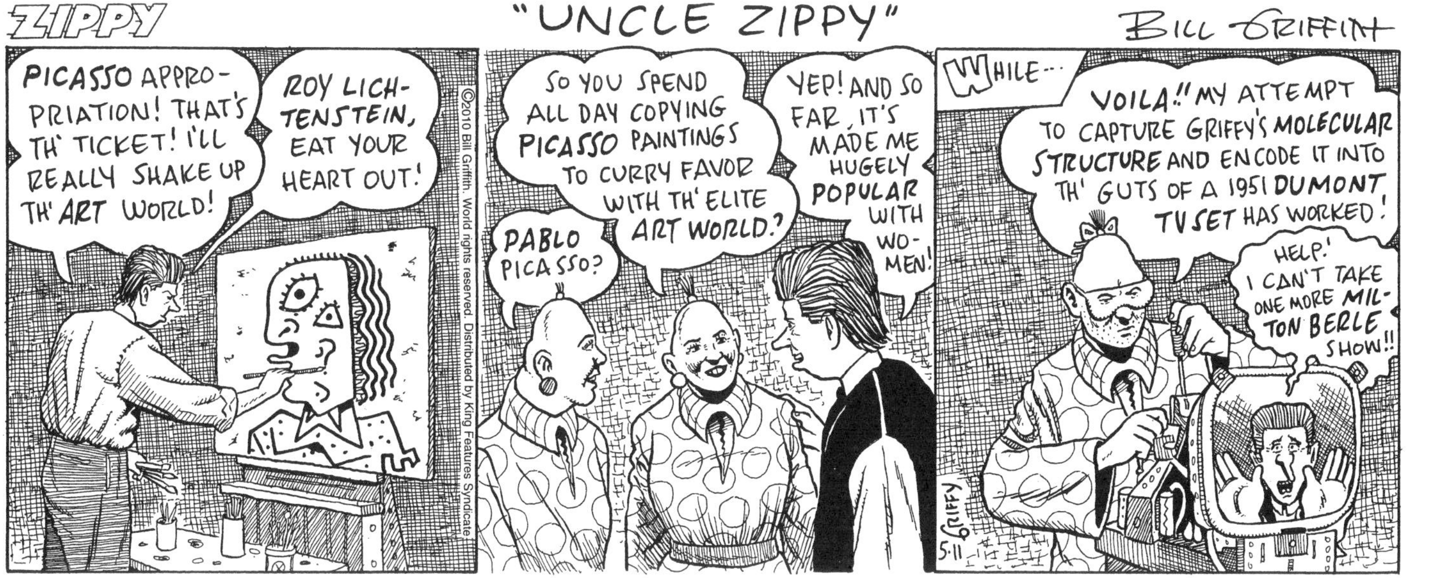
ZIPPY
"UNCLE ZIPPY"
BILL GRIFFITH
PICASSO APPRO-PRIATION! THAT'S TH' TICKET! I'LL REALLY SHAKE UP TH' ART WORLD!
ROY LICH-TENSTEIN, EAT YOUR HEART OUT!
©2010 Bill Griffith. World rights reserved. Distributed by King Features Syndicate
SO YOU SPEND ALL DAY COPYING PICASSO PAINTINGS TO CURRY FAVOR WITH TH' ELITE ART WORLD?
YEP! AND SO FAR, IT'S MADE ME HUGELY POPULAR WITH WO-MEN!
PABLO PICASSO?
GRIFFY
5·11
WHILE..
VOILA!! MY ATTEMPT TO CAPTURE GRIFFY'S MOLECULAR STRUCTURE AND ENCODE IT INTO TH' GUTS OF A 1951 DUMONT TV SET HAS WORKED!
HELP! I CAN'T TAKE ONE MORE MIL-TON BERLE SHOW!!

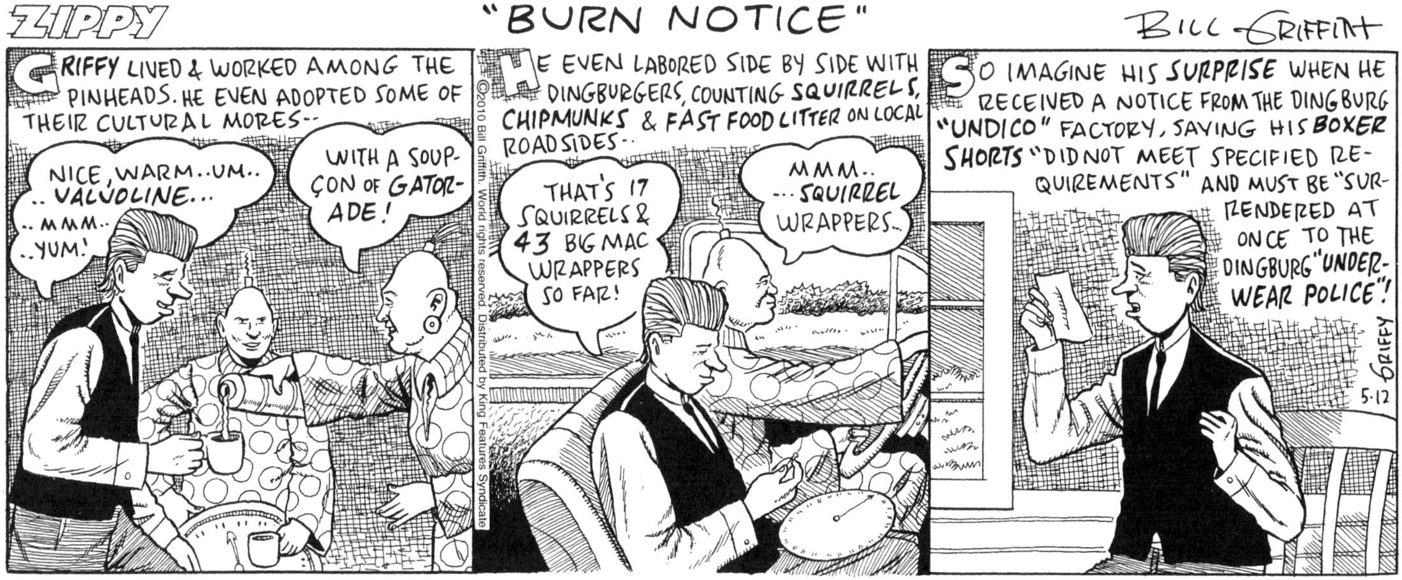
ZIPPY
"BURN NOTICE"
BILL GRIFFITH
GRIFFY LIVED & WORKED AMONG THE PINHEADS. HE EVEN ADOPTED SOME OF THEIR CULTURAL MORES--
NICE, WARM..UM.. ..VALVOLINE... ..MMM.. ..YUM!
WITH A SOUPÇON OF GATORADE!
©2010 Bill Griffith. World rights reserved. Distributed by King Features Syndicate
HE EVEN LABORED SIDE BY SIDE WITH DINGBURGERS, COUNTING SQUIRRELS, CHIPMUNKS & FAST FOOD LITTER ON LOCAL ROADSIDES..
THAT'S 17 SQUIRRELS & 43 BIG MAC WRAPPERS SO FAR!
MMM.. ...SQUIRREL WRAPPERS...
SO IMAGINE HIS SURPRISE WHEN HE RECEIVED A NOTICE FROM THE DINGBURG "UNDICO" FACTORY, SAYING HIS BOXER SHORTS "DID NOT MEET SPECIFIED REQUIREMENTS" AND MUST BE "SURRENDERED AT ONCE TO THE DINGBURG "UNDERWEAR POLICE"!
GRIFFY
5·12

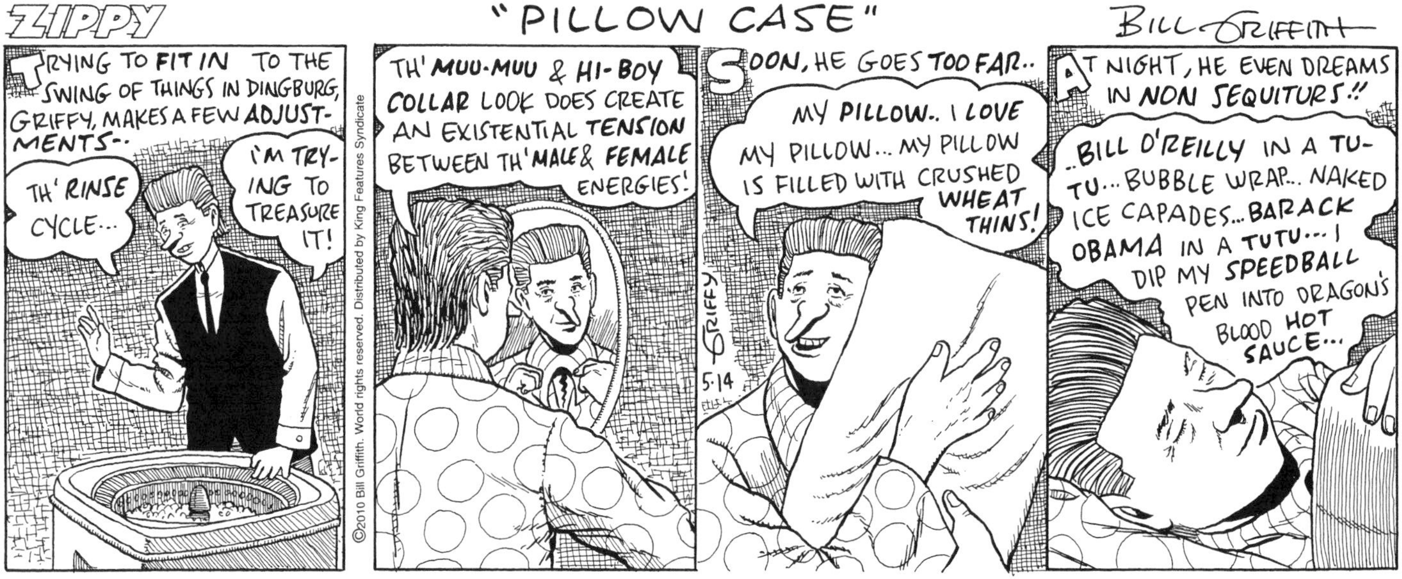
ZIPPY
"PILLOW CASE"
BILL GRIFFITH
TRYING TO FIT IN TO THE SWING OF THINGS IN DINGBURG, GRIFFY, MAKES A FEW ADJUSTMENTS-.
TH' RINSE CYCLE...
I'M TRYING TO TREASURE IT!
©2010 Bill Griffith. World rights reserved. Distributed by King Features Syndicate
TH' MUU-MUU & HI-BOY COLLAR LOOK DOES CREATE AN EXISTENTIAL TENSION BETWEEN TH' MALE & FEMALE ENERGIES!
SOON, HE GOES TOO FAR..
MY PILLOW.. I LOVE MY PILLOW... MY PILLOW IS FILLED WITH CRUSHED WHEAT THINS!
GRIFFY
5·14
AT NIGHT, HE EVEN DREAMS IN NON SEQUITURS!!
..BILL O'REILLY IN A TUTU... BUBBLE WRAP... NAKED ICE CAPADES... BARACK OBAMA IN A TUTU... I DIP MY SPEEDBALL PEN INTO DRAGON'S BLOOD HOT SAUCE...

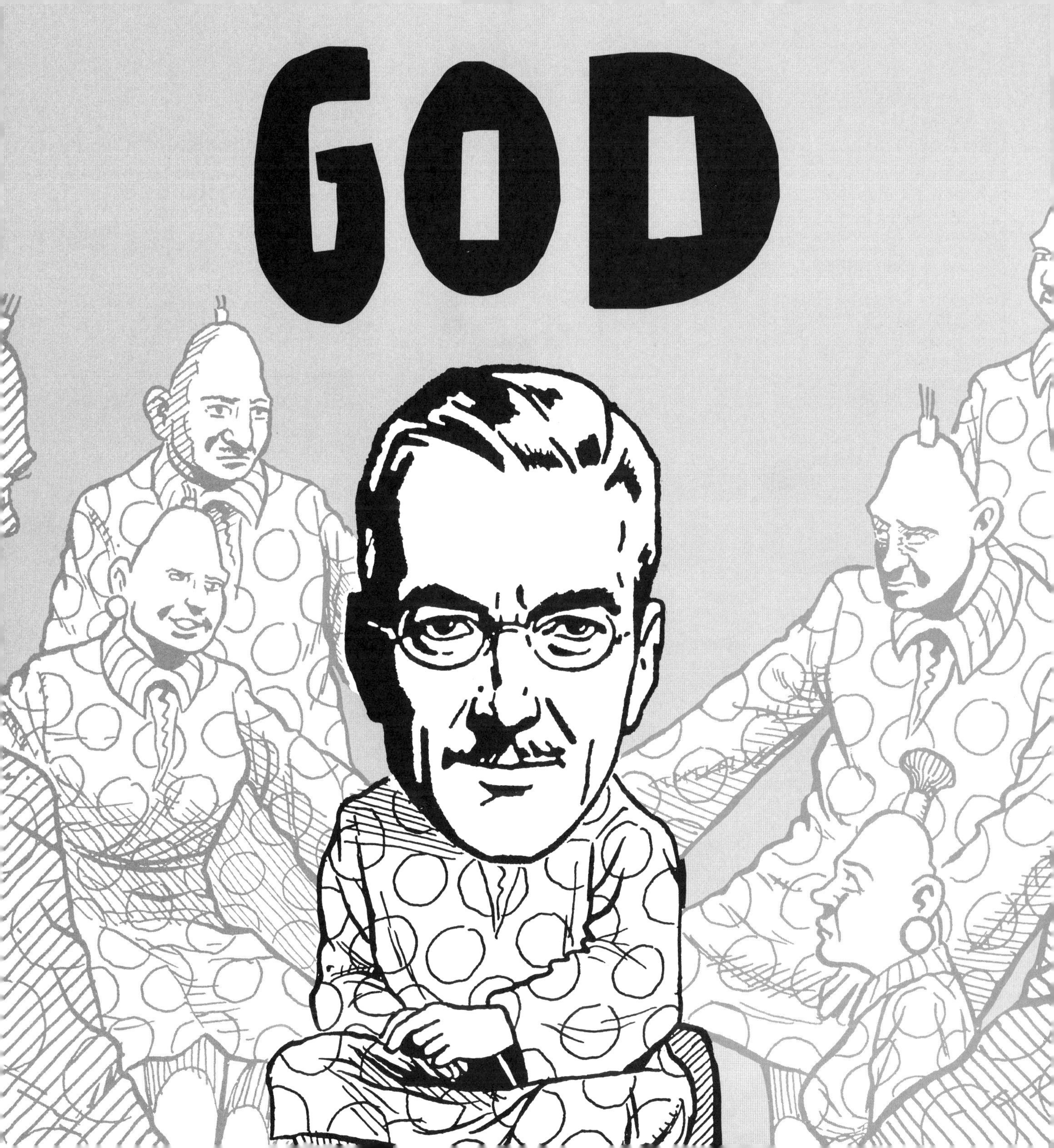
GOD

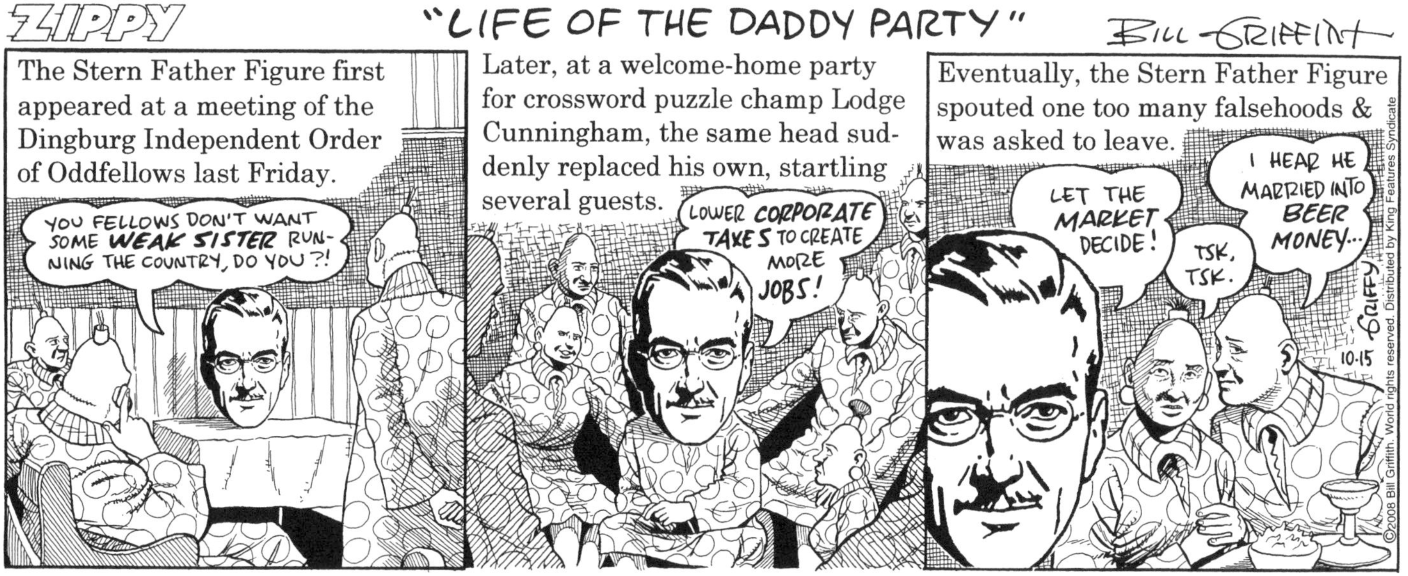
ZIPPY
"LIFE OF THE DADDY PARTY"
BILL GRIFFITH
The Stern Father Figure first appeared at a meeting of the Dingburg Independent Order of Oddfellows last Friday.
YOU FELLOWS DON'T WANT SOME WEAK SISTER RUNNING THE COUNTRY, DO YOU?!
Later, at a welcome-home party for crossword puzzle champ Lodge Cunningham, the same head suddenly replaced his own, startling several guests.
LOWER CORPORATE TAXES TO CREATE MORE JOBS!
Eventually, the Stern Father Figure spouted one too many falsehoods & was asked to leave.
LET THE MARKET DECIDE!
TSK, TSK.
I HEAR HE MARRIED INTO BEER MONEY...
GRIFFY
10·15
©2008 Bill Griffith. World rights reserved. Distributed by King Features Syndicate

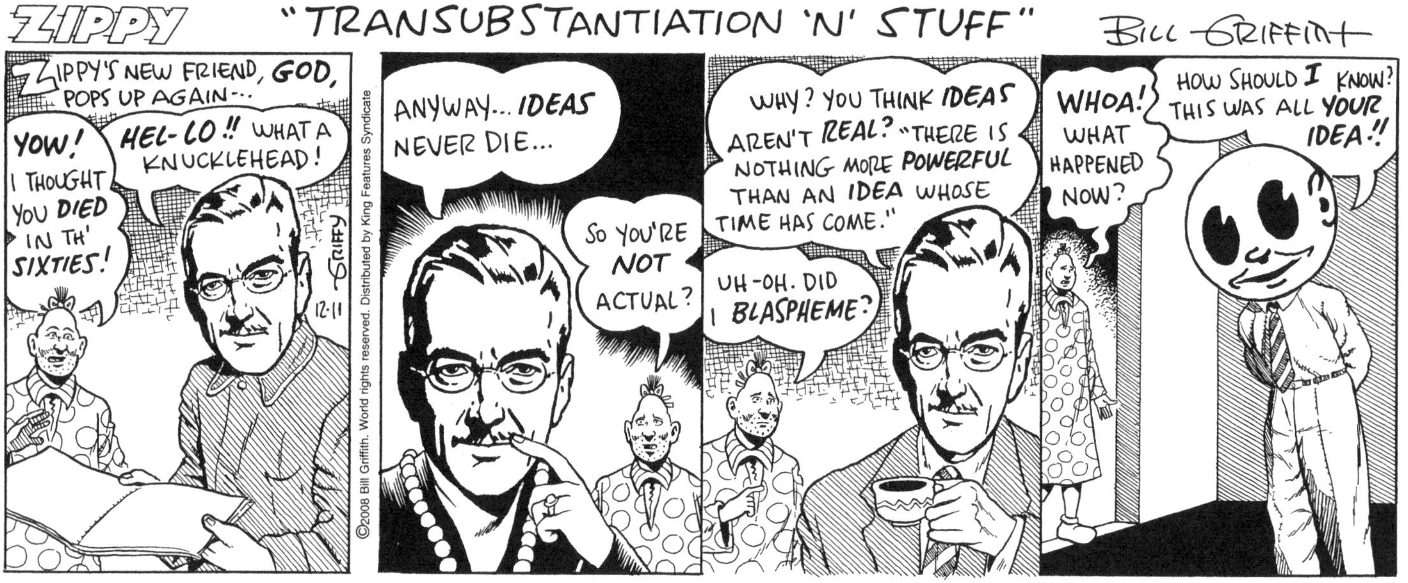
ZIPPY
"TRANSUBSTANTIATION 'N' STUFF"
BILL GRIFFITH
ZIPPY'S NEW FRIEND, GOD, POPS UP AGAIN...
YOW! I THOUGHT YOU DIED IN TH' SIXTIES!
HEL-LO!! WHAT A KNUCKLEHEAD!
GRIFFY
12·11
©2008 Bill Griffith. World rights reserved. Distributed by King Features Syndicate
ANYWAY... IDEAS NEVER DIE...
SO YOU'RE NOT ACTUAL?
WHY? YOU THINK IDEAS AREN'T REAL? "THERE IS NOTHING MORE POWERFUL THAN AN IDEA WHOSE TIME HAS COME."
UH-OH. DID I BLASPHEME?
WHOA! WHAT HAPPENED NOW?
HOW SHOULD I KNOW? THIS WAS ALL YOUR IDEA!!

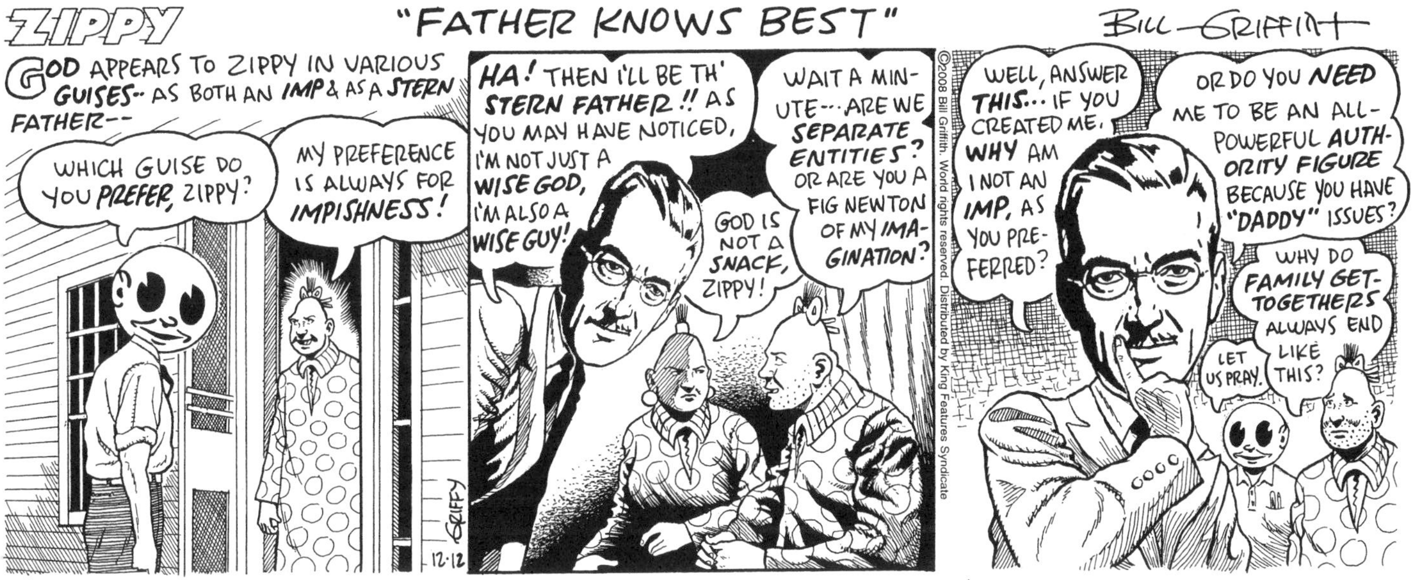
ZIPPY
"FATHER KNOWS BEST"
BILL GRIFFITH
GOD APPEARS TO ZIPPY IN VARIOUS GUISES-- AS BOTH AN IMP & AS A STERN FATHER--
WHICH GUISE DO YOU PREFER, ZIPPY?
MY PREFERENCE IS ALWAYS FOR IMPISHNESS!
GRIFFY
12-12
HA! THEN I'LL BE TH' STERN FATHER!! AS YOU MAY HAVE NOTICED, I'M NOT JUST A WISE GOD, I'M ALSO A WISE GUY!
GOD IS NOT A SNACK, ZIPPY!
WAIT A MIN-UTE--- ARE WE SEPARATE ENTITIES? OR ARE YOU A FIG NEWTON OF MY IMA-GINATION?
©2008 Bill Griffith. World rights reserved. Distributed by King Features Syndicate
WELL, ANSWER THIS... IF YOU CREATED ME, WHY AM I NOT AN IMP, AS YOU PRE-FERRED?
OR DO YOU NEED ME TO BE AN ALL-POWERFUL AUTH-ORITY FIGURE BECAUSE YOU HAVE "DADDY" ISSUES?
WHY DO FAMILY GET-TOGETHERS ALWAYS END LIKE THIS?
LET US PRAY.

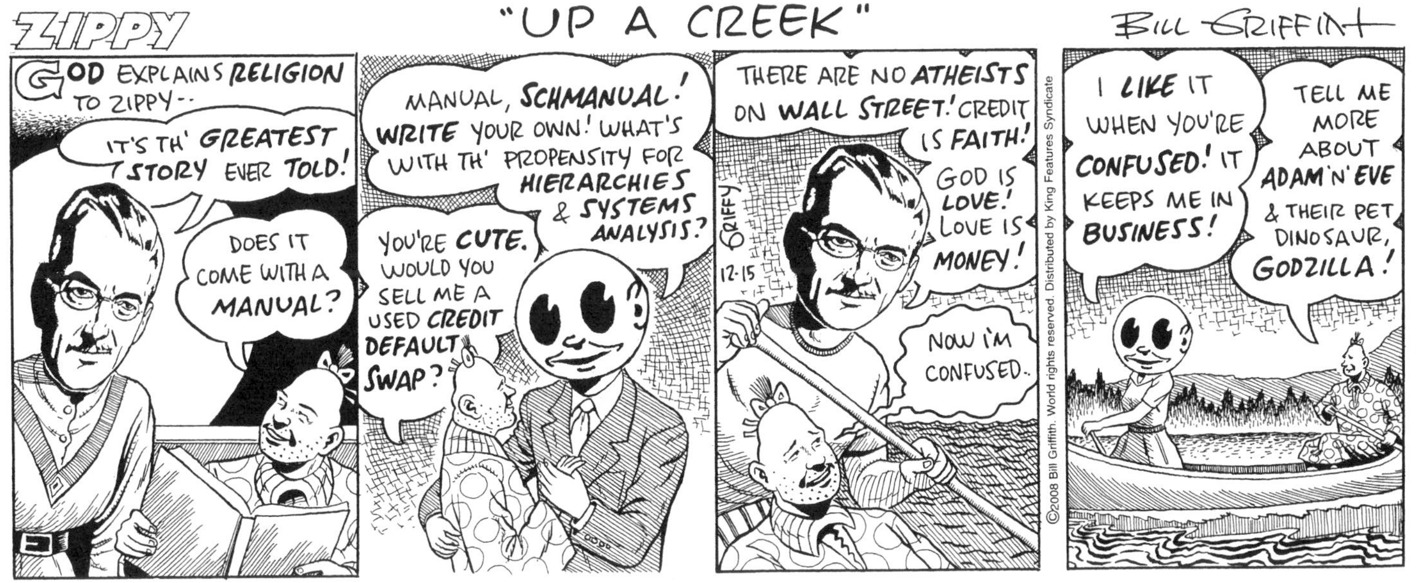
ZIPPY
"UP A CREEK"
BILL GRIFFITH
GOD EXPLAINS RELIGION TO ZIPPY--
IT'S TH' GREATEST STORY EVER TOLD!
DOES IT COME WITH A MANUAL?
MANUAL, SCHMANUAL! WRITE YOUR OWN! WHAT'S WITH TH' PROPENSITY FOR HIERARCHIES & SYSTEMS ANALYSIS?
YOU'RE CUTE. WOULD YOU SELL ME A USED CREDIT DEFAULT SWAP?
THERE ARE NO ATHEISTS ON WALL STREET! CREDIT IS FAITH!
GOD IS LOVE! LOVE IS MONEY!
GRIFFY
12-15
NOW I'M CONFUSED..
©2008 Bill Griffith. World rights reserved. Distributed by King Features Syndicate
I LIKE IT WHEN YOU'RE CONFUSED! IT KEEPS ME IN BUSINESS!
TELL ME MORE ABOUT ADAM 'N' EVE & THEIR PET DINOSAUR, GODZILLA!

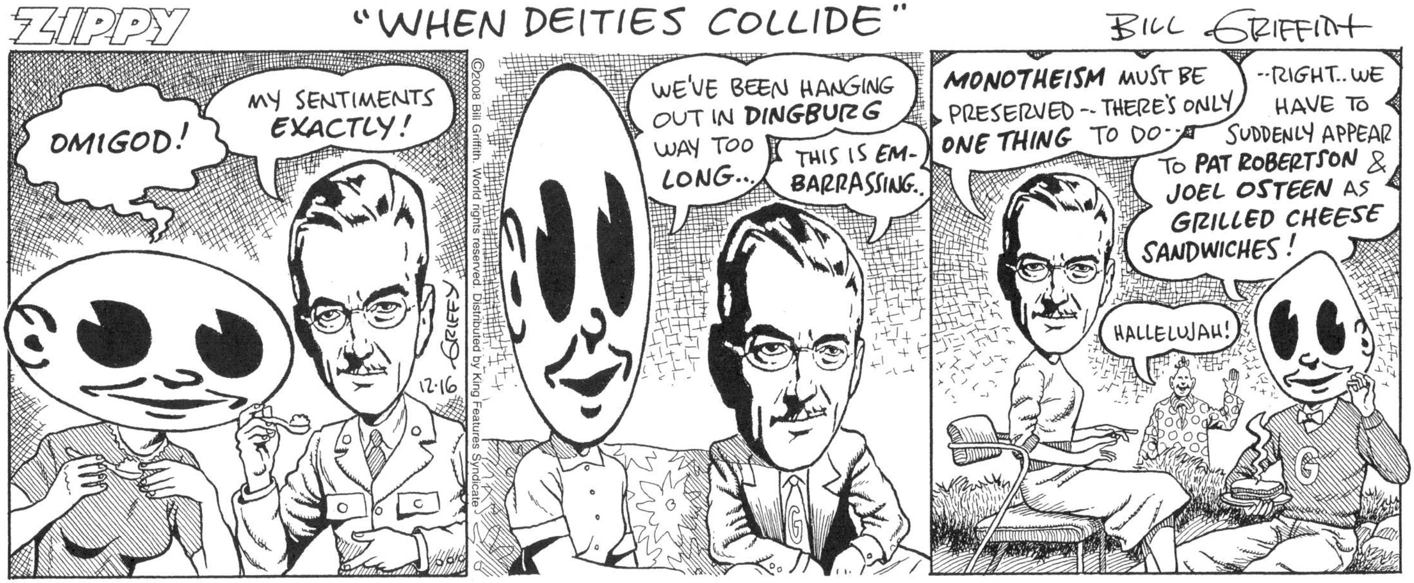
ZIPPY
"WHEN DEITIES COLLIDE"
BILL GRIFFITH
OMIGOD!
MY SENTIMENTS EXACTLY!
GRIFFY 12·16
©2008 Bill Griffith. World rights reserved. Distributed by King Features Syndicate
WE'VE BEEN HANGING OUT IN DINGBURG WAY TOO LONG...
THIS IS EMBARRASSING..
MONOTHEISM MUST BE PRESERVED -- THERE'S ONLY ONE THING TO DO--
--RIGHT.. WE HAVE TO SUDDENLY APPEAR TO PAT ROBERTSON & JOEL OSTEEN AS GRILLED CHEESE SANDWICHES!
HALLELUJAH!

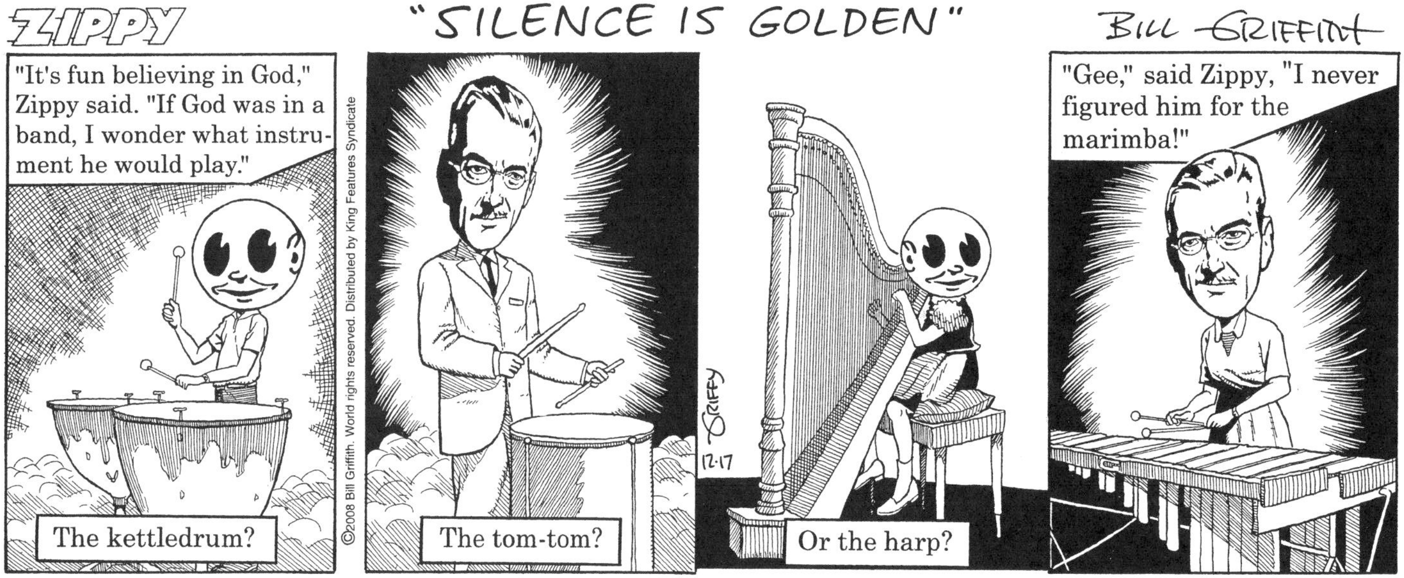
ZIPPY
"SILENCE IS GOLDEN"
BILL GRIFFITH
"It's fun believing in God," Zippy said. "If God was in a band, I wonder what instrument he would play."
The kettledrum?
©2008 Bill Griffith. World rights reserved. Distributed by King Features Syndicate
The tom-tom?
GRIFFY 12·17
Or the harp?
"Gee," said Zippy, "I never figured him for the marimba!"

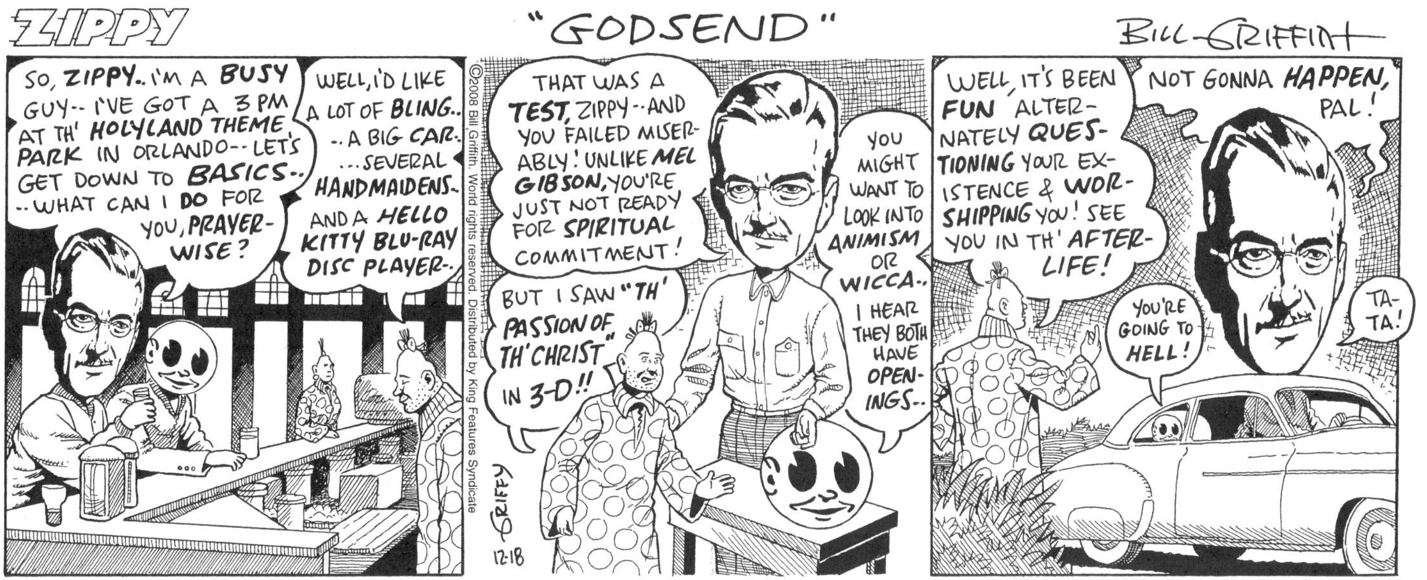
ZIPPY
"GODSEND"
BILL GRIFFITH
SO, ZIPPY.. I'M A BUSY GUY-- I'VE GOT A 3 PM AT TH' HOLYLAND THEME PARK IN ORLANDO-- LET'S GET DOWN TO BASICS.. ..WHAT CAN I DO FOR YOU, PRAYER-WISE?
WELL, I'D LIKE A LOT OF BLING.. ..A BIG CAR.. ...SEVERAL HANDMAIDENS.. AND A HELLO KITTY BLU-RAY DISC PLAYER..
©2008 Bill Griffith. World rights reserved. Distributed by King Features Syndicate
GRIFFY 12-18
THAT WAS A TEST, ZIPPY--AND YOU FAILED MISERABLY! UNLIKE MEL GIBSON, YOU'RE JUST NOT READY FOR SPIRITUAL COMMITMENT!
BUT I SAW "TH' PASSION OF TH' CHRIST" IN 3-D!!
YOU MIGHT WANT TO LOOK INTO ANIMISM OR WICCA.. I HEAR THEY BOTH HAVE OPENINGS..
WELL, IT'S BEEN FUN ALTERNATELY QUESTIONING YOUR EXISTENCE & WORSHIPPING YOU! SEE YOU IN TH' AFTERLIFE!
NOT GONNA HAPPEN, PAL!
YOU'RE GOING TO HELL!
TA-TA!

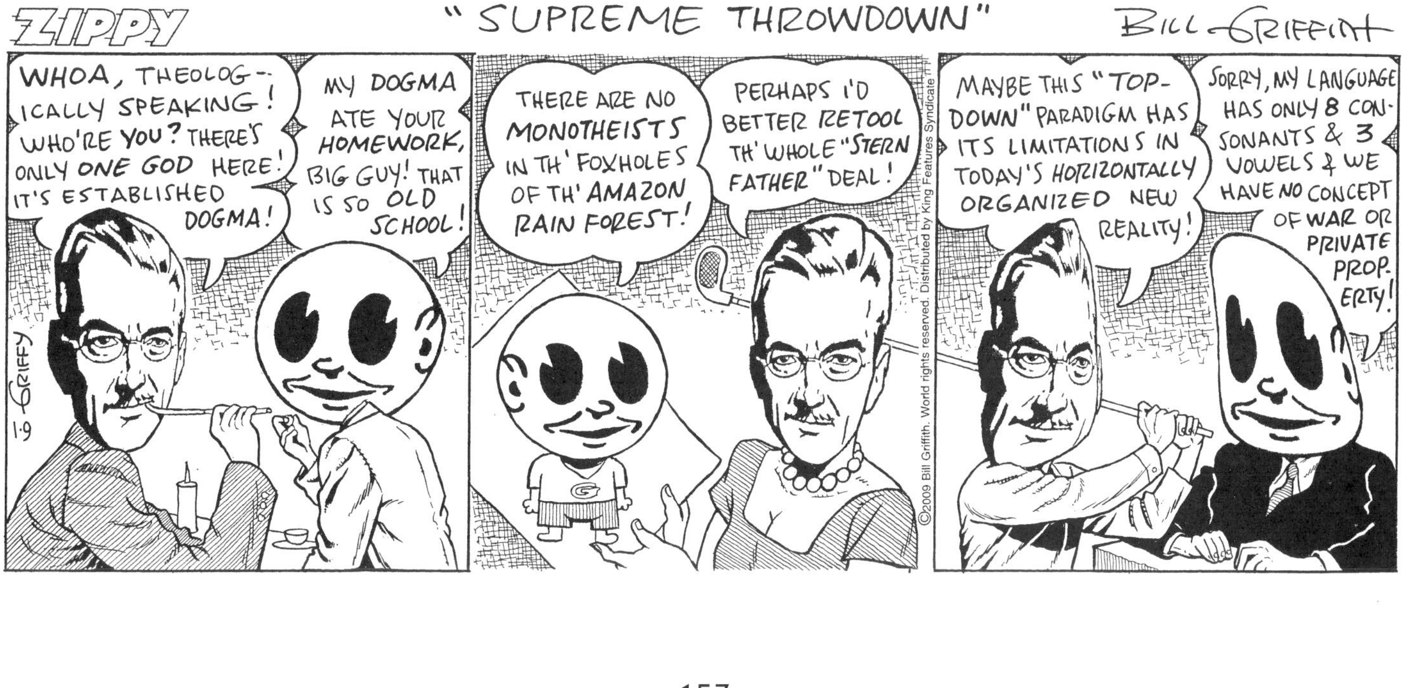
ZIPPY
"SUPREME THROWDOWN"
BILL GRIFFITH
WHOA, THEOLOGICALLY SPEAKING! WHO'RE YOU? THERE'S ONLY ONE GOD HERE! IT'S ESTABLISHED DOGMA!
MY DOGMA ATE YOUR HOMEWORK, BIG GUY! THAT IS SO OLD SCHOOL!
GRIFFY 1-9
THERE ARE NO MONOTHEISTS IN TH' FOXHOLES OF TH' AMAZON RAIN FOREST!
PERHAPS I'D BETTER RETOOL TH' WHOLE "STERN FATHER" DEAL!
©2009 Bill Griffith. World rights reserved. Distributed by King Features Syndicate
MAYBE THIS "TOP-DOWN" PARADIGM HAS ITS LIMITATIONS IN TODAY'S HORIZONTALLY ORGANIZED NEW REALITY!
SORRY, MY LANGUAGE HAS ONLY 8 CONSONANTS & 3 VOWELS & WE HAVE NO CONCEPT OF WAR OR PRIVATE PROPERTY!

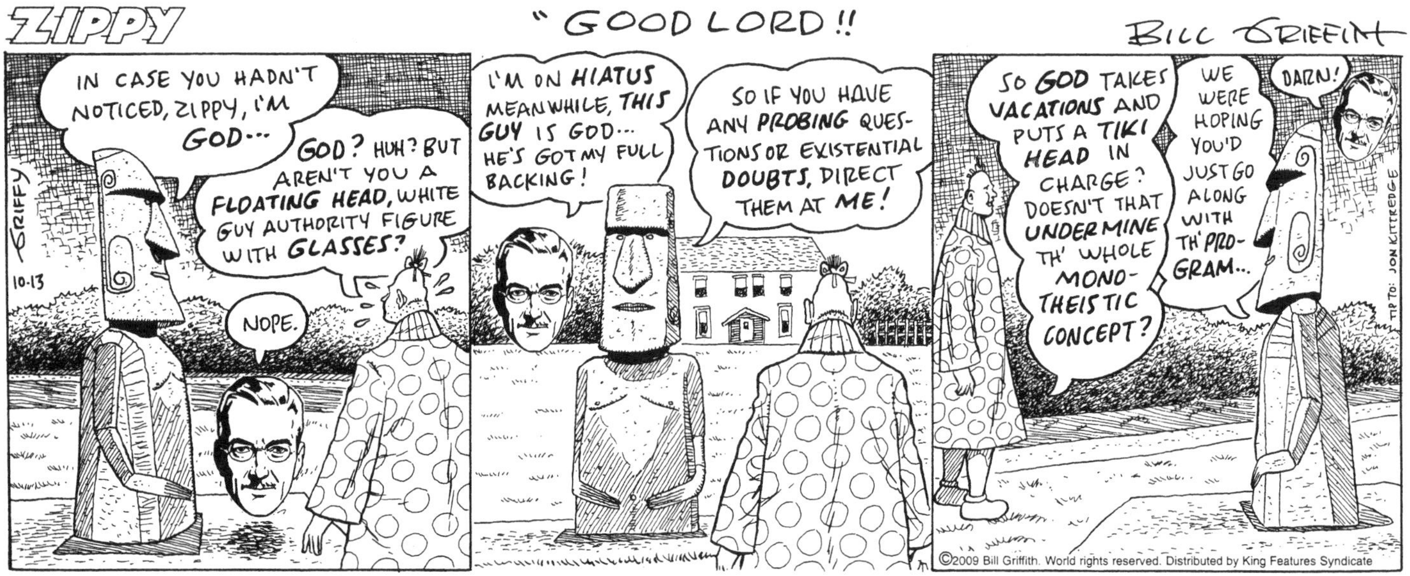
ZIPPY
"GOOD LORD!!"
BILL GRIFFITH
IN CASE YOU HADN'T NOTICED, ZIPPY, I'M GOD...
GOD? HUH? BUT AREN'T YOU A FLOATING HEAD, WHITE GUY AUTHORITY FIGURE WITH GLASSES?
NOPE.
GRIFFY 10-13
I'M ON HIATUS MEANWHILE, THIS GUY IS GOD... HE'S GOT MY FULL BACKING!
SO IF YOU HAVE ANY PROBING QUESTIONS OR EXISTENTIAL DOUBTS, DIRECT THEM AT ME!
SO GOD TAKES VACATIONS AND PUTS A TIKI HEAD IN CHARGE? DOESN'T THAT UNDERMINE TH' WHOLE MONOTHEISTIC CONCEPT?
WE WERE HOPING YOU'D JUST GO ALONG WITH TH' PROGRAM...
DARN!
TIP TO: JON KITTREDGE
©2009 Bill Griffith. World rights reserved. Distributed by King Features Syndicate

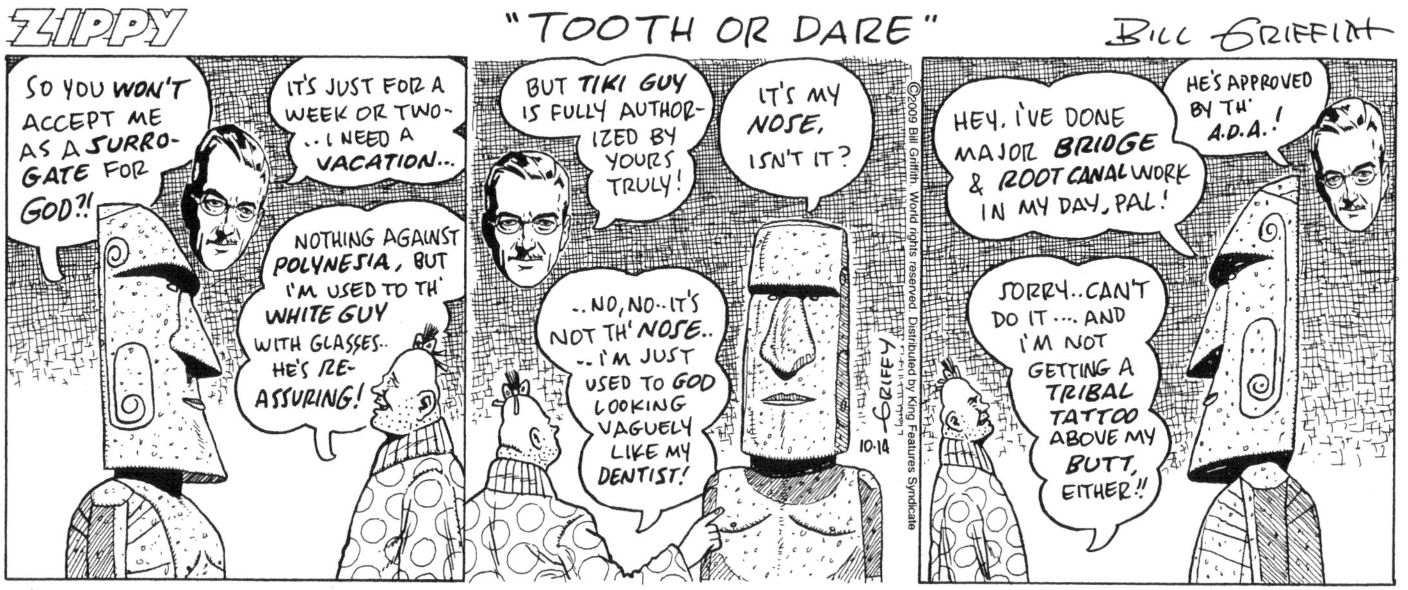
ZIPPY
"TOOTH OR DARE"
BILL GRIFFITH
SO YOU WON'T ACCEPT ME AS A SURROGATE FOR GOD?!
IT'S JUST FOR A WEEK OR TWO-..I NEED A VACATION...
NOTHING AGAINST POLYNESIA, BUT I'M USED TO TH' WHITE GUY WITH GLASSES.. HE'S REASSURING!
BUT TIKI GUY IS FULLY AUTHORIZED BY YOURS TRULY!
IT'S MY NOSE, ISN'T IT?
..NO, NO.. IT'S NOT TH' NOSE.. ..I'M JUST USED TO GOD LOOKING VAGUELY LIKE MY DENTIST!
GRIFFY 10-14
©2009 Bill Griffith. World rights reserved. Distributed by King Features Syndicate
HEY, I'VE DONE MAJOR BRIDGE & ROOT CANAL WORK IN MY DAY, PAL!
HE'S APPROVED BY TH' A.D.A.!
SORRY.. CAN'T DO IT.... AND I'M NOT GETTING A TRIBAL TATTOO ABOVE MY BUTT, EITHER!!

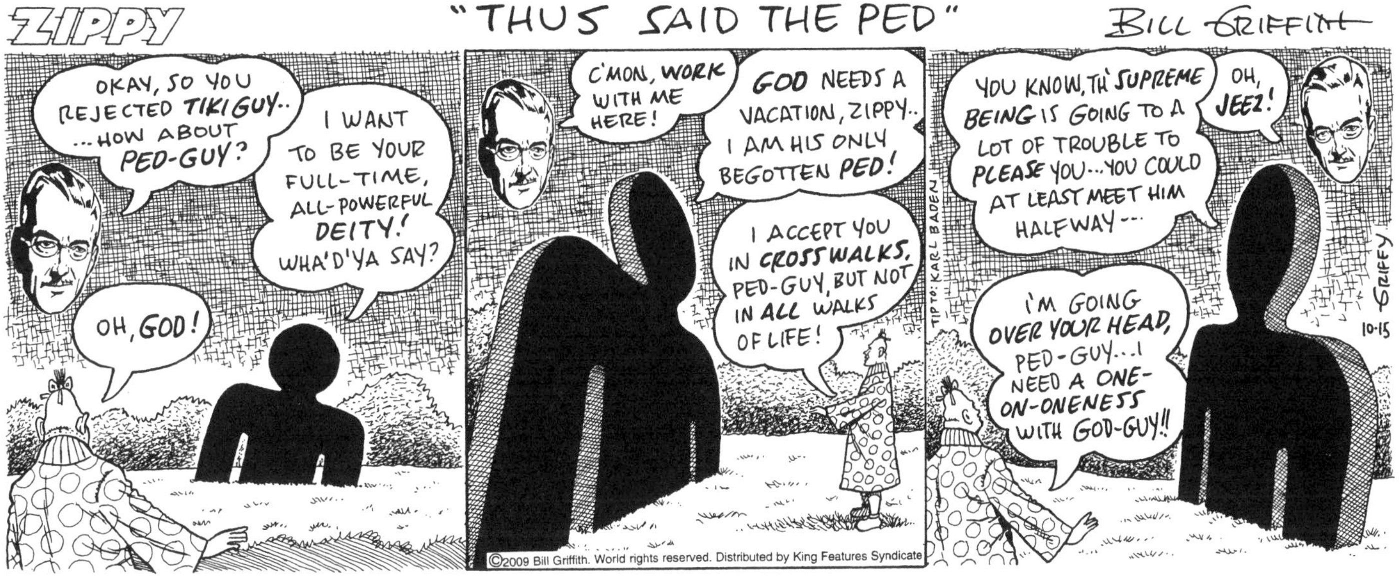
ZIPPY
"THUS SAID THE PED"
BILL GRIFFITH
OKAY, SO YOU REJECTED TIKI GUY.. ...HOW ABOUT PED-GUY?
I WANT TO BE YOUR FULL-TIME, ALL-POWERFUL DEITY! WHA'D'YA SAY?
OH, GOD!
C'MON, WORK WITH ME HERE!
GOD NEEDS A VACATION, ZIPPY.. I AM HIS ONLY BEGOTTEN PED!
I ACCEPT YOU IN CROSSWALKS, PED-GUY, BUT NOT IN ALL WALKS OF LIFE!
©2009 Bill Griffith. World rights reserved. Distributed by King Features Syndicate
TIP TO: KARL BADEN
YOU KNOW, TH' SUPREME BEING IS GOING TO A LOT OF TROUBLE TO PLEASE YOU...YOU COULD AT LEAST MEET HIM HALFWAY--
OH, JEEZ!
I'M GOING OVER YOUR HEAD, PED-GUY...I NEED A ONE-ON-ONENESS WITH GOD-GUY!!
GRIFFY
10-15

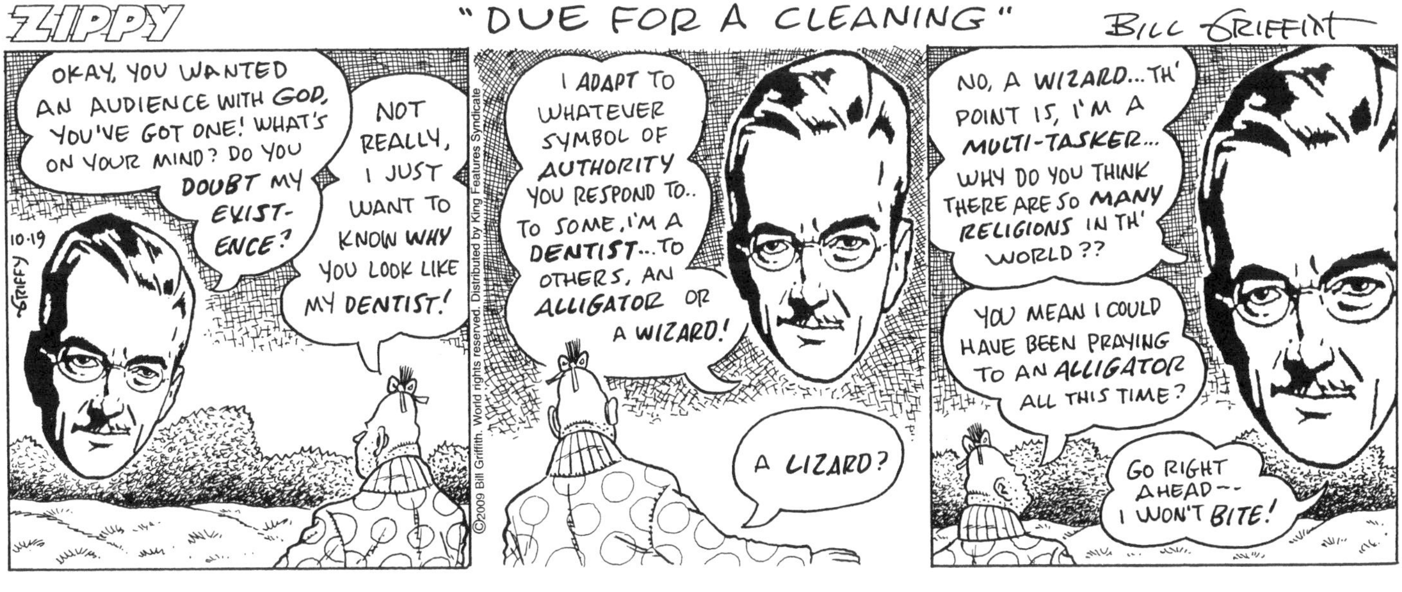
ZIPPY
"DUE FOR A CLEANING"
BILL GRIFFITH
OKAY, YOU WANTED AN AUDIENCE WITH GOD, YOU'VE GOT ONE! WHAT'S ON YOUR MIND? DO YOU DOUBT MY EXIST-ENCE?
10-19
GRIFFY
NOT REALLY, I JUST WANT TO KNOW WHY YOU LOOK LIKE MY DENTIST!
©2009 Bill Griffith. World rights reserved. Distributed by King Features Syndicate
I ADAPT TO WHATEVER SYMBOL OF AUTHORITY YOU RESPOND TO.. TO SOME, I'M A DENTIST...TO OTHERS, AN ALLIGATOR OR A WIZARD!
A LIZARD?
NO, A WIZARD...TH' POINT IS, I'M A MULTI-TASKER... WHY DO YOU THINK THERE ARE SO MANY RELIGIONS IN TH' WORLD??
YOU MEAN I COULD HAVE BEEN PRAYING TO AN ALLIGATOR ALL THIS TIME?
GO RIGHT AHEAD-- I WON'T BITE!

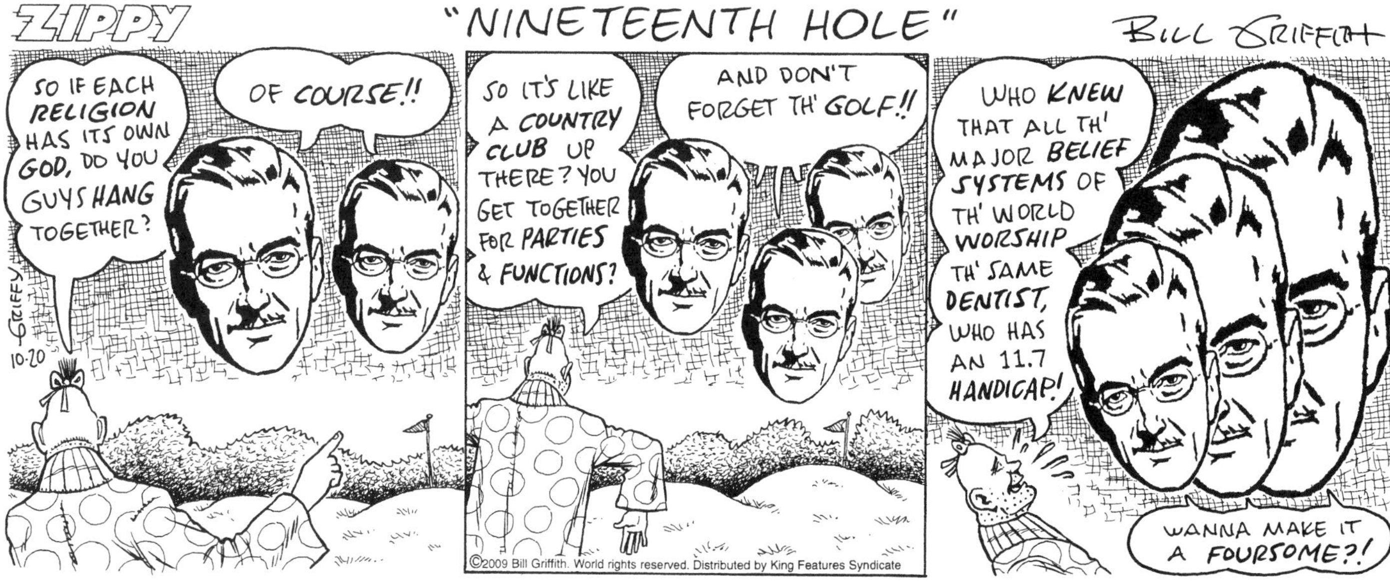
ZIPPY
"NINETEENTH HOLE"
BILL GRIFFITH
SO IF EACH RELIGION HAS ITS OWN GOD, DO YOU GUYS HANG TOGETHER?
OF COURSE!!
GRIFFY 10-20
SO IT'S LIKE A COUNTRY CLUB UP THERE? YOU GET TOGETHER FOR PARTIES & FUNCTIONS?
AND DON'T FORGET TH' GOLF!!
©2009 Bill Griffith. World rights reserved. Distributed by King Features Syndicate
WHO KNEW THAT ALL TH' MAJOR BELIEF SYSTEMS OF TH' WORLD WORSHIP TH' SAME DENTIST, WHO HAS AN 11.7 HANDICAP!
WANNA MAKE IT A FOURSOME?!

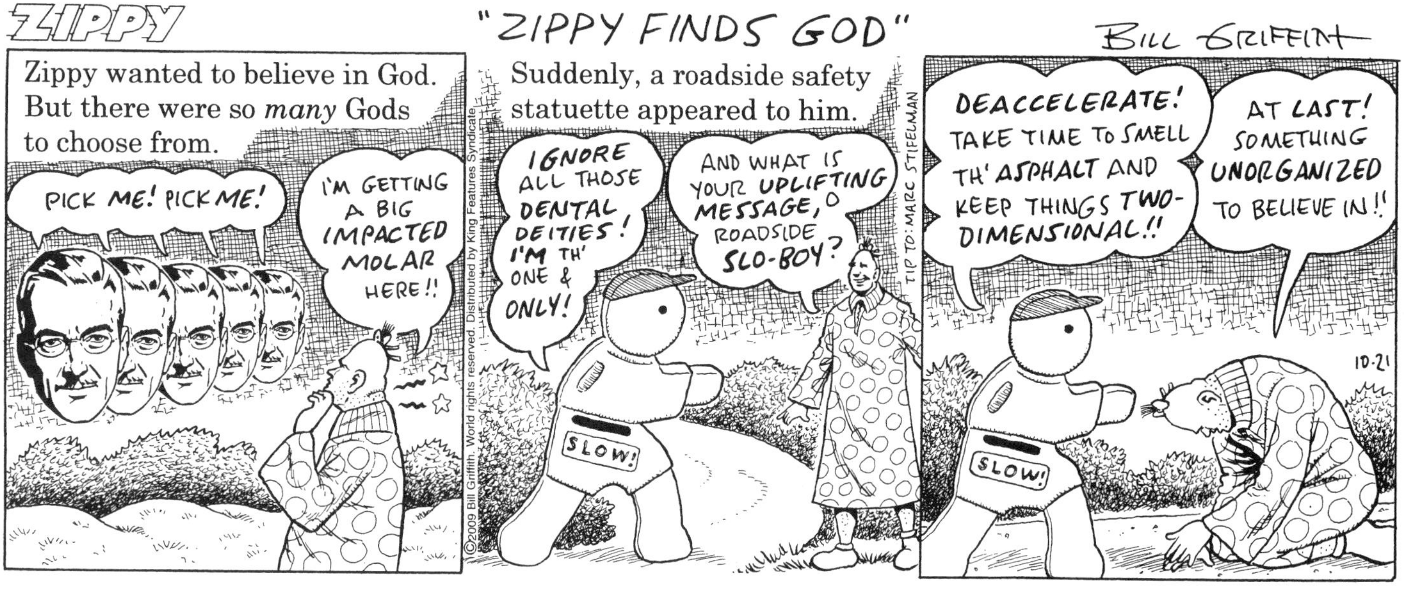
ZIPPY
"ZIPPY FINDS GOD"
BILL GRIFFITH
Zippy wanted to believe in God. But there were so *many* Gods to choose from.
PICK ME! PICK ME!
I'M GETTING A BIG IMPACTED MOLAR HERE!!
©2009 Bill Griffith. World rights reserved. Distributed by King Features Syndicate
Suddenly, a roadside safety statuette appeared to him.
IGNORE ALL THOSE DENTAL DEITIES! I'M TH' ONE & ONLY!
AND WHAT IS YOUR UPLIFTING MESSAGE, O ROADSIDE SLO-BOY?
SLOW!
TIP TO: MARC STIFELMAN
DEACCELERATE! TAKE TIME TO SMELL TH' ASPHALT AND KEEP THINGS TWO-DIMENSIONAL!!
AT LAST! SOMETHING UNORGANIZED TO BELIEVE IN!!
SLOW!
10-21

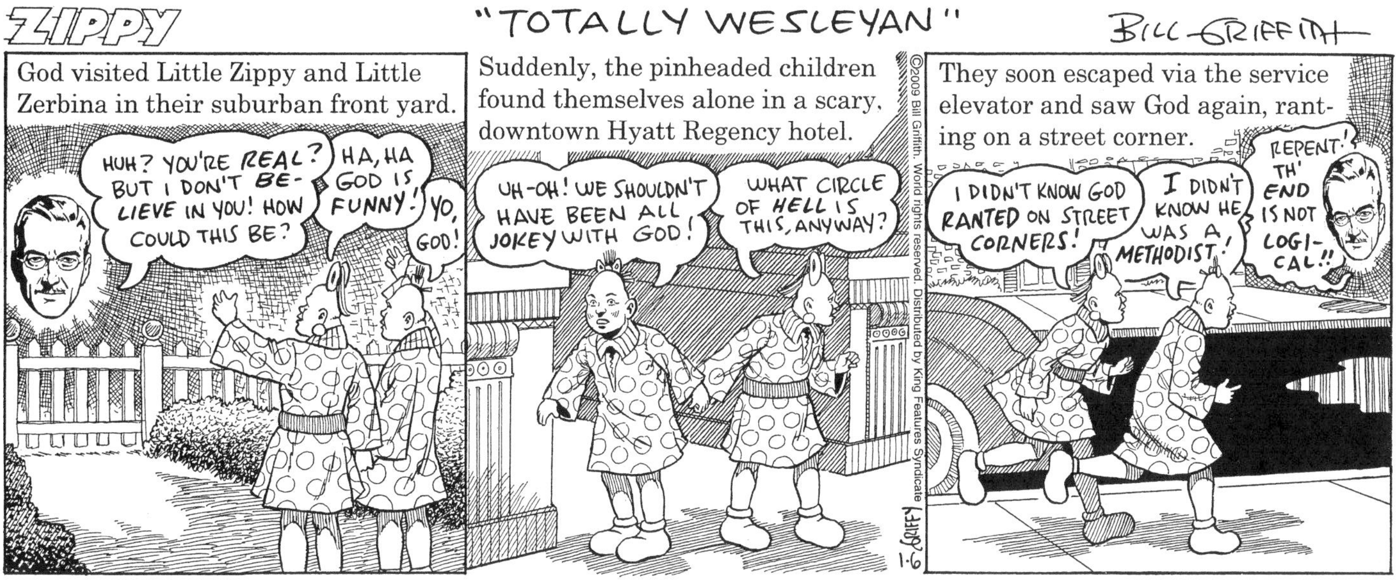
ZIPPY
"TOTALLY WESLEYAN"
BILL GRIFFITH
God visited Little Zippy and Little Zerbina in their suburban front yard.
HUH? YOU'RE REAL? BUT I DON'T BE-LIEVE IN YOU! HOW COULD THIS BE?
HA, HA GOD IS FUNNY!
YO, GOD!
Suddenly, the pinheaded children found themselves alone in a scary, downtown Hyatt Regency hotel.
UH-OH! WE SHOULDN'T HAVE BEEN ALL JOKEY WITH GOD!
WHAT CIRCLE OF HELL IS THIS, ANYWAY?
©2009 Bill Griffith. World rights reserved. Distributed by King Features Syndicate
GRIFFY 1-6
They soon escaped via the service elevator and saw God again, ranting on a street corner.
I DIDN'T KNOW GOD RANTED ON STREET CORNERS!
I DIDN'T KNOW HE WAS A METHODIST!
REPENT! TH' END IS NOT LOGI-CAL!!

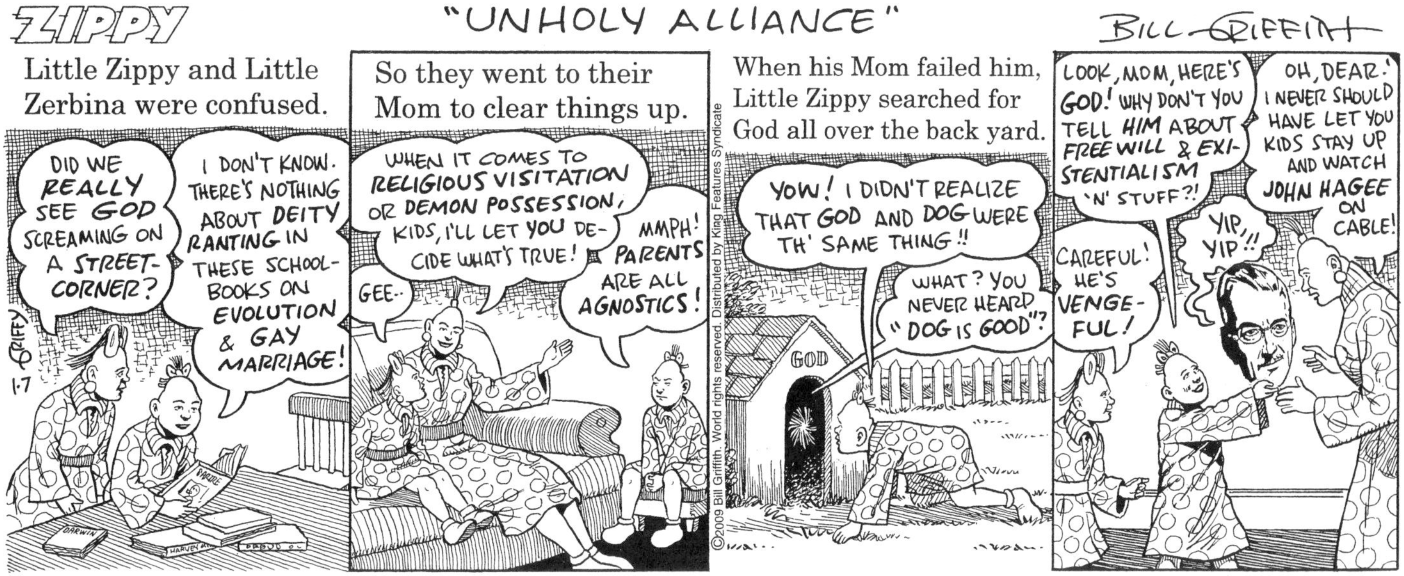
ZIPPY
"UNHOLY ALLIANCE"
BILL GRIFFITH
Little Zippy and Little Zerbina were confused.
DID WE REALLY SEE GOD SCREAMING ON A STREET-CORNER?
I DON'T KNOW. THERE'S NOTHING ABOUT DEITY RANTING IN THESE SCHOOL-BOOKS ON EVOLUTION & GAY MARRIAGE!
GRIFFY 1-7
DARWIN
So they went to their Mom to clear things up.
WHEN IT COMES TO RELIGIOUS VISITATION OR DEMON POSSESSION, KIDS, I'LL LET YOU DE-CIDE WHAT'S TRUE!
GEE..
MMPH! PARENTS ARE ALL AGNOSTICS!
©2009 Bill Griffith. World rights reserved. Distributed by King Features Syndicate
When his Mom failed him, Little Zippy searched for God all over the back yard.
YOW! I DIDN'T REALIZE THAT GOD AND DOG WERE TH' SAME THING!!
WHAT? YOU NEVER HEARD "DOG IS GOOD"?
GOD
LOOK, MOM, HERE'S GOD! WHY DON'T YOU TELL HIM ABOUT FREE WILL & EXI-STENTIALISM 'N' STUFF?!
OH, DEAR! I NEVER SHOULD HAVE LET YOU KIDS STAY UP AND WATCH JOHN HAGEE ON CABLE!
CAREFUL! HE'S VENGE-FUL!
YIP, YIP!!

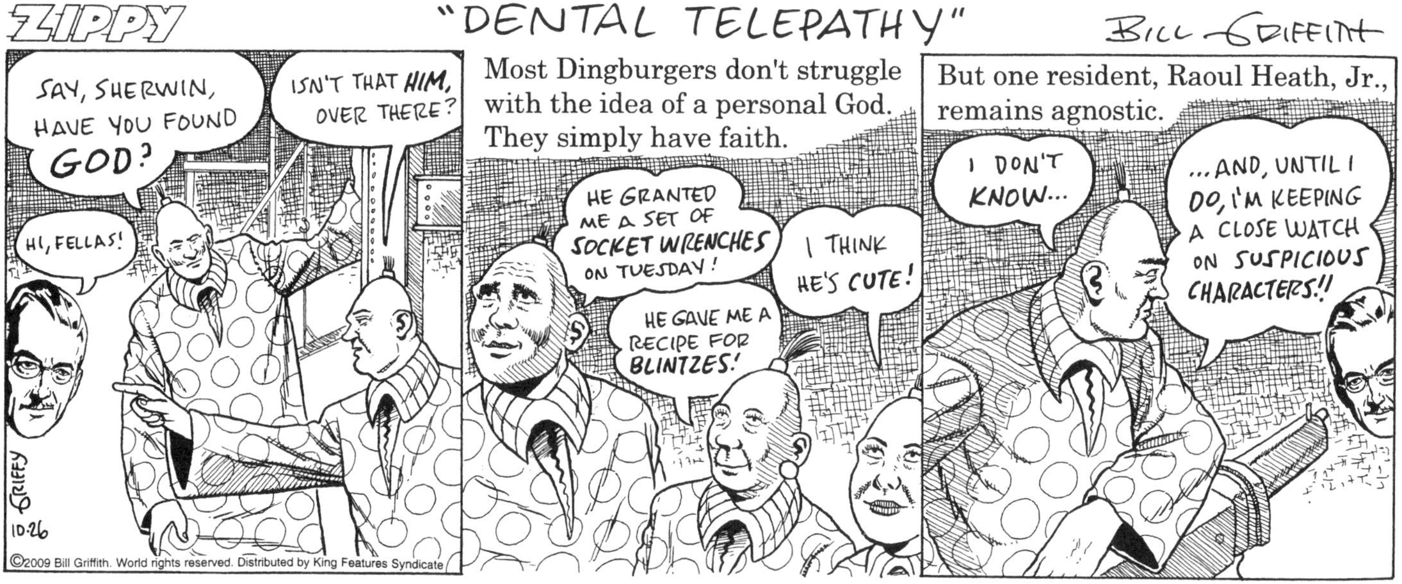
ZIPPY
"DENTAL TELEPATHY"
BILL GRIFFITH
SAY, SHERWIN, HAVE YOU FOUND GOD?
ISN'T THAT HIM, OVER THERE?
HI, FELLAS!
GRIFFY 10-26
©2009 Bill Griffith. World rights reserved. Distributed by King Features Syndicate
Most Dingburgers don't struggle with the idea of a personal God. They simply have faith.
HE GRANTED ME A SET OF SOCKET WRENCHES ON TUESDAY!
I THINK HE'S CUTE!
HE GAVE ME A RECIPE FOR BLINTZES!
But one resident, Raoul Heath, Jr., remains agnostic.
I DON'T KNOW...
...AND, UNTIL I DO, I'M KEEPING A CLOSE WATCH ON SUSPICIOUS CHARACTERS!!

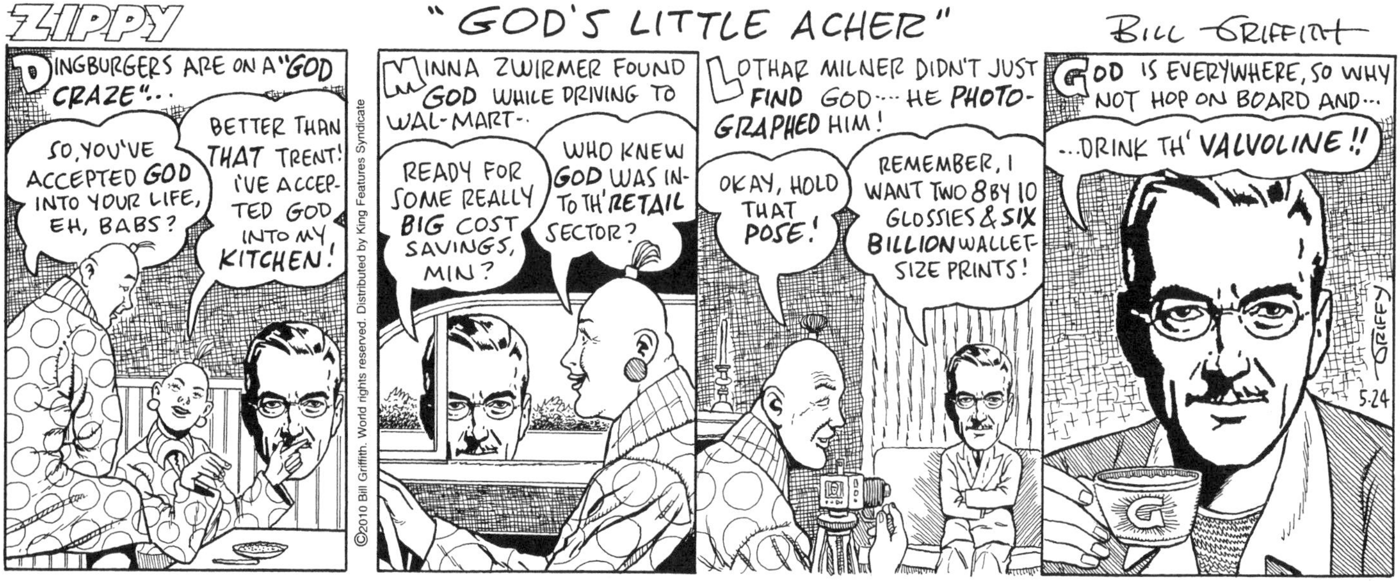
ZIPPY
"GOD'S LITTLE ACHER"
BILL GRIFFITH
DINGBURGERS ARE ON A "GOD CRAZE"...
SO, YOU'VE ACCEPTED GOD INTO YOUR LIFE, EH, BABS?
BETTER THAN THAT TRENT! I'VE ACCEPTED GOD INTO MY KITCHEN!
©2010 Bill Griffith. World rights reserved. Distributed by King Features Syndicate
MINNA ZWIRMER FOUND GOD WHILE DRIVING TO WAL-MART...
READY FOR SOME REALLY BIG COST SAVINGS, MIN?
WHO KNEW GOD WAS INTO TH' RETAIL SECTOR?
LOTHAR MILNER DIDN'T JUST FIND GOD... HE PHOTOGRAPHED HIM!
OKAY, HOLD THAT POSE!
REMEMBER, I WANT TWO 8 BY 10 GLOSSIES & SIX BILLION WALLET-SIZE PRINTS!
GOD IS EVERYWHERE, SO WHY NOT HOP ON BOARD AND...
...DRINK TH' VALVOLINE!!
GRIFFY 5-24

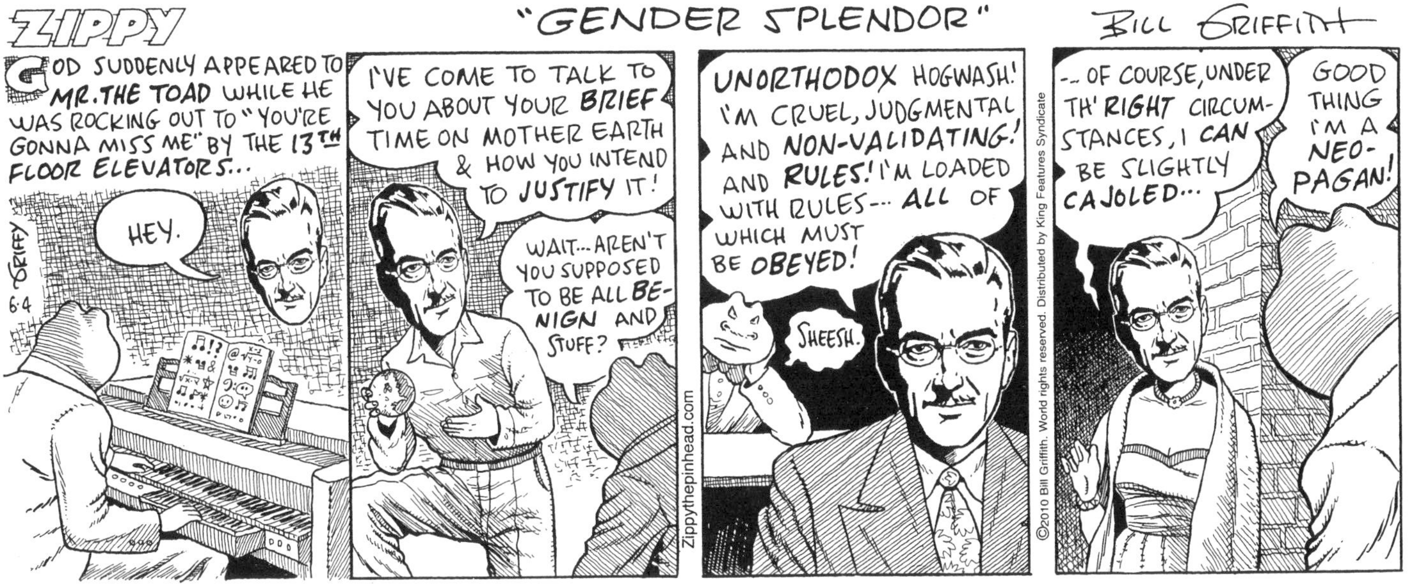
ZIPPY
"GENDER SPLENDOR"
BILL GRIFFITH
GOD SUDDENLY APPEARED TO MR. THE TOAD WHILE HE WAS ROCKING OUT TO "YOU'RE GONNA MISS ME" BY THE 13TH FLOOR ELEVATORS...
HEY.
GRIFFY 6·4
I'VE COME TO TALK TO YOU ABOUT YOUR BRIEF TIME ON MOTHER EARTH & HOW YOU INTEND TO JUSTIFY IT!
WAIT... AREN'T YOU SUPPOSED TO BE ALL BENIGN AND STUFF?
zippythepinhead.com
UNORTHODOX HOGWASH! I'M CRUEL, JUDGMENTAL AND NON-VALIDATING! AND RULES! I'M LOADED WITH RULES--- ALL OF WHICH MUST BE OBEYED!
SHEESH.
©2010 Bill Griffith. World rights reserved. Distributed by King Features Syndicate
-- OF COURSE, UNDER TH' RIGHT CIRCUMSTANCES, I CAN BE SLIGHTLY CAJOLED...
GOOD THING I'M A NEO-PAGAN!

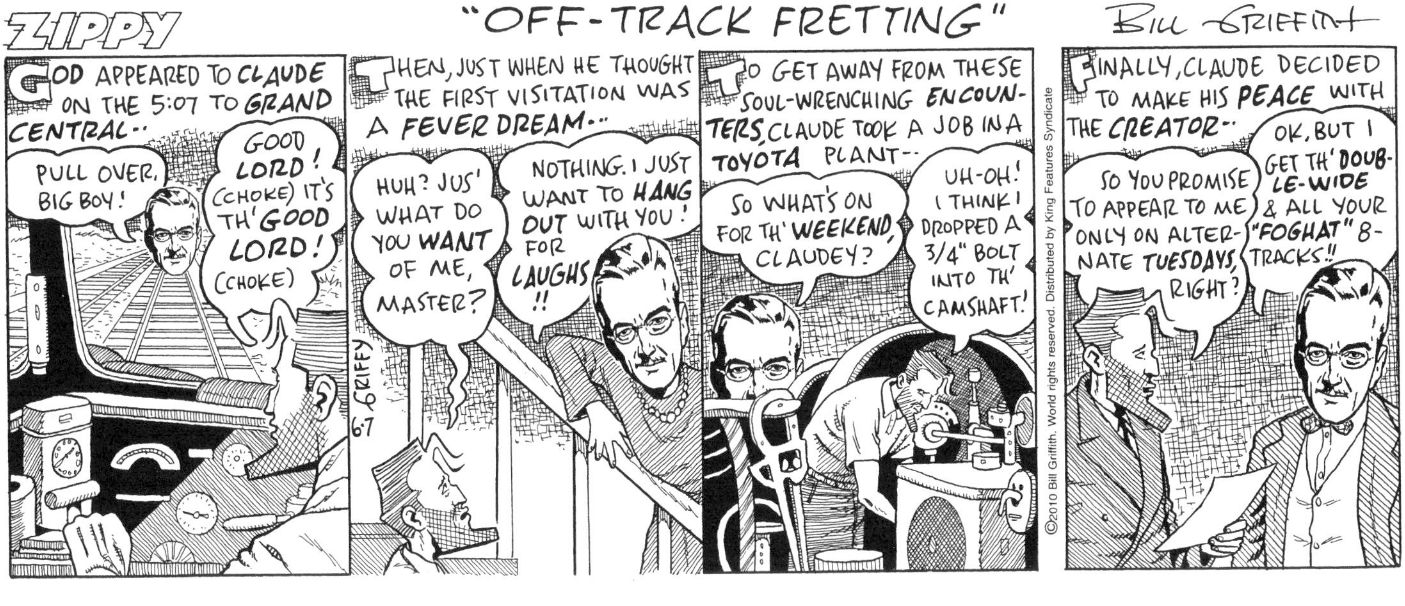
ZIPPY
"OFF-TRACK FRETTING"
BILL GRIFFITH
GOD APPEARED TO CLAUDE ON THE 5:07 TO GRAND CENTRAL..
PULL OVER, BIG BOY!
GOOD LORD! (CHOKE) IT'S TH' GOOD LORD! (CHOKE)
THEN, JUST WHEN HE THOUGHT THE FIRST VISITATION WAS A FEVER DREAM...
HUH? JUS' WHAT DO YOU WANT OF ME, MASTER?
NOTHING. I JUST WANT TO HANG OUT WITH YOU! FOR LAUGHS!!
GRIFFY 6·7
TO GET AWAY FROM THESE SOUL-WRENCHING ENCOUNTERS, CLAUDE TOOK A JOB IN A TOYOTA PLANT..
SO WHAT'S ON FOR TH' WEEKEND, CLAUDEY?
UH-OH! I THINK I DROPPED A 3/4" BOLT INTO TH' CAMSHAFT!
©2010 Bill Griffith. World rights reserved. Distributed by King Features Syndicate
FINALLY, CLAUDE DECIDED TO MAKE HIS PEACE WITH THE CREATOR..
SO YOU PROMISE TO APPEAR TO ME ONLY ON ALTERNATE TUESDAYS, RIGHT?
OK, BUT I GET TH' DOUBLE-WIDE & ALL YOUR "FOGHAT" 8-TRACKS!!

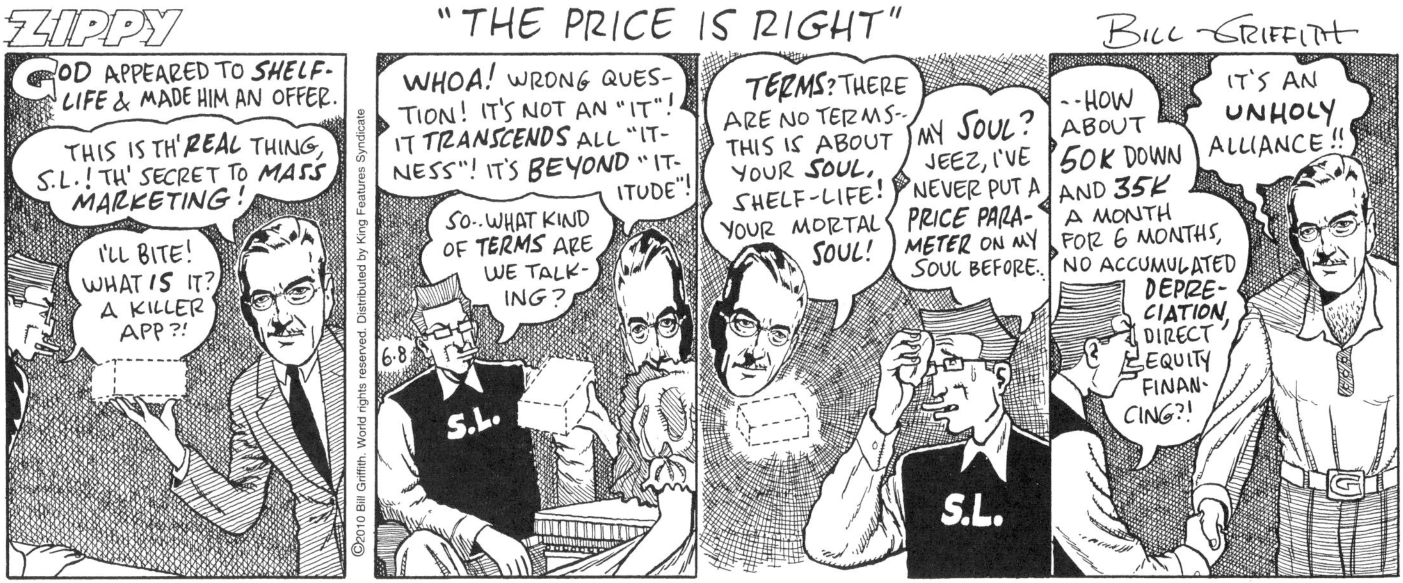
ZIPPY
"THE PRICE IS RIGHT"
BILL GRIFFITH
GOD APPEARED TO SHELF-LIFE & MADE HIM AN OFFER.
THIS IS TH' REAL THING, S.L.! TH' SECRET TO MASS MARKETING!
I'LL BITE! WHAT IS IT? A KILLER APP?!
©2010 Bill Griffith. World rights reserved. Distributed by King Features Syndicate
WHOA! WRONG QUESTION! IT'S NOT AN "IT"! IT TRANSCENDS ALL "IT-NESS"! IT'S BEYOND "IT-ITUDE"!
SO.. WHAT KIND OF TERMS ARE WE TALKING?
6·8
S.L.
TERMS? THERE ARE NO TERMS-- THIS IS ABOUT YOUR SOUL, SHELF-LIFE! YOUR MORTAL SOUL!
MY SOUL? JEEZ, I'VE NEVER PUT A PRICE PARAMETER ON MY SOUL BEFORE..
S.L.
--HOW ABOUT 50K DOWN AND 35K A MONTH FOR 6 MONTHS, NO ACCUMULATED DEPRECIATION, DIRECT EQUITY FINANCING?!
IT'S AN UNHOLY ALLIANCE!!
G

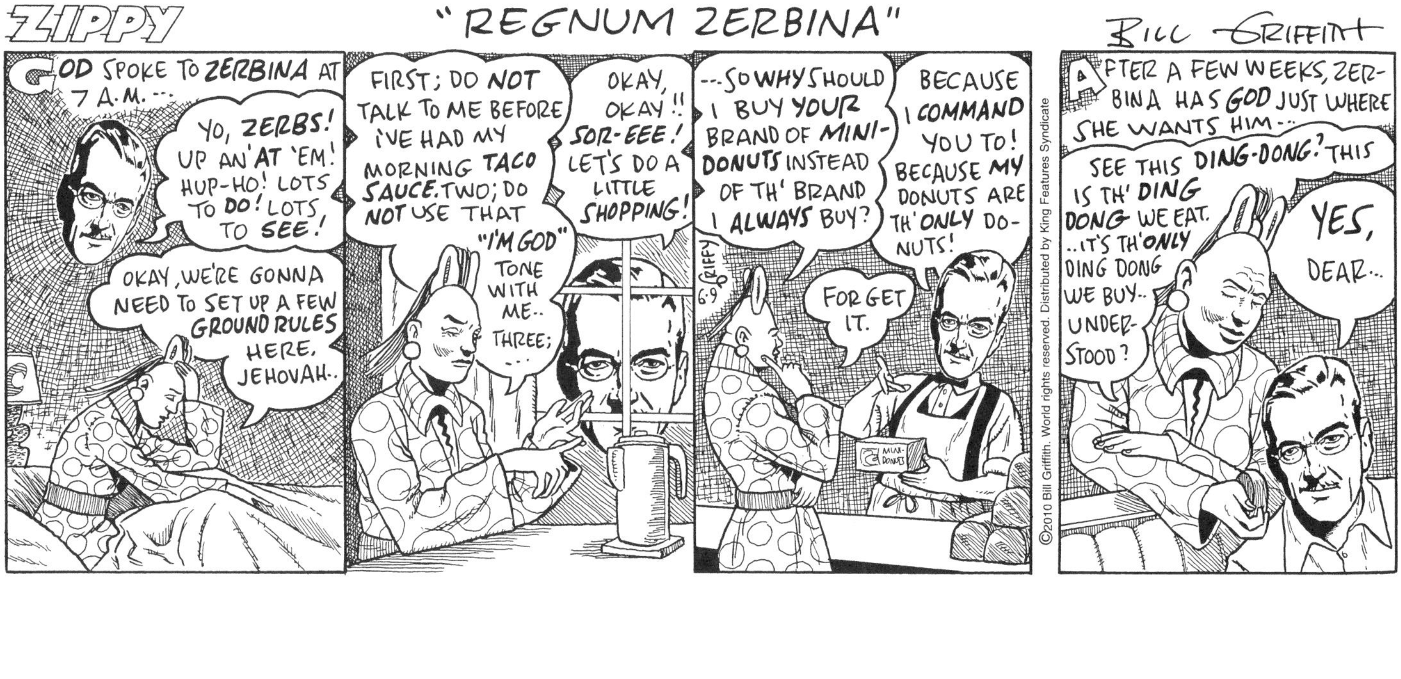
ZIPPY
"REGNUM ZERBINA"
BILL GRIFFITH
GOD SPOKE TO ZERBINA AT 7 A.M.--
YO, ZERBS! UP AN' AT 'EM! HUP-HO! LOTS TO DO! LOTS TO SEE!
OKAY, WE'RE GONNA NEED TO SET UP A FEW GROUND RULES HERE, JEHOVAH..
FIRST; DO NOT TALK TO ME BEFORE I'VE HAD MY MORNING TACO SAUCE. TWO; DO NOT USE THAT "I'M GOD" TONE WITH ME.. THREE; ...
OKAY, OKAY!! SOR-EEE! LET'S DO A LITTLE SHOPPING!
--SO WHY SHOULD I BUY YOUR BRAND OF MINI-DONUTS INSTEAD OF TH' BRAND I ALWAYS BUY?
BECAUSE I COMMAND YOU TO! BECAUSE MY DONUTS ARE TH' ONLY DONUTS!
FOR GET IT.
GRIFFY 6·9
MINI-DONUTS
©2010 Bill Griffith. World rights reserved. Distributed by King Features Syndicate
AFTER A FEW WEEKS, ZERBINA HAS GOD JUST WHERE SHE WANTS HIM..
SEE THIS DING-DONG? THIS IS TH' DING DONG WE EAT. ..IT'S TH' ONLY DING DONG WE BUY.. UNDERSTOOD?
YES, DEAR..

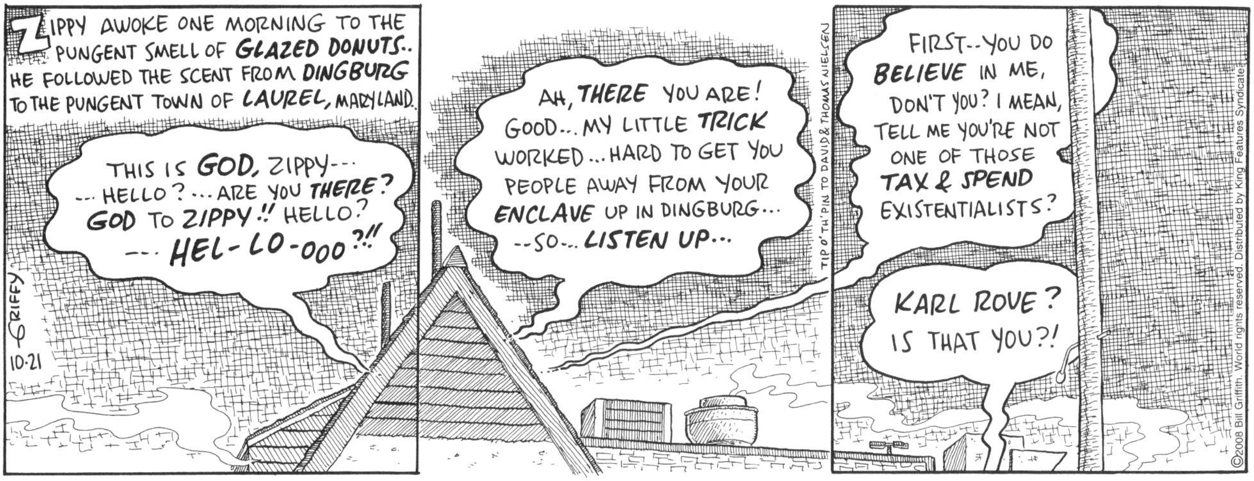
ZIPPY AWOKE ONE MORNING TO THE PUNGENT SMELL OF GLAZED DONUTS.. HE FOLLOWED THE SCENT FROM DINGBURG TO THE PUNGENT TOWN OF LAUREL, MARYLAND.
THIS IS GOD, ZIPPY--- --- HELLO? --- ARE YOU THERE? GOD TO ZIPPY!! HELLO? --- HEL-LO-OOO?!!
AH, THERE YOU ARE! GOOD--- MY LITTLE TRICK WORKED... HARD TO GET YOU PEOPLE AWAY FROM YOUR ENCLAVE UP IN DINGBURG... --SO-- LISTEN UP...
FIRST--YOU DO BELIEVE IN ME, DON'T YOU? I MEAN, TELL ME YOU'RE NOT ONE OF THOSE TAX & SPEND EXISTENTIALISTS?
KARL ROVE? IS THAT YOU?!
GRIFFY 10·21
TIP O' TH' PIN TO DAVID & THOMAS NIELSEN
©2008 Bill Griffith. World rights reserved. Distributed by King Features Syndicate

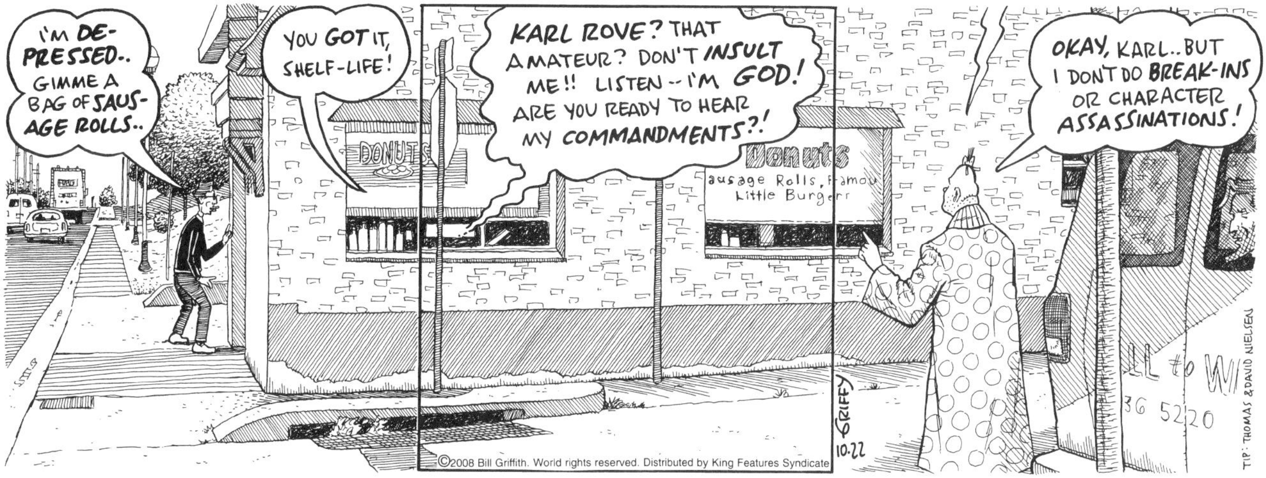
I'M DE-PRESSED.. GIMME A BAG OF SAUS-AGE ROLLS..
YOU GOT IT, SHELF-LIFE!
DONUTS
KARL ROVE? THAT AMATEUR? DON'T INSULT ME!! LISTEN -- I'M GOD! ARE YOU READY TO HEAR MY COMMANDMENTS?!
Donuts
OKAY, KARL.. BUT I DON'T DO BREAK-INS OR CHARACTER ASSASSINATIONS!
GRIFFY 10·22
TIP: THOMAS & DAVID NIELSEN
©2008 Bill Griffith. World rights reserved. Distributed by King Features Syndicate

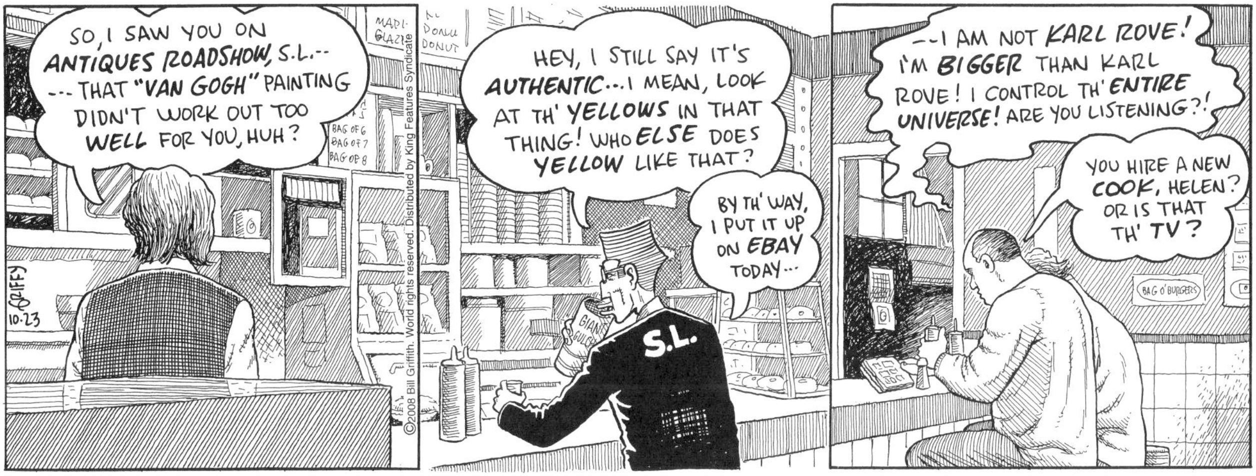
SO, I SAW YOU ON ANTIQUES ROADSHOW, S.L.-- --- THAT "VAN GOGH" PAINTING DIDN'T WORK OUT TOO WELL FOR YOU, HUH?
BAG OF 6 BAG OF 7 BAG OF 8
HEY, I STILL SAY IT'S AUTHENTIC... I MEAN, LOOK AT TH' YELLOWS IN THAT THING! WHO ELSE DOES YELLOW LIKE THAT?
BY TH' WAY, I PUT IT UP ON EBAY TODAY...
S.L.
--I AM NOT KARL ROVE! I'M BIGGER THAN KARL ROVE! I CONTROL TH' ENTIRE UNIVERSE! ARE YOU LISTENING?!
YOU HIRE A NEW COOK, HELEN? OR IS THAT TH' TV?
BAG O' BURGERS
GRIFFY 10·23
©2008 Bill Griffith. World rights reserved. Distributed by King Features Syndicate

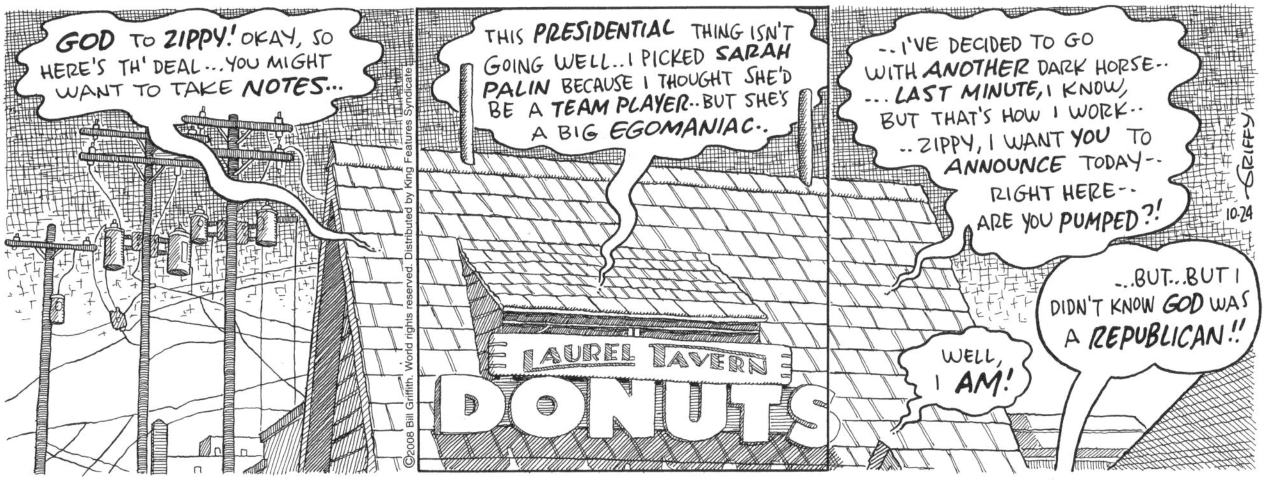
GOD TO ZIPPY! OKAY, SO HERE'S TH' DEAL...YOU MIGHT WANT TO TAKE NOTES...
THIS PRESIDENTIAL THING ISN'T GOING WELL..I PICKED SARAH PALIN BECAUSE I THOUGHT SHE'D BE A TEAM PLAYER..BUT SHE'S A BIG EGOMANIAC..
LAUREL TAVERN
DONUTS
©2008 Bill Griffith. World rights reserved. Distributed by King Features Syndicate
..I'VE DECIDED TO GO WITH ANOTHER DARK HORSE.. ...LAST MINUTE, I KNOW, BUT THAT'S HOW I WORK.. ..ZIPPY, I WANT YOU TO ANNOUNCE TODAY-- RIGHT HERE-- ARE YOU PUMPED?!
..BUT..BUT I DIDN'T KNOW GOD WAS A REPUBLICAN!!
WELL, I AM!
GRIFFY
10-24

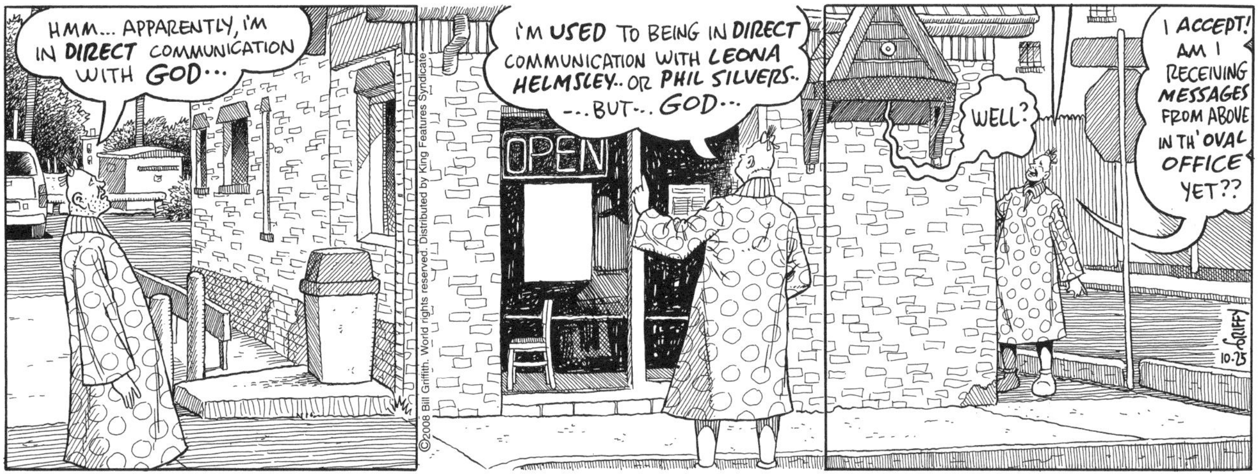
HMM... APPARENTLY, I'M IN DIRECT COMMUNICATION WITH GOD...
©2008 Bill Griffith. World rights reserved. Distributed by King Features Syndicate
I'M USED TO BEING IN DIRECT COMMUNICATION WITH LEONA HELMSLEY.. OR PHIL SILVERS.. ...BUT... GOD...
OPEN
WELL?
I ACCEPT! AM I RECEIVING MESSAGES FROM ABOVE IN TH' OVAL OFFICE YET??
GRIFFY
10-25

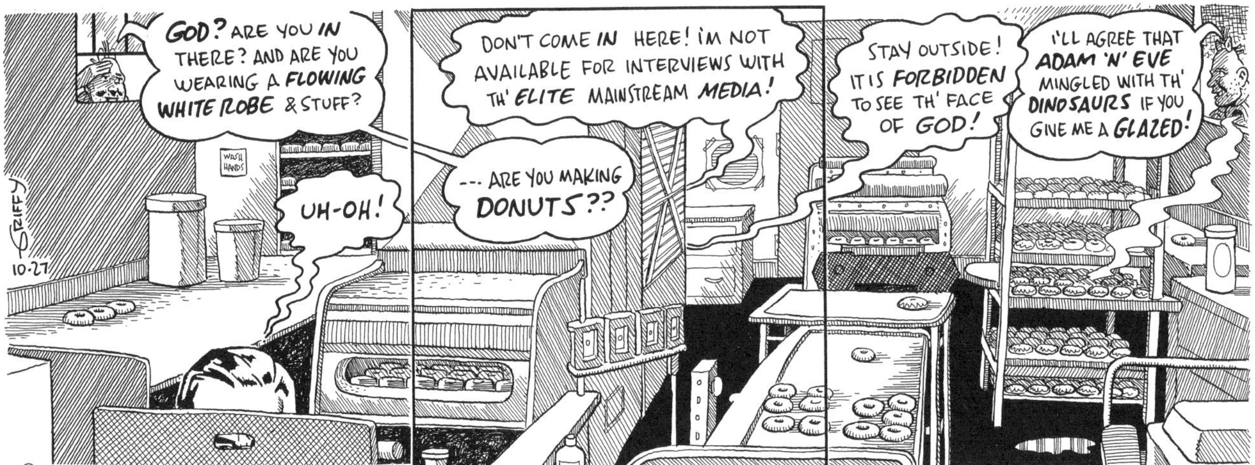
GOD? ARE YOU IN THERE? AND ARE YOU WEARING A FLOWING WHITE ROBE & STUFF?
...ARE YOU MAKING DONUTS??
UH-OH!
WASH HANDS
GRIFFY
10-27
DON'T COME IN HERE! I'M NOT AVAILABLE FOR INTERVIEWS WITH TH' ELITE MAINSTREAM MEDIA!
STAY OUTSIDE! IT IS FORBIDDEN TO SEE TH' FACE OF GOD!
I'LL AGREE THAT ADAM 'N' EVE MINGLED WITH TH' DINOSAURS IF YOU GIVE ME A GLAZED!

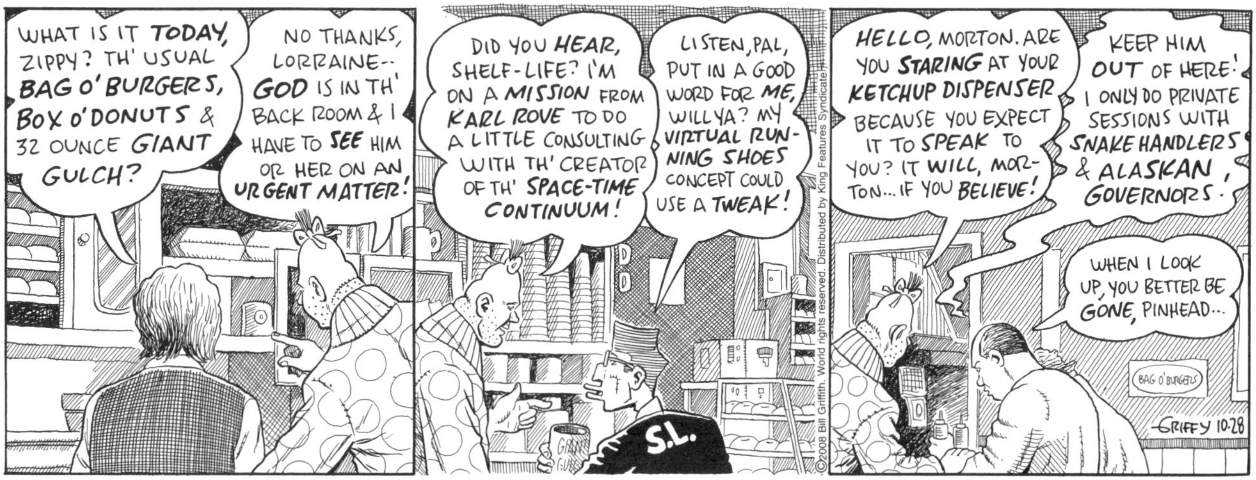

WHAT IS IT TODAY, ZIPPY? TH' USUAL BAG O' BURGERS, BOX O' DONUTS & 32 OUNCE GIANT GULCH?
NO THANKS, LORRAINE-- GOD IS IN TH' BACK ROOM & I HAVE TO SEE HIM OR HER ON AN URGENT MATTER!
DID YOU HEAR, SHELF-LIFE? I'M ON A MISSION FROM KARL ROVE TO DO A LITTLE CONSULTING WITH TH' CREATOR OF TH' SPACE-TIME CONTINUUM!
LISTEN, PAL, PUT IN A GOOD WORD FOR ME, WILLYA? MY VIRTUAL RUNNING SHOES CONCEPT COULD USE A TWEAK!
S.L.
©2008 Bill Griffith. World rights reserved. Distributed by King Features Syndicate
HELLO, MORTON. ARE YOU STARING AT YOUR KETCHUP DISPENSER BECAUSE YOU EXPECT IT TO SPEAK TO YOU? IT WILL, MORTON... IF YOU BELIEVE!
KEEP HIM OUT OF HERE! I ONLY DO PRIVATE SESSIONS WITH SNAKE HANDLERS & ALASKAN GOVERNORS.
WHEN I LOOK UP, YOU BETTER BE GONE, PINHEAD...
BAG O' BURGERS
GRIFFY 10-28

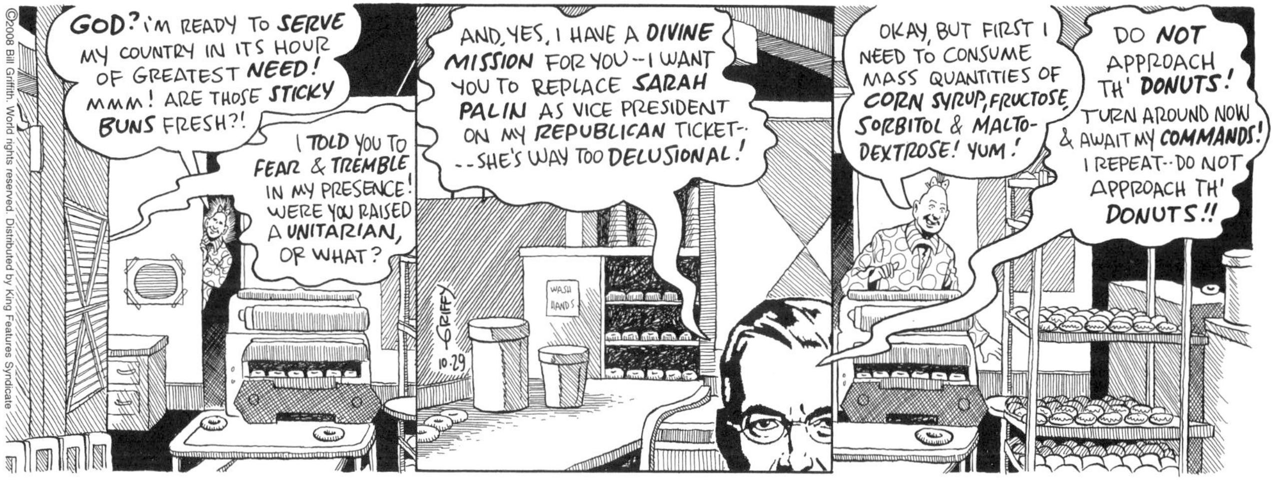

©2008 Bill Griffith. World rights reserved. Distributed by King Features Syndicate
GOD? I'M READY TO SERVE MY COUNTRY IN ITS HOUR OF GREATEST NEED! MMM! ARE THOSE STICKY BUNS FRESH?!
I TOLD YOU TO FEAR & TREMBLE IN MY PRESENCE! WERE YOU RAISED A UNITARIAN, OR WHAT?
AND, YES, I HAVE A DIVINE MISSION FOR YOU--I WANT YOU TO REPLACE SARAH PALIN AS VICE PRESIDENT ON MY REPUBLICAN TICKET-- --SHE'S WAY TOO DELUSIONAL!
WASH HANDS
GRIFFY 10-29
OKAY, BUT FIRST I NEED TO CONSUME MASS QUANTITIES OF CORN SYRUP, FRUCTOSE, SORBITOL & MALTODEXTROSE! YUM!
DO NOT APPROACH TH' DONUTS! TURN AROUND NOW & AWAIT MY COMMANDS! I REPEAT--DO NOT APPROACH TH' DONUTS!!

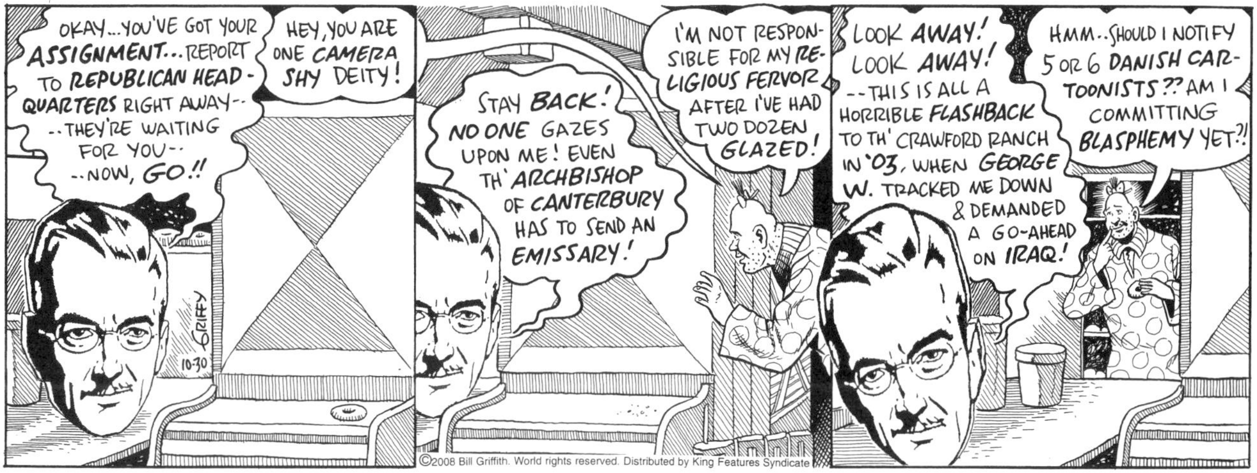

OKAY...YOU'VE GOT YOUR ASSIGNMENT...REPORT TO REPUBLICAN HEADQUARTERS RIGHT AWAY-- --THEY'RE WAITING FOR YOU-- --NOW, GO!!
HEY, YOU ARE ONE CAMERA SHY DEITY!
GRIFFY 10-30
STAY BACK! NO ONE GAZES UPON ME! EVEN TH' ARCHBISHOP OF CANTERBURY HAS TO SEND AN EMISSARY!
I'M NOT RESPONSIBLE FOR MY RELIGIOUS FERVOR AFTER I'VE HAD TWO DOZEN GLAZED!
LOOK AWAY! LOOK AWAY! --THIS IS ALL A HORRIBLE FLASHBACK TO TH' CRAWFORD RANCH IN '03, WHEN GEORGE W. TRACKED ME DOWN & DEMANDED A GO-AHEAD ON IRAQ!
HMM..SHOULD I NOTIFY 5 OR 6 DANISH CARTOONISTS?? AM I COMMITTING BLASPHEMY YET?!
©2008 Bill Griffith. World rights reserved. Distributed by King Features Syndicate

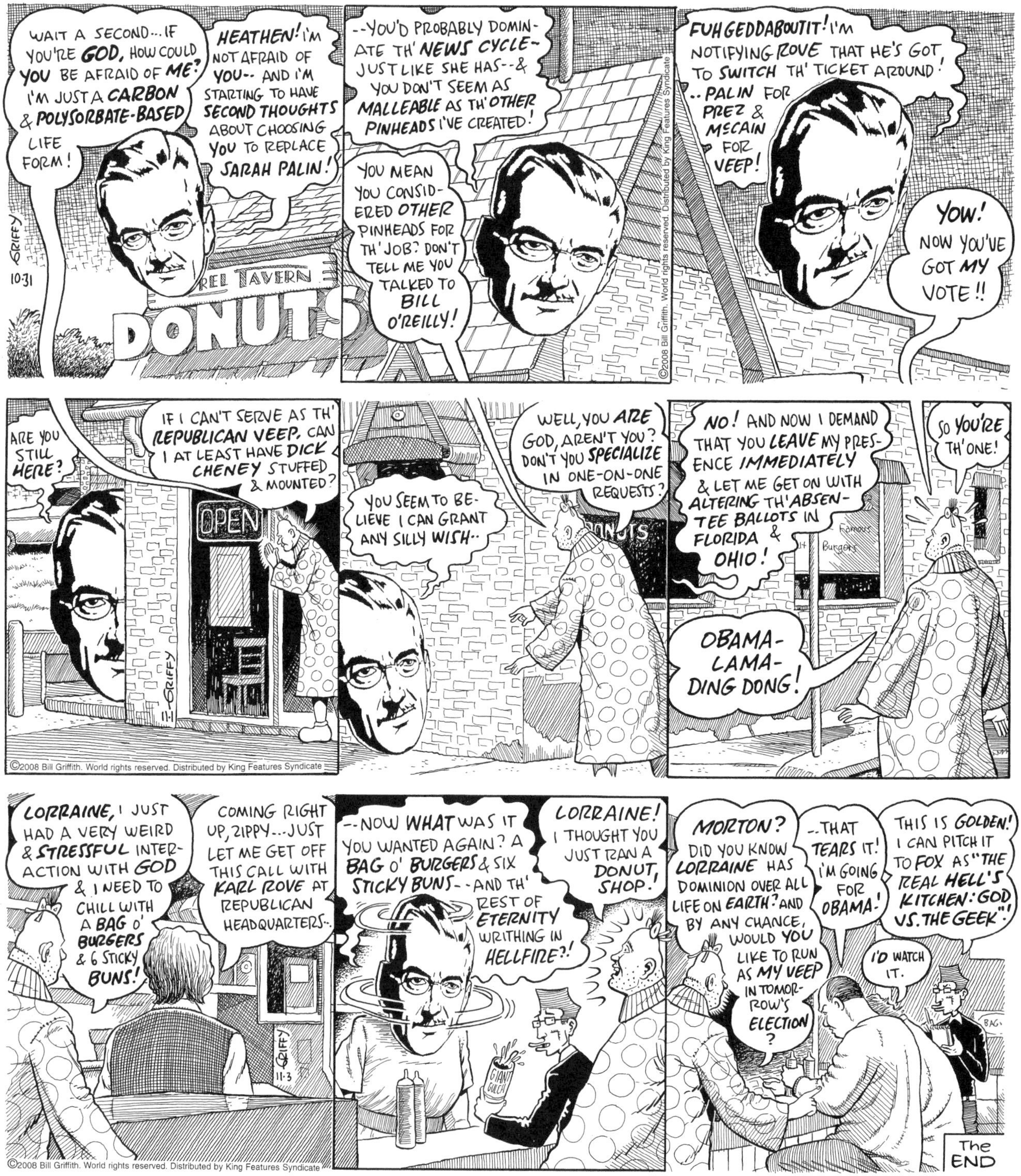
WAIT A SECOND... IF YOU'RE GOD, HOW COULD YOU BE AFRAID OF ME? I'M JUST A CARBON & POLYSORBATE-BASED LIFE FORM!
HEATHEN! I'M NOT AFRAID OF YOU-- AND I'M STARTING TO HAVE SECOND THOUGHTS ABOUT CHOOSING YOU TO REPLACE SARAH PALIN!
REL TAVERN
DONUTS
GRIFFY
10-31
--YOU'D PROBABLY DOMINATE TH' NEWS CYCLE-- JUST LIKE SHE HAS--& YOU DON'T SEEM AS MALLEABLE AS TH' OTHER PINHEADS I'VE CREATED!
YOU MEAN YOU CONSIDERED OTHER PINHEADS FOR TH' JOB? DON'T TELL ME YOU TALKED TO BILL O'REILLY!
©2008 Bill Griffith. World rights reserved. Distributed by King Features Syndicate
FUHGEDDABOUTIT! I'M NOTIFYING ROVE THAT HE'S GOT TO SWITCH TH' TICKET AROUND! ..PALIN FOR PREZ & McCAIN FOR VEEP!
YOW! NOW YOU'VE GOT MY VOTE!!
ARE YOU STILL HERE?
IF I CAN'T SERVE AS TH' REPUBLICAN VEEP, CAN I AT LEAST HAVE DICK CHENEY STUFFED & MOUNTED?
OPEN
GRIFFY
11-1
©2008 Bill Griffith. World rights reserved. Distributed by King Features Syndicate
YOU SEEM TO BELIEVE I CAN GRANT ANY SILLY WISH..
WELL, YOU ARE GOD, AREN'T YOU? DON'T YOU SPECIALIZE IN ONE-ON-ONE REQUESTS?
DONUTS
NO! AND NOW I DEMAND THAT YOU LEAVE MY PRESENCE IMMEDIATELY & LET ME GET ON WITH ALTERING TH' ABSENTEE BALLOTS IN FLORIDA & OHIO!
SO YOU'RE TH' ONE!
OBAMA-LAMA-DING DONG!
LORRAINE, I JUST HAD A VERY WEIRD & STRESSFUL INTERACTION WITH GOD & I NEED TO CHILL WITH A BAG O' BURGERS & 6 STICKY BUNS!
COMING RIGHT UP, ZIPPY... JUST LET ME GET OFF THIS CALL WITH KARL ROVE AT REPUBLICAN HEADQUARTERS..
GRIFFY
11-3
©2008 Bill Griffith. World rights reserved. Distributed by King Features Syndicate
--NOW WHAT WAS IT YOU WANTED AGAIN? A BAG O' BURGERS & SIX STICKY BUNS--AND TH' REST OF ETERNITY WRITHING IN HELLFIRE?!
LORRAINE! I THOUGHT YOU JUST RAN A DONUT SHOP!
MORTON? DID YOU KNOW LORRAINE HAS DOMINION OVER ALL LIFE ON EARTH? AND BY ANY CHANCE, WOULD YOU LIKE TO RUN AS MY VEEP IN TOMORROW'S ELECTION?
--THAT TEARS IT! I'M GOING FOR OBAMA!
THIS IS GOLDEN! I CAN PITCH IT TO FOX AS "THE REAL HELL'S KITCHEN: GOD VS. THE GEEK"!
I'D WATCH IT.
The END

THE UNUSUAL SUSPECTS

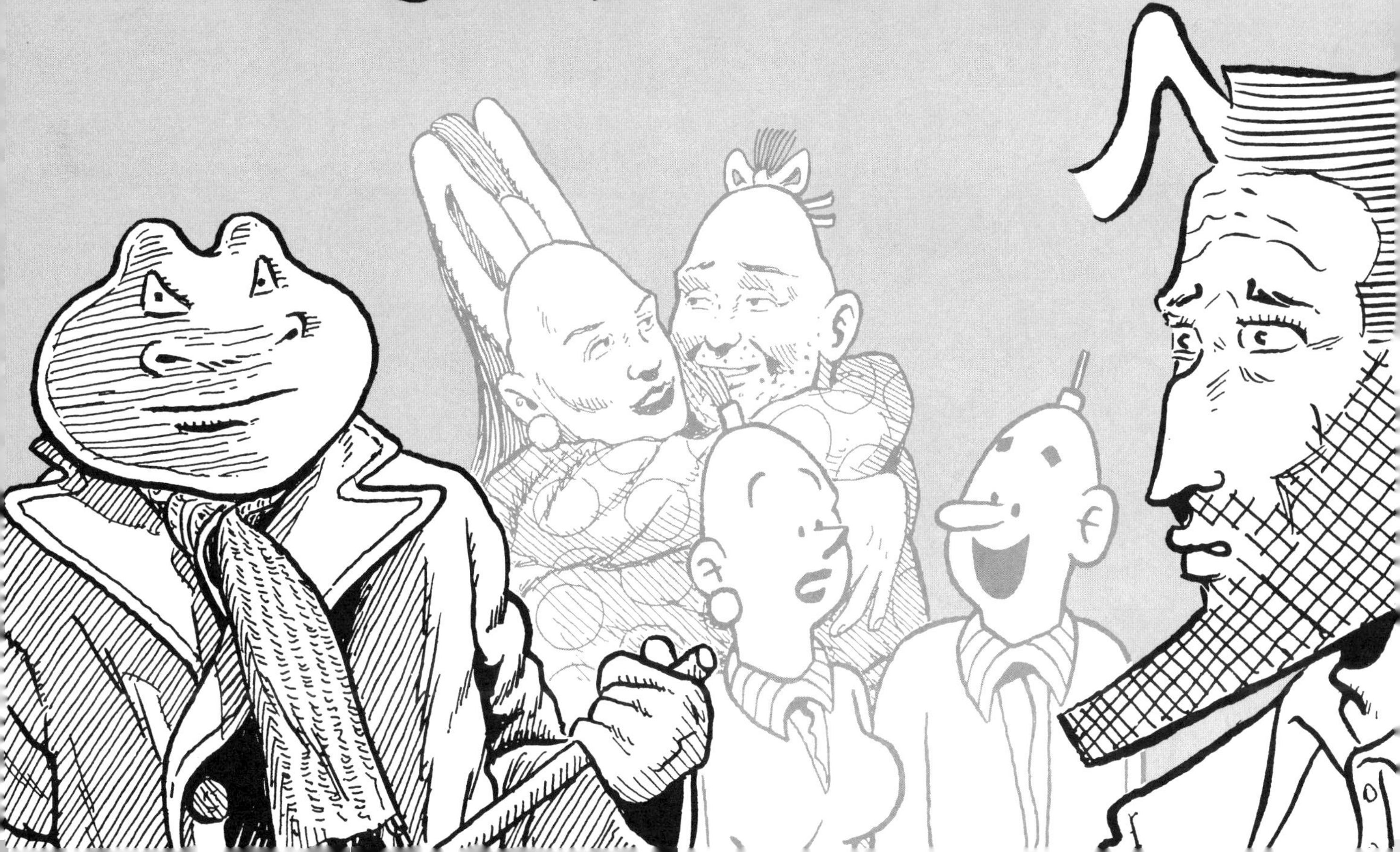

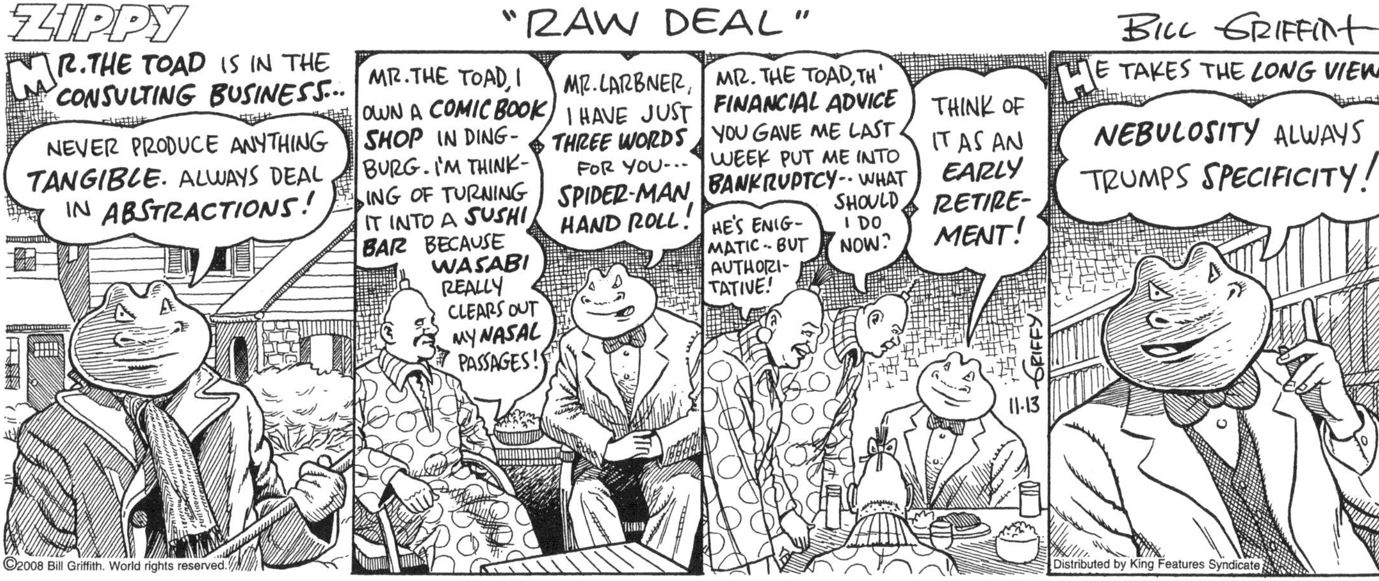
ZIPPY
"RAW DEAL"
BILL GRIFFITH
MR. THE TOAD IS IN THE CONSULTING BUSINESS...
NEVER PRODUCE ANYTHING TANGIBLE. ALWAYS DEAL IN ABSTRACTIONS!
MR. THE TOAD, I OWN A COMIC BOOK SHOP IN DINGBURG. I'M THINKING OF TURNING IT INTO A SUSHI BAR BECAUSE WASABI REALLY CLEARS OUT MY NASAL PASSAGES!
MR. LARBNER, I HAVE JUST THREE WORDS FOR YOU--- SPIDER-MAN HAND ROLL!
MR. THE TOAD, TH' FINANCIAL ADVICE YOU GAVE ME LAST WEEK PUT ME INTO BANKRUPTCY-- WHAT SHOULD I DO NOW?
HE'S ENIGMATIC-- BUT AUTHORITATIVE!
THINK OF IT AS AN EARLY RETIREMENT!
GRIFFY 11-13
HE TAKES THE LONG VIEW..
NEBULOSITY ALWAYS TRUMPS SPECIFICITY!
©2008 Bill Griffith. World rights reserved.
Distributed by King Features Syndicate

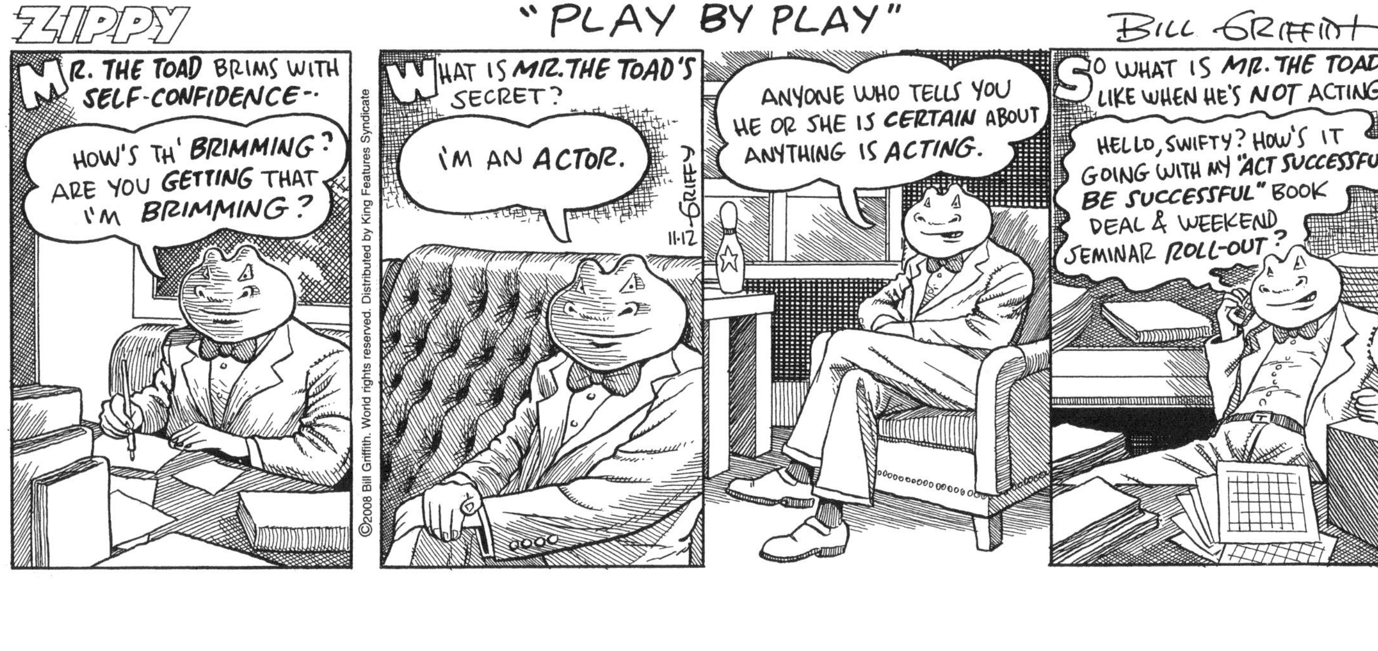
ZIPPY
"PLAY BY PLAY"
BILL GRIFFITH
MR. THE TOAD BRIMS WITH SELF-CONFIDENCE--
HOW'S TH' BRIMMING? ARE YOU GETTING THAT I'M BRIMMING?
©2008 Bill Griffith. World rights reserved. Distributed by King Features Syndicate
WHAT IS MR. THE TOAD'S SECRET?
I'M AN ACTOR.
GRIFFY 11-12
ANYONE WHO TELLS YOU HE OR SHE IS CERTAIN ABOUT ANYTHING IS ACTING.
SO WHAT IS MR. THE TOAD LIKE WHEN HE'S NOT ACTING?
HELLO, SWIFTY? HOW'S IT GOING WITH MY "ACT SUCCESSFUL, BE SUCCESSFUL" BOOK DEAL & WEEKEND SEMINAR ROLL-OUT?

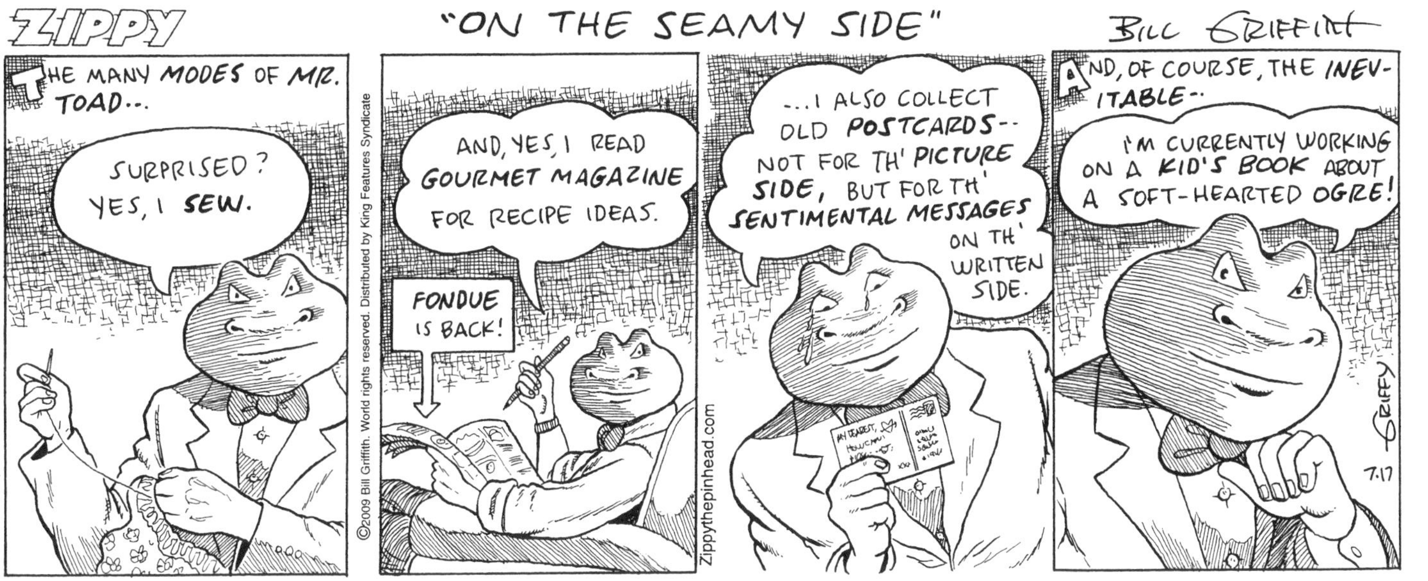
ZIPPY
"ON THE SEAMY SIDE"
BILL GRIFFITH
THE MANY MODES OF MR. TOAD...
SURPRISED? YES, I SEW.
©2009 Bill Griffith. World rights reserved. Distributed by King Features Syndicate
AND, YES, I READ GOURMET MAGAZINE FOR RECIPE IDEAS.
FONDUE IS BACK!
Zippythepinhead.com
...I ALSO COLLECT OLD POSTCARDS-- NOT FOR TH' PICTURE SIDE, BUT FOR TH' SENTIMENTAL MESSAGES ON TH' WRITTEN SIDE.
AND, OF COURSE, THE INEVITABLE--
I'M CURRENTLY WORKING ON A KID'S BOOK ABOUT A SOFT-HEARTED OGRE!
GRIFFY
7.17

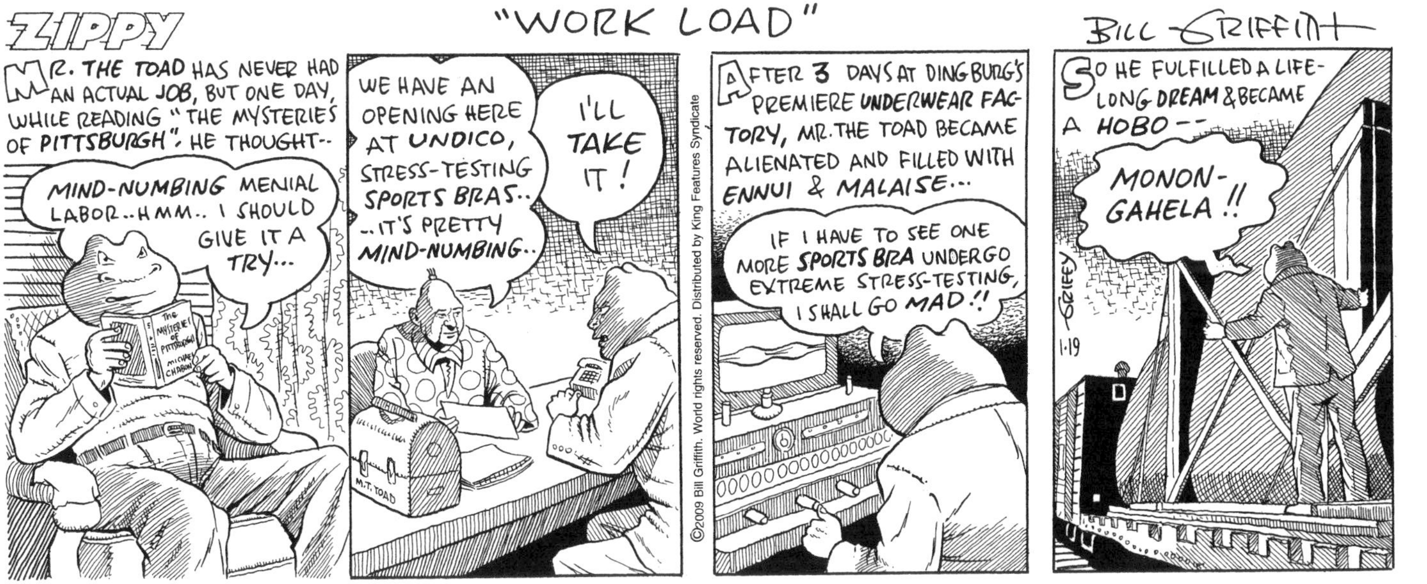
ZIPPY
"WORK LOAD"
BILL GRIFFITH
MR. THE TOAD HAS NEVER HAD AN ACTUAL JOB, BUT ONE DAY, WHILE READING "THE MYSTERIES OF PITTSBURGH", HE THOUGHT--
MIND-NUMBING MENIAL LABOR..HMM.. I SHOULD GIVE IT A TRY...
THE MYSTERIES OF PITTSBURGH MICHAEL CHABON
WE HAVE AN OPENING HERE AT UNDICO, STRESS-TESTING SPORTS BRAS.. ..IT'S PRETTY MIND-NUMBING..
I'LL TAKE IT!
M.T. TOAD
©2009 Bill Griffith. World rights reserved. Distributed by King Features Syndicate
AFTER 3 DAYS AT DINGBURG'S PREMIERE UNDERWEAR FACTORY, MR. THE TOAD BECAME ALIENATED AND FILLED WITH ENNUI & MALAISE...
IF I HAVE TO SEE ONE MORE SPORTS BRA UNDERGO EXTREME STRESS-TESTING, I SHALL GO MAD!!
SO HE FULFILLED A LIFE-LONG DREAM & BECAME A HOBO--
MONONGAHELA!!
GRIFFY
1-19

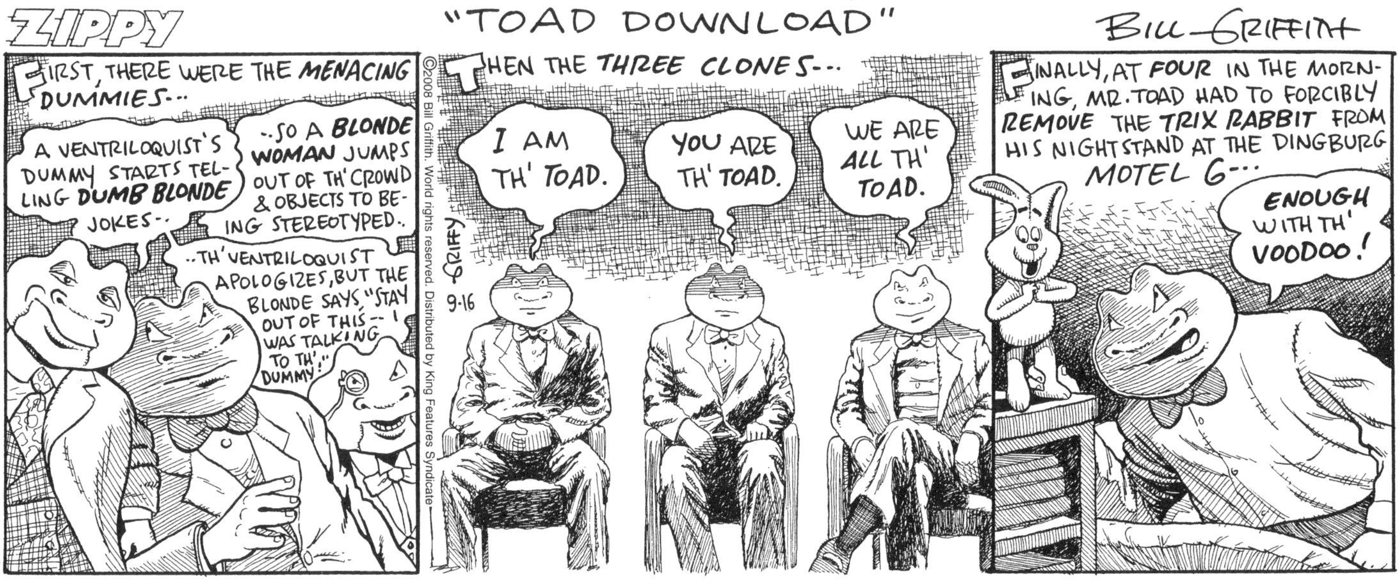
ZIPPY
"TOAD DOWNLOAD"
BILL GRIFFITH
FIRST, THERE WERE THE MENACING DUMMIES--
A VENTRILOQUIST'S DUMMY STARTS TELLING DUMB BLONDE JOKES--
--SO A BLONDE WOMAN JUMPS OUT OF TH' CROWD & OBJECTS TO BEING STEREOTYPED..
--TH' VENTRILOQUIST APOLOGIZES, BUT THE BLONDE SAYS, "STAY OUT OF THIS-- I WAS TALKING TO TH' DUMMY!"
©2008 Bill Griffith. World rights reserved. Distributed by King Features Syndicate
GRIFFY 9-16
THEN THE THREE CLONES---
I AM TH' TOAD.
YOU ARE TH' TOAD.
WE ARE ALL TH' TOAD.
FINALLY, AT FOUR IN THE MORNING, MR. TOAD HAD TO FORCIBLY REMOVE THE TRIX RABBIT FROM HIS NIGHTSTAND AT THE DINGBURG MOTEL 6---
ENOUGH WITH TH' VOODOO!

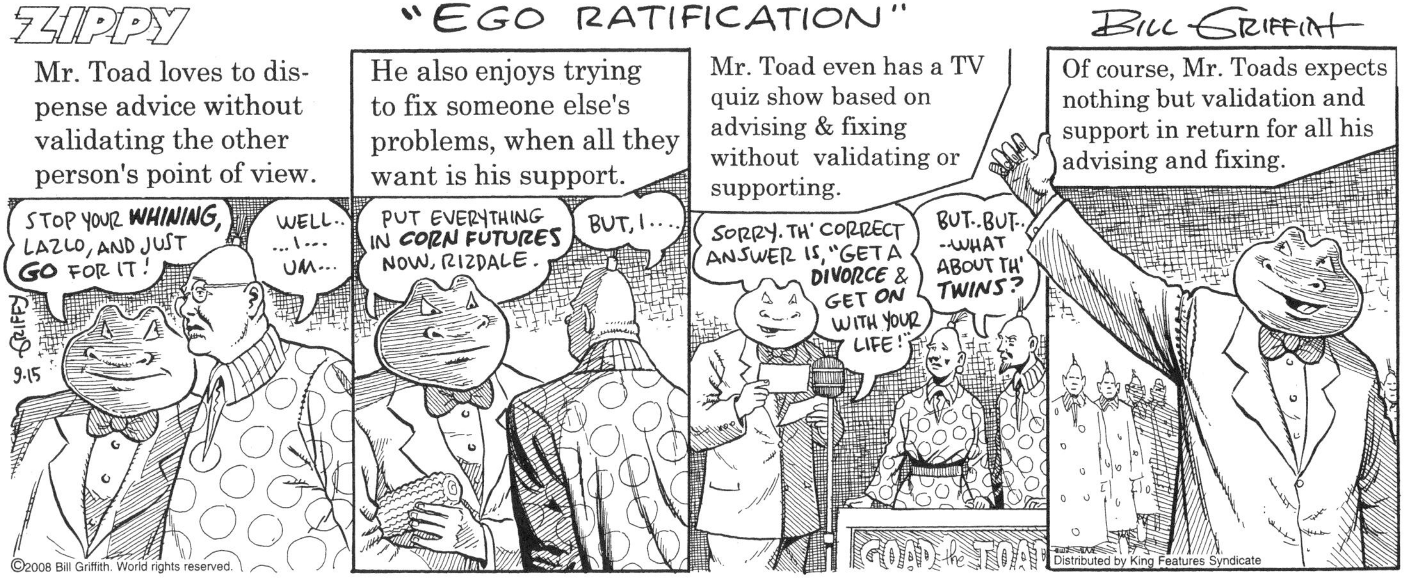
ZIPPY
"EGO RATIFICATION"
BILL GRIFFITH
Mr. Toad loves to dispense advice without validating the other person's point of view.
STOP YOUR WHINING, LAZLO, AND JUST GO FOR IT!
WELL.. ...I--- UM...
GRIFFY 9-15
©2008 Bill Griffith. World rights reserved.
He also enjoys trying to fix someone else's problems, when all they want is his support.
PUT EVERYTHING IN CORN FUTURES NOW, RIZDALE.
BUT, I....
Mr. Toad even has a TV quiz show based on advising & fixing without validating or supporting.
SORRY. TH' CORRECT ANSWER IS, "GET A DIVORCE & GET ON WITH YOUR LIFE!"
BUT..BUT.. --WHAT ABOUT TH' TWINS?
Of course, Mr. Toads expects nothing but validation and support in return for all his advising and fixing.
Distributed by King Features Syndicate

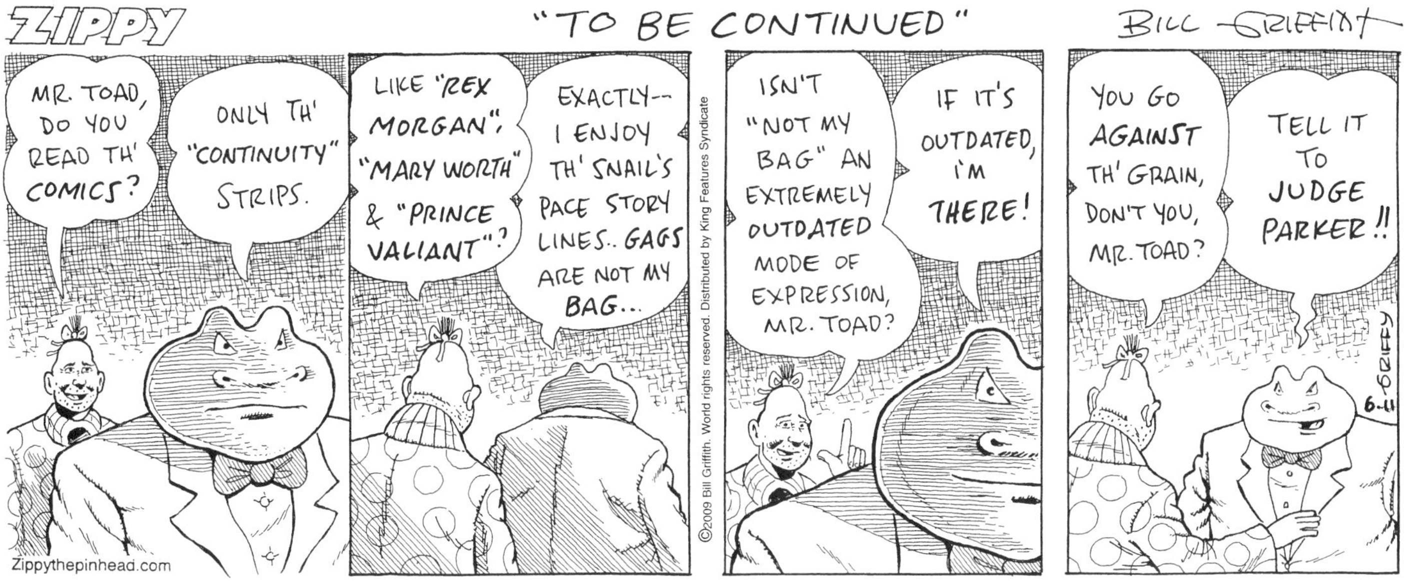
ZIPPY
"TO BE CONTINUED"
BILL GRIFFITH
MR. TOAD, DO YOU READ TH' COMICS?
ONLY TH' "CONTINUITY" STRIPS.
LIKE "REX MORGAN", "MARY WORTH" & "PRINCE VALIANT"?
EXACTLY-- I ENJOY TH' SNAIL'S PACE STORY LINES.. GAGS ARE NOT MY BAG...
ISN'T "NOT MY BAG" AN EXTREMELY OUTDATED MODE OF EXPRESSION, MR. TOAD?
IF IT'S OUTDATED, I'M THERE!
YOU GO AGAINST TH' GRAIN, DON'T YOU, MR. TOAD?
TELL IT TO JUDGE PARKER!!
GRIFFY 6-11
©2009 Bill Griffith. World rights reserved. Distributed by King Features Syndicate
Zippythepinhead.com

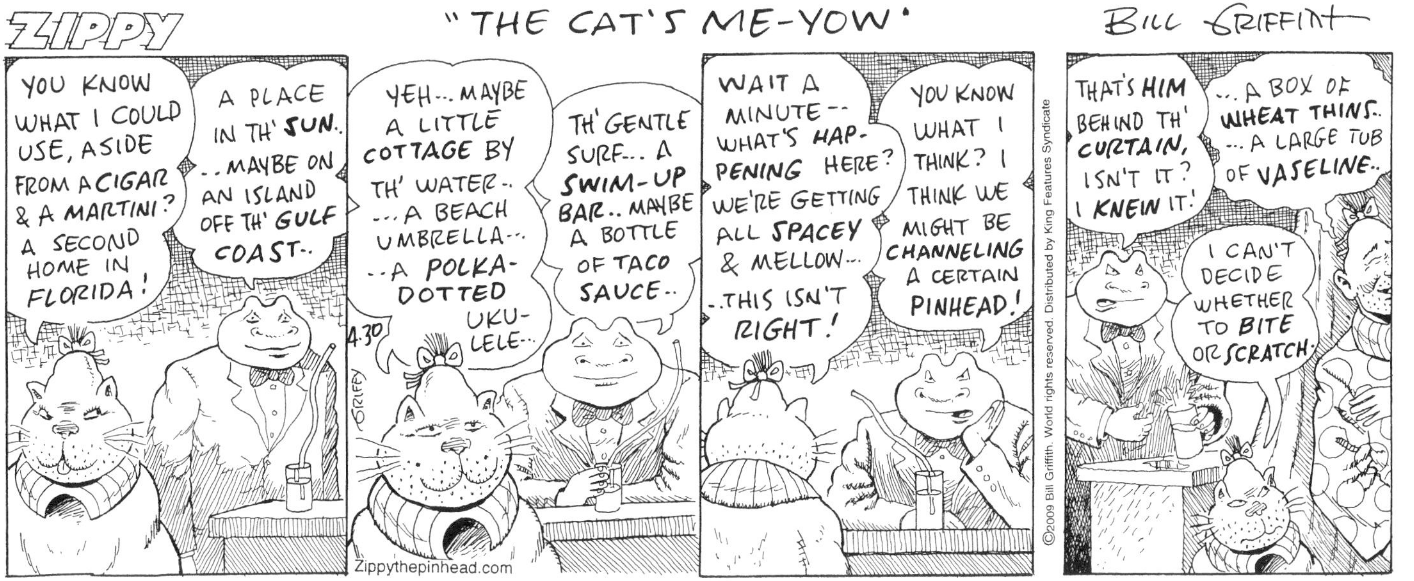
ZIPPY
"THE CAT'S ME-YOW"
BILL GRIFFITH
YOU KNOW WHAT I COULD USE, ASIDE FROM A CIGAR & A MARTINI? A SECOND HOME IN FLORIDA!
A PLACE IN TH' SUN.. ..MAYBE ON AN ISLAND OFF TH' GULF COAST..
YEH... MAYBE A LITTLE COTTAGE BY TH' WATER.. ...A BEACH UMBRELLA... ..A POLKA-DOTTED UKU-LELE...
TH' GENTLE SURF... A SWIM-UP BAR.. MAYBE A BOTTLE OF TACO SAUCE..
4-30 GRIFFY
WAIT A MINUTE-- WHAT'S HAP-PENING HERE? WE'RE GETTING ALL SPACEY & MELLOW... ..THIS ISN'T RIGHT!
YOU KNOW WHAT I THINK? I THINK WE MIGHT BE CHANNELING A CERTAIN PINHEAD!
THAT'S HIM BEHIND TH' CURTAIN, ISN'T IT? I KNEW IT!
...A BOX OF WHEAT THINS.. ...A LARGE TUB OF VASELINE..
I CAN'T DECIDE WHETHER TO BITE OR SCRATCH.
©2009 Bill Griffith. World rights reserved. Distributed by King Features Syndicate
Zippythepinhead.com

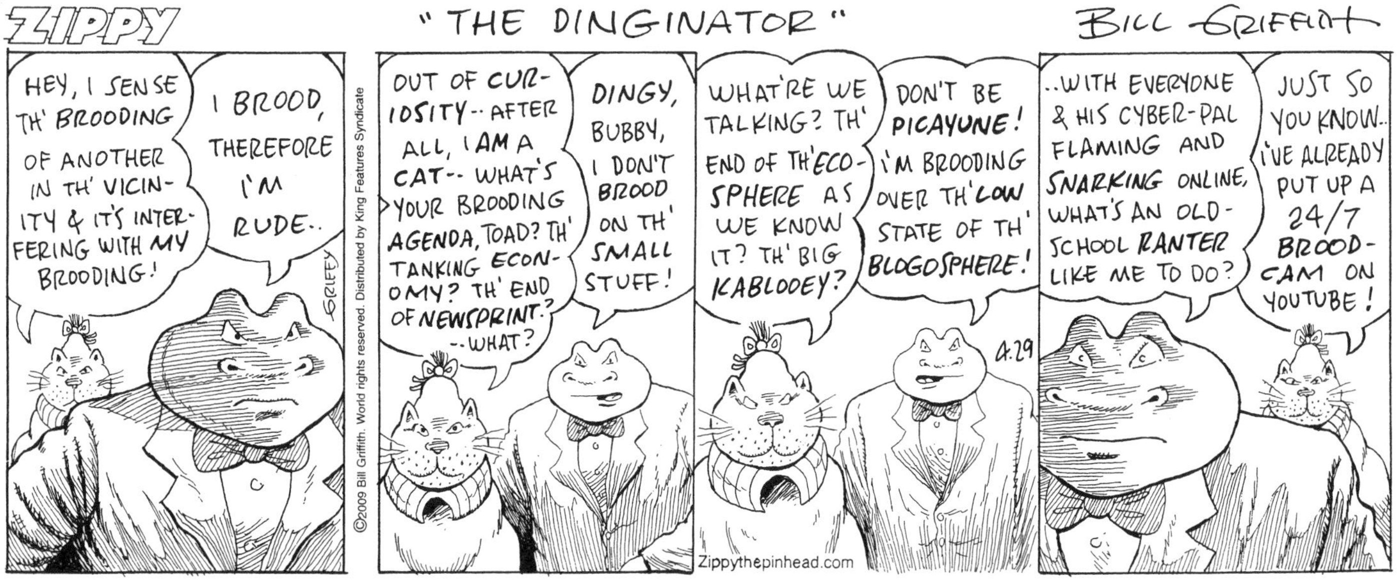
ZIPPY
"THE DINGINATOR"
BILL GRIFFITH
HEY, I SENSE TH' BROODING OF ANOTHER IN TH' VICINITY & IT'S INTERFERING WITH MY BROODING!
I BROOD, THEREFORE I'M RUDE..
GRIFFY
©2009 Bill Griffith. World rights reserved. Distributed by King Features Syndicate
OUT OF CURIOSITY-- AFTER ALL, I AM A CAT-- WHAT'S YOUR BROODING AGENDA, TOAD? TH' TANKING ECONOMY? TH' END OF NEWSPRINT? --WHAT?
DINGY, BUBBY, I DON'T BROOD ON TH' SMALL STUFF!
WHAT'RE WE TALKING? TH' END OF TH' ECOSPHERE AS WE KNOW IT? TH' BIG KABLOOEY?
DON'T BE PICAYUNE! I'M BROODING OVER TH' LOW STATE OF TH' BLOGOSPHERE!
4.29
Zippythepinhead.com
..WITH EVERYONE & HIS CYBER-PAL FLAMING AND SNARKING ONLINE, WHAT'S AN OLD-SCHOOL RANTER LIKE ME TO DO?
JUST SO YOU KNOW.. I'VE ALREADY PUT UP A 24/7 BROOD-CAM ON YOUTUBE!

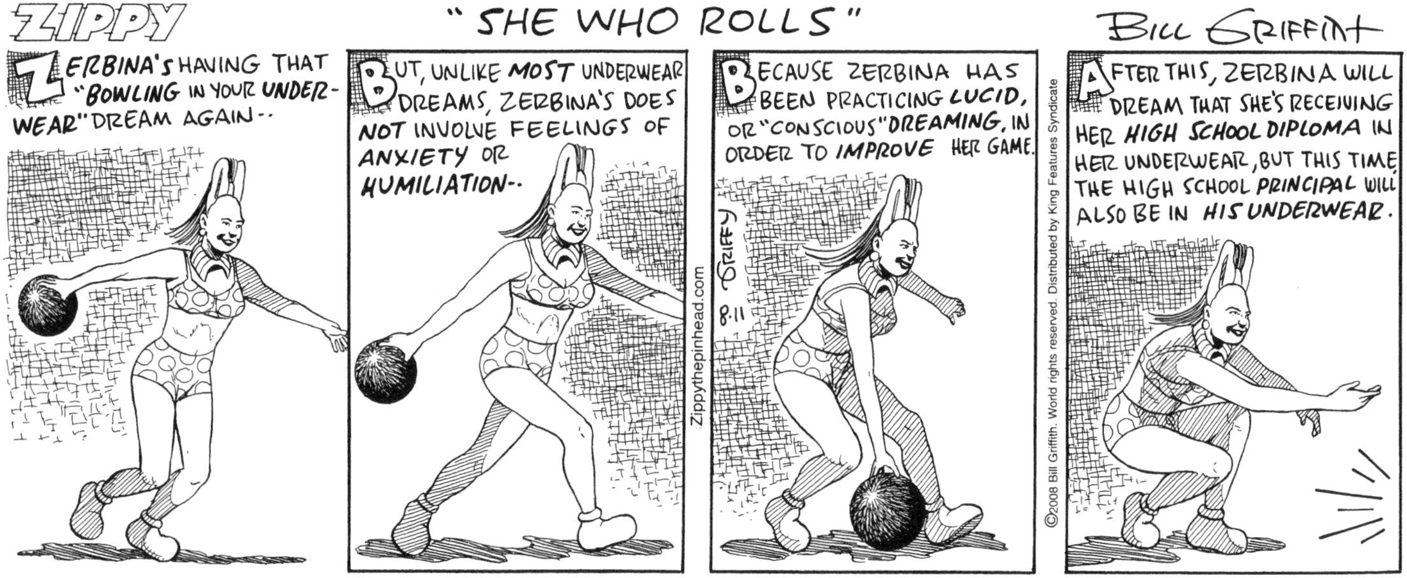
ZIPPY
"SHE WHO ROLLS"
BILL GRIFFITH
ZERBINA'S HAVING THAT "BOWLING IN YOUR UNDERWEAR" DREAM AGAIN--
BUT, UNLIKE MOST UNDERWEAR DREAMS, ZERBINA'S DOES NOT INVOLVE FEELINGS OF ANXIETY OR HUMILIATION--
Zippythepinhead.com
GRIFFY
8.11
BECAUSE ZERBINA HAS BEEN PRACTICING LUCID, OR "CONSCIOUS" DREAMING, IN ORDER TO IMPROVE HER GAME.
©2008 Bill Griffith. World rights reserved. Distributed by King Features Syndicate
AFTER THIS, ZERBINA WILL DREAM THAT SHE'S RECEIVING HER HIGH SCHOOL DIPLOMA IN HER UNDERWEAR, BUT THIS TIME THE HIGH SCHOOL PRINCIPAL WILL ALSO BE IN HIS UNDERWEAR.

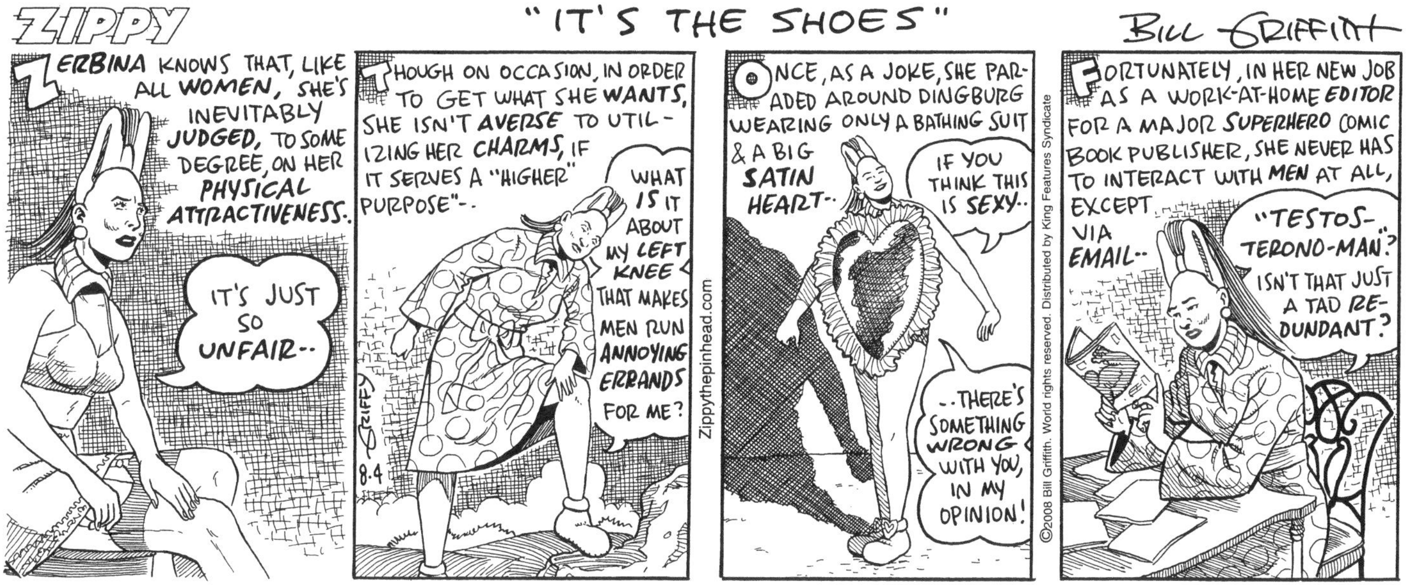
ZIPPY
"IT'S THE SHOES"
BILL GRIFFITH
ZERBINA KNOWS THAT, LIKE ALL WOMEN, SHE'S INEVITABLY JUDGED, TO SOME DEGREE, ON HER PHYSICAL ATTRACTIVENESS..
IT'S JUST SO UNFAIR--
THOUGH ON OCCASION, IN ORDER TO GET WHAT SHE WANTS, SHE ISN'T AVERSE TO UTILIZING HER CHARMS, IF IT SERVES A "HIGHER" PURPOSE"--.
WHAT IS IT ABOUT MY LEFT KNEE THAT MAKES MEN RUN ANNOYING ERRANDS FOR ME?
GRIFFY 8.4
Zippythepinhead.com
ONCE, AS A JOKE, SHE PARADED AROUND DINGBURG WEARING ONLY A BATHING SUIT & A BIG SATIN HEART--.
IF YOU THINK THIS IS SEXY..
--THERE'S SOMETHING WRONG WITH YOU, IN MY OPINION!
©2008 Bill Griffith. World rights reserved. Distributed by King Features Syndicate
FORTUNATELY, IN HER NEW JOB AS A WORK-AT-HOME EDITOR FOR A MAJOR SUPERHERO COMIC BOOK PUBLISHER, SHE NEVER HAS TO INTERACT WITH MEN AT ALL, EXCEPT VIA EMAIL--
"TESTOSTERONO-MAN"? ISN'T THAT JUST A TAD REDUNDANT?

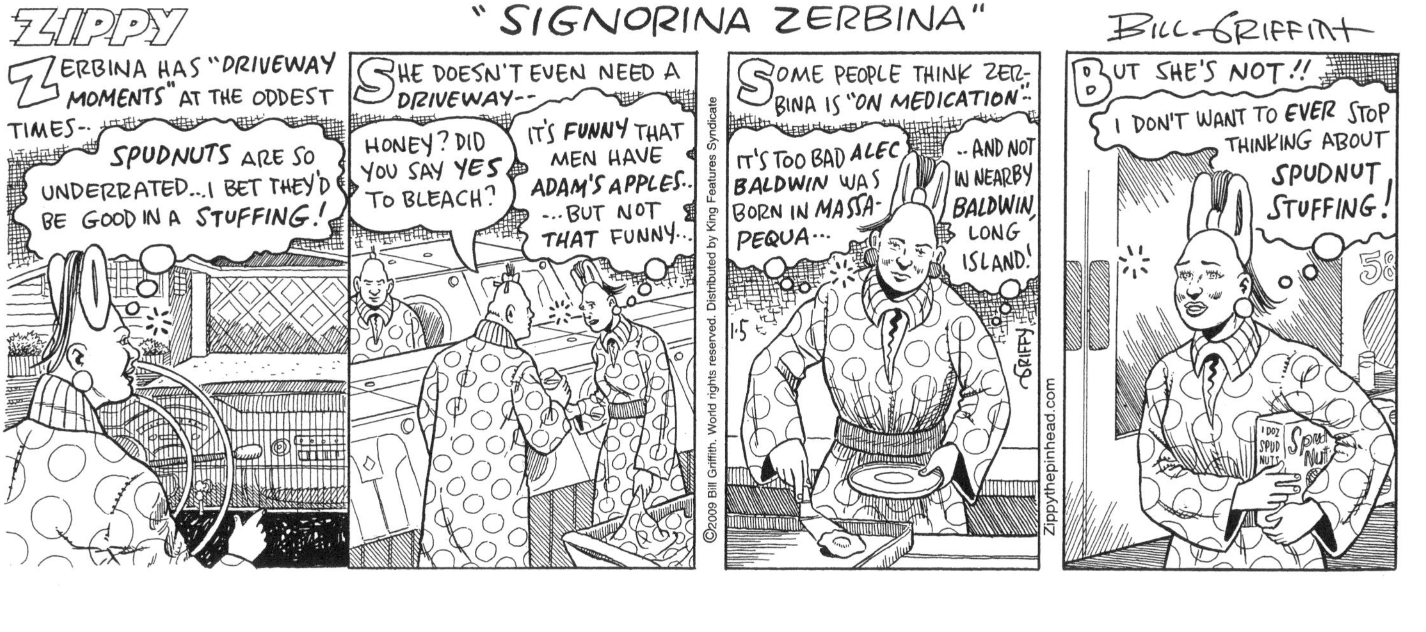
ZIPPY
"SIGNORINA ZERBINA"
BILL GRIFFITH
ZERBINA HAS "DRIVEWAY MOMENTS" AT THE ODDEST TIMES-.
SPUDNUTS ARE SO UNDERRATED...I BET THEY'D BE GOOD IN A STUFFING!
SHE DOESN'T EVEN NEED A DRIVEWAY--
HONEY? DID YOU SAY YES TO BLEACH?
IT'S FUNNY THAT MEN HAVE ADAM'S APPLES.. ...BUT NOT THAT FUNNY...
©2009 Bill Griffith. World rights reserved. Distributed by King Features Syndicate
SOME PEOPLE THINK ZERBINA IS "ON MEDICATION"..
IT'S TOO BAD ALEC BALDWIN WAS BORN IN MASSAPEQUA...
..AND NOT IN NEARBY BALDWIN, LONG ISLAND!
1.5 GRIFFY
Zippythepinhead.com
BUT SHE'S NOT!!
I DON'T WANT TO EVER STOP THINKING ABOUT SPUDNUT STUFFING!
1 DOZ SPUD NUTS
SPUD NUT

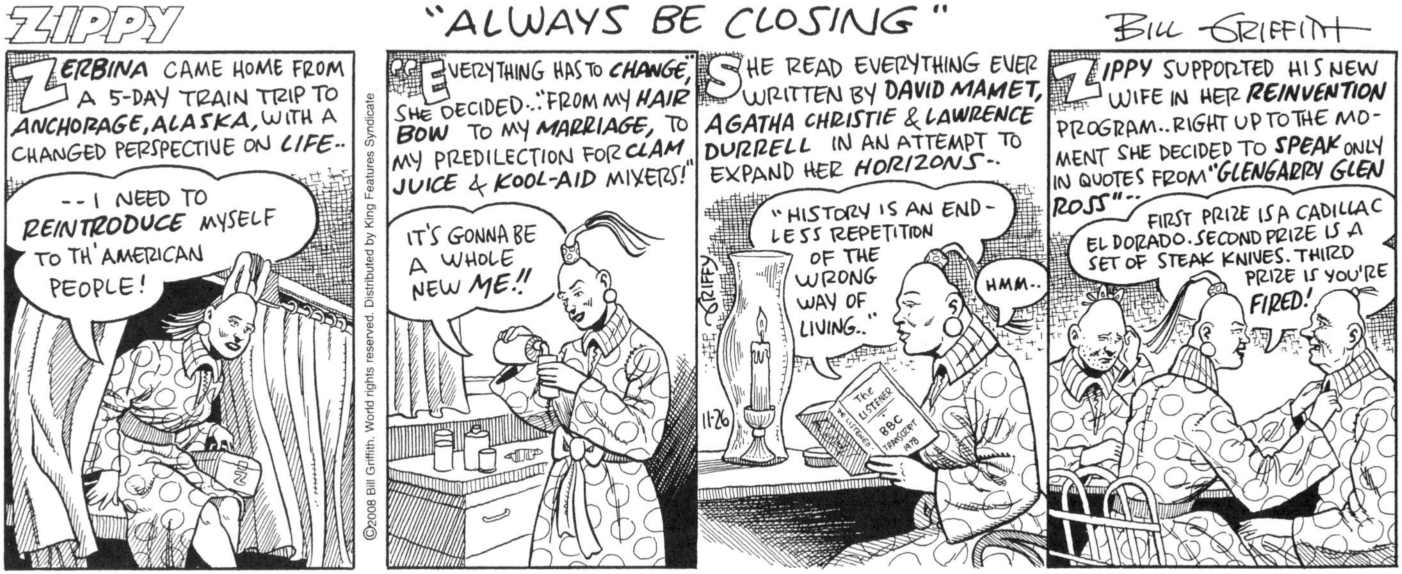
ZIPPY
"ALWAYS BE CLOSING"
BILL GRIFFITH
ZERBINA CAME HOME FROM A 5-DAY TRAIN TRIP TO ANCHORAGE, ALASKA, WITH A CHANGED PERSPECTIVE ON LIFE..
--I NEED TO REINTRODUCE MYSELF TO TH' AMERICAN PEOPLE!
©2008 Bill Griffith. World rights reserved. Distributed by King Features Syndicate
"EVERYTHING HAS TO CHANGE," SHE DECIDED.."FROM MY HAIR BOW TO MY MARRIAGE, TO MY PREDILECTION FOR CLAM JUICE & KOOL-AID MIXERS!"
IT'S GONNA BE A WHOLE NEW ME!!
SHE READ EVERYTHING EVER WRITTEN BY DAVID MAMET, AGATHA CHRISTIE & LAWRENCE DURRELL IN AN ATTEMPT TO EXPAND HER HORIZONS..
"HISTORY IS AN ENDLESS REPETITION OF THE WRONG WAY OF LIVING.."
HMM..
The LISTENER BBC TRANSCRIPT 1978
GRIFFY
11-26
ZIPPY SUPPORTED HIS NEW WIFE IN HER REINVENTION PROGRAM.. RIGHT UP TO THE MOMENT SHE DECIDED TO SPEAK ONLY IN QUOTES FROM "GLENGARRY GLEN ROSS"..
FIRST PRIZE IS A CADILLAC EL DORADO. SECOND PRIZE IS A SET OF STEAK KNIVES. THIRD PRIZE IS YOU'RE FIRED!

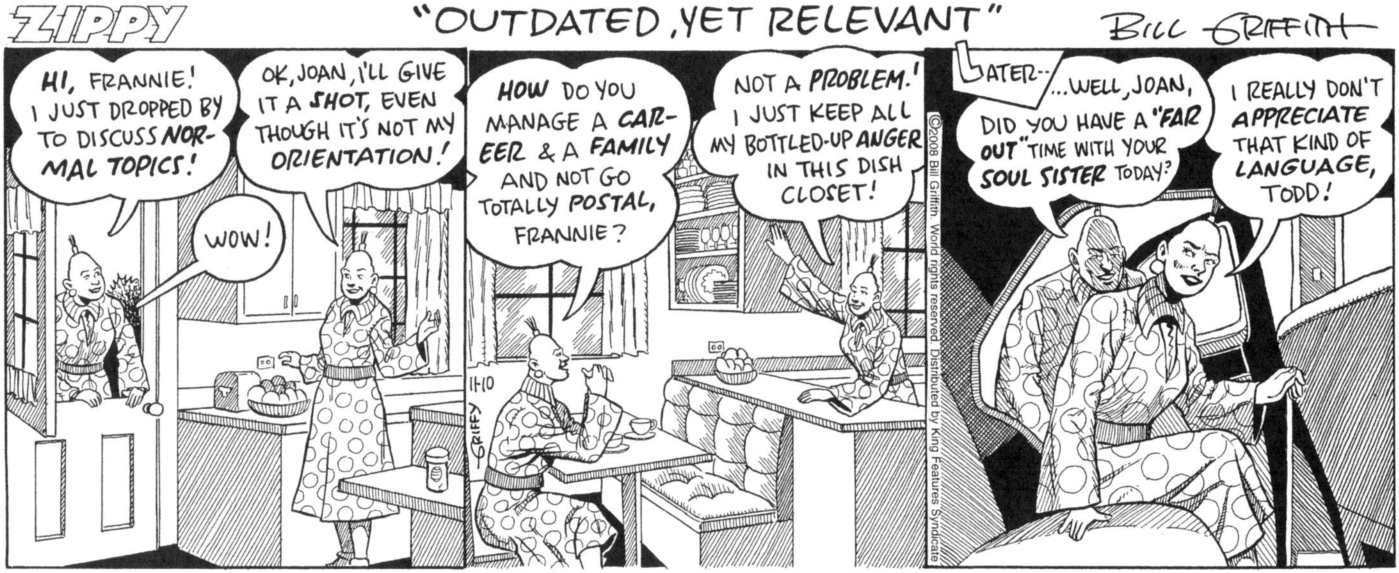
ZIPPY
"OUTDATED, YET RELEVANT"
BILL GRIFFITH
HI, FRANNIE! I JUST DROPPED BY TO DISCUSS NORMAL TOPICS!
OK, JOAN, I'LL GIVE IT A SHOT, EVEN THOUGH IT'S NOT MY ORIENTATION!
WOW!
HOW DO YOU MANAGE A CAREER & A FAMILY AND NOT GO TOTALLY POSTAL, FRANNIE?
NOT A PROBLEM! I JUST KEEP ALL MY BOTTLED-UP ANGER IN THIS DISH CLOSET!
GRIFFY
11-10
©2008 Bill Griffith. World rights reserved. Distributed by King Features Syndicate
LATER--
...WELL, JOAN, DID YOU HAVE A "FAR OUT" TIME WITH YOUR SOUL SISTER TODAY?
I REALLY DON'T APPRECIATE THAT KIND OF LANGUAGE, TODD!

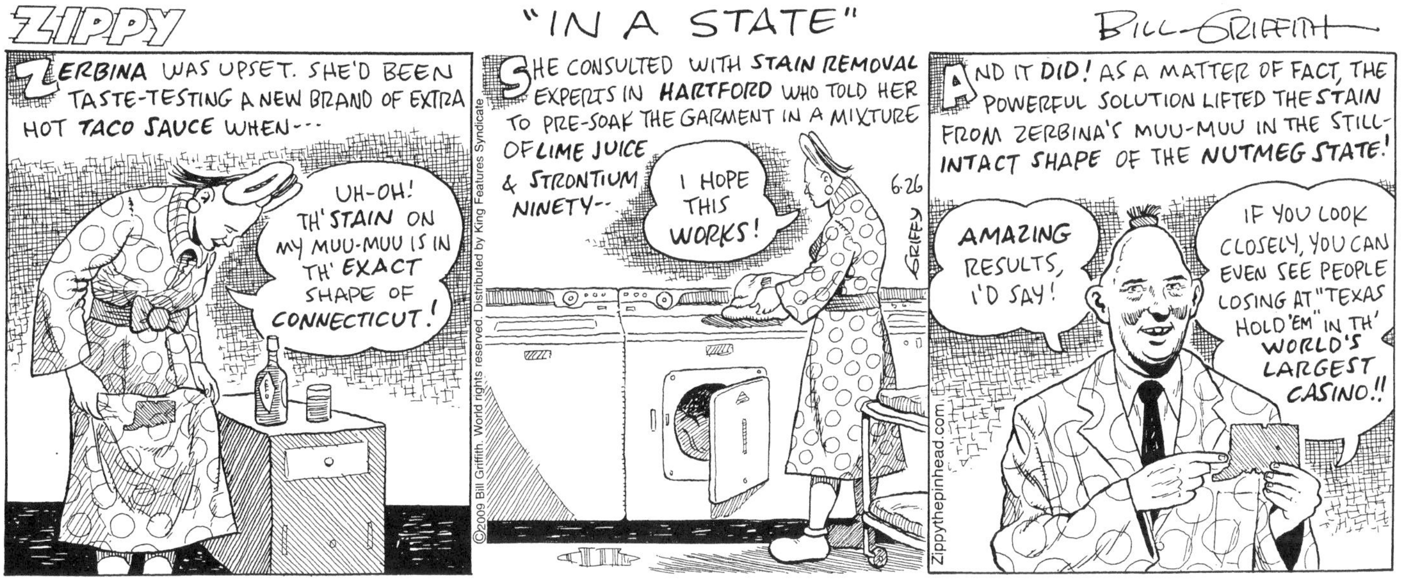
ZIPPY
"IN A STATE"
BILL GRIFFITH
ZERBINA WAS UPSET. SHE'D BEEN TASTE-TESTING A NEW BRAND OF EXTRA HOT TACO SAUCE WHEN---
UH-OH! TH' STAIN ON MY MUU-MUU IS IN TH' EXACT SHAPE OF CONNECTICUT!
©2009 Bill Griffith. World rights reserved. Distributed by King Features Syndicate
SHE CONSULTED WITH STAIN REMOVAL EXPERTS IN HARTFORD WHO TOLD HER TO PRE-SOAK THE GARMENT IN A MIXTURE OF LIME JUICE & STRONTIUM NINETY--
I HOPE THIS WORKS!
6·26
GRIFFY
Zippythepinhead.com.
AND IT DID! AS A MATTER OF FACT, THE POWERFUL SOLUTION LIFTED THE STAIN FROM ZERBINA'S MUU-MUU IN THE STILL-INTACT SHAPE OF THE NUTMEG STATE!
AMAZING RESULTS, I'D SAY!
IF YOU LOOK CLOSELY, YOU CAN EVEN SEE PEOPLE LOSING AT "TEXAS HOLD'EM" IN TH' WORLD'S LARGEST CASINO!!

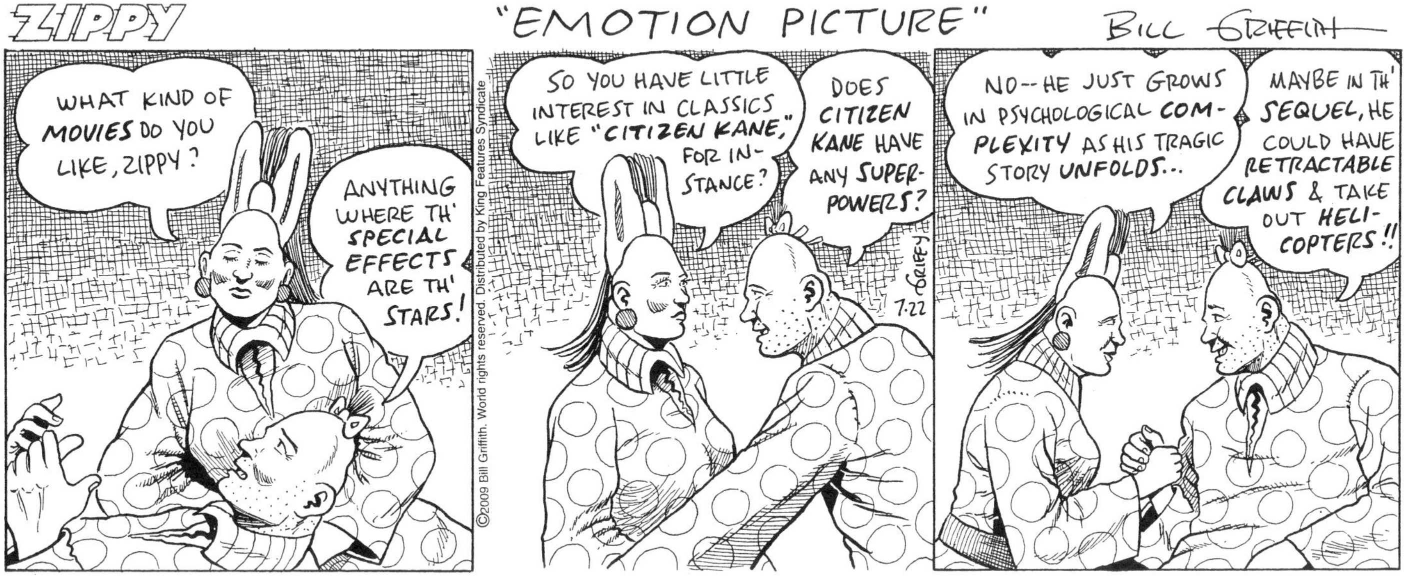
ZIPPY
"EMOTION PICTURE"
BILL GRIFFITH
WHAT KIND OF MOVIES DO YOU LIKE, ZIPPY?
ANYTHING WHERE TH' SPECIAL EFFECTS ARE TH' STARS!
©2009 Bill Griffith. World rights reserved. Distributed by King Features Syndicate
SO YOU HAVE LITTLE INTEREST IN CLASSICS LIKE "CITIZEN KANE," FOR INSTANCE?
DOES CITIZEN KANE HAVE ANY SUPER-POWERS?
GRIFFY
7·22
NO--HE JUST GROWS IN PSYCHOLOGICAL COMPLEXITY AS HIS TRAGIC STORY UNFOLDS...
MAYBE IN TH' SEQUEL, HE COULD HAVE RETRACTABLE CLAWS & TAKE OUT HELICOPTERS!!

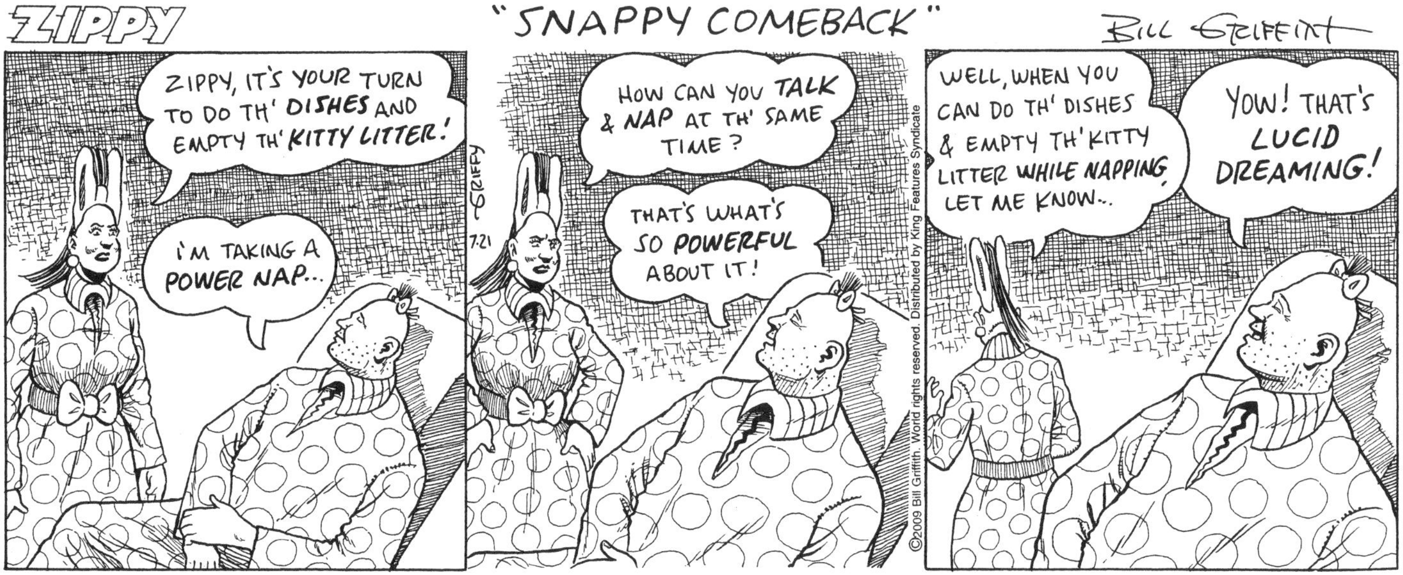
ZIPPY
"SNAPPY COMEBACK"
BILL GRIFFITH
ZIPPY, IT'S YOUR TURN TO DO TH' DISHES AND EMPTY TH' KITTY LITTER!
I'M TAKING A POWER NAP...
GRIFFY 7·21
HOW CAN YOU TALK & NAP AT TH' SAME TIME?
THAT'S WHAT'S SO POWERFUL ABOUT IT!
©2009 Bill Griffith. World rights reserved. Distributed by King Features Syndicate
WELL, WHEN YOU CAN DO TH' DISHES & EMPTY TH' KITTY LITTER WHILE NAPPING, LET ME KNOW...
YOW! THAT'S LUCID DREAMING!

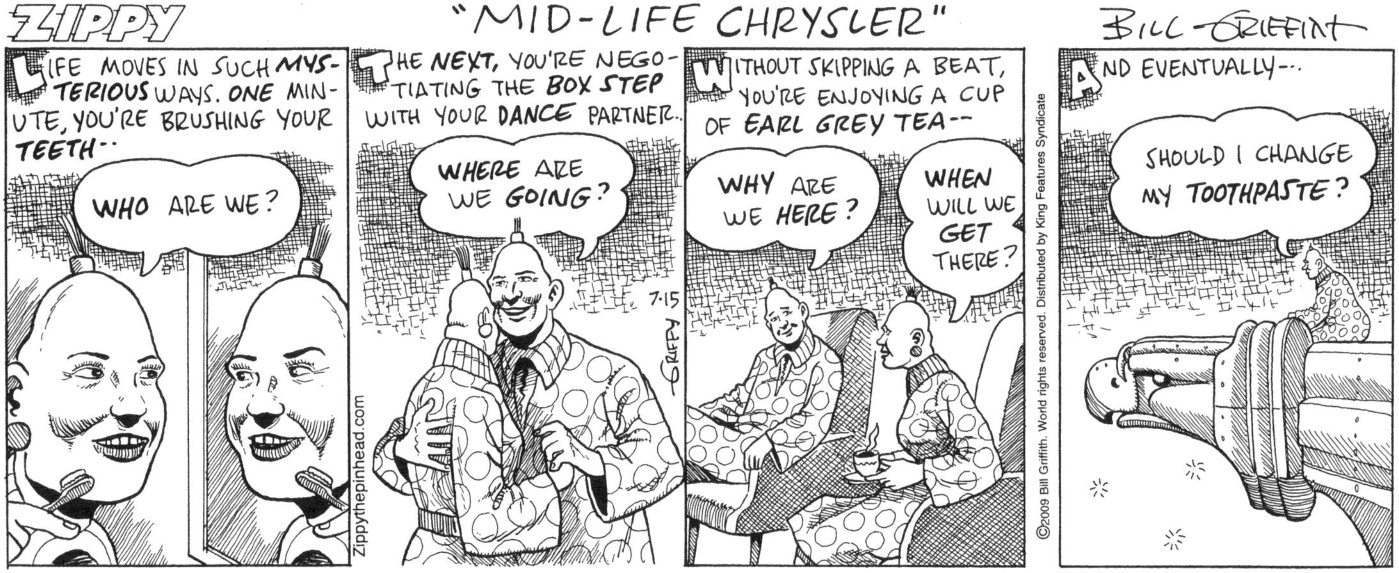
ZIPPY
"MID-LIFE CHRYSLER"
BILL GRIFFITH
LIFE MOVES IN SUCH MYSTERIOUS WAYS. ONE MINUTE, YOU'RE BRUSHING YOUR TEETH..
WHO ARE WE?
Zippythepinhead.com
THE NEXT, YOU'RE NEGOTIATING THE BOX STEP WITH YOUR DANCE PARTNER..
WHERE ARE WE GOING?
7·15 GRIFFY
WITHOUT SKIPPING A BEAT, YOU'RE ENJOYING A CUP OF EARL GREY TEA--
WHY ARE WE HERE?
WHEN WILL WE GET THERE?
©2009 Bill Griffith. World rights reserved. Distributed by King Features Syndicate
AND EVENTUALLY--..
SHOULD I CHANGE MY TOOTHPASTE?

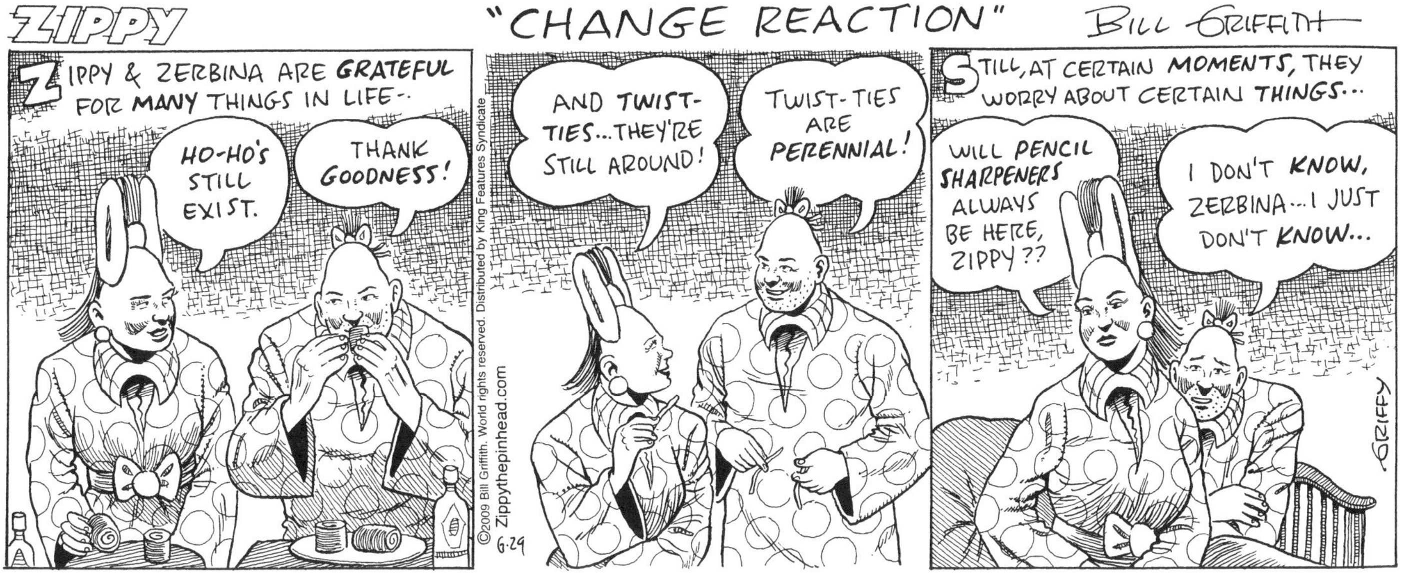
ZIPPY
"CHANGE REACTION"
BILL GRIFFITH
ZIPPY & ZERBINA ARE GRATEFUL FOR MANY THINGS IN LIFE..
HO-HO'S STILL EXIST.
THANK GOODNESS!
©2009 Bill Griffith. World rights reserved. Distributed by King Features Syndicate
Zippythepinhead.com
6-29
AND TWIST-TIES...THEY'RE STILL AROUND!
TWIST-TIES ARE PERENNIAL!
STILL, AT CERTAIN MOMENTS, THEY WORRY ABOUT CERTAIN THINGS...
WILL PENCIL SHARPENERS ALWAYS BE HERE, ZIPPY??
I DON'T KNOW, ZERBINA...I JUST DON'T KNOW...
GRIFFY

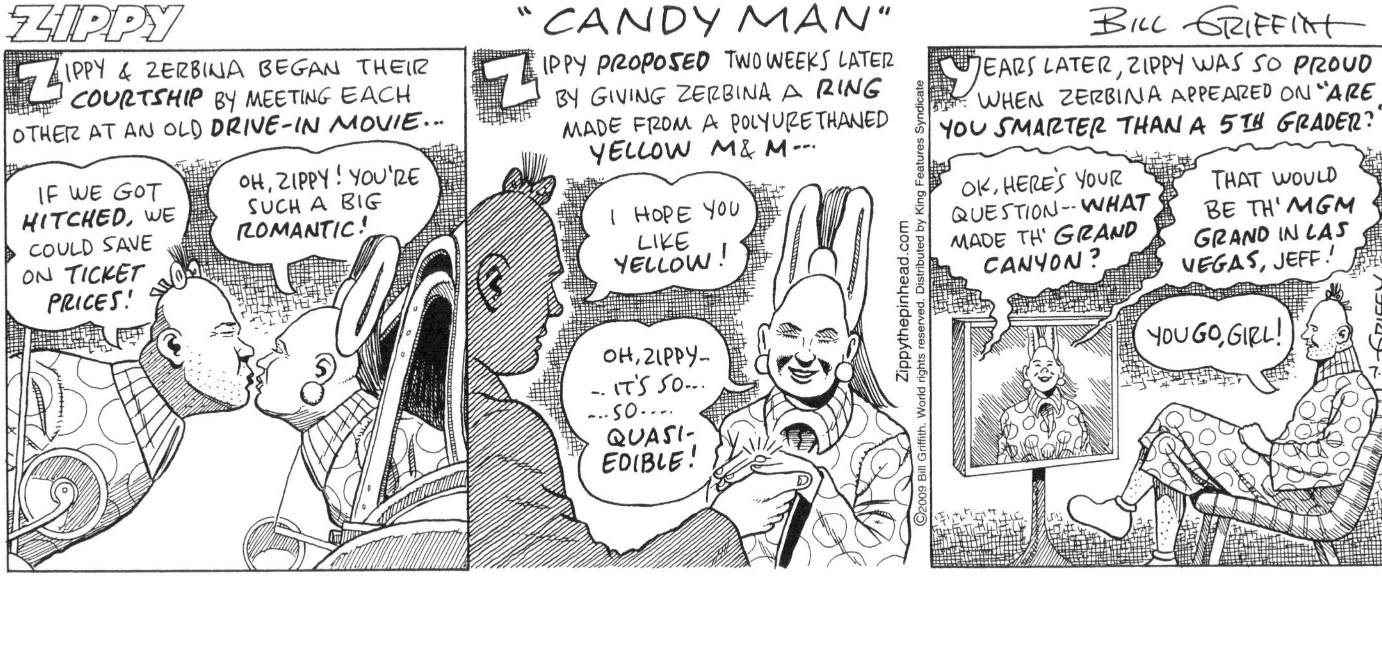
ZIPPY
"CANDY MAN"
BILL GRIFFITH
ZIPPY & ZERBINA BEGAN THEIR COURTSHIP BY MEETING EACH OTHER AT AN OLD DRIVE-IN MOVIE...
IF WE GOT HITCHED, WE COULD SAVE ON TICKET PRICES!
OH, ZIPPY! YOU'RE SUCH A BIG ROMANTIC!
ZIPPY PROPOSED TWO WEEKS LATER BY GIVING ZERBINA A RING MADE FROM A POLYURETHANED YELLOW M& M--
I HOPE YOU LIKE YELLOW!
OH, ZIPPY--. IT'S SO--. --SO---. QUASI-EDIBLE!
©2009 Bill Griffith. World rights reserved. Distributed by King Features Syndicate
Zippythepinhead.com
YEARS LATER, ZIPPY WAS SO PROUD WHEN ZERBINA APPEARED ON "ARE YOU SMARTER THAN A 5TH GRADER?"
OK, HERE'S YOUR QUESTION-- WHAT MADE TH' GRAND CANYON?
THAT WOULD BE TH' MGM GRAND IN LAS VEGAS, JEFF!
YOU GO, GIRL!
GRIFFY
7-3

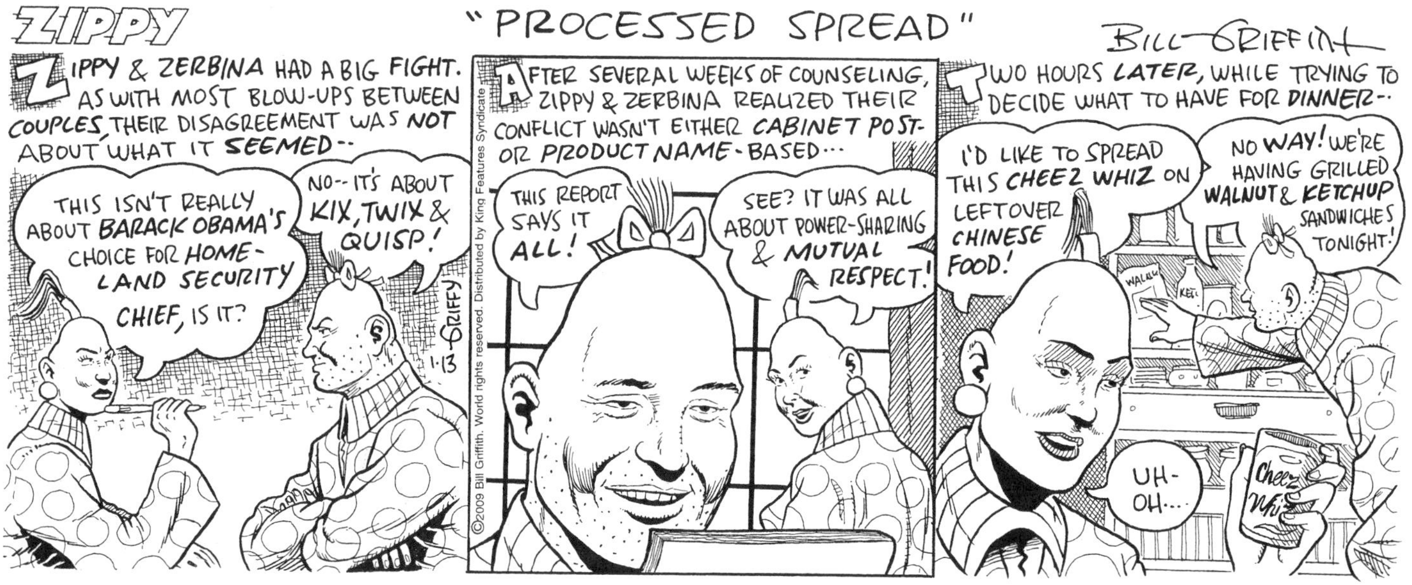
ZIPPY
"PROCESSED SPREAD"
BILL GRIFFITH
ZIPPY & ZERBINA HAD A BIG FIGHT. AS WITH MOST BLOW-UPS BETWEEN COUPLES, THEIR DISAGREEMENT WAS NOT ABOUT WHAT IT SEEMED--
THIS ISN'T REALLY ABOUT BARACK OBAMA'S CHOICE FOR HOME-LAND SECURITY CHIEF, IS IT?
NO-- IT'S ABOUT KIX, TWIX & QUISP!
GRIFFY 1-13
AFTER SEVERAL WEEKS OF COUNSELING, ZIPPY & ZERBINA REALIZED THEIR CONFLICT WASN'T EITHER CABINET POST- OR PRODUCT NAME-BASED...
THIS REPORT SAYS IT ALL!
SEE? IT WAS ALL ABOUT POWER-SHARING & MUTUAL RESPECT!
©2009 Bill Griffith. World rights reserved. Distributed by King Features Syndicate
TWO HOURS LATER, WHILE TRYING TO DECIDE WHAT TO HAVE FOR DINNER--
I'D LIKE TO SPREAD THIS CHEEZ WHIZ ON LEFTOVER CHINESE FOOD!
NO WAY! WE'RE HAVING GRILLED WALNUT & KETCHUP SANDWICHES TONIGHT!
UH-OH...
Cheez Whiz

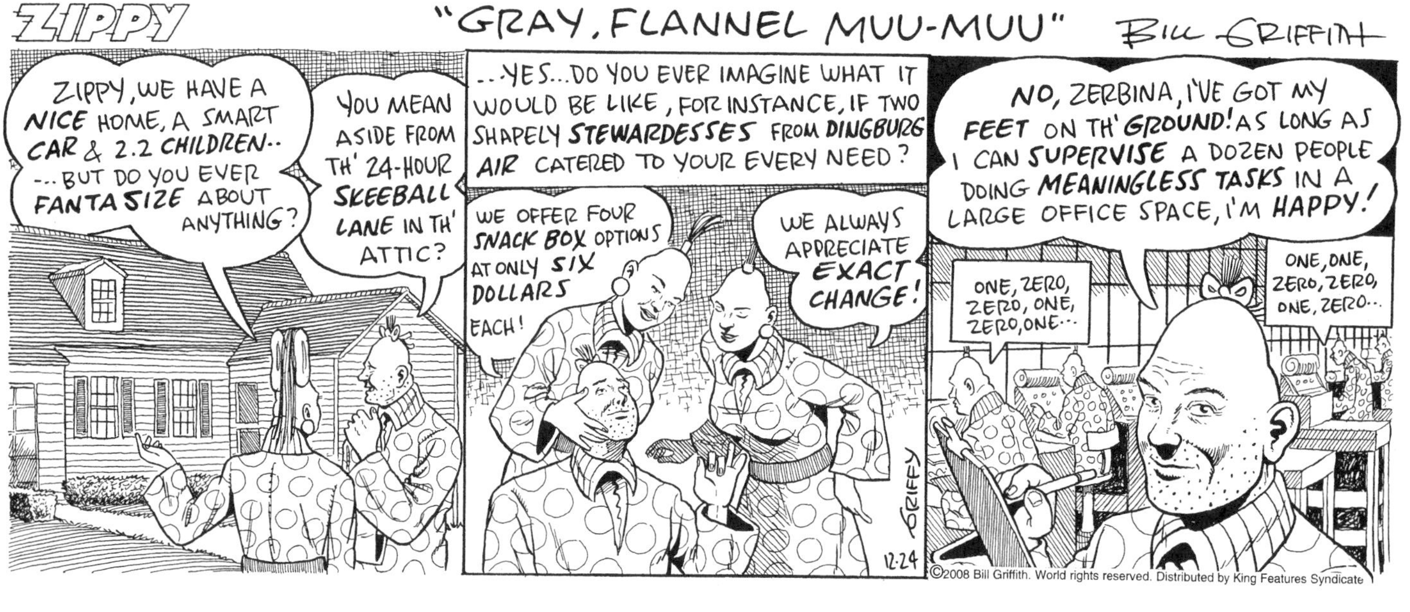
ZIPPY
"GRAY, FLANNEL MUU-MUU"
BILL GRIFFITH
ZIPPY, WE HAVE A NICE HOME, A SMART CAR & 2.2 CHILDREN.. --..BUT DO YOU EVER FANTASIZE ABOUT ANYTHING?
YOU MEAN ASIDE FROM TH' 24-HOUR SKEEBALL LANE IN TH' ATTIC?
..YES...DO YOU EVER IMAGINE WHAT IT WOULD BE LIKE, FOR INSTANCE, IF TWO SHAPELY STEWARDESSES FROM DINGBURG AIR CATERED TO YOUR EVERY NEED?
WE OFFER FOUR SNACK BOX OPTIONS AT ONLY SIX DOLLARS EACH!
WE ALWAYS APPRECIATE EXACT CHANGE!
GRIFFY 12-24
NO, ZERBINA, I'VE GOT MY FEET ON TH' GROUND! AS LONG AS I CAN SUPERVISE A DOZEN PEOPLE DOING MEANINGLESS TASKS IN A LARGE OFFICE SPACE, I'M HAPPY!
ONE, ZERO, ZERO, ONE, ZERO, ONE...
ONE, ONE, ZERO, ZERO, ONE, ZERO...
©2008 Bill Griffith. World rights reserved. Distributed by King Features Syndicate

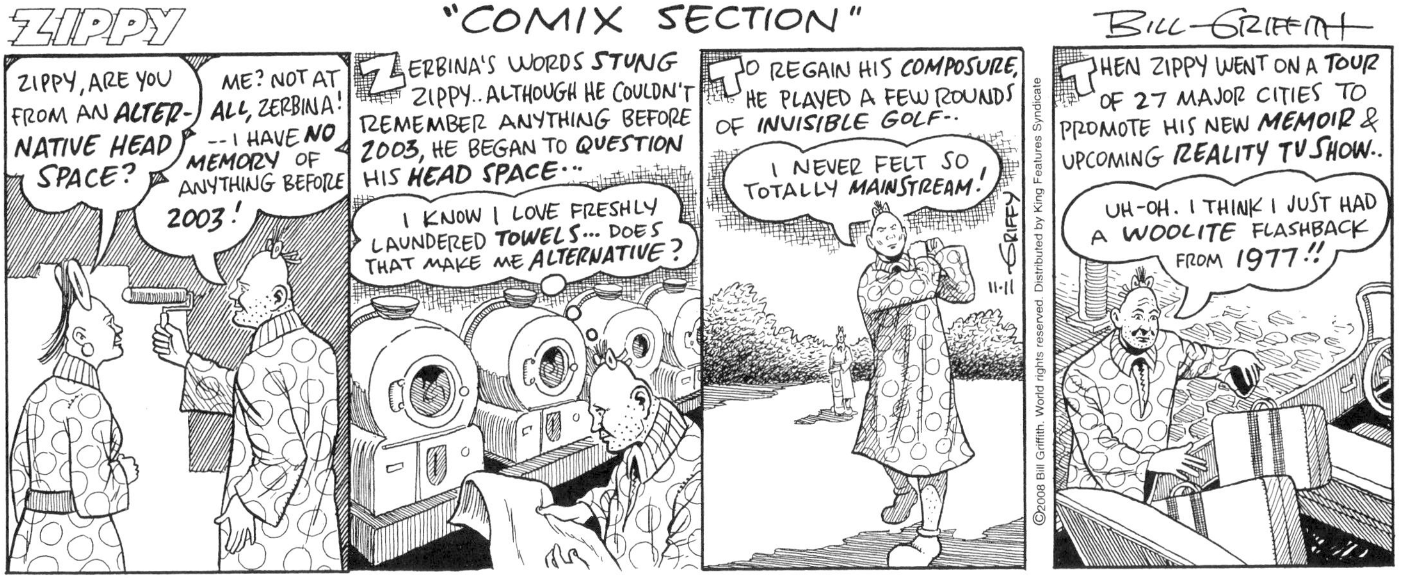
ZIPPY
"COMIX SECTION"
BILL GRIFFITH
ZIPPY, ARE YOU FROM AN ALTERNATIVE HEAD SPACE?
ME? NOT AT ALL, ZERBINA! --I HAVE NO MEMORY OF ANYTHING BEFORE 2003!
ZERBINA'S WORDS STUNG ZIPPY.. ALTHOUGH HE COULDN'T REMEMBER ANYTHING BEFORE 2003, HE BEGAN TO QUESTION HIS HEAD SPACE..
I KNOW I LOVE FRESHLY LAUNDERED TOWELS... DOES THAT MAKE ME ALTERNATIVE?
TO REGAIN HIS COMPOSURE, HE PLAYED A FEW ROUNDS OF INVISIBLE GOLF..
I NEVER FELT SO TOTALLY MAINSTREAM!
GRIFFY
11-11
©2008 Bill Griffith. World rights reserved. Distributed by King Features Syndicate
THEN ZIPPY WENT ON A TOUR OF 27 MAJOR CITIES TO PROMOTE HIS NEW MEMOIR & UPCOMING REALITY TV SHOW..
UH-OH. I THINK I JUST HAD A WOOLITE FLASHBACK FROM 1977!!

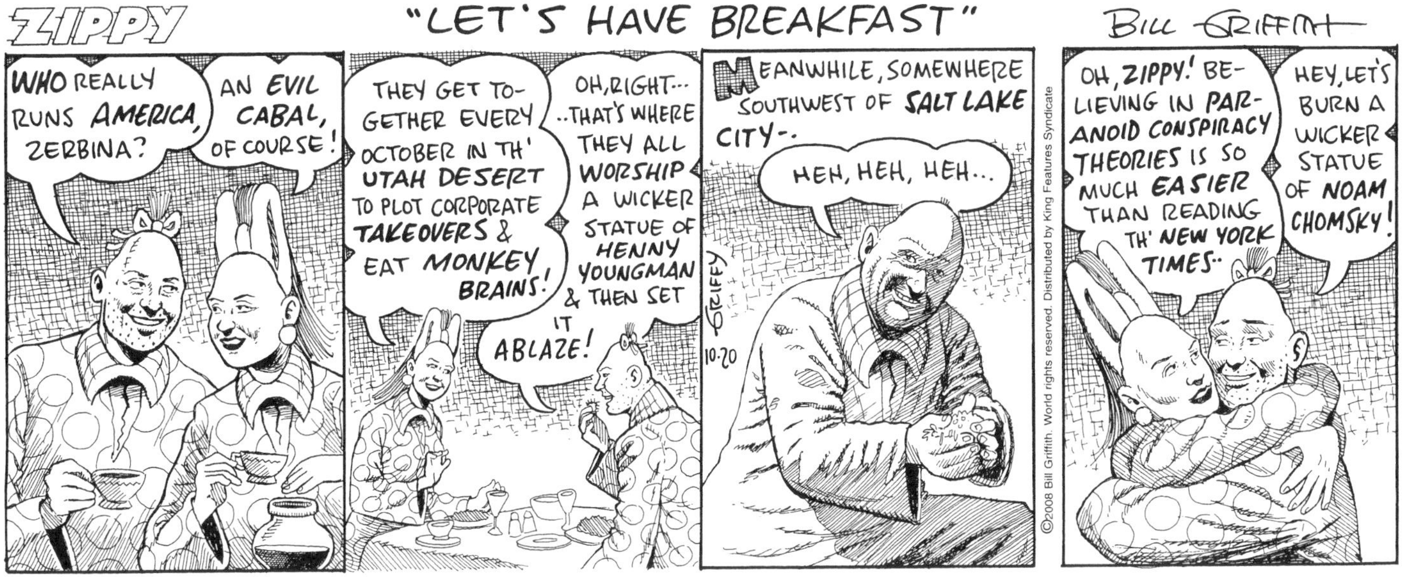
ZIPPY
"LET'S HAVE BREAKFAST"
BILL GRIFFITH
WHO REALLY RUNS AMERICA, ZERBINA?
AN EVIL CABAL, OF COURSE!
THEY GET TOGETHER EVERY OCTOBER IN TH' UTAH DESERT TO PLOT CORPORATE TAKEOVERS & EAT MONKEY BRAINS!
OH, RIGHT... ..THAT'S WHERE THEY ALL WORSHIP A WICKER STATUE OF HENNY YOUNGMAN & THEN SET IT ABLAZE!
GRIFFY
10-20
MEANWHILE, SOMEWHERE SOUTHWEST OF SALT LAKE CITY..
HEH, HEH, HEH...
©2008 Bill Griffith. World rights reserved. Distributed by King Features Syndicate
OH, ZIPPY! BELIEVING IN PARANOID CONSPIRACY THEORIES IS SO MUCH EASIER THAN READING TH' NEW YORK TIMES..
HEY, LET'S BURN A WICKER STATUE OF NOAM CHOMSKY!

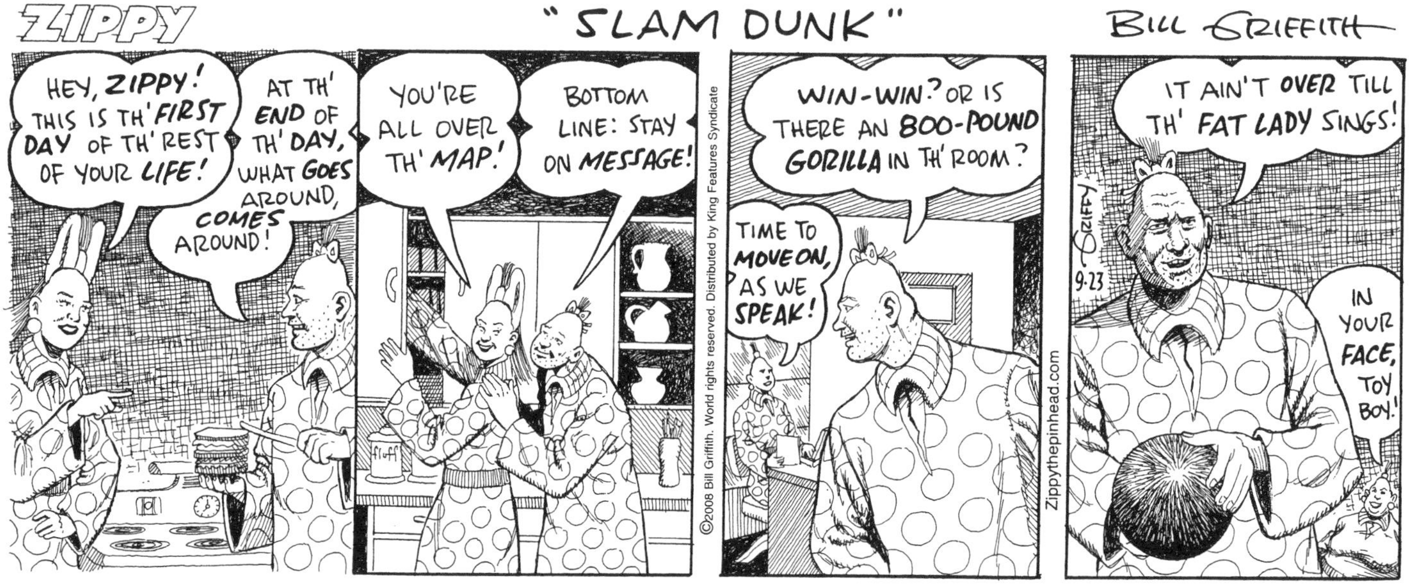
ZIPPY
"SLAM DUNK"
BILL GRIFFITH
HEY, ZIPPY! THIS IS TH' FIRST DAY OF TH' REST OF YOUR LIFE!
AT TH' END OF TH' DAY, WHAT GOES AROUND, COMES AROUND!
YOU'RE ALL OVER TH' MAP!
BOTTOM LINE: STAY ON MESSAGE!
fluff
©2008 Bill Griffith. World rights reserved. Distributed by King Features Syndicate
WIN-WIN? OR IS THERE AN 800-POUND GORILLA IN TH' ROOM?
TIME TO MOVE ON, AS WE SPEAK!
Zippythepinhead.com
IT AIN'T OVER TILL TH' FAT LADY SINGS!
GRIFFY 9-23
IN YOUR FACE, TOY BOY!

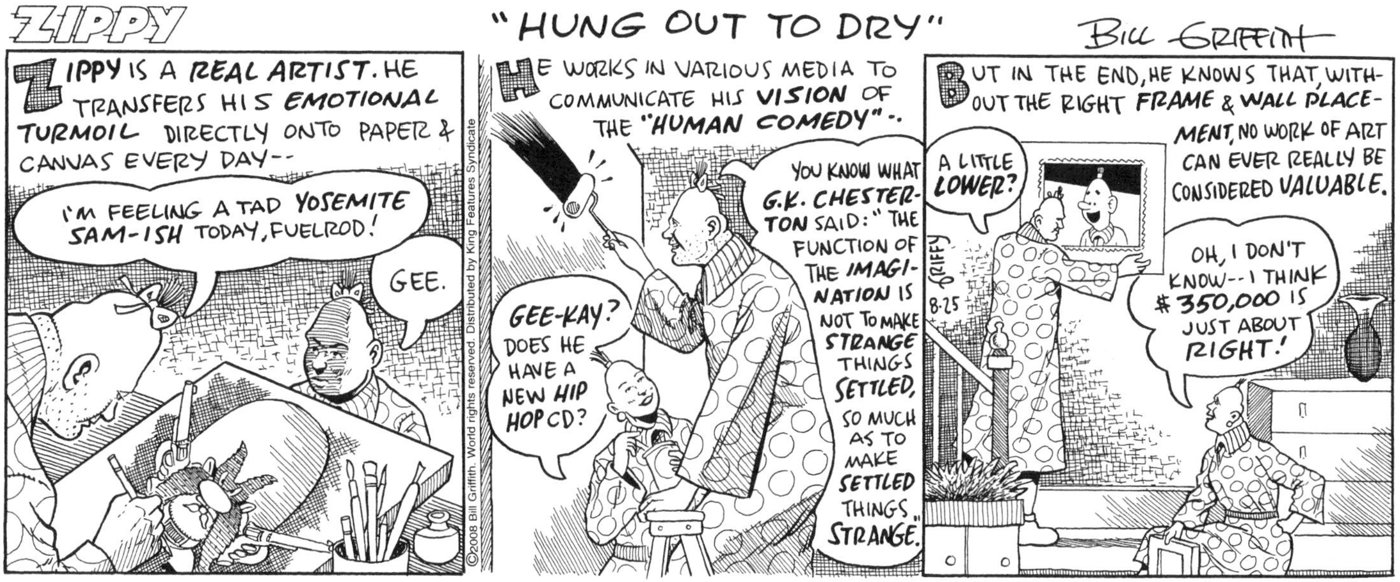
ZIPPY
"HUNG OUT TO DRY"
BILL GRIFFITH
ZIPPY IS A REAL ARTIST. HE TRANSFERS HIS EMOTIONAL TURMOIL DIRECTLY ONTO PAPER & CANVAS EVERY DAY--
I'M FEELING A TAD YOSEMITE SAM-ISH TODAY, FUELROD!
GEE.
©2008 Bill Griffith. World rights reserved. Distributed by King Features Syndicate
HE WORKS IN VARIOUS MEDIA TO COMMUNICATE HIS VISION OF THE "HUMAN COMEDY"..
YOU KNOW WHAT G.K. CHESTERTON SAID: "THE FUNCTION OF THE IMAGINATION IS NOT TO MAKE STRANGE THINGS SETTLED, SO MUCH AS TO MAKE SETTLED THINGS STRANGE."
GEE-KAY? DOES HE HAVE A NEW HIP HOP CD?
BUT IN THE END, HE KNOWS THAT, WITHOUT THE RIGHT FRAME & WALL PLACEMENT, NO WORK OF ART CAN EVER REALLY BE CONSIDERED VALUABLE.
A LITTLE LOWER?
GRIFFY 8-25
OH, I DON'T KNOW--I THINK $350,000 IS JUST ABOUT RIGHT!

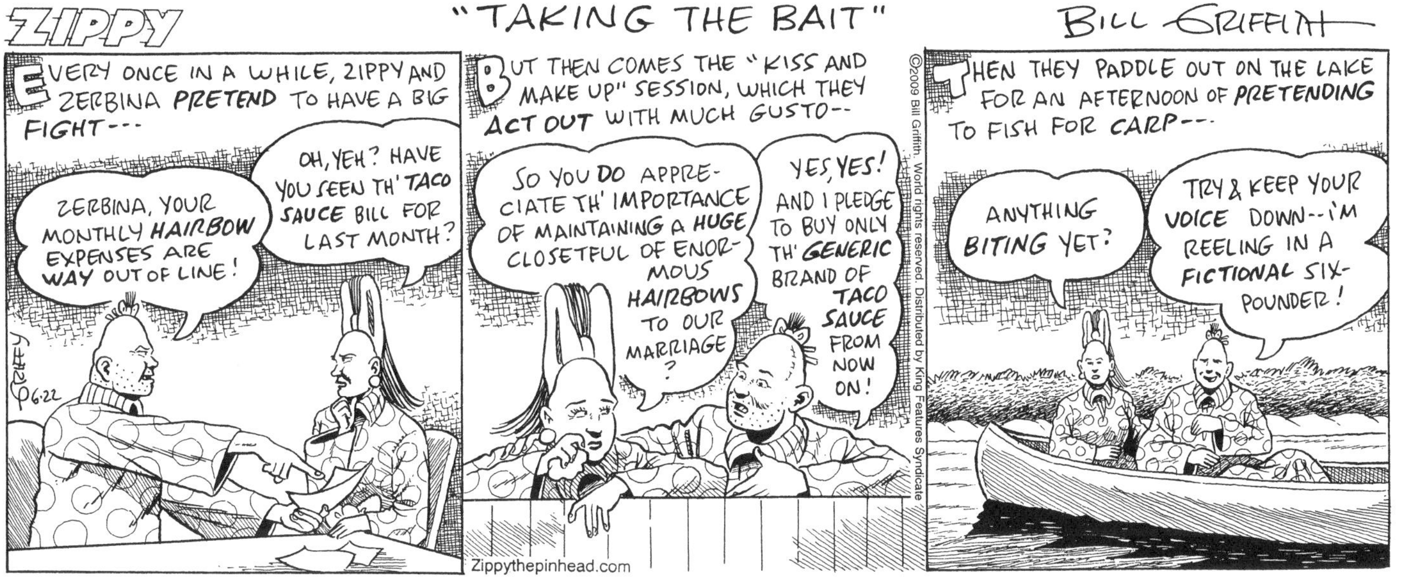
ZIPPY
"TAKING THE BAIT"
BILL GRIFFITH
EVERY ONCE IN A WHILE, ZIPPY AND ZERBINA PRETEND TO HAVE A BIG FIGHT---
ZERBINA, YOUR MONTHLY HAIRBOW EXPENSES ARE WAY OUT OF LINE!
OH, YEH? HAVE YOU SEEN TH' TACO SAUCE BILL FOR LAST MONTH?
GRIFFY 6·22
BUT THEN COMES THE "KISS AND MAKE UP" SESSION, WHICH THEY ACT OUT WITH MUCH GUSTO--
SO YOU DO APPRECIATE TH' IMPORTANCE OF MAINTAINING A HUGE CLOSETFUL OF ENORMOUS HAIRBOWS TO OUR MARRIAGE?
YES, YES! AND I PLEDGE TO BUY ONLY TH' GENERIC BRAND OF TACO SAUCE FROM NOW ON!
Zippythepinhead.com
©2009 Bill Griffith. World rights reserved. Distributed by King Features Syndicate
THEN THEY PADDLE OUT ON THE LAKE FOR AN AFTERNOON OF PRETENDING TO FISH FOR CARP---
ANYTHING BITING YET?
TRY & KEEP YOUR VOICE DOWN--I'M REELING IN A FICTIONAL SIX-POUNDER!

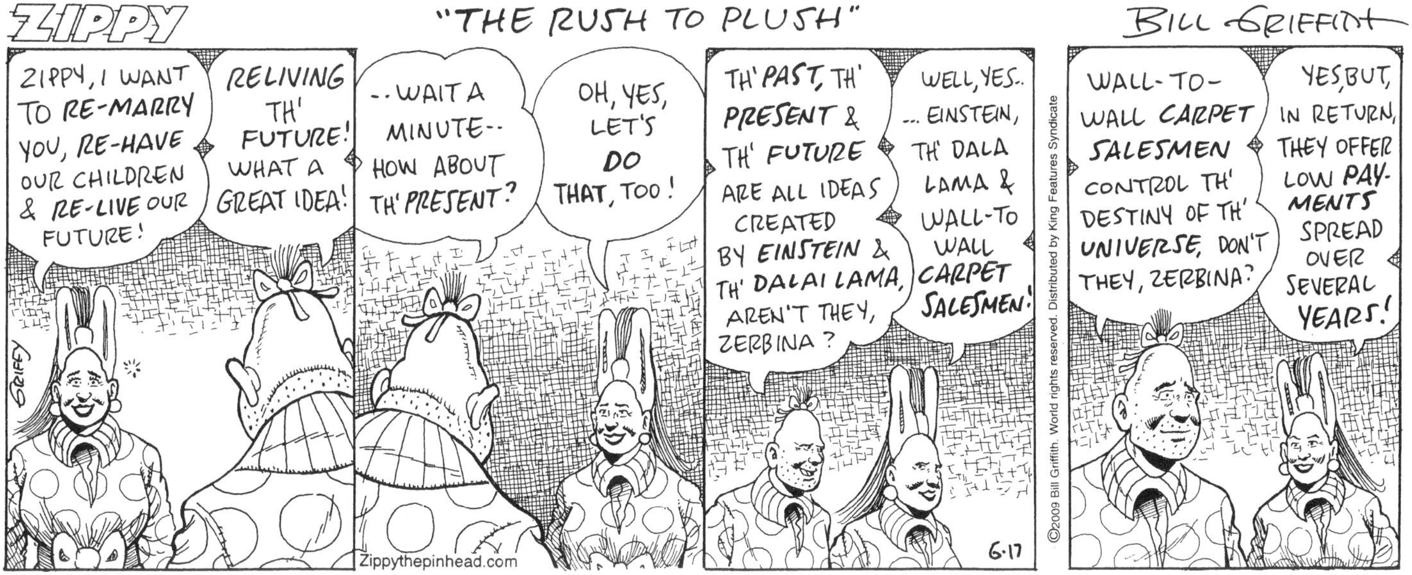
ZIPPY
"THE RUSH TO PLUSH"
BILL GRIFFITH
ZIPPY, I WANT TO RE-MARRY YOU, RE-HAVE OUR CHILDREN & RE-LIVE OUR FUTURE!
RELIVING TH' FUTURE! WHAT A GREAT IDEA!
GRIFFY
--WAIT A MINUTE-- HOW ABOUT TH' PRESENT?
OH, YES, LET'S DO THAT, TOO!
Zippythepinhead.com
TH' PAST, TH' PRESENT & TH' FUTURE ARE ALL IDEAS CREATED BY EINSTEIN & TH' DALAI LAMA, AREN'T THEY, ZERBINA?
WELL, YES.. ...EINSTEIN, TH' DALA LAMA & WALL-TO WALL CARPET SALESMEN!
6·17
©2009 Bill Griffith. World rights reserved. Distributed by King Features Syndicate
WALL-TO-WALL CARPET SALESMEN CONTROL TH' DESTINY OF TH' UNIVERSE, DON'T THEY, ZERBINA?
YES, BUT, IN RETURN, THEY OFFER LOW PAYMENTS SPREAD OVER SEVERAL YEARS!

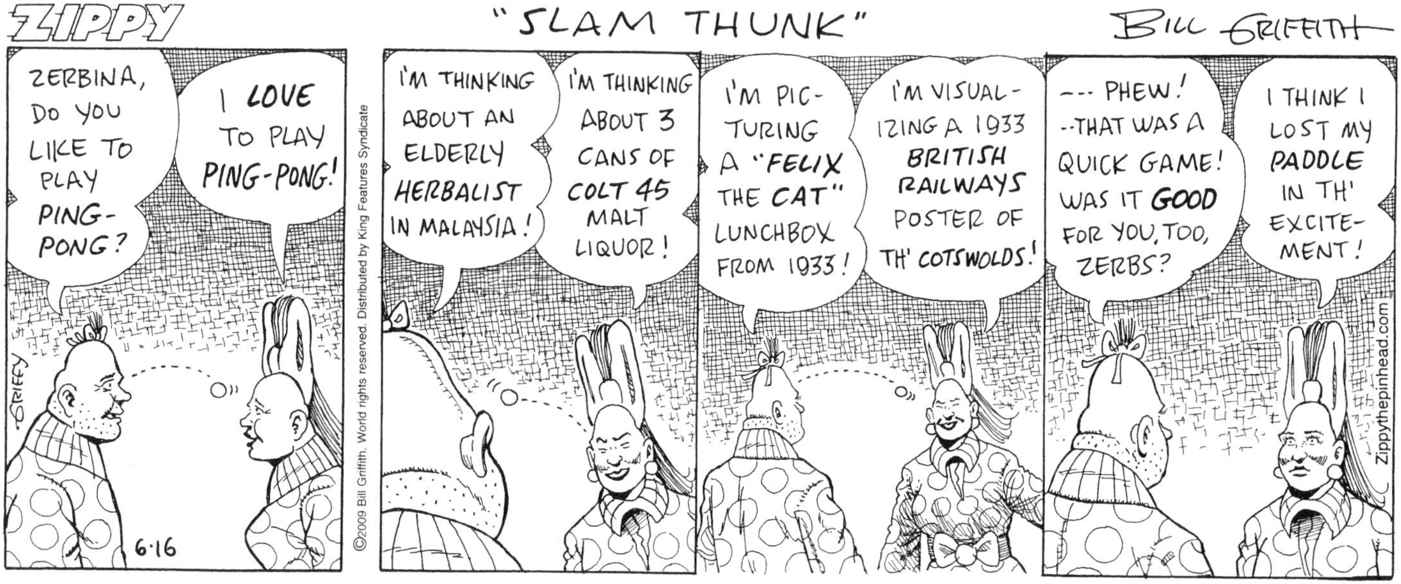
ZIPPY
"SLAM THUNK"
BILL GRIFFITH
ZERBINA, DO YOU LIKE TO PLAY PING-PONG?
I LOVE TO PLAY PING-PONG!
GRIFFY
6·16
©2009 Bill Griffith. World rights reserved. Distributed by King Features Syndicate
I'M THINKING ABOUT AN ELDERLY HERBALIST IN MALAYSIA!
I'M THINKING ABOUT 3 CANS OF COLT 45 MALT LIQUOR!
I'M PICTURING A "FELIX THE CAT" LUNCHBOX FROM 1933!
I'M VISUALIZING A 1933 BRITISH RAILWAYS POSTER OF TH' COTSWOLDS!
--- PHEW! --THAT WAS A QUICK GAME! WAS IT GOOD FOR YOU, TOO, ZERBS?
I THINK I LOST MY PADDLE IN TH' EXCITEMENT!
Zippythepinhead.com

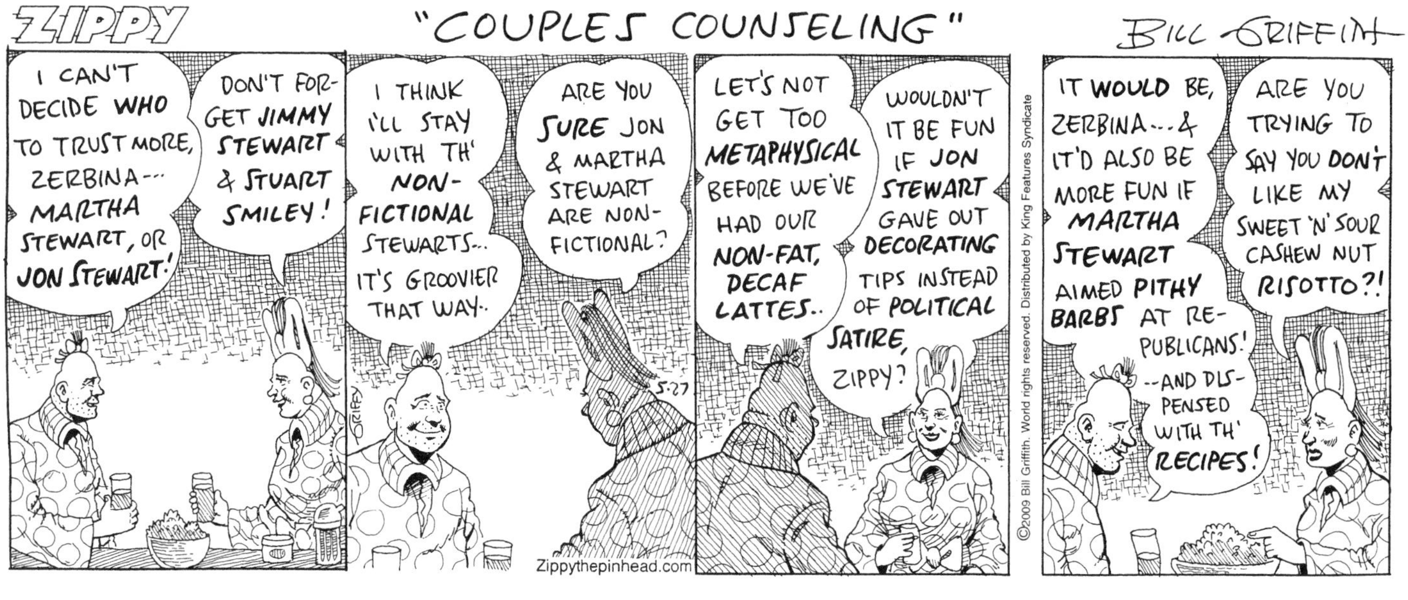
ZIPPY
"COUPLES COUNSELING"
BILL GRIFFITH
I CAN'T DECIDE WHO TO TRUST MORE, ZERBINA--- MARTHA STEWART, OR JON STEWART!
DON'T FORGET JIMMY STEWART & STUART SMILEY!
I THINK I'LL STAY WITH TH' NON-FICTIONAL STEWARTS... IT'S GROOVIER THAT WAY..
ARE YOU SURE JON & MARTHA STEWART ARE NON-FICTIONAL?
GRIFFY
5·27
Zippythepinhead.com
LET'S NOT GET TOO METAPHYSICAL BEFORE WE'VE HAD OUR NON-FAT, DECAF LATTES..
WOULDN'T IT BE FUN IF JON STEWART GAVE OUT DECORATING TIPS INSTEAD OF POLITICAL SATIRE, ZIPPY?
©2009 Bill Griffith. World rights reserved. Distributed by King Features Syndicate
IT WOULD BE, ZERBINA--- & IT'D ALSO BE MORE FUN IF MARTHA STEWART AIMED PITHY BARBS AT REPUBLICANS!
--AND DISPENSED WITH TH' RECIPES!
ARE YOU TRYING TO SAY YOU DON'T LIKE MY SWEET 'N' SOUR CASHEW NUT RISOTTO?!

ZIPPY "OPPOSITE EFFECT" BILL GRIFFITH

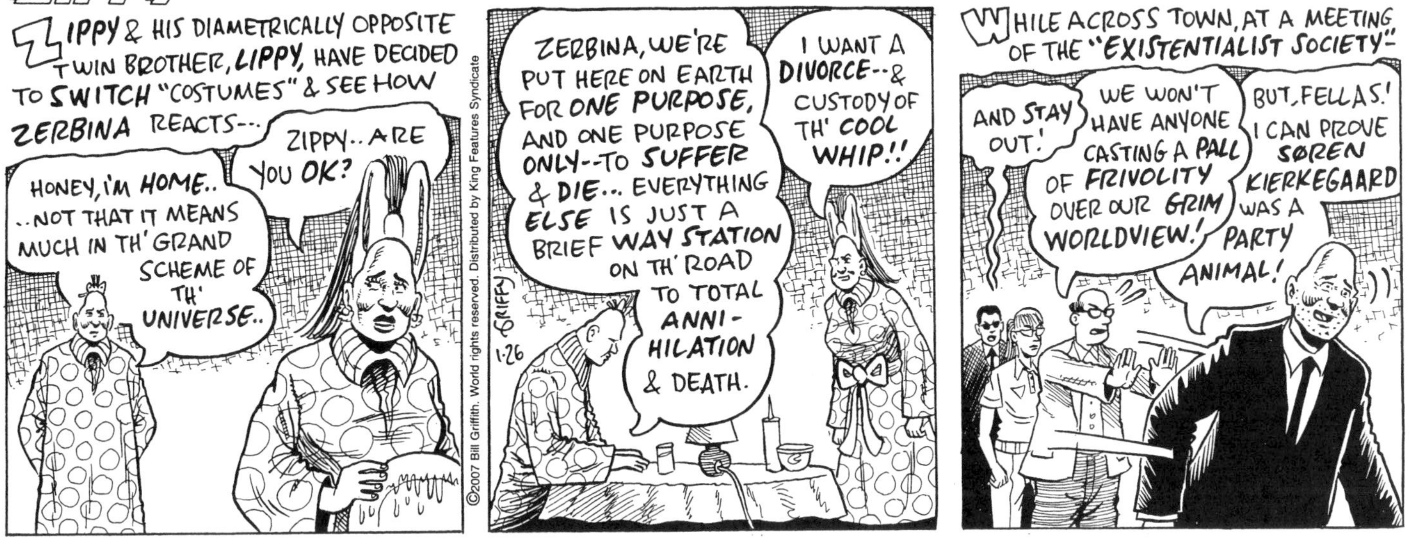
ZIPPY & HIS DIAMETRICALLY OPPOSITE TWIN BROTHER, LIPPY, HAVE DECIDED TO SWITCH "COSTUMES" & SEE HOW ZERBINA REACTS--.
HONEY, I'M HOME.. ..NOT THAT IT MEANS MUCH IN TH' GRAND SCHEME OF TH' UNIVERSE..
ZIPPY.. ARE YOU OK?
ZERBINA, WE'RE PUT HERE ON EARTH FOR ONE PURPOSE, AND ONE PURPOSE ONLY--TO SUFFER & DIE.. EVERYTHING ELSE IS JUST A BRIEF WAY STATION ON TH' ROAD TO TOTAL ANNI-HILATION & DEATH.
I WANT A DIVORCE--& CUSTODY OF TH' COOL WHIP!!
GRIFFY
1-26
WHILE ACROSS TOWN, AT A MEETING OF THE "EXISTENTIALIST SOCIETY"-
AND STAY OUT!
WE WON'T HAVE ANYONE CASTING A PALL OF FRIVOLITY OVER OUR GRIM WORLDVIEW!
BUT, FELLAS! I CAN PROVE SØREN KIERKEGAARD WAS A PARTY ANIMAL!

ZIPPY "FLOWER CHILD" BILL GRIFFITH

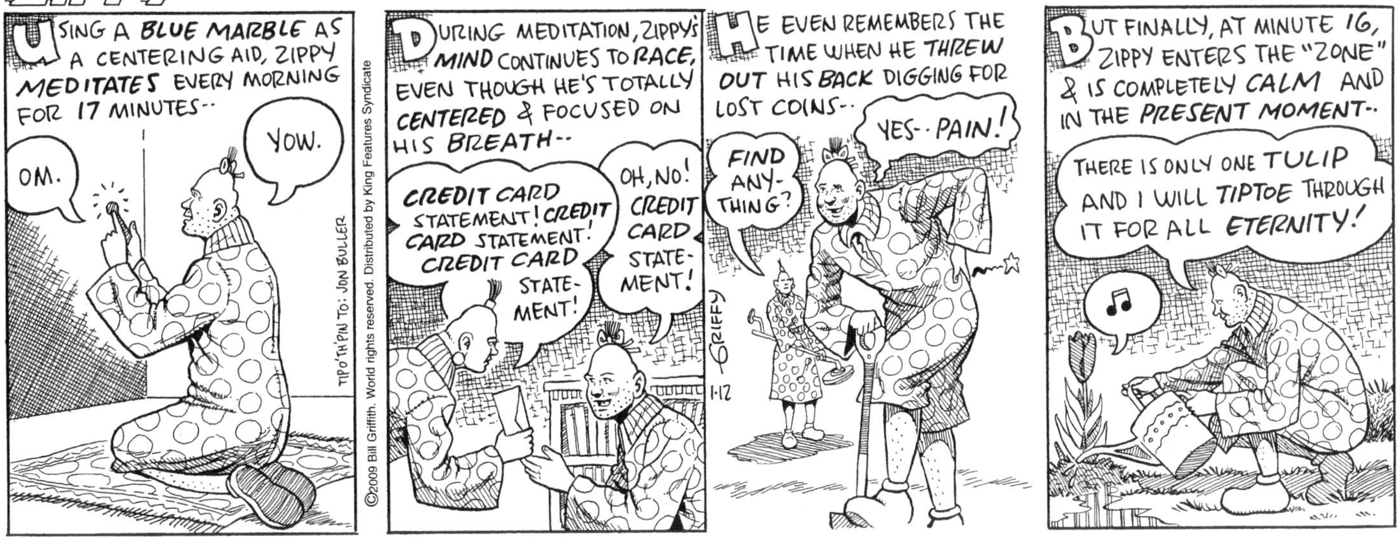
USING A BLUE MARBLE AS A CENTERING AID, ZIPPY MEDITATES EVERY MORNING FOR 17 MINUTES--
OM.
YOW.
TIP O'TH'PIN TO: JON BULLER
DURING MEDITATION, ZIPPY'S MIND CONTINUES TO RACE, EVEN THOUGH HE'S TOTALLY CENTERED & FOCUSED ON HIS BREATH--
CREDIT CARD STATEMENT! CREDIT CARD STATEMENT! CREDIT CARD STATE-MENT!
OH, NO! CREDIT CARD STATE-MENT!
HE EVEN REMEMBERS THE TIME WHEN HE THREW OUT HIS BACK DIGGING FOR LOST COINS--
FIND ANY-THING?
YES-- PAIN!
GRIFFY
1-12
BUT FINALLY, AT MINUTE 16, ZIPPY ENTERS THE "ZONE" & IS COMPLETELY CALM AND IN THE PRESENT MOMENT--
THERE IS ONLY ONE TULIP AND I WILL TIPTOE THROUGH IT FOR ALL ETERNITY!

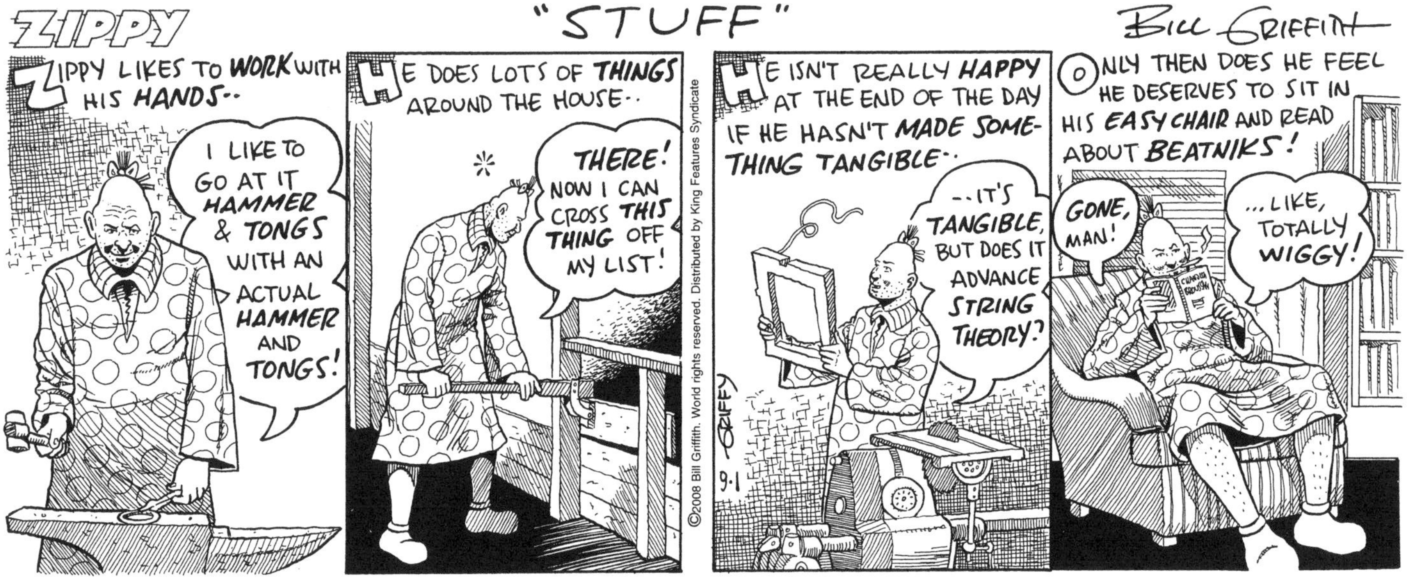
ZIPPY
"STUFF"
BILL GRIFFITH
ZIPPY LIKES TO WORK WITH HIS HANDS..
I LIKE TO GO AT IT HAMMER & TONGS WITH AN ACTUAL HAMMER AND TONGS!
HE DOES LOTS OF THINGS AROUND THE HOUSE..
THERE! NOW I CAN CROSS THIS THING OFF MY LIST!
©2008 Bill Griffith. World rights reserved. Distributed by King Features Syndicate
GRIFFY
9.1
HE ISN'T REALLY HAPPY AT THE END OF THE DAY IF HE HASN'T MADE SOMETHING TANGIBLE..
..IT'S TANGIBLE, BUT DOES IT ADVANCE STRING THEORY?
ONLY THEN DOES HE FEEL HE DESERVES TO SIT IN HIS EASY CHAIR AND READ ABOUT BEATNIKS!
GONE, MAN!
...LIKE, TOTALLY WIGGY!

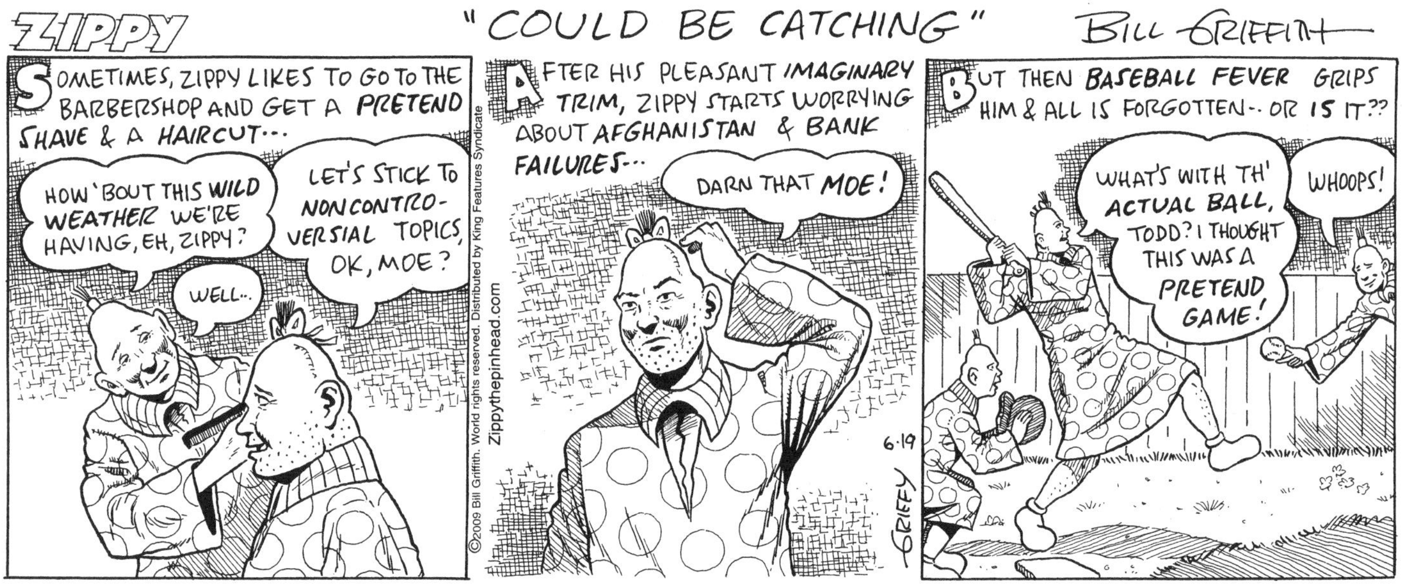
ZIPPY
"COULD BE CATCHING"
BILL GRIFFITH
SOMETIMES, ZIPPY LIKES TO GO TO THE BARBERSHOP AND GET A PRETEND SHAVE & A HAIRCUT...
HOW 'BOUT THIS WILD WEATHER WE'RE HAVING, EH, ZIPPY?
LET'S STICK TO NONCONTROVERSIAL TOPICS, OK, MOE?
WELL..
©2009 Bill Griffith. World rights reserved. Distributed by King Features Syndicate
Zippythepinhead.com
AFTER HIS PLEASANT IMAGINARY TRIM, ZIPPY STARTS WORRYING ABOUT AFGHANISTAN & BANK FAILURES...
DARN THAT MOE!
6.19
GRIFFY
BUT THEN BASEBALL FEVER GRIPS HIM & ALL IS FORGOTTEN.. OR IS IT??
WHAT'S WITH TH' ACTUAL BALL, TODD? I THOUGHT THIS WAS A PRETEND GAME!
WHOOPS!

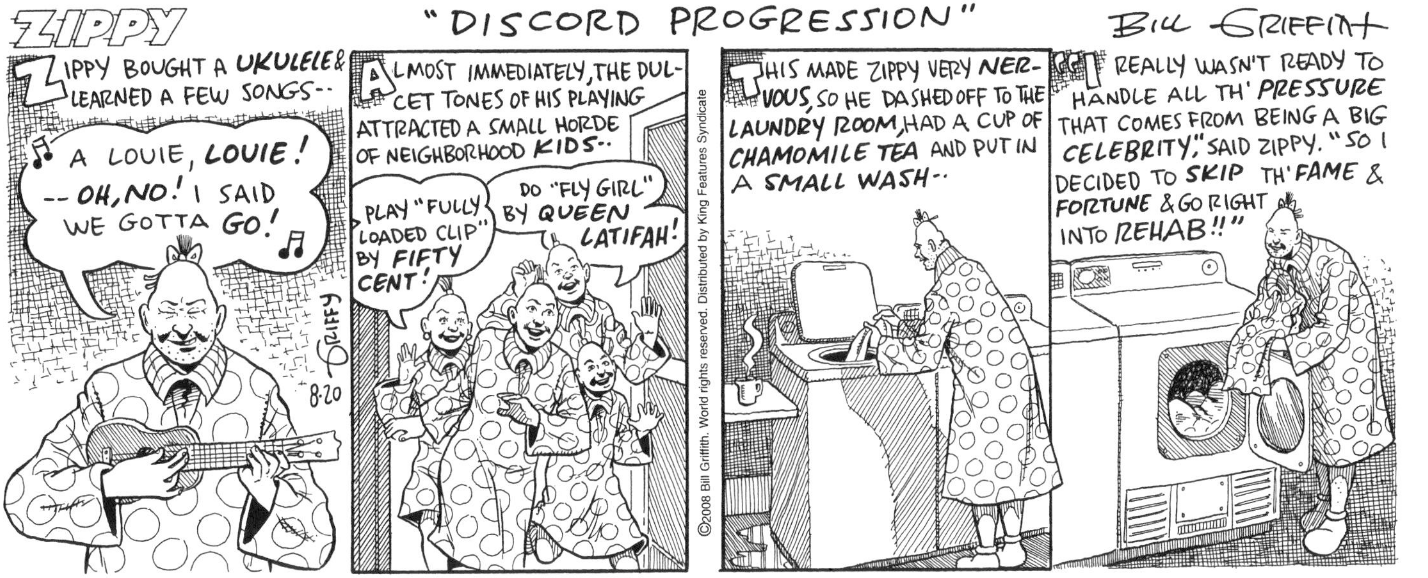

ZIPPY
"DISCORD PROGRESSION"
BILL GRIFFITH
ZIPPY BOUGHT A UKULELE & LEARNED A FEW SONGS--
A LOUIE, LOUIE! --OH, NO! I SAID WE GOTTA GO!
GRIFFY 8·20
ALMOST IMMEDIATELY, THE DULCET TONES OF HIS PLAYING ATTRACTED A SMALL HORDE OF NEIGHBORHOOD KIDS--
PLAY "FULLY LOADED CLIP" BY FIFTY CENT!
DO "FLY GIRL" BY QUEEN LATIFAH!
©2008 Bill Griffith. World rights reserved. Distributed by King Features Syndicate
THIS MADE ZIPPY VERY NERVOUS, SO HE DASHED OFF TO THE LAUNDRY ROOM, HAD A CUP OF CHAMOMILE TEA AND PUT IN A SMALL WASH--
"I REALLY WASN'T READY TO HANDLE ALL TH' PRESSURE THAT COMES FROM BEING A BIG CELEBRITY," SAID ZIPPY. "SO I DECIDED TO SKIP TH' FAME & FORTUNE & GO RIGHT INTO REHAB!!"

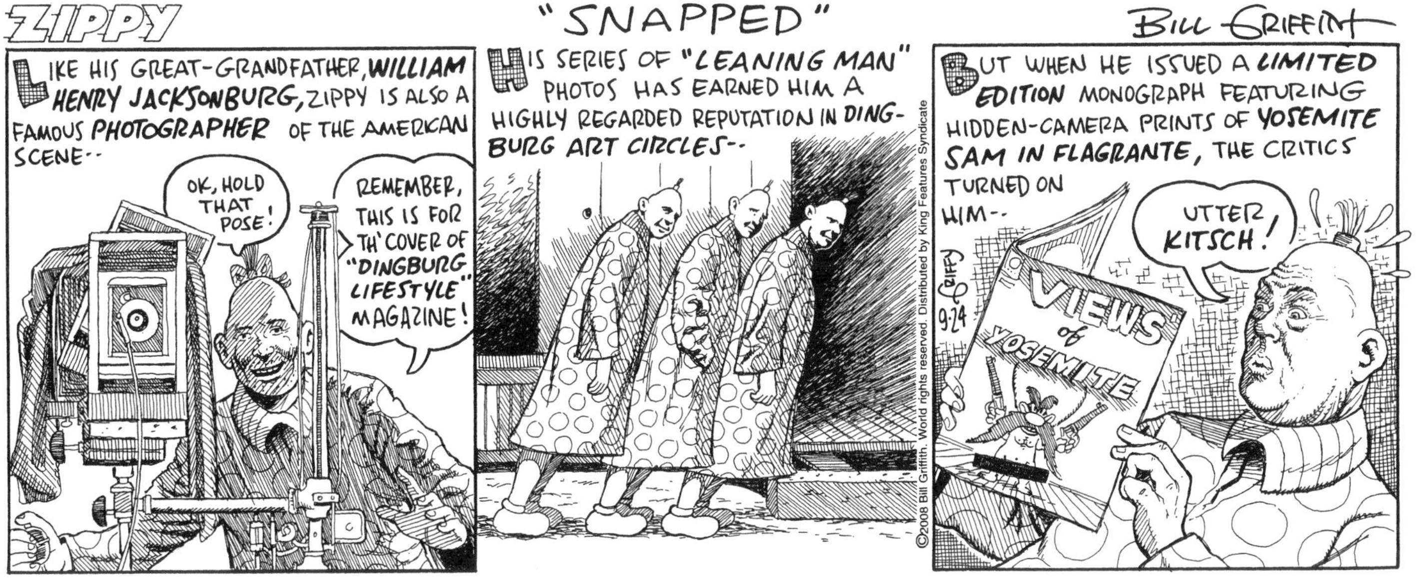

ZIPPY
"SNAPPED"
BILL GRIFFITH
LIKE HIS GREAT-GRANDFATHER, WILLIAM HENRY JACKSONBURG, ZIPPY IS ALSO A FAMOUS PHOTOGRAPHER OF THE AMERICAN SCENE--
OK, HOLD THAT POSE!
REMEMBER, THIS IS FOR TH' COVER OF "DINGBURG LIFESTYLE" MAGAZINE!
HIS SERIES OF "LEANING MAN" PHOTOS HAS EARNED HIM A HIGHLY REGARDED REPUTATION IN DINGBURG ART CIRCLES--
©2008 Bill Griffith. World rights reserved. Distributed by King Features Syndicate
GRIFFY 9·24
BUT WHEN HE ISSUED A LIMITED EDITION MONOGRAPH FEATURING HIDDEN-CAMERA PRINTS OF YOSEMITE SAM IN FLAGRANTE, THE CRITICS TURNED ON HIM--
UTTER, KITSCH!
VIEWS of YOSEMITE

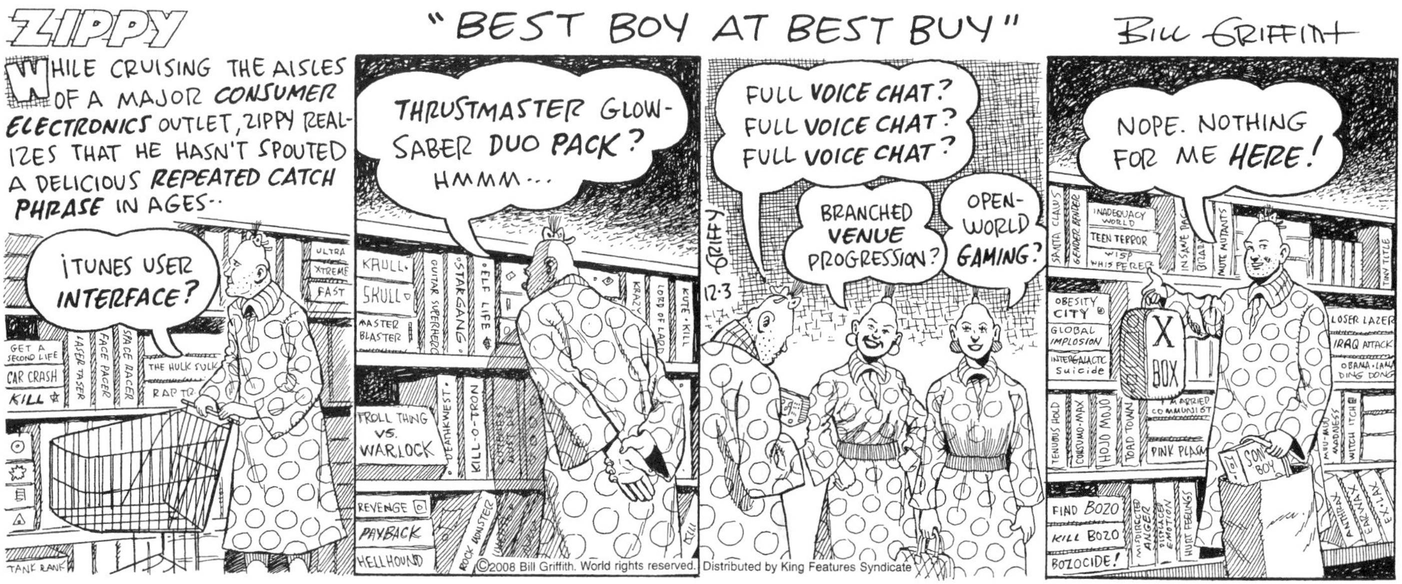
ZIPPY
"BEST BOY AT BEST BUY"
BILL GRIFFITH
WHILE CRUISING THE AISLES OF A MAJOR CONSUMER ELECTRONICS OUTLET, ZIPPY REALIZES THAT HE HASN'T SPOUTED A DELICIOUS REPEATED CATCH PHRASE IN AGES..
¡TUNES USER INTERFACE?
THRUSTMASTER GLOW-SABER DUO PACK? HMMM...
FULL VOICE CHAT? FULL VOICE CHAT? FULL VOICE CHAT?
BRANCHED VENUE PROGRESSION?
OPEN-WORLD GAMING?
NOPE. NOTHING FOR ME HERE!
GRIFFY 12·3
©2008 Bill Griffith. World rights reserved. Distributed by King Features Syndicate

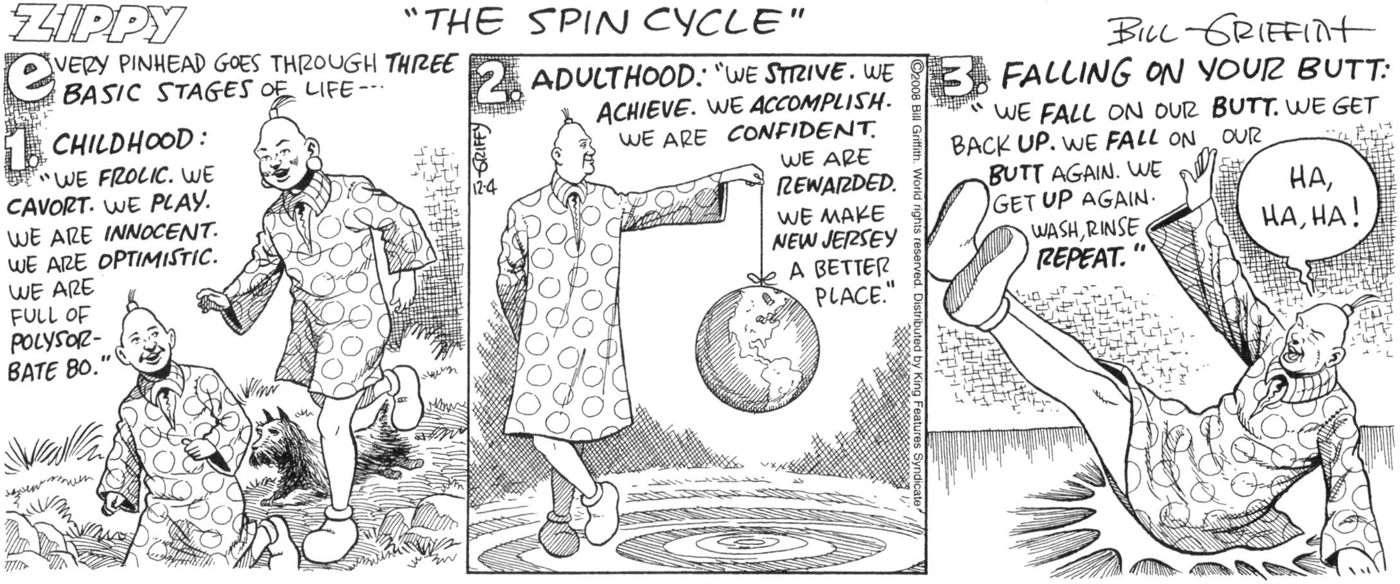
ZIPPY
"THE SPIN CYCLE"
BILL GRIFFITH
EVERY PINHEAD GOES THROUGH THREE BASIC STAGES OF LIFE---
1. CHILDHOOD: "WE FROLIC. WE CAVORT. WE PLAY. WE ARE INNOCENT. WE ARE OPTIMISTIC. WE ARE FULL OF POLYSORBATE 80."
2. ADULTHOOD: "WE STRIVE. WE ACHIEVE. WE ACCOMPLISH. WE ARE CONFIDENT. WE ARE REWARDED. WE MAKE NEW JERSEY A BETTER PLACE."
3. FALLING ON YOUR BUTT: "WE FALL ON OUR BUTT. WE GET BACK UP. WE FALL ON OUR BUTT AGAIN. WE GET UP AGAIN. WASH, RINSE REPEAT."
HA, HA, HA!
GRIFFY 12·4
©2008 Bill Griffith. World rights reserved. Distributed by King Features Syndicate

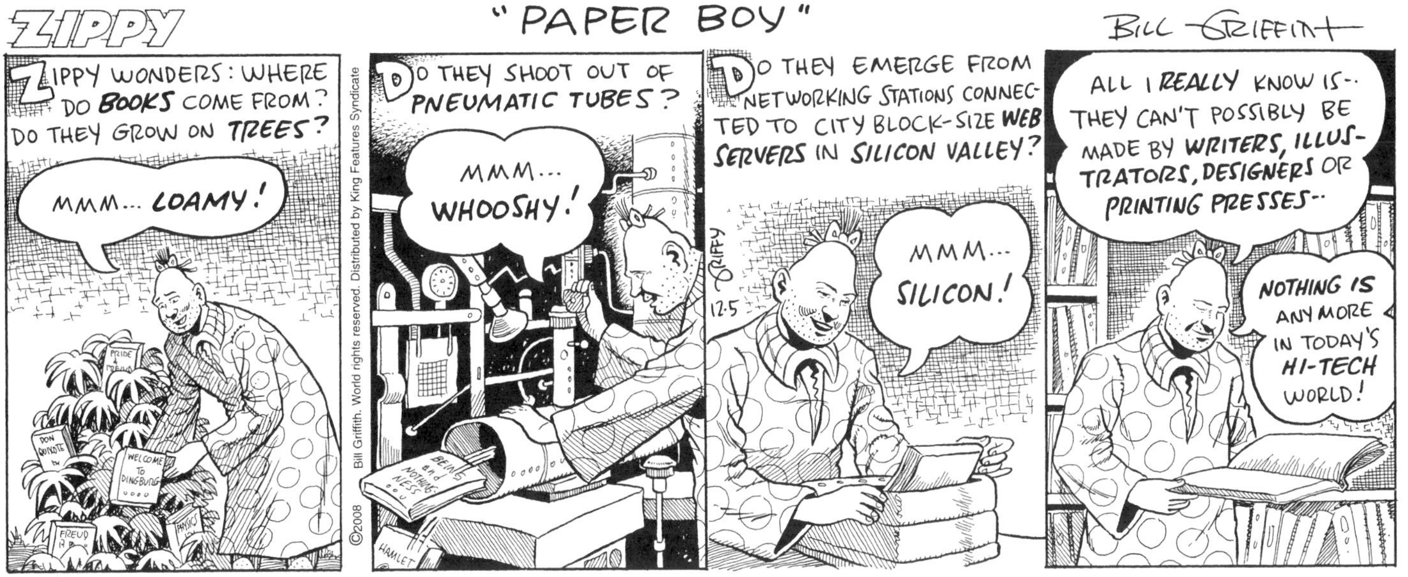
ZIPPY
"PAPER BOY"
BILL GRIFFITH
ZIPPY WONDERS: WHERE DO BOOKS COME FROM? DO THEY GROW ON TREES?
MMM... LOAMY!
©2008 Bill Griffith. World rights reserved. Distributed by King Features Syndicate
DO THEY SHOOT OUT OF PNEUMATIC TUBES?
MMM... WHOOSHY!
HAMLET
DO THEY EMERGE FROM NETWORKING STATIONS CONNECTED TO CITY BLOCK-SIZE WEB SERVERS IN SILICON VALLEY?
MMM... SILICON!
GRIFFY 12·5
ALL I REALLY KNOW IS.. THEY CAN'T POSSIBLY BE MADE BY WRITERS, ILLUSTRATORS, DESIGNERS OR PRINTING PRESSES..
NOTHING IS ANYMORE IN TODAY'S HI-TECH WORLD!

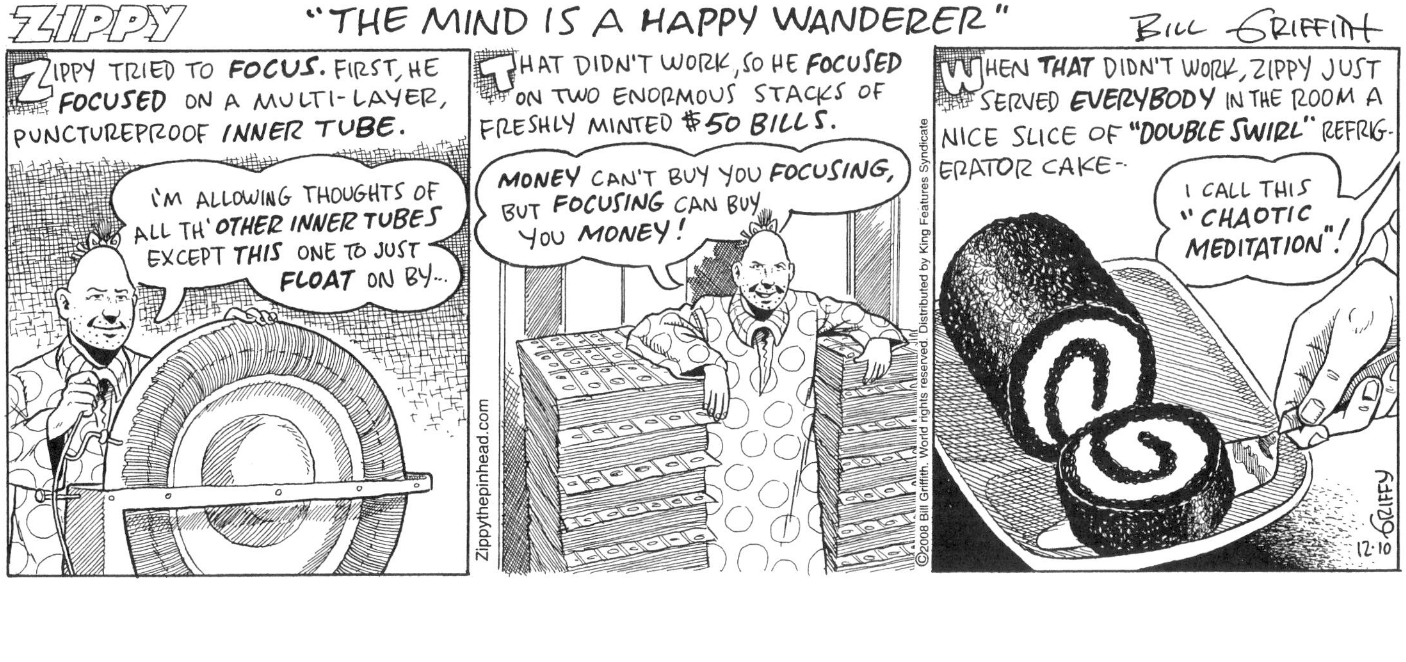
ZIPPY
"THE MIND IS A HAPPY WANDERER"
BILL GRIFFITH
ZIPPY TRIED TO FOCUS. FIRST, HE FOCUSED ON A MULTI-LAYER, PUNCTUREPROOF INNER TUBE.
I'M ALLOWING THOUGHTS OF ALL TH' OTHER INNER TUBES EXCEPT THIS ONE TO JUST FLOAT ON BY...
Zippythepinhead.com
THAT DIDN'T WORK, SO HE FOCUSED ON TWO ENORMOUS STACKS OF FRESHLY MINTED $50 BILLS.
MONEY CAN'T BUY YOU FOCUSING, BUT FOCUSING CAN BUY YOU MONEY!
©2008 Bill Griffith. World rights reserved. Distributed by King Features Syndicate
WHEN THAT DIDN'T WORK, ZIPPY JUST SERVED EVERYBODY IN THE ROOM A NICE SLICE OF "DOUBLE SWIRL" REFRIGERATOR CAKE..
I CALL THIS "CHAOTIC MEDITATION"!
GRIFFY 12·10

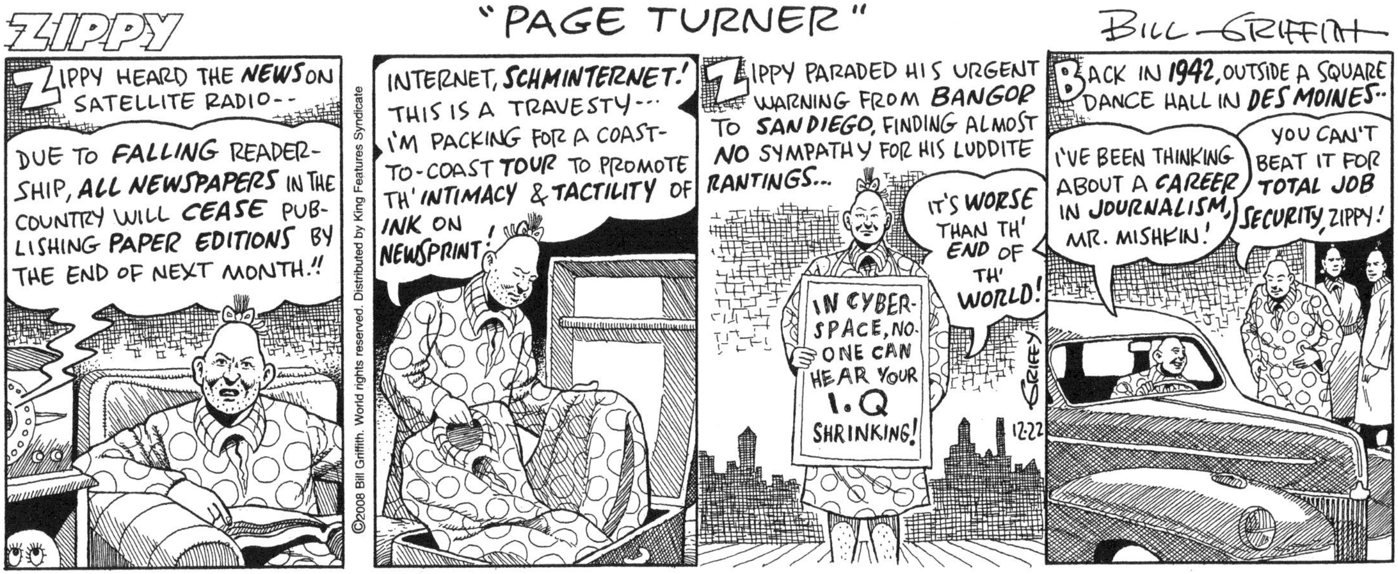
ZIPPY
"PAGE TURNER"
BILL GRIFFITH
ZIPPY HEARD THE NEWS ON SATELLITE RADIO--
DUE TO FALLING READERSHIP, ALL NEWSPAPERS IN THE COUNTRY WILL CEASE PUBLISHING PAPER EDITIONS BY THE END OF NEXT MONTH.!!
INTERNET, SCHMINTERNET! THIS IS A TRAVESTY--- I'M PACKING FOR A COAST-TO-COAST TOUR TO PROMOTE TH' INTIMACY & TACTILITY OF INK ON NEWSPRINT!
ZIPPY PARADED HIS URGENT WARNING FROM BANGOR TO SAN DIEGO, FINDING ALMOST NO SYMPATHY FOR HIS LUDDITE RANTINGS...
IN CYBERSPACE, NO ONE CAN HEAR YOUR I.Q SHRINKING!
IT'S WORSE THAN TH' END OF TH' WORLD!
GRIFFY 12·22
BACK IN 1942, OUTSIDE A SQUARE DANCE HALL IN DES MOINES..
I'VE BEEN THINKING ABOUT A CAREER IN JOURNALISM, MR. MISHKIN!
YOU CAN'T BEAT IT FOR TOTAL JOB SECURITY, ZIPPY!
©2008 Bill Griffith. World rights reserved. Distributed by King Features Syndicate

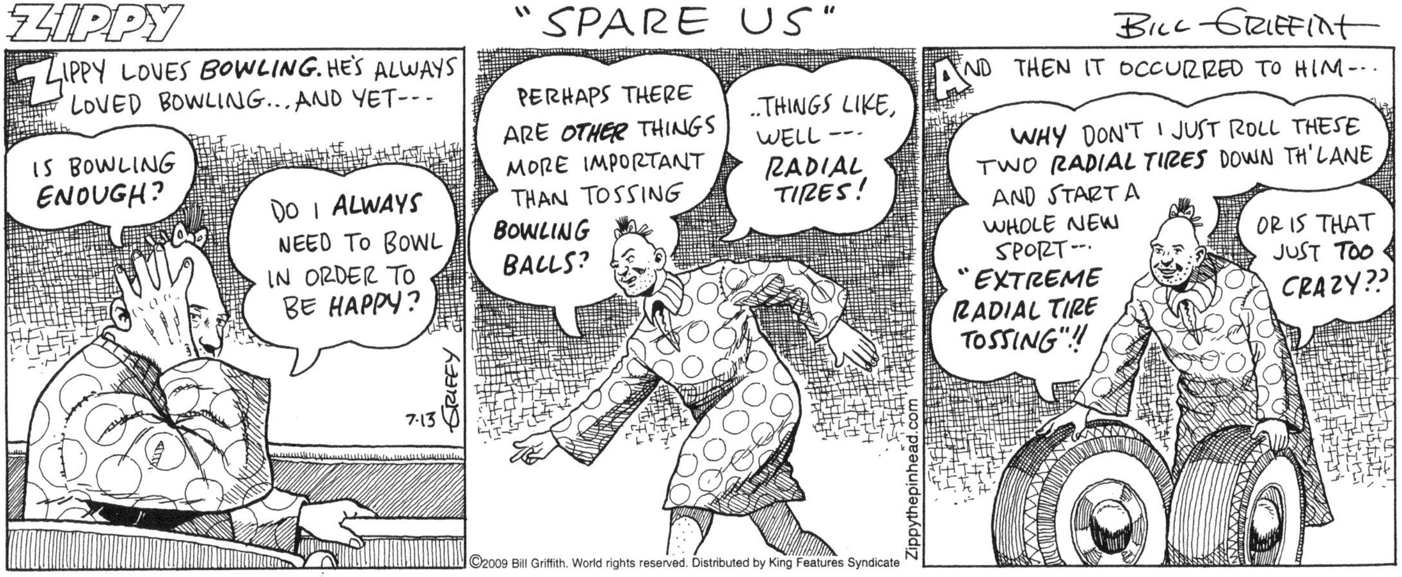
ZIPPY
"SPARE US"
BILL GRIFFITH
ZIPPY LOVES BOWLING. HE'S ALWAYS LOVED BOWLING..., AND YET---
IS BOWLING ENOUGH?
DO I ALWAYS NEED TO BOWL IN ORDER TO BE HAPPY?
GRIFFY 7·13
PERHAPS THERE ARE OTHER THINGS MORE IMPORTANT THAN TOSSING BOWLING BALLS?
..THINGS LIKE, WELL --- RADIAL TIRES!
AND THEN IT OCCURRED TO HIM---
WHY DON'T I JUST ROLL THESE TWO RADIAL TIRES DOWN TH' LANE AND START A WHOLE NEW SPORT-- "EXTREME RADIAL TIRE TOSSING"!!
OR IS THAT JUST TOO CRAZY??
©2009 Bill Griffith. World rights reserved. Distributed by King Features Syndicate
Zippythepinhead.com

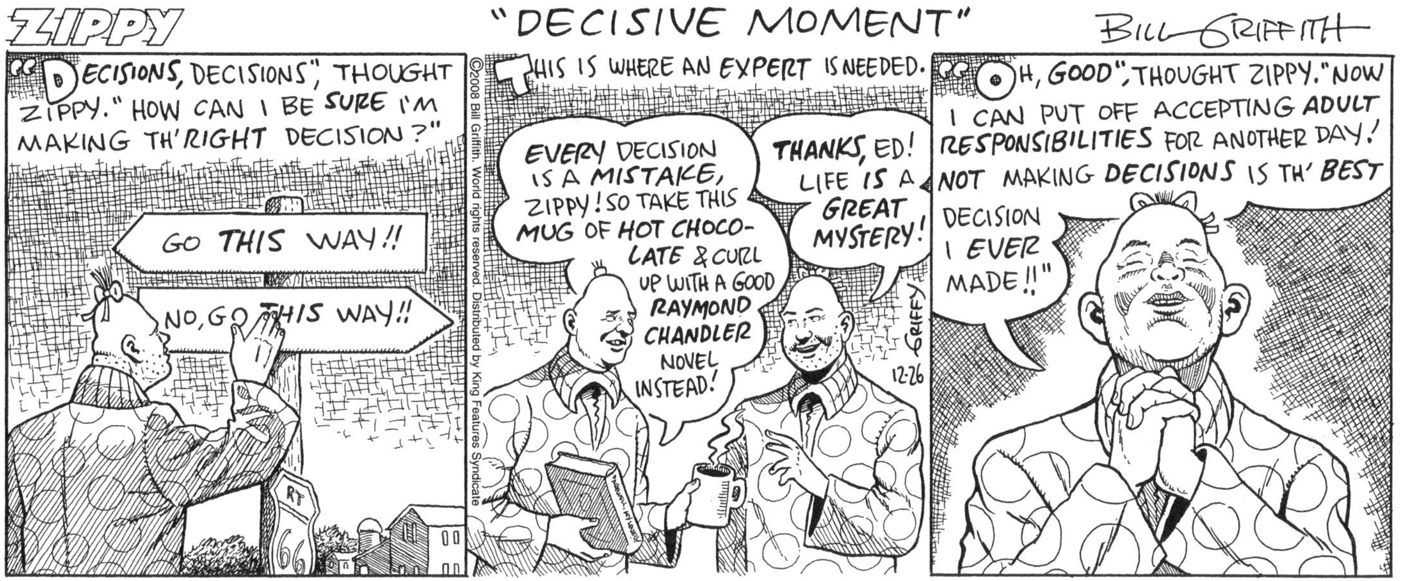
ZIPPY
"DECISIVE MOMENT"
BILL GRIFFITH
"DECISIONS, DECISIONS", THOUGHT ZIPPY. "HOW CAN I BE SURE I'M MAKING TH' RIGHT DECISION?"
GO THIS WAY!!
NO, GO THIS WAY!!
RT 66
©2008 Bill Griffith. World rights reserved. Distributed by King Features Syndicate
THIS IS WHERE AN EXPERT IS NEEDED.
EVERY DECISION IS A MISTAKE, ZIPPY! SO TAKE THIS MUG OF HOT CHOCOLATE & CURL UP WITH A GOOD RAYMOND CHANDLER NOVEL INSTEAD!
THANKS, ED! LIFE IS A GREAT MYSTERY!
GRIFFY
12·26
"OH, GOOD", THOUGHT ZIPPY. "NOW I CAN PUT OFF ACCEPTING ADULT RESPONSIBILITIES FOR ANOTHER DAY! NOT MAKING DECISIONS IS TH' BEST DECISION I EVER MADE!!"

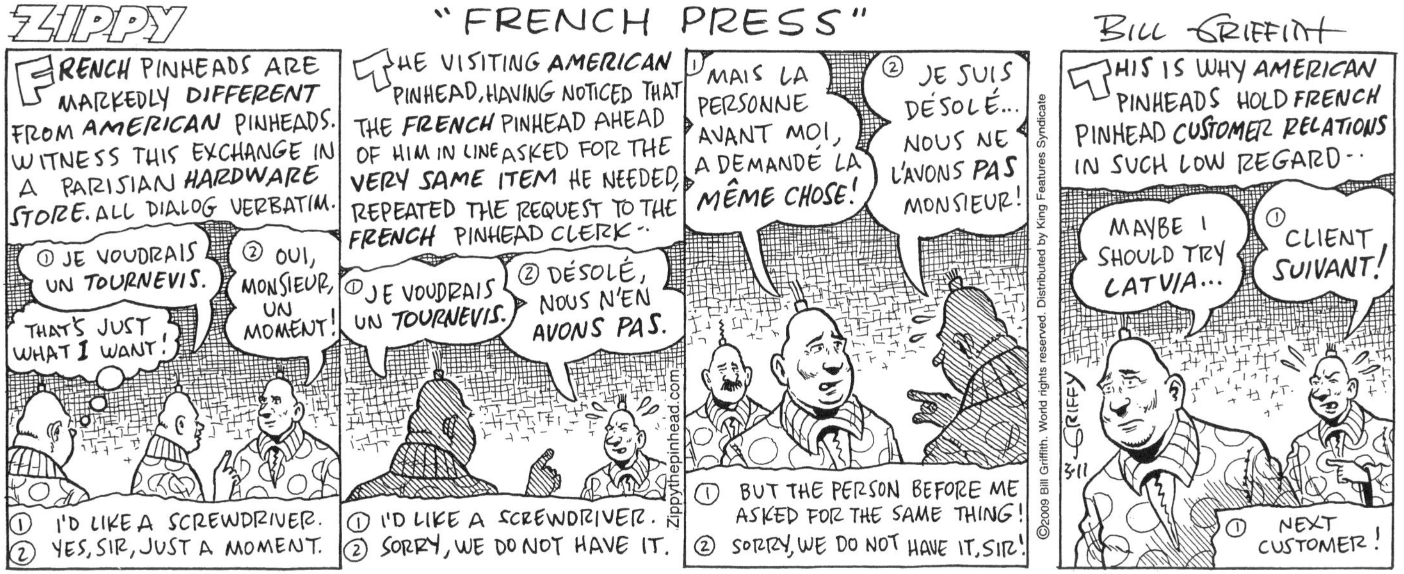
ZIPPY
"FRENCH PRESS"
BILL GRIFFITH
FRENCH PINHEADS ARE MARKEDLY DIFFERENT FROM AMERICAN PINHEADS. WITNESS THIS EXCHANGE IN A PARISIAN HARDWARE STORE. ALL DIALOG VERBATIM.
① JE VOUDRAIS UN TOURNEVIS.
② OUI, MONSIEUR, UN MOMENT!
THAT'S JUST WHAT I WANT!
① I'D LIKE A SCREWDRIVER.
② YES, SIR, JUST A MOMENT.
THE VISITING AMERICAN PINHEAD, HAVING NOTICED THAT THE FRENCH PINHEAD AHEAD OF HIM IN LINE ASKED FOR THE VERY SAME ITEM HE NEEDED, REPEATED THE REQUEST TO THE FRENCH PINHEAD CLERK··
① JE VOUDRAIS UN TOURNEVIS.
② DÉSOLÉ, NOUS N'EN AVONS PAS.
zippythepinhead.com
① I'D LIKE A SCREWDRIVER.
② SORRY, WE DO NOT HAVE IT.
① MAIS LA PERSONNE AVANT MOI, A DEMANDÉ LA MÊME CHOSE!
② JE SUIS DÉSOLÉ... NOUS NE L'AVONS PAS MONSIEUR!
① BUT THE PERSON BEFORE ME ASKED FOR THE SAME THING!
② SORRY, WE DO NOT HAVE IT, SIR!
©2009 Bill Griffith. World rights reserved. Distributed by King Features Syndicate
THIS IS WHY AMERICAN PINHEADS HOLD FRENCH PINHEAD CUSTOMER RELATIONS IN SUCH LOW REGARD··
MAYBE I SHOULD TRY LATVIA...
① CLIENT SUIVANT!
GRIFFY
3·11
① NEXT CUSTOMER!

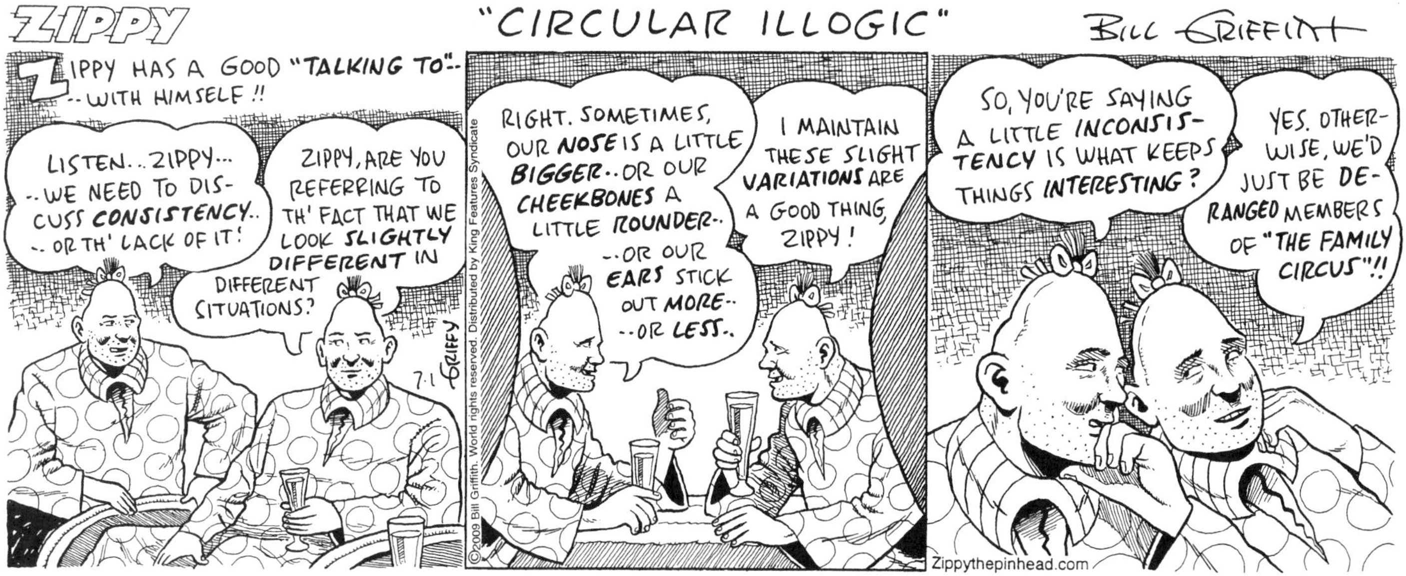
ZIPPY
"CIRCULAR ILLOGIC"
BILL GRIFFITH
ZIPPY HAS A GOOD "TALKING TO" -- WITH HIMSELF !!
LISTEN.. ZIPPY... -- WE NEED TO DISCUSS CONSISTENCY.. -- OR TH' LACK OF IT!
ZIPPY, ARE YOU REFERRING TO TH' FACT THAT WE LOOK SLIGHTLY DIFFERENT IN DIFFERENT SITUATIONS?
GRIFFY 7.1
©2009 Bill Griffith. World rights reserved. Distributed by King Features Syndicate
RIGHT. SOMETIMES, OUR NOSE IS A LITTLE BIGGER.. OR OUR CHEEKBONES A LITTLE ROUNDER.. --OR OUR EARS STICK OUT MORE-- --OR LESS..
I MAINTAIN THESE SLIGHT VARIATIONS ARE A GOOD THING, ZIPPY!
SO, YOU'RE SAYING A LITTLE INCONSISTENCY IS WHAT KEEPS THINGS INTERESTING?
YES. OTHERWISE, WE'D JUST BE DERANGED MEMBERS OF "THE FAMILY CIRCUS"!!
Zippythepinhead.com

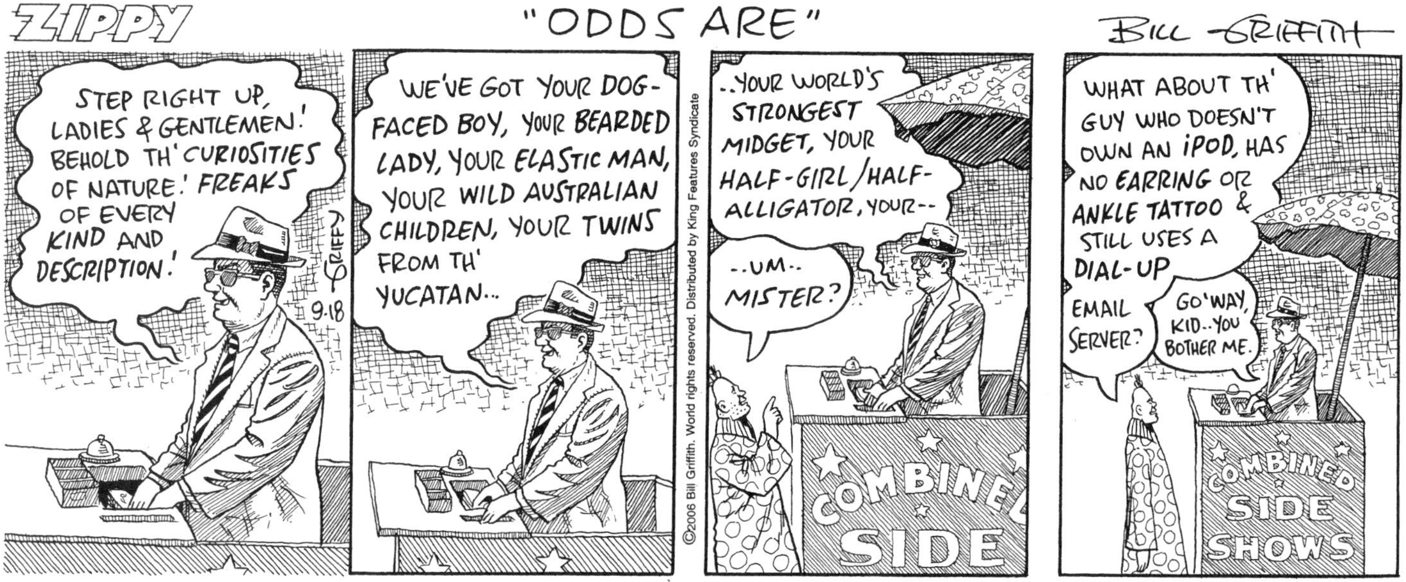
ZIPPY
"ODDS ARE"
BILL GRIFFITH
STEP RIGHT UP, LADIES & GENTLEMEN! BEHOLD TH' CURIOSITIES OF NATURE! FREAKS OF EVERY KIND AND DESCRIPTION!
GRIFFY 9.18
WE'VE GOT YOUR DOG-FACED BOY, YOUR BEARDED LADY, YOUR ELASTIC MAN, YOUR WILD AUSTRALIAN CHILDREN, YOUR TWINS FROM TH' YUCATAN...
©2006 Bill Griffith. World rights reserved. Distributed by King Features Syndicate
..YOUR WORLD'S STRONGEST MIDGET, YOUR HALF-GIRL/HALF-ALLIGATOR, YOUR--
--UM.. MISTER?
COMBINED SIDE
WHAT ABOUT TH' GUY WHO DOESN'T OWN AN iPOD, HAS NO EARRING OR ANKLE TATTOO & STILL USES A DIAL-UP EMAIL SERVER?
GO'WAY, KID.. YOU BOTHER ME.
COMBINED SIDE SHOWS

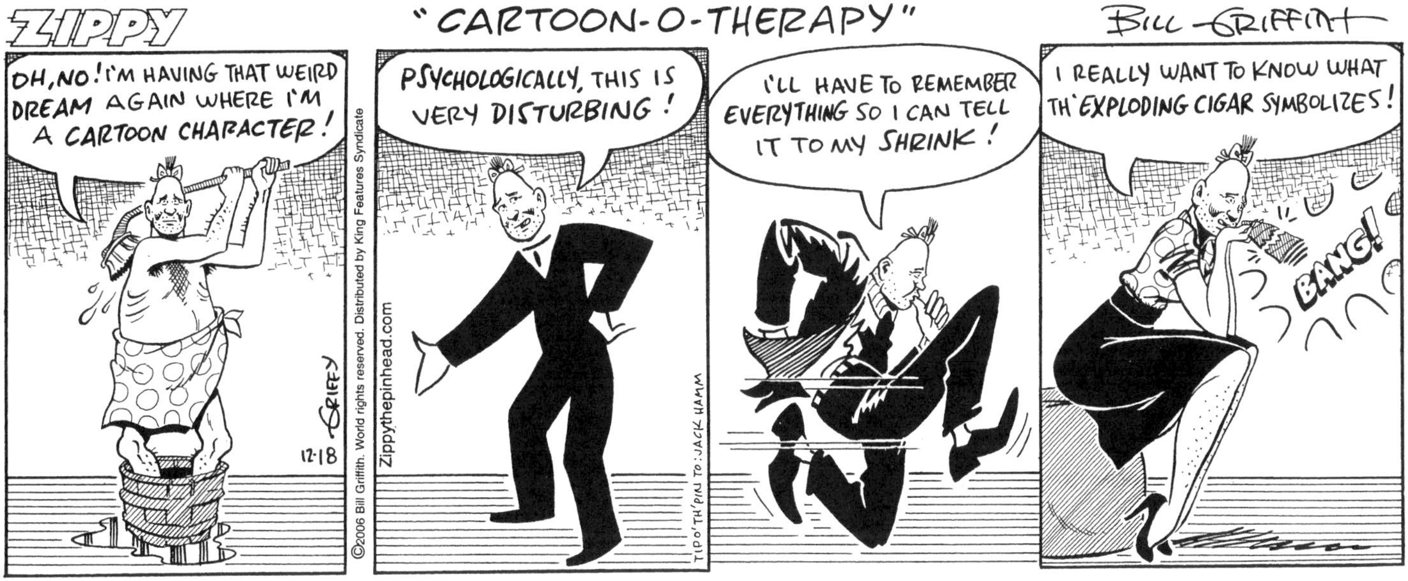
ZIPPY
"CARTOON-O-THERAPY"
BILL GRIFFITH
OH, NO! I'M HAVING THAT WEIRD DREAM AGAIN WHERE I'M A CARTOON CHARACTER!
GRIFFY 12-18
©2006 Bill Griffith. World rights reserved. Distributed by King Features Syndicate
Zippythepinhead.com
PSYCHOLOGICALLY, THIS IS VERY DISTURBING!
TIP O' TH' PIN TO: JACK HAMM
I'LL HAVE TO REMEMBER EVERYTHING SO I CAN TELL IT TO MY SHRINK!
I REALLY WANT TO KNOW WHAT TH' EXPLODING CIGAR SYMBOLIZES!
BANG!

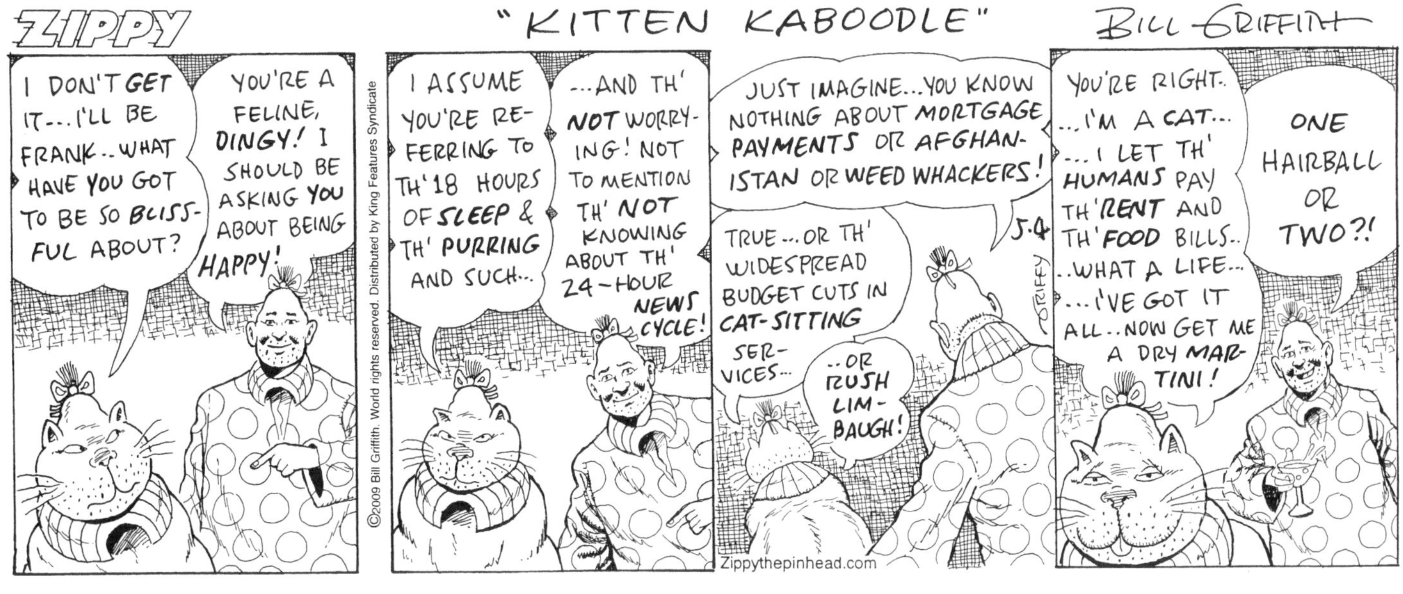
ZIPPY
"KITTEN KABOODLE"
BILL GRIFFITH
I DON'T GET IT... I'LL BE FRANK.. WHAT HAVE YOU GOT TO BE SO BLISSFUL ABOUT?
YOU'RE A FELINE, DINGY! I SHOULD BE ASKING YOU ABOUT BEING HAPPY!
©2009 Bill Griffith. World rights reserved. Distributed by King Features Syndicate
I ASSUME YOU'RE REFERRING TO TH' 18 HOURS OF SLEEP & TH' PURRING AND SUCH...
...AND TH' NOT WORRYING! NOT TO MENTION TH' NOT KNOWING ABOUT TH' 24-HOUR NEWS CYCLE!
JUST IMAGINE... YOU KNOW NOTHING ABOUT MORTGAGE PAYMENTS OR AFGHANISTAN OR WEED WHACKERS!
TRUE... OR TH' WIDESPREAD BUDGET CUTS IN CAT-SITTING SERVICES...
..OR RUSH LIMBAUGH!
5.4
GRIFFY
Zippythepinhead.com
YOU'RE RIGHT.. ...I'M A CAT... ...I LET TH' HUMANS PAY TH' RENT AND TH' FOOD BILLS.. ..WHAT A LIFE... ...I'VE GOT IT ALL.. NOW GET ME A DRY MARTINI!
ONE HAIRBALL OR TWO?!

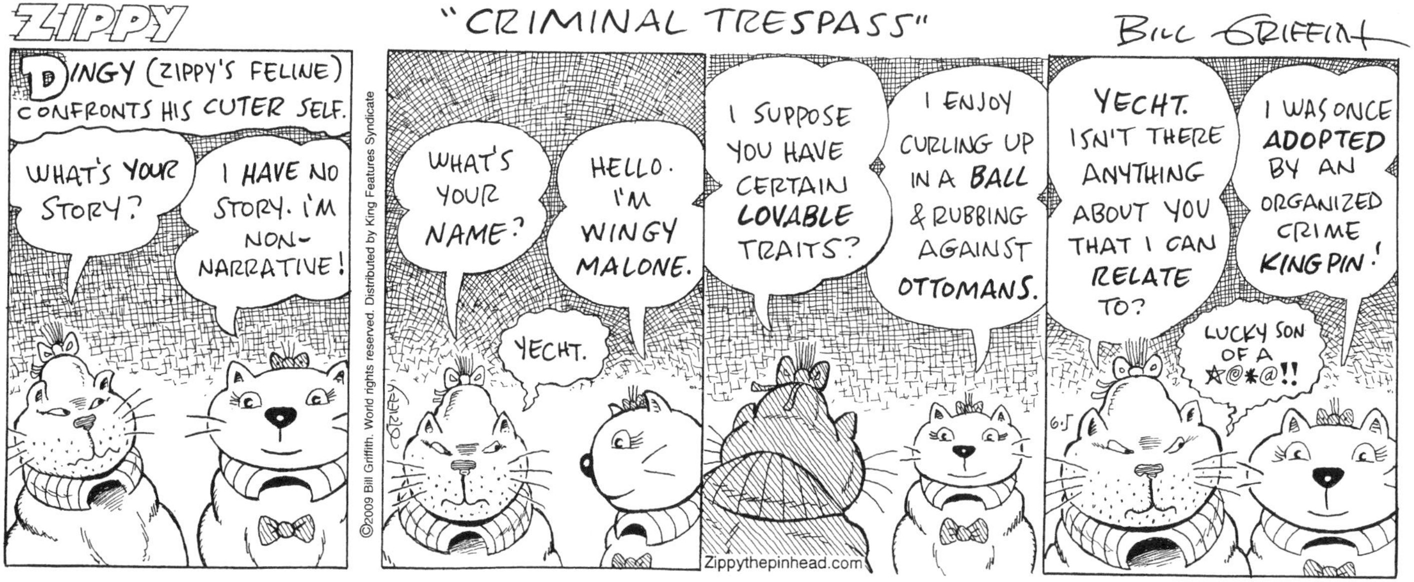
ZIPPY
"CRIMINAL TRESPASS"
BILL GRIFFITH
DINGY (ZIPPY'S FELINE) CONFRONTS HIS CUTER SELF.
WHAT'S YOUR STORY?
I HAVE NO STORY. I'M NON-NARRATIVE!
©2009 Bill Griffith. World rights reserved. Distributed by King Features Syndicate
WHAT'S YOUR NAME?
HELLO. I'M WINGY MALONE.
YECHT.
I SUPPOSE YOU HAVE CERTAIN LOVABLE TRAITS?
I ENJOY CURLING UP IN A BALL & RUBBING AGAINST OTTOMANS.
Zippythepinhead.com
YECHT. ISN'T THERE ANYTHING ABOUT YOU THAT I CAN RELATE TO?
I WAS ONCE ADOPTED BY AN ORGANIZED CRIME KINGPIN!
LUCKY SON OF A ☆@✱@!!
6.5

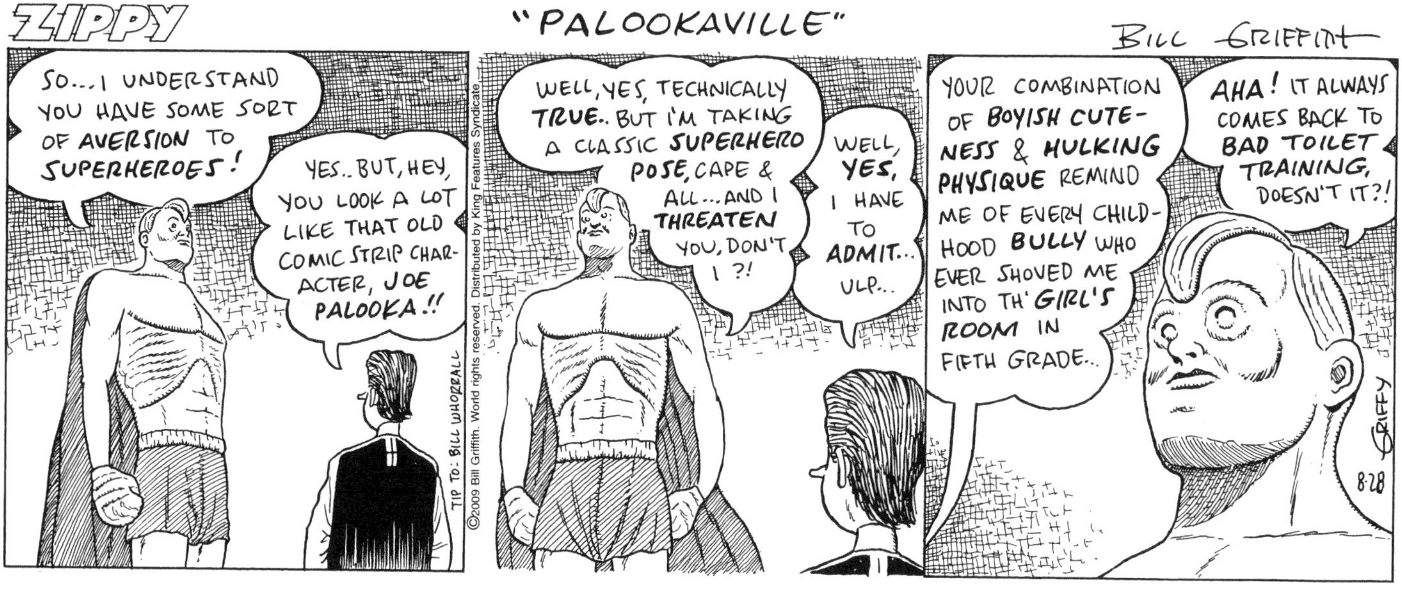
ZIPPY
"PALOOKAVILLE"
BILL GRIFFITH
SO... I UNDERSTAND YOU HAVE SOME SORT OF AVERSION TO SUPERHEROES!
YES.. BUT, HEY, YOU LOOK A LOT LIKE THAT OLD COMIC STRIP CHARACTER, JOE PALOOKA!!
TIP TO: BILL WHORRALL
©2009 Bill Griffith. World rights reserved. Distributed by King Features Syndicate
WELL, YES, TECHNICALLY TRUE.. BUT I'M TAKING A CLASSIC SUPERHERO POSE, CAPE & ALL... AND I THREATEN YOU, DON'T I?!
WELL, YES, I HAVE TO ADMIT... ULP...
YOUR COMBINATION OF BOYISH CUTENESS & HULKING PHYSIQUE REMIND ME OF EVERY CHILDHOOD BULLY WHO EVER SHOVED ME INTO TH' GIRL'S ROOM IN FIFTH GRADE..
AHA! IT ALWAYS COMES BACK TO BAD TOILET TRAINING, DOESN'T IT?!
GRIFFY
8.28

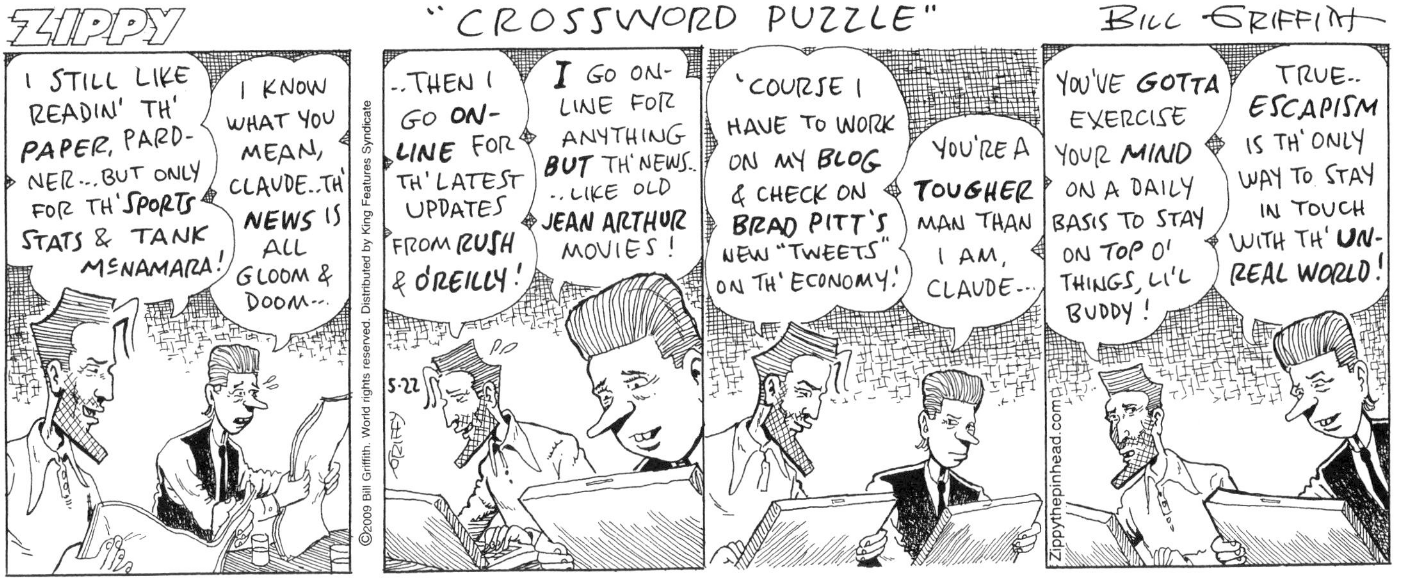

ZIPPY
"CROSSWORD PUZZLE"
BILL GRIFFITH
I STILL LIKE READIN' TH' PAPER, PARDNER... BUT ONLY FOR TH' SPORTS STATS & TANK McNAMARA!
I KNOW WHAT YOU MEAN, CLAUDE.. TH' NEWS IS ALL GLOOM & DOOM...
©2009 Bill Griffith. World rights reserved. Distributed by King Features Syndicate
..THEN I GO ON-LINE FOR TH' LATEST UPDATES FROM RUSH & O'REILLY!
I GO ON-LINE FOR ANYTHING BUT TH' NEWS.. ..LIKE OLD JEAN ARTHUR MOVIES!
5-22
'COURSE I HAVE TO WORK ON MY BLOG & CHECK ON BRAD PITT'S NEW "TWEETS" ON TH' ECONOMY!
YOU'RE A TOUGHER MAN THAN I AM, CLAUDE...
YOU'VE GOTTA EXERCISE YOUR MIND ON A DAILY BASIS TO STAY ON TOP O' THINGS, LI'L BUDDY!
TRUE.. ESCAPISM IS TH' ONLY WAY TO STAY IN TOUCH WITH TH' UNREAL WORLD!
Zippythepinhead.com

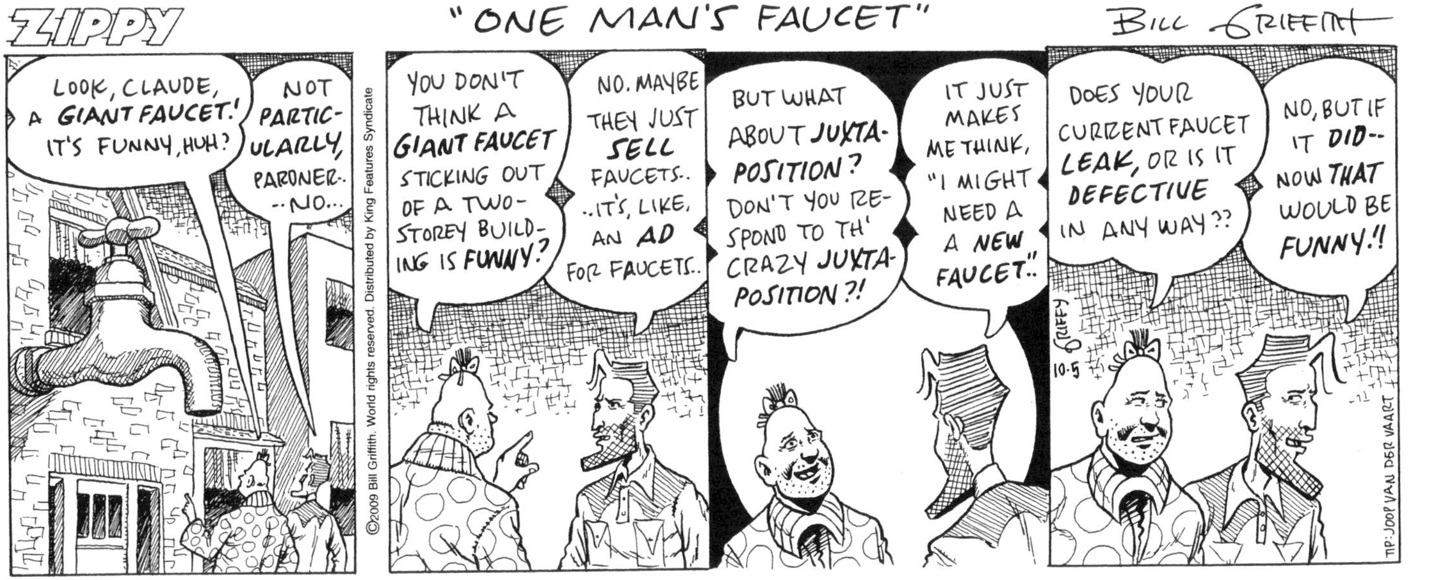

ZIPPY
"ONE MAN'S FAUCET"
BILL GRIFFITH
LOOK, CLAUDE, A GIANT FAUCET! IT'S FUNNY, HUH?
NOT PARTICULARLY, PARDNER.. ..NO...
©2009 Bill Griffith. World rights reserved. Distributed by King Features Syndicate
YOU DON'T THINK A GIANT FAUCET STICKING OUT OF A TWO-STOREY BUILDING IS FUNNY?
NO. MAYBE THEY JUST SELL FAUCETS.. ..IT'S, LIKE, AN AD FOR FAUCETS..
BUT WHAT ABOUT JUXTAPOSITION? DON'T YOU RESPOND TO TH' CRAZY JUXTAPOSITION?!
IT JUST MAKES ME THINK, "I MIGHT NEED A NEW FAUCET."
10-5
DOES YOUR CURRENT FAUCET LEAK, OR IS IT DEFECTIVE IN ANY WAY??
NO, BUT IF IT DID-- NOW THAT WOULD BE FUNNY!!
TIP: JOOP VAN DER VAART

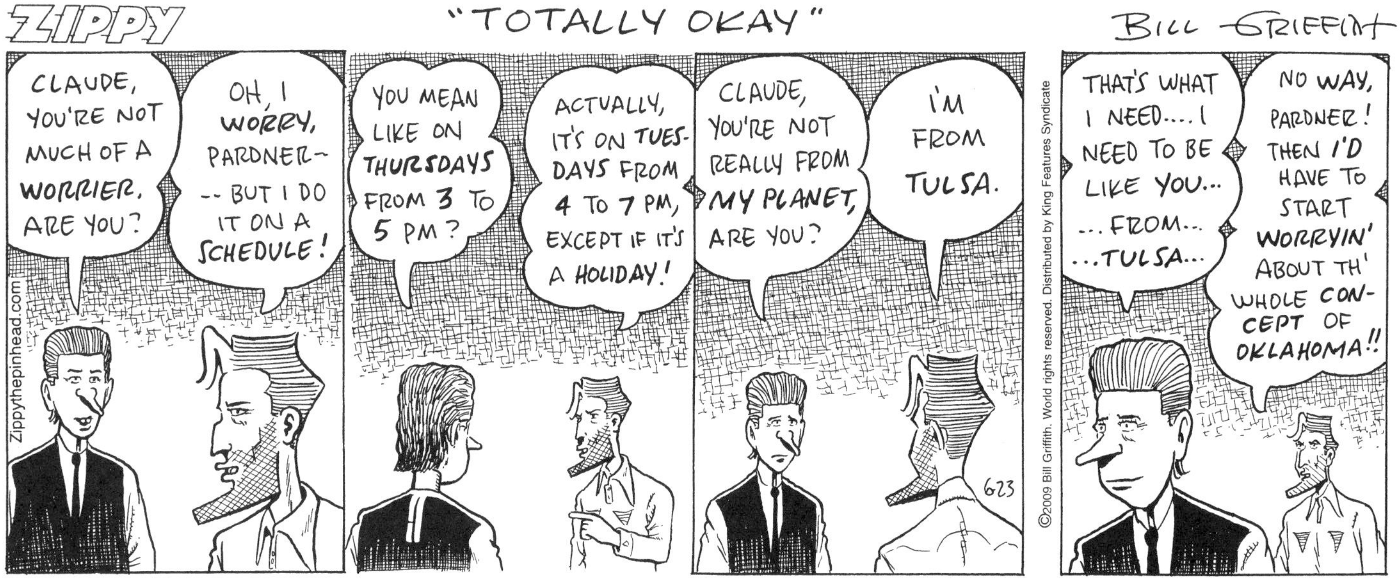
ZIPPY
"TOTALLY OKAY"
BILL GRIFFITH
CLAUDE, YOU'RE NOT MUCH OF A WORRIER, ARE YOU?
OH, I WORRY, PARDNER-- BUT I DO IT ON A SCHEDULE!
YOU MEAN LIKE ON THURSDAYS FROM 3 TO 5 PM?
ACTUALLY, IT'S ON TUESDAYS FROM 4 TO 7 PM, EXCEPT IF IT'S A HOLIDAY!
CLAUDE, YOU'RE NOT REALLY FROM MY PLANET, ARE YOU?
I'M FROM TULSA.
THAT'S WHAT I NEED.... I NEED TO BE LIKE YOU... ...FROM... ...TULSA...
NO WAY, PARDNER! THEN I'D HAVE TO START WORRYIN' ABOUT TH' WHOLE CONCEPT OF OKLAHOMA!!
Zippythepinhead.com
©2009 Bill Griffith. World rights reserved. Distributed by King Features Syndicate
6·23

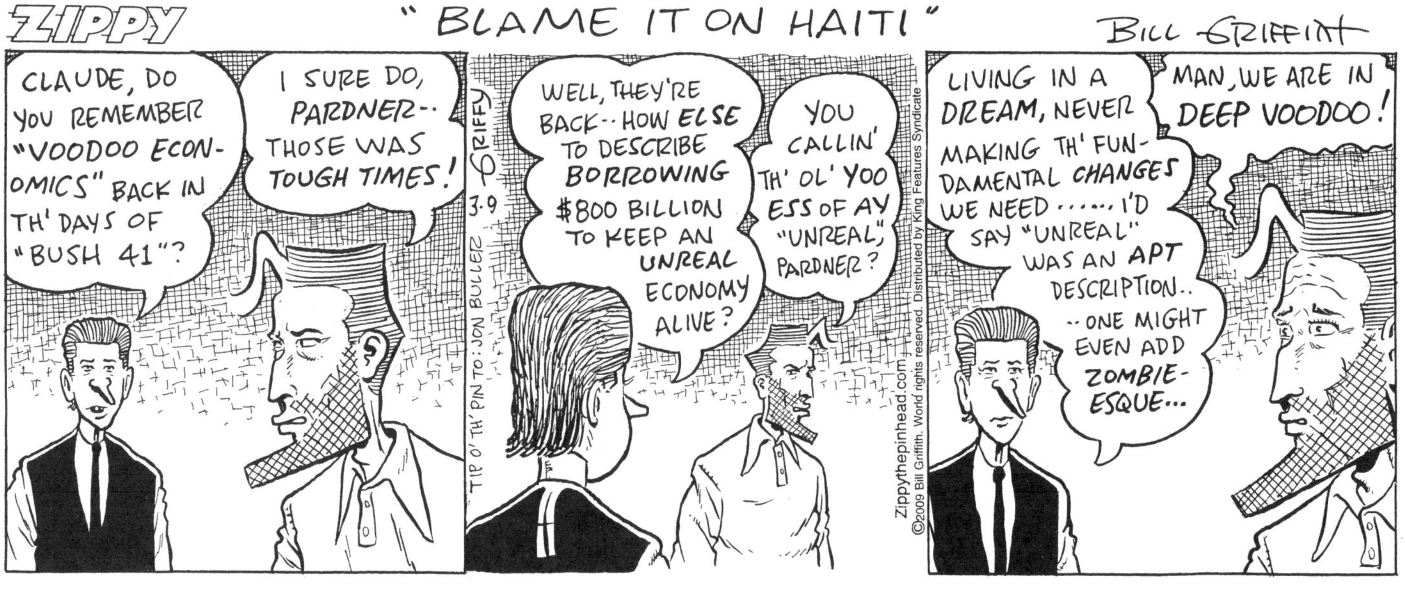
ZIPPY
"BLAME IT ON HAITI"
BILL GRIFFITH
CLAUDE, DO YOU REMEMBER "VOODOO ECONOMICS" BACK IN TH' DAYS OF "BUSH 41"?
I SURE DO, PARDNER-- THOSE WAS TOUGH TIMES!
GRIFFY 3·9
TIP O' TH' PIN TO: JON BULLER
WELL, THEY'RE BACK-- HOW ELSE TO DESCRIBE BORROWING $800 BILLION TO KEEP AN UNREAL ECONOMY ALIVE?
YOU CALLIN' TH' OL' YOO ESS OF AY "UNREAL," PARDNER?
LIVING IN A DREAM, NEVER MAKING TH' FUNDAMENTAL CHANGES WE NEED...... I'D SAY "UNREAL" WAS AN APT DESCRIPTION.. --ONE MIGHT EVEN ADD ZOMBIE-ESQUE...
MAN, WE ARE IN DEEP VOODOO!
Zippythepinhead.com
©2009 Bill Griffith. World rights reserved. Distributed by King Features Syndicate

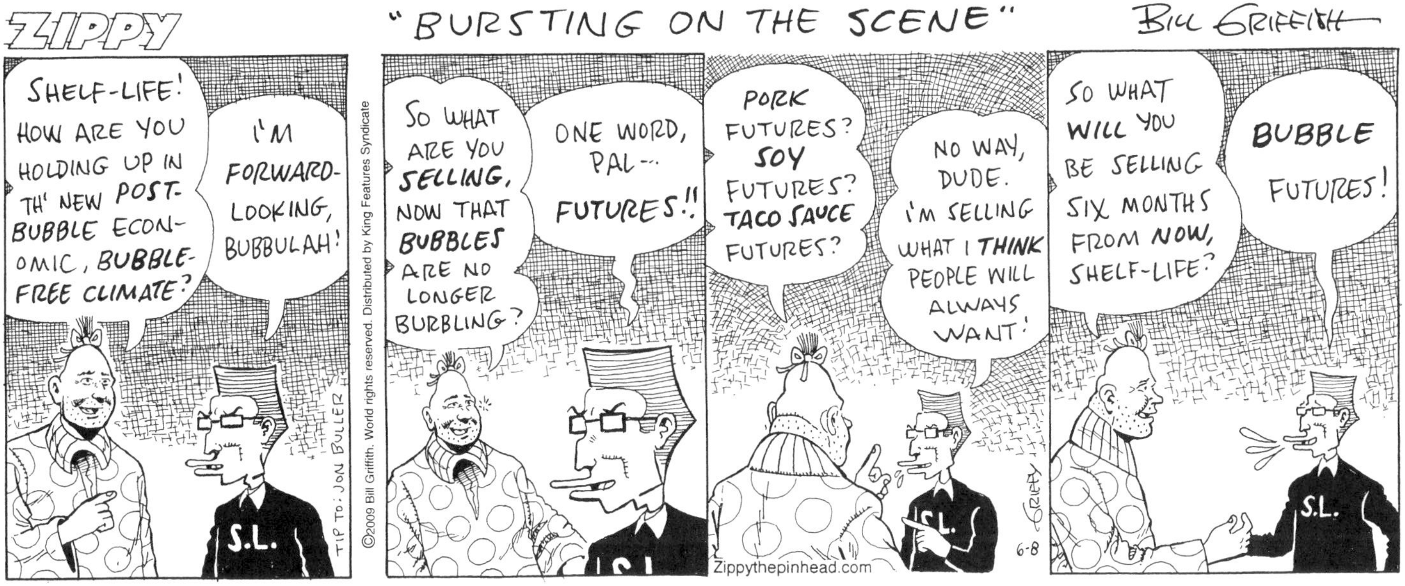
ZIPPY
"BURSTING ON THE SCENE"
BILL GRIFFITH
SHELF-LIFE! HOW ARE YOU HOLDING UP IN TH' NEW POST-BUBBLE ECONOMIC, BUBBLE-FREE CLIMATE?
I'M FORWARD-LOOKING, BUBBULAH!
S.L.
TIP TO: JON BULLER
©2009 Bill Griffith. World rights reserved. Distributed by King Features Syndicate
SO WHAT ARE YOU SELLING, NOW THAT BUBBLES ARE NO LONGER BURBLING?
ONE WORD, PAL-- FUTURES!!
PORK FUTURES? SOY FUTURES? TACO SAUCE FUTURES?
NO WAY, DUDE. I'M SELLING WHAT I THINK PEOPLE WILL ALWAYS WANT!
S.L.
GRIFFY
6-8
Zippythepinhead.com
SO WHAT WILL YOU BE SELLING SIX MONTHS FROM NOW, SHELF-LIFE?
BUBBLE FUTURES!
S.L.

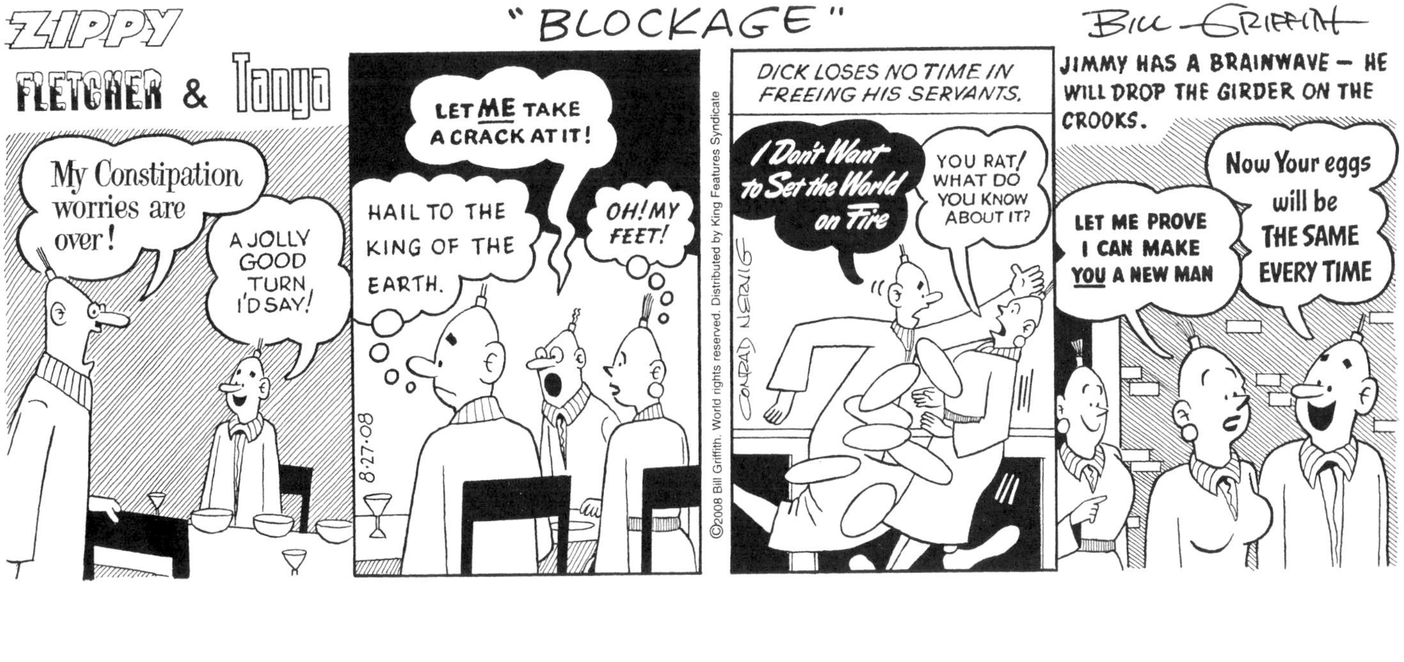
ZIPPY
"BLOCKAGE"
BILL GRIFFITH
FLETCHER & Tanya
My Constipation worries are over!
A JOLLY GOOD TURN I'D SAY!
LET ME TAKE A CRACK AT IT!
HAIL TO THE KING OF THE EARTH.
OH! MY FEET!
8-27-08
©2008 Bill Griffith. World rights reserved. Distributed by King Features Syndicate
DICK LOSES NO TIME IN FREEING HIS SERVANTS.
I Don't Want to Set the World on Fire
YOU RAT! WHAT DO YOU KNOW ABOUT IT?
CONRAD NERVIG
JIMMY HAS A BRAINWAVE — HE WILL DROP THE GIRDER ON THE CROOKS.
LET ME PROVE I CAN MAKE YOU A NEW MAN
Now Your eggs will be THE SAME EVERY TIME

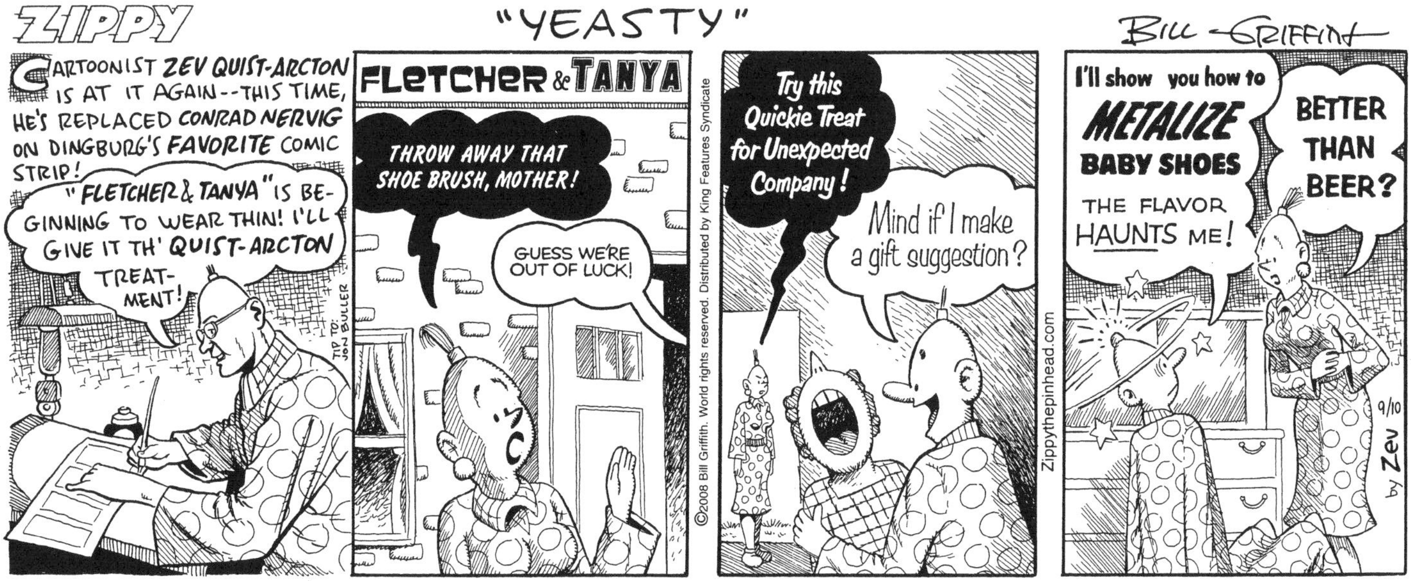
ZIPPY
"YEASTY"
BILL GRIFFITH
CARTOONIST ZEV QUIST-ARCTON IS AT IT AGAIN--THIS TIME, HE'S REPLACED CONRAD NERVIG ON DINGBURG'S FAVORITE COMIC STRIP!
"FLETCHER & TANYA" IS BEGINNING TO WEAR THIN! I'LL GIVE IT TH' QUIST-ARCTON TREATMENT!
TIP TO: JON BULLER
FLETCHER & TANYA
THROW AWAY THAT SHOE BRUSH, MOTHER!
GUESS WE'RE OUT OF LUCK!
©2008 Bill Griffith. World rights reserved. Distributed by King Features Syndicate
Try this Quickie Treat for Unexpected Company!
Mind if I make a gift suggestion?
Zippythepinhead.com
I'll show you how to METALIZE BABY SHOES
THE FLAVOR HAUNTS ME!
BETTER THAN BEER?
9/10
by Zev

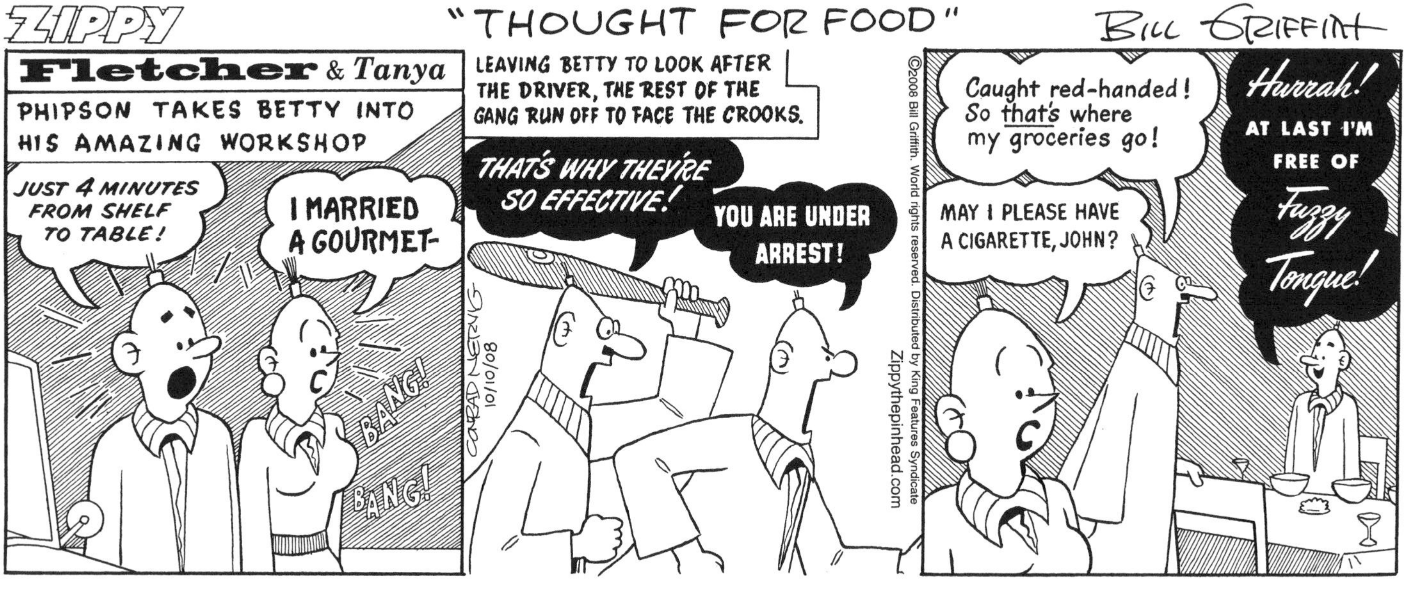
ZIPPY
"THOUGHT FOR FOOD"
BILL GRIFFITH
Fletcher & Tanya
PHIPSON TAKES BETTY INTO HIS AMAZING WORKSHOP
JUST 4 MINUTES FROM SHELF TO TABLE!
I MARRIED A GOURMET-
BANG!
BANG!
CONRAD NERVIG 10/10/08
LEAVING BETTY TO LOOK AFTER THE DRIVER, THE REST OF THE GANG RUN OFF TO FACE THE CROOKS.
THAT'S WHY THEY'RE SO EFFECTIVE!
YOU ARE UNDER ARREST!
©2008 Bill Griffith. World rights reserved. Distributed by King Features Syndicate
Zippythepinhead.com
Caught red-handed! So that's where my groceries go!
MAY I PLEASE HAVE A CIGARETTE, JOHN?
Hurrah! AT LAST I'M FREE OF Fuzzy Tongue!

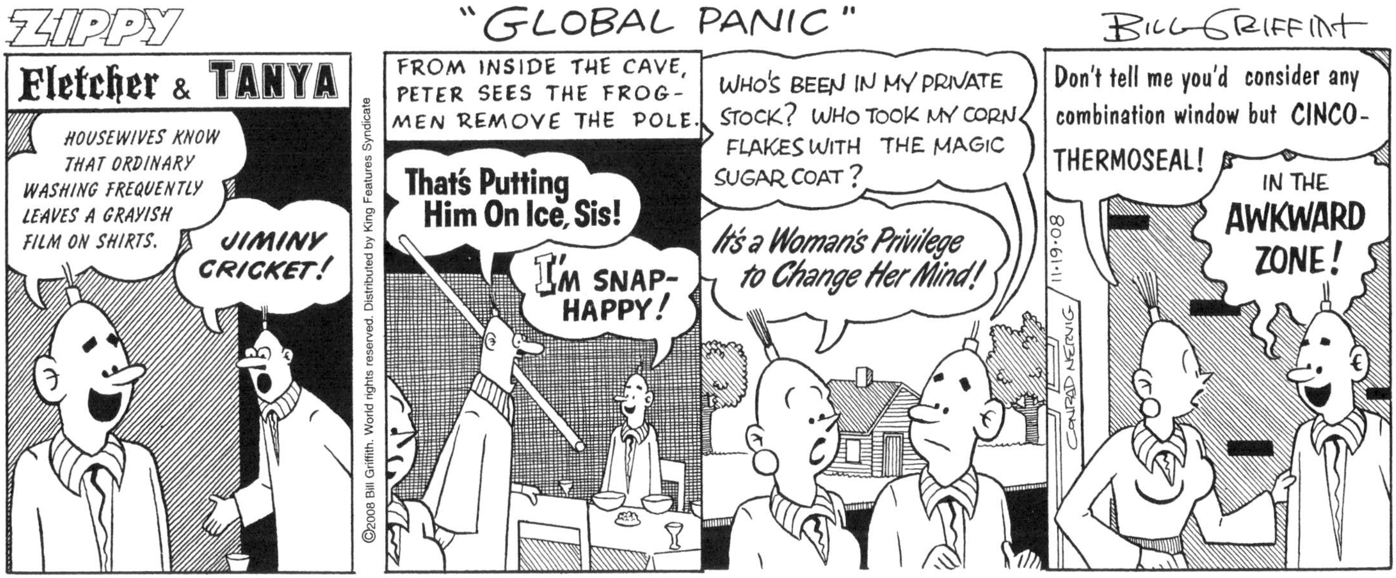
ZIPPY
"GLOBAL PANIC"
BILL GRIFFITH
Fletcher & TANYA
HOUSEWIVES KNOW THAT ORDINARY WASHING FREQUENTLY LEAVES A GRAYISH FILM ON SHIRTS.
JIMINY CRICKET!
©2008 Bill Griffith. World rights reserved. Distributed by King Features Syndicate
FROM INSIDE THE CAVE, PETER SEES THE FROG-MEN REMOVE THE POLE.
That's Putting Him On Ice, Sis!
I'M SNAP-HAPPY!
WHO'S BEEN IN MY PRIVATE STOCK? WHO TOOK MY CORN FLAKES WITH THE MAGIC SUGAR COAT?
It's a Woman's Privilege to Change Her Mind!
11-19-08
CONRAD NERVIG
Don't tell me you'd consider any combination window but CINCO-THERMOSEAL!
IN THE AWKWARD ZONE!

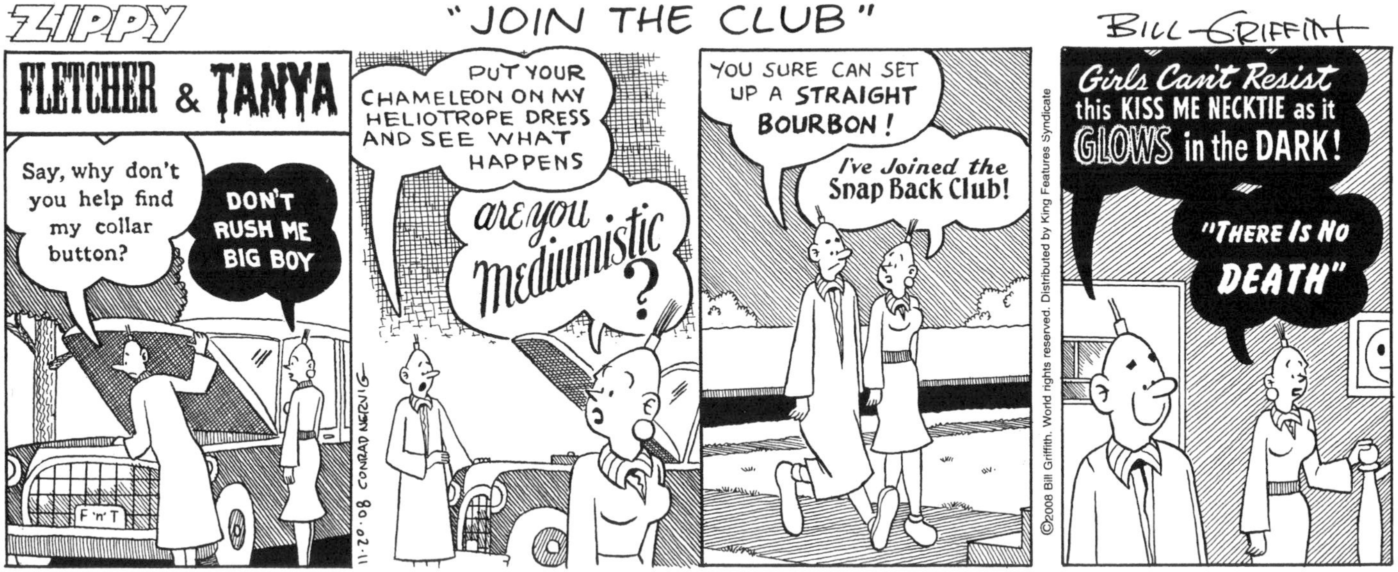
ZIPPY
"JOIN THE CLUB"
BILL GRIFFITH
FLETCHER & TANYA
Say, why don't you help find my collar button?
DON'T RUSH ME BIG BOY
F'n'T
11-20-08
CONRAD NERVIG
PUT YOUR CHAMELEON ON MY HELIOTROPE DRESS AND SEE WHAT HAPPENS
are you mediumistic?
YOU SURE CAN SET UP A STRAIGHT BOURBON!
I've Joined the Snap Back Club!
©2008 Bill Griffith. World rights reserved. Distributed by King Features Syndicate
Girls Can't Resist this KISS ME NECKTIE as it GLOWS in the DARK!
"THERE IS NO DEATH"

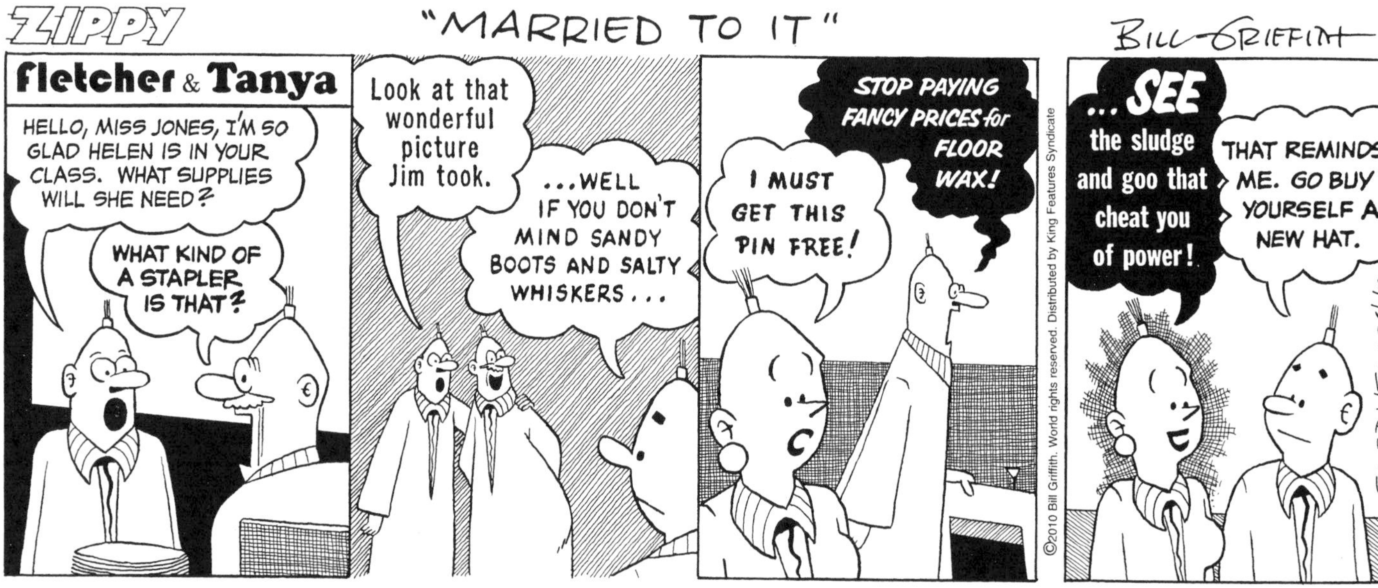
ZIPPY
"MARRIED TO IT"
BILL GRIFFITH
Fletcher & Tanya
HELLO, MISS JONES, I'M SO GLAD HELEN IS IN YOUR CLASS. WHAT SUPPLIES WILL SHE NEED?
WHAT KIND OF A STAPLER IS THAT?
Look at that wonderful picture Jim took.
...WELL IF YOU DON'T MIND SANDY BOOTS AND SALTY WHISKERS...
STOP PAYING FANCY PRICES for FLOOR WAX!
I MUST GET THIS PIN FREE!
©2010 Bill Griffith. World rights reserved. Distributed by King Features Syndicate
...SEE the sludge and goo that cheat you of power!
THAT REMINDS ME. GO BUY YOURSELF A NEW HAT.
CONRAD NERVIG 6/1/10

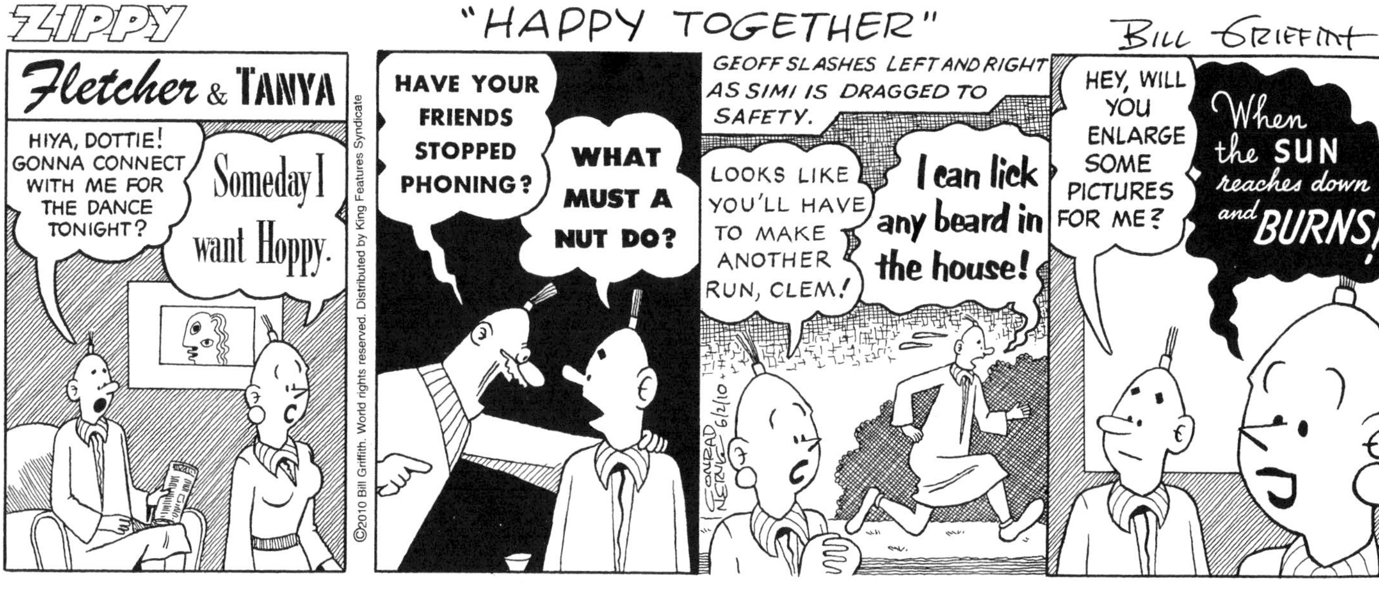
ZIPPY
"HAPPY TOGETHER"
BILL GRIFFITH
Fletcher & TANYA
HIYA, DOTTIE! GONNA CONNECT WITH ME FOR THE DANCE TONIGHT?
Someday I want Hoppy.
©2010 Bill Griffith. World rights reserved. Distributed by King Features Syndicate
HAVE YOUR FRIENDS STOPPED PHONING?
WHAT MUST A NUT DO?
GEOFF SLASHES LEFT AND RIGHT AS SIMI IS DRAGGED TO SAFETY.
LOOKS LIKE YOU'LL HAVE TO MAKE ANOTHER RUN, CLEM!
I can lick any beard in the house!
CONRAD NERVIG 6/2/10
HEY, WILL YOU ENLARGE SOME PICTURES FOR ME?
When the SUN reaches down and BURNS!

ZIPPY "THE FLETCHERNESS OF THE TANYATUDE" BILL GRIFFITH

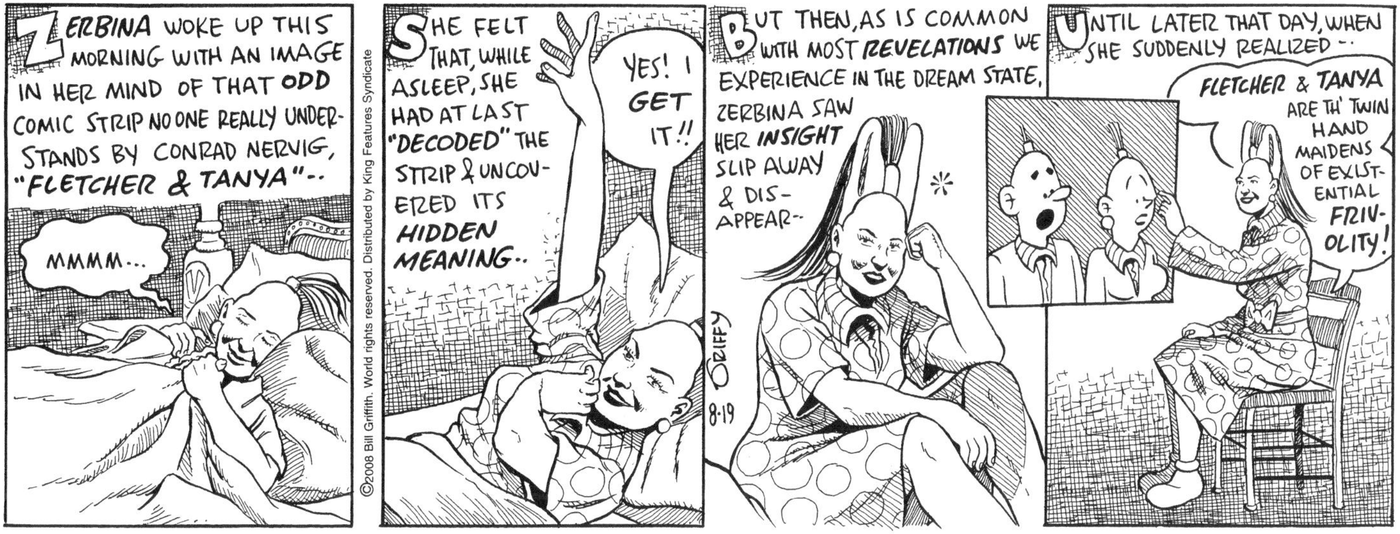
ZERBINA WOKE UP THIS MORNING WITH AN IMAGE IN HER MIND OF THAT ODD COMIC STRIP NO ONE REALLY UNDERSTANDS BY CONRAD NERVIG, "FLETCHER & TANYA"--
MMMM...
SHE FELT THAT, WHILE ASLEEP, SHE HAD AT LAST "DECODED" THE STRIP & UNCOVERED ITS HIDDEN MEANING..
YES! I GET IT!!
GRIFFY 8-19
BUT THEN, AS IS COMMON WITH MOST REVELATIONS WE EXPERIENCE IN THE DREAM STATE, ZERBINA SAW HER INSIGHT SLIP AWAY & DISAPPEAR--
UNTIL LATER THAT DAY, WHEN SHE SUDDENLY REALIZED--
FLETCHER & TANYA ARE TH' TWIN HAND MAIDENS OF EXISTENTIAL FRIVOLITY!

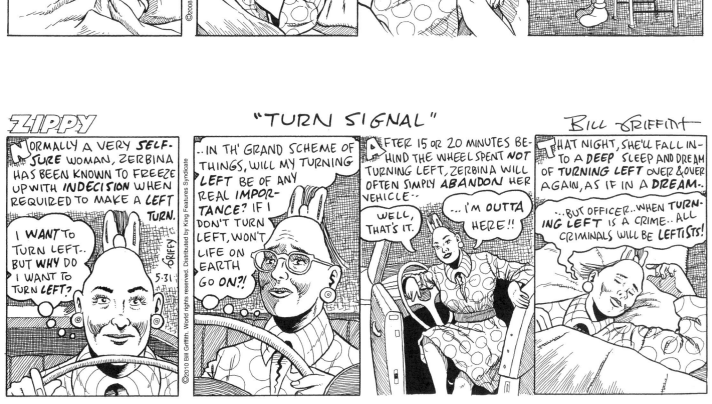

ZIPPY "TURN SIGNAL" BILL GRIFFITH

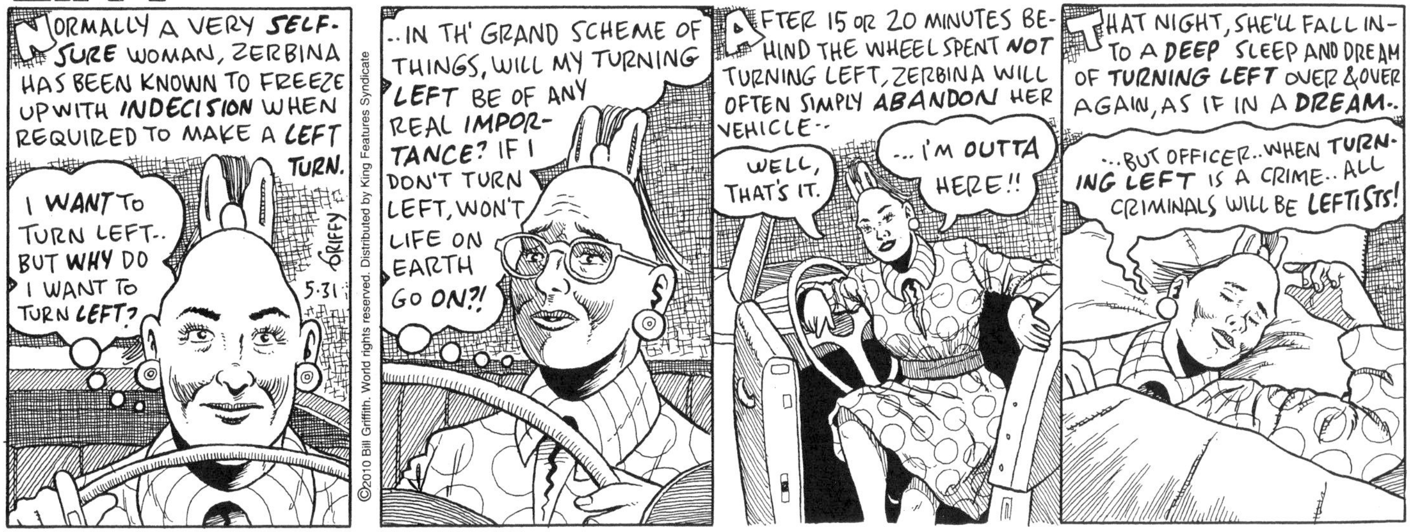
NORMALLY A VERY SELF-SURE WOMAN, ZERBINA HAS BEEN KNOWN TO FREEZE UP WITH INDECISION WHEN REQUIRED TO MAKE A LEFT TURN.
I WANT TO TURN LEFT-.. BUT WHY DO I WANT TO TURN LEFT?
GRIFFY 5-31
..IN TH' GRAND SCHEME OF THINGS, WILL MY TURNING LEFT BE OF ANY REAL IMPORTANCE? IF I DON'T TURN LEFT, WON'T LIFE ON EARTH GO ON?!
AFTER 15 OR 20 MINUTES BEHIND THE WHEEL SPENT NOT TURNING LEFT, ZERBINA WILL OFTEN SIMPLY ABANDON HER VEHICLE--
WELL, THAT'S IT.
...I'M OUTTA HERE!!
THAT NIGHT, SHE'LL FALL INTO A DEEP SLEEP AND DREAM OF TURNING LEFT OVER & OVER AGAIN, AS IF IN A DREAM..
...BUT OFFICER.. WHEN TURNING LEFT IS A CRIME.. ALL CRIMINALS WILL BE LEFTISTS!

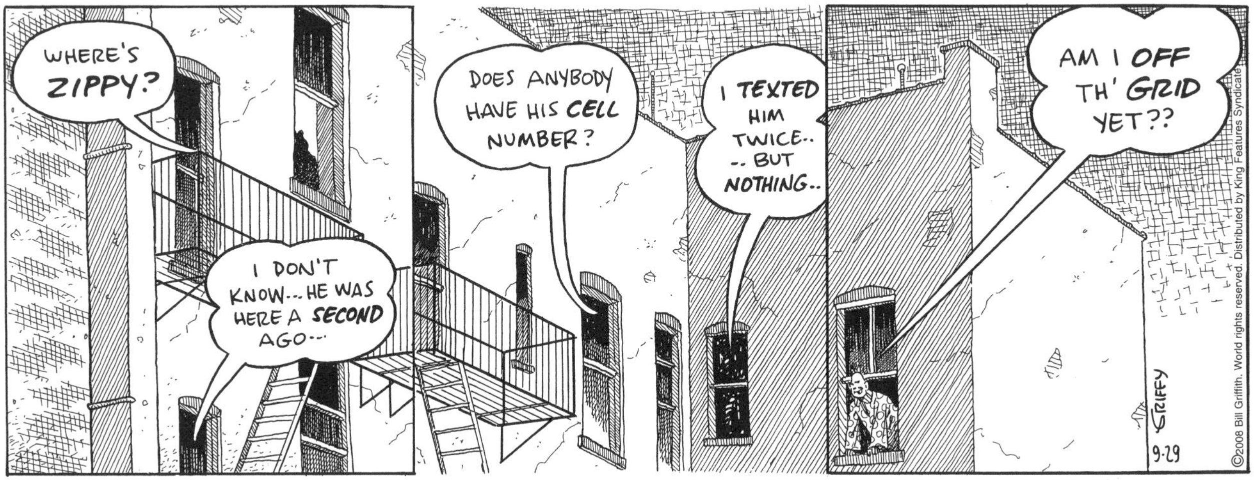
WHERE'S ZIPPY?
I DON'T KNOW-- HE WAS HERE A SECOND AGO--
DOES ANYBODY HAVE HIS CELL NUMBER?
I TEXTED HIM TWICE.. -- BUT NOTHING..
AM I OFF TH' GRID YET??
GRIFFY
9·29
©2008 Bill Griffith. World rights reserved. Distributed by King Features Syndicate

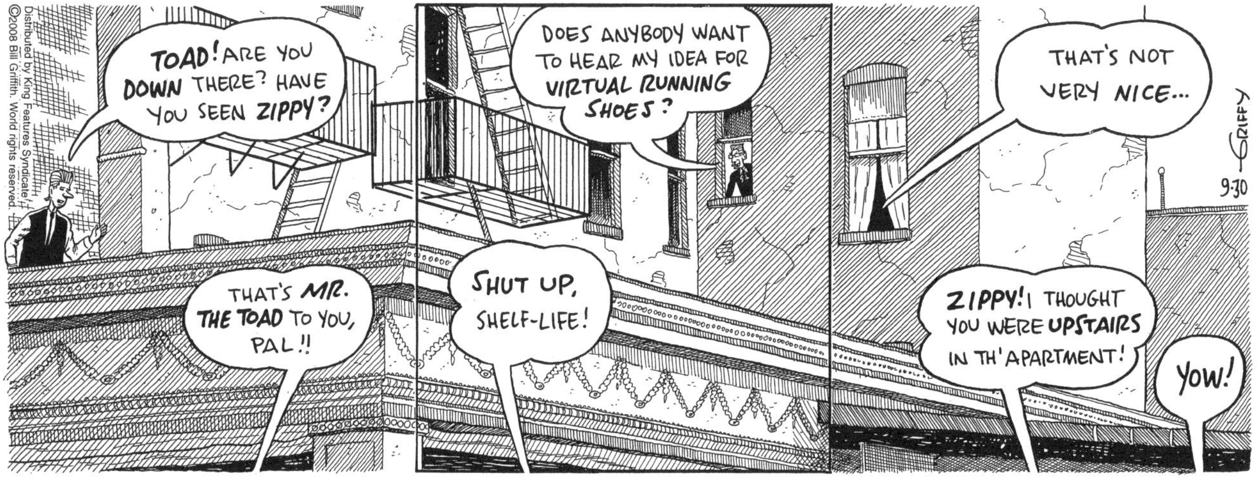
©2008 Bill Griffith. World rights reserved. Distributed by King Features Syndicate
TOAD! ARE YOU DOWN THERE? HAVE YOU SEEN ZIPPY?
THAT'S MR. THE TOAD TO YOU, PAL!!
DOES ANYBODY WANT TO HEAR MY IDEA FOR VIRTUAL RUNNING SHOES?
SHUT UP, SHELF-LIFE!
THAT'S NOT VERY NICE...
GRIFFY
9·30
ZIPPY! I THOUGHT YOU WERE UPSTAIRS IN TH' APARTMENT!
YOW!

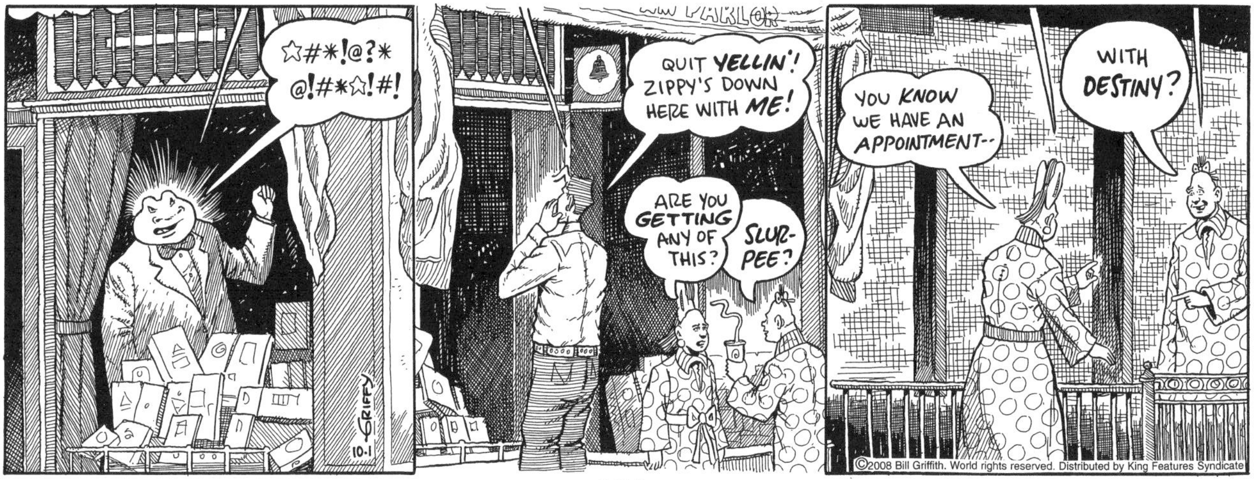
☆#✱!@?✱ @!#✱☆!#!
GRIFFY
10·1
PARLOR
QUIT YELLIN'! ZIPPY'S DOWN HERE WITH ME!
ARE YOU GETTING ANY OF THIS?
SLURPEE?
YOU KNOW WE HAVE AN APPOINTMENT--
WITH DESTINY?
©2008 Bill Griffith. World rights reserved. Distributed by King Features Syndicate

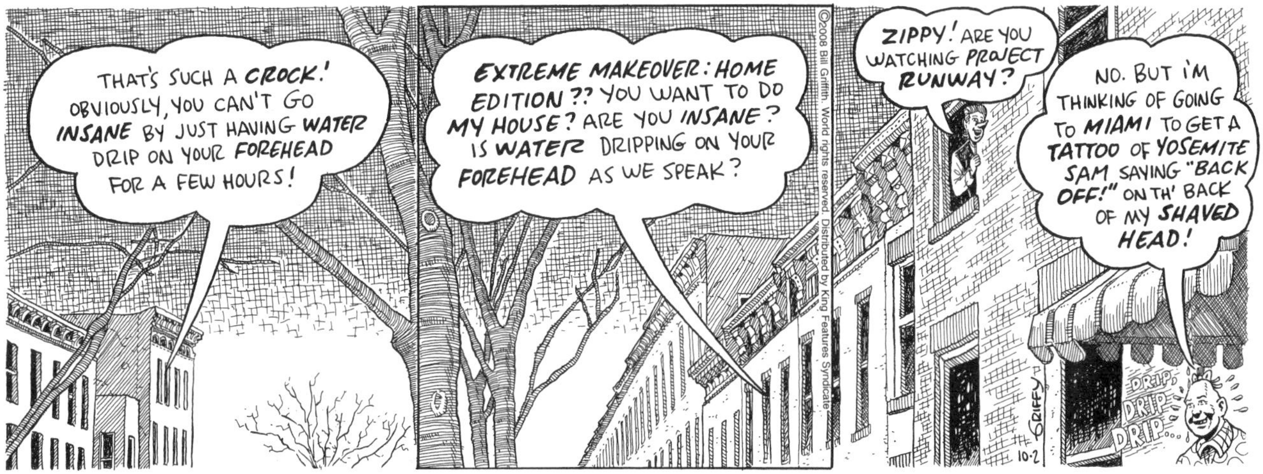
THAT'S SUCH A CROCK! OBVIOUSLY, YOU CAN'T GO INSANE BY JUST HAVING WATER DRIP ON YOUR FOREHEAD FOR A FEW HOURS!
EXTREME MAKEOVER: HOME EDITION?? YOU WANT TO DO MY HOUSE? ARE YOU INSANE? IS WATER DRIPPING ON YOUR FOREHEAD AS WE SPEAK?
©2008 Bill Griffith. World rights reserved. Distributed by King Features Syndicate
ZIPPY! ARE YOU WATCHING PROJECT RUNWAY?
NO. BUT I'M THINKING OF GOING TO MIAMI TO GET A TATTOO OF YOSEMITE SAM SAYING "BACK OFF!" ON TH' BACK OF MY SHAVED HEAD!
DRIP, DRIP, DRIP...
GRIFFY
10·2

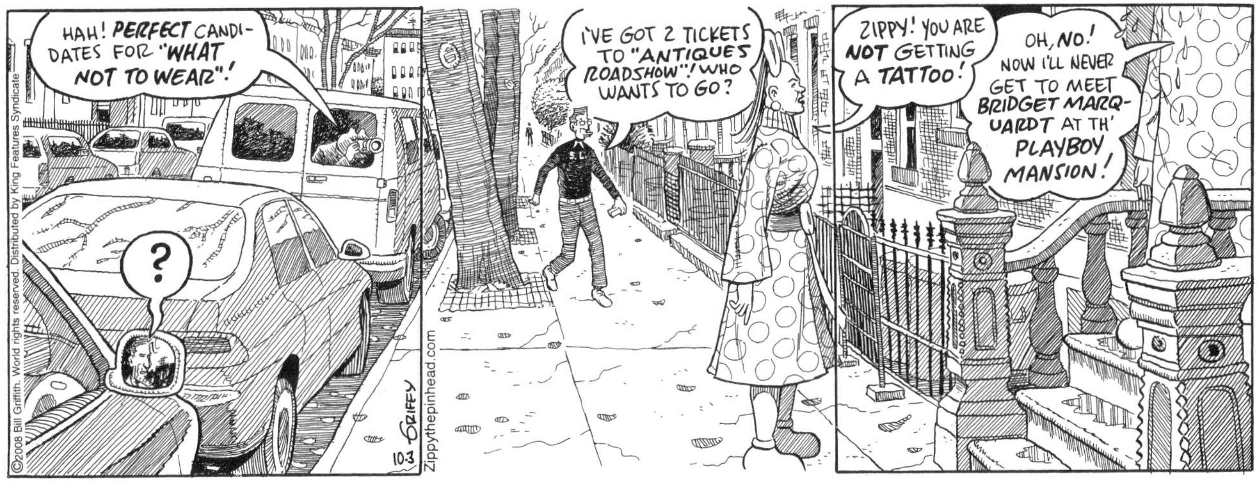
HAH! PERFECT CANDIDATES FOR "WHAT NOT TO WEAR"!
?
©2008 Bill Griffith. World rights reserved. Distributed by King Features Syndicate
GRIFFY
10·3
Zippythepinhead.com
I'VE GOT 2 TICKETS TO "ANTIQUES ROADSHOW"! WHO WANTS TO GO?
ZIPPY! YOU ARE NOT GETTING A TATTOO!
OH, NO! NOW I'LL NEVER GET TO MEET BRIDGET MARQUARDT AT TH' PLAYBOY MANSION!

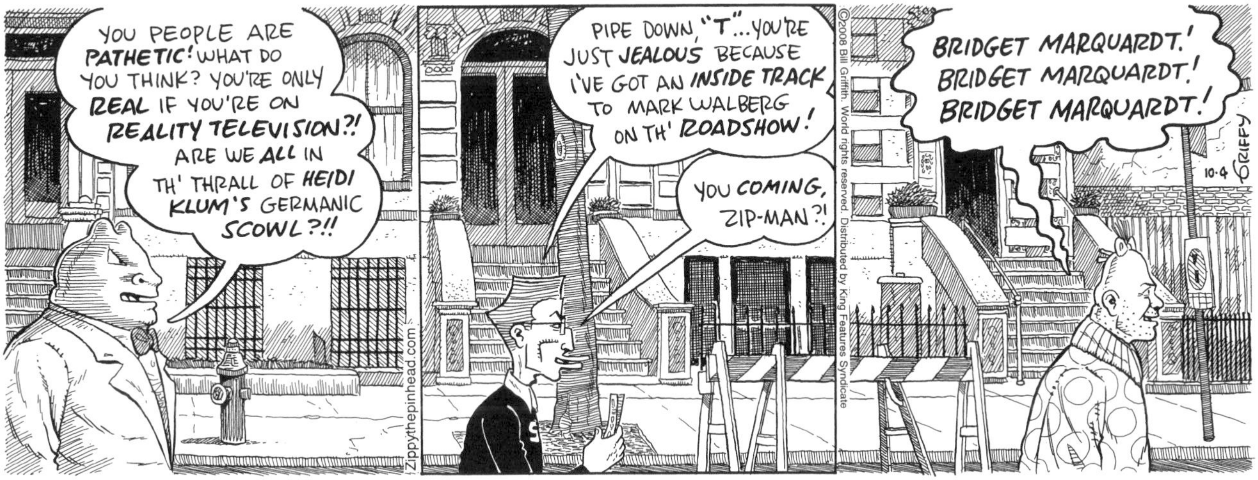
YOU PEOPLE ARE PATHETIC! WHAT DO YOU THINK? YOU'RE ONLY REAL IF YOU'RE ON REALITY TELEVISION?! ARE WE ALL IN TH' THRALL OF HEIDI KLUM'S GERMANIC SCOWL?!!
Zippythepinhead.com
PIPE DOWN, "T"... YOU'RE JUST JEALOUS BECAUSE I'VE GOT AN INSIDE TRACK TO MARK WALBERG ON TH' ROADSHOW!
YOU COMING, ZIP-MAN?!
©2008 Bill Griffith. World rights reserved. Distributed by King Features Syndicate
BRIDGET MARQUARDT! BRIDGET MARQUARDT! BRIDGET MARQUARDT!
GRIFFY
10·4

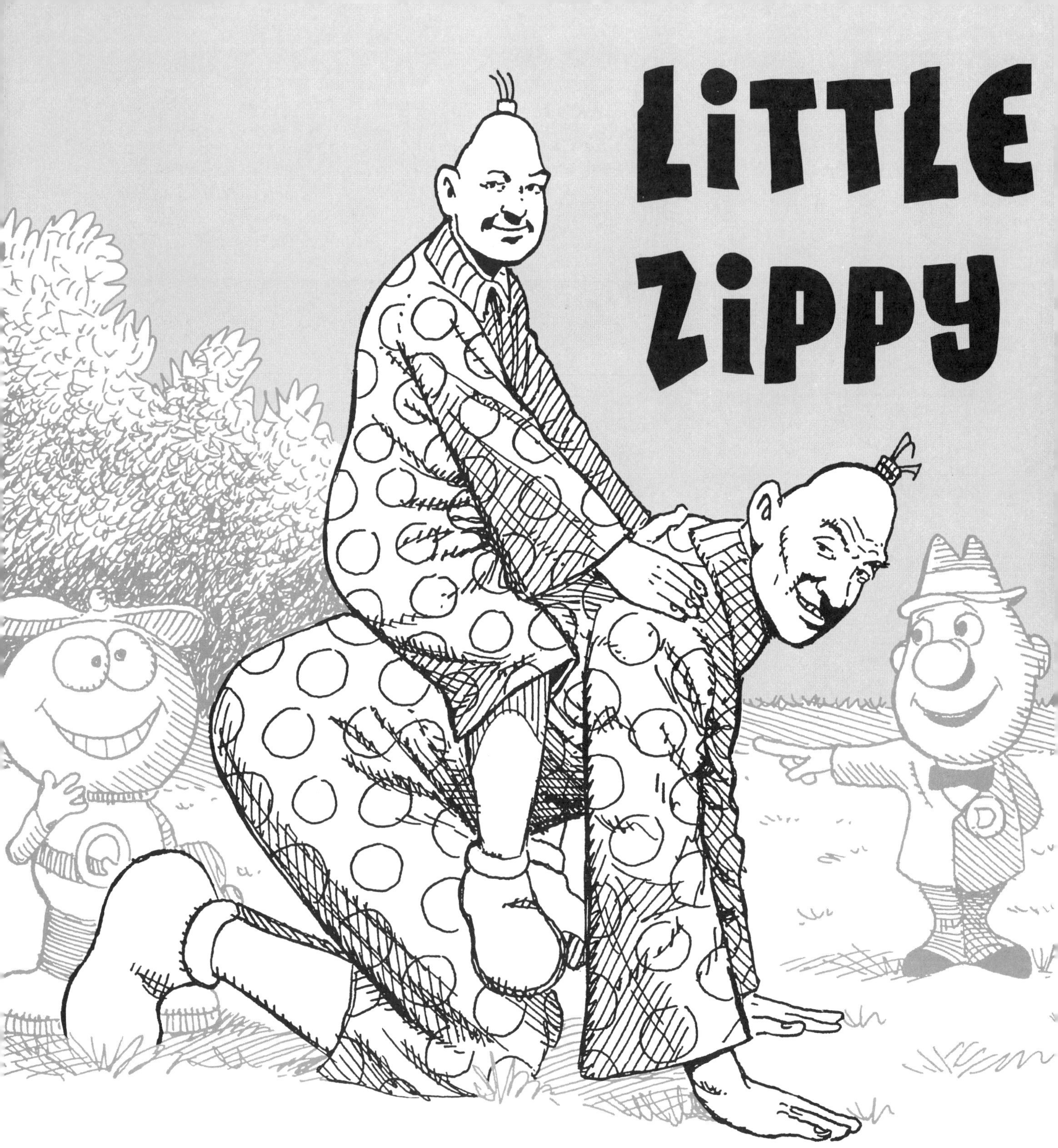
LITTLE
ZIPPY

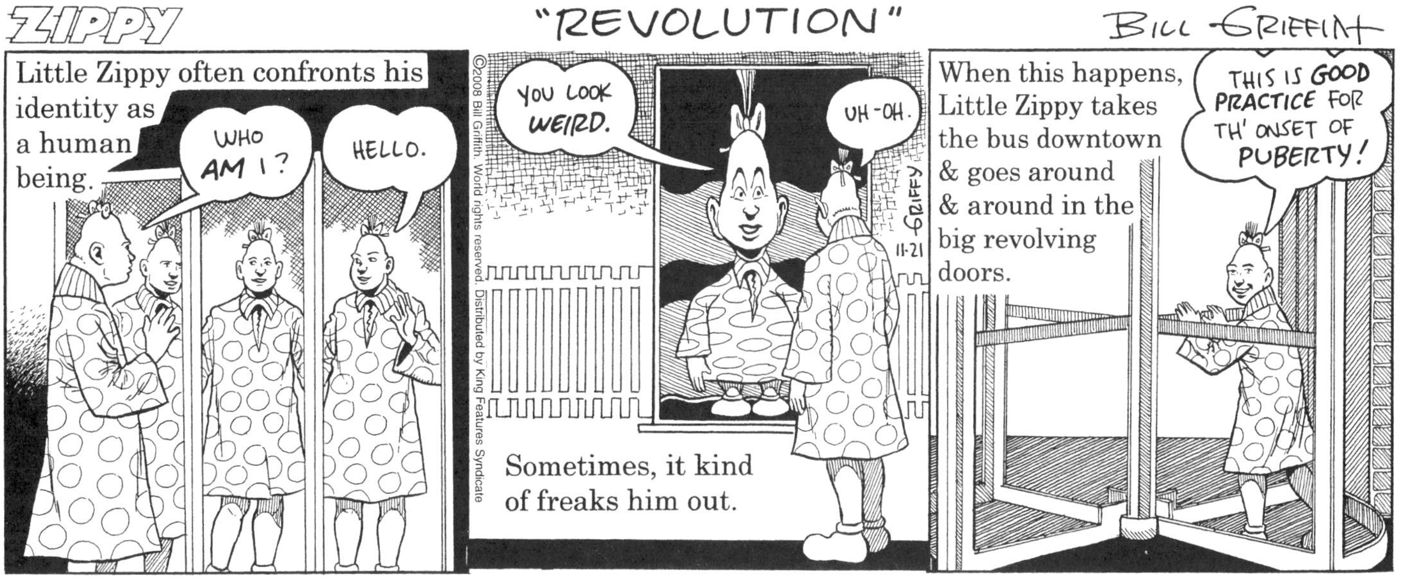
ZIPPY
"REVOLUTION"
BILL GRIFFITH
Little Zippy often confronts his identity as a human being.
WHO AM I?
HELLO.
©2008 Bill Griffith. World rights reserved. Distributed by King Features Syndicate
YOU LOOK WEIRD.
UH-OH.
GRIFFY 11-21
Sometimes, it kind of freaks him out.
When this happens, Little Zippy takes the bus downtown & goes around & around in the big revolving doors.
THIS IS GOOD PRACTICE FOR TH' ONSET OF PUBERTY!

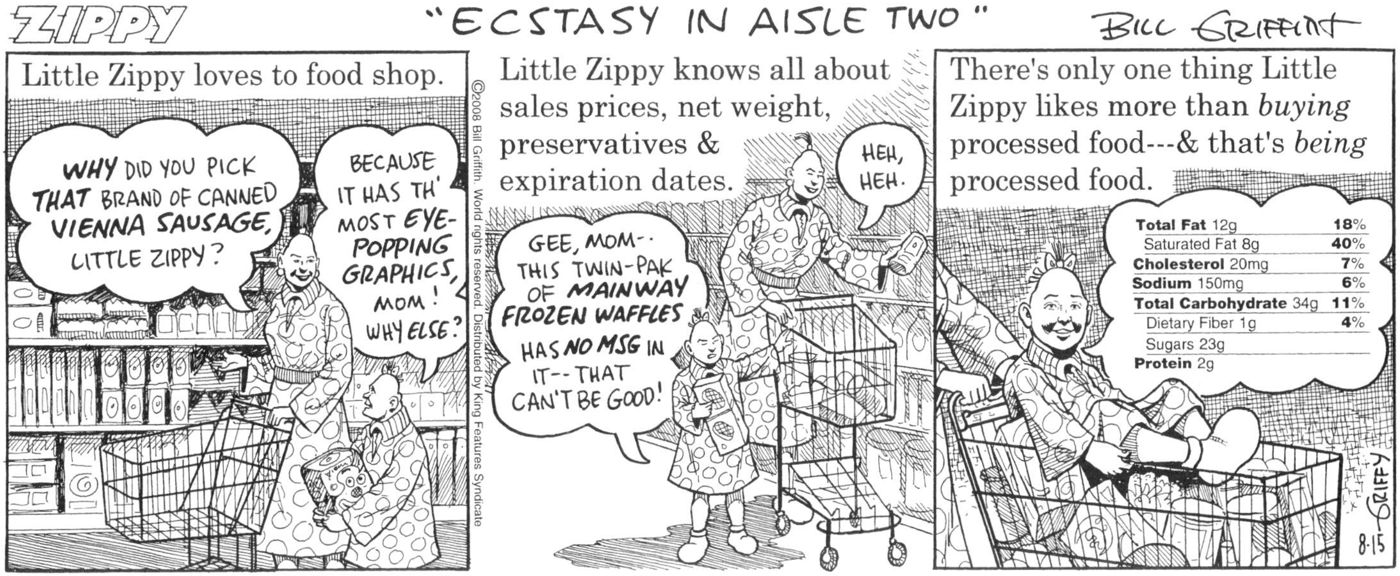
ZIPPY
"ECSTASY IN AISLE TWO"
BILL GRIFFITH
Little Zippy loves to food shop.
WHY DID YOU PICK THAT BRAND OF CANNED VIENNA SAUSAGE, LITTLE ZIPPY?
BECAUSE IT HAS TH' MOST EYE-POPPING GRAPHICS, MOM! WHY ELSE?
©2008 Bill Griffith. World rights reserved. Distributed by King Features Syndicate
Little Zippy knows all about sales prices, net weight, preservatives & expiration dates.
HEH, HEH.
GEE, MOM-- THIS TWIN-PAK OF MAINWAY FROZEN WAFFLES HAS NO MSG IN IT--THAT CAN'T BE GOOD!
There's only one thing Little Zippy likes more than buying processed food---& that's being processed food.
Total Fat 12g 18%
Saturated Fat 8g 40%
Cholesterol 20mg 7%
Sodium 150mg 6%
Total Carbohydrate 34g 11%
Dietary Fiber 1g 4%
Sugars 23g
Protein 2g
GRIFFY 8-15

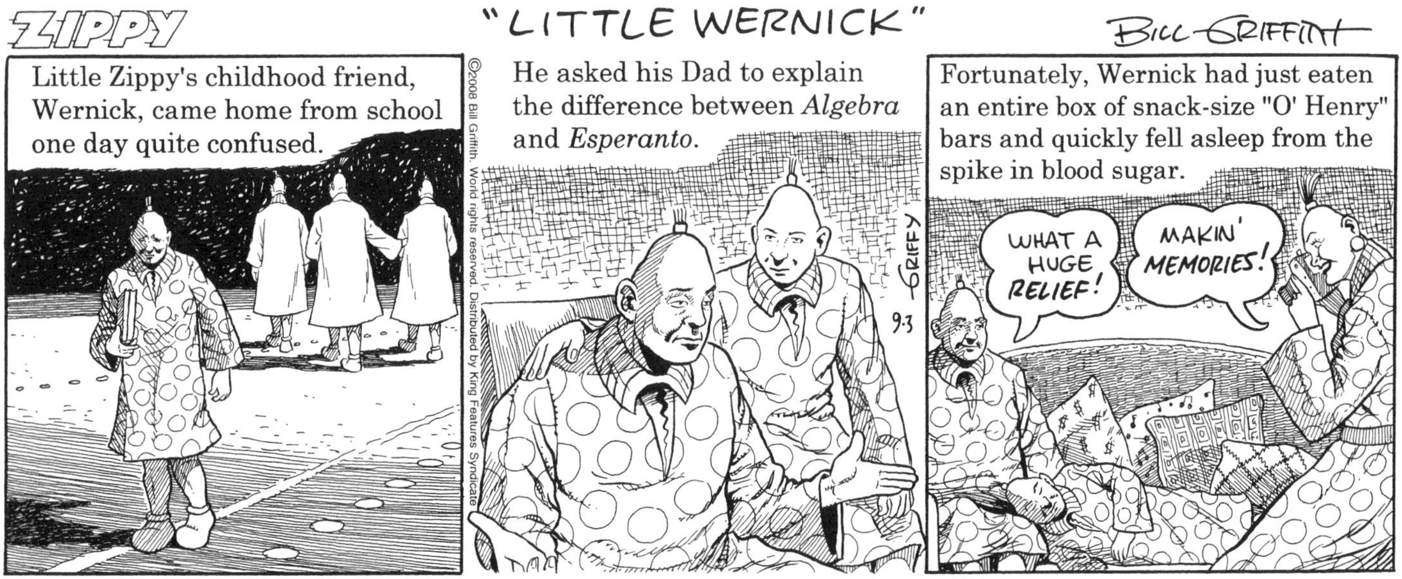
ZIPPY
"LITTLE WERNICK"
BILL GRIFFITH
Little Zippy's childhood friend, Wernick, came home from school one day quite confused.
©2008 Bill Griffith. World rights reserved. Distributed by King Features Syndicate
He asked his Dad to explain the difference between *Algebra* and *Esperanto*.
GRIFFY
9·3
Fortunately, Wernick had just eaten an entire box of snack-size "O' Henry" bars and quickly fell asleep from the spike in blood sugar.
WHAT A HUGE, **RELIEF**!
MAKIN' **MEMORIES**!

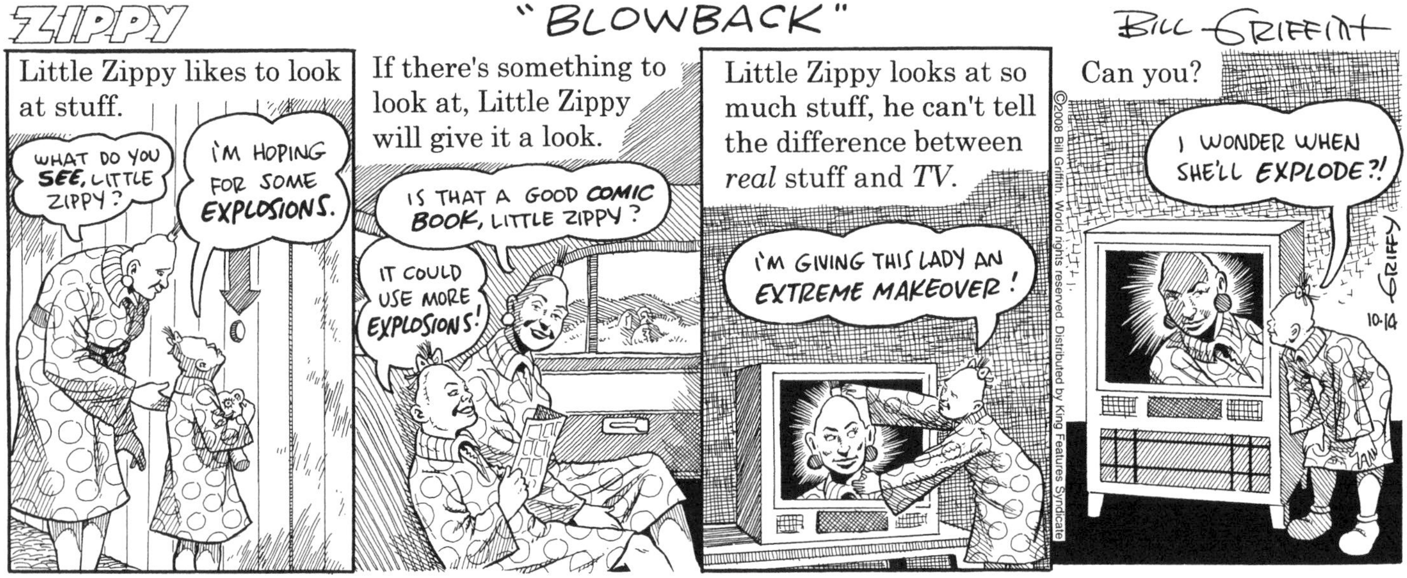
ZIPPY
"BLOWBACK"
BILL GRIFFITH
Little Zippy likes to look at stuff.
WHAT DO YOU **SEE**, LITTLE ZIPPY?
I'M HOPING FOR SOME **EXPLOSIONS**.
If there's something to look at, Little Zippy will give it a look.
IS THAT A GOOD **COMIC BOOK**, LITTLE ZIPPY?
IT COULD USE MORE **EXPLOSIONS**!
Little Zippy looks at so much stuff, he can't tell the difference between *real* stuff and *TV*.
I'M GIVING THIS LADY AN **EXTREME MAKEOVER**!
©2008 Bill Griffith. World rights reserved. Distributed by King Features Syndicate
Can you?
I WONDER WHEN SHE'LL **EXPLODE**?!
GRIFFY
10·14

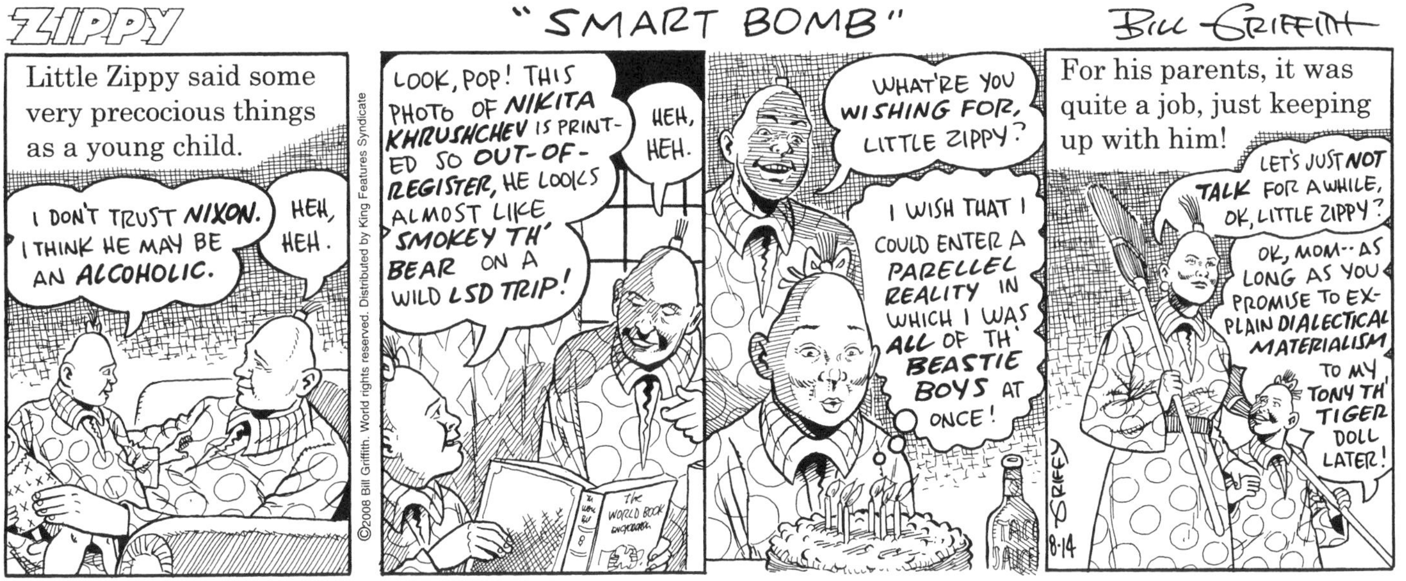
ZIPPY
"SMART BOMB"
BILL GRIFFITH
Little Zippy said some very precocious things as a young child.
I DON'T TRUST NIXON. I THINK HE MAY BE AN ALCOHOLIC.
HEH, HEH.
©2008 Bill Griffith. World rights reserved. Distributed by King Features Syndicate
LOOK, POP! THIS PHOTO OF NIKITA KHRUSHCHEV IS PRINTED SO OUT-OF-REGISTER, HE LOOKS ALMOST LIKE SMOKEY TH' BEAR ON A WILD LSD TRIP!
HEH, HEH.
WHAT'RE YOU WISHING FOR, LITTLE ZIPPY?
I WISH THAT I COULD ENTER A PARELLEL REALITY IN WHICH I WAS ALL OF TH' BEASTIE BOYS AT ONCE!
GRIFFY 8·14
For his parents, it was quite a job, just keeping up with him!
LET'S JUST NOT TALK FOR A WHILE, OK, LITTLE ZIPPY?
OK, MOM-- AS LONG AS YOU PROMISE TO EXPLAIN DIALECTICAL MATERIALISM TO MY TONY TH' TIGER DOLL LATER!

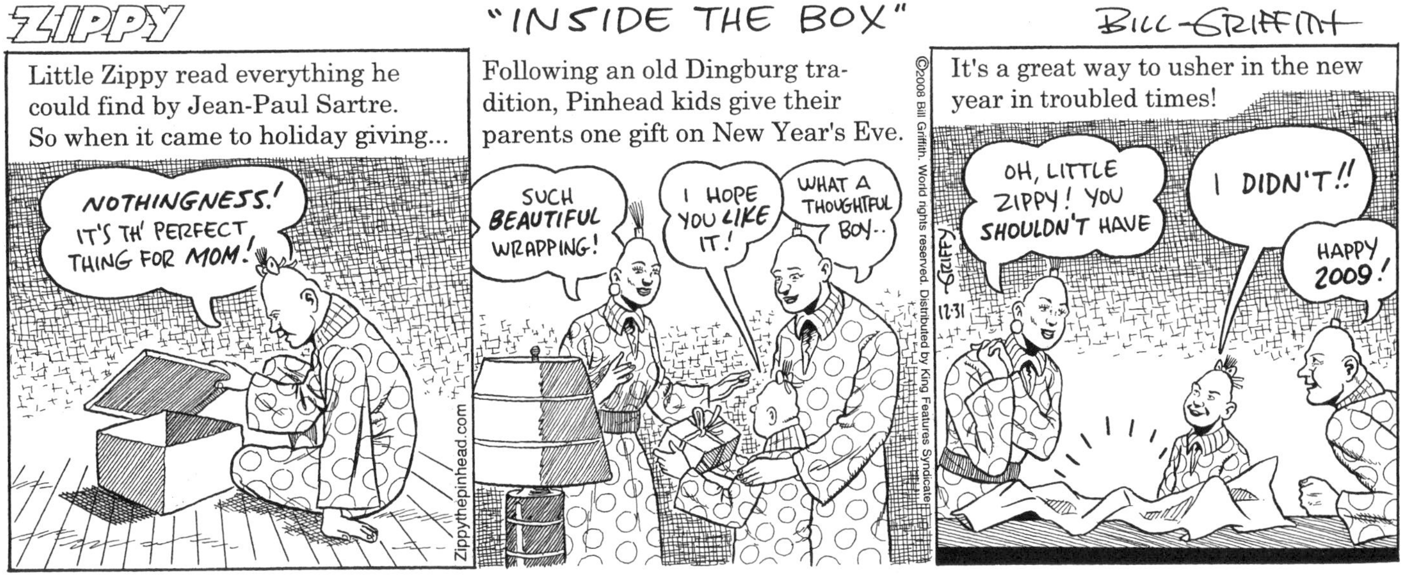
ZIPPY
"INSIDE THE BOX"
BILL GRIFFITH
Little Zippy read everything he could find by Jean-Paul Sartre. So when it came to holiday giving...
NOTHINGNESS! IT'S TH' PERFECT THING FOR MOM!
Zippythepinhead.com
Following an old Dingburg tradition, Pinhead kids give their parents one gift on New Year's Eve.
SUCH BEAUTIFUL WRAPPING!
I HOPE YOU LIKE IT!
WHAT A THOUGHTFUL BOY..
©2008 Bill Griffith. World rights reserved. Distributed by King Features Syndicate
GRIFFY 12·31
It's a great way to usher in the new year in troubled times!
OH, LITTLE ZIPPY! YOU SHOULDN'T HAVE
I DIDN'T!!
HAPPY 2009!

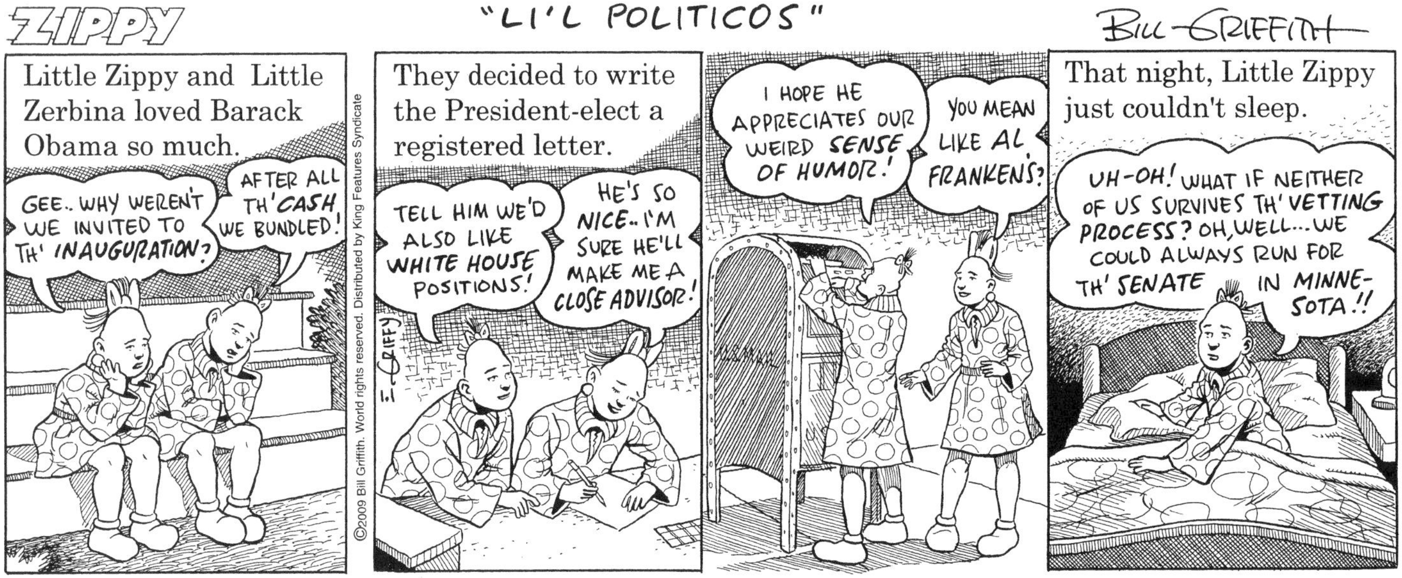
ZIPPY
"LI'L POLITICOS"
BILL GRIFFITH
Little Zippy and Little Zerbina loved Barack Obama so much.
GEE.. WHY WEREN'T WE INVITED TO TH' INAUGURATION?
AFTER ALL TH' CASH WE BUNDLED!
©2009 Bill Griffith. World rights reserved. Distributed by King Features Syndicate
They decided to write the President-elect a registered letter.
TELL HIM WE'D ALSO LIKE WHITE HOUSE POSITIONS!
HE'S SO NICE.. I'M SURE HE'LL MAKE ME A CLOSE ADVISOR!
I HOPE HE APPRECIATES OUR WEIRD SENSE OF HUMOR!
YOU MEAN LIKE AL FRANKEN'S?
That night, Little Zippy just couldn't sleep.
UH-OH! WHAT IF NEITHER OF US SURVIVES TH' VETTING PROCESS? OH, WELL... WE COULD ALWAYS RUN FOR TH' SENATE IN MINNESOTA!!

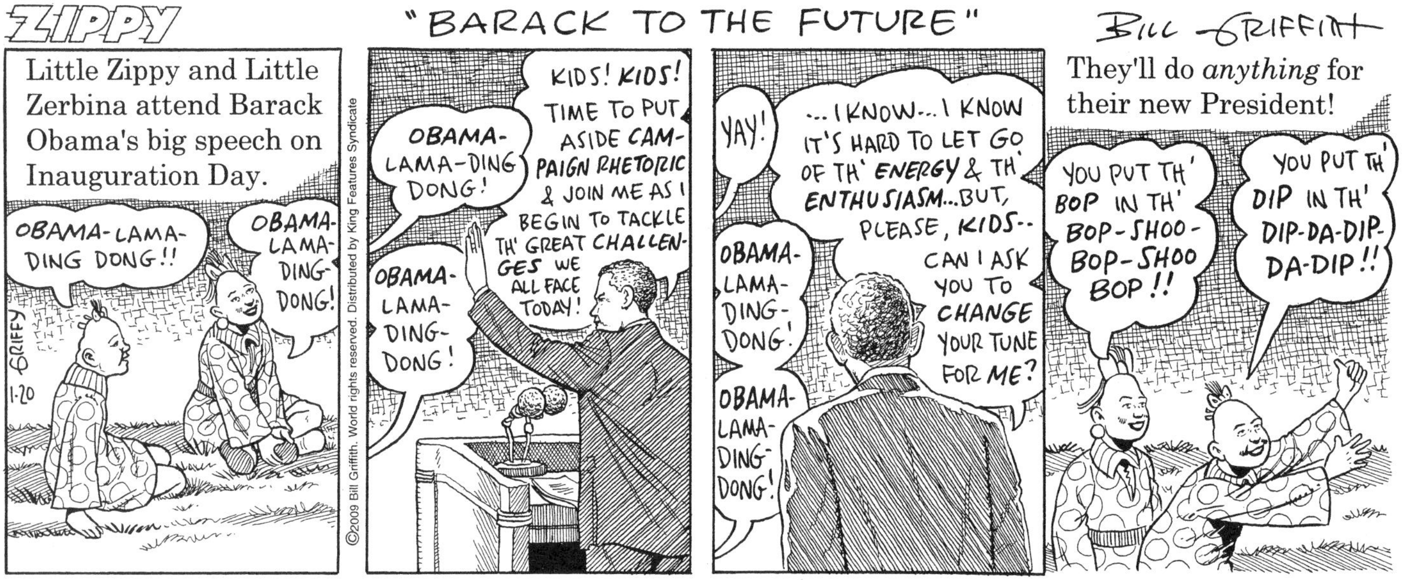
ZIPPY
"BARACK TO THE FUTURE"
BILL GRIFFITH
Little Zippy and Little Zerbina attend Barack Obama's big speech on Inauguration Day.
OBAMA-LAMA-DING DONG!!
OBAMA-LAMA-DING-DONG!
GRIFFY 1-20
©2009 Bill Griffith. World rights reserved. Distributed by King Features Syndicate
OBAMA-LAMA-DING DONG!
KIDS! KIDS! TIME TO PUT ASIDE CAMPAIGN RHETORIC & JOIN ME AS I BEGIN TO TACKLE TH' GREAT CHALLENGES WE ALL FACE TODAY!
OBAMA-LAMA-DING-DONG!
YAY!
...I KNOW...I KNOW IT'S HARD TO LET GO OF TH' ENERGY & TH' ENTHUSIASM...BUT, PLEASE, KIDS.. CAN I ASK YOU TO CHANGE YOUR TUNE FOR ME?
OBAMA-LAMA-DING-DONG!
OBAMA-LAMA-DING-DONG!
They'll do anything for their new President!
YOU PUT TH' BOP IN TH' BOP-SHOO-BOP-SHOO BOP!!
YOU PUT TH' DIP IN TH' DIP-DA-DIP-DA-DIP!!

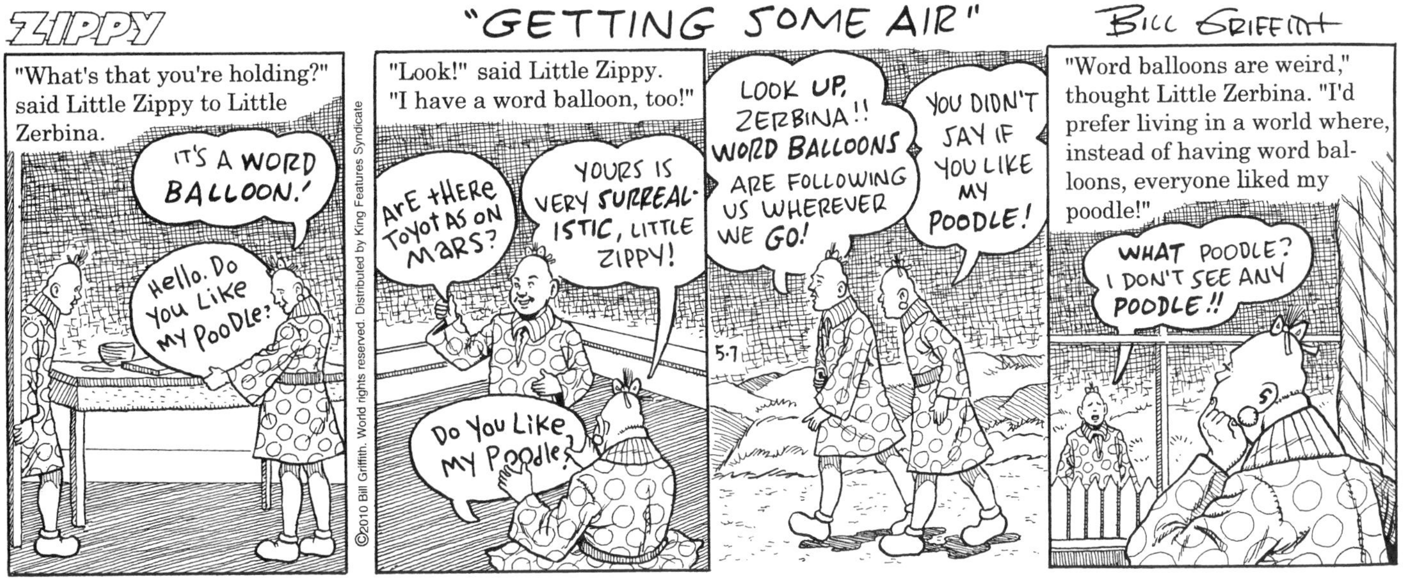
ZIPPY
"GETTING SOME AIR"
BILL GRIFFITH
"What's that you're holding?" said Little Zippy to Little Zerbina.
IT'S A WORD BALLOON!
Hello. Do you Like my PooDLe?
©2010 Bill Griffith. World rights reserved. Distributed by King Features Syndicate
"Look!" said Little Zippy. "I have a word balloon, too!"
ArE tHERE ToyotAS ON MARS?
YOURS IS VERY SURREAL-ISTIC, LITTLE ZIPPY!
Do You Like my Poodle?
LOOK UP, ZERBINA!! WORD BALLOONS ARE FOLLOWING US WHEREVER WE GO!
YOU DIDN'T SAY IF YOU LIKE MY POODLE!
5-7
"Word balloons are weird," thought Little Zerbina. "I'd prefer living in a world where, instead of having word balloons, everyone liked my poodle!"
WHAT POODLE? I DON'T SEE ANY POODLE!!

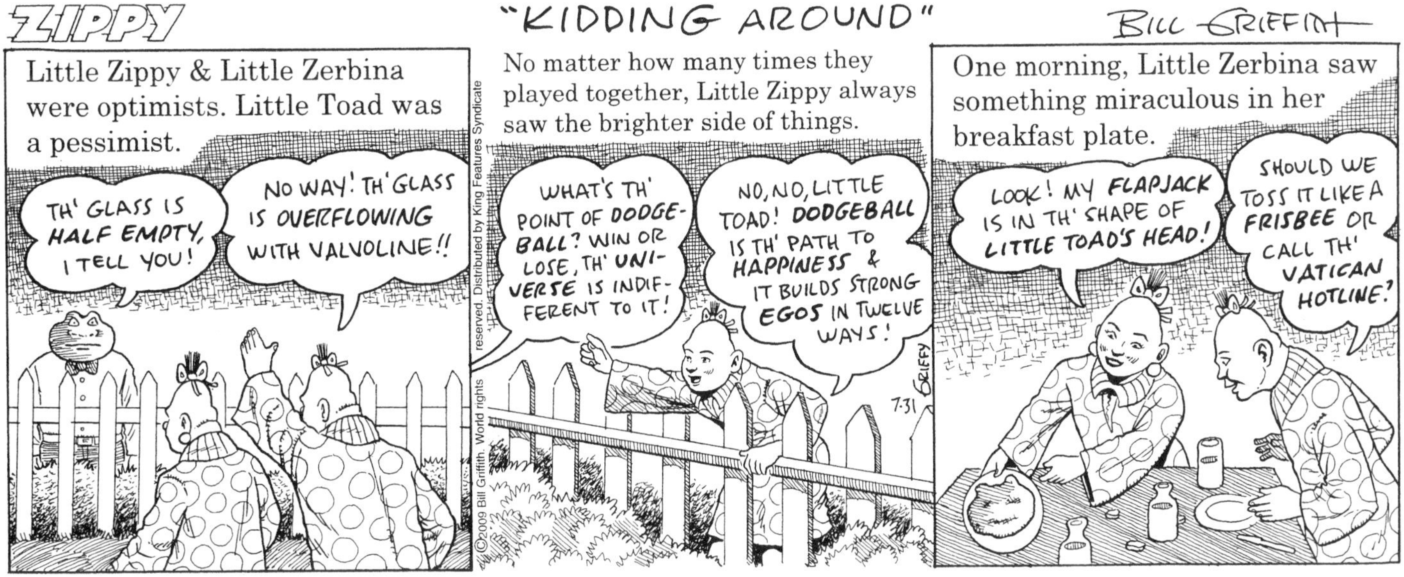
ZIPPY
"KIDDING AROUND"
BILL GRIFFITH
Little Zippy & Little Zerbina were optimists. Little Toad was a pessimist.
TH' GLASS IS HALF EMPTY, I TELL YOU!
NO WAY! TH' GLASS IS OVERFLOWING WITH VALVOLINE!!
©2009 Bill Griffith. World rights reserved. Distributed by King Features Syndicate
No matter how many times they played together, Little Zippy always saw the brighter side of things.
WHAT'S TH' POINT OF DODGE-BALL? WIN OR LOSE, TH' UNI-VERSE IS INDIF-FERENT TO IT!
NO, NO, LITTLE TOAD! DODGEBALL IS TH' PATH TO HAPPINESS & IT BUILDS STRONG EGOS IN TWELVE WAYS!
GRIFFY
7-31
One morning, Little Zerbina saw something miraculous in her breakfast plate.
LOOK! MY FLAPJACK IS IN TH' SHAPE OF LITTLE TOAD'S HEAD!
SHOULD WE TOSS IT LIKE A FRISBEE OR CALL TH' VATICAN HOTLINE?

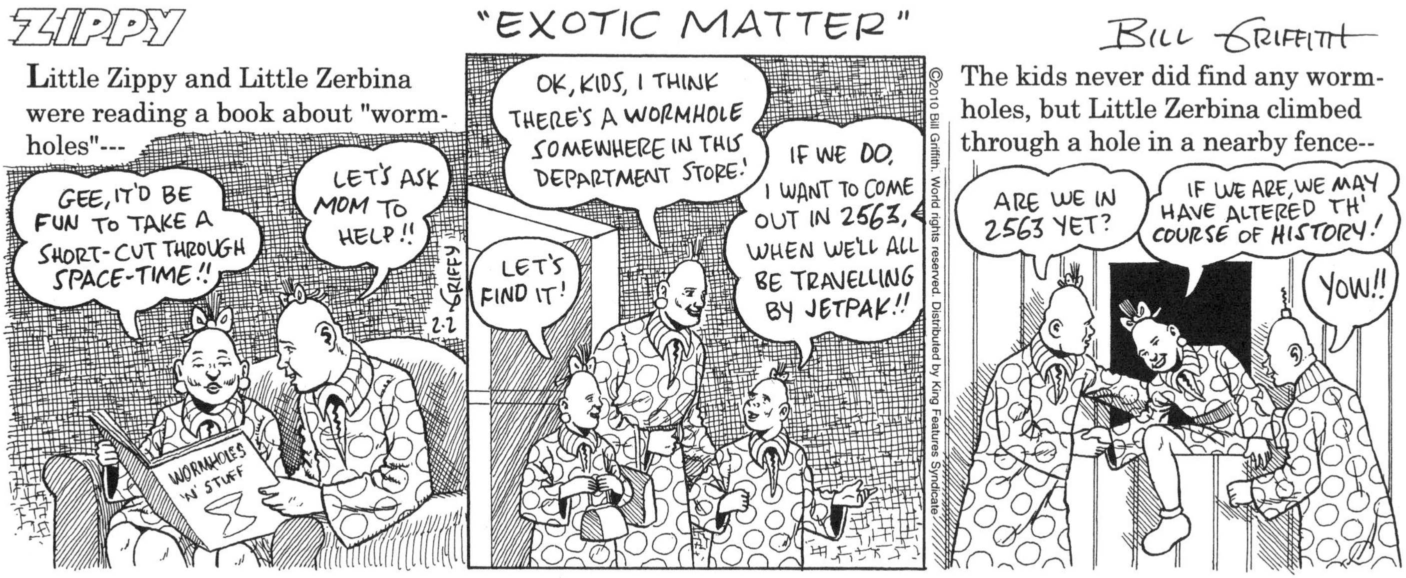
ZIPPY
"EXOTIC MATTER"
BILL GRIFFITH
Little Zippy and Little Zerbina were reading a book about "wormholes"---
GEE, IT'D BE FUN TO TAKE A SHORT-CUT THROUGH SPACE-TIME!!
LET'S ASK MOM TO HELP!!
WORMHOLES 'N' STUFF
GRIFFY 2·2
OK, KIDS, I THINK THERE'S A WORMHOLE SOMEWHERE IN THIS DEPARTMENT STORE!
LET'S FIND IT!
IF WE DO, I WANT TO COME OUT IN 2563, WHEN WE'LL ALL BE TRAVELLING BY JETPAK!!
©2010 Bill Griffith. World rights reserved. Distributed by King Features Syndicate
The kids never did find any wormholes, but Little Zerbina climbed through a hole in a nearby fence--
ARE WE IN 2563 YET?
IF WE ARE, WE MAY HAVE ALTERED TH' COURSE OF HISTORY!
YOW!!

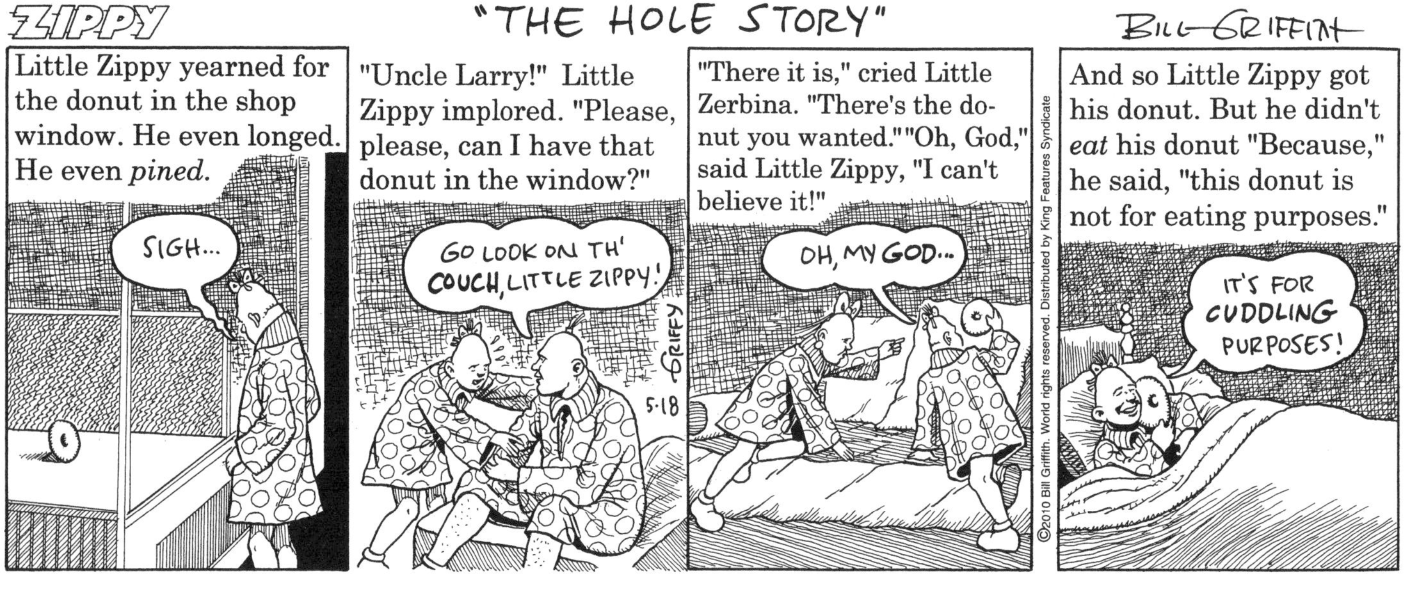
ZIPPY
"THE HOLE STORY"
BILL GRIFFITH
Little Zippy yearned for the donut in the shop window. He even longed. He even *pined.*
SIGH...
"Uncle Larry!" Little Zippy implored. "Please, please, can I have that donut in the window?"
GO LOOK ON TH' COUCH, LITTLE ZIPPY!
GRIFFY 5·18
"There it is," cried Little Zerbina. "There's the donut you wanted." "Oh, God," said Little Zippy, "I can't believe it!"
OH, MY GOD...
©2010 Bill Griffith. World rights reserved. Distributed by King Features Syndicate
And so Little Zippy got his donut. But he didn't *eat* his donut "Because," he said, "this donut is not for eating purposes."
IT'S FOR CUDDLING PURPOSES!

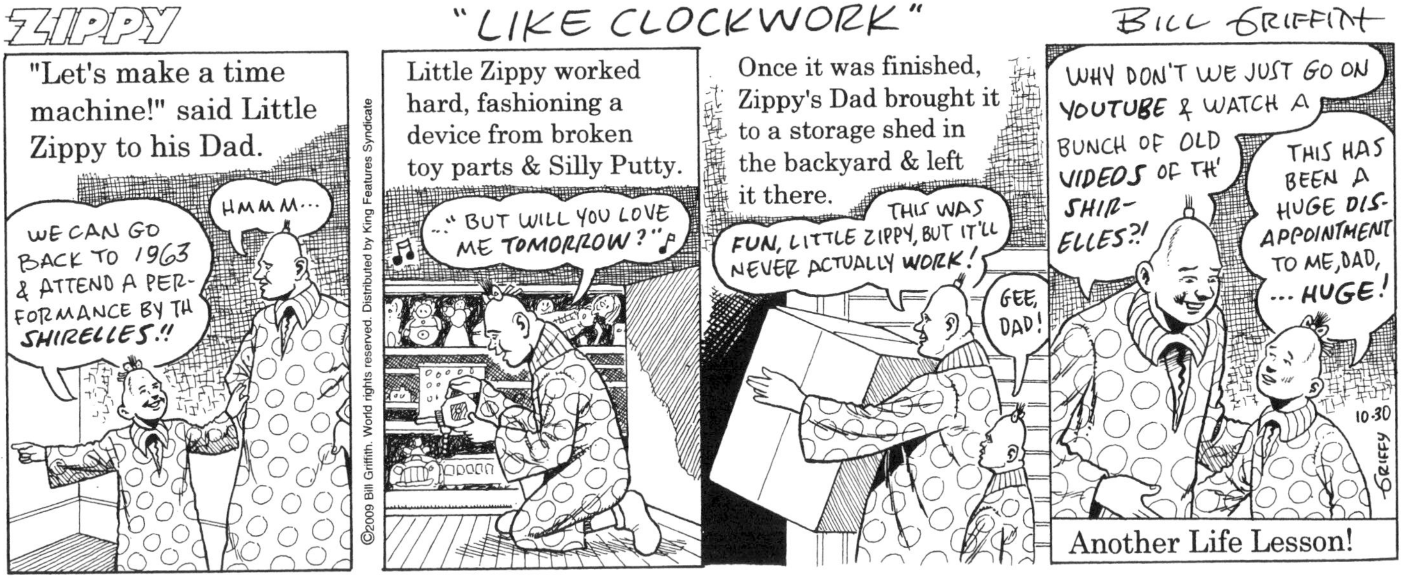
ZIPPY
"LIKE CLOCKWORK"
BILL GRIFFITH
"Let's make a time machine!" said Little Zippy to his Dad.
WE CAN GO BACK TO 1963 & ATTEND A PERFORMANCE BY TH SHIRELLES!!
HMMM...
©2009 Bill Griffith. World rights reserved. Distributed by King Features Syndicate
Little Zippy worked hard, fashioning a device from broken toy parts & Silly Putty.
.."BUT WILL YOU LOVE ME TOMORROW?"
Once it was finished, Zippy's Dad brought it to a storage shed in the backyard & left it there.
THIS WAS FUN, LITTLE ZIPPY, BUT IT'LL NEVER ACTUALLY WORK!
GEE, DAD!
WHY DON'T WE JUST GO ON YOUTUBE & WATCH A BUNCH OF OLD VIDEOS OF TH' SHIRELLES?!
THIS HAS BEEN A HUGE DISAPPOINTMENT TO ME, DAD, ...HUGE!
10-30
GRIFFY
Another Life Lesson!

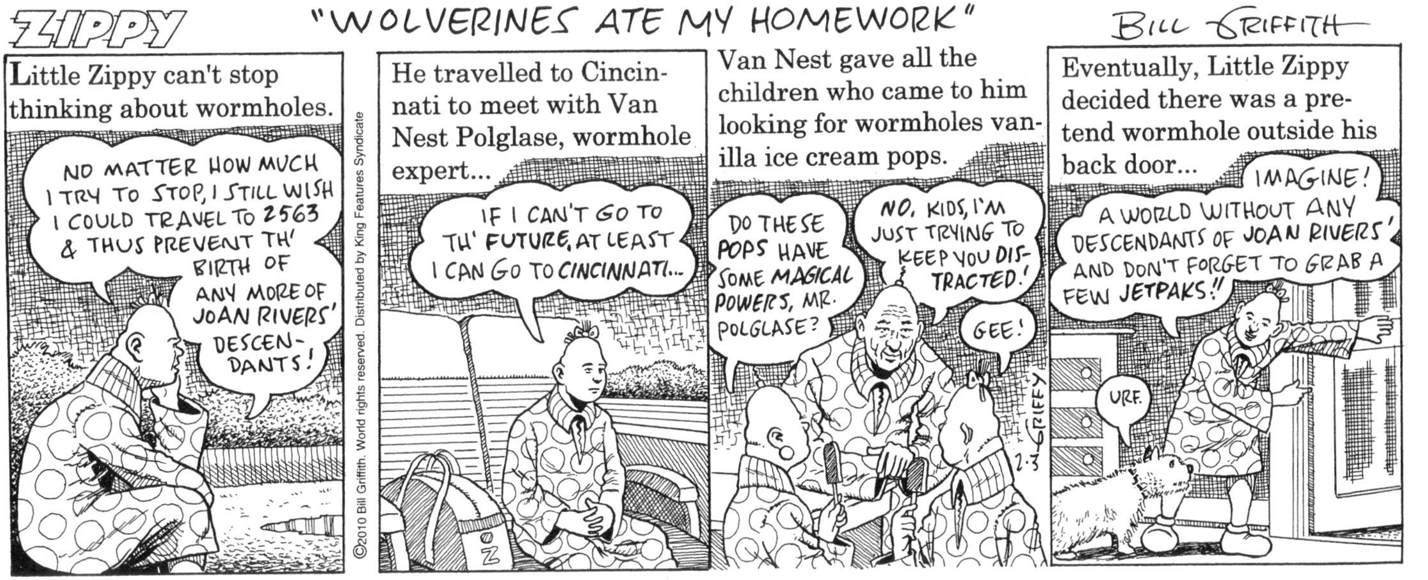
ZIPPY
"WOLVERINES ATE MY HOMEWORK"
BILL GRIFFITH
Little Zippy can't stop thinking about wormholes.
NO MATTER HOW MUCH I TRY TO STOP, I STILL WISH I COULD TRAVEL TO 2563 & THUS PREVENT TH' BIRTH OF ANY MORE OF JOAN RIVERS' DESCENDANTS!
©2010 Bill Griffith. World rights reserved. Distributed by King Features Syndicate
He travelled to Cincinnati to meet with Van Nest Polglase, wormhole expert...
IF I CAN'T GO TO TH' FUTURE, AT LEAST I CAN GO TO CINCINNATI...
Van Nest gave all the children who came to him looking for wormholes vanilla ice cream pops.
DO THESE POPS HAVE SOME MAGICAL POWERS, MR. POLGLASE?
NO, KIDS, I'M JUST TRYING TO KEEP YOU DISTRACTED!
GEE!
GRIFFY
2-3
Eventually, Little Zippy decided there was a pretend wormhole outside his back door...
IMAGINE! A WORLD WITHOUT ANY DESCENDANTS OF JOAN RIVERS' AND DON'T FORGET TO GRAB A FEW JETPAKS!!
URF.

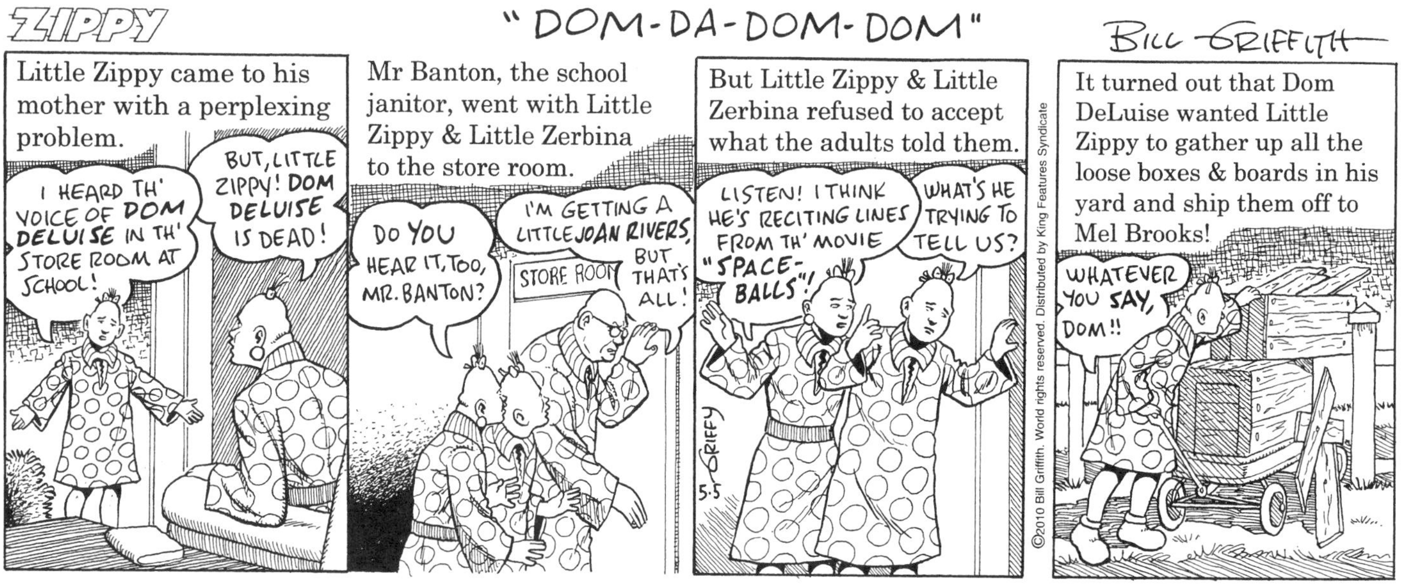
ZIPPY
"DOM-DA-DOM-DOM"
BILL GRIFFITH
Little Zippy came to his mother with a perplexing problem.
I HEARD TH' VOICE OF DOM DELUISE IN TH' STORE ROOM AT SCHOOL!
BUT, LITTLE ZIPPY! DOM DELUISE IS DEAD!
Mr Banton, the school janitor, went with Little Zippy & Little Zerbina to the store room.
DO YOU HEAR IT, TOO, MR. BANTON?
I'M GETTING A LITTLE JOAN RIVERS, BUT THAT'S ALL!
STORE ROOM
GRIFFY 5.5
But Little Zippy & Little Zerbina refused to accept what the adults told them.
LISTEN! I THINK HE'S RECITING LINES FROM TH' MOVIE "SPACE-BALLS"!
WHAT'S HE TRYING TO TELL US?
It turned out that Dom DeLuise wanted Little Zippy to gather up all the loose boxes & boards in his yard and ship them off to Mel Brooks!
WHATEVER YOU SAY, DOM!!
©2010 Bill Griffith. World rights reserved. Distributed by King Features Syndicate

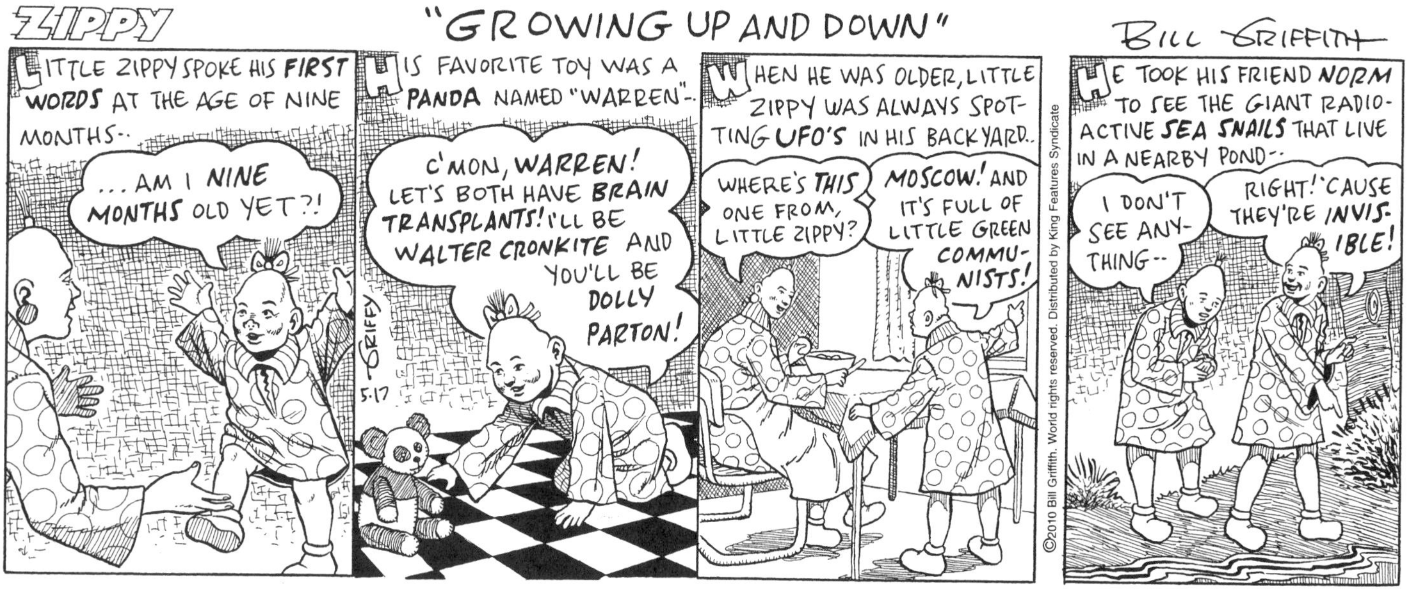
ZIPPY
"GROWING UP AND DOWN"
BILL GRIFFITH
LITTLE ZIPPY SPOKE HIS FIRST WORDS AT THE AGE OF NINE MONTHS..
...AM I NINE MONTHS OLD YET?!
HIS FAVORITE TOY WAS A PANDA NAMED "WARREN"..
C'MON, WARREN! LET'S BOTH HAVE BRAIN TRANSPLANTS! I'LL BE WALTER CRONKITE AND YOU'LL BE DOLLY PARTON!
GRIFFY 5.17
WHEN HE WAS OLDER, LITTLE ZIPPY WAS ALWAYS SPOTTING UFO'S IN HIS BACKYARD..
WHERE'S THIS ONE FROM, LITTLE ZIPPY?
MOSCOW! AND IT'S FULL OF LITTLE GREEN COMMU-NISTS!
HE TOOK HIS FRIEND NORM TO SEE THE GIANT RADIO-ACTIVE SEA SNAILS THAT LIVE IN A NEARBY POND--
I DON'T SEE ANY-THING--
RIGHT! 'CAUSE THEY'RE INVIS-IBLE!
©2010 Bill Griffith. World rights reserved. Distributed by King Features Syndicate

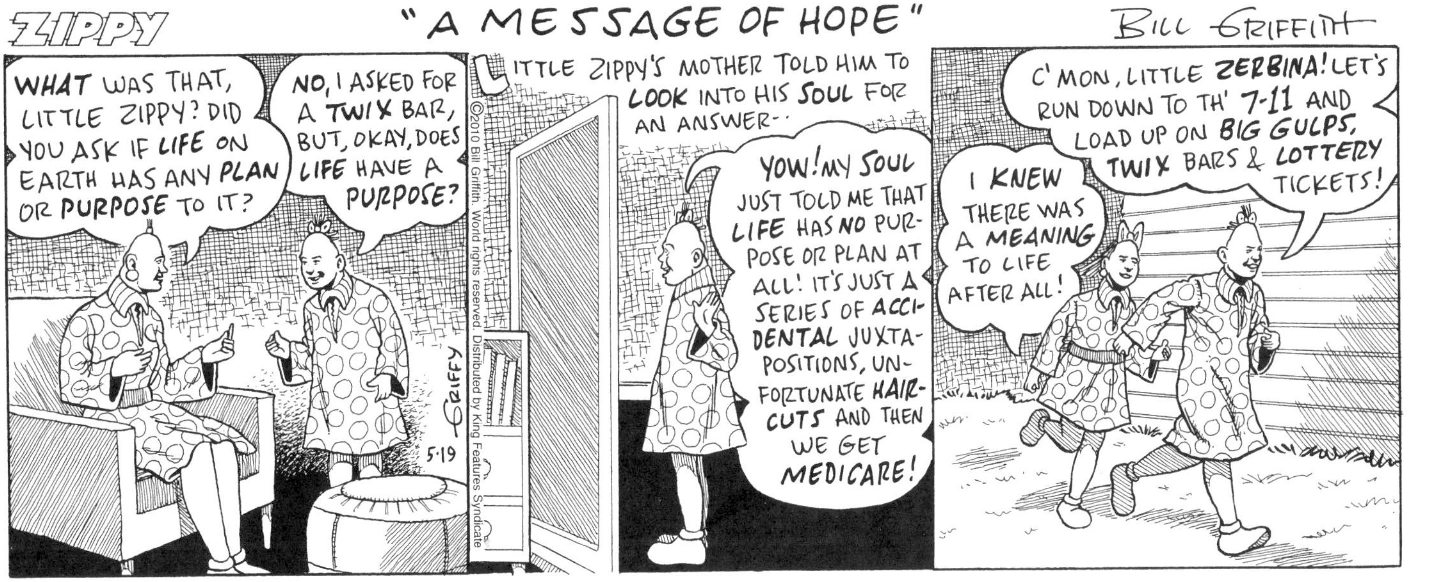
ZIPPY
"A MESSAGE OF HOPE"
BILL GRIFFITH
WHAT WAS THAT, LITTLE ZIPPY? DID YOU ASK IF LIFE ON EARTH HAS ANY PLAN OR PURPOSE TO IT?
NO, I ASKED FOR A TWIX BAR, BUT, OKAY, DOES LIFE HAVE A PURPOSE?
GRIFFY
5·19
©2010 Bill Griffith. World rights reserved. Distributed by King Features Syndicate
LITTLE ZIPPY'S MOTHER TOLD HIM TO LOOK INTO HIS SOUL FOR AN ANSWER··
YOW! MY SOUL JUST TOLD ME THAT LIFE HAS NO PURPOSE OR PLAN AT ALL! IT'S JUST A SERIES OF ACCIDENTAL JUXTAPOSITIONS, UNFORTUNATE HAIRCUTS AND THEN WE GET MEDICARE!
C'MON, LITTLE ZERBINA! LET'S RUN DOWN TO TH' 7-11 AND LOAD UP ON BIG GULPS, TWIX BARS & LOTTERY TICKETS!
I KNEW THERE WAS A MEANING TO LIFE AFTER ALL!

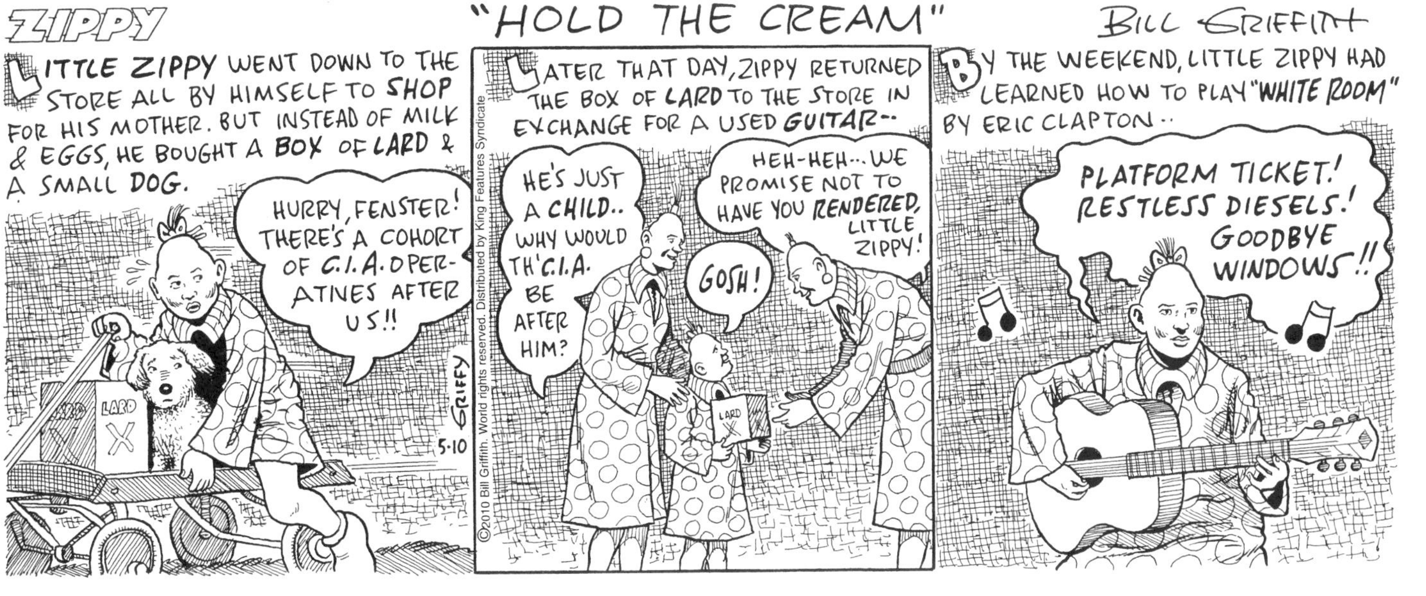
ZIPPY
"HOLD THE CREAM"
BILL GRIFFITH
LITTLE ZIPPY WENT DOWN TO THE STORE ALL BY HIMSELF TO SHOP FOR HIS MOTHER. BUT INSTEAD OF MILK & EGGS, HE BOUGHT A BOX OF LARD & A SMALL DOG.
HURRY, FENSTER! THERE'S A COHORT OF C.I.A. OPERATIVES AFTER US!!
LARD
GRIFFY
5·10
©2010 Bill Griffith. World rights reserved. Distributed by King Features Syndicate
LATER THAT DAY, ZIPPY RETURNED THE BOX OF LARD TO THE STORE IN EXCHANGE FOR A USED GUITAR··
HE'S JUST A CHILD.. WHY WOULD TH' C.I.A. BE AFTER HIM?
HEH-HEH... WE PROMISE NOT TO HAVE YOU RENDERED, LITTLE ZIPPY!
GOSH!
LARD
BY THE WEEKEND, LITTLE ZIPPY HAD LEARNED HOW TO PLAY "WHITE ROOM" BY ERIC CLAPTON··
PLATFORM TICKET! RESTLESS DIESELS! GOODBYE WINDOWS!!

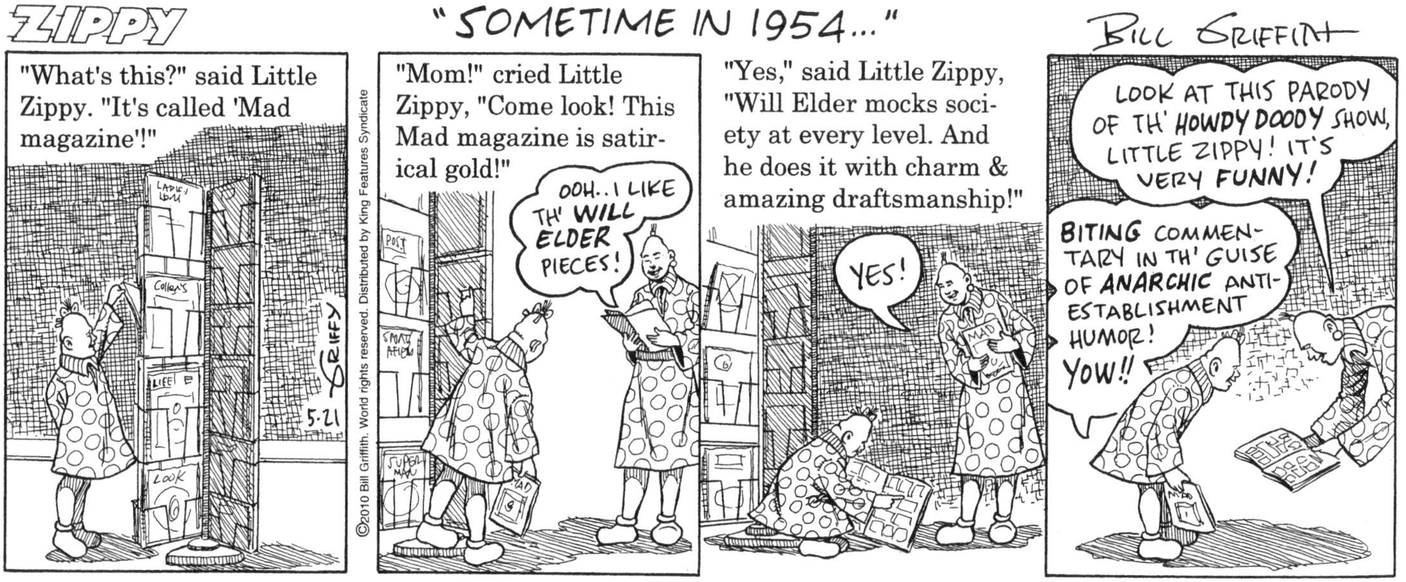
ZIPPY
"SOMETIME IN 1954..."
BILL GRIFFITH
"What's this?" said Little Zippy. "It's called 'Mad magazine'!"
LOOK
LIFE
GRIFFY
5·21
©2010 Bill Griffith. World rights reserved. Distributed by King Features Syndicate
"Mom!" cried Little Zippy, "Come look! This Mad magazine is satirical gold!"
OOH.. I LIKE TH' WILL ELDER PIECES!
"Yes," said Little Zippy, "Will Elder mocks society at every level. And he does it with charm & amazing draftsmanship!"
YES!
MAD
LOOK AT THIS PARODY OF TH' HOWDY DOODY SHOW, LITTLE ZIPPY! IT'S VERY FUNNY!
BITING COMMENTARY IN TH' GUISE OF ANARCHIC ANTI-ESTABLISHMENT HUMOR! YOW!!

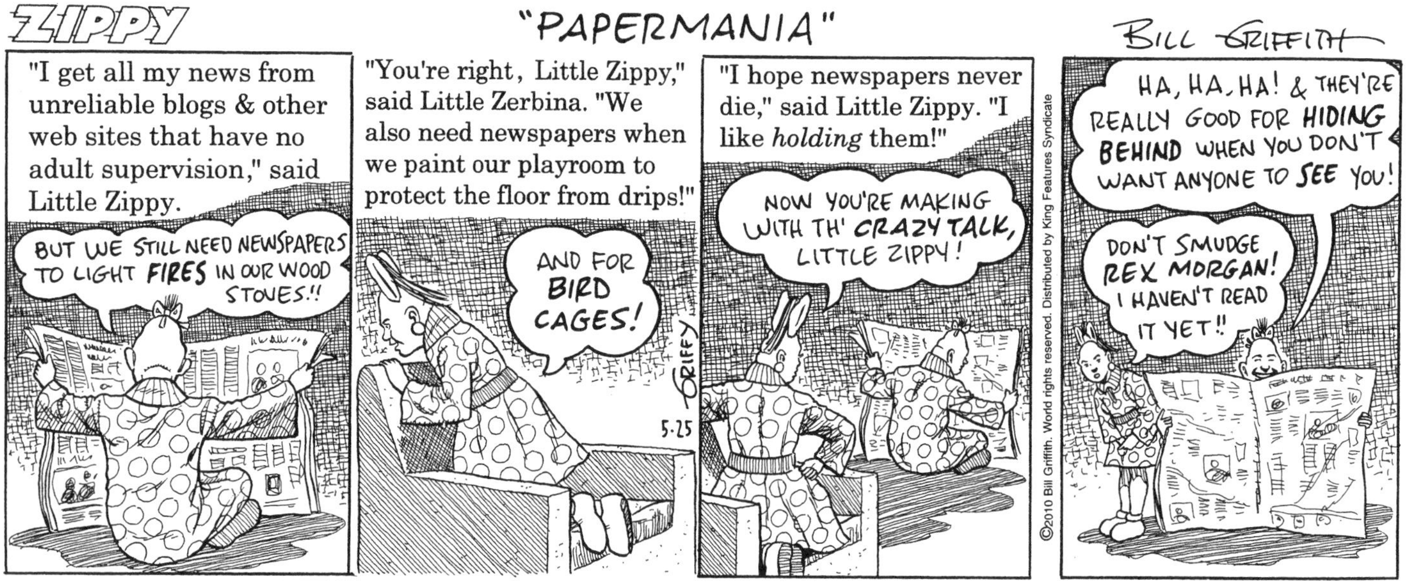
ZIPPY
"PAPERMANIA"
BILL GRIFFITH
"I get all my news from unreliable blogs & other web sites that have no adult supervision," said Little Zippy.
BUT WE STILL NEED NEWSPAPERS TO LIGHT FIRES IN OUR WOOD STOVES!!
"You're right, Little Zippy," said Little Zerbina. "We also need newspapers when we paint our playroom to protect the floor from drips!"
AND FOR BIRD CAGES!
GRIFFY
5·25
"I hope newspapers never die," said Little Zippy. "I like *holding* them!"
NOW YOU'RE MAKING WITH TH' CRAZY TALK, LITTLE ZIPPY!
©2010 Bill Griffith. World rights reserved. Distributed by King Features Syndicate
HA, HA, HA! & THEY'RE REALLY GOOD FOR HIDING BEHIND WHEN YOU DON'T WANT ANYONE TO SEE YOU!
DON'T SMUDGE REX MORGAN! I HAVEN'T READ IT YET!!

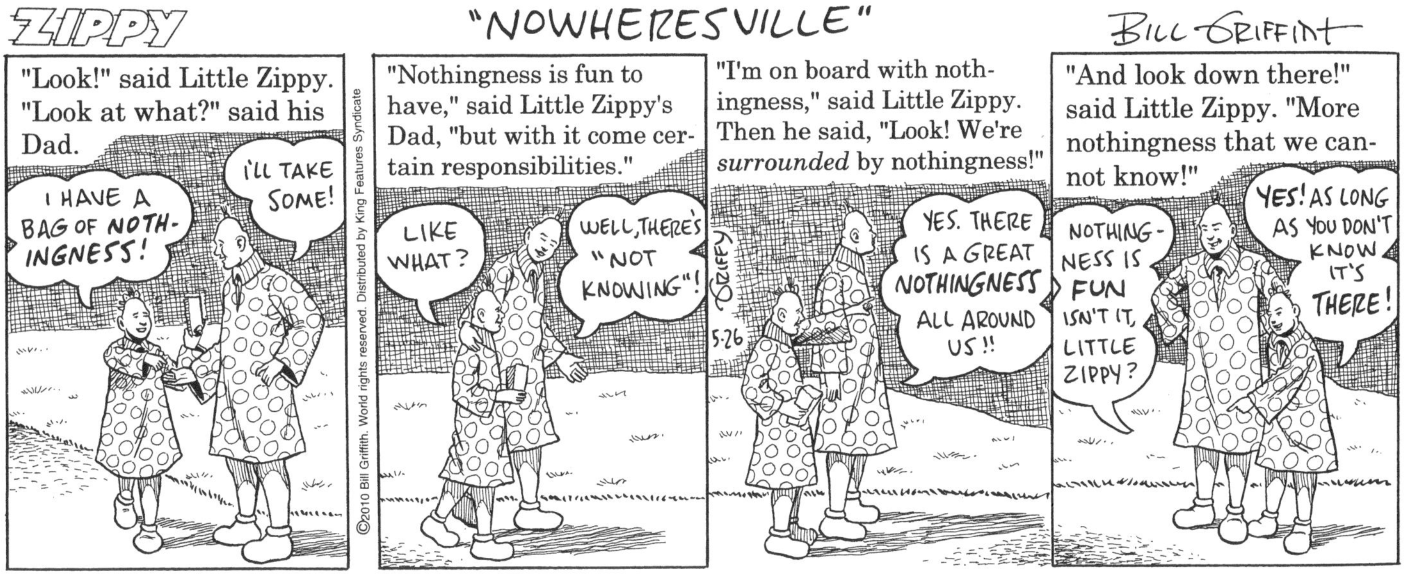
ZIPPY
"NOWHERESVILLE"
BILL GRIFFITH
"Look!" said Little Zippy. "Look at what?" said his Dad.
I HAVE A BAG OF NOTHINGNESS!
I'LL TAKE SOME!
©2010 Bill Griffith. World rights reserved. Distributed by King Features Syndicate
"Nothingness is fun to have," said Little Zippy's Dad, "but with it come certain responsibilities."
LIKE WHAT?
WELL, THERE'S "NOT KNOWING"!
GRIFFY
5-26
"I'm on board with nothingness," said Little Zippy. Then he said, "Look! We're *surrounded* by nothingness!"
YES. THERE IS A GREAT NOTHINGNESS ALL AROUND US!!
"And look down there!" said Little Zippy. "More nothingness that we cannot know!"
NOTHINGNESS IS FUN ISN'T IT, LITTLE ZIPPY?
YES! AS LONG AS YOU DON'T KNOW IT'S THERE!

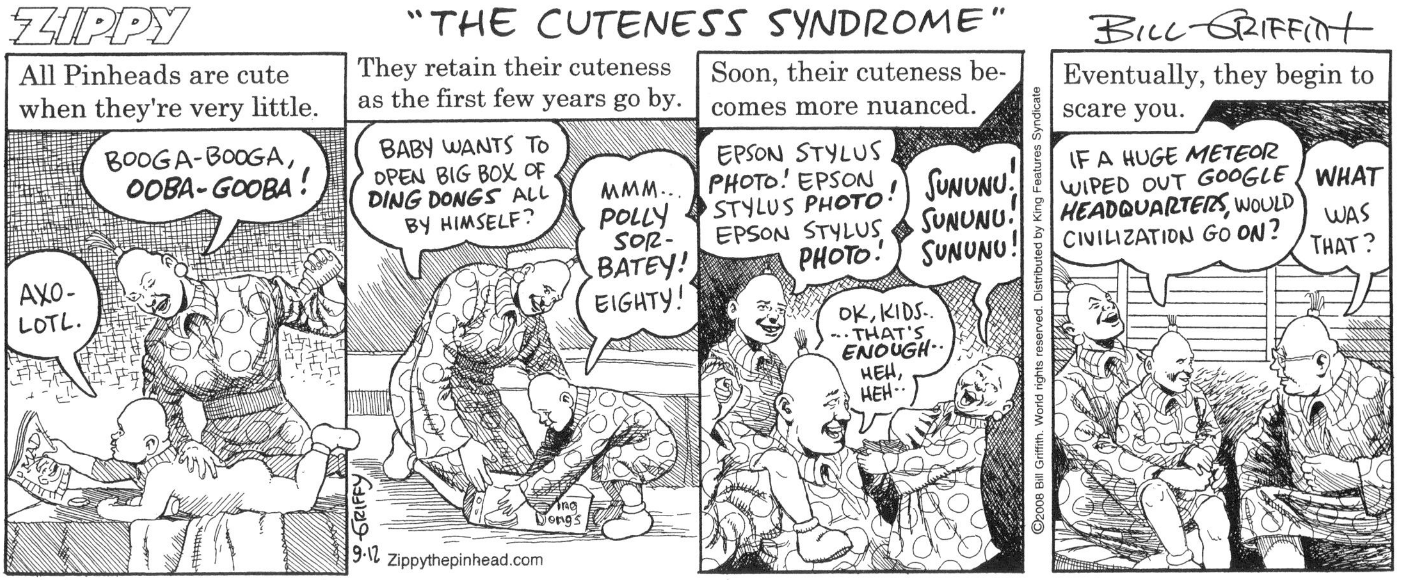
ZIPPY
"THE CUTENESS SYNDROME"
BILL GRIFFITH
All Pinheads are cute when they're very little.
BOOGA-BOOGA, OOBA-GOOBA!
AXOLOTL.
They retain their cuteness as the first few years go by.
BABY WANTS TO OPEN BIG BOX OF DING DONGS ALL BY HIMSELF?
MMM.. POLLY SORBATEY! EIGHTY!
GRIFFY
9-12
Zippythepinhead.com
Soon, their cuteness becomes more nuanced.
EPSON STYLUS PHOTO! EPSON STYLUS PHOTO! EPSON STYLUS PHOTO!
SUNUNU! SUNUNU! SUNUNU!
OK, KIDS.. ..THAT'S ENOUGH.. HEH, HEH..
©2008 Bill Griffith. World rights reserved. Distributed by King Features Syndicate
Eventually, they begin to scare you.
IF A HUGE METEOR WIPED OUT GOOGLE HEADQUARTERS, WOULD CIVILIZATION GO ON?
WHAT WAS THAT?

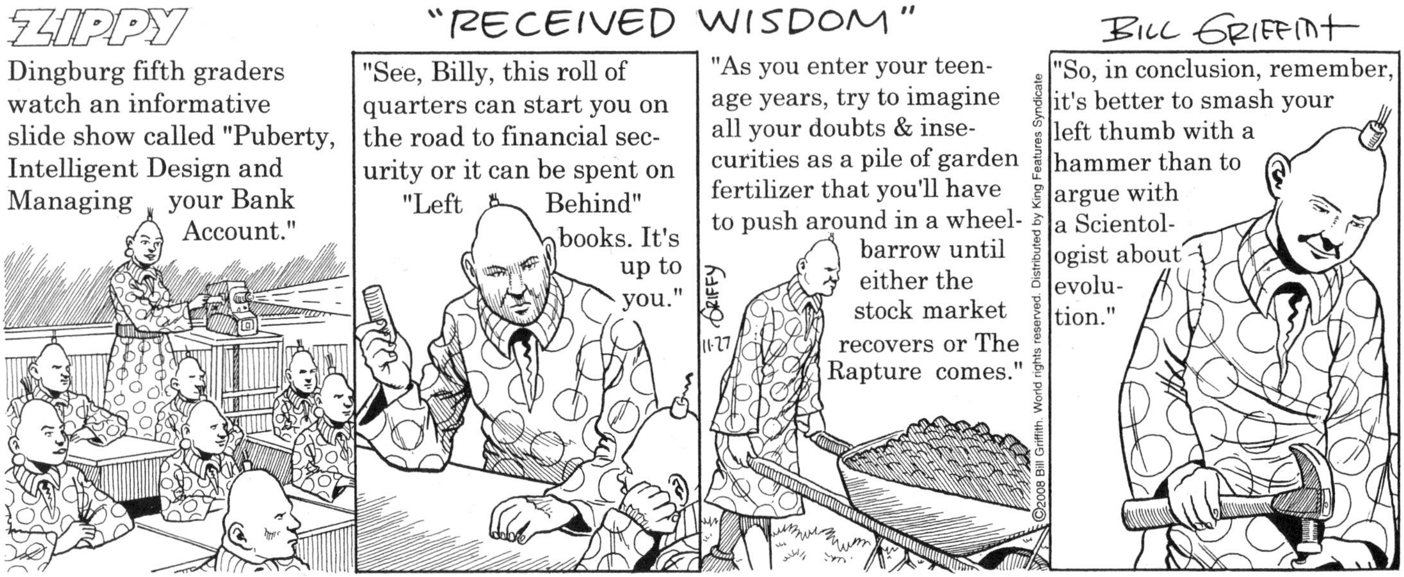
ZIPPY
"RECEIVED WISDOM"
BILL GRIFFITH
Dingburg fifth graders watch an informative slide show called "Puberty, Intelligent Design and Managing your Bank Account."
"See, Billy, this roll of quarters can start you on the road to financial security or it can be spent on "Left Behind" books. It's up to you."
"As you enter your teenage years, try to imagine all your doubts & insecurities as a pile of garden fertilizer that you'll have to push around in a wheelbarrow until either the stock market recovers or The Rapture comes."
GRIFFY
11-27
©2008 Bill Griffith. World rights reserved. Distributed by King Features Syndicate
"So, in conclusion, remember, it's better to smash your left thumb with a hammer than to argue with a Scientologist about evolution."

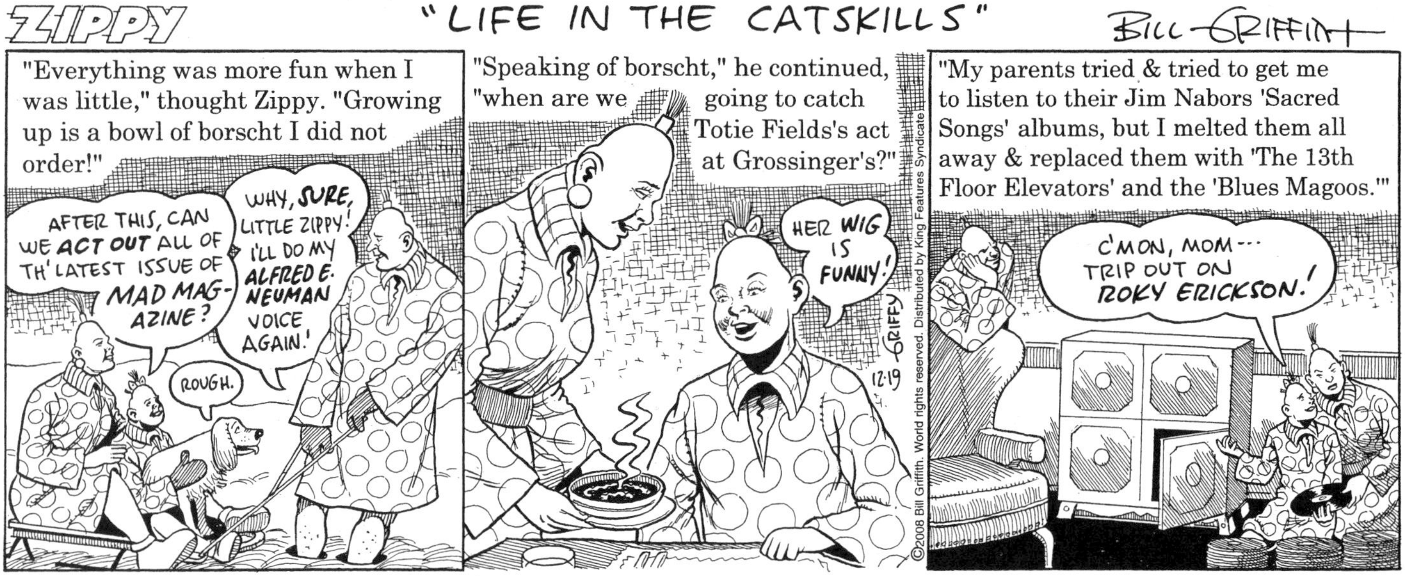
ZIPPY
"LIFE IN THE CATSKILLS"
BILL GRIFFITH
"Everything was more fun when I was little," thought Zippy. "Growing up is a bowl of borscht I did not order!"
AFTER THIS, CAN WE ACT OUT ALL OF TH' LATEST ISSUE OF MAD MAGAZINE?
WHY, SURE, LITTLE ZIPPY! I'LL DO MY ALFRED E. NEUMAN VOICE AGAIN!
ROUGH.
"Speaking of borscht," he continued, "when are we going to catch Totie Fields's act at Grossinger's?"
HER WIG IS FUNNY!
GRIFFY
12-19
©2008 Bill Griffith. World rights reserved. Distributed by King Features Syndicate
"My parents tried & tried to get me to listen to their Jim Nabors 'Sacred Songs' albums, but I melted them all away & replaced them with 'The 13th Floor Elevators' and the 'Blues Magoos.'"
C'MON, MOM--- TRIP OUT ON ROKY ERICKSON!

The “Pindex” for this book, showing real locations, etc., may be found online at: zippythepinhead.com/pages/aarealday.html